CAS PROFESSIONAL STANDARDS FOR HIGHER EDUCATION

Sixth Edition
2006

Laura A. Dean, Ph.D.
CAS Publications Editor
Assistant Professor, College Student Affairs Administration
University of Georgia

Council for the Advancement of Standards in Higher Education

Washington, DC

i

CAS Professional Standards for Higher Education
6th Edition

© Copyright 2006 by the Council for the Advancement of Standards in Higher Education

Library of Congress Cataloging-in-Publication Data
Dean, Laura A.
CAS Professional Standards for Higher Education
Includes bibliographic references.

ISBN 1-58328-037-5
1. Student Affairs, 2. Student Services, 3. Professional Standards, 4. Advising,
5. Counseling, 6. Higher Education, 7. Learning Assistance

Interior Design: Laura A. Dean, Athens, GA
Cover Design: Laura Dugan, HBP, Hagerstown, MD
Printing and Binding: HBP, Inc., Hagerstown, MD

This book is a revision of CAS Professional Standards previously published in 1986, 1997, 1999, 2001, and 2003.

CAS

Council for the Advancement of Standards in Higher Education

CAS Professional Standards for Higher Education

Table of Contents

Table of Contents, *continued*

* New or revised since 2003 edition

Appendices

Council for the Advancement of Standards in Higher Education

CAS President's Letter to the Profession

As President of the Council for the Advancement of Standards in Higher Education, I am thrilled and honored to introduce the 6th edition of the CAS Professional Standards for Higher Education. Since 1979 CAS has written and promulgated standards for programs and services in higher education. Complying with national standards is one of the means by which educators can assure high quality educational practices and subsequently student learning.

The establishment of standards is accomplished through the tedious process of what we refer to as consensus validity, where representatives of over 30 professional associations in higher education participate in the drafting, revising, and approval of standards and guidelines. This process also encompasses feedback from experts outside of CAS. Expert feedback, in conjunction with a consensus of a broad representation of higher education associations, is the collective wisdom of CAS. Hours of drafting committee and full board attention are devoted to each standard.

Recent research has indicated that CAS materials are used for guiding new programs, evaluating current programs, advocating for new initiatives, and guiding professional development. Since its inception, CAS has advocated for the value of self-assessment for its own merits. More recently, users of CAS standards have completed CAS self studies in conjunction with or in preparation for an accreditation study. The standards herein also provide an informed foundation upon which graduate students and new professionals can begin to ground their practice. As evidenced in this volume, CAS has been busy since the previous edition in creating new resources and standards while revising previous resources, all in an effort to provide the most appropriate guidance for today and tomorrow's context. We welcome your thoughts regarding our work and hope that you find our work as beneficial as we intend it to be.

CAS has also been busy in creating an additional resource that I think you will find helpful in your assessment efforts. The CAS standards dictate that educators "identify relevant and desirable student learning and development outcomes and provide programs and services that encourage the achievement of those outcomes. " To assist educators in assessing student learning, CAS has published a companion piece to this book called the Frameworks for Assessing Learning Development Outcomes. That book offers a brief synopsis on assessment, theoretical background of 16 learning domains, possible learning domain variables to measure, assessment examples, and websites and other resources on assessing learning.

It is recognized that national standards are one of the means by which a profession matures. The work of CAS recognizes the critical work of professional educators in higher education who offer educational programs and services that enhance student learning. I want to thank all of the many CAS representatives as well as those outside of CAS (functional area experts, readers, and editors) who worked diligently, in addition to their robust full-time employment, to make this publication and the national standards possible. Their diligence and wisdom is acknowledged and greatly appreciated.

Sincerely,

Jan Arminio, Ph.D.
CAS President
Professor, Counseling and College Student Personnel
Shippensburg University

CAS

Council for the Advancement of Standards in Higher Education

Editor's Note

This sixth edition of the CAS Professional Standards for Higher Education reflects the continuing commitment, creativity, and insight of the CAS Board of Directors and the organizations they represent. After nearly 30 years in existence, CAS continues to be at the forefront of important developments in higher education. This book includes five newly developed sets of standards and guidelines, nine sets revised since the last edition, and two new documents: the CAS Characteristics of Individual Excellence and the CAS Statement of Shared Ethical Principles. Along with revisions to nearly all of the functional area contextual statements, this represents an incredible amount of work and dedication on the part of the CAS Directors, the Executive Committee, and all those involved in reviewing and providing feedback on draft after draft. All of this culminates in the CAS process of examining each standard, line by line, as a full Board, until representatives from professional associations across higher education agree that the final version reflects the high quality of practice that will ultimately benefit the students who are, after all, the focus of our efforts.

Over the course of my career, CAS has served as a touchstone - for learning about the field as a graduate student, for implementing programs and services as a staff member and administrator, and now for teaching new professionals about quality practice as a faculty member. My service on the Board of Directors has been one of the highlights of my career and my most significant source of professional development; I have learned from an amazing array of colleagues, including a number who have helped to shape our profession.

I am particularly honored now to be taking over the role of Publications Editor from Ted Miller, who shepherded several iterations of this book with care, with an eye for detail and an ear for language, and with incredible dedication to its integrity and utility. Ted's impact on CAS, on student affairs, and on higher education has been significant, and along with the other CAS founders and long-term Directors, he has helped to define and advance our work. There is a plaque at my alma mater that reads "*We have all been warmed by fires we did not build and drunk from wells we did not dig.*" The foundation for CAS built by Ted and others gives us now the solid base on which we continue to build. It is my hope that I have honored the work of the Board, and the work that Ted did so ably for so long, in the production of this sixth edition of the "Blue Book." Ted literally "wrote the book" when it came to this publication; this edition still reflects his work, and his words, to a great extent.

I am grateful to the Board and the Executive Committee for their support, assistance, and trust in me. I am also grateful to the American College Counseling Association (ACCA) for their continued support of my role as the ACCA representative to the Board; by maintaining me as their Director over these ten years, they have allowed me to accept an increasing role in the work of CAS. Finally, I am grateful to the institutions in which I've worked as I've moved into the role of Editor. Peace College and now the University of Georgia have supported my involvement in CAS and my work as editor, and I am appreciative to them both. UGA in particular has provided assistance in multiple ways, and I extend my gratitude especially to the CSAA program faculty, the College of Education, and the students who assisted in the process, especially Steve Maddern for his technological expertise.

It is a bit daunting, a bit humbling, but always an honor to serve on CAS and to know that the work we do has an impact on students, professionals, and institutions across the country and beyond. I hope that this edition of the CAS Professional Standards, along with the other CAS publications, does justice to the work of the Board and provides professionals with information and strategies to improve their work and effectiveness. CAS is unique as a concept, as an entity, as an approach, and as a process. It is a consortium of professional associations that exists for the purpose of promoting quality programs and services for students in higher education; it is also a collaborative, consensus-oriented, hard-working, patient, funny, intelligent, dedicated, interested and interesting group of professionals that I am proud to call my colleagues and friends. My thanks go to them, and to all of you who work with us to be of service to our students and our institutions.

Laura A. Dean, Ph.D.
CAS Publications Editor
Assistant Professor, College Student Affairs Administration
University of Georgia
June 2006

PROLOGUE

This 2006 edition of CAS Professional Standards for Higher Education, often referred to as the CAS Blue Book or the CAS Book of Standards, is the sixth iteration of professional standards generated and promulgated by the Council for the Advancement of Standards in Higher Education (CAS). This edition contains 20 previously published functional area standards, along with 9 standards that have recently undergone major revision and 5 new standards that appear for the first time in this edition. This brings the total number of functional area standards to 34, in addition to the standard for Professional Preparation in Student Affairs at the master's level. CAS continues to attract interest from professionals across higher education, whether they are seeking to use existing professional standards or to develop new ones.

The standards that have been revised since the 2003 edition include those focused on Academic Advising, Clinical Health (formerly College Health), Commuter & Off-Campus Living, Housing & Residential Life, Multicultural Student Programs (formerly Minority Student Programs), Orientation, Campus Religious/Spiritual Programs (formerly Religious Programs), Student Conduct (formerly Judicial Programs), and Women Student Programs. As the field changes, so does our language, and several of these have been renamed to reflect more current philosophy and practice. Additionally, new standards have been developed in the areas of College Honor Societies, Education Abroad, Health Promotion, Internships, and Service-Learning. Again, the development of new standards reflects the evolving nature of our work in higher education. As has been increasingly true in previous editions, the breadth of CAS standards focuses attention not only on functions that comprise the traditional student affairs areas and directly support student learning and development, but also on other educational functions essential to institutional effectiveness that may be less focused on direct work with students. This expanded CAS vision reflects an increased emphasis on developing standards to guide professional practice throughout the whole of higher education.

Also included in this edition are two new documents, the CAS Characteristics of Individual Excellence and the CAS Statement of Shared Ethical Principles. Both the result of extended work within CAS, these materials extend the work of CAS to the consideration of the hallmarks of high quality professional practice and of the ethical values that we hold in common.

CAS was established over a quarter century ago for purposes of developing and promulgating standards of professional practice to guide higher education practitioners and their institutions, especially in regard to work with college students. Currently, the CAS Board of Directors is composed of delegates from 36 professional higher education associations in the United States and Canada. These organizations represent a full range of not-for-profit corporations concerned with student learning and development, many of which identify with the field of student affairs. In addition to the functional area practice standards, CAS has adopted and promulgated a set of master's level academic program standards to guide the graduate education of student affairs entry level professionals. Included in this publication are 35 sets of standards and guidelines, along with a description of the historical evolutions and contextual settings of the area.

As institutions of higher learning face new challenges, they often require faculty and staff members to implement their educational responsibilities in new and different ways. Approaches and strategies that were previously successful often need to be amended as institutions and programs evolve and student populations and characteristics change. Consequently, both educational and developmental needs brought to campus by students may change over time, requiring new and different approaches for those needs to be met effectively. As institutions and their constituents change, so to must the vehicles that guide practice within the shifting culture. As new developments occur that result in previously unrecognized or newly identified student needs, programs and services must change as well. In light of these factors, each CAS standard must be viewed as a living document that will shift over time as it reflects an evolving function.

The Council for the Advancement of Standards in Higher Education, a name adopted in 1992 to reflect the expanded context of the Council's higher education focus, was originally established in 1979 as a not-for-profit corporation called the Council for the Advancement of Standards for Student Services/Development Programs. Impetus for its existence was encouraged by a movement on the part of several national associations to develop accreditation standards for academic programs that prepare counselors and counselor educators. This movement, which culminated in the establishment of the Council for the Accreditation of Counseling and Related Educational Programs (CACREP) in 1980, provided the American College Personnel Association (ACPA) with impetus to create a set of preparation standards for use in master's level college student affairs administration programs. Rather than promulgating these standards as its own, ACPA sought out other professional associations interested in the development of standards for student affairs preparation and practice. The National Association of Student Personnel Administrators (NASPA) indicated an interest in the project, and the two associations jointly issued invitations to a meeting of interested professional associations. Seven student affairs- oriented organizations sent representatives to the exploratory meeting held in Alexandria, Virginia in June 1979. This meeting resulted in the creation of an inter-association consortium for purposes of developing and promulgating professional standards to guide both student affairs practice and academic preparation of those who administer student support programs and services. A subsequent organizational meeting in September 1979 resulted in the establishment of CAS as a not-for-profit corporate consortium of 11 charter member associations (see Appendix A).

Today, after nearly three decades of collaboration and a name change to reflect its expanded interests, the Council for the Advancement of Standards in Higher Education is composed of 36 member associations, and has generated and promulgated 34 sets of functional area standards and guidelines, one set of master's level academic preparation program standards for college student affairs administration, and statements regarding characteristics of individual excellence for professionals in higher education and the ethical principles that are held in common across the many areas of professional practice represented at CAS.

CAS Mission

CAS was founded to implement several profession-wide initiatives, with emphasis on the development and promulgation of professional standards. As CAS evolved, its raison d'être shifted as well. The following reflects the contemporary CAS mission.

- To establish, adopt, and disseminate unified and timely professional standards to guide student learning and development support programs and services and related higher education initiatives.
- To promote the assessment and improvement of higher education services and programs through self-study, evaluation, and the use of CAS standards.
- To establish, adopt, and disseminate unified and timely professional preparation standards for the education of student affairs practitioners.
- To promote the assessment and improvement of professional preparation graduate programs for student affairs administrators through the use of CAS standards for assessment, evaluation, and self-study purposes.

- To advance the use and importance of professional standards among practitioners and educators in higher education.
- To develop and provide materials to assist and support practitioners and educators in the use of professional standards in higher education.
- To promote and encourage public and private higher education systems and institutions to focus attention on the assurance of quality in all educational endeavors.
- To promote inter-association efforts to address the issues of quality assurance, student learning and development, and professional integrity in higher education.

As these purposes imply, CAS exists to accomplish several complementary tasks. A primary purpose is to provide a forum in which representatives from higher education organizations can meet and interact for purposes of seeking consensus on the fundamental principles of "best practice" that can lead to enhanced professional standards. The CAS initiative provides a forum wherein all voices can be heard in the creation of timely and useful standards to guide contemporary practice. This approach encourages the establishment of viable linkages among professional associations, most of which focus on highly specialized functions. This professional collaboration results in the creation of standards that represent a profession-wide perspective rather than a narrow and limited viewpoint.

Not only does the CAS initiative provide a vehicle for the development of functional area and academic preparation standards, but it also provides a well recognized and credible profession-wide entity to publish and promulgate standards and related materials and to encourage and educate practitioners to apply the standards effectively in their work with students. Further, and of special significance, the CAS consortium speaks with a single voice that bridges numerous specialty areas and can represent the profession-at-large on matters concerning professional standards and quality assurance.

CAS Rationale

As appears obvious in retrospect, CAS was created as a direct response to the emerging profession's need to establish standards to guide both practice and preparation. By the 1960s, the felt need for a profession-wide entity to speak as one voice for all was very apparent. An initial attempt to establish such a group, the Council of Student Personnel Associations in Higher Education (COSPA), was mounted in the late 1960s by 10 student affairs associations. This consortium is best remembered for its promotion of an enlightened approach to student affairs practice reflected in a statement published in 1972 by its Commission of Professional Development entitled "Student Development Services in Post-Secondary Education" (Rentz, 1994). Unfortunately, COSPA was dissolved in 1976, largely as a result of member disillusionment resulting from unresolved political issues.

CAS was established on a comparable consortial basis to that of the COSPA for an equally important, though less ambitious, purpose. Whereas COSPA was intended to function on a full range of professional issues, from the outset, CAS sought to avoid politicization and be driven by agreed-upon values rather than special interests. Consequently, the purposes and objectives of CAS are highly focused, which tends to protect the Council from internal strife resulting from member disagreement about its designated purpose and the processes used to accomplish its mission.

Although some may question the value of CAS's existence, it seems certain that without CAS working collaboratively and speaking collectively on behalf of practitioners and their functional area specialties, there would be no profession-wide criteria of good practice such as the CAS standards. In effect, CAS desires to represent every college and university educator and functional area specialist who believes the learning and development of all students to be the essence of higher education.

Although some professional associations or inter-association collectives may work unilaterally to establish standards of good practice for student support services, their products and models will inevitably fail to become part of the educational culture unless viewed as an enhancement to the educational interests of students. In other words, credibility within the whole of higher education is more effectively gained through collective action than through narrowly defined initiatives of individuals or associations. For standards of professional practice to be truly viable, they must reflect the interests and values of multiple professional organizations and the functional areas they champion. CAS strives to provide this collaborative avenue to establishing thoughtful, balanced, and achievable standards upon which all can rely.

Foundations for Standards and Guidelines
The initial full CAS publication, CAS Standards and Guidelines (CAS, 1986), was based on the premise that student support practitioners needed access to a comprehensive and valid set of criteria to judge support program quality and effectiveness. Further, it was viewed as essential that those standards represent best practices that any college or university program can reasonably achieve.

From the CAS perspective, virtually all functional areas of practice, no matter how specialized, have identifiable commonalties with other functions. For example, an institution's admission, academic advising, campus activities, and career services programs, although established to accomplish clearly different purposes, will each benefit from establishing a written mission statement that is compatible with the mission of the institution. Likewise, the same is true for human, fiscal, physical, and technological resources; legal responsibilities; campus and community relations; ethical considerations; and program evaluation among others. Consequently, CAS has incorporated a number of common criteria that have relevance for each and every functional area, no matter what its primary focus. These common criteria are referred to as "general standards" and will be found embedded in all functional area standards, along with criteria that relate to specialized aspects. These general standards are designed to overcome the "silo effect" so common throughout higher education in which autonomous administrative units, programs, and services function independently and sometimes inconsistently. In effect, the general standards make the CAS standards highly utilitarian and promote inter-departmental, inter-program, and inter-service cooperation and collaboration. Users are encouraged to view the CAS standards and guidelines as vehicles that interconnect administrative units. Because what these various functional units have in common (e.g., educational purpose, student learning and development) often exceeds their differences, the effective practitioner will find that collaboration between and among units can enhance the educational environment in many important ways.

All CAS standards use the auxiliary verbs "must" and "shall" and appear in bold print so that users can quickly identify them. As previously noted, all functional areas have specialty standards in addition to the general standards. Specialty standards are essential to accomplishing a support program's purpose and appear in bold print as do the general standards.

CAS standards are constructed to represent criteria that every higher education institution and its student support programs should be expected and able to meet with the application of reasonable effort and diligence. Although the standards are carefully worded for easy understanding, it is sometimes helpful to amplify them by providing additional information to facilitate the user's ability to interpret them accurately. Also, when programs are organizationally mature, there is need to provide users with additional criteria that may be used to make good programs even better. Consequently, as a supplement to its standards, CAS has established "guidelines" designed to clarify and amplify the standards. Guidelines may be used to guide enhanced practice when a program has previously achieved high levels of effectiveness. Guidelines use the auxiliary verbs "should" and "may" and are printed in lightface type to distinguish them from the standards.

In summary, CAS functional area standards and guidelines are basic statements that should be achievable by any program in any higher education institution when adequate and appropriate effort, energy, and resources are applied. Further, standards reflect a level of good practice generally agreed upon by the profession-at-large. In addition to the standards, guidelines are incorporated into each functional area to amplify and explain the standards and to guide enhanced practice. This dual presentation is most helpful because functional area programs in both early and advanced stages of development can use the CAS standards to good purpose. Most important is the fact that the CAS standards have been conceived and developed via a profession-wide process that can assure continuity and consistency of practice among all higher education institutions. In addition, each set of standards is reviewed on a five year staggered basis to assure currency and determine need for revision. When found wanting, the standard is submitted to a CAS committee for revision.

CAS Applications

The CAS standards and guidelines were established for institutions' student support programs and services to use for program development, program self-study, and staff development purposes. Although the standards have utility for institutional and program accreditation purposes, CAS has not sought to establish its own accrediting process. Rather, CAS takes the position that individualized institutional and program "self-regulation" is the preferred route to program quality and effectiveness. There is little doubt that CAS standards have utility for complementing regional or specialty accreditation self-studies. At this juncture, however, CAS views its profession-wide role as one to develop and promulgate professional standards to guide practice and to educate practitioners in the appropriate use of its standards.

CAS Role in Professional Practice

The professional role of the Council for the Advancement of Standards in Higher Education has become increasingly important during the past quarter century. The first order of business was to develop and promulgate professional standards of practice and preparation for student affairs and student support programs and services. However, CAS is viewed by many as an important professional development vehicle as well. CAS user surveys designed to determine how CAS influenced professional practice and the use of CAS materials were most revealing and are summarized below.

Many practitioners indicated that CAS standards are important because they speak to the issues of institutional change as practitioners struggle to meet the needs of ever changing student constituent bodies, not only in numbers but in age, gender, race, ethnicity, ability, sexual orientation, and long term goals as well. One respondent shared the perspective that,

". . . as each campus has examined its own situation, and looked to its peers for ideas, the CAS standards have guided not only implementation but review and evaluation. Most of this work was done in expansionary times. Now as we regroup, downsize, retrench, whatever institutions name it, we need to have some means by which to measure what we do. The CAS standards, in all of the functional areas, serve as an excellent tool to begin that process. They are flexible without being vague, broad without being limitless, and ideal for what we constantly face in higher education, change."

One comment that reflected the value of the CAS initiative for entry-level professionals was most telling.

"I can easily imagine that the standards would provide indispensable guidance for some of our younger or less experienced colleagues in graduate education. It must be like having a consultant's report at your finger tips that attests, 'Do at least this much well, and you will find success in your program'."

The CAS enterprise has led to a number of spin-offs in that some professional groups have expanded on the standards to meet sometimes highly specific professional needs. One example is in the area of learning assistance. As one respondent noted,

"No sooner than the first "Learning Assistance Program Standards were published, we were already talking about how to build upon that work. Whereas the CAS standards addressed broad basic elements that are essential to a comprehensive learning assistance program, practitioners in the field expressed interest in obtaining similar statements that addressed pedagogical components as well."

Consequently, the National Association for Developmental Education [NADE] responded to the challenge by creating "NADE Guides." These documents emulated the CAS standards assessment model and addressed the specific functions of tutoring services, adjunct instructional programs, developmental coursework, and the teaching/learning process. This developmental activity led to inter-association cooperation among learning assistance and developmental education organizations and paved a path for communication and collaboration in the revision of the CAS Learning Assistance Program Standards that follow in Part 2 of this volume. A related comment was made by a close observer of CAS initiatives.

"I have two general observations. First, CAS has filled a void that no other organization could accomplish. A network has been established to mutually equip the student affairs profession with standards of performance. Second, the CAS effort has attracted increased attention and offered increased value over the years. A genuine service has been provided to the academy by helping and guiding all students toward achieving holistic development."

Another CAS-sponsored survey was initiated in Spring 2000 and directed by Jan L. Arminio at Shippensburg University (Arminio & Gochenaur, 2004). CAS surveyed over 5,000 individual members from 22 CAS member associations. Of those responding, 62.5% had heard of CAS (i.e., 85 percent of responding vice presidents; 67% of functional area directors, 66% of new professionals, and 31% of faculty members). Participants in the study were asked if they measured learning outcomes and if so whether there was a connection between CAS standards and positive learning outcomes. Forty-one percent stated that there was a connection, 28% said there was a vague or indirect connection, 2% stated there was no connection, and 19% were unsure. Of those who stated that CAS has positively influenced their programs, 27% believed CAS positively influenced programs through assessing current programs, 22% in expanding current programs, 13% through clarifying mission and goals, 10% by justifying current programs, 8% by emphasizing student and staff training, 5% as a guide for new programs, and 4% to influence budget programs. Eighty-two percent of vice presidents and associate vice presidents for student affairs stated that CAS standards were positively associated with learning outcomes. A member of NACA noted, "CAS has closed the loop in student activities advising to see if student leaders learn or do not."

Future study is needed to answer other important questions about the influence of CAS and its initiatives. In an article published in the College Student Affairs Journal (2003), Don G. Creamer offers several CAS-related research questions that need to be addressed:

1. What is the level of use of CAS Standards by functional area and geographic area?
2. What is the type and frequency of use of CAS Standards and Guidelines?
3. How do CAS Standards shape professional practice?
4. What is the role of CAS in shaping educational programs and services?
5. Do practitioners perceive that the use of CAS Standards and Guidelines improves their performance?
6. Does CAS benefit professionals' learning and development?
7. Are programs and services that meet CAS Standards and Guidelines more effective in meeting learning goals than those that do not?
8. How does professional practice that is influenced by CAS in turn influence student learning?

There can be little doubt that the CAS initiative has been fruitful during its nearly thirty year existence. Although there is much work yet to do, the Council for the Advancement of Standards in Higher Education has made a professional difference and is prepared to continue its important efforts toward professionalizing programs and services in higher education.

Recent Developments

While continuing to develop and revise functional area standards, CAS has also continued to explore ways to improve and enhance its work. One of the most significant and potentially influential CAS initiatives was the 2003 revision of the CAS general standards that are incorporated into each functional area standard. This revision included a new, major emphasis on student learning and development, which is evident primarily in the Program component, Part Two, of each functional area standard. This section includes a table of 16 relevant student learning and development outcome domains designed to guide practitioners in their attempts to both emphasize and assess student learning and development. The example assessment indicators included in the table are intended to help practitioners identify behaviors that reflect student achievement in the various domains.

In 2006, in conjunction with this edition, CAS is also publishing a new companion book to the Standards. The *Frameworks for Assessing Learning and Development Outcomes* (FALDOs) were created to assist practitioners in developing sound and effective strategies for assessing outcomes. Based on the 16 student learning and development outcome domains described above, the FALDOs offer insight into the theoretical constructs of each domain, relevant variables, assessment examples, and information about assessment, evaluation, and research tools, as well as additional resources.

Finally, CAS has also used its collective voice and inter-association collaboration to develop two new statements related to the work of professionals in higher education. The first, the CAS Characteristics of Individual Excellence for Professional Practice in Higher Education, is designed to define a list of necessary attributes for professionals in higher education that is broader than competencies and includes other markers of professionalism. While CAS has historically focused on quality assurance with regard to programs and services, the Characteristics were created to suggest the hallmarks of quality on an individual basis. The second statement, the CAS Statement of Shared Ethical Principles, articulates those values which underlie the ethics statements of CAS member associations. By identifying the themes, the statement is designed to highlight the beliefs shared by professionals working across the range of functional areas in higher education. Like the standards themselves, the Characteristics of Individual Excellence and the Statement of Shared Ethical Principles seek to identify, articulate, and promulgate quality practices in the work that we do.

References

Arminio, J. & Gochenaur, P. (2004). After 16 years of publishing standards, do CAS standards make a difference? *College Student Affairs Journal, 23,* 51-65.

Council for the Advancement of Standards (CAS). (1986). *CAS standards and guidelines for student service/development programs.* Iowa City: American College Testing Program.

Council of Student Personnel Associations in Higher Education. (1994; 1972). Student development services in post-secondary education (pp. 428-447). In A. L. Rentz (Ed.), *Student affairs: A profession's heritage.* Washington, DC: American College Personnel Association.

Creamer, D. G. (2003). Research needed on the use of CAS standards and guidelines. *College Student Affairs Journal, 22:2,* 109-124.

CAS Context

A standard to guide practice is an essential characteristic of any established profession. It is vital during the evolution of a mature profession that a relevant set of standards be developed and promulgated by and for those working in that arena. The Council for the Advancement of Standards in Higher Education (CAS) was founded in 1979 as a profession-wide entity to establish standards to guide practice by student affairs, student development, and student support service providers employed by institutions of higher learning. Currently, 36 professional associations hold membership in CAS, representing nearly 100,000 higher education service providers. This book provides 35 functional area standards for use by the profession at large, as well as statements related to individual characteristics of excellence and to ethical principles. This edition of CAS Professional Standards represents the sixth major iteration of CAS standards, the first having been published under the auspices of the American College Testing Program (CAS, 1986).

During the twentieth century, college and university student support programs evolved from a few faculty members being assigned part-time to attend to students' needs beyond the classroom to the establishment of institutional divisions designed to complement the educational goals of academic affairs. Further, contemporary student support programs employ many full-time, well-qualified staff members, most with highly specialized knowledge and skills and with advanced degrees. There is little doubt that the complexity of the student support services enterprise has increased as organizational structures have expanded. It is largely in response to the increased complexity of role, function, and purpose that the CAS standards were developed. As the field matured and the responsibilities of its practitioners expanded, a complementary need for accountability increased. It is no longer feasible, let alone desirable, for practitioners to function on the basis of best guesses or intuition when creating environments conducive to student learning and development. Likewise, practitioners have demanded that standards be developed to guide the quality of practice. The CAS functional area standards and guidelines have been developed to meet these important professional needs. CAS was created as a bellwether for the profession at large. To ensure cross-fertilization of theories, research, and application strategies from the field as a whole, knowledgeable representatives from its member associations bring to the table the most current thinking in the functional areas they represent and champion. This commitment to collaboration among functional area specialties ensures that no single component will dominate the foundations that underlie the generation, revision, and presentation of each CAS standard. Although the standards reflect a broad range of interests, they are clearly values driven. Underlying them is a set of fundamental principles upon which CAS was founded and by which it is guided.

CAS Guiding Principles

The fundamental principles that undergird the work of CAS and guide its initiatives are organized into five categories. They were derived from theories and conceptual models implicit within human development, group dynamics, student learning, organizational management, and higher education administration that inform the work of student affairs administrators, student development educators, and student support service providers.

Students and Their Institutions

These initial eight principles are concerned with how students learn and the environmental conditions that institutions need to emphasize for learning and development to occur. The first four principles were derived from the 1938 and 1949 editions of the Student Personnel Point of View (Miller & Prince, 1976, p.4) and reflect fundamental "truths" upon which the CAS standards and guidelines are based. Principles five through eight reflect institutional perspectives that complement the student-focused viewpoint. When combined, these principles represent the presuppositions upon which student support programs and services are founded.

- The student must be considered as a whole person.
- Each student is a unique person and must be treated as such.
- The student's total environment is educational and must be used to achieve full development.
- Students seek higher education in responsible ways and will, when encouraged to do so, access appropriate educational resources when they are provided, made known, and relevant to students' felt educational and developmental needs.
- Institutions of higher learning are purposeful and function as social and cultural resources to provide opportunities for students to learn and develop in holistic ways.
- The primary responsibility for learning and development rests with the student.
- Institutions of higher learning reflect the diversity of the societies and cultures in which they exist.

• Institutions are responsible for creating learning environments that provide a choice of educational opportunities and challenge students to learn and develop while providing support to nurture their development.

Each CAS functional area standard was created to inform practitioners about the criteria that represent fundamental levels of programmatic and organizational quality that must be met if institutions are to be effective in facilitating student learning and development.

In effect, when a college or university provides programs and services that meet or exceed the CAS criteria, the institution will have effectively implemented an intentional educational environment conducive to the learning and development of its students. It is important to note that the CAS standards do not dictate that students, individually or collectively, must conform to a prescribed standard of involvement or behavior. Rather, they call for institutions and student support programs to meet a standard of programmatic and organizational efficiency and effectiveness sufficient to provide opportunity and encouragement for students to grow, develop, and achieve individual potentials. The institution and its educational programs are social resources that provide citizens opportunities to expand their horizons and capacities to serve society. The CAS standards have been developed and promulgated from a profession-wide point of view to provide institutions with a relevant, reasonable, and achievable set of voluntary professional standards.

Diversity and Multiculturalism

Issues of diversity in institutions of higher education can be fraught with dissension and discord. The CAS standards affirm the importance of affirming the existence of diversity and considering its influence when creating and implementing educational and developmental initiatives. In an increasingly complex and shrinking global environment, it is essential that students learn to function effectively and justly when exposed to ideas, beliefs, values, physical and mental abilities, sexual orientations, lifestyles, and cultures that differ from their own. Two principles in this regard are embedded in the CAS standards.

• Recognizing the ubiquitous nature of human diversity, institutions are committed to eliminating barriers that impede student learning and development, attending especially to establishing and maintaining diverse human relationships essential to survival in a global society.

• Justice and respect for differences bond individuals to community; thus education for multicultural awareness and positive regard for differences is essential to the development and maintenance of a health engendering society.

The CAS standards call for institutions and their student support programs to recognize the increasingly diverse societies to be served and the importance of enhancing students' capacities to function effectively within the context of constantly shifting environments and opinions. CAS recognizes that the spirit of affirmative action is inherent in the delivery of effective student support services and that discrimination against any student population or employment category is antithetical to belief in the dignity of the individual. This proposition is fundamental to student development theory and its applications to practice. The CAS standards reinforce the fact that those responsible for creating educational environments need to be open to and accepting of differences, and that they must recognize how such environments are important for enhancing the quality of the education provided and the learning achieved. Further, the standards consistently call for personnel whose demographic characteristics reflect those of the institution's constituencies. In addition, all students must have access to the educational and co-curricular resources available to the academic community at large; no student, for any reason, should be denied access to them.

Organization, Leadership, and Human Resources

The CAS standards reflect the belief that form follows function; consequently, the structure of an organization should mirror the purposes for which it was established. It is essential that institutions, programs, and services be based on a mutually determined, clearly and publicly stated, and well understood purpose. Without a clearly defined mission, an institution and its programs are virtually rudderless and will ultimately founder. Unmistakably defined lines of authority must be drawn, detailed duties and job responsibilities described, and policies and procedures established to guide the desired processes. Those who lead and administer programs of student support must remember that because theory without practice is empty, and practice without theory is blind, it is essential that the theory embraced be connected to the purposes sought in pursuit of quality practice. Three basic principles concerned with these factors also underlie the CAS standards.

• Capable, credible, knowledgeable, and experienced leadership is essential for institutional success; organizational units are most successful when their missions and outcome expectations are effectively documented and understood by all concerned.

• Effective programs and services require well-qualified staff members who understand and support the student learning and development outcomes the programs are intended to promote.

- Student learning and personal development will be enhanced when staff members at all levels of responsibility possess appropriate, relevant, and adequate educational preparation and practical experience.

CAS standards do not prescribe organization or administrative structures to which institutions and programs are expected to adhere. CAS is guided by the belief that every institution is unique and must establish the frame of administrative reference most appropriate to its particular mission. Consequently, the standards do not prescribe specific requirements, but rather provide fundamental criteria that practitioners can use to judge the effectiveness of their current or projected structures. For example, certain elements clearly are essential to functional success, including employing leaders who possess viable visions of how and what is to be achieved and are suitably positioned for access to the highest administrative levels. Leaders and staff members alike must possess effective managerial skills, be properly titled, and be well qualified by both education and experience. Under-educated and under-experienced staff members, good intentions notwithstanding, will virtually always fail to accomplish the program's objectives over the long term.

Health Engendering Environments

Institutional environments of quality combine educational philosophies and values in conjunction with adequate physical facilities, human resources, and fiscal support to create positive input on the education and development of students. The establishment of effective, health generating environments is an important aspect of the CAS standards.

- Student support and developmental programs and services prosper in benevolent environments that provide students with appropriate levels of challenge and support.

The primary purpose of education has always been to promote change, both in individuals and in society. College and university student support programs are primarily educational enterprises. Clearly, the Student Learning Imperative (ACPA, 1996) prevails throughout each CAS functional area standard because an important purpose of the standards is to provide criteria that can be used to judge a program's capacity and effectiveness in creating learning and development opportunities. The establishment of educational environments conducive to student learning and development is essential if an institution of higher learning is to achieve its educational purposes.

Ethical Considerations

A major component in each CAS standard incorporates the fundamental ethical expectations to which all student support practitioners must adhere to ensure fair and equitable practice. Just as a mission statement is essential to provide programs with direction, ethical standards are essential to guide the behavior of staff members in ways that enhance the overall integrity of both the program and its host institution.

- Because special mentoring relationships exist between students and those who facilitate their learning and development, support service providers must exemplify impeccable ethical behavior in both their professional relationships and personal lives.

As an essential task of every profession's emergence, it establishes and codifies ethical standards to guide the behavior of its members. The CAS standards provide the essential ethical foundations upon which to build humane, ethical practice. Without a clearly defined code of ethics, support service staff members would have little or no guidance for establishing and maintaining a reasonable level of effective moral and ethical behavior. The best of intentions are insufficient if they are not founded on a solid ethical base that can be understood and acknowledged by all concerned. Practitioners can be informed by their own association's ethical codes, the relevant criteria in the CAS standards, and the CAS Statement of Shared Ethical Principles.

Putting CAS Standards to Work

CAS standards and guidelines are conceived and crafted with care to be instructive and useful to practitioners and educational leaders. Based upon professional judgment and societal expectations, they include principles that are fundamental to student learning and development and guidelines for practice for particular functional areas.

Because CAS believes in the importance of self-assessment, the standards and guidelines, as well as other CAS-related materials, are offered as criteria that can be used in multiple ways toward the goal of assuring and enhancing quality practice. As noted in the CAS Preamble (below), they can be used for design of new programs and services, for determining the efficacy of programs, for staff development, or for programmatic assessment as part of an institutional self-study. CAS does not prescribe or proscribe ways of using the standards; rather, they are intended to be tools for practitioners to use to improve practice.

Self-Study Process

The most thorough and, perhaps, productive use of the standards involves a self-study process for program evaluation. This process involves others at the institution in examining evidence to determine collectively whether the program is in compliance with the standards. Involvement of others serves several purposes; it ensures a broader and more objective perspective, increases knowledge and awareness of the program across the institution, and develops support for implementation of identified improvements.

For each set of standards and guidelines, CAS provides a Self-Assessment Guide (SAG) that includes a comprehensive self-study process for program evaluation. Seven basic steps to using a SAG are suggested for implementing a functional area self-study. The following, in summary form, is the recommended self-study process.

1. Establish and Prepare the Self-Assessment Team

Division and functional area leaders need first to determine the functional area or areas to be evaluated. This may be dictated by institutional program review cycles or planning for accreditation processes, or it may result from internal divisional goals and needs.

It is desirable to involve the full staff in the initial planning stage of the self-study process, including support staff members and knowledgeable students and faculty members when feasible. This approach provides opportunity for shared ownership in the evaluation. For a self-study of a single functional area, a representative group of three to five members, including one or more knowledgeable individuals from outside the area under review, should be selected to compose the primary self-study team. Initially, the team should familiarize itself with the relevant CAS functional area standard by examining it carefully before making individual or group judgments. It is important that all members come to understand and interpret the standard in similar fashion. Team training should be conducted to ensure that members' interpretive differences are resolved before initiating the study. Likewise, ground rules for the study should be established and agreed upon. Team members should realize and accept that disagreement is natural, healthy, and probably inevitable, but the resulting debates will usually strengthen the team's ultimate consensus on the matter. Finally, the team should discuss whether any of the guidelines (included with the standards to indicate areas where practice can be enhanced beyond the minimum expectations) should be treated as a standard for self-study purposes. For example, a functional area guideline might include the statement "facilities should include a private office where individual consultations can be held." The study team may decide that this guideline statement, which is not a CAS standard compliance requirement, is imperative at their institution and should therefore be treated as a standard for purposes of their self-study. If

so decided, a criterion measure statement such as "private office space is available for staff members to use for consultation purposes" would be inserted as a criterion measure to be rated along with the other criterion measures included in the SAG and evaluated accordingly.

2. Initiating the Self-Study

It is suggested that team members use the CAS Functional Area Self-Assessment Guide (SAG) to implement the self-study. When used, the initial step is for members to rate the criterion measures individually and then collectively to make judgments about how well the program meets the criteria. The SAG provides a 4-point scale from Not Met to Fully Met for rating the criterion measures, which reflect the essence of the standards.

3. Identify and Summarize Evaluative Evidence

Judging the program by rating it against the standard's criterion measures and identifying program strengths and weaknesses does not represent a completed self-study. Rather, the process requires documentation of the evidence that supports each criterion measure rating. The nature of such documentary evidence may be quantitative, qualitative, or, most typically, a combination of the two. For example, quantitative measures might include the staff-to-student ratio for a given activity, an analysis of the cost-effectiveness of a given activity, or the results of a developmental task assessment of student learning and development outcome achievement. Qualitative documentation, on the other hand, might include notes on the process used to develop the program's mission or outcome objectives or structured interviews with students. Essential documentation includes relevant publications (e.g., student and staff handbooks), program descriptions (e.g., career decision-making workshop outlines), program evaluation data (e.g., program assessment results), institutional data (e.g., student profiles), and self-study initiated research (e.g., student survey or focus group results). No self-study can be considered complete without relevant data and related documentation to support and validate the team's judgments. These data can be collected over time and stored in a database for self-study purposes. Such data also have utility for preparing annual reports.

Following the rating and review procedure, it is desirable for the study team to invite the full staff to review and discuss the team's interim assessment of program compliance with the standards. This approach provides opportunity to inform all staff members of the team's evaluation and permits all staff members to explore together how well the program appears to be accomplishing its stated purpose. Through this process, team members may be exposed to alternative interpretations of the study results-to-date and obtain additional insight into the program from the perspective of others.

The Program section of the CAS standards for every functional area includes learning and development outcome domains for which programs must demonstrate outcomes. The CAS Frameworks for Assessing Learning and Development Outcomes (FALDOs), the companion publication to this book, are designed to assist practitioners in designing effective assessments of the designated outcomes.

4. Identify Discrepancies

Study team members should compare their ratings and interpretations of program characteristics, accomplishments, strengths, and shortcomings against the criteria expressed in the standard. Further, the study team should carefully review each criterion measure and related practice that the study team rated as Not Done, Unsatisfactory, or where rated discrepancies of two or more were noted. A specific rationale should be prepared for each shortcoming identified.

When discrepancies are noted between the assessment criteria and actual practice, it is possible to identify existing operational problems that need resolution. For example, each standard calls for the existence of a program mission statement consistent with the nature and goals of the institution. If the program has no written mission statement or an outdated one, then the discrepancy between the standard and actual program practice clearly calls for the creation of a current, relevant program mission statement that is consistent with the institution's mission.

5. Determine Appropriate Corrective Action

The self-study team should describe in detail the adjustments that need to be implemented for the program to achieve the quality and effectiveness to which it aspires. For example, returning to the example of the program mission, the action required would call for program staff members to draft a statement delineating the elements they believe are agreed upon, circulate them for review and comment, and then prepare and disseminate a final program mission statement to guide the program and its services.

An important point to note in regard to corrective action is the importance of subdividing the overall task into manageable parts that can be accomplished in step-by-step fashion. Trying to revise a total functional area in one step is neither a desirable nor an effective approach to program development. It is important that the study team list specific actions identified in the self-study that require implementation. It is also desirable to set priorities on the list by order of importance, need, and achievability of the desired change.

6. Recommend Steps for Program Enhancement

Even excellent programs can be further refined to provide more desirable and effective outcomes. Action in this regard is particularly relevant for programs in which self-study team members identified selected guidelines calling for enhanced functioning. Unless staff members are satisfied with meeting basic standards only, additional initiatives can be implemented to enhance program quality and effectiveness. This can be accomplished by listing each specific action identified in the self-study that would enhance and strengthen services and setting priorities among them for follow-up purposes.

7. Prepare an Action Plan

As the self-study process comes to closure, it is important for staff members to identify and establish priorities to influence the program's future directions. This represents a process of comparing past performance with desired outcomes and can best be accomplished by carefully reviewing the actual self-study process that was conducted to ensure that all relevant program issues are addressed. The post-self-assessment action plan should acknowledge the program's strengths as well as its shortcomings as it moves toward establishing a strategic approach for correcting deficiencies and initiating enhancements. The primary goal of this final step is to identify and set priorities for future actions and directions, after comparing the results of the self-study with the outcomes to which the program aspires.

The process for preparing a final program action plan consists of preparing a comprehensive action plan for implementing program changes, identifying resources (i.e., human, fiscal, physical) that are essential to program enhancement, establishing dates by which specific actions are to be completed, identifying responsible parties to complete the action steps, and setting a tentative start-up date for initiating a subsequent self-study.

For those interested in obtaining additional information and training on the self-assessment process described above, CAS has prepared an e-learning program that is incorporated into the CAS Self-Assessment Guides CD ROM; information is available on the CAS website, www.cas.edu.

Other Uses of the CAS Standards

In addition to the model presented for full program self-study, the CAS standards are a resource that can be used for a number of other purposes. The uses outlined below are representative; since the standards and guidelines are tools to be used by practitioners, there are not really "wrong" ways to use them, as long as the values and spirit underlying them are honored.

Design of New Programs and Services

As student and institutional needs change, the opportunity may arise to develop a new program or service on campus, or to restructure existing areas. In doing so, it is helpful to have criteria to serve as an outline to guide planning. The functional area standards and guidelines can serve as a helpful resource when such planning is needed.

Staff Development

Staff members can study the various criteria to determine how well they and their colleagues are implementing the standards in their daily work with students. The relevant functional area standards can be used as an orientation device to assist new professionals in understanding their area, as a point of discussion for supervisors and staff to discuss program strengths and weaknesses, as a resource for educating others at the institution about what is involved in a sound program, or as the format by which annual program reports are prepared. The more the CAS standards are used within a division or institution, the more it will lead to a common language and shared perception of the elements of good practice.

The most comprehensive staff development program, using one of the functional area standards and guidelines as a training device, may require from six to twelve hours of meeting time during which staff members share responsibility for leading discussions about the standard's various components. This approach is particularly valuable when a program self-study is in the offing. In such an instance, staff members can both learn how CAS standards can be used to guide and influence good practice and how they can provide a vehicle for implementing a program self-study. Training staff members before conducting a self-study typically produces a more comprehensive and valuable program evaluation.

Academic Preparation

The CAS standards have another valuable educational function when used as a resource in formal academic preparation programs, especially in an introductory course concerned with student support functions common to institutions of higher learning. The 34 CAS functional area standards and their accompanying contextual statements, as well as the statements regarding individual

characteristics and shared ethical principles, all presented in Part 2 of this book, provide an excellent primer for those entering the fields of student affairs and higher education administration. The contextual statements summarize the roles and functions of key program and service units, their primary purposes, historical perspectives, and relevant resources available to explore the areas in greater detail. These succinct summary statements provide an introduction for those unfamiliar with the areas under study. The CAS standards provide an in-depth description of the characteristics common to and expected of the various functional areas.

For students who desire to examine a given functional area in greater detail or participate in a practicum, internship, or externship experience, the CAS Self-Assessment Guide (SAG) provides a unique resource for obtaining a comprehensive understanding. Each functional area SAG includes the standards, guidelines, and criterion measures that can be used to judge the level of compliance a program exhibits in regard to the standards. Using a SAG, students can readily identify a program's strengths and shortcomings. Further, the SAG has utility as a vehicle for both students and supervisors to use for examining together and discussing the various components of the area under study. For learning the basics of student support functions, there is no better information available than that provided by the CAS standards and the complementary Self-Assessment Guides that operationalize the various standards. The *Frameworks for Assessing Learning and Development Outcomes* (FALDOs, published as a companion to this book) offer insight and assistance into developing strategies for the assessment of student learning and development.

Credibility and Accountability

Any profession, along with its practitioners, must exhibit a reasonable level of credibility if it is to survive. Professional entities lacking user confidence will be at best underutilized and may ultimately disappear. In effect, credibility is essential to the existence of all service agencies, including those associated with higher education. Through publication of and adherence to standards of professional practice, institutions seek to assure potential student users and the general public of their competence and credibility. Both laypersons and professionals alike attribute credibility to programs, professions, and institutions that meet stringent standards; compliance with such standards demonstrates that quality is present.

Various means have been established to ensure

accountability and quality assurance. Institutional and academic program credibility is typically established through accreditation, a voluntary process by which agencies encourage and assist institutions and their sub-units (e.g., colleges, schools, departments, and programs) to evaluate and improve their programs and services (Eaton, 2001). The institutions and programs that voluntarily meet or exceed acceptable standards of quality and effectiveness are made public by the accrediting body. It is not uncommon for institutions not possessing accreditation status to be denied federal aid or other resources available to accredited institutions. Graduates of non-accredited institutions may be denied admission to graduate schools or certain employment opportunities. Accreditation is intended to assure the public that an institution and its programs do indeed provide quality education.

However, the general public cannot be assured that individuals who have diplomas, certificates, or degrees from accredited institutions and programs are, in fact, effective practitioners. Consequently, various structures have been established by professional and governmental oversight agencies to judge the professional qualifications of service providers in education, health, and social service areas.

Three primary methods have been established to enable individuals to document their professional qualifications: registry, certification, and licensure. CAS, which is a consortium of higher education professional associations, focuses minimal attention on these credentialing options, although some have encouraged CAS to expand its focus into registry and certification, which are often initiated by non-governmental professional bodies. Licensure, on the other hand, is largely the province of governments. For instance, licenses based on generally comparable criteria are required of physicians, psychologists, and lawyers in all states; counselors, morticians, and engineers, on the other hand, require licenses in only some states and are judged by diverse criteria from state to state. A recent employment criterion trend in some states has been to require college counselors and psychologists to be licensed in order to be eligible for employment. Although not yet fully tested in the courts, such initiatives are likely to increase during the coming decades.

As demand for accountability in higher education increases, so too does demand for practitioner accountability. CAS endorses self-regulation as the most viable approach to program accountability, calling for each institution to initiate a program of self-assessment for its student support programs, services, and personnel. Whether student support units are administratively assigned to student affairs, academic affairs, business affairs, or elsewhere in the organizational hierarchy,

CAS encourages program review and evaluation on a continuing basis using the CAS standards. From this perspective, self-regulation becomes a preferred strategy to establish and maintain credibility. When deemed appropriate and desirable, the various functional areas could invite representatives from peer institutions to review their self-assessment reports as part of the validation process. Self-regulation requires institutions and their leaders to establish their own policies and procedures for institutional assessment and evaluation and to adhere to them when evaluating quality and effectiveness. Thus, through continuing assessment, institutions can compile and maintain in databases the internal documentation required by regional accrediting bodies and governmental oversight agencies. Self-regulation provides institutions and their student support programs with tools to achieve and evidence quality assurance. In effect, if institutions accept responsibility for initiating meaningful and well considered assessment processes and procedures, there is less likelihood that external oversight agencies, governmental or otherwise, will seek to do so.

Example Applications

The following is a summary of examples of how CAS standards have been applied in practice and for purposes of professional staff development.

Institutional Program Review

From an institutional perspective, many practitioners view the CAS standards as a staple for conducting comprehensive program reviews. One institution's policy requires that a standard external to the institution be used to implement periodic comprehensive program reviews. Because CAS standards are readily available, easily understood, and simple to use, they are often the standard of choice for administrative unit reviews. The fact that operational versions of the standards in the form of CAS Self-Assessment Guides (SAGs) are also available has increased both the availability and ease with which the standards can be used for program review purposes. In addition, the very presence of the CAS standards typically informs practitioners that professional practice is neither ad hoc nor layman's work. Rather, it consists of the application of the collective wisdom of the profession and is subject to assessment and regulation.

Program Development and Advocacy

From a programmatic perspective, the CAS standards have special utility, especially for emerging student support areas. For example, educators responsible for guiding programs of learning assistance and developmental education tend to exhibit strong commitment to promoting the use of professional standards in their ranks. Many leaders in this arena literally "invented" their programs and learned from each other what worked best to produce quality outcomes. During the past decade, the CAS Learning Assistance Programs Standards and Guidelines has become a shared document among learning assistance practitioners. Leaders in this arena have indicated that the CAS standards provided a common ground to unite those responsible for ensuring that students received the special attention and support they needed to be successful.

From another program-specific perspective, two important uses of the standards in addition to the self-assessment function were identified, one as a guide for initiating new programs and the other for advocacy. On virtually a weekly basis, the National Clearinghouse for Commuter Programs (NCCP) receives requests from institutions desiring to establish on-campus commuter programs. Most practitioners interested in such initiatives fail initially to comprehend the scope of the functions essential to a comprehensive program. Often, the initiator is interested in establishing a particular type of program (e.g., peer mentoring, orientation for commuters) or service (e.g., off-campus housing referral, commuter newsletter). When such requests are made, the CAS standards are readily available as a professionally sanctioned tool that provides guidance to those interested in providing support for such populations.

Advocacy was a second use noted, because it is often helpful when consulting with colleagues about student support programs to make a case for broadening the administrators' understanding of what is required to meet the basic essentials. All too often, campus administrators tend to limit their initial thinking about a new program to relatively mundane issues such as access, and not to think in terms of how a new program could help students become better integrated into the campus community or enhance their learning and development. The CAS standards have great utility for opening institutional leaders' eyes to the importance of comprehensive programming and grasping a broader view.

From another professional association perspective, the Association of Fraternity Advisors [AFA] discovered that standards can be extremely beneficial in relating association purpose to the broader mission of higher education and those of various institutions. Association leaders determined that when colleagues utilized the CAS standards to establish or reorganize various student support services, those program changes were not challenged because the standards provided a recognized level of credibility that did not exist prior to the availability of the CAS standards.

Professional Preparation

From the perspective of graduate education, many preparation programs have integrated the CAS standards into their curricula. Often, the concept of quality assurance is quite vague to graduate students, especially at the master's level. However, the idea of applying standards to practice is more concrete and students can quickly come to understand the role, function, and utility of professional standards. Thus, even beginning students can begin to internalize the professional interests of self-regulation and improvement. Many college student affairs academic programs have incorporated the CAS standards into their practicum and internship experiential components. Students complete a "mini-self-study" of the functional areas to which they are assigned as part of their practical field-work experiences. This not only ensures that future practitioners know about the existence of the CAS standards, but also provides them with direct experience that enhances their ability to put the standards into practice as they move into entry level positions.

CAS Initiatives

The Council for the Advancement of Standards in Higher Education was established as a profession-wide collaborative body to develop and promulgate professional standards and to inform those responsible for providing higher education with information about how to use standards effectively. CAS functional area standards were created as living, evolving documents. The Council established a five-year review program to ensure that each standard undergoes regular review and updating. Protocols to guide the development of new and the revision of existing standards are in place and appear in Appendix B. These protocols identify the processes, participants, and procedures used by CAS to create and review its standards. Completion of a typical standard review takes approximately one year from initiation to Board adoption. It takes slightly longer to complete a new standard because an initial draft must be written before the CAS review process can be initiated. Because of the complex and often laborious nature of standards development, the process is very time consuming. Historically, by the time a functional area standard has undergone the long and arduous development and review, the CAS Board of Directors has nearly always been unanimous in its decision to adopt a new or revised standard.

In the rich discussions that emerge around the Board table, other issues or needs are sometimes identified. When ideas emerge that are found to be within the scope and purpose of CAS, projects to support and enhance the work of CAS are undertaken. This is the genesis of the projects that have developed into the SAGs, the

FALDOs, the Characteristics of Individual Excellence, the Statement of Shared Ethical Principles, and the CAS National Symposium.

In addition to its primary purpose to develop and promulgate professional standards, CAS takes seriously its responsibility to inform and educate the higher education community and the public about the importance of professional standards and their utility for institutional and program self-assessment. Over the years, CAS Board members have represented the Council in numerous conferences, workshops, and instructional activities designed to inform members of the higher education community about CAS initiatives and instruct practitioners in using the standards. Most of the CAS member associations have periodically included CAS-related presentations and training workshops in their conference programs. On several occasions, CAS representatives have made presentations at the annual American Association of Higher Education Assessment Forum, and in 2002 CAS was represented at the European Association of Institutional Research in Prague. Likewise, CAS has sponsored a series of assessment workshops designed to instruct higher education personnel in the use of CAS standards in combination with regional accrediting criteria when implementing institutional accreditation self-studies. In 2006, CAS initiated the first CAS National Symposium to further educate participants on the implementation of the CAS approach and materials.

The CAS standards provide an important tool that expresses to students, faculty, and administrators alike the complex and vital nature of student support programs and services and their relationship to student learning and development. There are ample indications within higher education that there exists a lack of understanding about the importance of creating supportive, health engendering environments for students as an important condition that enhances the higher education experiences. Over the years, those providing students with basic educational support services have often been viewed as secondary or supplemental participants in achieving the academic mission, rather than integral to it. The creation of clearly articulated professional standards has gone far to deepen the understanding of faculty and administrative colleagues and to increase their confidence in the valuable educational and developmental role that student support service providers offer students.

Note: The preceding section was adapted from previous editions and was originally authored by Ted K. Miller.

CAS **Preamble**
Approved by CAS Board of Directors
November 18, 1994
Washington, DC

Let us raise a standard to which the wise and honest can repair.   George Washington, 1787

The CAS *Purpose*

The Council for the Advancement of Standards in Higher Education (CAS) develops and promulgates standards that enhance the quality of a student's total learning experience in higher education. CAS is a consortium of associations in higher education whose representatives achieve consensus on the nature and application of standards that guide the work of practitioners. CAS derives its authority from the prestige and traditional influence of its member associations and from the consensus of those members in establishing requirements for high-quality practice.

The CAS philosophy is grounded in beliefs about excellence in higher education, collaboration between teacher and learner, ethics in educational practice, student development as a major goal of higher education, and student responsibility for learning. Taken together, these beliefs about practice shape the vision for all CAS endeavors.

The beliefs about excellence require that all programs and services in institutions of higher education function at optimum level.

The beliefs about collaboration require that learning be accomplished in concert by students and educators.

The beliefs about ethics require that all programs and services be carried out in an environment of integrity and high ideals.

The beliefs about student development require that the student be considered as a whole person in the context of a diverse population and a diversity of institutions, that outcomes of education be comprehensive, and that the total environment be structured to create opportunities for student involvement and learning.

The beliefs about responsibility require that the institution recognize the rights and responsibilities of students as its citizens and that it provide an array of resources and learning opportunities that enable students to exercise their responsibility to take full advantage of them.

CAS collectively develops, examines, and endorses standards and guidelines for program and service areas in higher education. The CAS approach to ensuring quality educational experiences is anchored in the assumption that its standards and guidelines can be used in a variety of ways to enhance institutional quality. They can, for example, be used for design of programs and services, for determination of the efficacy of programs, for staff development designed to enhance the skills of those providing professional services, for programmatic self-assessment to assure institutional effectiveness, and for self-regulation purposes.

Background

The Council for the Advancement of Standards in Higher Education was established in 1979 as the Council for the Advancement of Standards for Student Services/Development Programs, a consortium of professional associations representing student affairs practitioners committed to assuring quality programs and services for students. Members of nearly 32 established professional associations have directed their interests, talents, and resources to develop and promulgate professional standards and guidelines based on state-of-the-art thinking about educational programs and services. From the beginning, CAS has employed an open process of consensus-building among the representatives of member associations as the primary tool for producing its standards and guidelines.

The Council published the original set of 16 functional area standards and the academic preparation standards in 1986, with a grant from American College Testing (ACT). In 1988, CAS developed a Self-Assessment Guide (SAG) for each set of functional area standards to facilitate program assessment and evaluation. Each SAG is an operational version of a functional area standard designed to provide practitioners with a detailed instrument for self-assessment.

The Council's current name and expanded mission were adopted in 1992, to be inclusive of all programs for students in higher education, including those serving undergraduate, graduate, traditional, and nontraditional students. CAS now oversees the development of standards for new service areas and the systematic review and periodic revision of existing standards and guidelines.

The CAS Approach to Self-Regulation and Self-Assessment

Self-regulation is an internally motivated and directed institutional process devoted to the creation, maintenance, and enhancement of high-quality programs and services. CAS believes this approach is preferable to externally motivated regulation, because those within an institution generally have the clearest perceptions of its mission, goals, resources, and capabilities. The essential elements of self-regulation include:

- Institutional culture that values involvement of all its members in decision making,
- Quality indicators that are determined by the institution,
- Use of standards and guidelines in quality assurance,
- Collection and analysis of data on institutional performance, and
- Commitment to continuing improvement that presupposes freedom to explore and develop alternative directions for the future.

The success of self-regulation depends on mutual respect between an institution and its members. Within the self-regulated institution, individual accomplishments are valued, goals are based on shared vision, systems are open and interactive, processes are carried out in a climate of mutual trust and caring, conflicts are mediated in the best interests of the entire community, and achievements are recognized and rewarded. Such an environment stimulates individual and group initiatives and fosters self-determination of goals. In a self-regulating environment, members identify quality indicators in consultation with a variety of internal and external constituencies and stakeholders, including professional associations.

These indicators may include professionally derived standards, such as those of CAS, which comprise the views of many professional practitioners and professional associations. Self-regulation relies on the willingness and capacity of the organization to examine itself meticulously, faithfully, and reliably, and then to assemble the pertinent results of that examination into coherent reports that constituents can comprehend and use. Such reports are essential for recording the evidence assembled in self-study, for displaying synthesis and analysis of information, for fostering the broad participation of members in the self-regulation process, and for registering benchmark results and conclusions for future reference.

Finally, the self-regulation process relies on the institution's capacity to modify its own practices as needed. A culture that supports self-regulation must operate in a climate that permits members to make independent choices among reasonable alternatives. These choices constitute a commitment to constant improvement of educational practices and of the health of the organization.

References

American College Personnel Association (ACPA). (March/April 1996). Special issue: The student learning imperative. *Journal of College Student Development, 37*(2).

Council for the Advancement of Standards (CAS). (1986). *CAS standards and guidelines for student service/development programs.* Iowa City: American College Testing Program.

Eaton, J. S. (March/April 2001). Regional accreditation reform: Who is served? *Change Magazine,* 39-45.

Miller, T. K., & Prince, J. S. (1976). *The future of student affairs: A guide to student development for tomorrow's higher education.* San Francisco: Jossey-Bass.

CAS Characteristics of Individual Excellence for Professional Practice in Higher Education

CAS Contextual Statement

Defining competencies of student affairs and other professionals in higher education who plan, implement, and offer programs and services is the mark of a maturing profession. A number of authors and organizations have framed competencies in several broad areas. For example, Pope, Reynolds, and Mueller (2004) identified competencies in the areas of 1) administration and management, 2) multicultural awareness, knowledge, and skills, 3) helping and advising, 4) assessment and research, 5) teaching and training, 6) ethics and professional standards, and 7) translation and use of theory to guide practice. This document seeks to define a list of necessary attributes for professionals in higher education that is broader than competencies and includes other markers of professionalism. These characteristics of excellence can be used in an evaluative format, both self evaluation and in the context of "360 degree" (Tornow, London, & Associates, 1998) or supervisory format.

There are numerous purposes for the creation and use of this document. One purpose is to move the student affairs profession and other professionals within the higher education context to more concrete, concise, and agreed upon characteristics that are expected of professionals who provide, implement, and facilitate programs and services in higher education. Another purpose is to assist in the enculturation of new professionals into the profession by defining what it means to be a professional in higher education. This document also seeks to clarify the context within which people are choosing to work. In response to the literature on supervision that indicates that supervision in higher education is often irregular and when it does occur stresses operational tasks rather than professional development (Arminio & Creamer, 2001; Saunders, Cooper, Winston, & Chernow, 2000; Winston & Creamer, 1997), this document was created to provide aspirational expectations for higher education professionals (Carpenter, 2003).

Because it is the intent of this document to honor individual differences that people bring to their practice, when perceived differences from the expected characteristics are identified these differences need to be discussed. It is through these discussions with supervisors and colleagues that such differences can be acknowledged and their implications explored.

This document offers direction for professional development whether prompted by self evaluation or from supervisory evaluation. In either case, this document is intended to be used in collaboration and discussion with a supervisor, supervisees, students, and/or colleagues. From these discussions an individual professional development plan can be created and then movement toward accomplishing that plan be evaluated.

References

Arminio, J. & Creamer, D. G. (2001). What quality supervisors say about quality supervision. *College Student Affairs Journal, 21*, 35-44.

Carpenter, D. S. (2003). Professionalism. In S. R. Komives & D. Woodard Jr (Eds.). *Student services: A handbook for the profession* (4th edition; pp. 573-592). San Francisco: Jossey-Bass.

Pope, R. L., Reynolds, A. L., & Mueller, J. A. (2004). *Multicultural competence in student affairs.* San Francisco: Jossey-Bass.

Saunders, S. A., Cooper, D. L. Winston, R. B. Jr., & Chernow, E. (2000). Supervising staff in student affairs: Exploration of the synergistic approach. *Journal of College Student Development, 41*, 1281-191.

Tornow, W. W., London, M., & Associates (1998). *Maximizing the value of 360-degree feedback.* San Francisco: Jossey bass.

Winston, R. B., Jr., & Creamer, D. G. (1997). *Improving staffing practices in student affairs.* San Francisco: Jossey-Bass.

CAS Characteristics of Individual Excellence for Professional Practice in Higher Education

Evaluating individual professional practice in higher education requires the identification of ideal performance characteristics that describe excellence in professional practice. This document has evolved from multi-faceted professional competencies that are inherent in the purpose, development, and application of the CAS Standards and Guidelines. It assumes a philosophy and practice of life-long learning and professional development shared by individual practitioners and their institutions. Characteristics are grouped into **General Knowledge and Skills**, **Interactive Competencies**, and **Self Mastery**.

General Knowledge and Skills

General Knowledge:

1. Understands and supports the broad responsibility of the institution for enhancing the collegiate experience for all students

2. Possesses appropriate knowledge of relevant theories, literature, and philosophies on which to base informed professional practice

3. Knows values, historical context, and current issues of one's profession

4. Has developed, can articulate, and acts consistently with a sound educational philosophy consistent with the institution's mission

5. Understands and respects similarities and differences of people in the institutional environment

6. Understands relevant legal issues

General Skills:

7. Manages and influences campus environments that promote student success

8. Works to create campus and related educational environments that are safe and secure

9. Effectively utilizes language through speaking, writing, and other means of communication

10. Engages disparate audiences effectively

11. Teaches effectively directly or through example

12. Thinks critically about complex issues

13. Works collaboratively

14. Is trustworthy and maintains confidentiality

15. Exercises responsible stewardship of resources

16. Engages in evaluation and assessment to determine outcomes and identify areas for improvement

17. Uses technology effectively for educational and institutional purposes

18. Bases decisions on appropriate data

19. Models effective leadership

Interactive Competencies

With Students:

20. Counsels, advises, supervises, and leads individuals and groups effectively

21. Knows the developmental effects of college on students

22. Knows characteristics of students attending institutions of higher education

23. Knows students who attend the institution, use services, and participants in programs

24. Interacts effectively with a diverse range of students

25. Provides fair treatment to all students and works to change aspects of the environment that do not promote fair treatment

26. Values differences among groups of students and between individuals; helps students understand the interdependence among people both locally and globally

27. Actively and continually pursues insight into the cultural heritage of students

28. Encourages student learning through successful experiences as well as failures

With Colleagues and the Institution:

29. Supervises others effectively

30. Manages fiscal, physical, and human resources responsibly and effectively

31. Judges the performance of self and others fairly

32. Contributes productively in partnerships and team efforts

33. Demonstrates loyalty and support of the institution where employed

34. Behaves in ways that reflect integrity, responsibility, honesty, and with accurate representation of self, others, and program

35. Creates and maintains campus relationships characterized by integrity and responsibility

36. Effectively creates and maintains networks among colleagues locally, regionally, nationally, and internationally

37. Contributes to campus life and supports activities that promote campus community

continued

18

Self Mastery

38. Commits to excellence in all work

39. Intentionally employs self reflection to improve practice and gain insight

40. Responds to the duties of one's role and also to the spirit of one's responsibilities

41. Views his or her professional life as an important element of personal identity

42. Strives to maintain personal wellness and a healthy lifestyle

43. Maintains position-appropriate appearance

44. Stays professionally current by reading literature, building skills, attending conferences, enhancing technological literacy, and engaging in other professional development activities

45. Manages personal life so that overall professional effectiveness is maintained

46. Belongs to and contributes to activities of relevant professional associations

47. Assumes proper accountability for individual and organizational mistakes

48. Espouses and follows a written code of professional ethical standards

49. Abides by laws and institutional policies and works to change policies that are incongruent with personal and professional principles

50. Re-evaluates continued employment when personal, professional, and institutional goals and values are incompatible and inhibit the pursuit of excellence

Developed and approved in 2006

CAS Statement of Shared Ethical Principles

The Council for the Advancement of Standards in Higher Education (CAS) has served as a voice for quality assurance and promulgation of standards in higher education for over twenty five years. CAS was established to promote inter-association efforts to address quality assurance, student learning, and professional integrity. It was believed that a single voice would have greater impact on the evaluation and improvement of services and programs than would many voices speaking for special interests by individual practitioners or by single-interest organizations.

CAS includes membership of over 35 active professional associations and has established standards in over 30 functional areas. It has succeeded in providing a platform through which representatives from across higher education can jointly develop and promulgate standards of good practice that are endorsed not just by those working in a particular area, but by representatives of higher education association.

CAS often cites George Washington, who said, "Let us raise a standard to which the wise and honest can repair." CAS has raised standards; it is now time to focus on the attributes, such as wisdom and honesty, of those professionals who would use the standards. Professionals working to provide services in higher education share more than a commitment to quality assurance and standards of practice. A review of the ethical statements of member associations demonstrates clearly that there are elements of ethical principles and values that are shared across the professions in higher education.

Most of the member associations represented in CAS are guided by ethical codes of professional practice enforced through the prescribed channels of its association. CAS acknowledges and respects the individual codes and standards of ethical conduct of their organizations. From these codes, CAS has created a statement of shared ethical principles that focuses on seven basic principles that form the foundation for CAS member association codes: autonomy, non-malfeasance, beneficence, justice, fidelity, veracity, and affiliation. This statement is not intended to replace or supplant the code of ethics of any professional association; rather, it is intended to articulate those shared ethical principles. It is our hope that by articulating those shared beliefs, CAS can promulgate a better understanding of the professions of those in service to students and higher education.

Principle I - Autonomy
We take responsibility for our actions and both support and empower an individual's and group's freedom of choice.

- We strive for quality and excellence in the work that we do
- We respect one's freedom of choice
- We believe that individuals, ourselves and others, are responsible for their own behavior and learning
- We promote positive change in individuals and in society through education
- We foster an environment where people feel empowered to make decisions
- We hold ourselves and others accountable
- We study, discuss, investigate, teach, conduct research, and publish freely within the academic community
- We engage in continuing education and professional development

Principle II – Non-Malfeasance
We pledge to do no harm.

- We collaborate with others for the good of those whom we serve
- We interact in ways that promote positive outcomes
- We create environments that are educational and supportive of the growth and development of the whole person
- We exercise role responsibilities in a manner that respects the rights and property of others without exploiting or abusing power

Principle III - Beneficence
We engage in altruistic attitudes and actions that promote goodness and contribute to the health and welfare of others.

- We treat others courteously
- We consider the thoughts and feelings of others
- We work toward positive and beneficial outcomes

Principle IV - Justice
We actively promote human dignity and endorse equality and fairness for everyone.

- We treat others with respect and fairness,

preserving their dignity, honoring their differences, promoting their welfare

- We recognize diversity and embrace a cross-cultural approach in support of the worth, dignity, potential, and uniqueness of people within their social and cultural contexts
- We eliminate barriers that impede student learning and development or discriminate against full participation by all students
- We extend fundamental fairness to all persons
- We operate within the framework of laws and policies
- We respect the rights of individuals and groups to express their opinions
- We assess students in a valid, open, and fair manner and one consistent with learning objectives
- We examine the influence of power on the experience of diversity to reduce marginalization and foster community

Principle V - Fidelity

We are faithful to an obligation, trust, or duty.

- We maintain confidentiality of interactions, student records, and information related to legal and private matters
- We avoid conflicts of interest or the appearance thereof
- We honor commitments made within the guidelines of established policies and procedures
- We demonstrate loyalty and commitment to institutions that employ us
- We exercise good stewardship of resources

Principle VI - Veracity

We seek and convey the truth in our words and actions.

- We act with integrity and honesty in all endeavors and interactions
- We relay information accurately
- We communicate all relevant facts and information while respecting privacy and confidentiality

Principle VII – Affiliation

We actively promote connected relationships among all people and foster community.

- We create environments that promote connectivity
- We promote authenticity, mutual empathy, and engagement within human interactions

When professionals act in accordance with ethical principles, program quality and excellence are enhanced and ultimately students are better served. As professionals providing services in higher education, we are committed to upholding these shared ethical principles, for the benefit of our students, our professions, and higher education.

Some concepts for this code were taken from:

Kitchner, K. 1985). Ethical principles and ethical decisions in student affairs. In H. Canon & R. Brown (Eds.), *Applied ethics in student services* (New Directions in Student Services, No. 30, pp. 17-30). San Francisco: Jossey-Bass.

Developed and adopted in 2006

THE ROLE of the *CAS* GENERAL STANDARDS in FUNCTIONAL AREA STANDARDS AND GUIDELINES

The Council for the Advancement of Standards in Higher Education (CAS) was established in 1979 as a consortium of professional associations whose members championed student learning and development in a variety of functional areas. From the outset, CAS identified its primary mission as the development and promulgation of professional standards that higher education practitioners could use to guide, develop, and assess programs and services. By 1986, with a repayable grant from the American College Testing Program (ACT), CAS had created 16 sets of functional area standards and published them in the first *CAS "Blue Book."* It was clear by the time of the initial publication that there were a number of characteristics common to all functional areas, commonalties that demanded inclusion in all current and future CAS standards. As a result, a set of *boilerplate, General Standards* were devised that CAS Board members unanimously agreed were relevant to all the student learning and development programs championed by CAS member associations. As the CAS General Standards evolved over the years, the Council consistently held to the principle that the fundamental commonalities underlying student learning and development are of the essence and must be maintained within the context of all CAS standards.

The most recent major revision of the General Standards was adopted by the CAS Board of Directors in 2002. A significant feature of this revision was the increased emphasis placed on achievable, observable, and assessable outcomes associated with student learning and development. Earlier versions of the CAS General Standards included a list of developmental domains (e.g., intellectual growth, effective communication, realistic self-appraisal, clarified values, career choices, leadership, and meaningful interpersonal relationships among others) for functional area programs to consider in their educational efforts. The 2002 revision, however, reaffirmed and reinforced the importance of the specified outcome domains by building into the General Standards a stated expectation that all functional area programs must place emphasis on identifying relevant learning outcomes and assessing their achievement by students.

Those who use CAS standards for program evaluation, development, and enhancement will note the importance of the 16 specified outcome domains and the fact that they are viewed as highly desirable for all functional areas to pursue. To facilitate assessment of the various outcome domains, the General Standards include a table listing the 16 domains along with examples of assessment indicators that can be used to guide the assessment process. The indicators represent examples of observable student behaviors that practitioners can use to judge learning and developmental achievement. CAS has now also published the *Frameworks for Assessing Learning and Development Outcomes* to further assist practitioners in implementing outcomes assessment activities. In effect, the General Standards recognize the potential educational impact that functional area programs can have upon student learning and development and reflect the need for them to emphasize and influence that learning as a significant part of their missions. It is anticipated that over time the student learning and development emphases among student support programs and services will increase and that ultimately these programs that currently complement formal academic learning will become coordinate in status as a recognized vehicle for student learning and development.

Although the CAS General Standards were not designed to stand alone, they are presented here to remind and inform educators about the commonalities that exist among the many student support programs and services throughout higher education. There can be little doubt that if those who lead and practice in such programs combine their collective powers to make an educational difference in the lives of the students they serve, the resulting educational trust will carry student support programs and services to new heights of achievement for all concerned.

Contributors:
Current edition: Laura A. Dean, University of Georgia, ACCA
Previous editions: Ted K. Miller, University of Georgia,
ACPA/CAS

CAS General Standards
CAS Standards and Guidelines

Part 1. MISSION

Each program and service in higher education must incorporate student learning and student development in its mission. The program and service must enhance overall educational experiences. The program and service must develop, record, disseminate, implement, and regularly review its mission and goals. Mission statements must be consistent with the mission and goals of the institution and with the standards in this document. The program and service must operate as an integral part of the institution's overall mission.

Part 2. PROGRAM

The formal education of students consists of the curriculum and the co-curriculum, and must promote student learning and development that is purposeful and holistic. Programs and services must identify relevant and desirable student learning and development outcomes and provide programs and services that encourage the achievement of those outcomes.

Relevant and desirable outcomes include: intellectual growth, effective communication, realistic self-appraisal, enhanced self-esteem, clarified values, career choices, leadership development, healthy behaviors, meaningful interpersonal relationships, independence, collaboration, social responsibility, satisfying and productive lifestyles, appreciation of diversity, spiritual awareness, and achievement of personal and educational goals.

Each program and service must provide evidence of its impact on the achievement of student learning and development outcomes.

The table below offers examples of evidence of achievement of student learning and development.

Student Learning and Development Outcome Domains

Intellectual growth
Examples of achievement indicators
> Produces personal and educational goal statements; Employs critical thinking in problem solving; Uses complex information from a variety of sources including personal experience and observation to form a decision or opinion; Obtains a degree; Applies previously understood information and concepts to a new situation or setting; Expresses appreciation for literature, the fine arts, mathematics, sciences, and social sciences

Effective communication
Examples of achievement indicators
> Writes and speaks coherently and effectively; Writes and speaks after reflection; Able to influence others through writing, speaking, or artistic expression; Effectively articulates abstract ideas; Uses appropriate syntax; Makes presentations or gives performances

Enhanced self-esteem
Examples of achievement indicators
> Shows self-respect and respect for others; Initiates actions toward achievement of goals; Takes reasonable risks; Demonstrates assertive behavior; Functions without need for constant reassurance from others

Realistic self-appraisal
Examples of achievement indicators
> Articulates personal skills and abilities; Makes decisions and acts in congruence with personal values; Acknowledges personal strengths and weaknesses; Articulates rationale for personal behavior; Seeks feedback from others; Learns from past experiences

Clarified values
Examples of achievement indicators
> Articulates personal values; Acts in congruence with personal values; Makes decisions that reflect personal values; Demonstrates willingness to scrutinize personal beliefs and values; Identifies personal, work, and lifestyle values and explains how they influence decision-making

Career choices
Examples of achievement indicators
> Articulates career choices based on assessment of interests, values, skills, and abilities; Documents knowledge, skills, and accomplishmens resulting from formal education, work experience, community service, and volunteer experiences; Makes the connections between classroom and out-of-classroom learning; Can construct a resume with clear job objectives and evidence of related knowledge, skills, and accomplishments; Articulates the characteristics of a preferred work environment; Comprehends the world of work; Takes steps to initiate a job search or seek advanced education

Leadership development
Examples of achievement indicators
> Articulates leadership philosophy or style; Serves in a leadership position in a student organization; Comprehends the dynamics of a group; Exhibits democratic principles as a leader; Exhibits ability to visualize a group purpose and desired outcomes

Healthy behavior
Examples of achievement indicators
> Chooses behaviors and environments that promote health and reduce risk; Articulates the relationship between health and wellness and accomplishing life-long goals; Exhibits behaviors that advance a healthy community

Meaningful interpersonal relationships
Examples of achievement indicators
> Develops and maintains satisfying interpersonal

relationships; Establishes mutually rewarding relationships with friends and colleagues; Listens to and considers others' points of view; Treats others with respect

Independence
Examples of achievement indicators
Exhibits self-reliant behaviors; Functions autonomously; Exhibits ability to function interdependently; Accepts supervision as needed; Manages time effectively

Collaboration
Examples of achievement indicators
Works cooperatively with others; Seeks the involvement of others; Seeks feedback from others; Contributes to achievement of a group goal; Exhibits effective listening skills

Social responsibility
Examples of achievement indicators
Understands and participates in relevant governance systems; Understands, abides by, and participates in the development, maintenance, and/or orderly change of community, social, and legal standards or norms; Appropriately challenges the unfair, unjust, or uncivil behavior of other individuals or groups; Participates in service/volunteer activities

Satisfying and productive lifestyles
Examples of achievement indicators
Achieves balance between education, work, and leisure time; Articulates and meets goals for work, leisure, and education; Overcomes obstacles that hamper goal achievement; Functions on the basis of personal identity, ethical, spiritual, and moral values; Articulates long-term goals and objectives

Appreciating diversity
Examples of achievement indicators
Understands one's own identity and culture; Seeks involvement with people different from oneself; Seeks involvement in diverse interests; Articulates the advantages and challenges of a diverse society; Challenges appropriately the abusive use of stereotypes by others; Understands the impact of diversity on one's own society

Spiritual awareness
Examples of achievement indicators
Develops and articulates personal belief system; Understands roles of spirituality in personal and group values and behaviors

Personal and educational goals
Examples of achievement indicators
Sets, articulates, and pursues individual goals; Articulates personal and educational goals and objectives; Uses personal and educational goals to guide decisions; Understands the effect of one's personal and educational goals on others

Programs and services must be (a) intentional, (b) coherent, (c) based on theories and knowledge of learning and human development, (d) reflective of developmental and demographic profiles of the student population, and (e) responsive to needs of individuals, special populations, and communities.

Part 3. LEADERSHIP
Effective and ethical leadership is essential to the success of all organizations. Institutions must appoint, position, and empower leaders within the administrative structure to accomplish stated missions. Leaders at various levels must be selected on the basis of formal education and training, relevant work experience, personal skills and competencies, relevant professional credentials, as well as potential for promoting learning and development in students, applying effective practices to educational processes, and enhancing institutional effectiveness. Institutions must determine expectations of accountability for leaders and fairly assess their performance.

Leaders of programs and services must exercise authority over resources for which they are responsible to achieve their respective missions.

Leaders must:
- articulate a vision for their organization
- set goals and objectives based on the needs and capabilities of the population served
- promote student learning and development
- prescribe and practice ethical behavior
- recruit, select, supervise, and develop others in the organization
- manage financial resources
- coordinate human resources
- plan, budget for, and evaluate personnel and programs
- apply effective practices to educational and administrative processes
- communicate effectively
- initiate collaborative interaction between individuals and agencies that possess legitimate concerns and interests in the functional area

Leaders must identify and find means to address individual, organizational, or environmental conditions that inhibit goal achievement.

Leaders must promote campus environments that result in multiple opportunities for student learning and development.

Leaders must continuously improve programs and services in response to changing needs of students and other constituents, and evolving institutional priorities.

Part 4. ORGANIZATION and MANAGEMENT

Guided by an overarching intent to ensure student learning and development, programs and services must be structured purposefully and managed effectively to achieve stated goals. Evidence of appropriate structure must include current and accessible policies and procedures, written performance expectations for all employees, functional workflow graphics or organizational charts, and clearly stated service delivery expectations.

Evidence of effective management must include use of comprehensive and accurate information for decisions, clear sources and channels of authority, effective communication practices, decision-making and conflict resolution procedures, responsiveness to changing conditions, accountability and evaluation systems, and recognition and reward processes. Programs and services must provide channels within the organization for regular review of administrative policies and procedures.

Part 5. HUMAN RESOURCES

The program and service must be staffed adequately by individuals qualified to accomplish its mission and goals. Within established guidelines of the institution, programs and services must establish procedures for staff selection, training, and evaluation; set expectations for supervision; and provide appropriate professional development opportunities. The program and service must strive to improve the professional competence and skills of all personnel it employs.

Professional staff members must hold an earned graduate degree in a field relevant to the position they hold or must possess an appropriate combination of educational credentials and related work experience.

Degree or credential-seeking interns must be qualified by enrollment in an appropriate field of study and by relevant experience. These individuals must be trained and supervised adequately by professional staff members holding educational credentials and related work experience appropriate for supervision.

Student employees and volunteers must be carefully selected, trained, supervised, and evaluated. They must be trained on how and when to refer those in need of assistance to qualified staff members and have access to a supervisor for assistance in making these judgments. Student employees and volunteers must be provided clear and precise job descriptions, pre-service training based on assessed needs, and continuing staff development.

Each organizational unit must have technical and support staff members adequate to accomplish its mission. Staff members must be technologically proficient and qualified to perform their job functions, be knowledgeable of ethical and legal uses of technology, and have access to training. The level of staffing and workloads must be adequate and appropriate for program and service demands.

Salary levels and fringe benefits for all staff members must be commensurate with those for comparable positions within the institution, in similar institutions, and in the relevant geographic area.

Programs and services must institute hiring and promotion practices that are fair, inclusive, and non-discriminatory. Programs and services must employ a diverse staff to provide readily identifiable role models for students and to enrich the campus community.

Program and services must create and maintain position descriptions for all staff members and provide regular performance planning and appraisals.

Programs and services must have a system for regular staff evaluation and must provide access to continuing education and professional development opportunities, including in-service training programs and participation in professional conferences and workshops.

Part 6. FINANCIAL RESOURCES

Each program and service must have adequate funding to accomplish its mission and goals. Funding priorities must be determined within the context of the stated mission, goals, objectives, and comprehensive analysis of the needs and capabilities of students and the availability of internal or external resources.

Programs and services must demonstrate fiscal responsibility and cost effectiveness consistent with institutional protocols.

Part 7. FACILITIES, TECHNOLOGY, and EQUIPMENT

Each program and service must have adequate, suitably located facilities, adequate technology, and equipment to support its mission and goals efficiently and effectively. Facilities, technology, and equipment must be evaluated regularly and be in compliance with relevant federal, state/provincial, and local requirements to provide for access, health, safety, and security.

Part 8. LEGAL RESPONSIBILITIES

Staff members must be knowledgeable about and responsive to laws and regulations that relate to their respective responsibilities. Staff members must inform users of programs and services and officials, as appropriate, of legal obligations and limitations including constitutional, statutory, regulatory, and case law; mandatory laws and orders emanating from federal, state/provincial, and local governments; and the institution's policies.

Staff members must use reasonable and informed practices to limit the liability exposure of the institution, its officers, employees, and agents. Staff members must be informed about institutional policies regarding personal liability and related insurance coverage options.

The institution must provide access to legal advice for staff members as needed to carry out assigned responsibilities.

The institution must inform staff and students in a timely and systematic fashion about extraordinary or changing legal obligations and potential liabilities.

Part 9. EQUITY and ACCESS

Staff members must ensure that services and programs are provided on a fair and equitable basis. Facilities, programs, and services must be accessible. Hours of operation and delivery of and access to programs and services must be responsive to the needs of all students and other constituents. Each program and service must adhere to the spirit and intent of equal opportunity laws.

Programs and services must be open and readily accessible to all students and must not discriminate except where sanctioned by law and institutional policy. Discrimination must be avoided on the bases of age; color; creed; cultural heritage; disability; ethnicity; gender identity; nationality; political affiliation; religious affiliation; sex; sexual orientation; or social, economic, marital, or veteran status.

Consistent with their mission and goals, programs and services must take affirmative action to remedy significant imbalances in student participation and staffing patterns.

As the demographic profiles of campuses change and new instructional delivery methods are introduced, institutions must recognize the needs of students who participate in distance learning for access to programs and services offered on campus. Institutions must provide appropriate services in ways that are accessible to distance learners and assist them in identifying and gaining access to other appropriate services in their geographic region.

Part 10. CAMPUS and EXTERNAL RELATIONS

Programs and services must establish, maintain, and promote effective relations with relevant individuals, campus offices, and external agencies.

Part 11. DIVERSITY

Within the context of each institution's unique mission, diversity enriches the community and enhances the collegiate experience for all; therefore, programs and services must nurture environments where commonalties and differences among people are recognized and honored.

Programs and services must promote educational experiences that are characterized by open and continuous communication that deepens understanding of one's own identity, culture, and heritage, and that of others. Programs and services must educate and promote respect about commonalties and differences in their historical and cultural contexts.

Programs and services must address the characteristics and needs of a diverse population when establishing and implementing policies and procedures.

Part 12. ETHICS

All persons involved in the delivery of programs and services must adhere to the highest principles of ethical behavior. Programs and services must develop or adopt and implement appropriate statements of ethical practice. Programs and services must publish these statements and ensure their periodic review by relevant constituencies.

Staff members must ensure that privacy and confidentiality are maintained with respect to all communications and records to the extent that such records are protected under the law and appropriate statements of ethical practice. Information contained in students' education records must not be disclosed without written consent except as allowed by relevant laws and institutional policies. Staff members must disclose to appropriate authorities information judged to be of an emergency nature, especially when the safety of the individual or others is involved, or when otherwise required by institutional policy or relevant law.

All staff members must be aware of and comply with the provisions contained in the institution's human subjects research policy and in other relevant institutional policies addressing ethical practices and confidentiality of research data concerning individuals.

Staff members must recognize and avoid personal conflict of interest or appearance thereof in their transactions with students and others.

Staff members must strive to insure the fair, objective, and impartial treatment of all persons with whom they deal. Staff members must not participate in nor condone any form of harassment that demeans persons or creates an intimidating, hostile, or offensive campus environment.

When handling institutional funds, all staff members must ensure that such funds are managed in accordance with established and responsible accounting procedures and the fiscal policies or processes of the institution.

Staff members must perform their duties within the limits of their training, expertise, and competence. When these limits are exceeded, individuals in need of further assistance must be referred to persons possessing appropriate qualifications.

Staff members must use suitable means to confront and otherwise hold accountable other staff members who exhibit unethical behavior.

Staff members must be knowledgeable about and practice ethical behavior in the use of technology.

Part 13. ASSESSMENT and EVALUATION

Programs and services must conduct regular assessment and evaluations. Programs and services must employ effective qualitative and quantitative methodologies as appropriate, to determine whether and to what degree the stated mission, goals, and student learning and development outcomes are being met. The process must employ sufficient and sound assessment measures to ensure comprehensiveness. Data collected must include responses from students and other affected constituencies.

Programs and services must evaluate periodically how well they complement and enhance the institution's stated mission and educational effectiveness.

Results of these evaluations must be used in revising and improving programs and services and in recognizing staff performance.

General Standards were revised and adopted in 2002

THE ROLE of ACADEMIC ADVISING
CAS Standards Contextual Statement

Academic advising is an essential element of a student's collegiate experience. Advising evolves from the institution's culture, values, and practices and is delivered in accordance with these factors. Advising practice draws from various theories and strategies in the social sciences, humanities, and education (e.g., teaching and counseling, the psychology of learning, communication studies, theories of decision making and information transfer, and story telling as a mechanism for understanding human experiences.) "In recent years, increasing political, social and economic demands, along with newly developed technologies, have spurred changes in educational delivery systems, student access, and faculty roles. As a result of these changes, more specialized student support opportunities have emerged, including adaptations in academic advising. And as White (2000) noted with a growing 'number of majors available on college campuses, an increasingly complex and rapidly shifting work environment…, and a dizzyingly extensive array of out-of-class educational experiences to choose from, college students are demanding more and better advising'"(NACADA, 2005).

Academic advising is one of the very few institutional functions that connect all students to the institution. As higher educational curricula become increasingly complex and as educational options expand, pressure to make the academic experience as meaningful as possible for students has increased as well. Higher education, in turn, has responded with renewed attention to the need for quality academic advising.

"Once almost exclusively a faculty function, today academic advising has come forward as a specialization within the higher education community. While remaining a role that faculty members play, academic advising has emerged as an area of expertise in and of itself" (NACADA, 2005). Habley (2005) expounds the notion that "advising bears the distinction of being the only structured activity on campus in which all students have the opportunity for on-going, one-to-one interaction with a concerned representative of the institution, and this fact is a source of its tremendous potential today" (NACADA, 2005). This, coupled with increasing educational options, has brought pressure to make the student educational experiences as meaningful as possible.

The establishment of the National Academic Advising Association (NACADA) following the first national conference on advising in 1977 was a significant turning point in according recognition to those within higher education who consider their work in academic advising as purposeful and unique. Today, NACADA flourishes with membership numbering more than 9100 and national and regional meetings that attract more than 6000 participants annually. The NACADA Statement of Core Values, last revised in 2004, meets the need for ethical principles to guide advising practice and provides a professional framework for all academic advisors to examine their behaviors.

Academic advising became a significant category within professional literature during the 1980s, and this trend continues today. NACADA publishes the *NACADA Journal*, a juried research journal, along with books, monographs, videos and CDs that examine various aspects of advising. Some of the most referenced resources in the field include *Academic Advising: A comprehensive handbook, The Status of Academic Advising: The Findings from the ACT Sixth National Survey,* the *Guide to Assessment in Academic Advising,* and the resources found on the Web from the *NACADA Clearinghouse of Academic Advising Resources.* Information about NACADA's publications, as well as a link to the *Clearinghouse,* can be located electronically via the NACADA web site on the World Wide Web at www.nacada.ksu.edu. The NACADA Executive Office is an excellent source of general information.

Academic advising is a crucial component of all students' experiences in higher education. Within this context, students can find meaning in their lives, make significant decisions about the future, be supported to achieve to their maximum potential, and access all that higher education has to offer. When practiced with competence and dedication, academic advising can enhance retention rates. In an age often characterized by impersonality and detachment, academic advising provides a vital personal connection that students need.

References, Readings, and Resources

Campbell, S., Nutt, C., Robbins, R. Kirk-Kuwaye, M. and Higa, L. (2005). *Guide to Assessment in Academic Advising.* Manhattan, KS: National Academic Advising Association.

Gordon, V.M., & Habley, W. R. (Eds.). (2000). *Academic advising: A comprehensive handbook.* San Francisco: Jossey-Bass.

Habley, W. R. (2004). *The Status of Academic Advising: Findings from the ACT Sixth National Survey.* Manhattan, KS: National Academic Advising Association.

Habley, W.R. (August, 2005). Foundations of academic advising. Presentation. 2005 NACADA Summer Institute.

NACADA. (2004). Statement of Core Values. Retrieved January 24, 2006 from http://www.nacada.ksu.edu/Clearinghouse/AdvisingIssues/Core-Values.htm

NACADA. (2005). The History and Definitions of Academic Advising. In *What is Academic Advising: Foundation of Academic Advising CD Series.* Manhattan, KS: National Academic Advising Association.

NACADA. (2006). Clearinghouse of Academic Advising Resources. Retrieved January 24, 2005 from http://www.nacada.ksu.edu/Resources/index.htm.

White, E. R. (2000). Developing Mission, Goals, and Objectives for the Advising Program. In V.N. Gordon & W.R. Habley (Eds.), *Academic advising: A comprehensive handbook* (pp. 180-191). San Francisco: Jossey-Bass.

Contributors: Eric R. White, The Pennsylvania State University, NACADA
Charlie Nutt, NACADA, with input from Marsha Miller, NACADA
Previous editions: Linda C. Higginson, The Pennsylvania State University

ACADEMIC ADVISING PROGRAMS
CAS Standards and Guidelines

Part 1. MISSION

The primary purpose of the Academic Advising Program (AAP) is to assist students in the development of meaningful educational plans.

AAP must incorporate student learning and student development in its mission. AAP must enhance overall educational experiences. AAP must develop, record, disseminate, implement, and regularly review its mission and goals. Its mission statement must be consistent with the mission and goals of the institution and with the standards in this document. AAP must operate as an integral part of the institution's overall mission.

The institution must have a clearly written mission statement pertaining to academic advising that must include program goals and expectations of advisors and advisees.

Part 2. PROGRAM

The formal education of students is purposeful, holistic, and consists of the curriculum and the co-curriculum. The Academic Advising Program (AAP) must identify relevant and desirable student learning and development outcomes and provide programs and services that encourage the achievement of those outcomes.

Relevant and desirable outcomes include: intellectual growth, effective communication, realistic self-appraisal, enhanced self-esteem, clarified values, career choices, leadership development, healthy behaviors, meaningful interpersonal relations, independence, collaboration, social responsibility, satisfying and productive lifestyles, appreciation of diversity, spiritual awareness, and achievement of personal and educational goals.

AAP must provide evidence of its impact on the achievement of student learning and development outcomes.

The table below offers examples of achievement of student learning and development outcomes.

Student Learning & Development Outcome Domains

Intellectual growth

Examples of achievement indicators

Examines information about academic majors and minors; Understands the requirements of an academic degree plan, as well as institutional policies and procedures; Employs critical thinking in problem solving on selection of major and course selection; Uses complex information from a variety of sources including personal experience and observation to form a decision or opinion; Declares a major; Achieves educational goals; Applies previously understood information and concepts to a new situation or setting; Demonstrates understanding of a general education and expresses appreciation for literature, the fine arts, mathematics, sciences, and social sciences

Personal and educational goals

Examples of achievement indicators

Sets, articulates, and pursues individual goals; Articulates personal and educational goals and objectives; Uses personal and educational goals to guide decisions; Produces a schedule of classes in consultation with advisors; Understands the effect of one's personal and education goals on others

Enhanced self-esteem

Examples of achievement indicators

Shows self-respect and respect for others; Initiates actions toward achievement of goals; Evaluates reasonable risks with regard to academic course selection and course load when conferring with advisors

Realistic self-appraisal

Examples of achievement indicators

Evaluates personal and academic skills, abilities, and interests and uses this appraisal to establish appropriate educational plans; Makes decisions and acts in congruence with personal values and other personal and life demands; Focuses on areas of academic ability and interest and mitigates academic weaknesses; Uses information on degree program requirements, course load, and course availability to construct a course schedule; Seeks opportunities for involvement in co-curricular activities; Seeks feedback from advisors; Learns from past experiences; Seeks services for personal needs (e.g., writing labs and counseling)

Clarified values

Examples of achievement indicators

Demonstrates ability to evaluate personal values and beliefs regarding academic integrity and other ethical issues; Articulates personal values; Acts in congruence with personal values; Identifies personal, work, and lifestyle values and explains how they influence decision-making in regard to course selection, course load, and major and minor selections

Career choices
Examples of achievement indicators

Describes career choice and choices of academic major and minor based on interests, values, skills, and abilities; Documents knowledge, skills, and accomplishments resulting from formal education, work experience, community service, and volunteer experiences; Makes the connections between classroom and out-of-classroom learning; Identifies the purpose and role of career services in the development and attainment of academic and career goals

Independence
Examples of achievement indicators

Operates autonomously by attending advising sessions or programs or by seeking the advice of advisors in a timely fashion; Correctly interprets and applies degree audit information; Selects, schedules, and registers for courses in consultation with advisors

Effective communication
Examples of achievement indicators

Communicates personal and academic strengths and weaknesses that affect academic plans; Demonstrates ability to use campus technology resources; Composes appropriate questions when inquiring about particular requirements, departments, and resources

Leadership development
Examples of achievement indicators

Articulates leadership philosophy or style; Serves in a leadership position in student, community, or professional organizations; Comprehends the dynamics of a group; Exhibits democratic principles as a leader; Exhibits ability to visualize a group purpose and desired outcomes

Healthy behavior
Examples of achievement indicators

Exhibits personal behaviors that promote a healthy lifestyle; Articulates the relationship between health and wellness and accomplishing life long-goals; Exhibits behaviors that advance a healthy campus and community

Meaningful interpersonal relationships
Examples of achievement indicators

Develops relationships with academic advisors, faculty members, students, and other institution staff to be engaged with the institution in meaningful ways; Listens to and considers others' points of view; Treats others with respect

Collaboration
Examples of achievement indicators

Works cooperatively with others; Seeks the involvement of others; Seeks feedback from others; Contributes to achievement of group goals; Exhibits effective listening skills

Social responsibility
Examples of achievement indicators

Understands the requirements of the codes of conduct; Understands and practices principles of academic integrity; Understands and participates in relevant governance systems; Understands, abides by, and participates in the development, maintenance, and orderly change of community, social, and legal standards or norms; Appropriately challenges the unfair, unjust, or uncivil behavior of other individuals or groups; Participates in service and volunteer activities

Satisfying and productive lifestyles
Examples of achievement indicators

Achieves balance among academic course load requirements, work, and leisure time; Develops plans to satisfy academic requirements, work expectations, and leisure pursuits; Identifies and works to overcome obstacles that hamper goal achievement; Functions on the basis of personal identity, ethical, spiritual, and moral values; Articulates long-term goals and objectives

Appreciating diversity
Examples of achievement indicators

Selects course offerings that will increase understanding of one's own and others' identity and cultures; Seeks involvement with people different from oneself; Demonstrates an appreciation for diversity and the impact it has on society

Spiritual awareness
Examples of achievement indicators

Identifies campus and community spiritual and religious resources, including course offerings; Develops and articulates personal belief system; Understands roles of spirituality in personal and group values and behaviors

Both students and advisors must assume shared responsibility in the advising process. AAP must assist students to make the best academic decisions possible by encouraging identification and assessment of alternatives and consideration of the consequences of their decisions.

The ultimate responsibility for making decisions about educational plans and life goals should rest with the individual student.

AAP must be guided by a set of written goals and objectives that are directly related to its stated mission.

AAP must:

- promote student growth and development
- assist students in assessing their interests and abilities, examining their educational goals, making decisions and developing short-term and long-term plans to meet their objectives
- discuss and clarify educational, career, and life goals
- provide accurate and timely information and interpret institutional, general education, and major requirements
- assist students to understand the educational context within which they are enrolled
- advise on the selection of appropriate courses and other educational experiences
- clarify institutional policies and procedures
- evaluate and monitor student academic progress and the impact on achievement of goals
- reinforce student self-direction and self-sufficiency
- direct students with educational, career or personal concerns, or skill/learning deficiencies to other resources and programs on the campus when necessary
- make students aware of and refer to educational, institutional, and community resources and services (e.g., internship, study abroad, honors, service-learning, research opportunities)
- collect and distribute relevant data about student needs, preferences, and performance for use in institutional decisions and policy

AAP should provide information about student experiences and concerns regarding their academic program to appropriate decision makers.

AAP must be (a) intentional, (b) coherent, (c) based on theories and knowledge of teaching, learning and human development, (d) reflective of developmental and demographic profiles of the student population, and (e) responsive to the needs of individuals, special populations, and communities.

AAP should make available to academic advisors all pertinent research (e.g., about students, the academic advising program, and perceptions of the institution).

The academic advisor must review and use available data about students' academic and educational needs, performance, and aspirations.

AAP must identify environmental conditions that may positively or negatively influence student academic achievement and propose interventions that may neutralize negative conditions.

AAP must provide current and accurate advising information to students and academic advisors.

AAP should employ the latest technologies for delivery of advising information.

Academic advising conferences must be available to students each academic term.

Academic advisors should offer conferences in a format that is convenient to the student, i.e., in person, by telephone, or on-line. Advising conferences may be carried out individually or in groups.

Academic advising caseloads must be consistent with the time required for the effective performance of this activity.

The academic status of the student being advised should be taken into consideration when determining caseloads. For example, first year, undecided, under-prepared, and honors students may require more advising time than upper division students who have declared their majors.

Academic advisors should allow an appropriate amount of time for students to discuss plans, programs, courses, academic progress, and other subjects related to their educational programs.

When determining workloads it should be recognized that advisors may work with students not officially assigned to them and that contacts regarding advising may extend beyond direct contact with the student.

Part 3. LEADERSHIP

Effective and ethical leadership is essential to the success of all organizations. Institutions must appoint, position, and empower Academic Advising Program (AAP) leaders within the administrative structure to accomplish stated missions. Leaders at various levels must be selected on the basis of formal education and training, relevant work experience as an advisor, personal skills and competencies, knowledge of the literature of academic advising, relevant professional credentials, as well as potential for promoting learning and development in students, applying effective practices to educational processes, and enhancing institutional effectiveness. Institutions must determine expectations of accountability for AAP leaders and fairly assess their performance.

AAP leaders must exercise authority over resources for which they are responsible to achieve their respective missions.

AAP leaders must:

- articulate a vision for their organization
- set goals and objectives based on the needs and capabilities of the population served
- promote student learning and development
- prescribe and practice ethical behavior
- recruit, select, supervise, and develop others in the organization
- manage financial resources
- coordinate human resources
- plan, budget for, and evaluate personnel and programs
- apply effective practices to educational and administrative processes
- communicate effectively
- initiate collaborative interactions between individuals and agencies that possess legitimate concerns and interests in academic advising

AAP leaders must identify and find means to address individual, organizational, or environmental conditions that inhibit goal achievement.

AAP leaders must promote campus environments that result in multiple opportunities for student learning and development.

AAP leaders must continuously improve programs and services in response to changing needs of students and other constituents and evolving institutional priorities.

Part 4. ORGANIZATION and MANAGEMENT

Guided by an overarching intent to ensure student learning and development, Academic Advising Programs (AAP) must be structured purposefully and managed effectively to achieve stated goals. Evidence of appropriate structure must include current and accessible policies and procedures, written performance expectations for all employees, functional workflow graphics or organizational charts, and clearly stated service delivery expectations.

Evidence of effective management practices must include use of comprehensive and accurate information for decisions, clear sources and channels of authority, effective communication practices, decision-making and conflict resolution procedures, responsiveness to changing conditions, accountability and evaluation systems, and recognition and reward processes. AAP must provide channels within the organization for regular review of administrative policies and procedures.

The design of AAP must be compatible with the institution's organizational structure and its students' needs. Specific advisor responsibilities must be clearly delineated, published, and disseminated to both advisors and advisees.

Students, faculty advisors, and professional staff must be informed of their respective advising responsibilities.

AAP may be a centralized or decentralized function within an institution, with a variety of people throughout the institution assuming responsibilities.

AAP must provide the same services to distance learners as it does to students on campus. The distance education advising must provide for appropriate real time or delayed interaction between advisors and students.

Part 5. HUMAN RESOURCES

The Academic Advising Program (AAP) must be staffed adequately by individuals qualified to accomplish its mission and goals. Within established guidelines of the institution, AAP must establish procedures for staff selection, training, and evaluation; set expectations for supervision; and provide appropriate professional development opportunities. AAP must strive to improve the professional competence and skills of all personnel it employs.

Academic advising personnel may be full-time or part-time professionals who have advising as their primary function or may be faculty whose responsibilities include academic advising. Paraprofessionals (e.g., graduate students, interns, or assistants) or peer advisors may also assist advisors.

An academic advisor must hold an earned graduate degree in a field relevant to the position held or must possess an appropriate combination of educational credentials and related work experience.

Academic advisors should have an understanding of student development, student learning, career development, and other relevant theories in education, social sciences, and humanities.

Academic advisors should have a comprehensive knowledge of the institution's programs, academic requirements, policies and procedures, majors, minors, and support services.

Academic advisors should demonstrate an interest and effectiveness in working with and assisting students and a willingness to participate in professional activities.

Sufficient personnel must be available to address students' advising needs without unreasonable delay.

Degree or credential-seeking interns must be qualified by enrollment in an appropriate field of study and by relevant experience. These individuals must be trained and supervised adequately by professional staff members holding educational credentials and related work experience appropriate for supervision.

Student employees and volunteers must be carefully selected, trained, supervised, and evaluated. They must be trained on how and when to refer those in need of assistance to qualified staff members and have access to a supervisor for assistance in making these judgments. Student employees and volunteers must be provided clear and precise job descriptions, pre-service training based on assessed needs, and continuing staff development.

AAP must have technical and support staff members adequate to accomplish its mission. Staff members must be technologically proficient and qualified to perform their job functions, be knowledgeable of ethical and legal uses of technology, and have access to training. The level of staffing and workloads must be adequate and appropriate for program and service demands.

Support personnel should maintain student records, organize resource materials, receive students, make appointments, and handle correspondence and other operational needs. Technical staff may be used in research, data collection, systems development, and special projects.

Technical and support personnel must be carefully selected and adequately trained, supervised, and evaluated.

AAP staff must recognize the limitations of their positions and be familiar with institutional resources to make appropriate referrals.

Salary levels and fringe benefits for all AAP staff members must be commensurate with those for comparable positions within the institution, in similar institutions, and in the relevant geographic area.

AAP must institute hiring and promotion practices that are fair, inclusive, and non-discriminatory. AAP must employ a diverse staff to provide readily identifiable role models for students and to enrich the campus community.

AAP must create and maintain position descriptions for all staff members and provide regular performance planning and appraisals.

AAP must have a system for regular staff evaluation and must provide access to continuing education and professional development opportunities, including in-service training programs and participation in professional conferences and workshops.

AAP must strive to improve the professional competence and skills of all personnel it employs.

Continued professional development should include areas such as the following and how they relate to academic advising:
- theories of student development, student learning, career development, and other relevant theories in education, social sciences, and humanities
- academic policies and procedures, including institutional transfer policies and curricular changes
- legal issues including US Family Education and Records Privacy Act (FERPA)/Canadian Freedom Of Information and Protection of Privacy (FOIPP) and other privacy laws and policies
- technology and software training (e.g., degree audit, web registration)
- institutional resources (e.g., research opportunities, career services, internship opportunities, counseling and health services, tutorial services)
- ADA compliance issues

Part 6. FINANCIAL RESOURCES

The Academic Advising Program (AAP) must have adequate funding to accomplish its mission and goals. Funding priorities must be determined within the context of the stated mission, goals, objectives, and comprehensive analysis of the needs and capabilities of students and the availability of internal and external resources.

AAP must demonstrate fiscal responsibility and cost effectiveness consistent with institutional protocols.

Special consideration should be given to providing funding for the professional development of advisors.

Financial resources should be sufficient to provide high-quality print and web-based information for students and training materials for advisors. Sufficient financial resources should be provided to promote the academic advising program.

Part 7. FACILITIES, TECHNOLOGY, and EQUIPMENT

The Academic Advising Program (AAP) must have adequate, suitably located facilities, adequate technology, and equipment to support its mission and goals efficiently and effectively. Facilities, technology, and equipment must be evaluated regularly and be in compliance with relevant federal, state, provincial, and local requirements to provide for access, health, safety, and security.

AAP must assure that online and technology-assisted advising includes appropriate mechanisms for obtaining approvals, consultations, and referrals.

Data about students maintained on individual workstations and departmental or institutional servers must be secure and must comply with institutional policies on data stewardship.

Academic advisors must have access to computing equipment, local networks, student data bases, and the Internet. Privacy and freedom from visual and auditory distractions must be considered in designing appropriate facilities.

Part 8. LEGAL RESPONSIBILITIES

The Academic Advising Program (AAP) staff members must be knowledgeable about and responsive to laws and regulations that relate to their respective responsibilities. Staff members must inform users of programs and services and officials, as appropriate, of legal obligations and limitations including constitutional, statutory, regulatory, and case law; mandatory laws and orders emanating from federal, state, provincial, and local governments; and the institution's policies.

Academic advisors must use reasonable and informed practices to limit the liability exposure of the institution, its officers, employees, and agents. Academic advisors must be informed about institutional policies regarding personal liability and related insurance coverage options.

The institution must provide access to legal advice for academic advisors as needed to carry out assigned responsibilities.

The institution must inform academic advisors and students, in a timely and systematic fashion, about extraordinary or changing legal obligations and potential liabilities.

Part 9. EQUITY and ACCESS

The Academic Advising Program (AAP) staff members must ensure that services and programs are provided on a fair and equitable basis. Facilities, programs, and services must be accessible. Hours of operation and delivery of and access to programs and services must be responsive to the needs of all students and other constituents. AAP must adhere to the spirit and intent of equal opportunity laws.

AAP must be open and readily accessible to all students and must not discriminate except where sanctioned by law and institutional policy. Discrimination must especially be avoided on the basis of age; color; creed; cultural heritage; disability; ethnicity; gender identity; nationality; political affiliation; religious affiliation; sex; sexual orientation; or social, economic, marital, or veteran status.

Consistent with the mission and goals, AAP must take affirmative action to remedy significant imbalances in student participation and staffing patterns.

As the demographic profiles of campuses change and new instructional delivery methods are introduced, institutions must recognize the needs of students who participate in distance learning for access to programs and services offered on campus. Institutions must provide appropriate services in ways that are accessible to distance learners and assist them in identifying and gaining access to other appropriate services in their geographic region.

Part 10. CAMPUS and EXTERNAL RELATIONS

The Academic Advising Program (AAP) must establish, maintain, and promote effective relations with relevant campus offices and external agencies.

Academic advising is integral to the educational process and depends upon close working relationships with other institutional agencies and the administration. AAP should be fully integrated into other processes of the institution. Academic advisors should be consulted when there are modifications to or closures of academic programs.

For referral purposes, AAP should provide academic advisors a comprehensive list of relevant external agencies, campus offices, and opportunities.

Part 11. DIVERSITY

Within the context of the institution's unique mission, diversity enriches the community and enhances the collegiate experience for all; therefore the Academic Advising Program (AAP) must nurture environments where similarities and differences among people are recognized and honored.

AAP must promote educational experiences that are characterized by open and continuous communication that deepen understanding of one's own identity, culture and heritage, and that of others. AAP must educate and promote respect about commonalties and differences in historical and cultural contexts.

AAP must address the characteristics and needs of a diverse population when establishing and implementing policies and procedures.

Part 12. ETHICS

All persons involved in the delivery of the Academic Advising Program (AAP) must adhere to the highest of principles of ethical behavior. AAP must develop or adopt and implement appropriate statements of ethical practice. AAP must publish these statements and ensure their periodic review by relevant constituencies.

Advisors must uphold policies, procedures, and values of their departments and institutions.

Advisors should consider ethical standards or other statements from relevant professional associations.

AAP staff members must ensure that privacy and confidentiality are maintained with respect to all communications and records to the extent that such records are protected under the law and appropriate statements of ethical practice. Information contained in students' education records must not be disclosed without written consent except as allowed by relevant laws and institutional polices. AAP staff members must disclose to appropriate authorities information judged to be of an emergency nature, especially when the safety of the individual or others is involved, or when otherwise required by institutional policy or relevant law.

When emergency disclosure is required, AAP should inform the student that it has taken place, to whom, and why.

All AAP staff members must be aware of and comply with the provisions contained in the institution's human subjects research policy and in other relevant institutional policies addressing ethical practices and confidentiality of research data concerning individuals.

All AAP staff members must recognize and avoid personal conflict of interest or appearance thereof in their transactions with students and others.

All AAP staff members must strive to ensure the fair, objective, and impartial treatment of all persons with whom they deal. AAP staff members must not participate in nor condone any form of harassment that demeans persons or creates intimidating, hostile, or offensive campus environment.

When handling institutional funds, all AAP staff members must ensure that such funds are managed in accordance with established and responsible accounting procedures and the fiscal policies or processes of the institution.

AAP staff members must perform their duties within the limits of their training, expertise, and competence. When these limits are exceeded, individuals in need of further assistance must be referred to persons possessing appropriate qualifications.

AAP staff members must use suitable means to confront and otherwise hold accountable other staff members who exhibit unethical behavior.

AAP staff members must be knowledgeable about and practice ethical behavior in the use of technology.

Part 13. ASSESSMENT and EVALUATION

The Academic Advising Program (AAP) must conduct regular assessment and evaluations. AAP must employ effective qualitative and quantitative methodologies as appropriate, to determine whether and to what degree the stated mission, goals, and student learning and development outcomes are being met. The process must employ sufficient and sound assessment measures to ensure comprehensiveness. Data collected must include responses from students and other affected constituencies.

AAP must evaluate periodically how well they complement and enhance the institution's stated mission and educational effectiveness.

Results of these evaluations must be used in revising and improving programs and services and in recognizing staff performance and the performance of academic advisors.

General Standards revised in 2002; AAP content developed/revised in 1986, 1997, & 2005

THE ROLE of COLLEGE ADMISSION PROGRAMS
CAS Standards Contextual Statement

When colonial colleges were founded, their primary mission was similar to the English tradition of providing liberal education and professional study for young men of intellectual and financial ability. Admission programs focused on identifying and admitting young men for the ministry. However, as other colleges were subsequently founded, chartered, and funded, their missions changed to address changes in student needs, ages, religions, social class, identities, and proximity to campus.

The role of admissions professionals and the process of admissions today might best be understood by considering two competing forces: service to the institution and service to prospective students. In general, the overall responsibility of admissions professionals is to help students understand the process of transition to college, admission criteria, and the competitiveness of their credentials. These tasks are typically accomplished through personal interactions, group presentations, publications, and other recruitment and counseling strategies.

The admissions professional must also have a firm understanding of the institution's mission, enrollment goals, fiscal priorities, and student and departmental needs. When performing well, the successful admissions professional serves a vital role establishing good matches between students and institutions. Just as changes in demographics, finances, laws, and shifts in the competitiveness of their credentials have affected prospective college students, the role of the admissions officer has also changed over time, from the functions suggested by titles such as registrar, counselor, dean and director, marketer, and recruiter to that of enrollment manager.

In general, admission professionals . . .

- provide information and assistance to prospective students (first time students as well as potential transfer students), families, and secondary school and community college counselors on the academic, financial, curricular, and co-curricular offerings of their institutions
- evaluate the qualifications of applicants
- develop, implement, and coordinate the institution's strategic marketing or recruitment plans
- work with the college faculty and administration to develop, implement, and evaluate enrollment policies and goals for the institution
- establish cooperative relationships with secondary school and community college counselors and other relevant constituencies
- work in concert with other campus offices to ensure that students are not only recruited but retained and eventually graduate

The admissions professional today is faced with many challenges: diverse students and student needs, high college costs, limited financial aid, and intense competition for students. They must also apply new technologies to deliver messages about the institution. Today, admission policies range from being "open-admission" to highly competitive and selective. Similarly, the hundreds of thousands of applicants present varying ability levels, financial concerns, personal challenges, and academic interests, and admission officers must be prepared to serve them all. Admissions offices must have appropriate and adequate staff, policies, and skills in human relations to manage their important roles.

As the new century approaches, admissions professionals recognize the benefits of cooperating with other student affairs professionals to enhance students' educational experiences. During the past decade, enrollment management models have been developed to bring greater sophistication in efforts to recruit, retain, educate, and graduate students. On today's campuses, models for admissions offices may include such areas as admissions, recruitment or outreach, financial assistance, orientation, housing, transfer counseling, and academic advising—all reporting to a central administrator. Enrollment management assumes the establishment of activities based on an understanding of market research, student impact research, and organizational theory. Enrollment management paradigms are viewed as on-going processes that can enable college and university administrators to exert greater influence over factors that shape their enrollments. Clearly, today's admissions professionals must continue to respect students and their need for quality counseling and support throughout the whole admission process, while they also address institutional expectations. The Admission Program Standards and Guidelines that follow have been designed to facilitate the admission professional's response to these increasingly complex demands.

References, Readings, and Resources

American Association of Collegiate Registrars and Admissions Officers. (1997). The college admission handbook. Washington, DC: Author.

American Association of Collegiate Registrars and Admissions Officers (AACRAO), The College Entrance Examination Board (CEEB), The Educational Testing Services (ETS), and the National Association of College Admission Counselors (NACAC). (1995). Challenges in college admissions: A report of a survey of undergraduate admissions policies, practices, and procedures. Washington, DC: Authors.

Fetter, J. (1995) Questions and admissions: Reflections on 100,000 admissions decisions at Stanford. Stanford, CA: Stanford University Press.

Goodchild, L. F., & Wechsler, H. W. (eds.) (1989). The statutes of Harvard, 1646. ASHE Reader on The History of Higher Education. pp. 89-90. Needham Heights, MA: Ginn Press.

Hossler, E. & Litten, L. (1993). *Mapping the higher education landscape.* New York: The College Entrance Examination Board.

Loeb, J. (1992). *Academic standards in higher education.* New York: The College Entrance Examination Board.

National Association for College Admission Counseling. (1993). *Achieving diversity: Strategies for the recruitment and retention of traditionally underrepresented students.* Alexandria, VA: Author.

Steinberg, J. (2002). *The gatekeepers: Inside the admissions process of a premier college.* London: Penguin Books.

American Association of Collegiate Registrars and Admission Officers (AACRAO)
One Dupont Circle, NW, Suite 330,
Washington, DC 20036-1171
202-293-9161; 202-872-8857 (fax);
http://www.reg.uci.edu/aacrao
Publisher of *College and University.*

The College Board
45 Columbus Avenue, New York, NY 10023
212-713-8000; http://www.collegeboard.org
Publisher of *The College Review*

The National Association for College Admission Counseling (NACAC)
1631 Prince Street, Alexandria, Virginia 22314-2818
703-836-2222; 703-836-8015 (fax); http://www.nacac.com
Publisher of the *Journal of College Admission*

The National Association of Graduate Admissions Professionals (NAGAP)
www.nagap.org
Publisher of the *NAGAP Journal*

Contributors:
Current edition: Jan Arminio, Shippensburg University, NACA
Previous editions: Joyce Smith, NACAC

ADMISSION PROGRAMS
CAS Standards and Guidelines

Part 1. MISSION

The Admission Programs (AP) in higher education must incorporate student learning and student development in its mission. The program must enhance overall educational experiences. The program and service must develop, record, disseminate, implement and regularly review its mission and goals. Mission statements must be consistent with the mission and goals of the institution and with the standards in this document. The AP must operate as an integral part of the institution's overall mission.

College and university AP must:

- address the abilities needs and expectations of prospective students as they move from secondary to postsecondary education, from one postsecondary institution to another, or as they return from a period of non-enrollment to formal learning
- establish, promulgate, and implement admission criteria that accurately represent the mission, goals, and purposes of the institution, and that accommodate the abilities, needs, and interests of potential students
- reflect the mission, goals, policies, procedures, facilities, and characteristics of the parent institution, and must be compatible with the ability of the institution to bring adequate resources to bear upon the relevant needs and aspirations of all students accepted for enrollment
- develop and regularly review institutional goals for admission with appropriate individuals within the institution; such goals must be consistent with good admission practices and with the nature and mission of the institution

Generally, in higher education, the terms "admission," "admission program," and "admission counselor" refer respectively to the processes, the agencies, and the institutional agents involved in the many activities that are related to the formal entry of students into postsecondary institutions. These generally include recruitment, counseling, selection, enrollment, orientation, advisement, and retention of students. In practice, institutions may establish separate agencies to provide these programs and services.

The AP should provide or ensure personalized counseling that is responsive to the needs and expectations of each prospective student and his or her family, with particular attention given to the transition process.

Admission criteria should also reflect a variable approach which includes the student's academic record (e.g., grade point average, test scores, class rank), personal characteristics, and extracurricular involvement.

Part 2. PROGRAM

The formal education of students consists of the curriculum and the co-curriculum, and must promote student learning and development that is purposeful and holistic. The Admission Programs (AP) must identify relevant and desirable student learning and development outcomes and provide programs and services that encourage the achievement of those outcomes.

Relevant and desirable outcomes include: intellectual growth, effective communication, realistic self-appraisal, enhanced self-esteem, clarified values, career choices, leadership development, healthy behaviors, meaningful interpersonal relationships, independence, collaboration, social responsibility, satisfying and productive lifestyles, appreciation of diversity, spiritual awareness, and achievement of personal and educational goals.

AP must provide evidence of its impact on the achievement of student learning and development outcomes.

The table below offers examples of evidence of achievement of student learning and development.

Student Learning and Development Outcome Domains

Intellectual growth
Examples of achievement indicators
 Produces personal and educational goal statements; Employs critical thinking in problem solving; Uses complex information from a variety of sources including personal experience and observation to form a decision or opinion; Obtains a degree; Applies previously understood information and concepts to a new situation or setting; Expresses appreciation for literature, the fine arts, mathematics, sciences, and social sciences

Effective communication
Examples of achievement indicators
 Writes and speaks coherently and effectively; Writes and speaks after reflection; Able to influence others through writing, speaking or artistic expression; Effectively

articulates abstract ideas; Uses appropriate syntax; Makes presentations or gives performances

Enhanced self-esteem

Examples of achievement indicators

Shows self-respect and respect for others; Initiates actions toward achievement of goals; Takes reasonable risks; Demonstrates assertive behavior; Functions without need for constant reassurance from others

Realistic self-appraisal

Examples of achievement indicators

Articulates personal skills and abilities; Makes decisions and acts in congruence with personal values; Acknowledges personal strengths and weaknesses; Articulates rationale for personal behavior; Seeks feedback from others; Learns from past experiences

Clarified values

Examples of achievement indicators

Articulates personal values; Acts in congruence with personal values; Makes decisions that reflect personal values; Demonstrates willingness to scrutinize personal beliefs and values; Identifies personal, work, and lifestyle values and explains how they influence decision-making

Career choices

Examples of achievement indicators

Articulates career choices based on assessment of interests, values, skills, and abilities; Documents knowledge, skills, and accomplishments resulting from formal education, work experience, community service, and volunteer experiences; Makes the connections between classroom and out-of-classroom learning; Can construct a resume with clear job objectives and evidence of related knowledge, skills, and accomplishments; Articulates the characteristics of a preferred work environment; Comprehends the world of work; Takes steps to initiate a job search or seek advanced education

Leadership development

Examples of achievement indicators

Articulates leadership philosophy or style; Serves effectively in a leadership position in a student organization; Comprehends the dynamics of a group; Exhibits democratic principles as a leader; Exhibits ability to visualize a group purpose and desired outcomes

Healthy behavior

Examples of achievement indicators

Chooses behaviors and environments that promote health and reduce risk; Articulates the relationship between health and wellness and accomplishing life- long goals; Exhibits behaviors that advance a healthy community

Meaningful interpersonal relationships

Examples of achievement indicators

Develops and maintains satisfying interpersonal relationships; Establishes mutually rewarding relationships with friends and colleagues; Listens to and considers others' points of view; Treats others with respect

Independence

Examples of achievement indicators

Exhibits self-reliant behaviors; Functions autonomously; Exhibits ability to function interdependently; Accepts supervision as needed; Manages time effectively

Collaboration

Examples of achievement indicators

Works cooperatively with others; Seeks the involvement of others; Seeks feedback from others; Contributes to achievement of a group goal; Exhibits effective listening skills

Social responsibility

Examples of achievement indicators

Understands and participates in relevant governance systems; Understands, abides by, and participates in the development, maintenance, and/or orderly change of community, social, and legal standards or norms; Appropriately challenges the unfair, unjust, or uncivil behavior of other individuals or groups; Participates in service/volunteer activities

Satisfying and productive lifestyles

Examples of achievement indicators

Achieves balance between education, work, and leisure time; Articulates and meets goals for work, leisure, and education; Overcomes obstacles that hamper goal achievement; Functions on the basis of personal identity, ethical, spiritual, and moral values; Articulates long-term goals and objectives

Appreciating diversity

Examples of achievement indicators

Understands ones own identity and culture; Seeks involvement with people different from oneself; Seeks involvement in diverse interests; Articulates the advantages and challenges of a diverse society; Challenges appropriately the abusive use of stereotypes by others; Understands the impact of diversity on one's own society

Spiritual awareness

Examples of achievement indicators

Develops and articulates personal belief system; Understands roles of spirituality in personal and group values and behaviors

Personal and educational goals

Examples of achievement indicators

Sets, articulates, and pursues individual goals; Articulates personal and educational goals and objectives; Uses personal and educational goals to guide decisions; Understands the effect of one's personal and educational goals on others

AP must be (a) intentional, (b) coherent, (c) based on theories and knowledge of learning and human development, (d) reflective of developmental and demographic profiles of the student population, and (e) responsive to special needs of individuals.

AP must:

- **provide programs and services designed to establish, meet, and maintain desired enrollment**
- **promote and maintain integrity, timeliness, and accuracy in program delivery**
- **promote deliberate educational planning opportunities for all relevant constituencies**
- **provide oral and written information for all relevant constituencies**
- **promote and provide equal access to all eligible prospective students interested in and capable of pursuing an education at the institution**

Admission priorities, preferences, and objectives must be stated clearly in the formal admission policies and procedures of the institution. This statement must be easily obtainable by individuals seeking admission. Not every student is suited for a particular postsecondary institution. Proper student-institutional matches are a major factor in the persistence of students toward graduation.

The distribution of current and complete information is an important priority for admission offices. Students and parents require comprehensive information on admission policies, requirements and procedures, as well as on institutional program offerings, selection criteria, acceptance decisions and financial aid opportunities. All admission personnel should be well informed and able to share such information in a variety of contexts in the interest of deliberate planning.

All admission professional staff members should be expected to perform the admission counseling function. This includes the following activities and interventions:

- assistance and direction of students engaged in the admission process to encourage an appropriate match between student interests and available postsecondary opportunities
- acquisition and dissemination of timely, accurate and relevant information regarding postsecondary opportunities,

- curriculum choices and future educational plans
- promotion and development of individual problem-solving practices by students
- referral of students to appropriate institutional or other resources in response to particular needs
- encouragement of students toward deliberate choices and realistic expectations regarding institutional and personal standards of performance
- effective work with students of different levels of ability
- acknowledgment and positive use of proper interest in the student on the part of high school counselors, faculty, administrators, and students' families
- facilitation of proper exchange of non-restricted information among high schools, postsecondary institutions, families, students, and others involved in the admission process
- encouragement of students to engage in effective life planning
- provision of opportunities for a personal interview to students who are being considered for enrollment where appropriate
- making available to prospective students information regarding financial aid opportunities and deadlines; standard financial aid forms should be available through the admission office as well as through any financial aid office
- providing to students who are offered admission information about academic advising and counseling, and student orientation programs and activities

AP may be accomplished through practices which may include but are not limited to:

- recruitment, marketing, and public relations activities (e.g., high school visits, college fairs, direct mail campaigns, publications, alumni relations and assistance, dissemination of admission and financial aid information)
- admission counseling (e.g., evaluation of student credentials, selection, and notification)
- pre-enrollment counseling (e.g., academic advisement and orientation)
- establishment of institutional policies regarding advanced placement, prior college level credit, or credit for equivalent experience

Part 3. LEADERSHIP

Effective and ethical leadership is essential to the success of all organizations. Institutions must appoint, position, and empower Admission Programs (AP) leaders within the administrative structure to accomplish stated missions. Leaders at various levels must be selected on the basis of formal education and training, relevant work experience, personal skills and competencies, relevant professional credentials, as well as potential for promoting learning and development in students, applying

effective practices to educational processes, and enhancing institutional effectiveness. Institutions must determine expectations of accountability for leaders and fairly assess their performance.

Leaders of AP must exercise authority over resources for which they are responsible to achieve their respective missions.

Leaders must:
- articulate a vision for their organization
- set goals and objectives based on the needs and capabilities of the population served
- promote student learning and development
- prescribe and practice ethical behavior
- recruit, select, supervise, and develop others in the organization
- manage financial resources
- coordinate human resources
- plan, budget for, and evaluate personnel and programs
- apply effective practices to educational and administrative processes
- communicate effectively
- initiate collaborative interaction between individuals and agencies that possess legitimate concerns and interests in the functional area

AP leaders must identify and find means to address individual, organizational, or environmental conditions that inhibit goal achievement. Leaders must promote campus environments that result in multiple opportunities for student learning and development.

AP leaders must continuously improve the admissions programs in response to changing needs of students and other constituents, and evolving institutional priorities.

Part 4. ORGANIZATION and MANAGEMENT

Guided by an overarching intent to ensure student learning and development, Admission Programs (AP) must be structured purposefully and managed effectively to achieve stated goals. Evidence of appropriate structure must include current and accessible policies and procedures, written performance expectations for all employees, functional workflow graphics or organizational charts, and clearly stated service delivery expectations.

Evidence of effective management must include use of comprehensive and accurate information for decisions, clear sources and channels of authority,

effective communication practices, decision-making and conflict resolution procedures, responsiveness to changing conditions, accountability and evaluation systems, and recognition and reward processes. AP must provide channels within the organization for regular review of administrative policies and procedures.

The institution must appoint or designate a leader in the AP. This leader must be positioned in the institutional organization so that the needs of students and the operations of admission are both well-represented and advocated at the highest levels of administration.

The specific title and lines of accountability may vary among institutions in light of particular settings and institutional needs. Selection of the chief admission officer should be based on personal characteristics as well as formal training.

The lead admission officer should be able to develop, advocate, and implement a statement of the mission goals and objectives for the admission program on campus.

The lead admission officer should create an effective system to manage the programs, services, and personnel of the admission office. He or she should plan, organize, staff, lead, and regularly assess programs. The leader should also be able to coordinate the admission program with other institutional services and with institutional development activities.

The lead admission officer should attract and select qualified staff members who are capable of making informed decisions about policies, procedures, personnel, budgets, facilities and equipment. He or she should assume responsibility for program and staff development, assessment, and improvement.

Administrative policies and organization structures should be written, properly disseminated and posted, and modified when necessary .

Admission programs, policies, and procedures should minimally include:
- an organizational chart which depicts areas of accountability and reporting relationships for units and personnel as appropriate
- job descriptions that accurately reflect the duties and responsibilities for all admission program personnel
- clearly stated criteria used in the decision making process for admission to the institution and the source of authority for the criteria employed
- steps for appealing, evaluating, or revising policies and procedures

Part 5. HUMAN RESOURCES

Admission Programs (AP) must be staffed adequately by individuals qualified to accomplish its mission and goals. Within established guidelines of the institution, programs and services must establish regular procedures for staff selection, training, and evaluation; set expectations for supervision; and provide appropriate professional development opportunities. AP must strive to improve the professional competence and skills of all personnel it employs.

Professional admissions staff members must hold an earned graduate degree in a field relevant to the position they hold or must possess an appropriate combination of educational credentials and related work experience.

Degree or credential-seeking interns must be qualified by enrollment in an appropriate field of study and by relevant experience. These individuals must be trained and supervised adequately by professional staff members holding educational credentials and related work experience appropriate for supervision.

Student employees and volunteers must be carefully selected, trained, supervised, and evaluated. They must be trained on how and when to refer those in need of assistance to qualified staff members and have access to a supervisor for assistance in making these judgments. Student employees and volunteers must be provided clear and precise job descriptions, pre-service training based on assessed needs, and continuing staff development.

AP must have technical and support staff members adequate to accomplish its mission. Staff members must be technologically proficient and qualified to perform their job functions, be knowledgeable of ethical and legal uses of technology, and have access to training. The level of staffing and workloads must be adequate and appropriate for program and service demands.

Salary levels and fringe benefits for all staff members must be commensurate with those for comparable positions within the institution, in similar institutions, and in the relevant geographic area.

AP must institute hiring and promotion practices that are fair, inclusive, and non-discriminatory. Programs and services must employ a diverse staff to provide readily identifiable role models for students and to enrich the campus community.

AP must create and maintain position descriptions for all staff members and provide regular performance planning and appraisals.

AP must have a system for regular staff evaluation and must provide access to continuing education and professional development opportunities, including in-service training programs and participation in professional conferences and workshops.

PROFESSIONAL STAFF

The senior admission officer should be an experienced and effective manager and have substantial work experience in admission-related employment.

Professional staff members should be competent to provide assistance to the prospective student and to work effectively to assist each student with his or her educational goals. This assistance may include, but should not be limited to, the following:

- ethical and objective presentation of the institution's programs and opportunities; careful and concerned analysis of each student's goals
- establishment of a clear understanding of likely student-institution compatibility
- responsible decision-making in the selection of an institution
- knowledgeable guidance and counseling on all admission issues and concerns; interpretation of tasks and statistical data
- explanation of and placing in a proper context any relevant governmental policy or practice on education

The professional staff should be knowledgeable in the areas of marketing, financial aid, and testing, and should demonstrate knowledge and sensitivity to the needs of traditionally under-represented students and students with a special talent. Activities in these special areas of concern should contribute positively to the reputation of the institution and its position in the higher education marketplace.

Each admission staff member should be specifically trained to articulate the institution's unique and essential aspects. This training should be supplemental to formal outside training. While no specific timeline is prescribed, a minimum of two weeks' specialized training is recommended. Included in this training should be:

- a thorough tour of the campus
- familiarization with the college catalog, all academic programs, freshman and transfer admission policies, and all service and social aspects of the institution
- systematic orientation to relevant other facets of the institution
- familiarization with clerical and financial aid operations

Institutions should provide ongoing opportunities for career-related information and professional growth to the entire admission staff. This process will promote effective admission services and encourage the continued involvement of admission personnel in the field. Numerous avenues promote professional growth. These include in-service workshops, membership and participation in professional organizations, and the development of an admission library. A library should include current scholarly literature, research findings, trade journals, and newspapers.

Continuing education is essential for all admission officers. It is important to be alert to changes within the field and to be able to integrate changes into daily practice when appropriate. Every admission officer should be:
- willing to seek out and implement new ideas
- able to translate new ideas into practical methods for improving the overall operation of the admission function
- willing to seek out and use new conceptual frameworks and equipment that bring information to students more clearly and effectively
- aware of relevant developments in the broad context of formal education and able to incorporate these developments in his or her work

For formal training in preparation for professional admission work, suggested areas for graduate work include student services administration and higher education management. Additional course work may include computer literacy, research and statistical methods, counseling, enrollment management, legal issues relating to admission and higher education, leadership skills, transcript evaluation, and public relations.

SUPPORT STAFF

Support staff members such as administrative assistants, transcript evaluators, and office assistants, should possess the academic background, experience, personal interest, and competence necessary for effective performance of their responsibilities. Support staff should be skilled in interpersonal communications, public relations, referral techniques, and dissemination of information.

Training in procedures, policies, and good office practices should be included in the employment orientation for clerical and support staff. Such training will promote a consistent presentation of the institution and dependable performance of staff.

An annual admission staff workshop to plan and review admission programs is recommended. Topics and components of the workshop may include current issues in college admission, team development, marketing, computer operations, and financial aid issues and status.

Part 6. FINANCIAL RESOURCES

The Admission Program (AP) must have adequate funding to accomplish its mission and goals. Funding priorities must be determined within the context of the stated mission, goals, objectives and comprehensive analysis of the needs and capabilities of students and the availability of internal or external resources.

AP must demonstrate fiscal responsibility and cost effectiveness consistent with institutional protocols.

The institution must prescribe policies governing:
- **in-kind consideration in lieu of cash payment, reimbursement, or remuneration for approved admission-related activity or participation**
- **any necessary external contractual agreements (e.g., professional consultation fees, special mailings)**
- **travel, accommodations, and all expenditures authorized for recruitment purposes; reimbursements for out-of-pocket expenses**

Institutions should provide support for an admission program that offers prospective students ample opportunities to:
- inquire about the entrance requirements and nature of the institution
- inquire about and receive counseling regarding the institution's admission process and apply for admission
- receive financial aid information and forms
- be interviewed as applicants for admission
- receive assistance in orientation and academic advisement

Institutional admission offices should be able to respond in a timely manner to requests for information, literature, programs and services upon the request of prospective students.

Part 7. FACILITIES, TECHNOLOGY, and EQUIPMENT

Admission Programs (AP) must have adequate, suitably located facilities, adequate technology, and equipment to support its mission and goals efficiently and effectively. Facilities, technology, and equipment must be evaluated regularly and be in compliance with relevant federal, state, provincial, and local requirements to provide for access, health, safety, and security.

Sufficient office space should be allocated for confidential interviews and counseling, processing of all relevant documents, files, and staff supervision.

Office space should be adequate and properly equipped for the secure and confidential storage of student records as appropriate.

Security measures, facilities, and equipment appropriate for handling cash or negotiable paper should be provided when necessary.

The admission office should be readily accessible to prospective students, parents, and others who have need for admission services or personnel.

Special concern for providing readily accessible and nearby parking, or the availability of convenient public transportation, is strongly recommended.

Campus maps and highly visible signage that will assist visitors and prospective students to locate the admission office are strongly recommended.

Part 8. LEGAL RESPONSIBILITIES

Admission Program (AP) staff members must be knowledgeable about and responsive to laws and regulations that relate to their respective responsibilities. Staff members must inform users of programs and services and officials, as appropriate, of legal obligations and limitations including constitutional, statutory, regulatory, and case law; mandatory laws and orders emanating from federal, state/provincial and local governments; and the institution's policies.

Staff members must use reasonable and informed practices to limit the liability exposure of the institution, its officers, employees, and agents. Staff members must be informed about institutional policies regarding personal liability and related insurance coverage options.

The institution must provide access to legal advice for staff members as needed to carry out assigned responsibilities.

The institution must inform staff and students in a timely and systematic fashion about extraordinary or changing legal obligations and potential liabilities.

Part 9. EQUITY and ACCESS

Staff members must ensure that Admission Programs (AP) are provided on a fair and equitable basis. Facilities, programs, and services must be accessible. Hours of operation and delivery of and access to programs and services must be responsive to the needs of all students and other constituents. Each program and service must adhere to the spirit and intent of equal opportunity laws.

AP must be open and readily accessible to all students and must not discriminate except where sanctioned by law and institutional policy. Discrimination must be avoided on the bases of age; color; creed; cultural heritage; disability; ethnicity; gender identity; nationality; political affiliation; religious affiliation; sex; sexual orientation; or social, economic, marital, or veteran status.

Consistent with their mission and goals, programs and services must take affirmative action to remedy significant imbalances in student participation and staffing patterns.

As the demographic profiles of campuses change and new instructional delivery methods are introduced, institutions must recognize the needs of students who participate in distance learning for access to programs and services offered on campus. Institutions must provide appropriate services in ways that are accessible to distance learners and assist them in identifying and gaining access to other appropriate services in their geographic region.

Part 10. CAMPUS and EXTERNAL RELATIONS

Admission Programs (AP) must establish, maintain, and promote effective relations with relevant campus offices and external agencies.

Institutional organizational functions and constituencies linked to admission typically include financial aid, student development, student activities, athletics, student accounts, academic support, counseling, career planning and placement, the registrar, records, the faculty, the alumni, and institutional advancement. Residents of the larger community in which the institution is located may also have special interests regarding institutional admission practices.

Students with special needs should be identified and referral made to the appropriate office. Special needs may include those with learning disabilities, physical handicaps, deficiencies in certain academic skills, and those who come from educationally disadvantaged backgrounds. Financial aid and admission decisions should be made independently. However, the financial aid office should have access to appropriate information in the student's admission file. After financial aid has been allocated, the admission office should have access to information regarding the amount and characteristics of the financial aid award. Admission decisions should be based on the establishment or a match between the student's needs and the characteristics of the institution. A student's apparent ability to pay for the services of the institution should not affect the admission decision.

Part 11. DIVERSITY

Within the context of each institution's unique

mission, diversity enriches the community and enhances the collegiate experience for all; therefore, Admission Programs (AP) must nurture environments where commonalties and differences among people are recognized and honored.

AP must promote educational experiences that are characterized by open and continuous communication that deepens understanding of one's own identity, culture, and heritage, and that of others. AP must educate and promote respect about commonalties and differences in their historical and cultural contexts.

AP must address the characteristics and needs of a diverse population when establishing and implementing policies and procedures.

Part 12. ETHICS
All persons involved in the delivery of Admission Programs (AP) must adhere to the highest principles of ethical behavior. AP must develop or adopt and implement appropriate statements of ethical practice. AP must publish these statements and ensure their periodic review by relevant constituencies.

Staff members must ensure that privacy and confidentiality are maintained with respect to all communications and records to the extent that such records are protected under the law and appropriate statements of ethical practice. Information contained in students' education records must not be disclosed without written consent except as allowed by relevant laws and institutional policies. Staff members must disclose to appropriate authorities information judged to be of an emergency nature, especially when the safety of the individual or others is involved, or when otherwise required by institutional policy or relevant law.

All staff members must be aware of and comply with the provisions contained in the institution's human subjects research policy and in other relevant institutional policies addressing ethical practices and confidentiality of research data concerning individuals.

Staff members must recognize and avoid personal conflict of interest or appearance thereof in their transactions with students and others.

Staff members must strive to ensure the fair, objective, and impartial treatment of all persons with whom they deal. Staff members must not participate in nor condone any form of harassment that demeans persons or creates an intimidating, hostile, or offensive campus environment.

When handling institutional funds, all staff members must ensure that such funds are managed in accordance with established and responsible accounting procedures and the fiscal policies or processes of the institution.

Staff members must perform their duties within the limits of their training, expertise, and competence. When these limits are exceeded, individuals in need of further assistance must be referred to persons possessing appropriate qualifications.

Staff members must use suitable means to confront and otherwise hold accountable other staff members who exhibit unethical behavior.

Staff members must be knowledgeable about and practice ethical behavior in the use of technology.

Staff members must not participate in any form of harassment that demeans persons or creates an intimidating, hostile, or offensive campus environment.

AP staff members must perform their duties within the limits of their training, expertise, and competence. When these limits are exceeded, individuals in need of further assistance must be referred to persons possessing appropriate qualifications.

Staff members must use suitable means to confront and otherwise hold accountable other staff members who exhibit unethical behavior.

Staff members must maintain the highest principles of ethical behavior in the use of technology.

All printed material including application forms, financial aid information, and promotional literature must accurately represent the institution's goals, services, programs, and policies.

As professional AP members, admission personnel must receive compensation in the form of a fixed salary, rather than commissions or bonuses on the number of students recruited or enrolled.

Admission officers must insure timely and fair administration of policies regarding: admission decisions; proper notification; wait-listing; evaluating student competencies, credentials, and prior credits; and confidentiality in keeping with federal and state laws.

Promotional publications, written communications, and presentations must:
- state entrance requirements clearly and precisely
- include a current and accurate admission calendar
- provide precise information on opportunities for financial aid
- offer accurate and detailed information regarding special programs
- include realistic descriptions, illustrations, and photographs of the campus and community

Development of admission criteria must be centered around the probability of academic success. When evaluating applicants, particularly those with special talents, admission officers must be guided by their best judgment and should make exception to established admission policies only after a thorough and prudent evaluation of all relevant circumstances including where appropriate, consultation with relevant other agencies.

In some cases applicants may possess outstanding talent in drama, music, athletics, art, or other areas. These students might not meet all established criteria for academic success. However, in some cases a special talent can motivate a student to perform well in a secondary school program. Where this is possible, admission officers are encouraged to acknowledge the special talent when evaluating the applicant.

In some cases, the applicants may possess special needs. For instance, students with learning disabilities or those from academically disadvantaged backgrounds might be admitted. Ethical practices would insist that the appropriate support services be available for these students if they are admitted.

Any comparisons made between or among institutions must be based on accurate and appropriate data. General comments of a disparaging nature about other institutions must be avoided.

Part 13. ASSESSMENT and EVALUATION

Admission Programs (AP) must conduct regular assessment and evaluations. Programs and services must employ effective qualitative and quantitative methodologies as appropriate, to determine whether and to what degree the stated mission, goals, and student learning and development outcomes are being met. The process must employ sufficient and sound

assessment measures to ensure comprehensiveness. Data collected must include responses from students and other affected constituencies.

AP must evaluate periodically how well they complement and enhance the institution's stated mission and educational effectiveness.

Results of these evaluations must be used in revising and improving programs and services and in recognizing staff performance.

Each institution should require that its admission offices, programs, and staff be evaluated regularly. This evaluation should determine the effectiveness of services to students and their families, achievement of departmental and institutional goals and direction toward more efficient cost-effective operations. The periodic study of needs, interests, and expectations of prospective and current students and others served by the program may be conducted in conjunction with these evaluations. Data collected from the study should be used to determine the effectiveness of institutional admission policies and programs. Marketing and recruitment techniques used by the admission office should be regularly reviewed.

General Standards revised in 2002; AP content developed/ revised in 1987 & 1997

THE ROLE of ALCOHOL, TOBACCO, and OTHER DRUG PROGRAMS
CAS Standards Contextual Statement

Abuse of alcohol and other drugs has historically been a major concern for institutions of higher education. Many colleges and universities have employed professional staff members to administer campus-based alcohol, tobacco, and other drug programs directed at prevention of associated problems. Most of these programs were initially established to respond to student needs, but increasingly are being developed to serve the entire campus, including faculty members, staff members, and their families. Campus administrators are now recognizing that the behaviors of all community members affect the nature of the problem and that efforts at education and prevention must be addressed to the whole college community. There has been a national movement to broaden the prevention efforts to include both the individual and the environmental approach.

Major factors that helped focus attention on the problems of alcohol and other drug abuse include:
- 1981 creation of the Inter-Association Task Force onAlcohol and Other Substance Issues, a consortium of professional associations
- 1984 creation of National Collegiate Alcohol Awareness Week
- 1985 promulgation of Guidelines for Beverage Alcohol Marketing on College and University Campuses
- 1986 passage by Congress of the Drug Free School and Communities Act and the establishment of the FIPSE (Fund for the Improvement of Post-Secondary Education) grant program for IHEs
- 1987 establishment by the US Department of Education of the Network of Colleges and Universities Committed to the Elimination of Drug and Alcohol Abuse, now called The Network: Addressing Collegiate Alcohol and Other Drug Issues.
- 1990 development of Standards and Guidelines for Alcohol and Drug Programs by the Council for the Advancement of Standards in Higher Education
- 1993 establishment of the Higher Education Center by the US Department of Education
- 2003 NIAAA College Drinking Report

Alcohol, Tobacco, and Other Drug Programs (ATODP) play an important role in challenging individual behaviors detrimental to the maintenance of civility in an increasingly complex microcosm of society, the college campus. ATODP staff members serve as counselors, advisers, educational programmers, change agents, and collaborators for many campus constituencies exploring appropriate venues to discuss, formulate, and educate campus groups about program mission and philosophy; policy enforcement; intervention strategies; treatment, referral, and support groups; healthy alternative activities; resource needs; target population needs; and appropriate assessment, evaluation, and research efforts. The professional staff member who is primarily responsible for the ATODP program generally serves as its campus spokesperson and must also handle public relations issues.

The institution's chief administrative officer and all other campus leaders must support a comprehensive campus ATODP for it to be effective. Those who voice support for these programs must view the problems as solvable and believe that confronting the problems created by alcohol and other drug abuse is a major responsibility facing educational institutions. Any effective strategy to combat these issues must emphasize the necessity for individual action, choice, and assumption of responsibility.

References, Readings, and Resources

Anderson, D.S., & Milgram, G.G. (1996). *Promising practices: Campus alcohol strategies.* George Mason University (Topical areas comprising policies and implementation, assessment and evaluation, training, peer-based initiatives, environmental and targeted strategies, enforcement, curriculum, awareness and information, support and intervention services, and staffing and resources).

Coombs, R.H., & Ziedonis, D. (1995). *Handbook on drug abuse prevention: A Comprehensive strategy to prevent the abuse of alcohol and other drugs.* Boston: Allyn & Bacon.

Wechsler, H., Dowdall, G., Davenport, A., & Castillo, S. (July, 1995). Correlates of college student binge drinking. *American Journal of Public Health,* 85, 7.

Journal of Drug Education: Baywood Publishing Co., Inc., P.O. Box 337, Amityville, NY 11701

The U.S. Department of Education's Higher Education Center publications, www.edc.org/hec

AMA Office of Alcohol & Other Drug Abuse www.ama-assn.org/ama/pub/category/3337.html

BACCHUS and GAMMA Peer Education Network www.bacchusgamma.org

National Clearinghouse for Alcohol and Drug Information (NCADI) www.health.org

National Institute of Drug Abuse (NIDA) www.drugabuse.gov

National Institute on Alcohol Abuse and Alcoholism (NIAAA) www.collegedrinkingprevention.gov

Contributor: Carole Middlebrooks, University of Georgia, The Network

ALCOHOL, TOBACCO, and OTHER DRUGS PROGRAMS

CAS Standards and Guidelines

For the purpose of this document the term "alcohol, tobacco, and other drug use or abuse" includes: (1) the illegal use of alcohol, tobacco, prescription medications and other drugs (2) the high-risk use and/or abuse of alcohol, tobacco, prescription medications, over-the-counter medications and nutritional supplements.

Part 1. MISSION

The Alcohol, Tobacco, and Other Drugs Program (ATODP) must incorporate student learning and student development in its mission. The program must enhance overall educational experiences. The program must develop, record, disseminate, implement and regularly review its mission and goals. Mission statements must be consistent with the mission and goals of the institution and with the standards in this document. The program must operate as an integral part of the institution's overall mission.

The goals of ATODP must:

- acknowledge and mitigate the inherent risks to the total community associated with alcohol, tobacco, and other drug use
- develop, disseminate, interpret, and support the enforcement of campus regulations that are consistent with institutional policies and local, state/provincial, and federal law
- promote healthy choices concerning the use of alcohol, tobacco, and other drugs, emphasizing the elimination of illegal use, high-risk behavior, harmful use, and related violence
- promote a safe, healthy, and learning conducive environment
- define ATODP policies and practices for prevention, education, training, intervention, evaluation, referral and treatment
- develop shared ownership of the issue by involving all entities of the campus community including governing boards, administrators, faculty and staff members, students, and community leaders
- protect the legal rights of students

Part 2. PROGRAM

The formal education of students consists of the curriculum and the co-curriculum, and must promote student learning and development that is purposeful and holistic. The Alcohol, Tobacco, and Other Drugs Program (ATODP) must identify relevant and desirable student learning and development outcomes and provide programs and services that encourage the achievement of those outcomes. The programs must provide evidence of student learning and development outcomes.

Relevant and desirable outcomes include: intellectual growth, effective communication, realistic self-appraisal, enhanced self-esteem, clarified values, career choices, leadership development, healthy behaviors, meaningful interpersonal relations, independence, collaboration, social responsibility, satisfying and productive lifestyles, appreciation of diversity, spiritual awareness, and achievement of personal and educational goals.

The program must provide evidence of its impact on the achievement of student learning and development outcomes.

The table below offers examples of achievement of student learning and development outcomes.

Student Learning and Development Outcome Domains

Intellectual Growth
Examples of achievement indicators
Clarifies personal and educational goal statements; Cites examples of critical thinking through means of logic and reasoning; Uses complex information from a variety of sources including personal experience and observation to form a decision or opinion; Completes educational goals; Applies previously understood information and concepts to a new situation or setting; Expresses respect for literature, the fine arts, sciences and social sciences

Effective communication
Examples of achievement indicators
Writes coherently and effectively; Speaks coherently and effectively; Expresses themselves effectively through a variety of mediums; Effectively articulates abstract ideas; Uses appropriate syntax; Exhibits the ability to make presentations

Enhanced self-esteem
Examples of achievement indicators
Shows self-respect and respect for others; Initiates actions toward achievement of goals; Takes reasonable risks; Develops intrapersonal and interpersonal skills

Realistic self-appraisal

Examples of achievement indicators

Articulates personal skills and abilities; Acts in congruence with personal values; Acknowledges personal strengths and weaknesses; Articulates rationale for personal behavior; Seeks feedback from others; Learns from experience

Values clarification

Examples of achievement indicators

Demonstrates willingness to identify and analyze personal beliefs, values, and choices; Examines impact of choices on self and others; Identifies personal, work, lifestyle, values, and can explain how they influence decision-making

Career choices

Examples of achievement indicators

Takes steps to explore future direction; Documents knowledge, skills, and accomplishments resulting from formal education, work experience, community service, and volunteer experiences; Makes the connections between classroom and out-of-classroom learning; Articulates the characteristics of a preferred work environment

Leadership development

Examples of achievement indicators

Participates in a student organization, athletics, study group or support group; Demonstrates the ability to effectively work with others to accomplish a goal

Healthy behavior

Examples of achievement indicators

Chooses behaviors and environments that promote health and reduce risk; Participates in health-promoting activities; Exercises regularly; Eats nutritious meals; Avoids unhealthy substances; Chooses behaviors that contribute to a healthy community; Articulates the importance of a healthy lifestyle; Identifies personal risk factors that impede optimal physical and emotional health; Recognizes mental health and/or substance abuse concerns and accesses resources

Meaningful interpersonal relationships

Examples of achievement indicators

Learns and refines skills to establish and cultivate interpersonal relationships; Establishes mutually rewarding relationships with friends and colleagues; Listens to others and accepts their right to their own beliefs and choices; Negotiates interpersonal conflict effectively; Treats others with respect

Independence

Examples of achievement indicators

Exhibits self-reliant behaviors; Demonstrates reliability and time management skills; Seeks advice and support appropriately

Collaboration

Examples of achievement indicators

Works cooperatively with others; Seeks the involvement of others; Seeks feedback from others; Contributes to achievement of a group goal; Possesses effective listening skills; Demonstrates time management

Social responsibility

Examples of achievement indicators

Abides by institutional, legal policies and laws; Respects others' right to a safe, healthy, and low risk living and learning environment; Challenges unfair, unjust, uncivil or discriminatory behavior of individuals or groups; Participates in service/volunteer activities on-campus or in the community; Understands and participates in relevant governance systems

Satisfying and productive lifestyles

Examples of achievement indicators

Achieves balance between education, work, and leisure time; Articulates and meets goals for work, leisure, and education; Develops skills to manage obstacles that hamper goal achievement; Functions on the basis of personal identity, ethical, spiritual, and moral values

Appreciating diversity

Examples of achievement indicators

Understands one's own personal identity and cultural background; Seeks involvement with people of various cultures, lifestyles, and experiences; Seeks involvement in diverse activities; Articulates the advantages and challenges of a diverse society; Challenges behavior that does not tolerate diversity

Spiritual awareness

Examples of achievement indicators

Identifies and develops personal beliefs; Understands roles of spirituality in personal and group values and behaviors

Personal and educational goals

Examples of achievement indicators

Sets, articulates, and pursues healthy individual goals; Uses personal goals to guide decisions; Understands how personal goals and behavior affect others

The ATODP must be (a) intentional, (b) coherent, (c) based on theories and knowledge of learning and human development, and evidence-based prevention and public health models (d) reflective of developmental and demographic profiles of the student population, (e) collaborative with related campus and community agencies, and (f) responsive to needs of individuals, special populations and communities.

The ATODP must involve students, faculty members, staff, and community constituents to reduce heavy and high-risk use of alcohol, tobacco, prescription medication and other drugs.

The ATODP must include:
- **environmental management strategies**
- **institutional policies**
- **enforcement strategies**
- **bi-annual review**
- **community collaboration**
- **training and education**
- **assistance and referral**
- **student leadership**

The ATODP staff must serve as positive role models for ethical and healthy behaviors.

Because faculty and staff members' behaviors often serve as models for students, resources should be available on-campus to assist supervisors in dealing with employees who exhibit high risk behavior related to alcohol, tobacco, and other drugs.

The ATODP must develop and provide education on policies, laws, prevention, intervention and treatment resources, and training for students, including student organizations.

The ATODP education and training program should address the cultural and economic context in which society promotes and condones alcohol, tobacco, and other drug use, including traditions and rituals conducive to high-risk drinking. Other topics may include: legal, physiological, psychological, and social aspects and effects of alcohol, tobacco, and other drug use, abuse, and dependency; high-risk uses of alcohol; risk factors for groups including risk factors for groups as identified through assessment; differences between actual student use and perceptions of student use; and the impact of alcohol, tobacco, and other drug use related to physiological and behavioral differences linked with gender. Techniques and protocols for identifying and referring students with problems to appropriate campus entities should also be included.

The ATODP should develop, provide, and advocate strategies that model practical applications of prevention theories and research results, including environmental approaches, risk reduction approaches, social norms approaches, student assistance programs, curricular infusion projects, development of on-campus task forces, and the development of campus and community coalitions.

The ATODP should provide training for faculty and staff members in identifying, intervening, and referring students with alcohol, tobacco, and other drug problems.

The ATODP should use public health prevention strategies that are evidenced-based and have demonstrated effectiveness in reducing heavy and high-risk drinking and other drug use in college populations.

The ATODP should advocate for incorporating alcohol, tobacco, and other drugs information within relevant courses and expanding campus library holdings.

The ATODP must provide access to support services for students with alcohol or other drug related concerns.

Student involvement in assistance services may be voluntary upon self-initiation or referral, or mandatory upon referral by judicial authorities or other entities.

The student assistance services program should include confidential individual assessment for students to explore and evaluate their attitudes, perceptions, and behaviors; the consequences, risk factors, and relationship to alcohol or other drugs; and make decisions based on the student's individual situation.

Student assistance services should provide, with peer involvement, a coordinated system across the campus for intervention and referral services for students. This system should include training programs on alcohol abuse and other drug use and referral skills.

Student assistance services should identify and maintain contacts with campus and community entities that offer effective treatment, education, and support to students, family members, and friends. Such services may include structured education and counseling sessions for individuals and groups; community service work; disability support services; self-help groups such as Alcoholics Anonymous, Narcotics Anonymous, Al-Anon and Adult Children of Alcoholics; support groups; and detoxification and inpatient therapy.

Part 3. LEADERSHIP
Effective and ethical leadership is essential to the success of all organizations. Institutions must appoint, position, and empower leaders within the administrative structure to accomplish stated missions. Leaders at various levels must be selected on the basis of formal education and training, relevant work experience, personal skills and competencies, relevant professional credentials, as well as potential for promoting learning and development in students, applying effective practices to educational processes, and enhancing institutional effectiveness. Institutions must determine expectations of accountability for leaders and fairly assess their performance.

The Alcohol, Tobacco, and Other Drugs Program (ATODP) leaders must exercise authority over resources for which they are responsible to achieve their respective missions.

ATODP leaders must:
- articulate a vision and mission statement for their program
- gather relevant data and review current literature
- set goals and objectives based on the needs and capabilities of the population served that will enhance program and institutional effectiveness
- promote student learning and development
- develop strategic, operational, and resource utilization plans and policies
- prescribe and practice ethical behavior
- recruit, select, supervise, and develop others in the program
- manage financial resources
- coordinate human resources
- plan, budget for, manage, and evaluate personnel and programs
- apply effective practices in educational and administrative processes
- communicate effectively
- initiate collaborative interaction between the program and individuals or agencies that possess legitimate concerns and interests in the ATODP
- ensure compliance with all institutional, state/provincial, and federal regulations and policies
- advocate for the advancement of the ATODP in the institution

ATODP leaders should provide institutional leaders with information on ATODP issues on their campus to engender support.

ATODP leaders must institute processes that improve programs and services in response to changing needs of students and other constituents, and evolving institutional priorities.

ATODP leaders must promote campus environments that result in multiple opportunities for student learning and development.

ATODP leaders must identify and find means to address individual, organizational, or environmental conditions that inhibit goal achievement.

Part 4. ORGANIZATION and MANAGEMENT
Guided by an overarching intent to ensure student learning and development, the Alcohol, Tobacco, and Other Drugs Program (ATODP) must be structured purposefully and managed effectively to achieve stated goals. Evidence of appropriate structure must include current and accessible policies and procedures, written performance expectations for all employees, functional work flow graphics or organizational charts, and clearly stated service delivery expectations.

Evidence of effective management must include use of comprehensive and accurate information for decisions, clear sources and channels of authority, effective communication practices, decision-making and conflict resolution procedures, responsiveness to changing conditions, accountability and evaluation systems, and recognition and reward processes. The ATODP must provide channels within the organization for regular review of administrative policies and procedures.

The ATODP director or coordinator must be placed within the institution's organizational structures so as to be able to promote cooperative interaction with appropriate campus and community entities and to develop the support of high-level administrators.

The scope and structure of the ATODP should be defined by the size, nature, complexity, and philosophy of the institution.

The ATODP should maintain an advisory board, preferably appointed by the executive officer, comprised of knowledgeable members of the campus and community, for advice and support on polices and programs.

The ATODP must collaborate in the development of policies to:
- maintain consistency with federal, state/provincial, and local laws and regulations
- promote an educational, social and living environment free from the abuse of alcohol, tobacco, legal drugs, and the use of illegal drugs
- define geographic jurisdictions and demographic characteristics of populations to whom policies pertain
- define individual and group behaviors and group activities that are prohibited both on campus property and at off-campus events controlled by the institution
- specify the potential consequences for using or possessing, distributing or manufacturing different amounts and/or categories of alcohol, tobacco, and other drugs
- establish protocols and procedures for the involvement of campus law enforcement, campus judicial programs, and other campus entities

- establish protocols and procedures for referring individuals with alcohol, tobacco, or other drug problems to appropriate sources for assistance
- define campus procedures on the availability and marketing of alcoholic beverages, if permitted
- define appropriate procedures for any permitted use of alcohol or tobacco

Part 5. HUMAN RESOURCES

The Alcohol, Tobacco, and Other Drugs Program (ATODP) must be staffed adequately by individuals qualified to accomplish its mission and goals. Within established guidelines of the institution, programs and services must establish procedures for staff selection, training, and evaluation; set expectations for supervision, and provide appropriate professional development opportunities. The program and service must strive to improve the professional competence and skills of all personnel it employs.

Professional staff members who provide clinical services must hold an earned graduate degree or appropriate license in a field relevant to the position description or must possess an appropriate combination of educational credentials and related work experience.

The ATODP should be supervised by professional staff members who have earned a master's degree from an accredited institution in fields of study such as health education, student services/development, psychology, social work, counseling, education, public health, or other appropriate health-related area, and who have relevant training and experience. Such training and experience should include prevention and intervention, assessment and treatment issues and strategies, and supervised work with older adolescents and adults of all ages.

The ATODP prevention specialist must hold a minimum of a bachelor's degree in a related field and have relevant training and experience.

Training and experience should include an understanding of prevention and intervention strategies as well as work experience with college students.

Degree or credential seeking interns, or others in training, must be qualified by enrollment in an appropriate field of study and by relevant experience. These individuals must be trained and supervised adequately by professional staff members holding educational credential and related work experience appropriate for supervision.

Student employees and volunteers must be carefully selected, trained, supervised, and evaluated. They must be trained on how and when to refer those in need of assistance to qualified staff members and have access to a supervisor for assistance in making these judgments. Student employees and volunteers must be provided clear and precise job descriptions, pre-service training based on assessed needs, and continuing staff development.

The ATODP must have support and technical staff members adequate to accomplish its mission. Staff members must be technologically proficient and qualified to perform their job functions, be knowledgeable of ethical and legal uses of technology, and have access to training. The level of staffing and workloads must be adequate and appropriate for program and service demands.

Salary levels and fringe benefits for all staff members must be commensurate with those for comparable positions within the institution, in similar institutions, and in the relevant geographic area.

ATODP must institute hiring and promotion practices which are fair, inclusive, and non-discriminatory. Programs and services must employ a diverse staff to provide readily identifiable role models for students and to enrich the campus community.

ATODP must create and maintain position descriptions for all staff members and provide regular performance planning and appraisals.

The ATODP must have regular systems of staff selection and evaluation, and must provide access to continuing education and professional development opportunities, including in-service training programs and participation in professional conferences and workshops.

The ATODP should provide training on problem recognition and referral procedures for professional and support staff, pre-professionals, and paraprofessionals.

Part 6. FINANCIAL RESOURCES

The Alcohol, Tobacco, and Other Drugs Program (ATODP) must have adequate funding to accomplish its mission and goals. Funding priorities must be determined within the context of the stated mission, goals, objectives, and comprehensive analysis of the needs and capabilities of students and the availability of internal and external resources.

The ATODP must demonstrate fiscal responsibility and cost effectiveness consistent with institutional protocols.

The institution should provide sufficient baseline funding for the ATODP so that staff members may spend the majority of their time on planning, programming, providing services, and evaluation rather than on seeking new or continuing funding sources.

Part 7. FACILITIES, TECHNOLOGY, and EQUIPMENT

The Alcohol, Tobacco, and Other Drugs Program (ATODP) must have adequate, suitably located facilities, adequate technology and equipment to support its mission and goals efficiently and effectively. Facilities, technology, and equipment must be evaluated regularly and be in compliance with relevant federal, state/provincial, and local requirements to provide for access, health, safety, and security.

Facilities for the ATODP should support a range of services, including prevention, education, assessment, intervention, programming, and a resource center.

Office space should be physically separate from human resources, campus security, and judicial programs.

Facilities and furnishings should ensure secure confidential files.

The ATODP should be provided facilities that ensure confidentiality and a location in which students, faculty, and staff might access and read information on alcohol, tobacco, and other drugs.

The ATODP should possess, or have access to, equipment and services such as audio-visual equipment and services, printing services, campus and community media resources, and computers.

Part 8. LEGAL RESPONSIBILITIES

Alcohol, Tobacco, and Other Drugs Program (ATODP) staff members must be knowledgeable about and responsive to law and regulations that relate to their respective responsibilities. Staff members must inform users of programs and services and officials, as appropriate, of legal obligations and limitations including constitutional, statutory, regulatory, and case law; mandatory laws and orders emanating from federal, state/provincial and local governments; and the institution's policies.

Staff members must use reasonable and informed practices to limit the liability exposure of the institution, its officers, employees, and agents. ATODP staff members must be informed about institutional policies regarding personal liability and related insurance coverage options.

The institution must provide access to legal advice for staff members as needed to carry out assigned responsibilities.

ATODP staff members must be aware of and seek advice from the institution's legal counsel on privacy and disclosure of student information and parental notification.

The institution must inform staff and students, in a timely and systematic fashion, about extraordinary or changing legal obligations and potential liabilities.

Part 9. EQUITY AND ACCESS

Alcohol, Tobacco, and Other Drugs Program (ATODP) staff members must ensure that services and programs are provided on a fair and equitable basis. ATODP must be accessible. Hours of operation and access to programs must be responsive to the needs of all students and other constituents. The ATODP must adhere to the spirit and intent of equal opportunity laws.

The ATODP must be open and readily accessible to all students and must not discriminate except where sanctioned by law and institutional policy. Discrimination must be avoided on the bases of age; color; creed; cultural heritage; disability; ethnicity; gender identity; nationality; political affiliation; religious affiliation; sex; sexual orientation; or social, economic, marital, or veteran status.

Consistent with its mission and goals, the ATODP program must take affirmative action to remedy significant imbalances in student participation and staffing patterns.

As the demographic profiles of campuses change and new instructional delivery methods are introduced, institutions must recognize the needs of students who participate in distance learning for access to programs and services offered on campus. Institutions must provide appropriate services in ways that are accessible to distance learners and assist them in identifying and gaining access to other appropriate services in their geographic region.

Part 10. CAMPUS and EXTERNAL RELATIONS

The Alcohol, Tobacco, and Other Drugs Program

(ATODP) must establish, maintain, and promote effective relations with relevant campus offices, community agencies and leaders and other external agencies.

The ATODP must gather and disseminate information to the campus community, including students, their parents, staff, and faculty on alcohol, tobacco, and other drug problems, risk reduction strategies, resources and related topics.

The ATODP must maintain effective working relationships with various campus offices and community groups and agencies to promote a healthy environment in which the use or abuse of alcohol and use of other drugs does not interfere with the learning, performance, or social aspects of college life.

These campus offices may include senior administrators; medical services; health promotion and prevention services; counseling; law enforcement and safety; judicial programs; residential life; campus information and visitor services; fraternity and sorority life; athletics; student and other campus media; disability support services, student activities offices and student organizations; academic departments; personnel services; and community relations and public affairs. Community agencies may include relevant local, state/provincial, and federal agencies and authorities such as the state liquor store control authority, state alcohol agency, the office of highway traffic safety, mayor and council, neighborhood associations, faith community, family, parents or guardians, school systems, area health care and treatment providers, support groups, as well as representatives from the local chamber of commerce and the hospitality industry.

The ATODP should engage the campus and community in the issues of access and availability of alcohol, tobacco, and other drugs, and in the enforcement of the law.

The ATODP must work with campus and community resources to encourage staff members to utilize appropriate screening protocols.

Part 11. DIVERSITY

Within the context of the institution's unique mission, diversity enriches the community and enhances the collegiate experience for all; therefore, the Alcohol, Tobacco, and Other Drugs Program (ATODP) must nurture environments where commonalities and differences among people are recognized and honored.

The ATODP must promote cultural educational experiences that are characterized by open and continuous communication that deepens understanding of one's own identity, and promote respect about commonalities and differences in their historical and cultural contexts.

The ATODP must address the characteristics and needs of a diverse population when establishing and implementing policies and procedures.

Part 12. ETHICS

All persons involved in the delivery of Alcohol, Tobacco, and Other Drugs Program (ATODP) must adhere to the highest principles of ethical behavior. The ATODP must develop or adopt and implement statements of ethical practice. The programs must publish these statements and ensure their periodic review by relevant constituencies.

ATODP staff members must ensure that privacy and confidentiality are maintained with respect to all communications and records to the extent that such records are protected under the law and appropriate statements of ethical practice. Information contained in students' educational records must not be disclosed without written consent except as allowed by relevant laws and institutional policies. Staff members must disclose to appropriate authorities information judged to be of an emergency nature, especially when the safety of the individual or others is involved, or when otherwise required by institutional policy or relevant law.

All staff members must be aware of and comply with the provisions contained in the institution's human subjects research policy and in other relevant institutional policies addressing ethical practices and confidentiality of research data concerning individuals.

Staff members must recognize and avoid personal conflict of interest or appearance thereof in their transactions with students and others.

Staff members must strive to insure the fair, objective, and impartial treatment of all persons with whom they deal. Staff members must not participate in any form of harassment that demeans persons or creates an intimidating, hostile, or offensive campus environment.

When handling institutional funds, ATODP staff members must ensure that such funds are managed in accordance with established and responsible accounting procedures and the fiscal policies or processes of the institution.

Staff members must perform their duties within the limits of their training, expertise, and competence. When these limits are exceeded, individuals in need of further assistance must be referred to persons possessing appropriate qualifications.

Staff members must use suitable means to confront and otherwise hold accountable other staff members who exhibit unethical behavior.

Staff members must be knowledgeable about and practice ethical behavior in the use of technology.

Part 13. ASSESSMENT and EVALUATION

Alcohol, Tobacco, and Other Drugs Programs (ATODP) must conduct regular assessment and evaluations. ATODP must employ effective qualitative and quantitative methodologies as appropriate, to determine whether and to what degree the stated mission, goals, and student learning and development outcomes are being met. The process must employ sufficient and sound assessment measures to ensure comprehensiveness. Data collected must include responses from students and other affected constituencies.

Programs and services must evaluate periodically how well they complement and enhance the institution's stated mission and educational effectiveness.

Results of these evaluations must be used in revising and improving programs and services and in recognizing staff performance.

The ATODP must assess systematically the following campus factors:
- attitudes, beliefs, and behaviors regarding alcohol, tobacco, and other drug use, abuse, and dependency
- consequences of alcohol, tobacco, or other drug use or abuse upon social skills; academic and work performance; property damage; policy violations; health, counseling, and disciplinary caseloads; and other indicators of problems
- perceptions of campus alcohol, tobacco, and other drug use norms
- features of the environment that abet high-risk alcohol use, tobacco, and other drug use marketing and promotion that promotes heavy or underage consumption of alcohol; inconsistent enforcement of campus policy and community law; lack of availability of alcohol-free social and recreational options on campus and in the surrounding community

The ATODP should assess the norms, behaviors, and behavioral consequences of specific focus populations.

The ATODP and other campus entities must exchange general and non-confidential assessment results of mutual application and benefit.

General Standards revised in 2002; ATODP content developed/ revised in 1990, 1997, & 2003

THE ROLE of CAMPUS ACTIVITIES
CAS Standards Contextual Statement

One of the first noted formal campus organizations established for the purpose of bringing students together (primarily for debating important issues of the day) was the Oxford Union founded in 1823. The Union's clubs also provided educational opportunities beyond the classroom, through such group activities as discussions of literature and poetry and involvement in hobbies and recreational activities. Today, numerous clubs and organizations (hundreds on some campuses) offer students opportunities to learn through their involvement in campus life. There is little debate now that the collegiate experience involves what occurs outside the classroom and that a college education includes more than what goes on in the classroom.

Campus activities describes in part the combined efforts of clubs and organizations established for and/or by students, including, but not limited to, governance, leadership, service, cultural, social, diversity, recreational, artistic, political and religious activities. Many of these efforts focus on programs that serve to educate, develop, or entertain club, organization, or group members, their guests, and the campus community.

Theory of involvement contends that the amount of energy—both physical and psychological—that students expend at their institution positively affects their development during college. Studies indicate that students who are involved in campus life devote considerable energy to their academic programs, spend considerable time on campus, participate actively in student organizations, and interact frequently with other students (Astin, 1996; Kuh, Douglas, Lund, Ramin-Gyurmek, 1994). Campus activities is one of the vehicles for involving students with the institution.

Though students' efforts are the backbone of campus activities, campus activity advisors serve as the catalysts for these efforts. They plan and implement training for student leaders and group members to assist them in attaining their goals, primarily regarding working with others; provide continuity for student clubs and organizations from year to year; educate students about institution policy, related legal matters, and fiscal responsibility; mediate conflicts between individuals and groups; encourage innovation and responsibility in program implementation; provide opportunities to practice leadership and organizational skills; integrate knowledge gained in the classroom with actual practice; and instruct about ethics, diversity, and other critical values.

The role of campus activity advisors is certainly linked to the quality of a student's involvement experience and thus a student's development. The CAS Standards and Guidelines that follow offer direction for campus activity advisors to create quality campus activity programs that are engaging, developmental, and experiential.

References, Readings, and Resources

Astin, A. W. (1996a). Involvement in learning revisited: Lessons we have learned. *Journal of College Student Development, 37*, 123-134.

Boatman, S. (1997). Leadership programs in campus activities. *The management of campus activities*. Columbia, SC: National Association of Campus Activities Education Foundation.

Cuyjet, M. J. (1996). Program development and group advising. In S. R. Komives & D. B. Woodward, Jr. (Eds*.), Student services: A handbook for the profession* (3rd ed., pp. 397-414). San Francisco: Jossey-Bass.

Julian, F. (1997). Law and campus life. *The management of student activities*. Columbia, SC: National Association for Campus Activities.

Kuh, G. D., Douglas, K. B., Lund, J. P., & Ramin-Gyurmek, J. (1994) *Student learning outside the classroom: Transcending artificial boundaries*. ASHE-ERIC Higher Education Report No. 8, Washington, DC: The George Washington University, Graduate School of Education and Human Development.

Meabon, D., Krehbiel, L., & Suddick, D. (1996). Financing campus activities. *The management of student activities*. Columbia, SC: National Association for Campus Activities.

Metz, N. D. (1996). *Student development in college unions and student activities*. Bloomington, IN: Association of College Unions International.

Nejman, M. R. (1995). *Diversity, student activities, and their roles in community colleges: Developing an effective program to achieve unity through diversity*. Columbia, SC: National Association for Campus Activities.

Roberts, D. C. (2003). Community Building and Programming. In S. R. Komives & D. B. Woodard (Eds.), *Student Services: A handbook for the profession* (4th ed.) (pp. 539-554). San Francisco: Jossey Bass.

Skipper, T. L. & Argo, R. (Eds.). (2003). *Involvement in campus activities and the retention of first-year college students*. Columbia, SC: National Resource Center for the First-Year Experience & Students in Transition and National Association of Campus Activities.

American College Personnel Association, Commission for Students, Their Activities and Their Community. One Dupont Circle, N.W., Suite 300, Washington, DC 20036-1110. (202) 835-2272; Webpage: http://www.myacpa.org

Association of College Unions International (ACUI), One City Center. 120 W. Seventh Street, Suite 200, Bloomington, IN 47404-3925; Webpage: www.acui.org

National Association for College Activities. 13 Harbison Way, Columbia, SC 29212-3401. (803) 732-6222; Web Page: www.naca.org

Contributor: Jan Arminio, Shippensburg University, NACA

CAMPUS ACTIVITIES PROGRAMS
CAS Standards and Guidelines

Part 1. MISSION

The Campus Activities Program (CAP) must incorporate student learning and student development in its mission. The CAP must enhance overall educational experiences. The CAP must develop, record, disseminate, implement and regularly review its mission and goals. Mission statements must be consistent with the mission and goals of the institution and with the standards in this document. The CAP must operate as an integral part of the institution's overall mission.

The CAP must complement the institution's academic programs. The purposes must enhance the overall educational experiences of students through development of, exposure to, and participation in social, cultural, multicultural, intellectual, recreational, community service, and campus governance programs.

Campus activities programs should provide environments in which students and student organizations are afford opportunities and are offered assistance to:

- participate in co-curricular activities; participate in campus governance
- develop leadership abilities
- develop healthy interpersonal relationships; use leisure time productively
- explore activities in individual and group settings for self-understanding and growth
- learn about varied cultures and experiences, ideas and issues, art and musical forms, and styles of life
- design and implement programs to enhance social, cultural, multi-cultural, intellectual, recreational, community service, and campus governance involvement; comprehend institutional policies and procedures and their relationship to individual and group interests and activities; and learn of and use campus facilities and other resources

Campus activities programs should be planned and implemented collaboratively by students, professional staff, and faculty. Such programs should reflect the institution's ideals and should serve to achieve its goals. These programs especially serve to enhance the appropriate recruitment and retention of students, to strengthen campus and community relations, and to reinforce accurate images of the institution. Programs should be comprehensive and should reflect and promote the diversity of student interests and needs, allowing especially for the achievement by students of a sense of self-worth and pride.

Part 2. PROGRAM

The formal education of students consists of the curriculum and the co-curriculum, and must promote student learning and development that is purposeful and holistic. The Campus Activities Program (CAP) must identify relevant and desirable student learning and development outcomes and provide programs and services that encourage the achievement of those outcomes.

Relevant and desirable outcomes include: intellectual growth, effective communication, realistic self-appraisal, enhanced self-esteem, clarified values, career choices, leadership development, healthy behaviors, meaningful interpersonal relationships, independence, collaboration, social responsibility, satisfying and productive lifestyles, appreciation of diversity, spiritual awareness, and achievement of personal and educational goals.

The CAP must provide evidence of its impact on the achievement of student learning and development outcomes.

The table below offers examples of evidence of achievement of student learning and development.

Student Learning and Development Outcome Domains

Intellectual growth
Examples of achievement indicators

Produces personal and educational goal statements; Employs critical thinking in problem solving; Uses complex information from a variety of sources including personal experience and observation to form a decision or opinion; Obtains a degree; Applies previously understood information and concepts to a new situation or setting; Expresses appreciation for literature, the fine arts, mathematics, sciences, and social sciences

Effective communication
Examples of achievement indicators

Writes and speaks coherently and effectively; Writes and speaks after reflection; Able to influence others through writing, speaking or artistic expression; Effectively articulates abstract ideas; Uses appropriate syntax; Makes presentations or gives performances

Enhanced self-esteem

Examples of achievement indicators

Shows self-respect and respect for others; Initiates actions toward achievement of goals; Takes reasonable risks; Demonstrates assertive behavior; Functions without need for constant reassurance from others

Realistic self-appraisal

Examples of achievement indicators

Articulates personal skills and abilities; Makes decisions and acts in congruence with personal values; Acknowledges personal strengths and weaknesses; Articulates rationale for personal behavior; Seeks feedback from others; Learns from past experiences

Clarified values

Examples of achievement indicators

Articulates personal values; Acts in congruence with personal values; Makes decisions that reflect personal values; Demonstrates willingness to scrutinize personal beliefs and values; Identifies personal, work, and lifestyle values and explains how they influence decision-making

Career choices

Examples of achievement indicators

Articulates career choices based on assessment of interests, values, skills, and abilities; Documents knowledge, skills, and accomplishments resulting from formal education, work experience, community service, and volunteer experiences; Makes the connections between classroom and out-of-classroom learning; Can construct a resume with clear job objectives and evidence of related knowledge, skills and accomplishments; Articulates the characteristics of a preferred work environment; Comprehends the world of work; Takes steps to initiate a job search or seek advanced education

Leadership development

Examples of achievement indicators

Articulates leadership philosophy or style; Serves in a leadership position in a student organization; Comprehends the dynamics of a group; Exhibits democratic principles as a leader; Exhibits ability to visualize a group purpose and desired outcomes

Healthy behavior

Examples of achievement indicators

Chooses behaviors and environments that promote health and reduce risk; Articulates the relationship between health and wellness and accomplishing life-long goals; Exhibits behaviors that advance a healthy community

Meaningful interpersonal relationships

Examples of achievement indicators

Develops and maintains satisfying interpersonal relationships; Establishes mutually rewarding relationships with friends and colleagues; Listens to and considers others' points of view; Treats others with respect

Independence

Examples of achievement indicators

Exhibits self-reliant behaviors; Functions autonomously; Exhibits ability to function interdependently; Accepts supervision as needed; Manages time effectively

Collaboration

Examples of achievement indicators

Works cooperatively with others; Seeks the involvement of others; Seeks feedback from others; Contributes to achievement of a group goal; Exhibits effective listening skills

Social responsibility

Examples of achievement indicators

Understands and participates in relevant governance systems; Understands, abides by, and participates in the development, maintenance, and/or orderly change of community, social, and legal standards or norms; Appropriately challenges the unfair, unjust, or uncivil behavior of other individuals or groups; Participates in service/volunteer activities

Satisfying and productive lifestyles

Examples of achievement indicators

Achieves balance between education, work, and leisure time; Articulates and meets goals for work, leisure, and education; Overcomes obstacles that hamper goal achievement; Functions on the basis of personal identity, ethical, spiritual, and moral values; Articulates long-term goals and objectives

Appreciating diversity

Examples of achievement indicators

Understands one's own identity and culture; Seeks involvement with people different from oneself; Seeks involvement in diverse interests; Articulates the advantages and challenges of a diverse society; Challenges appropriately the abusive use of stereotypes by others; Understands the impact of diversity on one's own society

Spiritual awareness

Examples of achievement indicators

Develops and articulates personal belief system; Understands roles of spirituality in personal and group values and behaviors

Personal and educational goals
Examples of achievement indicators

Sets, articulates, and pursues individual goals; Articulates personal and educational goals and objectives; Uses personal and educational goals to guide decisions; Understands the effect of one's personal and educational goals on others

The CAP must be (a) intentional, (b) coherent, (c) based on theories and knowledge of learning and human development, (d) reflective of developmental and demographic profiles of the student population, and (e) responsive to needs of individuals, special populations, and communities.

Campus activities must include social, cultural, multicultural, intellectual, recreational, governance, leadership, group development, campus and community service, and entertainment programs. Effective administrative support and individual and group advising must be provided.

The CAP should be based on valid indicators of student needs and interests, such as results of needs assessment surveys, research findings, professional literature, and judgments of professionals.

The CAP should be of broad scope, inclusive of all educational domains for student learning and development. Representative programming includes activities that:

- reinforce classroom instruction and complement academic learning
- offer instruction and experience in social skills and social interactions
- provide opportunities for individual participation in group membership and leadership
- develop citizenship through participation in campus and community affairs
- foster campus and community inter-group participation in common concerns and interests
- promote physical and psychosocial well-being
- stimulate the cultural, intellectual, and social life of the campus community
- promote understanding of people of varied cultures and ethnic backgrounds
- raise awareness about and address the needs of women, persons with disabilities, and other special populations
- develop and disseminate activities calendars, organizational directories, student handbooks, and other materials on public events
- foster meaningful interactions between students and members of the faculty, administration, and staff

The CAP should be promoted and produced according to professional practices and protocols. They should blend into the fabric of the institution, adding richness and texture to on-going and integral functions. Programs may evolve from student self-governing bodies which may conduct a wide variety of activities and services, including executive, judicial, legislative, business functions, and educational programs consistent with institutional values and mission.

The CAP may involve recruiting, negotiating, and contracting with performers by students. Entertainment should reflect the values stated in the campus activities mission statement. Admission fees for activities should be maintained at levels that encourage wide- spread student attendance at events. Policies should discourage hospitality requirements allowing for the provision of alcohol for entertainers. A constituency based advisory system should be in place for activities planning, execution, and evaluation.

Part 3. LEADERSHIP
Effective and ethical leadership is essential to the success of all organizations. Institutions must appoint, position, and empower Campus Activities Program (CAP) leaders within the administrative structure to accomplish stated missions. CAP leaders at various levels must be selected on the basis of formal education and training, relevant work experience, personal skills and competencies, relevant professional credentials, as well as potential for promoting learning and development in students, applying effective practices to educational processes, and enhancing institutional effectiveness. Institutions must determine expectations of accountability for leaders and fairly assess their performance.

CAP leaders must exercise authority over resources for which they are responsible to achieve their respective missions.

CAP leaders must:
- **articulate a vision for their organization**
- **set goals and objectives based on the needs and capabilities of the population served**
- **promote student learning and development**
- **prescribe and practice ethical behavior**
- **recruit, select, supervise, and develop others in the organization**
- **manage financial resources**
- **coordinate human resources**
- **plan, budget for, and evaluate personnel and programs**
- **apply effective practices to educational and administrative processes**
- **communicate effectively**
- **initiate collaborative interaction between**

individuals and agencies that possess legitimate concerns and interests in the functional area

CAP leaders must identify and find means to address individual, organizational, or environmental conditions that inhibit goal achievement.

CAP leaders must promote campus environments that result in multiple opportunities for student learning and development.

CAP leaders must continuously improve programs and services in response to changing needs of students and other constituents and evolving institutional priorities.

Part 4. ORGANIZATION and MANAGEMENT

Guided by an overarching intent to ensure student learning and development, Campus Activities Programs (CAP) must be structured purposefully and managed effectively to achieve stated goals. Evidence of appropriate structure must include current and accessible policies and procedures, written performance expectations for all employees, functional workflow graphics or organizational charts, and clearly stated service delivery expectations.

Evidence of effective management must include use of comprehensive and accurate information for decisions, clear sources and channels of authority, effective communication practices, decision-making and conflict resolution procedures, responsiveness to changing conditions, accountability and evaluation systems, and recognition and reward processes. CAP must provide channels within the organization for regular review of administrative policies and procedures.

The administrative leader of campus activities programs normally is responsible to the chief student affairs officer.

Part 5. HUMAN RESOURCES

The Campus Activities Program (CAP) must be staffed adequately by individuals qualified to accomplish its mission and goals. Within established guidelines of the institution, CAP must establish procedures for staff selection, training, and evaluation; set expectations for supervision, and provide appropriate professional development opportunities. The program must strive to improve the professional competence and skills of all personnel it employs.

CAP professional staff members must hold an earned graduate degree in a field relevant to the position they hold or must possess an appropriate combination of educational credentials and related work experience.

Professional staff members should be qualified by experience and formal graduate studies including at least a master's degree in college student affairs, higher education administration, or a related program. Graduate studies should include courses in the behavioral sciences, management, recreation, student affairs, student development, and research techniques. Institutions may require particular training and experience appropriate to serving distinctive campus populations and specialized campus or community needs.

The primary functions of full-time professional staff members include the administration and coordination of campus activities programs; assessment of student interests and needs; planning, implementing, and evaluating programs for students; advising student groups; and advising student self-governance organizations.

Depending upon the scope of campus activities programs, the activities staff may include an activities director, a program coordinator, organization and program advisors, orientation and leadership specialists, and a financial officer.

At least one professional staff member should be assigned to be responsible for campus activities programs at each institution. Qualifications of campus activities staff members include:
- ability to collaborate with faculty, administrative, staff colleagues, students and all other constituencies
- capacity to interpret student concerns and interests to the campus community
- expertise in the developmental education of students
- skill to create and deliver programs, activities, and services to students and to student groups
- skill for promoting student leadership
- capability of serving as a role model of ethical behavior
- commitment to professional and personal development
- knowledge of group dynamics and abilities to work effectively with groups

Degree or credential-seeking interns must be qualified by enrollment in an appropriate field of study and by relevant experience. These individuals must be trained and supervised adequately by professional CAP staff members holding educational credentials and related work experience appropriate for supervision.

Student employees and volunteers must be carefully selected, trained, supervised, and evaluated. They must be trained on how and when to refer those in need of assistance to qualified staff members and have access to a supervisor for assistance in making these judgments. Student employees and volunteers must be provided clear and precise job descriptions, pre-service training based on assessed needs, and continuing staff development.

Individuals such as part time professionals, graduate assistants, practicum and internship students, hourly wage employees, and volunteers may support full-time professional staff and assist with campus activities programs.

The CAP must have technical and support staff members adequate to accomplish its mission. CAP staff members must be technologically proficient and qualified to perform their job functions, be knowledgeable of ethical and legal uses of technology, and have access to training. The level of staffing and workloads must be adequate and appropriate for program and service demands.

Salary levels and fringe benefits for all CAP staff members must be commensurate with those for comparable positions within the institution, in similar institutions, and in the relevant geographic area.

The CAP must institute hiring and promotion practices that are fair, inclusive, and non-discriminatory. Programs and services must employ a diverse staff to provide readily identifiable role models for students and to enrich the campus community.

The CAP must create and maintain position descriptions for all CAP staff members and provide regular performance planning and appraisals.

The CAP must have a system for regular staff evaluation and must provide access to continuing education and professional development opportunities, including in-service training programs and participation in professional conferences and workshops.

Thorough training should be provided for student employees and volunteers to enable them to carry out their duties and responsibilities and to enhance their personal experiences with campus activities programs. Appropriate training should be offered for all staff members. Training in leadership, organizational planning, ethical decision making and communication skills should be emphasized. Staff members should develop resourcefulness, empathy, openness to serving a diverse student population, and creativity.

Joint ventures in staff development should be encouraged by colleagues in allied programs such as recreational sports, residence halls programming, and special programs for students

of traditionally under-represented groups and international students, regardless of whether they are administratively connected with campus activities programs.

Student participation in campus activities should be encouraged. Students should be trained in leadership concepts and skills, organizational development, ethical behavior, and other skill training particular to distinctive programming requirements, such as contracting for entertainment. Training should emphasize mutual sensitivity, recognizing diverse and special student or community population needs.

Part 6. FINANCIAL RESOURCES

The Campus Activities Program (CAP) must have adequate funding to accomplish its mission and goals. Funding priorities must be determined within the context of the stated mission, goals, objectives, and comprehensive analysis of the needs and capabilities of students and the availability of internal or external resources.

The CAP must demonstrate fiscal responsibility and cost effectiveness consistent with institutional protocols.

Methods for collecting and allocating fees must be clear and equitable. The authority and processes for decisions relevant to campus activities fees must be clearly established and funds be spent consistent with established priorities.

Funds for campus activities programs may be provided through state appropriations, institutional budgets, activities fees, user fees, membership and other specialized fees, revenues from programming or fund raising projects, grants, and foundation resources. Funds may be supplemented by income from ticket sales, sales of promotional items, and individual or group gifts consistent with institutional policies.

Students who have fiscal responsibility must be provided with information and training regarding institutional regulations and policies that govern accounting and handling of funds.

Adequate funding should be available for CAP including social, cultural, multicultural, intellectual, recreational, and campus governance programs.

Authority for decisions relevant to campus activities fees should rest in large part with students. Because of the amounts of money generated by campus activities and because of the transience of the student population, good business practice dictates that reasonable safeguards be established to ensure responsible management of and accounting for the funds involved. Student organizations may be required to maintain their funds with the institution's business office in which an account for each group is established and where bookkeeping and auditing services are provided. When possible, it is recommended that processes be established to permit individual student organizations to keep account of their own business transactions. Within this framework, the campus activities office works collaboratively with student organizations on matters of bookkeeping and budgeting, and other matters of fiscal accountability, including contract negotiations, consistent with institutional practices.

Mandatory activities fees normally are initiated by a vote of the student body. The fees, once approved through institutional processes, may be managed and allocations distributed by representative student governing bodies or by another allocations board or committee.

Finance committees of student organizations or student governments should work collaboratively with staff members to establish campus activities fees and priorities. Students and staff members should share responsibility for budget development and implementation according to mutually established program priorities. Specialized fees, generally applicable to college unions and residence halls governing groups and administered by their representative governing bodies, can be considered as part of the overall funding of the range of student activities available. In addition, professional staff members should educate students about the basics of financial management.

Part 7. FACILITIES, TECHNOLOGY, and EQUIPMENT

The Campus Activities Program (CAP) must have adequate, suitably located facilities, adequate technology, and equipment to support its mission and goals efficiently and effectively. Facilities, technology, and equipment must be evaluated regularly and be in compliance with relevant federal, state, provincial, and local requirements to provide for access, health, safety, and security.

Facilities should be located conveniently and designed with flexibility to serve the wide variety of functions associated with campus activities. Appropriate facilities, accessible to all clients, should be provided including student organization offices and adequately equipped public performance spaces.

The CAP may occur in college unions. [*See Standards and Guidelines for College Unions.*] In addition to their traditional programming, social and service facilities, unions typically house campus activities programs, student organization offices, and related meeting and work and storage rooms. Campus activities functions also may take place in the residence halls, recreation centers, fraternity and sorority houses, sports facilities, and other campus locations. Staff and student space should be designed to encourage maximum interaction among students and between staff members and students.

Part 8. LEGAL RESPONSIBILITIES

Campus Activities Program (CAP) staff members must be knowledgeable about and responsive to laws and regulations that relate to their respective responsibilities. CAP staff members must inform users of programs and services and officials, as appropriate, of legal obligations and limitations including constitutional, statutory, regulatory, and case law; mandatory laws and orders emanating from federal, state/provincial and local governments; and the institution's policies.

CAP staff members must use reasonable and informed practices to limit the liability exposure of the institution, its officers, employees, and agents. Staff members must be informed about institutional policies regarding personal liability and related insurance coverage options.

The institution must provide access to legal advice for CAP staff members as needed to carry out assigned responsibilities.

The institution must inform CAP staff and students in a timely and systematic fashion about extraordinary or changing legal obligations and potential liabilities.

Part 9. EQUITY and ACCESS

Campus Activities Program (CAP) staff members must ensure that services and programs are provided on a fair and equitable basis. Facilities, programs, and services must be accessible. Hours of operation and delivery of and access to programs and services must be responsive to the needs of all students and other constituents. The CAP must adhere to the spirit and intent of equal opportunity laws.

The CAP must be open and readily accessible to all students and must not discriminate except where sanctioned by law and institutional policy. Discrimination must be avoided on the bases of age; color; creed; cultural heritage; disability; ethnicity; gender identity; nationality; political affiliation; religious affiliation; sex; sexual orientation; or social, economic, marital, or veteran status.

Consistent with their mission and goals, the CAP must take affirmative action to remedy significant imbalances in student participation and staffing patterns.

As the demographic profiles of campuses change and new instructional delivery methods are introduced, institutions must recognize the needs of students who participate in distance learning for access to programs and services offered on campus. Institutions must provide appropriate services in ways that are accessible to distance learners and assist them in identifying and gaining access to other appropriate services in their geographic region.

Part 10. CAMPUS and EXTERNAL RELATIONS
The Campus Activities Program (CAP) must establish, maintain, and promote effective relations with relevant individuals, campus offices, and external agencies.

Campus activities programs should encourage faculty and staff members throughout the campus community to be involved in campus activities. Faculty members should serve as valuable resources related to their academic disciplines, especially as lecturers, performers, artists, and workshop facilitators. Faculty and staff members who serve as administrative advisors may work directly with organizations in program and leadership development and should be supported by the activities staff. Faculty, staff members, and administrators external to the program or institution may be important resources for activities programs. Faculty and staff members, administrators, and students may serve together on advisory boards to provide leadership for important initiatives.

Campus activities programs are highly visible to persons on and off campus and may be influential in forming public opinion about the institution and creating a positive environment for both communities. Cooperation between governmental and social organizations and campus activities programs on matters of mutual community concern strengthens the institution's role in the community, expands the resources available to both communities, and provides valuable developmental opportunities for students.

Part 11. DIVERSITY
Within the context of each institution's unique mission, diversity enriches the community and enhances the collegiate experience for all; therefore, the Campus Activities Program (CAP) must nurture environments where commonalties and differences among people are recognized and honored.

The CAP must promote educational experiences that are characterized by open and continuous communication that deepens understanding of one's own identity, culture, and heritage, and that of others. The CAP must educate and promote respect about commonalties and differences in their historical and cultural contexts.

The CAP must address the characteristics and needs of a diverse population when establishing and implementing policies and procedures.

The CAP must provide educational activities that sensitize all constituencies to an appreciation and understanding of cultural diversity among people. Activities programs must emphasize self assessment and personal responsibility for improving intercultural relations.

The CAP must provide educational programs that help students of traditionally under represented groups identify their unique needs, set appropriate goals, and learn how to achieve them. All students must be oriented to the culture of the institution. The program must give special attention to students from traditionally under-represented groups to ensure their best chances of success.

Part 12. ETHICS
All persons involved in the delivery of the Campus Activities Program (CAP) must adhere to the highest principles of ethical behavior. The CAP must develop or adopt and implement appropriate statements of ethical practice. The program must publish these statements and ensure their periodic review by relevant constituencies .

Applicable statements may include principles and standards pertaining to:
- civil and ethical conduct
- accuracy of information (i.e., accurate presentation of institutional goals, services, and policies to the public and the college or university community, and fair and accurate representation in publicity and promotions)
- conflict of interest
- role conflicts
- fiscal accountability
- fair and equitable administration of institutional policies; effective disclosure of and respect for relevant civil and criminal law
- student involvement in related institutional decisions
- free and open exchange of ideas through campus activities programs
- fulfillment of contractual arrangements and agreements

CAP staff members must ensure that privacy and confidentiality are maintained with respect to all communications and records to the extent that such records are protected under the law and appropriate statements of ethical practice. Information contained in students' education records must not be disclosed without written consent except as allowed by relevant laws and institutional policies. CAP staff members must disclose to appropriate authorities information judged to be of an emergency nature, especially when the safety of the individual or others is involved, or when otherwise required by institutional policy or relevant law.

All CAP staff members must be aware of and comply with the provisions contained in the institution's human subjects research policy and in other relevant institutional policies addressing ethical practices and confidentiality of research data concerning individuals.

CAP staff members must recognize and avoid personal conflict of interest or appearance thereof in their transactions with students and others.

CAP staff members must strive to insure the fair, objective, and impartial treatment of all persons with whom they deal. Staff members must not participate in nor condone any form of harassment that demeans persons or creates an intimidating, hostile, or offensive campus environment.

When handling institutional funds, all CAP staff members must ensure that such funds are managed in accordance with established and responsible accounting procedures and the fiscal policies or processes of the institution.

CAP staff members must perform their duties within the limits of their training, expertise, and competence. When these limits are exceeded, individuals in need of further assistance must be referred to persons possessing appropriate qualifications.

CAP staff members must use suitable means to confront and otherwise hold accountable other staff members who exhibit unethical behavior.

CAP staff members must be knowledgeable about and practice ethical behavior in the use of technology.

Part 13. ASSESSMENT and EVALUATION

The Campus Activities Program (CAP) must conduct regular assessment and evaluations. The CAP must employ effective qualitative and quantitative methodologies as appropriate, to determine whether and to what degree the stated mission, goals, and student learning and development outcomes are being met. The process must employ sufficient and sound assessment measures to ensure comprehensiveness.

Data collected must include responses from students and other affected constituencies.

The CAP must evaluate periodically how well they complement and enhance the institution's stated mission and educational effectiveness.

Results of these evaluations must be used in revising and improving programs and services and in recognizing staff performance.

Campus activities programs should be evaluated regularly and the findings should be disseminated to appropriate campus agencies and constituencies. Evaluation procedures should yield evidence relative to student success and retention, the achievement of program goals, quality and scope of program offerings, responsiveness to expressed interests, program attendance and effectiveness, cost effectiveness, quality and appearance of facilities, equipment use and maintenance, and staff performance. Data sources should include students, staff, alumni, faculty, administrators, community members, and relevant documents and records. Instrumentation and methods should be scientifically designed and implemented. Records of program evaluations should be maintained in the office of the administrative leader of campus activities programs and should be accessible to planners of subsequent programs

General Standards revised in 2002; CAP content developed/ revised in 1986 &1997

THE ROLE of CAMPUS INFORMATION AND VISITOR SERVICES
CAS Standards Contextual Statement

The development of campus information and visitor services has been a direct result of the increasing diversity, size, complexity, and specialization of institutions of higher learning during the 20th century. This pattern has been particularly seen on campuses in the United States and has necessitated the establishment of information centers to address the many informational needs of campus communities. Often these centers have evolved into, or have been combined with, visitor services to become comprehensive gateway operations providing entry points to institutions for visitors, prospective students, alumni, and other community members. The common objective of campus information and visitor services is to bring people and campus services and resources together through increased accessibility to information.

Some of the earliest examples of visitor services and centers include the establishment in 1951 of the Visitor Center at the U.S. Military Academy at West Point and the creation of the Visitor Information Center at the University of California at Berkeley in 1965. Historically, the majority of these programs originated as extensions of institutional recruitment activities and efforts. The earliest example of specialized information and referral services on a campus can be traced to the 1970 establishment of the Campus Assistance Center at the University of Wisconsin-Madison. Specialized information and referral programs were often established as information and rumor control efforts responding to the rapid expansion of campuses, and increasing lack of trust in traditional institutional communication methods. By providing inquirers with the information and services they needed, or referring them to the appropriate resources when necessary, these programs were quickly judged to be very useful in providing improved communication within the campus community and improving the quality of campus life. These early campus information and visitor service programs quickly became permanent campus operations with philosophies focused on access and individualized service. During this early period, many of the programs established clear guidelines for assisting inquirers in a friendly, sensitive manner and assuring appropriate confidentiality. Campus information and visitor services programs have had a profound impact on their campus communities through their commitment to the principle of providing inquirers with clear, concise, thorough, and nonjudgmental information and referrals in the most welcoming environment possible.

By the late 1980s, the increasing need for accountability, outreach, and service to the broader campus community resulted in an increase in the number of campus information and visitor services operations. Institutional accessibility to appropriate and timely information is a critical component in reaching instructional,

research, and outreach priorities. For many constituents, especially during downtimes—evenings, weekends, and breaks—campus information and visitor services become the physical embodiment of an institution. Increasing emphasis on quality improvement and service within the higher education community has been another driving force in the growing number of campus information and visitor services. The increasing importance of computer-mediated (e.g., web and email) and mass communication (e.g., radio and cable television) in the provision of information by institutions, and the resulting need for support services that can assure the accuracy and relevance of rapidly expanding information, have also increased the importance of campus information and visitor services. By having access to an easily available and credible information and visitor service, inquirers are assisted in making well-informed choices, planning wise courses of action, and taking advantage of the available and/or unique resources of the institution and the surrounding community.

These standards and guidelines provide a framework for excellence in the provision of campus information and visitor services (CIVS). CIVS is the process of linking people who have campus-related questions to appropriate resources. Also, the process assists institutional planning by providing feedback to service providers and discovering gaps and duplication in campus programs and services. CIVS provide information to an inquirer in response to a direct request for such information. Inquiries comprise anything related to the campus community, such as directions to a campus building or event; how to contact a department, faculty or staff member; or whom to contact or where to go for issues of a personal nature, to resolve a problem, or to apply for admission. Inquirers may be current students, staff, faculty, alumni, prospective students and their families, other visitors, or anyone needing information about the institution. CIVS serve as a gateway to the institution, providing one-on-one information to inquirers within and about the campus. When a direct answer is not possible, then referral is made, with careful attention to the needs of the inquirer, assessment of appropriate resources and response modes, identification of programs and services capable of meeting those needs, provision of sufficient information about each program and service to help inquirers make informed choices, location of alternative resources when services are unavailable, and active linking of the inquirer to needed services when necessary.

References, Readings, and Resources

Hefferlin, J. B. L. (1971). *Information services for academic administration.* San Francisco: Jossey-Bass.

Alliance of Information and Referral Systems. (undated). *Out of the shadows: Information and referral bringing people and services together.* Seattle, Washington: Author.

Alliance of Information and Referral Systems. (undated). *The ABC's of I & R: A self-study guide for information and referral staff.* Seattle, Washington: Author.

Collegiate Information and Visitor Services Association (CIVSA), Rutgers - The State University of New Jersey Campus Information Services, 542 George Street New Brunswick, New Jersey. 08901. (732) 932-9342; (732) 932-9359 (fax); Publisher of *The Welcomer.* Web Site: www.civsa.org

Contributor: Matthew J. Weismantel, Rutgers University, CIVS

CAMPUS INFORMATION and VISITOR SERVICES

CAS Standards and Guidelines

Part 1. MISSION

The overall mission of Campus Information and Visitor Services (CIVS) is to facilitate access to the institution by providing accurate information and appropriate referrals. CIVS is a primary point of access to the institution. By providing comprehensive contact information and general descriptions for many aspects of the institution, CIVS must meet the introductory informational needs of the campus community: students, faculty, staff, prospective students and their family members, alumni, and general visitors. To accomplish this mission, CIVS must:

- provide accurate information and referrals
- provide a welcoming environment
- be readily accessible
- emphasize personal communication and interaction

CIVS must have a strong commitment to student learning and development, contributing generally to institutional and other agency missions, and because students are an integral part of mission delivery. This commitment must be reflected in its mission statement and demonstrated through quality supervision, staff development, and performance appraisals.

CIVS must incorporate student learning and student development in its mission. CIVS must enhance overall educational experiences. The service must develop, record, disseminate, implement, and regularly review its mission and goals. Mission statements must be consistent with the mission and goals of the institution and with the standards in this document. CIVS must operate as an integral part of the institution's overall mission.

Part 2. PROGRAM

Campus Information and Visitor Services (CIVS) must be responsive to the needs and interests of students, faculty, staff, alumni, prospective students, and other inquirers.

A broad array of information and services must be available to ensure that accurate resources are provided in a timely manner that accommodates the needs of inquirers.

These services may include telephone or other electronic means of contact, or a walk-in facility, such as a visitor or information center, in which the inquirer has one-to-one, human contact and easy access to information resources such as catalogs, calendars, booklets, schedules, fliers, maps, books, and brochures.

Multiple media approaches must be used to provide information.

Such approaches may include signage, maps, 24-hour recorded telephone information, emergency assistance, and up-to-date web-site listings and e-mail.

The formal education of students consists of the curriculum and the co-curriculum, and must promote student learning and development that is purposeful and holistic. CIVS must identify relevant and desirable student learning and development outcomes and provide programs and services that encourage the achievement of those outcomes.

Relevant and desirable outcomes include: intellectual growth, effective communication, realistic self-appraisal, enhanced self-esteem, clarified values, career choices, leadership development, healthy behaviors, meaningful interpersonal relationships, independence, collaboration, social responsibility, satisfying and productive lifestyles, appreciation of diversity, spiritual awareness, and achievement of personal and educational goals.

CIVS must provide evidence of its impact on the achievement of student learning and development outcomes.

The table below offers examples of evidence of achievement of student learning and development.

Student Learning and Development Outcome Domains

Intellectual growth
Examples of achievement indicators
Produces personal and educational goal statements; Employs critical thinking in problem solving; Uses complex information from a variety of sources including personal experience and observation to form a decision or opinion; Obtains a degree; Applies previously understood information and concepts to a new situation or setting; Expresses appreciation for literature, the fine arts, mathematics, sciences, and social sciences

Effective communication

Examples of achievement indicators

Writes and speaks coherently and effectively; Writes and speaks after reflection; Able to influence others through writing, speaking or artistic expression; Effectively articulates abstract ideas; Uses appropriate syntax; Makes presentations or gives performances

Enhanced self-esteem

Examples of achievement indicators

Shows self-respect and respect for others; Initiates actions toward achievement of goals; Takes reasonable risks; Demonstrates assertive behavior; Functions without need for constant reassurance from others

Realistic self-appraisal

Examples of achievement indicators

Articulates personal skills and abilities; Makes decisions and acts in congruence with personal values; Acknowledges personal strengths and weaknesses; Articulates rationale for personal behavior; Seeks feedback from others; Learns from past experiences

Clarified values

Examples of achievement indicators

Articulates personal values; Acts in congruence with personal values; Makes decisions that reflect personal values; Demonstrates willingness to scrutinize personal beliefs and values; Identifies personal, work, and lifestyle values and explains how they influence decision-making

Career choices

Examples of achievement indicators

Articulates career choices based on assessment of interests, values, skills, and abilities; Documents knowledge, skills and accomplishments resulting from formal education, work experience, community service, and volunteer experiences; Makes the connections between classroom and out-of-classroom learning; Can construct a resume with clear job objectives and evidence of related knowledge, skills and accomplishments; Articulates the characteristics of a preferred work environment; Comprehends the world of work; Takes steps to initiate a job search or seek advanced education

Leadership development

Examples of achievement indicators

Articulates leadership philosophy or style; Serves in a leadership position in a student organization; Comprehends the dynamics of a group; Exhibits democratic principles as a leader; Exhibits ability to visualize a group purpose and desired outcomes

Healthy behavior

Examples of achievement indicators

Chooses behaviors and environments that promote health and reduce risk; Articulates the relationship between health and wellness and accomplishing life-long goals; Exhibits behaviors that advance a healthy community.

Meaningful interpersonal relationships

Examples of achievement indicators

Develops and maintains satisfying interpersonal relationships; Establishes mutually rewarding relationships with friends and colleagues; Listens to and considers others' points of view; Treats others with respect

Independence

Examples of achievement indicators

Exhibits self-reliant behaviors; Functions autonomously; Exhibits ability to function interdependently; Accepts supervision as needed; Manages time effectively

Collaboration

Examples of achievement indicators

Works cooperatively with others; Seeks the involvement of others; Seeks feedback from others; Contributes to achievement of a group goal; Exhibits effective listening skills

Social responsibility

Examples of achievement indicators

Understands and participates in relevant governance systems; Understands, abides by, and participates in the development, maintenance, and/or orderly change of community, social, and legal standards or norms; Appropriately challenges the unfair, unjust, or uncivil behavior of other individuals or groups; Participates in service/volunteer activities

Satisfying and productive lifestyles

Examples of achievement indicators

Achieves balance between education, work, and leisure time; Articulates and meets goals for work, leisure, and education; Overcomes obstacles that hamper goal achievement; Functions on the basis of personal identity, ethical, spiritual, and moral values; Articulates long-term goals and objectives

Appreciating diversity

Examples of achievement indicators

Understands one's own identity and culture; Seeks involvement with people different from oneself; Seeks involvement in diverse interests; Articulates the advantages and challenges of a diverse society; Challenges appropriately the abusive use of stereotypes by others; Understands the impact of diversity on one's own society

Spiritual awareness
Examples of achievement indicators

> Develops and articulates personal belief system; Understands roles of spirituality in personal and group values and behaviors

Personal and educational goals
Examples of achievement indicators

> Sets, articulates, and pursues individual goals; Articulates personal and educational goals and objectives; Uses personal and educational goals to guide decisions; Understands the effect of one's personal and educational goals on others

CIVS must be (a) intentional, (b) coherent, (c) based on theories and knowledge of learning and human development, (d) reflective of developmental and demographic profiles of the student population, and (e) responsive to needs of individuals, special populations, and communities.

CIVS must provide specific information and referral to existing campus programs or, when such programs do not exist, actively link inquirers to alternative community and other programs that can meet their specific needs.

CIVS programs must be easily accessible to assist inquirers in making well-informed choices, plan wise courses of action, and take advantage of available institutional resources.

CIVS must develop and maintain an accurate information retrieval and delivery system of available campus and community resources. This system must be updated regularly to ensure timeliness, accuracy, and comprehensiveness of information.

CIVS must be available at locations and times that meet the needs of the inquirers.

CIVS must provide feedback to appropriate campus officials regarding conditions that may negatively influence an inquirer's interaction with the institution and propose interventions to remedy such conditions.

Feedback topics may include statistics, data analysis, relevant documentation of service use (identifying unmet needs, gaps, and services duplication), and inquirer characteristics.

CIVS must strive to assist inquirers in friendly, caring, sensitive and non-judgmental manner and provide clear, concise information. CIVS must protect the privacy of individuals within the campus community from inappropriate inquiry.

CIVS must establish and maintain a planned program of activities to increase campus and community awareness of its services, mission, goals, and objectives.

Campus information and visitor services may include a campus visitor center, a campus information center, a campus tour program, broadcast services, campus outreach, and student recruitment programs. Information and services may include:

- campus orientation and tour programs
- display and presentation space
- broadcast and electronic informational resources and support
- visitor reception space including appropriate support services and facilities adequate in size and scope to meet the volume of inquirers to be assisted

CIVS should be a principal provider of structure and content to the institution's on-line information systems.

A range of information should be provided to inquirers, including brief responses, such as names or phone numbers, as well as details about an organization's policies and procedures.

Program activities may include:

- participation in training programs of other offices and departments
- provision of printed materials such as brochures, posters, directional information and exhibits
- public service announcements
- hosting orientation tours
- information-based web site
- role as a resource for other campus and community support services

Part 3. LEADERSHIP
Effective and ethical leadership is essential to the success of all organizations. Institutions must appoint, position and empower Campus Information and Visitor Services (CIVS) leaders within the administrative structure to accomplish stated missions. CIVS leaders at various levels must be selected on the basis of formal education and training, relevant work experience, personal skills and competencies, relevant professional credentials, as well as potential for promoting learning and development in students, applying effective practices to educational processes, and enhancing institutional effectiveness. Institutions must determine expectations of accountability for leaders and fairly assess their performance.

CIVS leaders of programs and services must exercise authority over resources for which they are responsible to achieve their respective missions.

CIVS leaders must:
- articulate a vision for their organization
- set goals and objectives based on the needs and capabilities of the population served
- promote student learning and development
- prescribe and practice ethical behavior
- recruit, select, supervise, and develop others in the organization
- manage financial resources
- coordinate human resources
- plan, budget for, and evaluate personnel and programs
- apply effective practices to educational and administrative processes
- communicate effectively
- initiate collaborative interaction between individuals and agencies that possess legitimate concerns and interests in the functional area

CIVS leaders must identify and find means to address individual, organizational, or environmental conditions that inhibit goal achievement.

CIVS leaders must promote campus environments that result in multiple opportunities for student learning and development.

CIVS leaders must continuously improve programs and services in response to changing needs of students and other constituents, and evolving institutional priorities.

Part 4. ORGANIZATION and MANAGEMENT

Campus Information and Visitor Services (CIVS) is most effective in an atmosphere of staff teamwork and continuous improvement.

Guided by an overarching intent to ensure student learning and development, CIVS must be structured purposefully and managed effectively to achieve stated goals. Evidence of appropriate structure must include current and accessible policies and procedures, written performance expectations for all employees, functional workflow graphics or organizational charts, and clearly stated service delivery expectations.

Evidence of effective management must include use of comprehensive and accurate information for decisions, clear sources and channels of authority,

effective communication practices, decision-making and conflict resolution procedures, responsiveness to changing conditions, accountability and evaluation systems, and recognition and reward processes. CIVS must provide channels within the organization for regular review of administrative policies and procedures.

CIVS must have well developed policies regarding the type, breadth and currency of information contained in the information retrieval and delivery system. The information retrieval and delivery system used by campus information and visitor services must be organized according to a standardized search system. The information system must have the capacity to accept changes in a very short time frame for information that may change in between regularly scheduled updates.

Policies for the information retrieval and delivery system should include, but not be limited to, responsiveness to inquirers and proximity of the resource to the campus.

CIVS must develop and maintain accurate, up-to-date resource files that include information on available campus resources and procedures for verifying accuracy.

Informational resources should be profiled to include:
- legal name, common name, and acronym address (i.e., room, building name, street, city, zip code)
- email address
- telephone number, fax number, hours and days of service
- type and description of service(s) provided
- population(s) served
- date of last update
- internet address
- eligibility guidelines
- intake procedures
- required documents
- cost
- waiting period for service
- contact person
- auspices (i.e., city, state, private, social service, campus)

CIVS must establish and use a system of collecting and organizing inquirer data for appropriate referral and feedback to the campus community.

Campus information and visitor services should pursue meaningful research to review and improve programs and services. Members of the campus community should be involved in the review of these findings, as well as in the design and governance of campus information and visitor services.

Students, faculty, staff, and appropriate external agencies should be involved through committees, councils, and boards.

Part 5. HUMAN RESOURCES

Campus Information and Visitor Services (CIVS) must be staffed adequately by individuals qualified to accomplish its mission and goals. Within established guidelines of the institution, CIVS must establish procedures for staff selection, training, and evaluation; set expectations for supervision, and provide appropriate professional development opportunities. CIVS must strive to improve the professional competence and skills of all personnel it employs.

Continuing staff development experiences should include in-service training programs, professional conferences, workshops, and other continuing education activities.

CIVS staff positions must be filled based on a defined set of qualifications such as level of education, work experience, and personal characteristics (for example, integrity, communication skills, and leadership ability).

Professional staff members must hold an earned graduate degree in a field relevant to the position description they hold or must possess an appropriate combination of education and experience.

CIVS must intentionally seek to employ qualified students, paraprofessional employees, and recruit volunteers to assist in carrying out programs and services.

Degree or credential-seeking interns must be qualified by enrollment in an appropriate field of study and by relevant experience. These individuals must be trained and supervised adequately by professional staff members holding educational credentials and related work experience appropriate for supervision.

Student employees and volunteers must be carefully selected, trained, supervised, and evaluated. They must be trained on how and when to refer those in need of assistance to qualified staff members and have access to a supervisor for assistance in making these judgments. Student employees and volunteers must be provided clear and precise job descriptions, pre-service training based on assessed needs, and continuing staff development.

CIVS must have technical and support staff members adequate to accomplish its mission. Staff members must be technologically proficient and qualified to perform their job functions, be knowledgeable of ethical and legal uses of technology, and have access to training. The level of staffing and workloads must be adequate and appropriate for program and service demands.

A formal training program must be required for all staff, especially those who will be providing direct service.

Training programs should include experiences for initial employee orientations as well as on-the-job training, in-service group training, and individualized training based on employee needs.

Staff-training programs should include:

- strategies for understanding campus and community resources
- information retrieval, delivery and data collection
- overview of mission, vision, role, purpose, function, structure, policies, and procedures
- student development theory and practice
- customer service and basic communication skills such as interviewing, listening, empathy, clarification and problem solving; overcoming communication barriers (e.g., hearing impaired, speakers of English as a second language)

Salary levels and fringe benefits for all CIVS staff members must be commensurate with those for comparable positions within the institution, in similar institutions, and in the relevant geographic area.
CIVS must institute hiring and promotion practices that are fair, inclusive, and non-discriminatory.
CIVS must employ a diverse staff to provide readily identifiable role models for students and to enrich the campus community.

Every CIVS staff member must be expected to show respect for all inquirers.

CIVS must create and maintain position descriptions for all staff members and provide regular performance planning and appraisals.

CIVS must have a system for regular staff evaluation and must provide access to continuing education and professional development opportunities, including in-service training programs and participation in professional conferences and workshops.

Periodic formal written evaluations of CIVS staff must be conducted and kept on record.

Part 6. FINANCIAL RESOURCES

Campus Information and Visitor Services (CIVS) must have adequate funding to accomplish its mission and goals. Funding priorities must be determined within the context of the stated mission, goals, objectives, and comprehensive analysis of the needs and capabilities of students and the availability of internal or external resources.

CIVS must demonstrate fiscal responsibility and cost effectiveness consistent with institutional protocols.

Institutional funds for campus information and visitor services should be allocated on a permanent basis.

In addition to institutional commitment of general funds, other funding sources may be considered including state appropriations, federal resources, fees and generated revenue, local community funding, donations, and contributions.

Financial resources should be sufficient to provide high quality print and electronic information.

Part 7. FACILITIES, TECHNOLOGY and EQUIPMENT

Campus Information and Visitor Services (CIVS) must have adequate, suitably located facilities, adequate technology, and equipment to support its mission and goals efficiently and effectively. Facilities, technology, and equipment must be evaluated regularly and be in compliance with relevant federal, state, provincial, and local requirements to provide for access, health, safety, and security.

CIVS must play an active role in the design and decision- making process for campus signage.

The CIVS facility should include space for confidential interviewing, display for materials, visitor reception, and information and referral operations. State-of-the-art telephone and computer capability should also be included.

The CIVS facility should be accessible to and by public transportation and be at a location that can best represent the "front door" of the institution.

Part 8. LEGAL RESPONSIBILITIES

Campus Information and Visitor Services (CIVS) staff members must be knowledgeable about and responsive to laws and regulations that relate to their respective responsibilities. Staff members must inform users of programs and services and officials, as appropriate, of legal obligations and limitations including constitutional, statutory, regulatory, and case law; mandatory laws and orders emanating from

federal, state/provincial and local governments; and the institution's policies.

CIVS staff members must use reasonable and informed practices to limit the liability exposure of the institution, its officers, employees, and agents. Staff members must be informed about institutional policies regarding personal liability and related insurance coverage options.

The institution must provide access to legal advice for CIVS staff members as needed to carry out assigned responsibilities.

The institution must inform CIVS staff and students in a timely and systematic fashion about extraordinary or changing legal obligations and potential liabilities.

Part 9. EQUITY and ACCESS

Campus Information and Visitor Services (CIVS) staff members must ensure that services and programs are provided on a fair and equitable basis. Facilities, programs, and services must be accessible. Hours of operation and delivery of and access to programs and services must be responsive to the needs of all students and other constituents. CIVS must adhere to the spirit and intent of equal opportunity laws.

CIVS must be open and readily accessible to all students and must not discriminate except where sanctioned by law and institutional policy. Discrimination must especially be avoided on the basis of age; color; creed; cultural heritage; disability; ethnicity; gender identity; nationality; political affiliation; religious affiliation; sex; sexual orientation; or social, economic, marital, or veteran status.

Consistent with their mission and goals, CIVS must take affirmative action to remedy significant imbalances in student participation and staffing patterns.

As the demographic profiles of campuses change and new instructional delivery methods are introduced, institutions must recognize the needs of students who participate in distance learning for access to programs and services offered on campus. Institutions must provide appropriate services in ways that are accessible to distance learners and assist them in identifying and gaining access to other appropriate services in their geographic region.

Part 10. CAMPUS and EXTERNAL RELATIONS

Campus information and visitor services must establish, maintain, and promote effective relations with relevant individuals, campus offices, and external agencies.

CIVS should collaborate closely with campus offices and external agencies to ensure accuracy, timeliness, and reliability of information being provided to inquirers.

When appropriate, inquirers should be referred to other resources, and staff may actively participate in this linking process. This referral process is often integrated with information dissemination, intervention, and advocacy. Inquirers should be encouraged to re-contact the campus information and visitor service if additional information or assistance is needed.

Within institutional guidelines, CIVS should intervene and advocate for inquirers when information is inaccurate or misleading and/or inquirer needs have not been addressed satisfactorily. Follow-up on more complex problem situations should occur to determine the extent to which inquirer needs have been met.

Part 11. DIVERSITY

Within the context of each institution's unique mission, diversity enriches the community and enhances the collegiate experience for all; therefore, Campus Information and Visitor Services (CIVS) must nurture environments where commonalties and differences among people are recognized and honored.

CIVS must promote educational experiences that are characterized by open and continuous communication that deepens understanding of one's own identity, culture, and heritage, and that of others. CIVS must educate and promote respect about commonalties and differences in their historical and cultural contexts.

CIVS must address the characteristics and needs of a diverse population when establishing and implementing policies and procedures.

Part 12. ETHICS

All persons involved in the delivery of Campus Information and Visitor Services (CIVS) must adhere to the highest principles of ethical behavior. CIVS must develop or adopt and implement appropriate statements of ethical practice. CIVS must publish these statements and ensure their periodic review by relevant constituencies .

Ethical standards or other statements from relevant professional associations should be considered.

CIVS staff members must ensure that privacy and confidentiality are maintained with respect to all communications and records to the extent that such records are protected under the law and appropriate statements of ethical practice. Information contained in students' education records must not be disclosed without written consent except as allowed by relevant laws and institutional policies. Staff members must disclose to appropriate authorities information judged to be of an emergency nature, especially when the safety of the individual or others is involved, or when otherwise required by institutional policy or relevant law.

All CIVS staff members must be aware of and comply with the provisions contained in the institution's human subjects research policy and in other relevant institutional policies addressing ethical practices and confidentiality of research data concerning individuals.

CIVS staff members must recognize and avoid personal conflict of interest or appearance thereof in their transactions with students and others.

CIVS staff members must strive to insure the fair, objective, and impartial treatment of all persons with whom they deal. Staff members must not participate in nor condone any form of harassment that demeans persons or creates an intimidating, hostile, or offensive campus environment.

When handling institutional funds, all CIVS staff members must ensure that such funds are managed in accordance with established and responsible accounting procedures and the fiscal policies or processes of the institution.

CIVS staff members must perform their duties within the limits of their training, expertise, and competence. When these limits are exceeded, individuals in need of further assistance must be referred to persons possessing appropriate qualifications.

CIVS staff members must use suitable means to confront and otherwise hold accountable other staff members who exhibit unethical behavior.

CIVS staff members must be knowledgeable about and practice ethical behavior in the use of technology.

Part 13. ASSESSMENT and EVALUATION

Campus Information and Visitor Services (CIVS) must conduct regular assessment and evaluations. CIVS must employ effective qualitative and quantitative methodologies as appropriate, to determine whether and to what degree the stated mission, goals, and student learning and development outcomes are being met. The process must employ sufficient and sound assessment measures to ensure comprehensiveness. Data collected must include responses from students and other affected constituencies.

CIVS must evaluate periodically how well they complement and enhance the institution's stated mission and educational effectiveness.

Results of these evaluations must be used in revising and improving programs and services and in recognizing staff performance.

CIVS must maintain an on-going process to collect inquirer use and inquirer satisfaction information.

Information concerning customer type and customer use satisfaction should contribute to planning activities, information system development, and identification of duplications and gaps in university services.

Thorough assessment should focus on the extent to which inquirers can improve their information retrieval skills. All data collected by campus information and visitor services should be made available to appropriate institutional offices or agencies.

General Standards revised in 2002; CIVS content developed/ revised in 2000

THE ROLE of CAMPUS RELIGIOUS and SPIRITUAL PROGRAMS
CAS Standards Contextual Statement

The origins of religious programs at colleges and universities can be traced to their earliest beginnings in Colonial America. The first institutions of higher education were based on Protestant Christian values and had the education of clergy as one of their primary purposes. Religious and moral instruction served as the foundation of the curriculum and formed the cornerstone of a college life whose primary goal was to educate a new elite class of leaders and professionals for the young American nation (Cawthon & Jones, 2004; Hartley, 2004; Temkin & Evans, 1998).

During the 19th century, the purpose of higher education shifted away from religion toward scholarship and research, leading to a more secular culture on college campuses, where religion became marginalized (Hartley, 2004). The Morrill Land-Grant Act of 1862 and Morrill Act of 1890 made public education more available and led to the increased enrollment of students from a variety of religious and spiritual backgrounds (Butler, 1989). The creation of this new "modern" university, the weakening between institutions and their founding religious denominations, and increases in the number of non-Protestant students on college campuses, caused religious denominations to establish a variety of student organizations (e.g., Baptist Student Union, Catholic Newman Club, Jewish Hillel, Presbyterian Student Association, United Methodist Wesley Foundation) during a period from the early 1900s to 1950s. A number of independent ecumenical organizations (e.g., Campus Crusade for Christ, Fellowship of Christian Athletes, InterVarsity Fellowship) not associated with specific denominations originated during this period (Cawthon & Jones, 2004).

In defining terms such as spirituality and religion, individuals construct meanings that are as varied as the ways institutions structure programs related to this area. This standard can be used as a guide to help both assess the needs of students and to structure student religious programs to serve these needs. As students look toward more diverse options to fulfill their spiritual and religious development, institutions should continue to equip staff with knowledge of issues that surround these programs.

For the purposes of these standards, religion is defined by function, rather than substance. Spirituality, more nebulous but present and relevant as a concept and practice on college campuses, is not synonymous with religion. Spiritually-related activities are defined as outward signs of internal meaning making processes (Love, 2001).

A clear distinction should be made between two separate but related functions of an educational institution: providing for the academic study of religions, and for programs that promote the spiritual and moral development of its students. A distinction should also be made between accommodation and promotion of religions and faiths by public institutions. The courts have mandated an even-handed accommodation of religious beliefs, but prohibited the promotion of a particular religious belief. According to the courts, any public institution's program must meet the following conditions to avoid violating the "establishment" clause of the US Constitution: It must have a secular purpose; its principal or primary effect must be one that neither advances nor inhibits religion; and it must not foster an excessive entanglement of the public institution with religion.

Recently there has been a noticeable increase of interest in religious and spiritual matters on college campuses (Love, 2001). Manning contends that the factors impacting this increase include: (1) Generation X's shift from materialism, (2) Baby Boomers becoming more reflective as they age, or (3) a desire for concrete meaning in a post modern world (2001). The diversification of American higher education has led to an environment where various religious and spiritual faiths and practices are more accepted (Hartley, 2004). As college campuses have become more diverse ethnically and culturally, particularly with the increased enrollment of international students at American colleges and universities, there has been an increase in the presence of non-Judeo-Christian religious groups and organizations (e.g., Muslim Student Association, Pagan Student Association, Unitarian Universalist Association) (Temkin & Evans, 1998).

While people may argue the impetus for the increase in interest, the importance of it must not be missed. Love points out that spirituality exists in everyday life and not just religious practices and that spiritually-related activities are outward signs of meaning making processes (2001). Fowler believed this to be true when he set out to "operationalize a rich concept of faith and to begin to look more systematically at faith in a constructive-developmental perspective" (2001). Involvement with religiously-affiliated student organizations or clubs can also provide an avenue for students to develop leadership and interpersonal skills. Religious programs and services often provide significant out-of-classroom developmental opportunities for college students.

Campus Religious/Spiritual Programs may be structured differently on individual campuses according to the needs and limitations of each institution. There is no preferred organizational or programming structure. Organization structures range from coordinating committees to individual staff members that work directly with these programs. Institution type, size, goals and mission are just a few of the factors that impact the workings of religious/spiritual programs on a campus. One major difference among institutions is between public and private secular colleges and universities and private religiously affiliated colleges and universities. The later type of institution may expect staff to sign creeds, have specific religious training, and may have a religiously-oriented mission statement that states its preference towards a particular faith or denomination, while the former may have legal constraints or preferences that prevent them from engaging in the same expectations. In general the courts have held that the First Amendment provides protection to religious believers and non-believers, and that the state shall be neutral in its relations with persons who profess a belief or disbelief in any religion, *Everson v. Board of Education*, 330 US 1(1977). This is particularly applicable to public institutions. However, the legal standards related to dealing with religious/spiritual programs across higher education are in a constant state of change and evolution. Therefore, those who administer Campus Religious and Spiritual Programs (CRSP) must work to maintain familiarity with current relevant case law.

References, Readings, and Resources

Butler, J. (1989). An overview of religion on campus. In Butler, J. (Ed.). Religion on campus. *New Directions for Student Services,* No. 46. San Francisco: Jossey-Bass.

Cawthon, T. W., & Jones, C. (2004). A description of traditional and contemporary campus ministries. *College Student Affairs Journal, 23*(2), p. 158-172.

Fowler, J.W. (2001). Faith development theory and the postmodern challenges. *The International Journal for the Psychology of Religion, 11,* 159-172.

Hartley, H. V. III (2004). How college affects students' religious faith and practice: A review of the research. *College Student Affairs Journal, 23(*2), p. 111-129.

Love, P.G. (2001). Spirituality and student development: Theoretical connections. *New Directions for Student Services, 95,* 7-16.

Manning, K. (2001). Infusing soul into student affairs: Organizational theory and models. *New Directions for Student Services, 95,* 27-35.

Temkin, L., & Evans, N. J. (1998). Religion on campus: Suggestions for cooperation between student affairs and campus-based religious organizations. *NASPA Journal, 36*(1), p. 61- 69.

Association of College and University Religious Affairs – http://www. acuraonline.org

National Association of College and University Chaplains – http://www. nacuc.net

National Campus Ministry Association – http://www.campusministry. net

Contributors:
Current edition:
S. Bryan Rush, University of Georgia
Brad Harmon, University of Georgia
J.D. White, University of Georgia
Merrily Dunn, University of Georgia
Diane L. Cooper, University of Georgia

Previous editions:
Diane L. Cooper, University of Georgia

CAMPUS RELIGIOUS and/or SPIRITUAL PROGRAMS
CAS Standards and Guidelines

Part 1. MISSION

The purpose of Campus Religious and/or Spiritual Programs (CRSP) is to provide access to programs that enable interested students to pursue full spiritual growth and development and to foster a campus atmosphere in which interested members of the college community may freely express their religion, spirituality, and faith.

A private or religiously affiliated institution may state its preference for a particular faith or spiritual tradition and may directly use its own resources for this purpose.

Campus Religious and/or Spiritual Programs (CRSP) must incorporate student learning and student development in its mission. CRSP must enhance overall educational experiences. CRSP must develop, record, disseminate, implement, and regularly review its mission and goals. Mission statements must be consistent with the mission and goals of the institution and with the standards in this document. CRSP must operate as an integral part of the institution's overall mission.

Public institutions without formal religious and/or spiritual programs should make provisions for religious and spiritual programs indirectly, that is, through cooperation with off-campus agencies that provide religious services and programs.

The goals of religious or spiritual programs or services should provide opportunities for interested students to:
- receive the religious and/or spiritual support they seek
- articulate a personal philosophy
- acquire skills and knowledge to address issues of values, ethics, and morality
- examine the interaction of faith, intellectual inquiry, and social responsibility as bases for finding and affirming meaning and satisfaction in life
- participate in dialogue between and among representatives of the religious and/or spiritual and the secular
- participate with others in the expression of their faith(s)

Part 2. PROGRAM

The formal education of students consists of the curriculum and the co-curriculum, and must promote student learning and development that is purposeful and holistic. Campus Religious and/or Spiritual Programs (CRSP) must identify relevant and desirable student learning and development outcomes and provide programs and services that encourage the achievement of those outcomes.

Relevant and desirable outcomes include: intellectual growth, effective communication, realistic self-appraisal, enhanced self-esteem, clarified values, career choices, leadership development, healthy behaviors, meaningful interpersonal relationships, independence, collaboration, social responsibility, satisfying and productive lifestyles, appreciation of diversity, spiritual awareness, and achievement of personal and educational goals.

CRSP must provide evidence of its impact on the achievement of student learning and development outcomes.

The table below offers examples of evidence of achievement of student learning and development.

Student Learning and Development Outcome Domains

Spiritual awareness
Examples of achievement indicators
> Develops and articulates personal belief system; Understands roles of spirituality in personal and group values and behaviors

Clarified values
Examples of achievement indicators
> Articulates personal values; Acts in congruence with personal values; Makes decisions that reflect personal values; Demonstrates willingness to scrutinize personal beliefs and values; Identifies personal, work, and lifestyle values and explains how they influence decision-making

Social responsibility
Examples of achievement indicators
> Understands and participates in relevant organization governance systems; Understands, abides by, and participates in the development, maintenance, and/or orderly change of community, social, and legal standards or norms; Appropriately challenges the unfair, unjust, or uncivil behavior of other individuals or groups; Participates in service or volunteer activities

Satisfying and productive lifestyles
Examples of achievement indicators
> Functions on the basis of personal identity, ethical, spiritual, and moral values; Engages in spiritual development activities; Achieves balance between education, work and leisure time, and spiritual development; Articulates and meets goals for work, leisure and education; Overcomes personal obstacles that hamper goal achievement

Appreciating diversity
Examples of achievement indicators

Understands one's own spiritual identity, belief system and culture; Seeks involvement with people with different spiritual beliefs from oneself; Seeks involvement in diverse interests; Articulates the advantages and challenges of a diverse society; Challenges appropriately the abusive use of stereotypes by others; Understands the impact of diversity on one's own society

Realistic self-appraisal
Examples of achievement indicators

Makes decisions and acts in congruence with personal values and spiritual belief system; Acknowledges and articulates personal strengths and weaknesses; Articulates rationale for personal behavior; Seeks feedback from others; Learns from past experiences

Intellectual growth
Examples of achievement indicators

Uses complex information from a variety of sources including personal experience, spiritual beliefs, and observation to form a decision or opinion; Produces personal and educational goal statements; Employs critical thinking in problem solving; Applies previously understood information and concepts to a new situation or setting

Effective communication
Examples of achievement indicators

Effectively articulates abstract ideas and personal spiritual beliefs; Writes and speaks coherently and effectively; Writes and speaks after reflection; Able to influence others through writing, speaking, or artistic expression

Enhanced self-esteem
Examples of achievement indicators

Shows self-respect and respect for others' spiritual beliefs; Initiates actions toward achievement of goals; Functions without need for constant reassurance from others

Career choices
Examples of achievement indicators

Exhibits congruence between personal spiritual beliefs and career interests

Leadership development
Examples of achievement indicators

Articulates leadership philosophy or style; Serves effectively in a leadership position in a student organization; Comprehends the dynamics of a group; Exhibits democratic principles as a leader; Exhibits ability to visualize a group purpose and desired outcomes

Healthy behavior
Examples of achievement indicators

Chooses behaviors and environments that promote health and reduce risk; Articulates the relationship between health and wellness and spiritual practices; Exhibits behaviors that advance a healthy community

Meaningful interpersonal relationships
Examples of achievement indicators

Develops and maintains satisfying interpersonal relationships; Establishes mutually rewarding relationships with friends and colleagues; Listens to and considers others' points of view; Treats others with respect

Independence
Examples of achievement indicators

Exhibits self-reliant behaviors and the ability to make personal spiritual decisions with confidence and competence; Functions autonomously; Exhibits ability to function interdependently

Collaboration
Examples of achievement indicators

Works cooperatively with others; Seeks the involvement of others; Seeks feedback from others; Contributes to achievement of a group goal; Exhibits effective listening skills

Personal and educational goals
Examples of achievement indicators

Understands the role of spirituality in personal and educational goal setting; Sets, articulates, and pursues individual goals; Understands the effect of one's personal and educational goals on others

CRSP must be (a) intentional, (b) coherent, (c) based on theories and knowledge of learning and human development, (d) reflective of developmental and demographic profiles of the student population, and (e) responsive to needs of individuals, special populations, and communities.

CRSP will vary depending on the requirements and beliefs of specific denominations and faiths, as well as the needs and traditions of the particular institution.

To the extent either required or prohibited by constitutional, statutory, or regulatory provisions, institutions must provide reasonable opportunities for students to:

- **question, explore, understand, affiliate with or avoid, and express or reject various religious faiths and/or spiritual beliefs and practices**
- **seek individual counseling or group associations for the examination and application of religious**

and/or spiritual values and beliefs
- **worship communally and individually**
- **pray and meditate**

In public institutions, staff members may coordinate programs, while personnel associated with religious groups provide direct service to campus community.

In religiously affiliated and private secular colleges, religious programs and direct service may be provided by staff members of the institution.

The types of religious programs and activities offered may include:
- co-curricular religious studies
- opportunities for religious and/or spiritual nurturance
- service opportunities
- where appropriate by law, regulation, or policy, opportunity to propagate religions or faiths
- where appropriate by law, regulation, or policy, opportunity to practice rituals of religion or faith
- advocacy for particular ethical or moral policies in public life
- opportunities to relate religious and spiritual beliefs to academic and professional programs
- programs that mark significant events or experiences in the life of the community, e.g., death, tragedy, memorials, or celebrations

In addition, institutions may provide guidance services to promote spiritual or religious growth. Co-curricular programs (e.g., lectures, discussions, or service projects) that are designed to help students understand their faiths and the faiths of others may also be offered.

Part 3. LEADERSHIP

Effective and ethical leadership is essential to the success of all organizations. Institutions must appoint, position, and empower Campus Religious and/or Spiritual Programs (CRSP) leaders within the administrative structure to accomplish stated missions. CRSP leaders at various levels must be selected on the basis of formal education and training, relevant work experience, personal skills and competencies, relevant professional credentials, as well as potential for promoting learning and development in students, applying effective practices to educational processes, and enhancing institutional effectiveness. Institutions must determine expectations of accountability for leaders and fairly assess their performance.

Leaders of CRSP must exercise authority over resources for which they are responsible to achieve their respective missions.

CRSP leaders must:
- **articulate a vision for their organization**
- **set goals and objectives based on the needs and capabilities of the population served**
- **promote student learning and development**
- **prescribe and practice ethical behavior**
- **recruit, select, supervise, and develop others in the organization**
- **manage financial resources**
- **coordinate human resources**
- **plan, budget for, and evaluate personnel and programs**
- **apply effective practices to educational and administrative processes**
- **communicate effectively**
- **initiate collaborative interaction between individuals and agencies that possess legitimate concerns and interests in the functional area**

CRSP leaders must identify and find means to address individual, organizational, or environmental conditions that inhibit goal achievement.

CRSP leaders must promote campus environments that result in multiple opportunities for student learning and development.

CRSP leaders must continuously improve programs and services in response to changing needs of students and other constituents and evolving institutional priorities.

Part 4. ORGANIZATION and MANAGEMENT

Guided by an overarching intent to ensure student learning and development, Campus Religious and/or Spiritual Programs (CRSP) must be structured purposefully and managed effectively to achieve stated goals. Evidence of appropriate structure must include current and accessible policies and procedures, written performance expectations for all employees, functional workflow graphics or organizational charts, and clearly stated service delivery expectations.

Evidence of effective management must include use of comprehensive and accurate information for decisions, clear sources and channels of authority, effective communication practices, decision-making and conflict resolution procedures, responsiveness to changing conditions, accountability and evaluation systems, and recognition and reward processes. CRSP must provide channels within the organization for regular review of administrative policies and procedures.

CRSP activities, policies, and procedures should be scrutinized regularly in light of the growing body of law in the area of religion and higher education.

Part 5. HUMAN RESOURCES

Campus Religious and/or Spiritual Programs (CRSP) must be staffed adequately by individuals qualified to accomplish its mission and goals. Within established guidelines of the institution, CRSP must establish procedures for staff selection, training, and evaluation; set expectations for supervision; and provide appropriate professional development opportunities. CRSP must strive to improve the professional competence and skills of all personnel it employs.

At public institutions, religious programs may be coordinated by a professional person and/or a committee. Professional or volunteer persons named (and paid) by the religious and spiritual groups represented on the campus may carry out their respective activities. The title "director or "coordinator" of religious programs is more appropriate because of the predominantly educational and liaison functions of the position.

At private institutions, campus religious programs are typically coordinated by a professional in an appropriate field or a committee. Additional staff members may be employed by the institution. Religious groups may also provide additional staff for the institution. Religiously related institutions should permit on-campus programs of religions or spiritual beliefs other than those espoused by the institution. Titles for the director or coordinator at private institutions include chaplain, director of religious life or spiritual development, or other title specific to a religious or spiritual tradition.

CRSP professional staff members must hold an earned graduate degree in a field relevant to the position they hold or must possess an appropriate combination of educational credentials and related work experience.

When the coordinator of religious and/or spiritual programs represents a particular religious and/or spiritual body, that person should possess qualifications consistent with the particular body represented and appropriate for a higher education setting.

Any director or coordinator should have:
- an understanding of and a commitment to spiritual and religious development as a part of a student's human growth
- the ability to treat fairly all varieties of campus religious experience and personal faith
- awareness and understanding of the beliefs of religious and spiritual groups affiliated with that campus

Depending upon the legal constraints of the institution, the responsibilities of the director or coordinator for religious and/or spiritual programs may include:
- the development and communication of policies relating to religious and spiritual programs that are educationally sound and legally acceptable
- the development of procedures whereby students may organize for religious, spiritual, or moral purposes and participate in programs and activities aimed at their spiritual and/or religious growth
- the provision of access to campus facilities for those responsible for religious or spiritual programs
- the provision of opportunities for guidance in relation to students' religious or spiritual needs
- coordination with other campus decision makers on matters related to religious and/or spiritual activities such as scheduling and examinations

Degree or credential-seeking interns must be qualified by enrollment in an appropriate field of study and by relevant experience. These individuals must be trained and supervised adequately by professional staff members holding educational credentials and related work experience appropriate for supervision.

Student employees and volunteers must be carefully selected, trained, supervised, and evaluated. They must be trained on how and when to refer those in need of assistance to qualified staff members and have access to a supervisor for assistance in making these judgments. Student employees and volunteers must be provided clear and precise job descriptions, pre-service training based on assessed needs, and continuing staff development.

CRSP must have technical and support staff members adequate to accomplish its mission. Staff members must be technologically proficient and qualified to perform their job functions, be knowledgeable of ethical and legal uses of technology, and have access to training. The level of staffing and workloads must be adequate and appropriate for program and service demands.

Salary levels and fringe benefits for all CRSP staff members must be commensurate with those for comparable positions within the institution, in similar institutions, and in the relevant geographic area.

CRSP must institute hiring and promotion practices that are fair, inclusive, and non-discriminatory. Programs and services must employ a diverse staff to provide readily identifiable role models for students and to enrich the campus community.

Officials should be fair and equitable in relationships with all agencies participating in the program.

CRSP must create and maintain position descriptions for all staff members and provide regular performance planning and appraisals.

CRSP must have a system for regular staff evaluation and must provide access to continuing education and professional development opportunities, including in-service training programs and participation in professional conferences and workshops.

Affiliation with appropriate professional organizations is encouraged.

When a staff member represents a particular religious and/or spiritual body, that person should possess qualifications consistent with the particular body they represent and appropriate for a higher education setting.

Part 6. FINANCIAL RESOURCES

Campus Religious and/or Spiritual Programs (CRSP) must have adequate funding to accomplish its mission and goals. Funding priorities must be determined within the context of the stated mission, goals, objectives, and comprehensive analysis of the needs and capabilities of students, and the availability of internal or external resources.

All institutions must provide sufficient funding for any institutional staff member(s) and the operational costs related to religious and/or spiritual programs.

If this assignment accounts for only a part of an individual staff member's work load, the budget should clearly indicate the portion that is available for religious and spiritual programs.

CRSP must demonstrate fiscal responsibility and cost effectiveness consistent with institutional protocols.

Funding for personnel and programs of adjunct agencies (i.e., not directly provided by the institution) must be assumed by the sponsors of the adjunct agency.

Part 7. FACILITIES, TECHNOLOGY, and EQUIPMENT

Campus Religious and/or Spiritual Programs (CRSP) must have adequate, suitably located facilities, adequate technology, and equipment to support its mission and goals efficiently and effectively. Facilities, technology, and equipment must be evaluated regularly and be in compliance with relevant federal, state/provincial, and local requirements to provide for access, health, safety, and security.

Opportunity must be provided for all student religious and/or spiritual organizations to utilize campus facilities on the same basis as other student organizations.

In public institutions, whenever space is made permanently or exclusively available for specific staff of affiliated agencies, arrangements should be made whereby the institution is appropriately reimbursed for expenses.

Private institutions may provide facilities designed to suit the purpose(s) of a specific religious group(s).

Institutions should provide fair and equitable arrangements and facilities (including in campus centers, academic buildings, or residential units) for specific religious and/or spiritual groups' programming and practices.

Suitable areas should be provided for individual meditation and small group spiritual interaction.

The institution should provide for or coordinate student religious and/or spiritual dietary differences.

Part 8. LEGAL RESPONSIBILITIES

Campus Religious and/or Spiritual Programs (CRSP) staff members must be knowledgeable about and responsive to laws and regulations that relate to their respective responsibilities. CRSP staff members must inform users of programs and services and officials, as appropriate, of legal obligations and limitations including constitutional, statutory, regulatory, and case law; mandatory laws and orders emanating from federal, state/provincial and local governments; and the institution's policies.

CRSP staff members must use reasonable and informed practices to limit the liability exposure of the institution, its officers, employees, and agents. Staff members must be informed about institutional policies regarding personal liability and related insurance coverage options.

The institution must provide access to legal advice for CRSP staff members as needed to carry out assigned responsibilities.

The institution must inform CRSP staff and students in a timely and systematic fashion about extraordinary or changing legal obligations and potential liabilities.

Part 9. EQUITY and ACCESS

Campus Religious and/or Spiritual Programs (CRSP) staff members must ensure that services

and programs are provided on a fair and equitable basis. Facilities, programs, and services must be accessible. Hours of operation and delivery of and access to programs and services must be responsive to the needs of all students and other constituents. CRSP must adhere to the spirit and intent of equal opportunity laws.

CRSP programs must be open and readily accessible to all students and must not discriminate except where sanctioned by law and institutional policy. Discrimination must be avoided on the bases of age; color; creed; cultural heritage; disability; ethnicity; gender identity; nationality; political affiliation; religious affiliation; sex; sexual orientation; or social, economic, marital, or veteran status.

Consistent with their mission and goals, CRSP must take affirmative action to remedy significant imbalances in student participation and staffing patterns.

As the demographic profiles of campuses change and new instructional delivery methods are introduced, institutions must recognize the needs of students who participate in distance learning for access to programs and services offered on campus. Institutions must provide appropriate services in ways that are accessible to distance learners and assist them in identifying and gaining access to other appropriate services in their geographic region.

Part 10. CAMPUS and EXTERNAL RELATIONS
Campus Religious and/or Spiritual Programs (CRSP) must establish, maintain, and promote effective relations with relevant individuals, campus offices, and external agencies.

Because religion and/or spirituality may be concerns of many academic disciplines and may have an important impact on student development, staff assigned to religious programs should consult with and coordinate their programs with interested colleagues.

The CRSP director or coordinator may interact with faculty and staff formally through advisory councils or through informal contacts.

Continuing attention should be given to developing and improving relationships with both on-campus and off-campus constituencies. Specific religious and/or spiritual programs and action projects may arise from many sources (e.g., academic departments, on-campus functional areas such as residence halls and campus centers, and off-campus organizations, whether local, regional, national, and/or international).

The coordinator, faculty, staff, and administrators of the institution should meet with personnel from religious and/or spiritual groups on a periodic basis.

Part 11. DIVERSITY
Within the context of each institution's unique mission, diversity enriches the community and enhances the collegiate experience for all; therefore, Campus Religious and/or Spiritual Programs (CRSP) must nurture environments where commonalties and differences among people are recognized and honored.

CRSP must promote educational experiences that are characterized by open and continuous communication that deepens understanding of one's own identity, culture, and heritage, and that of others. CRSP must educate and promote respect about commonalties and differences in their historical and cultural contexts.

CRSP must address the characteristics and needs of a diverse population when establishing and implementing policies and procedures.

Part 12. ETHICS
All persons involved in the delivery of Campus Religious and/or Spiritual Programs (CRSP) must adhere to the highest principles of ethical behavior. CRSP must develop or adopt and implement appropriate statements of ethical practice. CRSP must publish these statements and ensure their periodic review by relevant constituencies.

CRSP staff members must ensure that privacy and confidentiality are maintained with respect to all communications and records to the extent that such records are protected under the law and appropriate statements of ethical practice. Information contained in students' education records must not be disclosed without written consent except as allowed by relevant laws and institutional policies. Staff members must disclose to appropriate authorities information judged to be of an emergency nature, especially when the safety of the individual or others is involved, or when otherwise required by institutional policy or relevant law.

All CRSP staff members must be aware of and comply with the provisions contained in the institution's human subjects research policy and in other relevant institutional policies addressing ethical practices and confidentiality of research data concerning individuals.

CRSP staff members must recognize and avoid personal conflict of interest or appearance thereof in their transactions with students and others.

CRSP staff members must strive to insure the fair, objective, and impartial treatment of all persons with whom they deal. Staff members must not participate in nor condone any form of harassment that demeans persons or creates an intimidating, hostile, or offensive campus environment.

Accommodation must be made so that students, faculty members, and staff from various religions and faiths may carry out the essential practices of their belief systems.

When handling institutional funds, all CRSP staff members must ensure that such funds are managed in accordance with established and responsible accounting procedures and the fiscal policies or processes of the institution.

CRSP staff members must perform their duties within the limits of their training, expertise, and competence. When these limits are exceeded, individuals in need of further assistance must be referred to persons possessing appropriate qualifications.

CRSP staff members must use suitable means to confront and otherwise hold accountable other staff members who exhibit unethical behavior.

CRSP staff members must be knowledgeable about and practice ethical behavior in the use of technology.

CRSP staff members must avoid any actions that favor one particular faith over another.

As the institution carries out its academic program, fair and reasonable consideration should be given to the need of campus members to participate in the basic activities of their faiths. Institutional policies and practices should be reviewed regularly so as to avoid undue interference with the exercise of religious and/or spiritual traditions.

Private institutions that sponsor or require particular religious activities must clearly state so in their pre-admission literature, thus permitting a potential student to exercise choice in this regard before admission.

CRSP staff members must work to provide reasonable access for all groups and points of view to any public forums sponsored by the institution.

Membership requirements for on-campus religious organizations at public institutions must be consistent with the group's stated purposes. All religious and/or spiritual organizations must be accorded the same rights and privileges and be held accountable in the same manner as any other campus organization.

CRSP staff members must attempt to protect students, through policy and practice, from undue influence or harassment from persons advocating particular religious positions or activities.

Part 13. ASSESSMENT and EVALUATION

Campus Religious and/or Spiritual Programs (CRSP) must conduct regular assessment and evaluations. CRSP must employ effective qualitative and quantitative methodologies as appropriate, to determine whether and to what degree the stated mission, goals, and student learning and development outcomes are being met. The process must employ sufficient and sound assessment measures to ensure comprehensiveness. Data collected must include responses from students and other affected constituencies.

Each institution should require evaluation of its religious program to determine the achievement of goals, the constituencies reached, and its overall effectiveness.

This evaluation may be made in concert with the periodic examination of the diverse needs and interests of students and other members of the campus community.

CRSP must evaluate periodically how well they complement and enhance the institution's stated mission and educational effectiveness.

Data should be collected from officers and advisors of campus religious and spiritual organizations to determine the effectiveness of policies affecting religious activity.

Results of these evaluations must be used in revising and improving programs and services and in recognizing staff performance.

General standards revised in 2002; CRSP (formerly Religious Programs) content developed/revised in 1986, 1997, & 2006

THE ROLE of CAREER SERVICES
CAS Standards Contextual Statement

The first evidence of assistance in career services dates to the 19th century, when commercial employment agencies began to place graduates of the nation's teacher training programs. More than 200 such agencies existed by the late 1800s. By the turn of the century, an increasing number of institutions had begun to realize their responsibility to help graduates find jobs. When the first institutional appointment and placement services were established, faculty members typically took responsibility for them on part-time bases. Soon, many institutions established programs staffed by full-time "appointment secretaries." By 1920, approximately 75 percent of the nation's normal schools had established placement services. As a direct result of the increasing number of college-sponsored placement services, the number of external agencies decreased.

The first professional associations focusing on job placement for college graduates, the National Institutional Teacher Placement Association and the National Association of Appointment Secretaries, were both established in 1924. The former organization, in 1927, evolved into the American Association for Employment in Education (AAEE) while the latter became the American College Personnel Association (ACPA) in 1931. In addition, others concerned with business and industrial placement established the Eastern College Placement Association and, by the 1940s, seven other regional associations had been formed.

A forerunner to a comprehensive national association, the Association of School and College Placement, was formed in 1940. This group published the *School and College Placement* magazine, now known as the *NACE Journal*. In 1956, the national association was incorporated as the College Placement Publications Council and its name shortened in 1957 to the College Placement Council. In 1995, the association became the National Association of Colleges and Employers (NACE). Today, NACE's core purpose is to facilitate the employment of the college educated; it works to meet this mission in a variety of ways, including by providing an important connection between college career services centers and HR/staffing offices focused on recruiting and hiring new college graduates.

Following World War II, the economy exploded and employers sought the nation's college graduates to meet expanding needs. By the mid-1950s, on-campus recruiting of college graduates had reached its apex, with more than 65 percent of the current career services centers having been established between 1947 and 1960. Over the years, the function of these offices shifted from solely providing placement activities to providing a broad range of career activities. Accordingly, this shift is reflected by office name changes from "placement office" to "career planning and placement office" to the currently preferred title, "career services center."

Today, the majority of colleges and universities have career centers. Their services often include career counseling; programming such as job-search workshops and networking events; career and job fairs; assistance with co-op, internship, and externship programs; on-campus recruiting; and job posting and resume referral services. In the typical center, many of these services are available electronically through the career center's web site.

In the 21st century, career services is tasked to meet increasingly complex and sophisticated challenges that include more diversity, globalization, and technology. Career services professionals need to be both culturally sensitive in working with students and knowledgeable about career options both in the United States and internationally. Today's traditional-age students, characterized by their high comfort level with and expectation of technology, and "virtual" students, created through distance learning options, require that career services professionals have an increasingly high level of technical competence. Today's career services professional must balance high-tech and high-touch service and delivery in serving students and employers. Similarly, alumni, who are working on second, third, and fourth careers, are turning to career services to provide services through non-traditional means.

An increasing focus in higher education on assessment and accountability necessitates career services professionals to find meaningful measures by which to demonstrate their value to students, faculty, administrators, parents, and employers. Developing productive relationships not only with employers but also with faculty and other campus constituencies has never been more important. Increased emphasis on the part of employers on internships/co-ops, electronic recruiting, and diversity recruiting require a corresponding emphasis on the part of career services professionals.

The 21st century career services leader requires a broader range of skills and competencies beyond those once considered traditional for professionals involved in the career planning and development field. These include leadership, managerial, technical financial, marketing, assessment, and analytical skills.

References, Readings, and Resources

Bryant, B.J. (Ed.). (2006). *The job search handbook for educators.* Columbus, OH: American Association for Employment in Education.

Bryant, B.J. (Ed.). (2006). *The job hunter's guide: services and career fairs for educators.* Columbus, OH: American Association for Employment in Education.

Bryant, B.J. (Ed.). (2005). *Educator supply and demand research report*. Columbus, OH: American Association for Employment in Education.

Bryant, B.J. (Ed.). (2004-2005). *Directory of Public School Systems in the U.S.* Columbus, OH: American Association for Employment in Education.

Celebrating 50 years of excellence: organization history. National Association of Colleges and Employers. www.naceweb.org/50thanniversary/history.htm

NACE Attracting New Professionals Task Force (2004). *Career services in higher education* (PowerPoint presentation). www.naceweb.org/committee/whitepapers/CS_Professionals.ppt. Bethlehem, PA: National Association of Colleges and Employers.

NACE Future Trends Task Force (2005). *The future of college recruiting and hiring: executive summary*. Bethlehem, PA: National Association of Colleges and Employers.

State of the Profession: 2005 NACE Career Services Benchmark Survey (2005). Bethlehem, PA: National Association of Colleges and Employers.

National Association of Colleges and Employers (NACE). 62 Highland Avenue, Bethlehem, PA 18017. Phone: 800/544-5272. FAX: 610/868-0208. E-mail: infocenter@naceweb.org. Web site: www.naceweb.org

American Association for Employment in Education (AAEE). 3040 Riverside Drive, Suite 125, Columbus, OH 43221. Phone: 614/485-1111. FAX: 614/485-9609. E-mail: aaee@osu.edu. Web site: www.aaee.org

American College Personnel Association, Commission on Career Development. One DuPont Circle, Suite 300, Washington, DC 20036-1188. Phone: 202/835-2272. FAX: 202/296-3286. E-mail: info@acpa.nche.edu. Web site: www.acpa.nche.edu

Contributors:
Alison Angell, Lesley University, AAEE
Patricia Carretta, George Mason University, NACE
Mimi Collins, National Association of Colleges and Employers
R. Samuel Ratcliffe, Virginia Military Institute

CAREER SERVICES
CAS Standards and Guidelines

Part 1. MISSION

The primary mission of Career Services (CS) is to assist students and other designated clients through all phases of their career development.

In addition, the mission of CS is:

- **to provide leadership to the institution on career development concerns**
- **to develop positive relationships with employers and external constituencies,**
- **to support institutional outcomes assessment and relevant research endeavors**

CS must incorporate student learning and student development in its mission. CS must enhance overall educational experiences. CS must develop, record, disseminate, implement, and regularly review its mission and goals. Mission statements must be consistent with the mission and goals of the institution and with the standards in this document. CS must operate as an integral part of the institution's overall mission.

The stated mission should include helping students and other designated clients:

- to develop self-knowledge related to career choice and work performance by identifying, assessing, and understanding their competencies, interests, values, and personal characteristics
- to obtain educational and occupational information to aid career and educational planning and to develop an understanding of the world of work
- to select personally suitable academic programs and experiential opportunities that enhance future educational and employment options
- to take personal responsibility for developing job-search competencies, future educational and employment plans, and career decisions
- to gain experience through student activities, community service, student employment, research or creative projects, cooperative education, internships, and other opportunities
- to link with alumni, employers, professional organizations, and others who can provide opportunities to develop professional interests and competencies, integrate academic learning with work, and explore future career possibilities
- to prepare for finding suitable employment by developing job-search skills, effective candidate presentation skills, and an understanding of the fit between their competencies and both occupational and job requirements

- to seek desired employment opportunities or entry into appropriate educational, graduate, or professional programs

CS must promote a greater awareness within the institution of the world of work and the need for and nature of career development over the life span.

Because of the expertise and knowledge on career-related matters, CS should be involved in key administrative decisions related to student services, institutional development, curriculum planning, and external relations.

Part 2. PROGRAM

The formal education of students consists of the curriculum and the co-curriculum, and must promote student learning and development that is purposeful and holistic. Career Services (CS) must identify relevant and desirable student learning and development outcomes and provide programs and services that encourage the achievement of those outcomes.

Relevant and desirable outcomes include: intellectual growth, effective communication, realistic self-appraisal, enhanced self-esteem, clarified values, career choices, leadership development, healthy behaviors, meaningful interpersonal relationships, independence, collaboration, social responsibility, satisfying and productive lifestyles, appreciation of diversity, spiritual awareness, and achievement of personal and educational goals.

CS must provide evidence of its impact on the achievement of student learning and development outcomes.

The table below offers examples of evidence of achievement of student learning and development.

Student Learning and Development Outcome Domains

Intellectual growth

Examples of achievement indicators

Produces personal and educational goal statements; Employs critical thinking in problem solving; Uses complex information from a variety of sources including personal experience and observation to form a decision or opinion; Obtains a degree; Applies previously understood information and concepts to a new situation or setting; Expresses appreciation for literature, the fine arts, mathematics, sciences, and social sciences

Effective communication

Examples of achievement indicators

Writes and speaks coherently and effectively; Writes and speaks after reflection; Able to influence others through writing, speaking or artistic expression; Effectively articulates abstract ideas; Uses appropriate syntax; Makes presentations or gives performances

Enhanced self-esteem

Examples of achievement indicators

Shows self-respect and respect for others; Initiates actions toward achievement of goals; Takes reasonable risks; Demonstrates assertive behavior; Functions without need for constant reassurance from others

Realistic self-appraisal

Examples of achievement indicators

Articulates personal skills and abilities; Makes decisions and acts in congruence with personal values; Acknowledges personal strengths and weaknesses; Articulates rationale for personal behavior; Seeks feedback from others; Learns from past experiences

Clarified values

Examples of achievement indicators

Articulates personal values; Acts in congruence with personal values; Makes decisions that reflect personal values; Demonstrates willingness to scrutinize personal beliefs and values; Identifies personal, work, and lifestyle values and explains how they influence decision-making

Career choices

Examples of achievement indicators

Articulates career choices based on assessment of interests, values, skills and abilities; Documents knowledge, skills and accomplishments resulting from formal education, work experience, community service, and volunteer experiences; Makes the connections between classroom and out-of-classroom learning; Can construct a resume with clear job objectives and evidence of related knowledge, skills, and accomplishments; Articulates the characteristics of a preferred work environment; Comprehends the world of work; Takes steps to initiate a job search or seek advanced education

Leadership development

Examples of achievement indicators

Articulates leadership philosophy or style; Serves in a leadership position in a student organization; Comprehends the dynamics of a group; Exhibits democratic principles as a leader; Exhibits ability to visualize a group purpose and desired outcomes

Healthy behavior

Examples of achievement indicators

Chooses behaviors and environments that promote health and reduce risk; Articulates the relationship between health and wellness and accomplishing life- long goals; Exhibits behaviors that advance a healthy community

Meaningful interpersonal relationships

Examples of achievement indicators

Develops and maintains satisfying interpersonal relationships; Establishes mutually rewarding relationships with friends and colleagues; Listens to and considers others' points of view; Treats others with respect

Independence

Examples of achievement indicators

Exhibits self-reliant behaviors; Functions autonomously; Exhibits ability to function interdependently; Accepts supervision as needed; Manages time effectively

Collaboration

Examples of achievement indicators

Works cooperatively with others; Seeks the involvement of others; Seeks feedback from others; Contributes to achievement of a group goal; Exhibits effective listening skills

Social responsibility

Examples of achievement indicators

Understands and participates in relevant governance systems; Understands, abides by, and participates in the development, maintenance, and/or orderly change of community, social, and legal standards or norms; Appropriately challenges the unfair, unjust, or uncivil behavior of other individuals or groups; Participates in service/volunteer activities

Satisfying and productive lifestyles

Examples of achievement indicators

Achieves balance between education, work and leisure time; Articulates and meets goals for work, leisure, and education; Overcomes obstacles that hamper goal achievement; Functions on the basis of personal identity, ethical, spiritual, and moral values; Articulates long-term goals and objectives

Appreciating diversity

Examples of achievement indicators

Understands one's own identity and culture; Seeks involvement with people different from oneself; Seeks involvement in diverse interests; Articulates the advantages and challenges of a diverse society; Challenges appropriately the abusive use of stereotypes by others; Understands the impact of diversity on one's own society

Spiritual awareness
Examples of achievement indicators
> Develops and articulates personal belief system; Understands roles of spirituality in personal and group values and behaviors

Personal and educational goals
Examples of achievement indicators
> Sets, articulates, and pursues individual goals; Articulates personal and educational goals and objectives; Uses personal and educational goals to guide decisions; Understands the effect of one's personal and educational goals on others

CS must be (a) intentional, (b) coherent, (c) based on theories and knowledge of learning and human development, (d) reflective of developmental and demographic profiles of the student population, and (e) responsive to needs of individuals, special populations, and communities.

CS must be based on an educational philosophy of teaching career development and related processes. CS must assist students and other designated clients to develop the skills necessary to compete in a rapidly changing, competency-based, global workplace.

Components of the CS must be clearly defined and articulated. To effectively accomplish its purpose, the program must include:
- **career counseling**
- **information and resources on careers and further education**
- **opportunities for career exploration through experiential learning**
- **job search services**
- **services to employers**
- **consultation and outcomes assessment**

CS must be delivered in a variety of formats in recognition of institutional settings, different learning styles, cultural differences, and special needs.

Program components of CS must be designed for and reflective of the career development needs and interests of students and other designated clients; current research, theories, and knowledge of career development and learning; contemporary career services practices and national standards of practice; economic trends, opportunities, and/or constraints; the varying needs and employment practices among small businesses, large corporations, government, and nonprofit organizations; and the priorities and resources of the institution.

CS must work collaboratively with academic divisions, departments, individual faculty members, student services, and other relevant constituencies of the institution to enhance students' career development.

CS must develop and implement intentional marketing strategies and outreach programming to promote awareness and encourage use of the services.

Program goals must be reviewed and updated regularly, and communicated, as appropriate, to students, administrators, faculty, staff, and employers and other constituencies.

CS should disseminate information on the availability, scope, and use of career services through institutional publications, campus media, presentations, outreach, and orientation programs.

Career Counseling
The institution must offer career counseling that assists students and other designated clients at any stage of their career development to:
- **understand the relationship between self-knowledge and career choice through assessment of interests, competencies, values, experience, personal characteristics, and desired lifestyles**
- **obtain and research occupational, educational, and employment information**
- **establish short-term and long-term career goals**
- **explore a full range of career and work possibilities**
- **make reasoned, informed career choices based on accurate self-knowledge and accurate information about the world of work**

Career counseling should:
- be available to students throughout their academic experience
- encourage students to take advantage of timely involvement in self-assessment, career decision making and career planning activities
- assist students to assess their skills, values, and interests by reflecting on past experiences
- assist students to integrate self-knowledge into their career planning
- recognize that students' career decision making is inextricably linked to additional psycho-social, personal, developmental and cultural issues and beliefs
- encourage and facilitate students' exploration of career interests through field visits, student employment, cooperative education, internships, shadowing experiences, research or creative projects, and informational interviews with working professionals

- be provided through a variety of formats, such as scheduled appointments, drop-in periods, group programs, career planning courses, outreach programs, and information technology

Career counseling should be offered through career services in order to link students' career exploration and decision making process with access to employers and employment information.

Information and Resources on Careers and Further Study

CS must help students and other designated clients to identify and access valid career information for their educational and career planning.

CS should provide information and resources:

- to help students assess and relate their interests, competencies, needs and expectations, education, experience, personal background, and desired lifestyle to the employment market
- for constituent groups on career and employment topics and the ethical obligations of students, employers, and others involved in the employment process
- on current employment opportunities and on employers to ensure that candidates have the widest possible choices of employment
- to help students identify and pursue future educational objectives

Information and resources must be:

- **comprehensive, enabling students and other designated clients to explore the widest range of information**
- **current and reflective of economic, occupational, and workplace trends**
- **accessible to clients**
- **organized in a system that is user-friendly, flexible, and adaptable to change**

The scope of information and resources available to clients should include:

- self-assessment and career planning
- occupational and job market information
- options for further study (e.g., community college articulation; graduate and professional school information)
- job search information
- experiential learning, internship, and job listings
- employer information

CS must provide access to information and resources on the internet.

Career information, resources, and means of delivery

must be compatible with the size and nature of the student population, the career and geographic interests of the students and scope of academic programs.

CS must provide information for students and other designated clients to identify and pursue future educational objectives in the context of lifelong learning.

Opportunities for Career Exploration through Experiential Learning

Experiential learning programs enable students to integrate their academic studies with work experiences and career exploration. The institution must provide experiential learning opportunities.

Experiential learning includes cooperative education, work-based learning, apprenticeships, student teaching, internships, work-study jobs, and other campus employment, volunteer experiences, service-learning, undergraduate research, and shadowing experiences.

Experiential learning programs administered through CS must:

- **provide students with opportunities to define both learning and career objectives and to reflect upon learning and other developmental aspects of their experience**
- **help students to identify employers for career development and potential employment**
- **teach students appropriate search and application techniques**
- **support institutional efforts to provide students with additional financial resources for attending college and/or opportunities for obtaining academic credit**
- **ensure adequate site supervision**

Experiential learning programs administered through CS should promote mentor/mentee relationships. When experiential learning opportunities are provided by other departments, CS should work closely with those departments.

Job Search Services

Job search services must assist students and other designated clients to:

- **develop job-search competencies**
- **present themselves effectively as candidates for employment**
- **obtain information on employment opportunities, trends, and prospective employers**
- **connect with employers through campus recruitment programs, job listings, referrals,**

direct application, networking, publications, and information technology

- **identify relevant career management issues (e.g., gender, age, sexual orientation, dual career, disability, cultural, mental health)**
- **access and effectively use career and employer resources on the internet**

Job search services may include offering site visits; campus recruiting; resume referrals; credential file services; information sessions; meetings with faculty members; pre-recruiting activities; student access to employer information; posting job openings; career and job fairs. Job search service should help students and other designated clients develop skills to uncover hidden job markets germane to their career interests.

CS must develop and implement marketing strategies that cultivate employment opportunities for students.

Services to Employers
Employers are both vital partners in the educational process and primary customers of career services. CS must offer services to employers that reflect student interests and employer needs.

Employer services may include: providing employers with information on academic departments and students within legal and policy guidelines; assisting in recruiting student populations; arranging experiential learning options such as shadowing experiences, internships, student teaching, or cooperative education; providing video conference interviewing; creating advertising and promotional vehicles; seeking input through career center advisory board membership; and organizing individual employer recruiting and college relations consultations.

CS must identify the range of employers it will serve (e.g., for profit, government, contract agencies, not-for-profit) and articulate policies that guide its working relationships with each of these constituencies.

CS must:
- **develop strategic objectives for employer services and job development that yield maximum opportunities for the institution's students and graduates**
- **inform, educate, and consult with employers on the nature of services provided and student candidates available**
- **encourage employer participation in programs that meet career and employment needs of students and other designated clients (e.g., career conferences, career and alumni fairs,**

cooperative education, and internships; career planning courses; classroom presentations)
- **develop and maintain relationships with employers who may provide career development and employment opportunities for students**
- **facilitate employer involvement and communication with faculty, students, and administrators concerning career and employment issues**
- **promote adherence to professional and ethical standards that model professional and ethical conduct for students**
- **enhance customer service and continuous improvement by using feedback from employers on key performance indicators and measures of services**

CS must provide timely, pertinent information to employers regarding:
- **the institutional student profile, academic programs and curricula, enrollments, and academic calendar**
- **class profile according to majors**
- **recruiting options available to reach targeted students**
- **policies, procedures, and instructions for using the services**
- **institutional non-discrimination policies with which employers must comply**

CS must treat employers fairly and equitably.

CS must develop policies for working with third-party recruiters and vendors.

Consultation and Outcomes Assessment
CS must provide consultative services to employers, faculty members, staff, administrators, students, and designated clients that are timely, knowledgeable, ethical, and responsive to constituent needs.

To develop effective long-term relationships with employers, CS must provide guidance to employers on how to develop effective college relations and recruiting strategies.

CS should provide guidance on:
- effective and appropriate strategies for reaching and attracting students
- student needs, issues and developmental perspectives
- cultivating relations with academic departments
- working with student leaders and student clubs and organizations

- timely corporate/organizational presence and participation in on-campus recruiting, fairs, and pre-recruiting
- using appropriate campus resources for visibility
- internship, co-op, and full-time hiring guidelines, processes, and programs
- promoting equal access for all students to all employment opportunities

To support the institution's mission and goals, CS must provide faculty and staff and administrative units with information, guidance, and support on career development and employment issues and linkages with the broader community.

CS should support faculty and staff and administrative units by:
- identifying and disseminating information on employment trends and top employing organizations and co-op and internship sponsors
- providing employer feedback on the preparation of students for jobs, the curriculum, and the hiring process
- raising awareness of appropriate ethical and legal guidelines for student referrals
- increasing awareness of career development issues and available resources
- providing and interpreting aggregate data on student learning and career-related outcomes for purposes such as accreditation, marketing, institutional development, and curriculum development

CS must consult with students and student groups regarding policy interpretation, program development, and relationships with employers.

Part 3. LEADERSHIP

Effective and ethical leadership is essential to the success of all organizations. Institutions must appoint, position, and empower Career Services (CS) leaders within the administrative structure to accomplish stated missions. CS leaders at various levels must be selected on the basis of formal education and training, relevant work experience, personal skills and competencies, relevant professional credentials, as well as potential for promoting learning and development in students, applying effective practices to educational processes, and enhancing institutional effectiveness. Institutions must determine expectations of accountability for leaders and fairly assess their performance.

Leaders of CS must exercise authority over resources for which they are responsible to achieve their respective missions.

CS leaders must:
- **articulate a vision for their organization**
- **set goals and objectives based on the needs and capabilities of the population served**
- **promote student learning and development**
- **prescribe and practice ethical behavior**
- **recruit, select, supervise, and develop others in the organization**
- **manage financial resources**
- **coordinate human resources**
- **plan, budget for, and evaluate personnel and programs**
- **apply effective practices to educational and administrative processes**
- **communicate effectively**
- **initiate collaborative interaction between individuals and agencies that possess legitimate concerns and interests in the functional area**

CS leaders must identify and find means to address individual, organizational, or environmental conditions that inhibit goal achievement.

CS leaders must promote campus environments that result in multiple opportunities for student learning and development.

CS leaders must continuously improve programs and services in response to changing needs of students and other constituents, and evolving institutional priorities.

If career components are offered through multiple units, the institution must designate a leader or leadership team to provide strategic direction and align career services with the mission of the institution and the needs of the constituencies served.

CS leaders should coordinate efforts with other units in the institution providing career components to integrate career services into the broader educational mission. Key constituencies served by each unit should be clearly identified and reflected in the mission and goals of the unit.

CS leaders must be advocates for the advancement of career services within the institution.

CS leaders should participate in institutional decisions about career services objectives and policies. CS leaders should participate in institutional decisions related to the identification and designation of clients served. Clients may include students, alumni, community members, and employers. Decisions about clients served should include type and scope of services offered and the fees, if any, that are charged.

Part 4. ORGANIZATION AND MANAGEMENT

Guided by an overarching intent to ensure student learning and development, Career Services (CS) must be structured purposefully and managed effectively to achieve stated goals. Evidence of appropriate structure must include current and accessible policies and procedures, written performance expectations for all employees, functional workflow graphics or organizational charts, and clearly stated service delivery expectations.

Evidence of effective management must include use of comprehensive and accurate information for decisions, clear sources and channels of authority, effective communication practices, decision-making and conflict resolution procedures, responsiveness to changing conditions, accountability and evaluation systems, and recognition and reward processes. CS must provide channels within the organization for regular review of administrative policies and procedures.

Other areas for consideration in determining structure and management of career services should include:
- size, nature and mission of the institution
- number and scope of academic-related services
- scope and intent of recruiting services
- philosophy and delivery system for services
- varied delivery methods (e.g., direct contact, technology)

CS should be integrated with, and complementary to, employment-related services.

Part 5. HUMAN RESOURCES

Career Services (CS) must be staffed adequately by individuals qualified to accomplish its mission and goals. Within established guidelines of the institution, CS must establish procedures for staff selection, training, and evaluation; set expectations for supervision, and provide appropriate professional development opportunities. CS must strive to improve the professional competence and skills of all personnel it employs.

CS staff must, in combination, have the competencies necessary to effectively perform the primary functions. Primary functions are program management and administration; program and event administration; career counseling and consultation; teaching/training/ educating; marketing/promoting/outreach; brokering/ connecting/linking; and information management.

The primary functions should include the following core competencies and knowledge domains.

Management and administration
Core Competencies

Needs assessment; program design, implementation and evaluation; strategic & operational planning; program integration and integrity; staffing; staff development and supervision; budget planning and administration; political sensitivity and negotiation skills; synthesize, interpret and report information

Knowledge Domains

Systems theory; organizational development; research design; statistics; accounting and budgeting procedures; revenue generation; principles; purchasing; staff selection; supervision; performance appraisals; management of information systems; customer service; marketing

Program and event administration
Core Competencies

Needs assessment; goal setting; program planning; implementation and evaluation; budget allocation; time management; problem solving; attention to detail

Knowledge Domains

Systems, logistics, and procedures; project management; customer service

Career counseling and consultation
Core Competencies

Needs assessment and diagnosis; intervention design and implementation; test administration and interpretation; counseling; feedback; evaluation; advising; empathy and interpersonal sensitivity; work with individuals and groups; use of career, occupational, and employment information

Knowledge Domains

Career development theories; adult development theory and unique issues for special populations; statistics; counseling processes; evaluation of person-job fit; job analysis; career decision making; behavior management; job search, interviews, and resumes

Teaching/ training/ educating
Core Competencies

Needs assessment; program/workshop design; researching, evaluating, and integrating information; effective teaching strategies; coaching; work with individuals and groups; use of technology for delivery of content

Knowledge Domains

Setting learning objectives; designing curricula and learning resources for specific content areas; experiential learning; career development and job search process; learning styles

Marketing/ promoting/ outreach
Core Competencies

Needs assessment and goal setting; written and interpersonal communication; public speaking; job development; effective use of print, web, personal presentation methods

Knowledge Domains
> Customer service; knowledge of institution and its academic programs; career services; employers' and faculty needs and expectations; recruiting and staffing methods, trends

Brokering/ connecting/ linking

Core Competencies
> Organize information, logistics, people, and processes toward a desired outcome; consulting; interpersonal skills

Knowledge Domains
> Systems and procedures; candidate/resume referral; recruiting and experiential learning operations; human resource selection practices

Information management

Core Competencies
> Organization and dissemination; storage and retrieval; computing systems and applications; data entry and analysis; acquisition of appropriate career resources; web design

Knowledge Domains
> Library/resources center organization; computer systems and applications; specific electronic management information systems.

CS professional staff members must hold an earned graduate degree in a field relevant to the position they hold or must possess an appropriate combination of educational credentials and related work experience.

Degree or credential-seeking interns must be qualified by enrollment in an appropriate field of study and by relevant experience. These individuals must be trained and supervised adequately by professional staff members holding educational credentials and related work experience appropriate for supervision.

Student employees and volunteers must be carefully selected, trained, supervised, and evaluated. They must be trained on how and when to refer those in need of assistance to qualified staff members and have access to a supervisor for assistance in making these judgments. Student employees and volunteers must be provided clear and precise job descriptions, pre-service training based on assessed needs, and continuing staff development.

Training should include customer service, program procedures, and information and resource utilization.

CS must have technical and support staff members adequate to accomplish its mission. Staff members must be technologically proficient and qualified to perform their job functions, be knowledgeable of ethical and legal uses of technology, and have access to training. The level of staffing and workloads must be adequate and appropriate for program and service demands.

Career information facilities should be staffed with persons who have the appropriate competencies to assist students and other designated clients in accessing and effectively using career information and resources. A technical support person or support service should be available to maintain computer and information technology systems for career services.

Salary levels and fringe benefits for all CS staff members must be commensurate with those for comparable positions within the institution, in similar institutions, and in the relevant geographic area.

CS must institute hiring and promotion practices that are fair, inclusive, and non-discriminatory. Programs and services must employ a diverse staff to provide readily identifiable role models for students and to enrich the campus community.

CS must create and maintain position descriptions for all staff members and provide regular performance planning and appraisals.

CS must have a system for regular staff evaluation and must provide access to continuing education and professional development opportunities, including in-service training programs and participation in professional conferences and workshops.

CS professional staff members must engage in continuing professional development activities to keep abreast of the research, theories, legislation, policies and developments that affect career services.

Staff training and development should be on-going and promote knowledge and skill development across program components.

All staff must be trained in legal, confidential, and ethical issues related to career services.

Part 6. FINANCIAL RESOURCES

Career Services (CS) must have adequate funding to accomplish its mission and goals. Funding priorities must be determined within the context of the stated mission, goals, objectives, and comprehensive analysis of the needs and capabilities of students, and the availability of internal or external resources.

CS must demonstrate fiscal responsibility and cost effectiveness consistent with institutional protocols.

CS should cultivate employer support of the institution, which may include scholarships and other forms of financial support, in coordination with development office efforts. While outside revenue may be generated to supplement the services it should not replace institutional funding. Revenue generated from employers, vendors, students, and other designated clients should be limited and reasonable to carry out stated objectives.

Part 7. FACILITIES, TECHNOLOGY, and EQUIPMENT

Career Services (CS) must have adequate, suitably located facilities, adequate technology, and equipment to support its mission and goals efficiently and effectively. Facilities, technology, and equipment must be evaluated regularly and be in compliance with relevant federal, state, provincial, and local requirements to provide for access, health, safety, and security.

CS must provide: private offices for professional staff in order to perform counseling or other confidential work; support staff work areas; reception and student registration area; career resource center; storage space sufficient to accommodate resources, supplies and equipment; technology resources for students and staff sufficient to support career services functions; access to conference rooms, computer labs and large group meeting rooms; private interview facilities for employers and students to accommodate the scope of the recruiting program; and reception spaces adequate to accommodate on-campus recruiting and career counseling services.

CS should be in a convenient location for students and employers and project a welcoming, professional atmosphere for its users. A private employer workspace should be available. Parking for visitors should be adequate and convenient.

Equipment and facilities must be secured to protect the confidentiality, security, and safety of records. Contracts with outside vendors must include adherence to ethics, confidentiality, security, institutional policies, as well as reflect support of career services programs, goals and standards.

Part 8. LEGAL RESPONSIBILITIES

Career Services (CS) staff members must be knowledgeable about and responsive to laws and regulations that relate to their respective responsibilities. Staff members must inform users of programs and services and officials, as appropriate, of legal obligations and limitations including constitutional, statutory, regulatory, and case law; mandatory laws and orders emanating from federal, state/provincial and local governments; and the institution's policies.

CS staff members must use reasonable and informed practices to limit the liability exposure of the institution, its officers, employees, and agents. Staff members must be informed about institutional policies regarding personal liability and related insurance coverage options.

The institution must provide access to legal advice for CS staff members as needed to carry out assigned responsibilities.

The institution must inform CS staff and students in a timely and systematic fashion about extraordinary or changing legal obligations and potential liabilities.

Career services staff members must be aware of and seek advice from the institution's legal counsel on: privacy and disclosure of student information contained in education records; defamation law regarding references and recommendations on the behalf of students and other designated clients; laws regarding employment referral practices of the career services office and others employed by the institution that refer students for employment; affirmative action regulations and laws regarding programs for special populations; liability issues pertaining to experiential learning programs; laws regarding eligibility to work; laws regarding contracts governing service provided by outside vendors; and laws regarding grant administration.

Career services must maintain appropriate records for future work with students and other designated clients.

Part 9. EQUITY and ACCESS

Career Services staff members must ensure that services and programs are provided on a fair and equitable basis. Facilities, programs and services must be accessible. Hours of operation and delivery of and access to programs and services must be responsive to the needs of all students and other constituents. CS must adhere to the spirit and intent of equal opportunity laws.

To respond to the needs of students and other designated clients, career services should provide services in-person, on-line, via telephone, e-mail, or other formats. CS should be responsive to the needs of all its constituencies through the establishment of office hours, customer service systems and on-line operations.

Policies and practices of CS must not discriminate on the basis of age, color, disability, sex, national origin, race, religious creed, sexual identity, and/or veteran status. Exceptions are appropriate only where provided by relevant law and institutional policy.

CS should ensure that employers who use career services adhere to the word and spirit of equal employment opportunity and affirmative action. CS staff should make every effort to inform or educate faculty members about issues relevant to discriminatory practices related to their referral of students directly to employers.

Consistent with their mission and goals, programs and services must take affirmative action to remedy significant imbalances in student participation and staffing patterns.

These groups may include traditionally under-represented, disabled, evening, part-time, commuter, and international students.

As the demographic profiles of campuses change and new instructional delivery methods are introduced, institutions must recognize the needs of students who participate in distance learning for access to programs and services offered on campus. Institutions must provide appropriate services in ways that are accessible to distance learners and assist them in identifying and gaining access to other appropriate services in their geographic region.

Part 10. CAMPUS and EXTERNAL RELATIONS
Career Services (CS) must establish, maintain, and promote effective relations with relevant individuals, campus offices, and external agencies.

As an integral function within the institution, CS must develop and maintain effective relationships with relevant stakeholders at the institution and in the community.

To achieve this, CS should develop institutional support for career development and employment programs by:
- participating fully in campus activities such as faculty organizations, committees, student orientation programs, classroom presentations, academic courses in career planning, and student organization programs
- arranging appropriate programs that use alumni experience and expertise
- establishing cooperative relationships with other offices and services to support the practice of mutual referrals, information exchange, resource sharing, and other program functions

- providing information and reports to the academic administration, faculty and key offices of the institution regarding career services for students, employers, and alumni
- developing informal or formal student, faculty, or employer advisory groups
- encouraging dialogues among employers, faculty members, and administrators concerning career issues and trends for students and graduates

In addition, CS should:
- encourage staff participation in and through professional associations and community activities related to career and employment issues (e.g., chambers of commerce, workforce development functions, employer open houses, workshops, federally mandated one stop centers, school-to-work efforts)
- raise issues and concerns with the legal counsel of the institution regarding compliance with laws as they pertain to employment, recruitment, supervision (e.g., interns)

Part 11. DIVERSITY
Within the context of each institution's unique mission, diversity enriches the community and enhances the collegiate experience for all; therefore, Career Services (CS) must nurture environments where commonalties and differences among people are recognized and honored.

CS must promote educational experiences that are characterized by open and continuous communication that deepens understanding of one's own identity, culture, and heritage, and that of others. CS must educate and promote respect about commonalties and differences in their historical and cultural contexts.

CS must address the characteristics and needs of a diverse population when establishing and implementing policies and procedures.

CS should work in conjunction with the institution's special services and minority organizations to enhance student's awareness and appreciation of cultural and ethnic differences. Collaborating departments and minority organizations should provide educational programs that help minority students, multicultural students, and individuals with disabilities to identify and address their unique needs related to career development and employment. CS should initiate partnerships and collaborative programming with other offices representing specific populations to ensure appropriate service delivery.

Part 12. ETHICS

All persons involved in the delivery of Career Services (CS) must adhere to the highest principles of ethical behavior. CS must develop or adopt and implement appropriate statements of ethical practice. CS must publish these statements and ensure their periodic review by relevant constituencies.

Ethical standards or other statements from relevant professional associations should be considered.

CS staff members must ensure that privacy and confidentiality are maintained with respect to all communications and records to the extent that such records are protected under the law and appropriate statements of ethical practice. Information contained in students' education records must not be disclosed without written consent except as allowed by relevant laws and institutional policies. Staff members must disclose to appropriate authorities information judged to be of an emergency nature, especially when the safety of the individual or others is involved, or when otherwise required by institutional policy or relevant law.

All CS staff members must be aware of and comply with the provisions contained in the institution's human subjects research policy and in other relevant institutional policies addressing ethical practices and confidentiality of research data concerning individuals.

CS staff members must recognize and avoid personal conflict of interest or appearance thereof in their transactions with students and others.

CS staff members must strive to insure the fair, objective, and impartial treatment of all persons with whom they deal. Staff members must not participate in nor condone any form of harassment that demeans persons or creates an intimidating, hostile, or offensive campus environment.

When handling institutional funds, all CS staff members must ensure that such funds are managed in accordance with established and responsible accounting procedures and the fiscal policies or processes of the institution.

CS staff members must perform their duties within the limits of their training, expertise, and competence. When these limits are exceeded, individuals in need of further assistance must be referred to persons possessing appropriate qualifications.

CS staff members must use suitable means to confront and otherwise hold accountable other staff members who exhibit unethical behavior.

CS staff members must be knowledgeable about and practice ethical behavior in the use of technology.

CS leaders/managers should provide guidance and education on these standards to all persons involved in providing career services, including, but not limited to, entry-level professionals, support staff, student staff, interns, graduate assistants, faculty and staff, employers, service providers, and other administrators.

Part 13. ASSESSMENT AND EVALUATION

Career Services (CS) must conduct regular assessment and evaluations. CS must employ effective qualitative and quantitative methodologies as appropriate, to determine whether and to what degree the stated mission, goals, and student learning and development outcomes are being met. The process must employ sufficient and sound assessment measures to ensure comprehensiveness. Data collected must include responses from students and other affected constituencies.

CS must evaluate periodically how well they complement and enhance the institution's stated mission and educational effectiveness.

Career services must conduct regular evaluations to improve programs and services, to adjust to changing client needs, and to respond to environmental threats and opportunities.

In order for institutions to employ comparable methods for evaluation, resources from recognized peers and professional associations should be consulted. CS should collaborate with institutional research units, state agencies, accrediting bodies, and other evaluative groups that generate and assess evaluation information. CS should promote institutional efforts to conduct relevant research on career development, institutional issues such as academic success and retention, student learning outcomes, employment trends, and career interests.

Evaluations should include:
- review of the strategic plan, mission, human resources needs, diversity efforts, and other areas covered in this document
- regular feedback from participants on events, programs, and services
- systematic needs assessment to guide program development
- first destination surveys at or following graduation

- employer and student feedback regarding experiential learning programs
- alumni follow-up surveys administered at specific times after graduation
- reports and satisfaction surveys from students and other constituencies interacting with career services such as employers, faculty, and other post-secondary institutionS

Results of these evaluations must be used in revising and improving programs and services and in recognizing staff performance.

CS should prepare and disseminate annual and special reports, including career services philosophy, goals and objectives, current programs and services, service delivery information, first destination information, and graduate follow-up information.

General Standards revised in 2002; CS content developed/ revised in 1986, 1997, & 2000

THE ROLE of CLINICAL HEALTH SERVICES
CAS Standards Contextual Statement

Clinical health services have a unique position within institutions of higher learning. Despite the absence of universal access to health care in our society, we recognize the need for it – and we struggle to achieve it. Clinical health services can play a role in ensuring access to medical care for college students, some of whom do not have health insurance, by providing convenient, barrier-free treatment of illness and injury; clinical health services also work with campus or community prevention programs to manage communicable diseases and address, with local public health departments, other public health needs on a college campus. Access to quality clinical health services (medical and nursing care) is an important aspect of creating a healthy campus community.

The complexity and comprehensiveness of health-related programs and services varies extensively by institutional type, mission, and student demographics. There are often constellations of other services that may or may not be administratively connected with the clinical health service, all focused on the same mission of promoting the health of students but with various non-clinical methodologies, such as health insurance, public safety, recreation, tutoring, personal and group counseling, public health policy, patient education, and health promotion.

In 1860, Edward Hitchcock, physician and Professor of Hygiene at Amherst College was charged with the task of using physical fitness and hygiene education to advance the health of students (Packwood, 1989). Later, in response to outbreaks and epidemics of communicable diseases, infirmaries were created to isolate students with infectious disease. In the 1950s, as veterans returned and took advantage of the GI Bill, physicals and immunizations were added. Societal and behavioral risk factors moved to the forefront in the 1960s and 1970s, and recognition of the impact of mental health concerns on students' ability to achieve their academic potential brought new institutional investments in counseling services.

The historical reasons for providing clinical health services on campus are as follows:

- a call from faculty to create a support system to maintain the student's health to permit persistence and engagement with academic studies, especially in locations with poor access to high quality medical care off campus

- the need for isolation and treatment of students with communicable diseases, especially prior to the advent of vaccines and antibiotics

- the need for experienced, specialized care for students with certain medical risks related to their academic programs, such as performance arts and veterinary medicine

- the confidentiality needs of a young adult when seeking medical or nursing services in the context of establishing a new relationship with parents

- the need for basic access to medical and nursing services for students who do not have health insurance or financial resources with which to pay for care, especially on campuses without a mandatory medical insurance access policy

Some of these historical reasons remain pertinent today. However, the financing and delivery of medical care has changed. Students who are insured are often covered for primary care and other medical services at a designated in-area facility. Yet, it is important to remember that still upwards of thirty percent of the population (especially graduate and professional students) is uninsured for any type of access to community medical services (ACHA, 2004).

Data suggest, though, that issues that pose a threat to the student's academic success are now more often psychosocial or behavioral rather than risks from infection or other diseases. Although data collected by the American College Health Association National College Health Assessment (ACHA-NCHA) show that colds, flu, sore throats and sinus infections still often rank in the top ten impediments to academic success, the great majority of health-related reasons for academic problems are not medical.

Our perception of the factors and influences that contribute to the health and well-being of an individual and affect the quality and student learning and engagement has changed in the past four decades; the nature and character of health-related services should change in parallel. The criterion against which to assess the continued value of any health-related service is its relationship to supporting student learning and creating a healthy campus community. Clinical health services are often compared to other primary care ambulatory medical services in the community. However, medical or nursing care is just one aspect of a vast array of possible health services financed by institutional appropriations or a "health fee." A public health model or an ecological model with an emphasis on primary prevention, societal intervention, and community creates a golden gateway to a future foundation. Some possible functional areas for coordinated efforts are counseling services, health promotion or wellness services, recreation services, disability services, clinical services, and possibility other services or programs depending upon the needs and capacities of the campus and the surrounding community. These areas will not necessarily report to the same director or campus administrator. The model, however, is not as important as the assessment and decision process through which leaders responsible for the connection of health and student learning came to a conscious choice and an intentional design for the services offered. Becoming more population-sensitive can enhance any model. This means that current campus and student needs are more important than the historical models that supported the original establishment of services. The most important aspect of any clinical health service will be its ability to create and maintain effective and collaborative relationships with the larger community of faculty and student affairs staff. These relationships are essential in maintaining an emphasis on assisting in a student's academic success and a focus on the population's needs for a health and safe campus community (Jackson & Weinstein, 1997).

Clinical health services will be one of a variety of methods used advance the health of students to the extent that such efforts enhance the learning environment at that institution of higher education. Clinical health services must make it a priority to first address health risks and problems prevalent in the population to impede academic success and a student's capacity to learn. These may include viral or bacterial infections and back injuries. They also need to deal increasingly with the health consequences of violence, racism, sexism, and heterosexist behaviors. Colleges must also meet the special needs of the physically and mentally challenged. As campuses and their clinical health services respond to a broad range of student needs, they must purposely create windows of opportunity that can be used to influence students who will become constructive members of society.

Although institutions differ in size and scope of services, there are universal concepts that affect the provision of medical care to college students. These standards are based in large measure upon The American College Health Association's Guidelines for a College Health Program. That publication maybe used in conjunction with these Standards.

References, Readings, and Resources

American College Health Association. (2004). American College Health Association - National College Health Assessment (ACHA-NCHA) Web Summary. Updated June 2004. Available at http://www.acha.org .

Jackson, M, Weinstein, H. (1997). The importance of healthy communities of higher education. *Journal of American College Health. 45*, 237-241.

Packwood, W. (1989). *College student personnel services.* Springfield, IL: Charles C. Thomas.

American College Health Association. (1999). *Guidelines for a college health program.* Baltimore, MD: Author.

Centers for Disease Control and Prevention. (1997) Youth risk behavior surveillance: national college health risk behavior survey-United States, *MMWR,* 46(6), 1-56.

Keeling, R.P. (2000). Beyond the campus clinic: A holistic approach to student health. *AAC&U Peer Review, 2*(3), 13-18.

Modeste, N. (1996). *Dictionary of public health promotion and education: Terms and concepts.* Thousand Oaks, CA, Sage Publications.

Neinstein, L.S. (2002). *Adolescent health care: A practical guide.* Philadelphia: Lippincott Williams & Wilkins.

Patrick, K. (1988). Student health: Medical care within institutions of higher education. *Journal of the American Medical Association, 260,* 3301-3305.

Swinford, P. (2002). Advancing the health of students: A viewpoint. *Journal of American College Health,* May 2002

United States Department of Human Services. (2000) *Healthy people 2010: National health promotion and disease prevention objectives.* DHHS (PHS) Pub. No. 91-50212. Washington, DC: U.S. Department of Health and Human Services.

American College Health Association [ACHA]. ACHA National Office, P.O. Box 28937. Baltimore, MD 21240-8937. (410) 859-1500; Fax (410) 859-1510. http://www.acha.org

National Association of Student Personnel Administrators [NASPA]. NASPA National Office, 1875 Connecticut Ave., N.W., Suite 418. Washington, DC 20009. (202) 265-7500. http://www.naspa.org

Contributors
Paula Swinford, University of Southern California, ACHA
Richard P. Keeling, MD, K&A, NYC, Public Director
Mary Hoban and Victor Lieno,, ACHA

CLINICAL HEALTH SERVICES
CAS Standards and Guidelines

Part 1. MISSION

The purpose of Clinical Health Services (CHS) is to provide, promote, support, and integrate individual healthcare, clinical preventive services, clinical treatment for illness, patient education, and public health responsibilities. Such services must take into consideration the health status of the student population and the learning environment. These services must be consistent with the educational mission of the institution and must comply with relevant legal requirements, state/provincial regulations, and professional standards. The mission must reflect the fundamental assumption that health and social justice are inextricable interconnected. CHS must serve as a method of advancing the health of the students, thereby enhancing the learning environment at the institution of higher education it serves.

The following characteristics exemplify CHS that are consistent with the environment of healthcare delivery and the environment of higher education:

- access to multiple data sources on the characteristics and health status of the population
- a spectrum of services, that supports the learning mission of the campus community and health in its broadest sense
- easy and equal access to services by all students
- advocacy for a healthy campus community by providing leadership on policy issues regarding health risks of the population in the context of the learning environment
- evidence of measures of quality, such as accreditation of services, the use of recognized standards, and data on service delivery and effectiveness
- significant student involvement in advising the program's mission, goals, services, funding, and evaluation
- providing leadership during a health-related crisis
- collaboration with other campus health-related programs and services

The CHS must incorporate student learning and student development in its mission. CHS must enhance overall educational experiences. CHS must develop, record, disseminate, implement, and regularly review its mission and goals. Mission statements must be consistent with the mission and goals of the institution with the standards in this document. CHS must operate as an integral part of the institution's overall mission.

Part 2. PROGRAM

The formal education of students consists of the curriculum and the co-curriculum, and must promote student learning and development that is purposeful and holistic. Clinical Health Services (CHS) must identify relevant and desirable student learning and development outcomes and provide services that encourage the achievement of those outcomes.

Relevant and desirable outcomes include: intellectual growth, effective communication, realistic self-appraisal, enhanced self-esteem, clarified values, career choices, leadership development, healthy behaviors, meaningful interpersonal relationships, independence, collaboration, social responsibility, satisfying and productive lifestyles, appreciation of diversity, spiritual awareness, and achievement of personal and educational goals.

CHS must provide evidence of its impact on the achievement of student learning and development outcomes.

The table below offers examples of achievement of student learning and development outcomes.

Student Learning and Development Outcome Domains

Intellectual growth
Examples of achievement indicators
> Produces personal and educational goal statements; Employs critical thinking in problem solving; Uses complex information from a variety of sources including personal experience and observation to form a decision or opinion; Obtains a degree; Applies previously understood information and concepts to a new situation or setting; Expresses appreciation for literature, the fine arts, mathematics, sciences, and social sciences

Effective communication
Examples of achievement indicators
> Writes and speaks coherently and effectively; Writes and speaks after reflection; Able to influence others through writing, speaking or artistic expression; Effectively articulates abstract ideas; Uses appropriate syntax; Makes presentations or gives performances

Enhanced self-esteem
Examples of achievement indicators
> Shows self-respect and respect for others; Initiates actions toward achievement of goals; Takes reasonable risks; Demonstrates assertive behavior; Functions without need for constant reassurance from others

Realistic self-appraisal

Examples of achievement indicators

Articulates personal skills and abilities; Makes decisions and acts in congruence with personal values; Acknowledges personal strengths and weaknesses; Articulates rationale for personal behavior; Seeks feedback from others; Learns from past experiences

Clarified values

Examples of achievement indicators

Articulates personal values; Acts in congruence with personal values; Makes decisions that reflect personal values; Demonstrates willingness to scrutinize personal beliefs and values; Identifies personal, work, and lifestyle values and explains how they influence decision-making

Career choices

Examples of achievement indicators

Articulates career choices based on assessment of interests, values, skills and abilities; Documents knowledge, skills, and accomplishments resulting from formal education, work experience, community service, and volunteer experiences; Makes the connections between classroom and out-of-classroom learning; Can construct a resume with clear job objectives and evidence of related knowledge, skills and accomplishments; Articulates the characteristics of a preferred work environment; Comprehends the world of work; Takes steps to initiate a job search or seek advanced education

Leadership development

Examples of achievement indicators

Articulates leadership philosophy or style; Serves in a leadership position in a student organization; Comprehends the dynamics of a group; Exhibits democratic principles as a leader; Exhibits ability to visualize a group purpose and desired outcomes

Healthy behavior

Examples of achievement indicators

Chooses behaviors and environments that promote health and reduce risk; Articulates the relationship between health and wellness and accomplishing life-long goals; Exhibits behaviors that advance a healthy community

Meaningful interpersonal relationships

Examples of achievement indicators

Develops and maintains satisfying interpersonal relationships; Establishes mutually rewarding relationships with friends and colleagues; Listens to and considers others' points of view; Treats others with respect

Independence

Examples of achievement indicators

Exhibits self-reliant behaviors; Functions autonomously; Exhibits ability to function interdependently; Accepts supervision as needed; Manages time and personal health effectively

Collaboration

Examples of achievement indicators

Works cooperatively with others; Seeks the involvement of others; Seeks feedback from others; Contributes to achievement of a group goal; Exhibits effective listening skills

Social responsibility

Examples of achievement indicators

Understands and participates in relevant governance systems; Understands, abides by, and participates in the development, maintenance, and/or orderly change of community, social, and legal standards or norms; Appropriately challenges the unfair, unjust, or uncivil behavior of other individuals or groups; Participates in service/volunteer activities

Satisfying and productive lifestyles

Examples of achievement indicators

Achieves balance between education, work, and leisure time and articulates the importance of such balance; Articulates and meets goals for work, leisure, and education; Overcomes obstacles that hamper goal achievement; Functions on the basis of personal identity, ethical, spiritual and moral values; Articulates long-term goals and objectives

Appreciating diversity

Examples of achievement indicators

Understands one's own identity and culture; Seeks involvement with people different from oneself; Seeks involvement in diverse interests; Articulates the advantages and challenges of a diverse society; Challenges appropriately the abusive use of stereotypes by others; Understands the impact of diversity on one's own society

Spiritual awareness

Examples of achievement indicators

Develops and articulates personal belief system; Understands roles of spirituality in personal and group values and behaviors

Personal and educational goals

Examples of achievement indicators

Sets, articulates, and pursues individual goals; Articulates personal and educational goals and objectives; Uses personal and educational goals to guide decisions; Understands the effect of one's personal and educational goals on others

CHS must be (a) intentional, (b) coherent, (c) based on theories and knowledge of learning and human development, (d) reflective of developmental and demographic profiles of the student population, and (e) responsive to needs of individuals, special populations, and communities.

CHS must acknowledge that health and social justice are inextricable interconnected.

CHS must establish appropriate policies and procedures for responding to emergency situations, especially where CHS facilities, personnel, and resources are not equipped to handle emergencies and/or when services are closed.

CHS must provide an infrastructure to support its services. The program must also create and maintain a network of services throughout the campus and surrounding communities.

Regardless of the size or scope of the institution, CHS must conform to a general level of acceptable practice that is theory-based and data-driven, and compliant with pertinent statutes, regulations, and professional standards.

In determining the scope of services to be offered, the following guidelines should apply:
- data on the affordability and accessibility of local healthcare resources, the insurance coverage of individual students, and the health status of the population should be collected and used to set priorities and tailor the CHS to the specific campus context
- CHS should contribute to the general education of students in the areas of behaviors and environments that promote physical, psychological, spiritual, and social health
- the scope and objectives of the services should be planned and outlined according to standards of practice utilizing data, goals and objectives, focus populations, assessment strategies and evaluative methodologies
- the educational goals of CHS should be consistent with nationally and internationally developed healthcare objectives
- documented evidence of organized strategic planning and implementation should be available
- CHS should create opportunities to address documented health issues and medical services needs within the student community it serves
- appropriate interdisciplinary and interagency collaboration should occur regularly

In determining the quality of services provided, the following guidelines should apply:
- access for all students to essential medical, nursing, and counseling services
- provision of services in accordance with standards of professional practice and ethical conduct and concern for the costs versus benefits to the health status of the population
- maintenance of accreditation, staff certification, and licensure where appropriate
- cost-effective and relevant services designed to address unique campus configurations
- coordination of services to ensure coverage with no duplication
- identification of less expensive alternative resources for individual healthcare when appropriate
- provision of appropriate referrals for additional or alternative treatments or assessments

Part 3. LEADERSHIP

Effective and ethical leadership is essential to the success of all organizations. Institutions must appoint, position, and empower Clinical Health Services (CHS) leaders within the administrative structure to accomplish stated mission. CHS leaders at various levels must be selected on the basis of formal education and training, relevant work experience, personal skills and competencies, relevant professional credentials, as well as potential for promoting learning and development in students, applying effective practices to educational processes and enhancing institutional effectiveness. Institutions must determine expectations of accountability for leaders and fairly assess their performance.

Leaders of CHS must exercise authority over resources for which they are responsible to achieve their respective missions.

CHS leaders must:
- **articulate a vision for their organization**
- **set goals and objectives based on the needs and capabilities of the population served**
- **promote student learning and development**
- **prescribe and practice ethical behavior**
- **recruit, select, supervise, and develop others in the organization**
- **manage financial resources,**
- **coordinate human resources**
- **plan, budget for, and evaluate personnel and services**
- **apply effective practices to educational and administrative processes**
- **communicate effectively**
- **initiate collaborative interaction between individuals and agencies that possess legitimate concerns and interests in the functional area**

CHS leaders must identify and find means to address individual, organizational, or environmental conditions that inhibit goal achievement.

CHS leaders must promote campus environments that result in multiple opportunities for student learning and development.

CHS leaders must continuously improve the program and services in response to changing needs of students and other constituents and evolving institutional priorities.

CHS leaders should continuously strive to eliminate duplicate coverage for care and contribute to a campus culture that supports health.

As the institution is legally constituted, the institution must have a defined governance structure that sets policy and is ultimately responsible for the clinical health services and its operations.

Part 4. ORGANIZATION and MANAGEMENT

Guided by an overarching intent to ensure student learning and development, Clinical Health Services (CHS) must be structured purposefully and managed effectively to achieve stated goals. Evidence of appropriate structure must include current and accessible policies and procedures, written performance expectations for all employees, functional workflow graphics or organizational charts, and clearly stated service delivery expectations.

CHS should be defined by the size, nature, complexity, and mission of the institution and by the documented needs and capabilities of the population it serves, as well as the availability of local community resources.

CHS should establish and maintain an advisory board with broad constituent representation, with specific duties and responsibilities for policy, budget, services, facilities, and resources.

CHS should make initial staff appointments, reappointments, and assignment or curtailment of clinical privileges based upon a professional review of credentials and as directed by institutional policy and state/provincial regulations and statutes.

Evidence of effective management must include use of comprehensive and accurate information for decisions, clear sources and channels of authority, effective communication practices, decision-making and conflict resolution procedures, responsiveness to changing conditions, accountability and evaluation systems, and recognition and reward processes. CHS must provide channels within the organization for regular review of administrative policies and procedures.

CHS should establish criteria and institute procedures for assessment and evaluation of medical access insurance policies.

The CHS director or coordinator must be placed within the institution's organizational structure to be able to promote cooperative interactions with appropriate campus and community entities.

Part 5. HUMAN RESOURCES

Clinical Health Services (CHS) must be staffed adequately by individuals qualified to accomplish its mission and goals. Within established guidelines of the institution, CHS must establish procedures for staff selection, training, and evaluation; set expectations for supervision, and provide appropriate professional development opportunities. CHS must strive to improve the professional competence and skills of all personnel it employs.

CHS should:

- strive to improve the professional competence and skill, as well as the quality of performance of all personnel it employs
- provide personnel with convenient access to on-line library resources that include materials pertinent to operational, administrative, institutional, and research services
- encourage participation of personnel in seminars, workshops, and other educational activities pertinent to its mission, goals, objectives, and the professional role
- verify participation in relevant external professional development programs, when attendance at such activities is required of professional personnel
- monitor the use of resources available to its personnel to identify that activities are relevant to the mission, goals, and objectives, and to maintain the licensure and/or certification of professional personnel
- identify continuing education activities based on quality improvement findings and the education criteria established by recognized professional authorities

Professional staff members must hold an earned graduate degree in a field relevant to the position they hold or must possess an appropriate combination of educational credentials and related work experience.

CHS must establish criteria and implement a procedure to review and verify credentials of staff.

Degree or credential-seeking interns must be qualified by enrollment in an appropriate filed of study and by relevant experience. These individuals must be trained and supervised adequately by professional staff members holding educational credentials and related work experience appropriate for supervision.

Student employees and volunteers must be carefully selected, trained, supervised, and evaluated. They must be trained on how and when to refer those in need of assistance to qualified staff members and have access to a supervisor for assistance in making these judgments. Student employees and volunteers must be provided clear and precise job descriptions, pre-service training based on assessed needs, and continuing staff development.

Student employees and volunteers must never have access to the personal health information of other students.

CHS must have technical and support staff members adequate to accomplish its mission. Staff members must be technologically proficient and qualified to perform their job functions, be knowledgeable of ethical and legal uses of technology, and have access to training. The level of staffing and workloads must be adequate and appropriate for program and service demands.

Salary levels and fringe benefits for all CHS staff members must be commensurate with those for comparable positions within the institution, in similar institutions, and in the relevant geographic area.

CHS must institute hiring and promotion practices that are fair, inclusive, and non-discriminatory. CHS must employ a diverse staff to provide readily identifiable role models for students and to enrich the campus community.

Staff members must take part in training sessions about gender, sexual orientation, racial, cultural, religious and/or spiritual, and ethnic sensitivity and should be aware of and involved in campus and community matters.

CHS must create and maintain position descriptions for all staff members and provide regular performance planning and appraisals.

CHS must have a system for staff evaluation and must provide access to continuing education and professional development opportunities, including in-service training programs and participation in professional conferences and workshops.

Specific aspects of the CHS for which staff should be assigned include business and financial management, community relations, and assessment.

Leaders should involve staff members in designing the organizational structure and in creating and reviewing policies and procedures that reinforce and foster health-engendering behaviors.

When CHS staff is involved in formal teaching or supervision, policies governing those activities must be consistent with the mission, goals, policies, and objectives of the institution.

When CHS staff is involved in research and publishing, policies governing those activities must be consistent with mission, goals, priorities, and objectives of the institution and capabilities of the program.

All CHS staff must be informed of the research policies of the institution and CHS.

Part 6. FINANCIAL RESOURCES

Clinical Health Services (CHS) must have adequate funding to accomplish its mission and goals. Funding priorities must be determined within the context of the stated mission, goals, objectives, and comprehensive analysis of the needs and capabilities of students and the availability of internal or external resources.

CHS must demonstrate fiscal responsibility and cost effectiveness consistent with institutional protocols.

Financial planning and projections should include budget data for both current and long-term expenditures that include capital expenditures and deferred maintenance costs.

Part 7. FACILITIES, TECHNOLOGY, and EQUIPMENT

Clinical Health Services (CHS) must have adequate, suitably located facilities, adequate technology, and equipment to support its mission and goals efficiently and effectively. Facilities, technology, and equipment must be evaluated regularly and be in compliance with relevant federal, state/provincial, and local requirements to provide for access, health, safety, and security.

CHS facilities should support a range of activities including clinical treatment, intervention and consultation, patient education and policy development. A safe, functional, and efficient environment is crucial to providing appropriate services and achieving desired outcomes.

Depending upon services offered, environmental conditions should include:

- necessary facilities, technology, and equipment to handle individual or campus emergencies
- regulations prohibiting smoking
- elimination of hazards that might lead to slipping, falling, electrical shock, burns, poisoning, or other trauma
- adequate reception areas, toilets, and telephones
- parking for guests, patients, and people with disabilities
- accommodations for persons with physical disabilities
- adequate lighting and ventilation
- clean and properly maintained facilities
- facilities that provide for confidentiality and privacy of services and records
- testing and proper maintenance of equipment
- a system for the proper identification, management, handling, transport, treatment, and disposition of hazardous materials and wastes whether solid, liquid, or gas
- appropriate alternative power sources in case of emergency
- technology to support services and facilities

CHS must ensure that facilities, technology, and equipment are accessible for persons with disabilities.

Part 8. LEGAL RESPONSIBILITIES

Clinical Health Services (CHS) staff members must be knowledgeable about and responsive to law and regulations that relate to their respective responsibilities. CHS staff members must inform users of programs and services and officials, as appropriate, of legal obligations and limitations including constitutional, statutory, regulatory, and case law; mandatory laws and orders emanating from federal, state/provincial and local governments; and the institution's policies.

Staff members must use reasonable and informed practices to limit the liability exposure of the institution, its officers, employees, and agents. Staff members must be informed about institutional policies regarding personal liability and related insurance coverage options.

The institution must provide access to legal advice for CHS staff members as needed to carry out assigned responsibilities and must inform CHS staff and students in a timely and systematic fashion about extraordinary or changing legal obligations and potential liabilities.

CHS must inform the institutional community of its policies and procedures addressing:

- **individual rights and responsibilities**
- **balancing protection of individual health and safety with individual rights to confidentiality and privacy**
- **risk management**
- **medical access insurance coverage**
- **informed consent**
- **access, release content, and maintenance of individual records in accordance with legal obligations and limitations**
- **research**
- **medical dismissal of students**

CHS must develop and maintain a systematic risk management program appropriate for the organization.

Risk management programs should focus on:

- methods by which individuals may be dismissed from or refused services
- methods of collecting unpaid accounts
- review of litigation related to the institution's CHS
- review of all deaths, trauma, or adverse events where there is health risk
- communication with the liability insurance carrier
- methods of dealing with inquiries from government agencies, attorneys, consumer advocate groups, reporters, and the media
- methods of managing a situation with an impaired staff member
- methods for complying with governmental regulations and contractual agreements
- methods of transporting students with medical emergencies
- maintenance of confidential records

Part 9. EQUITY and ACCESS

Clinical Health Services (CHS) staff members must ensure that services and programs are provided on a fair and equitable basis. Facilities, programs and services must be accessible. Hours of operation and delivery of and access to services must be responsive to the needs of all students and other constituents. CHS must adhere to the spirit and intent of equal opportunity laws.

CHS should accommodate the unique needs of individuals with disabilities and should encourage faculty, staff, and other students to develop awareness of and sensitivity to individuals with disabilities. Students with disabilities should be encouraged to self identify individual needs as soon as possible following admission (pre-matriculation) so that accommodations can be made.

For students with physical disabilities, CHS staff should advocate that the institution meet special needs through clinical health services, housing, food services, and counseling services. Whenever possible, the institution should eliminate architectural barriers that create difficulties for students with physical disabilities.

Policies and practices of CHS must open and readily accessible to all students and must not discriminate except where sanctioned by law and institutional policy. Discrimination must be avoided on the basis of age; color; creed; cultural heritage; disability; ethnicity; gender identity; nationality; political affiliation; religious affiliation; sex; sexual orientation; or social, economic, marital, or veteran status.

Students with special health risks may be identified by information provided on health history or behavioral assessment forms, or through screening, surveillance, and education services.

Students with chronic health conditions may be identified and informed of support services.

CHS may provide services directly or identify appropriate resources in the community to meet the special needs of these students.

Consistent with their mission and goals, CHS must take affirmative action to remedy significant imbalances in student participation and staffing patterns.

As the demographic profiles of campuses change and new instructional delivery methods are introduced, institutions must recognize the needs of students who participate in distance learning for access to programs and services offered on campus. Institutions must provide appropriate services in ways that are accessible to distance learners and assist them in identifying and gaining access to other appropriate services in their geographic region.

CHS must ensure that students are informed about the importance of medical and dental access insurance and how to make an informed decision based on their needs.

As a condition of enrollment, students may be required to provide evidence that they have adequate medical access through healthcare insurance coverage.

Medical access through insurance coverage should be available to all eligible students.

Part 10. CAMPUS and EXTERNAL RELATIONS
Clinical Health Services (CHS) must establish, maintain, and promote effective relations with relevant individuals, campus offices, and external agencies.

To ensure success, CHS must maintain good relations with students, faculty members, staff, alumni, the local community, contractors, and support agencies.

CHS must comply with these standards even when contracted for or outsourced by the Institution.

CHS staff should participate actively with their institution in designing policies and practices and developing further resources and services that have direct impact on the health status of the campus population.

CHS should review and assess health aspects of relevant institutional policies and practices. These issues may include but are not limited to drug use policies and treatment, blood-borne diseases, sexual harassment/assault, suicide and homicide threats, and discrimination of all types.

Policies on requirements for immunization prior to and during matriculation should be implemented and maintained to assure compliance, protect community health, and meet the needs of students at risk.

CHS should collaborate to minimize duplication of services with campus and community partners.

CHS should address the level and the priorities of campus services as determined by institution-specific population health status surveys, available community resources, user data and institutional context. CHS should review potential health hazards or problems related to academic activities.

CHS should identify and utilize community services, whenever appropriate, to build resource/service networks and create awareness within the community about special needs populations.

Part 11. DIVERSITY
Within the context of each institution's unique mission, diversity enriches the community and enhances the collegiate experience for all; therefore, Clinical Health Services (CHS) must nurture environments where commonalities and differences among people are recognized and honored.

CHS must promote educational experiences that are characterized by open and continuous communication that deepens understanding of one's own identity,

culture, and heritage, and that of others. CHS must educate and promote respect about commonalties and differences in their historical and cultural contexts.

CHS must address the characteristics and needs of a diverse population when establishing and implementing policies and procedures.

Every contact should be viewed as an opportunity to recognize and honor diversity to address specific concerns that might impact health and quality of life for the individual and community.

Students should be provided an environment of caring with an inclusive approach, which is essential for establishing levels of confidentiality, trust, and comfort.

CHS should establish procedures for students to discuss with staff their comfort or discomfort with various approaches in delivery of services.

Individuals should be accepted in a free and open manner and in an atmosphere of mutual respect to encourage candid discussion of sensitive personal issues. Staff members should demonstrate sensitivity and understanding to students from diverse backgrounds and cultures to provide satisfactory services.

Part 12. ETHICS

All persons in the delivery of Clinical Health Services (CHS) services must adhere to the highest principles of ethical behavior. CHS must develop or adopt and implement appropriate statements of ethical practice. CHS must publish these statements and ensure their periodic review by relevant constituencies.

CHS staff members must ensure that privacy and confidentiality are maintained with respect to all communications and records to the extent that such records are protected under the law and appropriate statements of ethical practice. Information contained in students' education records must not be disclosed without written consent except as allowed by relevant laws and institutional policies. Staff members must disclose to appropriate authorities information judged to be of an emergency nature, especially when the safety of the individual or others is involved, or when otherwise required by institutional policy or relevant law.

The task of media relations involving individual health status should be assigned to staff members who are knowledgeable about information that can be released.

Staff members should prevent visitors from entering the facility in any manner that would compromise confidentiality.

All CHS staff members must be aware of and comply with the provisions contained in the institution's human subjects research policy and in other relevant institutional policies addressing ethical practices and confidentiality of research data concerning individuals.

Staff members must recognize and avoid personal conflict of interest or appearance thereof in their transactions with students and others.

Products and services should not be promoted for any other reason than the individual's or the community's benefit.

CHS staff members must strive to ensure the fair, objective, and impartial treatment of all persons with whom they deal. Staff members must not participate in nor condone any form of harassment that demeans persons or creates an intimidating, hostile, or offensive campus environment.

When handling institutional funds, all CHS staff members must ensure that such funds are managed in accordance with established and responsible accounting procedures and the fiscal policies or processes of the institution.

CHS staff members must perform their duties within the limits of their training, expertise and competence. When these limits are exceeded, individuals in need of further assistance must be referred to persons possessing appropriate qualifications.

CHS members must use suitable means to confront and otherwise hold accountable other staff members who exhibit unethical behavior.

CHS staff members must be knowledgeable about and practice ethical behavior in the use of technology.

All marketing and advertising concerning the clinical health services must communicate the scope and range of services provided without deception.

Clinical health services should inform individuals of their basic rights and responsibilities regarding service. Such rights and responsibilities should include:
- service that is competent, considerate, and compassionate; recognizes basic human rights; safeguards personal dignity; and respects values and preferences

- provision of appropriate privacy, including protection from access to confidential information by faculty members, staff, student workers, and others
- ability to receive services from the staff member of choice
- accurate information regarding competencies and credentials of the clinical health services staff
- use of identified methods to express grievances and make suggestions
- information concerning individual health status and available services
- individual disclosure of complete and full information on health status that will be treated confidentially and for which the individual gives authority to approve or refuse release in compliance with applicable federal and state/provincial laws
- an explicit process to share necessary personal health information with mental health/counseling/psychotherapy services and other higher education faculty and staff on a need-to-know basis
- an explicit process for consent to share necessary personal health information with off-campus entities

Part 13. ASSESSMENT and EVALUATION

Clinical Health Services (CHS) must conduct regular assessment and evaluations. CHS must employ effective qualitative and quantitative methodologies as appropriate, to determine whether and to what degree the stated mission, goals, and student learning and development outcomes are being met. The process must employ sufficient and sound assessment measures to ensure comprehensiveness. Data collected must include responses from students and other affected constituencies.

CHS should maintain an active, organized, peer-based, quality management and improvement program that links peer review, quality improvement activities, and risk management in an organized, systematic way.

Periodically, the organization should assess user and non-user satisfaction with services and facilities provided by the clinical health services and incorporate findings into quality improvement.

To develop criteria used to evaluate services, staff members should understand, support and participate in programs of quality management and improvement. Data should be collected in an ongoing manner to identify unacceptable or unexpected trends or occurrences.

The quality improvement program should address administrative and cost issues and service outcomes.

CHS must evaluate periodically how well they complement and enhance the institution's stated mission and educational effectiveness. Results of these evaluations must be used in revision and improving services and in recognizing staff performance.

General Standards revised in 2002; CHS (formerly College Health Programs) developed/revised in 2001 & 2006

THE ROLE of COLLEGE HONOR SOCIETIES
CAS Standards Contextual Statement

The purposes of honor societies in colleges and universities are threefold. First, they exist primarily to recognize the attainment of scholarship of a superior quality. Second, a few societies recognize the development of leadership qualities and of commitment to service and excellence in research, in addition to a strong scholarship record. Third, to the degree that this recognition is coveted, they encourage the production of superior scholarship and leadership. To accomplish these objectives, it is clear that an honor society must define and maintain a truly high standard of eligibility for membership and achieve sufficient status by so doing that membership becomes something to be highly valued.

The honor society has followed the expansion and specialization of higher education in America. When Phi Beta Kappa was organized in 1776, there was no thought given to its field because all colleges then in existence were for the training of men for the service of the church and the state. With the expansion of education into new fields a choice had to be made, and Phi Beta Kappa elected to operate in the field of liberal arts and sciences. Although this was not finally decided until 1898, the trend was evident earlier; the 1880s saw the establishment of Tau Beta Pi in the field of engineering and Sigma Xi in scientific research.

Early in the 20th century, other honor societies came into being. Phi Kappa Phi was organized to accept membership from all academic fields in the university. A few others of this nature had origins in Black, Catholic, or Jesuit colleges and universities. These honor societies became known as general honor societies. Other variations have developed since that time. Leadership honor societies recognized meritorious attainments in all-around leadership and campus citizenship. Numerous societies drew membership from the various departments of study, recognizing good work in the student's special field of study. These societies are generally known as specialized honor societies. Another variation recognized scholastic achievement during the freshman or sophomore year. Yet another variation recognized achievement in associate degree programs.

The national organization of each honor society sets standards for establishing collegiate chapters and requirements for administering them. Chapters are chartered to institutions and have a dual relationship: maintain national honor society standards and requirements and abide by institutional policies and procedures.

The Association of College Honor Societies (ACHS) was founded in 1925 to join forces for the establishment and maintenance of useful functions and desirable standards, including criteria for membership, for governance of each member society, and for chapter operation. In addition to defining honor societies, similar student organizations with more liberal membership requirements were named Recognition Societies. Baird's Manual*, for many years the definitive reference of college organizations, adopted the ACHS definitions for classification of Honor Societies and Recognition Societies.

The standards and functions originally named in the early history of ACHS still have relevance today as ACHS fulfills a certifying function in assuring candidates for membership as well as institutions that member societies have met the high standards. The standards also serve a role for judging credibility of non-member societies.

The challenge in the 21st century is the same as when ACHS was founded: to use academic and operational standards to allay the confusion prevailing on campuses and among the public regarding the credibility and legitimacy of newly emerging honor societies. A plethora of Internet societies, for-profit societies, and an increasingly narrow focus of specialized societies gives rise to the need for the CAS standards to guide colleges and universities in setting regulations for official recognition of campus honor societies. Students, parents, and the public can use the standards as criteria for judging quality.

References, Readings, and Resources

Association of College Honor Societies. (2002*). ACHS Handbook, 2002-2005.* 4990 Northwind Dr., Ste. 140, East Lansing, MI 48823-5031. Web site: www.achsnatl.org.

Warren, J. W. (2000). *Prelude to the new millennium: Promoting honor for seventy-five years.* East Lansing, MI: Association of College Honor Societies. www.achsnatl.org/history.asp.

Note: *Baird's Manual of American College Fraternities*, last published in 1991 by Baird's Manual Foundation, was the authoritative reference work on college Greek-letter societies since first published in 1879.

Contributor: Dorothy I. Mitstifer, ACHS

College Honor Societies
CAS Standards and Guidelines

Part 1. MISSION

The mission of College Honor Societies (CHS) is to confer distinction for high achievement in undergraduate, graduate, and professional studies; in student leadership; in service; and in research.

CHS must incorporate student learning and student development in its mission.

CHS must enhance overall educational experiences. CHS must develop, record, disseminate, implement, and regularly review the mission and goals.

The mission statements of CHS must be consistent with the mission and goals of the institution and with the standards in this document. CHS must operate as integral parts of the institution's overall mission.

The following historical functions are properly served by CHS:
- foster a spirit of liberal education
- stimulate and encourage intellectual development
- stand for freedom of mind and spirit and for democracy of learning
- provide spiritual and intellectual leadership
- preserve valuable traditions and customs
- provide opportunities for members to associate in mutual understanding for the purpose of advancing society in the art of democratic living
- stimulate worthy attitudes for the improvement of the general welfare of the institution
- impose upon members high citizenship responsibilities and emphasize deeper study and discussion of the political-moral tradition—its characteristics, ideals, and possibilities

Part 2. PROGRAM

The formal education of students consists of the curriculum and the co-curriculum and must promote student learning and development that is purposeful and holistic. College Honor Societies (CHS) must identify relevant and desirable student learning and development outcomes and provide programs and services that encourage the achievement of those outcomes.

Relevant and desirable outcomes include: intellectual growth, effective communication, realistic self-appraisal, enhanced self-esteem, clarified values, career choices, leadership development, healthy behaviors, meaningful interpersonal relationships, independence, collaboration, social responsibility, satisfying and productive lifestyles, appreciation of diversity, spiritual awareness, and achievement of personal and educational goals.

CHS must provide evidence of their impact on the achievement of student learning and development outcomes.

The table below offers examples of evidence of achievement of student learning and development.

Student Learning and Development Outcome Domains

Intellectual growth
Examples of achievement indicators
   Produces personal and educational goal statements; Employs critical thinking in problem solving; Uses complex information from a variety of sources including personal experience and observation to form a decision or opinion; Obtains a degree; Applies previously understood information and concepts to a new situation or setting; Expresses appreciation for literature, the fine arts, mathematics, sciences, and social sciences

Effective communication
Examples of achievement indicators
   Writes and speaks coherently and effectively; Writes and speaks after reflection; Able to influence others through writing, speaking or artistic expression; Effectively articulates abstract ideas; Uses appropriate syntax; Makes presentations or gives performances

Enhanced self-esteem
Examples of achievement indicators
   Shows self-respect and respect for others; Initiates actions toward achievement of goals; Takes reasonable risks; Demonstrates assertive behavior; Functions without need for constant reassurance from others

Realistic self-appraisal
Examples of achievement indicators
   Articulates personal skills and abilities; Makes decisions and acts in congruence with personal values; Acknowledges personal strengths and weaknesses; Articulates rationale for personal behavior; Seeks feedback from others; Learns from past experiences

Clarified values
Examples of achievement indicators
   Articulates personal values; Acts in congruence with personal values; Makes decisions that reflect personal

values; Demonstrates willingness to scrutinize personal beliefs and values; Identifies personal, work, and lifestyle values and explains how they influence decision-making

Career choices

Examples of achievement indicators

Articulates career choices based on assessment of interests, values, skills and abilities; Documents knowledge, skills and accomplishments resulting from formal education, work experience, community service, and volunteer experiences; Makes the connections between classroom and out-of-classroom learning; Can construct a resume with clear job objectives and evidence of related knowledge, skills and accomplishments; Articulates the characteristics of a preferred work environment; Comprehends the world of work; Takes steps to initiate a job search or seek advanced education

Leadership development

Examples of achievement indicators

Articulates leadership philosophy or style; Serves in a leadership position in a student organization; Comprehends the dynamics of a group; Exhibits democratic principles as a leader; Exhibits ability to visualize a group purpose and desired outcomes

Healthy behavior

Examples of achievement indicators

Chooses behaviors and environments that promote health and reduce risk; Articulates the relationship between health and wellness and accomplishing life-long goals; Exhibits behaviors that advance a healthy community

Meaningful interpersonal relationships

Examples of achievement indicators

Develops and maintains satisfying interpersonal relationships; Establishes mutually rewarding relationships with friends and colleagues; Listens to and considers others' points of view; Treats others with respect

Independence

Examples of achievement indicators

Exhibits self-reliant behaviors; Functions autonomously; Exhibits ability to function interdependently; Accepts supervision as needed; Manages time effectively

Collaboration

Examples of achievement indicators

Works cooperatively with others; Seeks the involvement of others; Seeks feedback from others; Contributes to achievement of a group goal; Exhibits effective listening skills

Social responsibility

Examples of achievement indicators

Understands and participates in relevant governance systems; Understands, abides by, and participates in the development, maintenance, and/or orderly change of community, social, and legal standards or norms; Appropriately challenges the unfair, unjust, or uncivil behavior of other individuals or groups; Participates in service/volunteer activities

Satisfying and productive lifestyles

Examples of achievement indicators

Achieves balance between education, work and leisure time; Articulates and meets goals for work, leisure, and education; Overcomes obstacles that hamper goal achievement; Functions on the basis of personal identity, ethical, spiritual, and moral values; Articulates long-term goals and objectives

Appreciating diversity

Examples of achievement indicators

Understands one's own identity and culture; Seeks involvement with people different from oneself; Seeks involvement in diverse interests; Articulates the advantages and challenges of a diverse society; Challenges appropriately the abusive use of stereotypes by others; Understands the impact of diversity on one's own society

Spiritual awareness

Examples of achievement indicators

Develops and articulates personal belief system; Understands roles of spirituality in personal and group values and behaviors

Personal and educational goals

Examples of achievement indicators

Sets, articulates, and pursues individual goals; Articulates personal and educational goals and objectives; Uses personal and educational goals to guide decisions; Understands the effect of one's personal and educational goals on others

Programs of CHS must be (a) intentional, (b) coherent, (c) based on theories and knowledge of learning and human development, (d) reflective of developmental and demographic profiles of the student population, and (e) responsive to needs of individuals, special populations, and communities.

Programs of CHS must include the following elements:
- **educational programming that complements the academic curriculum**
- **opportunities for recognition by the institution**

- faculty, staff, and administrator involvement and interaction with students

The process for establishment of collegiate chapters of CHS must include:
- formal chartering of each chapter by institution and college/department petition
- approval by official action of the governing body of the national organization
- jointly defined relationship between the institution and the college honor society that must be formalized, documented, and disseminated
- candidate selection by the campus chapter
- membership invitation by the campus chapter

In order to maintain good standing with the national organization, CHS chapters must stay in compliance with national organization's policies.

The national organization of a college honor society must be governed by its membership and must include:
- officers/board members elected by the national membership
- chapter representation in the governing body
- national membership participation in approving and revising by-laws
- independent financial review and full financial disclosure

Classifications of CHS include general scholarship, general leadership, specialized scholarship, and freshman and sophomore and two year honor societies. Minimum scholastic qualifications in each classification of CHS should include:
- general scholarship – top 20%, not earlier than 5th semester
- general leadership – top 35%, not earlier than 5th semester
- specialized scholarship – top 35%, not earlier than 4th semester
- freshman and sophomore and two-year (associate degree) honor societies – adherence to the same high standards with the exception of semesters completed

"Recognition Societies" are those organizations with lower scholastic criteria.

Part 3. LEADERSHIP

Advisers (faculty or staff member) must represent the institution in advising chapters of College Honor Societies (CHS). The adviser must model leadership principles, establish a climate and structure that facilitates leadership development, determine expectations of accountability, and fairly assess student performance.

Chapter governance documents and the names of officers and advisers must be filed annually both with the institution and the national organization.

Institutions should maintain a centralized registry of CHS organizations.

Effective and ethical leadership is essential to the success of all organizations. Institutions must appoint, position, and empower advisers within the administrative structure to accomplish stated missions. Advisers of CHS must be selected on the basis of formal education and training, relevant work experience, personal skills and competencies, relevant professional credentials, as well as potential for promoting learning and development in students, applying effective practices to educational processes, and enhancing institutional effectiveness. Institutions must determine expectations of accountability for advisers and fairly assess their performance.

Leaders of CHS are elected by their peers to organize chapter activities.

Leaders of CHS should be students.

Leaders and advisers of CHS must exercise authority over resources for which they are responsible to achieve their respective missions.

Advisers must ensure that CHS leaders:
- articulate a vision for their organization
- set goals and objectives based on the needs and capabilities of the population served
- promote student learning and development
- prescribe and practice ethical behavior
- recruit, select, supervise, and develop others in the organization
- manage financial resources
- coordinate human resources
- plan, budget for, and evaluate personnel and programs
- apply effective practices to educational and administrative processes
- communicate effectively
- initiate collaborative interaction between individuals and agencies that possess legitimate concerns and interests in the functional area

Advisers must ensure that CHS leaders identify and find means to address individual, organizational, or environmental conditions to promote goal achievement.

Advisers must ensure that CHS leaders promote campus environments that result in multiple opportunities for student learning and development.

Advisers must ensure that CHS leaders continuously improve chapters, in response to the changing needs of students, and other constituents, and of evolving institutional priorities.

Part 4. ORGANIZATION AND MANAGEMENT

Guided by an overarching intent to ensure student learning and development, College Honor Societies (CHS) must be structured purposefully and managed effectively to achieve stated goals. Evidence of appropriate structure of the national organization must include current and accessible policies and procedures, written performance expectations for all volunteers, functional workflow graphics or organizational charts, and clearly stated service delivery expectations.

Evidence of effective management must include use of comprehensive and accurate information for decisions, clear sources and channels of authority, effective communication practices, decision-making and conflict resolution procedures, responsiveness to changing conditions, accountability and evaluation systems, and recognition and reward processes. CHS must provide channels within the organization for regular review of administrative policies and procedures.

Part 5. HUMAN RESOURCES

College Honor Societies (CHS) must be staffed adequately by honor society advisers, qualified to accomplish the mission and goals. Within established guidelines of the institution, CHS must establish procedures for adviser selection, training, and evaluation; set expectations and provide appropriate professional development opportunities. CHS must strive to improve the professional competence and skills of advisers.

CHS honor society advisers must be employed by the institution as faculty or staff members and hold an earned graduate degree in a field relevant to the position they hold or must possess an appropriate combination of educational credentials and related work experience.

With very few exceptions, faculty and staff are not employed as CHS advisers; most are volunteers.

Graduate student advisers of CHS must be qualified by enrollment in an appropriate field of study and by relevant experience. These individuals must be trained and supervised adequately by professional staff members holding educational credentials and related work experience appropriate for supervision.

Leaders and advisers must be carefully trained, supervised, and evaluated. They must be trained on how and when to refer those in need of assistance to qualified staff members and have access to a supervisor for assistance in making these judgments. Student leaders must be provided clear and precise job descriptions, pre-service training based on assessed needs, and continuing leadership development.

Degree or credential-seeking interns must be qualified by enrollment in an appropriate field of study and by relevant experience. These individuals must be trained and supervised adequately by professional staff members holding educational credentials and related work experience appropriate for supervision.

Student employees and volunteers must be carefully selected, trained, supervised, and evaluated. They must be trained on how and when to refer those in need of assistance to qualified staff members and have access to a supervisor for assistance in making these judgments. Student employees and volunteers must be provided clear and precise job descriptions, pre-service training based on assessed needs, and continuing staff development.

CHS must have technical and support staff to accomplish its mission. Support staff must be technologically proficient and qualified to perform their job functions, be knowledgeable of ethical and legal uses of technology, and have access to training.

The level of staffing and workloads must be adequate and appropriate for program and service demands.

Salary levels and fringe benefits for CHS advisers must be commensurate with those for comparable positions within the institution, in similar institutions, and in the relevant geographic area.

CHS must institute hiring and promotion practices that are fair, inclusive, and non-discriminatory. The **programs must employ a diverse staff to provide readily identifiable role models for students and to enrich the campus community.**

CHS must create and maintain position descriptions for advisers and leaders and provide regular performance planning and appraisals.

CHS must have a system for regular adviser evaluation and must provide access to continuing education and professional development opportunities, including in-service training programs and participation in professional conferences and workshops.

Part 6. FINANCIAL RESOURCES

College Honor Societies (CHS) must have adequate funding to accomplish the mission and goals. Funding priorities must be determined within the context of the stated mission, goals, objectives, and comprehensive analysis of the needs and capabilities of students and the availability of internal or external resources.

CHS must demonstrate fiscal responsibility and cost effectiveness consistent with institutional protocols.

Part 7. FACILITIES, TECHNOLOGY, AND EQUIPMENT

College Honor Societies (CHS) must have adequate suitably located facilities, technology, and equipment to support the mission and goals efficiently and effectively.

Meeting space for chapter activities and storage space for chapter materials (memorabilia, documents, files) should be available. Chapter files should be stored electronically and securely. Storage space for other chapter property should be available.

Facilities, technology, and equipment must be evaluated regularly and be in compliance with relevant federal state, provincial, and local requirements to provide for access, health, safety, and security.

Part 8. LEGAL RESPONSIBILITIES

Advisers of College Honor Societies (CHS) must be knowledgeable about and responsive to laws and regulations that relate to their respective responsibilities. Advisers must inform users of programs and services and officials, as appropriate, of legal obligations and limitations including constitutional, statutory, regulatory, and case law; mandatory laws and orders emanating from federal, state/provincial and local governments; and the institution's policies.

CHS advisers must use reasonable and informed practices to limit the liability exposure of the institution, its officers, employees, and agents. Advisers must be informed about national organization and institutional policies regarding personal liability and related insurance coverage options.

The institution must provide access to legal advice for honor society advisers as needed to carry out assigned responsibilities.

The institution must inform advisers and members of CHS in a timely and systematic fashion about extraordinary or changing legal obligations and potential liabilities.

Part 9. EQUITY and ACCESS

Advisers of College Honor Societies (CHS) must ensure that programs and services are provided on a fair and equitable basis. Advisors must ensure that invitations to membership in CHS are distributed on a fair and equitable basis. Facilities, programs, and services must be accessible. Hours of operation and delivery of and access to programs and services must be responsive to the needs of all students and other constituents. CHS must adhere to the spirit and intent of equal opportunity laws.

Policies and practices of CHS must not discriminate on the basis of age; color; creed; cultural heritage; disability; ethnicity; gender identity; nationality; political affiliation; religious affiliation; sex; sexual orientation; or social, economic, marital, or veteran status. Exceptions are appropriate only where provided by relevant law and institutional policy.

Consistent with their mission and goals, CHS must take affirmative action to remedy significant imbalances in student participation and advising patterns.

As the demographic profiles of campuses change and new instructional delivery methods are introduced, institutions must recognize the needs of students who participate in distance learning for access to programs and services offered on campus. Institutions must provide appropriate services in ways that are accessible to distance learners and assist them in identifying and gaining access to other appropriate services in their geographic region.

CHS must include outreach to underrepresented populations in membership recruitment activities.

Part 10. CAMPUS and EXTERNAL RELATIONS

College Honor Societies (CHS) must establish, maintain, and promote effective relations with relevant individuals, campus offices, and external agencies.

Part 11. DIVERSITY

Within the context of each institution's unique mission, diversity enriches the community and enhances the collegiate experience for all; therefore, College Honor Societies (CHS) must nurture environments where commonalties and differences among people are recognized and honored.

CHS must promote educational experiences that are characterized by open and continuous communication that deepens understanding of one's own identity, culture, and heritage, and that of others. CHS must educate and promote respect about commonalties and differences in their historical and cultural contexts.

CHS must address the characteristics and needs of a diverse population when establishing and implementing policies and procedures.

Part 12. ETHICS

All persons involved in the activities of College Honor Societies (CHS) must adhere to the highest principles of ethical behavior. CHS must develop or adopt and implement appropriate statements of ethical practice. CHS must publish these statements and ensure their periodic review by relevant constituencies.

Advisers of CHS must ensure that privacy and confidentiality are maintained with respect to all communications and records to the extent that such records are protected under the law and appropriate statements of ethical practice. Information contained in students' education records must not be disclosed without written consent except as allowed by relevant laws and institutional policies. Advisers must disclose to appropriate authorities information judged to be of an emergency nature, especially when the safety of the individual or others is involved, or when otherwise required by institutional policy or relevant law.

Advisers of CHS must be aware of and comply with the provisions contained in the institution's human subjects research policy and in other relevant institutional policies addressing ethical practices and confidentiality of research data concerning individuals.

Advisers of CHS must recognize and avoid personal conflict of interest or appearance thereof in their transactions with students and others.

Advisers of CHS must strive to ensure the fair, objective, and impartial treatment of all persons with whom they deal. Advisers must not participate in nor condone any form of harassment that demeans persons or creates an intimidating, hostile, or offensive campus environment.

When handling institutional funds, advisers of CHS must ensure that such funds are managed in accordance with established and responsible accounting procedures and the fiscal policies or processes of the institution.

Advisers of CHS must perform their duties within the limits of their training, expertise, and competence. When these limits are exceeded, individuals in need of further assistance must be referred to persons possessing appropriate qualifications.

Advisers of CHS must use suitable means to confront and otherwise hold accountable officers and members who exhibit unethical behavior.

Advisers of CHS must be knowledgeable about and practice ethical behavior in the use of technology.

Part 13. ASSESSMENT and EVALUATION

College Honor Societies (CHS) must conduct regular assessment and evaluations. CHS must employ effective qualitative and quantitative methodologies as appropriate to determine whether and to what degree the stated mission, goals, and student learning and development outcomes are being met. The process must employ sufficient and sound assessment measures to ensure comprehensiveness. Data collected must include responses from students and other affected constituencies.

CHS must evaluate periodically how well they complement and enhance the institution's stated mission and educational effectiveness.

Results of these evaluations must be used in revising and improving CHS and in recognizing adviser and leader performance.

CHS standards developed in 2005

THE ROLE of COLLEGE UNIONS
CAS Standards Contextual Statement

Today's college union is the campus community center, serving students, faculty, administrators, staff, alumni, and guests. It is a unifying force that brings together diverse people, provides a forum for divergent viewpoints, and creates an environment where all feel welcome.

The college union—which may refer to an organization, a program, or a building—evolved from the debating tradition of British universities. The earliest college union, founded at Cambridge University in 1815, was literally a "union" of three debating societies. The first US college union was organized at Harvard in 1832; like its British predecessors, it existed primarily for debating purposes. By the late 1800s, the Harvard Union had embraced the concept of being a general club. The first building erected explicitly for union purposes was Houston Hall at the University of Pennsylvania. Built in 1896, it housed lounges, dining rooms, reading and writing rooms, an auditorium, game rooms, and student offices; it was given to the university by the Houston family as a "place where all may meet on common ground."

In the 1930s, the success of civic recreational and cultural centers influenced college union leaders to view the union as the campus counterpart of the "community center," with an educational and recreational mission to perform. The most extensive period of union building construction took place following World War II, as enrollments surged and colleges and universities sought to better fulfill the needs of students and faculty. During the last half of the 20th Century, the college union movement has concentrated on building community, emphasizing its educational mission, and promoting student development and leadership.

Additionally, the contemporary college union offers many services used by all members of the campus community. College unions often include banks, post offices, child care, dining facilities, study lounges, computer labs, bookstores, and other services the campus community, and especially students, rely on during the course of the day while they are on campus. In providing these services, the college union allows its community to focus on academic and personal achievement.

The college union provides numerous educationally purposeful activities outside the classroom, which are "key to enhancing learning and personal development," according to The Student Learning Imperative (ACPA, 1994). The official Role of the College Union states that it is "an integral part of the educational mission of the college." The union contributes to the education of the student body at large through its cultural, educational, social, and recreational programs and by encouraging "self-directed activity, giving maximum opportunity for self-realization." But the union also educates the students involved in its governance and program boards

and those it employs. The role statement defines the union as "a student centered organization that values participatory decision making. Through volunteerism, its boards, committees, and student employment, the union offers firsthand experience in citizenship and educates students in leadership, social responsibility, and values." These models of college union governance foster student/ staff partnerships that form the foundation for student development and leadership training.

References, Readings, and Resources

American College Personnel Association [ACPA] (1994) The student learning imperative. Washington, DC: Author.

Butts, P. F. (1971). The college union idea. Bloomington, IN: Association of College Unions International.

McMillan, A., & Davis, N. T. (Eds.) (1989). College unions: Seventy-five years. Bloomington, IN: Association of College Unions International.

Metz, N. D. (Ed.) (1996). Student development in college unions and student activities. Bloomington, IN: Association of College Unions International.

Metz, N., & Sievers, C. S. (2002). Student leadership in college unions and student activities. Bloomington, IN: ACUI.

Mitchell, R. L. (1997). Metaphors, semaphores and two-by-fours: Reflections on a personal profession. Bloomington, IN: ACUI.

Maul, S. Y. (1994). Building community on campus. Bloomington, IN: ACUI.

Association of College Unions International (ACUI) Central Office, One City Centre, Suite 200, 120 W. Seventh St., Bloomington, IN 47404-3925. (812) 855-8550; www.acui.org

The Bulletin, ACUI publication, published bimonthly; available from the ACUI Central Office.

Contributors:
Current edition: Bob Rodda, College of Wooster, ACUI
Previous editions: Nancy Davis Metz, ACUI

COLLEGE UNIONS
CAS Standards and Guidelines

Part 1. MISSION

The College Union (CU) must incorporate student learning and student development in its mission. The CU must enhance overall educational experiences. The CU must develop, record, disseminate, implement and regularly review its mission and goals. Mission statements must be consistent with the mission and goals of the institution and with the standards in this document. The CU must operate as an integral part of the institution's overall mission.

The primary goals of the CU must be to maintain facilities, provide services, and promote programs that are responsive to student developmental needs and to the physical, social, recreational, and continuing education needs of the campus community.

The CU is a center for the campus community and, as such, is an integral part of the institution's educational environment. The union represents a building, an organization, and a program; it provides services, facilities, and educational and recreational programs that enhance the quality of college life.

Through the work of its staff and various committees the CU can be a "laboratory" where students can learn and practice leadership, programming, management, social responsibility, and interpersonal skills. As a center for the academic community, the union provides a place for increased interaction and understanding among individuals from diverse backgrounds.

To meet its goals, college unions should provide:

- food services
- leisure time and recreational opportunities
- social, cultural, and intellectual programs
- continuing education opportunities
- retail stores
- service agencies that are responsive to campus needs
- student leadership development programs and opportunities
- student employment
- student development programs

Part 2. PROGRAM

The formal education of students consists of the curriculum and the co-curriculum, and must promote student learning and development that is purposeful and holistic. The College Union (CU) must identify relevant and desirable student learning and development outcomes and provide programs and services that encourage the achievement of those outcomes.

Relevant and desirable outcomes include: intellectual growth, effective communication, realistic self-appraisal, enhanced self-esteem, clarified values, career choices, leadership development, healthy behaviors, meaningful interpersonal relationships, independence, collaboration, social responsibility, satisfying and productive lifestyles, appreciation of diversity, spiritual awareness, and achievement of personal and educational goals.

The CU must provide evidence of its impact on the achievement of student learning and development outcomes.

The table below offers examples of evidence of achievement of student learning and development.

Student Learning and Development Outcome Domains

Intellectual growth

Examples of achievement indicators

Produces personal and educational goal statements; Employs critical thinking in problem solving; Uses complex information from a variety of sources including personal experience and observation to form a decision or opinion; Obtains a degree; Applies previously understood information and concepts to a new situation or setting; Expresses appreciation for literature, the fine arts, mathematics, sciences, and social sciences

Effective communication

Examples of achievement indicators

Writes and speaks coherently and effectively; Writes and speaks after reflection; Able to influence others through writing, speaking or artistic expression; Effectively articulates abstract ideas; Uses appropriate syntax; Makes presentations or gives performances

Enhanced self-esteem

Examples of achievement indicators

Shows self-respect and respect for others; Initiates actions toward achievement of goals; Takes reasonable risks; Demonstrates assertive behavior; Functions without need for constant reassurance from others

Realistic self-appraisal

Examples of achievement indicators

Articulates personal skills and abilities; Makes decisions and acts in congruence with personal values; Acknowledges personal strengths and weaknesses; Articulates rationale for personal behavior; Seeks feedback from others; Learns from past experiences

Clarified values

Examples of achievement indicators

Articulates personal values; Acts in congruence with personal values; Makes decisions that reflect personal values; Demonstrates willingness to scrutinize personal beliefs and values; Identifies personal, work, and lifestyle values and explains how they influence decision-making

Career choices

Examples of achievement indicators

Articulates career choices based on assessment of interests, values, skills and abilities; Documents knowledge, skills and accomplishments resulting from formal education, work experience, community service ,and volunteer experiences; Makes the connections between classroom and out-of-classroom learning; Can construct a resume with clear job objectives and evidence of related knowledge, skills and accomplishments; Articulates the characteristics of a preferred work environment; Comprehends the world of work; Takes steps to initiate a job search or seek advanced education

Leadership development

Examples of achievement indicators

Articulates leadership philosophy or style; Serves in a leadership position in a student organization; Comprehends the dynamics of a group; Exhibits democratic principles as a leader; Exhibits ability to visualize a group purpose and desired outcomes

Healthy behavior

Examples of achievement indicators

Chooses behaviors and environments that promote health and reduce risk; Articulates the relationship between health and wellness and accomplishing life- long goals; Exhibits behaviors that advance a healthy community

Meaningful interpersonal relationships

Examples of achievement indicators

Develops and maintains satisfying interpersonal relationships; Establishes mutually rewarding relationships with friends and colleagues; Listens to and considers others' points of view; Treats others with respect

Independence

Examples of achievement indicators

Exhibits self-reliant behaviors; Functions autonomously; Exhibits ability to function interdependently; Accepts supervision as needed; Manages time effectively

Collaboration

Examples of achievement indicators

Works cooperatively with others; Seeks the involvement of others; Seeks feedback from others; Contributes to achievement of a group goal; Exhibits effective listening skills

Social responsibility

Examples of achievement indicators

Understands and participates in relevant governance systems; Understands, abides by, and participates in the development, maintenance, and/or orderly change of community, social, and legal standards or norms; Appropriately challenges the unfair, unjust, or uncivil behavior of other individuals or groups; Participates in service/volunteer activities

Satisfying and productive lifestyles

Examples of achievement indicators

Achieves balance between education, work and leisure time; Articulates and meets goals for work, leisure and education; Overcomes obstacles that hamper goal achievement; Functions on the basis of personal identity, ethical, spiritual, and moral values; Articulates long-term goals and objectives

Appreciating diversity

Examples of achievement indicators

Understands one's own identity and culture; Seeks involvement with people different from oneself; Seeks involvement in diverse interests; Articulates the advantages and challenges of a diverse society; Challenges appropriately the abusive use of stereotypes by others; Understands the impact of diversity on one's own society

Spiritual awareness

Examples of achievement indicators

Develops and articulates personal belief system; Understands roles of spirituality in personal and group values and behaviors

Personal and educational goals

Examples of achievement indicators

Sets, articulates, and pursues individual goals; Articulates personal and educational goals and objectives; Uses personal and educational goals to guide decisions; Understands the effect of one's personal and educational goals on others

The CU program must be (a) intentional, (b) coherent, (c) based on theories and knowledge of learning and human development, (d) reflective of developmental and demographic profiles of the student population, and (e) responsive to needs of individuals, special populations, and communities.

The CU activities and services must be appropriate to the size and diversity of the campus and must provide opportunities for student, staff, and faculty participation, interaction, and collaboration on policy establishment, facility operation, and program activities. The CU must strive to enhance intellectual and behavioral learning.

The program of college unions includes services, facilities and activity events. The college union should provide, in varying degrees, food services, meeting rooms, student and administrative offices, an information reception center, lounge(s), a merchandise counter or store, a lobby, public telephones, recreation facilities, and rest rooms.

Additional services and facilities provided by most unions include music listening rooms, table game rooms, space for exhibits, parking facilities, and conference rooms.

The union should include a balanced variety of activities, such as art, performing arts, music, cinematic arts, games and tournaments, outdoor recreation, lecture and literary events, crafts and hobbies, social and dance events, and activities addressing social responsibility and human relations. Program events should be diverse reflecting the richness of the community's cultures.

Part 3. LEADERSHIP

Effective and ethical leadership is essential to the success of all organizations. Institutions must appoint, position, and empower College Union (CU) leaders within the administrative structure to accomplish stated missions. CU leaders at various levels must be selected on the basis of formal education and training, relevant work experience, personal skills and competencies, relevant professional credentials, as well as potential for promoting learning and development in students, applying effective practices to educational processes, and enhancing institutional effectiveness. Institutions must determine expectations of accountability for CU leaders and fairly assess their performance.

CU leaders must exercise authority over resources for which they are responsible to achieve their respective missions.

CU leaders must:
- articulate a vision for their organization
- set goals and objectives based on the needs and capabilities of the population served
- promote student learning and development
- prescribe and practice ethical behavior

- recruit, select, supervise, and develop others in the organization
- manage financial resources
- coordinate human resources
- plan, budget for, and evaluate personnel and programs
- apply effective practices to educational and administrative processes
- communicate effectively
- initiate collaborative interaction between individuals and agencies that possess legitimate concerns and interests in the functional area

CU leaders must identify and find means to address individual, organizational, or environmental conditions that inhibit goal achievement.

CU leaders must promote campus environments that result in multiple opportunities for student learning and development.

CU leaders must continuously improve programs and services in response to changing needs of students and other constituents, and evolving institutional priorities.

Part 4. ORGANIZATION and MANAGEMENT

Guided by an overarching intent to ensure student learning and development, the College Union (CU) must be structured purposefully and managed effectively to achieve stated goals. Evidence of appropriate structure must include current and accessible policies and procedures, written performance expectations for all employees, functional workflow graphics or organizational charts, and clearly stated service delivery expectations.

Evidence of effective management must include use of comprehensive and accurate information for decisions, clear sources and channels of authority, effective communication practices, decision-making and conflict resolution procedures, responsiveness to changing conditions, accountability and evaluation systems, and recognition and reward processes. The CU must provide channels within the organization for regular review of administrative policies and procedures.

The CU must be organized to maintain its physical plant, to provide for cultural, intellectual, and recreational programming, to operate its business enterprises, and to deliver successfully the services inherent in the union's mission.

A variety of facilities, programs, and services may be incorporated within the building and operation. These include: food service; store and other revenue producing services; leisure time activities; social, cultural, and intellectual activities; building operations; and continuing education.

The CU must involve members of the campus community in its governance and programming structure and in the formulation of necessary union policies.

Operations involve day to-day undertakings such as fiscal controls, maintenance of physical plant and equipment, provision of services, supervision of personnel, planning, and public relations.

Involvement of the campus community should include students, faculty, staff, and alumni, as appropriate. Typically such involvement is through advisory, governing, and program boards. These boards might address issues such as (a) facility operating policies related to the use and/or rental of the union by campus and non-campus groups, (b) scheduling of controversial speakers and/or events, (c) budget planning and allocation of funds (d) employment policies, (e) space allocation priority setting, and (f) hours of operation.

Part 5. HUMAN RESOURCES

The College Union (CU) must be staffed adequately by individuals qualified to accomplish its mission and goals. Within established guidelines of the institution, the CU must establish procedures for staff selection, training, and evaluation; set expectations for supervision, and provide appropriate professional development opportunities. The CU must strive to improve the professional competence and skills of all personnel it employs.

CU professional staff members must hold an earned graduate degree in a field relevant to the position they hold or must possess an appropriate combination of educational credentials and related work experience.

Staff should include persons providing the necessary professional leadership to assume responsibility for the entire union as well as for specific programs.

Desirable qualities of staff members should include: (a) knowledge of and ability to use, management principles, including the effective management of volunteers; (b) skills in assessment, planning, training, and evaluation; (c) interpersonal skills; (d) technical skills; (e) understanding of union philosophy; (f) commitment to institutional mission; and (g) understanding of, and the ability to apply student development theory.

Graduate degrees should be earned in fields relevant to college unions including, but not limited to, student development, business administration, higher education administration, and recreation leadership.

Degree or credential-seeking interns must be qualified by enrollment in an appropriate field of study and by relevant experience. These individuals must be trained and supervised adequately by professional staff members holding educational credentials and related work experience appropriate for supervision.

Graduate students pursuing advanced degrees in student development, business administration, higher education institutional management, and recreation are among those to whom an internship or practicum in the college union can be valuable. Such experiences should provide a variety of opportunities within the union operation. Graduate assistantships also may allow persons pursuing careers in specific areas of the union field to expand their expertise. Graduate students frequently serve as program advisors or assist operations, recreation, or other department supervisors while pursuing advanced degrees. Others such as paraprofessional staff and volunteers may fulfill specific needs. The union should utilize volunteers in a manner consistent with its mission.

Student employees and volunteers must be carefully selected, trained, supervised, and evaluated. They must be trained on how and when to refer those in need of assistance to qualified staff members and have access to a supervisor for assistance in making these judgments. Student employees and volunteers must be provided clear and precise job descriptions, pre-service training based on assessed needs, and continuing staff development.

Student employees and volunteers may be an important part of the union's operation. Their work experience can be an important part of their educational experience as well as a source of income. A thorough training program should be provided for part time student helpers and volunteers and, depending on their assigned duties, might include leadership training, group facilitation skills, and communication skills. Volunteers should be adequately supervised and evaluated.

The CU must have technical and support staff members adequate to accomplish its mission. Staff members must be technologically proficient and qualified to perform their job functions, be knowledgeable of ethical and legal uses of technology, and have access to training. The level of staffing and workloads must be adequate and appropriate for program and service demands.

There should be adequate technical and clerical personnel to provide the services and maintain the facilities of the union. Included may be cooks, dishwashers, projectionists, stage hands, maintenance personnel, secretaries, bookkeepers, typists, attendants, receptionists, housekeepers, scheduling clerks, sales clerks, and cashiers.

Salary levels and fringe benefits for all CU staff members must be commensurate with those for comparable positions within the institution, in similar institutions, and in the relevant geographic area.

The CU must institute hiring and promotion practices that are fair, inclusive, and non-discriminatory. The CU must employ a diverse staff to provide readily identifiable role models for students and to enrich the campus community.

The CU must create and maintain position descriptions for all staff members and provide regular performance planning and appraisals.

The CU must have a system for regular staff evaluation and must provide access to continuing education and professional development opportunities, including in-service training programs and participation in professional conferences and workshops.

The CU must employ qualified professional, technical, and support staff members who have the ability to meet the varied educational, service, social, leisure, and recreational requirements inherent in the union's mission.

Specific aspects of the union's mission for which staff should be assigned include business operations (e.g., operations, program activities, cultural, recreational, theater, and arts and crafts) and special events.

Part 6. FINANCIAL RESOURCES

The College Union (CU) must have adequate funding to accomplish its mission and goals. Funding priorities must be determined within the context of the stated mission, goals, objectives and comprehensive analysis of the needs and capabilities of students and the availability of internal or external resources.

The CU must demonstrate fiscal responsibility and cost effectiveness consistent with institutional protocols.

The institution's budget commitment to the union should be sufficient to support the achievement of its mission and to provide appropriate services, facilities, and programs deemed

necessary to maintain standards and diversity of services commensurate with the image and reputation of the institution.

The union should have adequate financial resources to ensure reasonable pricing of services, adequate programming, adequate staffing, proper maintenance and professional development.

The institution should consider various methods and sources of financial support including, but not limited to: (a) income from sales, services, and rentals; (b) student activities or program fees; (c) fees for operation or debt service; and (d) direct institutional support (e.g., utilities subsidy, salary assistance, cleaning and maintenance, operating subsidy, and membership fees).

Part 7. FACILITIES, TECHNOLOGY, and EQUIPMENT

The College Union (CU) must have adequate, suitably located facilities, adequate technology, and equipment to support its mission and goals efficiently and effectively. Facilities, technology, and equipment must be evaluated regularly and be in compliance with relevant federal, state, provincial, and local requirements to provide for access, health, safety, and security.

The physical plant should be proportional in size to the campus population. Generally a college union should contain approximately 10 square feet of gross space for each student enrolled. Smaller colleges may require more square feet per student; large colleges may require less. Also to be considered is the nature of the student body. Colleges with a large number of commuter and/or part-time students or members of a special population might adjust facility requirements accordingly.

Part 8. LEGAL RESPONSIBILITIES

College Union (CU) staff members must be knowledgeable about and responsive to laws and regulations that relate to their respective responsibilities. CU staff members must inform users of programs and services and officials, as appropriate, of legal obligations and limitations including constitutional, statutory, regulatory, and case law; mandatory laws and orders emanating from federal, state/provincial and local governments; and the institution's policies.

CU staff members must use reasonable and informed practices to limit the liability exposure of the institution, its officers, employees, and agents. Staff members must be informed about institutional policies regarding personal liability and related insurance coverage options.

The institution must provide access to legal advice for CU staff members as needed to carry out assigned responsibilities.

The institution must inform CU staff and students in a timely and systematic fashion about extraordinary or changing legal obligations and potential liabilities.

Part 9. EQUITY and ACCESS

College Union (CU) staff members must ensure that services and programs are provided on a fair and equitable basis. Facilities, programs and services must be accessible. Hours of operation and delivery of and access to programs and services must be responsive to the needs of all students and other constituents. The CU program and services must adhere to the spirit and intent of equal opportunity laws.

The CU must be open and readily accessible to all students and must not discriminate except where sanctioned by law and institutional policy. Discrimination must be avoided on the bases of age; color; creed; cultural heritage; disability; ethnicity; gender identity; nationality; political affiliation; religious affiliation; sex; sexual orientation; or social, economic, marital, or veteran status.

Consistent with their mission and goals, the CU must take affirmative action to remedy significant imbalances in student participation and staffing patterns.

As the demographic profiles of campuses change and new instructional delivery methods are introduced, institutions must recognize the needs of students who participate in distance learning for access to programs and services offered on campus. Institutions must provide appropriate services in ways that are accessible to distance learners and assist them in identifying and gaining access to other appropriate services in their geographic region.

Part 10. CAMPUS and EXTERNAL RELATIONS

The College Union (CU) must establish, maintain, and promote effective relations with relevant individuals, campus offices, and external agencies.

The success of the CU is dependent on the maintenance of good relationships with students, faculty, administrators, alumni, the community at large, contractors, and support agencies. Staff members must encourage participation in union programs by relevant groups.

Each member of the campus community is a potential patron of the union's services, a potential member of the union organization, including its governing board, and a potential participant in the union's programming.

Students are the principal constituency of the union. Much of the vitality, variety, and spontaneity of the union's activities stem from student boards and committees.

Student government and other groups should have ongoing involvement with the union's programs, services, and operations.

Student publications also may be important for communicating information about union programs. Communications with students should be continuous.

The involvement of faculty, staff, and alumni is essential to the vitality of union programs and services.

Faculty members should be involved in policy making processes and program efforts of the union.

Alumni are potential sources of support and involvement, financial and otherwise.

The administrative staff of the institution is important to day-to-day operations of the union. In some instances important union services such as food, cleaning, repairs, bookstore, or accounting may be administered by a department of the college rather than by union staff; relations with those department heads and their representatives must be cultivated carefully. The support of other student affairs agencies as well as chief campus officials is important.

Technical and clerical staff members can be important as customers, members of the various committees, and members of the governing board.

Positive relations with lessees and contractors, (e.g., barbershops, boutiques, food services, bookstores) require close and continuing attention.

Part 11. DIVERSITY

Within the context of each institution's unique mission, diversity enriches the community and enhances the collegiate experience for all; therefore, the College Union (CU) must nurture environments where commonalties and differences among people are recognized and honored.

The CU must promote educational experiences that are characterized by open and continuous communication that deepens understanding of one's own identity, culture, and heritage, and that of others. The CU must educate and promote respect about commonalties and differences in their historical and cultural contexts.

The CU must address the characteristics and needs of a diverse population when establishing and implementing policies and procedures.

Part 12. ETHICS

All persons involved in the delivery of College Union (CU) programs and services must adhere to the highest principles of ethical behavior. The CU must develop or adopt and implement appropriate statements of ethical practice. The CU must publish these statements and ensure their periodic review by relevant constituencies.

CU staff members must ensure that privacy and confidentiality are maintained with respect to all communications and records to the extent that such records are protected under the law and appropriate statements of ethical practice. Information contained in students' education records must not be disclosed without written consent except as allowed by relevant laws and institutional policies. Staff members must disclose to appropriate authorities information judged to be of an emergency nature, especially when the safety of the individual or others is involved, or when otherwise required by institutional policy or relevant law.

All CU staff members must be aware of and comply with the provisions contained in the institution's human subjects research policy and in other relevant institutional policies addressing ethical practices and confidentiality of research data concerning individuals.

CU staff members must recognize and avoid personal conflict of interest or appearance thereof in their transactions with students and others.

CU staff members must strive to insure the fair, objective, and impartial treatment of all persons with whom they deal. Staff members must not participate in nor condone any form of harassment that demeans persons or creates an intimidating, hostile, or offensive campus environment.

When handling institutional funds, all CU staff members must ensure that such funds are managed in accordance with established and responsible accounting procedures and the fiscal policies or processes of the institution.

CU staff members must perform their duties within the limits of their training, expertise, and competence. When these limits are exceeded, individuals in need of further assistance must be referred to persons possessing appropriate qualifications.

CU staff members must use suitable means to confront and otherwise hold accountable other staff members who exhibit unethical behavior.

CU staff members must be knowledgeable about and practice ethical behavior in the use of technology.

Part 13. ASSESSMENT and EVALUATION

The College Union (CU) must conduct regular assessment and evaluations. The CU must employ effective qualitative and quantitative methodologies as appropriate, to determine whether and to what degree the stated mission, goals, and student learning and development outcomes are being met. The process must employ sufficient and sound assessment measures to ensure comprehensiveness. Data collected must include responses from students and other affected constituencies.

The CU must evaluate periodically how well they complement and enhance the institution's stated mission and educational effectiveness.

Results of these evaluations must be used in revising and improving programs and services and in recognizing staff performance.

Evaluation of union facilities, staff, programs, services, and governance must be continuous and must be within the context of the union's mission.

Evaluation may include goal related progress on such considerations as attendance at programs, cash flow, appearance of facilities, and vitality of volunteer groups.

Periodic reports, statistically valid research, and outside reviews should be utilized.

General Standards revised in 2002; CU content developed/ revised in 1986, 1997, & 1998.

THE ROLE of COMMUTER and OFF-CAMPUS LIVING PROGRAMS
CAS Standards Contextual Statement

Commuter and off-campus students, defined as those who do not live in institution-owned housing on campus, account for over 80 percent of college students in the U.S. (Jacoby, 2000). Commuter and off-campus students attend virtually every institution of higher education. Their numbers include students who live at home with their parents, in rental housing, or with their own families. They may attend college full time, part time, or alternate between the two. They may live near the campus or far away; they may commute by car, public transportation, walking, or bicycle. They may represent a small minority of students at a private, residential liberal arts college or the entire population of the community college or urban institution. The majority of commuter and off-campus students work, mostly off-campus, and some are employed the equivalent of full-time and/or at more than one job.

Regardless of differences in backgrounds, living arrangements, and educational goals, commuter and off-campus students face common needs and concerns, such as safe and reliable transportation, multiple life roles, integrating their off-campus support systems into their higher education experience, and developing a sense of belonging in their campus community. Whether they attend a predominantly residential or commuter institution, the fact that they reside off-campus profoundly affects the nature of their educational experience.

Despite the overwhelming numbers of commuter and off-campus students, the long-standing residential tradition of American higher education has often impeded effective, comprehensive institutional response to their wide range of lifestyles. Historically, the relationship of commuter and off-campus students to the institution has been neither well understood nor incorporated into the design of policies, programs, and practices. *The CAS Standards and Guidelines take the approach that all students must have equitable access to institutional services, engagement opportunities, and the total educational process regardless of place of residence.*

To begin to correct the inequities that have been built into policies and programs, institutions must critically and comprehensively examine their practices from the point of view of all types of commuter and off-campus students. These standards and guidelines provide a basis for institutional self-assessment and program development. In addition, because the commuter and off-campus student population is so diverse and because each institution's population is unique, it is important that each college and university regularly collect data about its commuter and off-campus students and the nature of their college experience.

References, Readings, and Resources

American College Personnel Association, Commission for Commuter Students and Adult Learners, One Dupont Circle NW, Suite 300, Washington DC 20036. (202) 835-2272. Http://www.acpa.nche.edu

Chickering, A.W. *Commuting Versus Resident Students.* San Francisco: Jossey-Bass, 1974.

Jacoby, B., (Ed.) *Involving Commuter Students in Learning.* New Directions for Higher Education #109, 2000.

Jacoby, B. "Engaging First-Year Commuter Students in Learning," *Metropolitan Universities*, 15:2, 2004.

Jacoby, B., and Garland, J. "Strategies for Enhancing Commuter Student Success," *Journal of College Student Retention*, 6(1), 2004.

Jacoby, B., *The Student as Commuter: Developing a Comprehensive Institutional Response.* ASHE-ERIC Higher Education Report No. 7, Washington, DC, School of Education and Human Development, The George Washington University, 1989.

Jacoby, B., and Girrell, K. "A model for improving service and programs for commuter students" (The SPAR Model), *NASPA Journal*, 18:3, Winter 1981.

\Schlossberg, N.K., Lynch, A.Q., and Chickering, A.W., *Improving Higher Education Environments for Adults*, Jossey-Bass, 1989.

Stewart, S.S. (Ed.), *Commuter Students: Enhancing Their Educational Experience*, Jossey-Bass, New Directions for Student Services # 24, 1983.

National Clearinghouse for Commuter Programs, Stamp Student Union, University of Maryland, College Park, MD 20742, (301) 405-0986, www.umd.edu/nccp

Contributor: Barbara Jacoby, University of Maryland, NCCP

COMMUTER and OFF-CAMPUS LIVING PROGRAMS
CAS Standards and Guidelines

Part 1. MISSION

The primary mission of Commuter and Off-Campus Living Programs (COCLP) is to ensure that all students have equitable access to programs, services, and engagement opportunities regardless of place of residence.

In addition, COCLP must:
- provide services and facilities to meet the basic needs of commuter and off-campus students as determined by institutional assessment
- ensure that all students benefit equitably from the institution's educational programs
- provide engagement opportunities to assist commuter and off-campus students and promote learning and development
- support the institution's vision for the student learning experience

COCLP must incorporate student learning and development in their mission.

COCLP must enhance overall educational experiences. The program must develop, record, disseminate, implement, and regularly review its mission and goals. Mission statements must be consistent with the mission and goals of the institution and with the standards in this document. COCLP must operate as an integral part of the institution's overall mission.

The COCLP mission should address not only programs and services but also education and advocacy on behalf of commuter and off-campus students.

Commuter and off-campus students may be defined differently at individual institutions; however, this document focuses on the equitable access of all students to institutional resources.

The number of commuter and off-campus students may range from a small minority to the entire student population. The commuter and off-campus students in any higher educational institution should have equitable benefits of the curricular and co-curricular programs and services offered, regardless of full-time or part-time credit load, family status, age, proximity to campus, day or evening enrollment, or dependent versus independent living status.

Part 2. PROGRAM

Commuter and Off-Campus Living Programs (COCLP) **must provide direct delivery of essential programs and services meeting a wide variety of needs and** interests, whether organized as a single office or distributed throughout the institution. In either case, these services and programs must be evaluated to ensure that all students have equitable access to programs, services, and engagement opportunities regardless of place of residence.

The formal education of students consists of the curriculum and the co-curriculum, and must promote student learning and development that is purposeful and holistic. COCLP must identify relevant and desirable student learning and development outcomes and provide programs and services that encourage the achievement of those outcomes.

Relevant and desirable outcomes include: intellectual growth, effective communication, realistic self-appraisal, enhanced self-esteem, clarified values, career choices, leadership development, healthy behaviors, meaningful interpersonal relationships, independence, collaboration, social responsibility, satisfying and productive lifestyles, appreciation of diversity, spiritual awareness, and achievement of personal and educational goals.

COCLP must provide evidence of their impact on the achievement of student learning and development outcomes.

The table below offers examples of evidence of achievement of student learning and development.

Student Learning and Development Outcome Domains

Intellectual growth
Examples of achievement indicators
> Produces personal and educational goal statements; Employs critical thinking in problem solving; Uses complex information from a variety of sources, including personal experience and observation, to form a decision or opinion, problem solving; Obtains a degree; Applies previously understood information and concepts to a new situation or setting; Expresses appreciation for literature, the fine arts, mathematics, sciences, and social sciences

Effective communication
Examples of achievement indicators
> Writes and speaks coherently and effectively; Writes and speaks after reflection; Able to influence others through writing, speaking or artistic expression; Effectively

articulates abstract ideas; Uses appropriate syntax; Makes presentations or gives performances

Enhanced self-esteem

Examples of achievement indicators

Shows self-respect and respect for others; Initiates actions toward achievement of goals; Takes reasonable risks; Demonstrates assertive behavior; Functions without need for constant reassurance from others

Realistic self-appraisal

Examples of achievement indicators

Articulates personal skills and abilities; Makes decisions and acts in congruence with personal values; Acknowledges personal strengths and weaknesses; Articulates rationale for personal behavior; Accepts personal accountability; Seeks feedback from others; Learns from past experiences

Clarified values

Examples of achievement indicators

Articulates personal values; Acts in congruence with personal values; Makes decisions that reflect personal values; Demonstrates willingness to scrutinize personal beliefs and values; Identifies personal, work, and lifestyle values and explains how they influence decision-making, acknowledging the values of others

Career choices

Examples of achievement indicators

Articulates career choices based on assessment of interests, values, skills and abilities; Documents knowledge, skills and accomplishments resulting from formal education, work experience, community service, and volunteer experiences; Makes the connections between classroom and out-of-classroom learning; Can construct a resume with clear job objectives and evidence of related knowledge, skills and accomplishments; Articulates the characteristics of a preferred work environment; Comprehends the world of work; Takes steps to initiate a job search or seek advanced education

Leadership development

Examples of achievement indicators

Articulates leadership philosophy or style; Serves in a leadership position in a student organization; Comprehends the dynamics of a group; Exhibits democratic principles as a leader; Exhibits ability to visualize a group purpose and desired outcomes

Healthy behavior

Examples of achievement indicators

Chooses behaviors and environments that promote health and reduce risk; Articulates the relationship between health

and wellness and accomplishing life-long goals; Exhibits behaviors that advance a healthy community

Meaningful interpersonal relationships

Examples of achievement indicators

Develops and maintains satisfying interpersonal relationships; Establishes mutually rewarding relationships with friends and colleagues; Listens to and considers others' points of view; Understands and practices empathy; Treats others with respect

Independence

Examples of achievement indicators

Exhibits self-reliant behaviors; Functions autonomously; Exhibits ability to function interdependently; Accepts supervision as needed; Manages time effectively

Collaboration

Examples of achievement indicators

Works cooperatively with others; Seeks the involvement of others; Seeks feedback from others; Contributes to achievement of a group goal; Exhibits effective listening skills

Social responsibility

Examples of achievement indicators

Understands and participates in relevant governance systems; Understands, abides by, and participates in the development, maintenance, and/or orderly change of community, social, and legal standards or norms; Appropriately challenges the unfair, unjust, or uncivil behavior of other individuals or groups; Participates in service/volunteer activities

Satisfying and productive lifestyles

Examples of achievement indicators

Achieves balance between education, work, and leisure time; Articulates and meets goals for work, leisure, and education; Overcomes obstacles that hamper goal achievement; Functions on the basis of personal identity, ethical, spiritual, and moral values; Articulates long-term goals and objectives

Appreciating diversity

Examples of achievement indicators

Understands one's own identity and culture; Seeks involvement with people different from oneself; Seeks involvement in diverse interests; Articulates the advantages and challenges of a diverse society; Appropriately challenges the abusive use of stereotypes by others and exhibits a willingness to consider feedback received from others; Understands the impact of diversity on one's own society

Spiritual awareness

Examples of achievement indicators

> Develops and articulates personal belief system; Understands roles of spirituality in personal and group values and behaviors

Personal and educational goals

Examples of achievement indicators

> Sets, articulates, and pursues individual goals; Articulates personal and educational goals and objectives; Uses personal and educational goals to guide decisions; Understands the effect of one's personal and educational goals on others

COCLP must be (a) intentional, (b) coherent, (c) based on theories and knowledge of learning and human development, (d) reflective of developmental and demographic profiles of the student population, and (e) responsive to needs of individuals, special populations, and communities.

COCLP must assist students with access to institutional resources and in meeting basic needs such as housing, transportation, parking, security, information and referral, facilities, food, computer and internet access, and childcare.

COCLP should assist students in making informed choices about housing and should provide information about available housing, tenants' rights and responsibilities, utilities, and legal advice and assistance.

Provisions should be made for parking; carpools; emergency vehicle assistance; and walkway, bike path, and parking lot security. Information about transportation alternatives to campus should be provided.

Information about campus services, programs, and current events should be disseminated in a variety of media and formats. Access to services such as course registration should be available via the internet and telephone as well as in traditional modes.

Students should have adequate study and lounge spaces in convenient locations around the campus. These should include access to computers, printers, copiers and lockers.

Food service should be available in convenient locations at hours when students are on campus, including evenings and weekends.

Institutions should address commuter and off-campus students' need for high-speed internet access for accomplishing course work, and should ensure equitable access to informational resources.

Institutions should provide adequate childcare services, either through the institution or through referrals to community childcare providers. On-campus facilities for infant feeding and changing should be available.

COCLP should work to ensure that all institutional services are available equitably to commuter and off-campus students, including scheduling of classes, events, campus employment, and office hours to accommodate students' varied schedules.

COCLP must provide programs that meet the specific needs of commuter and off-campus students and ensure that all students have equitable access to all educational, recreational, and social programming.

COCLP should provide educational programs that inform students of tenancy ordinances, tenants and landlord rights and responsibilities, legal advice and assistance, personal financial management, roommate and neighbor relations and conflict-resolution skills. Additional educational programs can include defensive driving, personal security, proper nutrition, and time management.

COCLP should offer programs, or encourage the institution to offer programs, that enable commuter and off-campus students to achieve learning and development outcomes. These include opportunities for interaction with faculty members and peers, activities scheduled at times convenient for commuter and off-campus students, peer mentoring, learning communities that do not require on-campus residence, experiential education, family-oriented activities, programs offered in off-campus locations with dense student populations, and programming using technology (e.g., virtual communities).

Institutions must include the commuter and off-campus student perspective at all appropriate levels of campus planning, policy making, budgeting, program delivery, and governance.

Commuter and off-campus student advocacy should focus on:

- access to comprehensive academic advising, student support services, and information
- recognition of the diverse subgroups of the commuter and off-campus student population, including students who are older, married, fully employed, part-time, evening, veterans, or who live at home with parents or guardian.
- equitable fee structure for campus services
- fair representation of all types of commuter and off-campus students in areas of campus employment, internships, and financial aid awards
- faculty and institutional research programs that enhance understanding of the demographic characteristics and unique needs of commuter and off-campus students
- inclusion of the commuter and off-campus student

perspective in community decision-making (e.g., transportation route planning, police coverage, and local ordinances)
- minimum standards for use as criteria for listing off-campus housing options

COCLP must collect data and encourage institutional research to understand the characteristics, needs, and experiences of commuter and off-campus students.

Research efforts may include demographic studies, needs assessments, retention studies, environmental assessments, involvement and satisfaction measures, longitudinal studies, and commuter-resident comparisons.

Part 3. LEADERSHIP

Effective and ethical leadership is essential to the success of all organizations. Institutions must appoint, position, and empower Commuter and Off-Campus Living Programs (COCLP) leaders within the administrative structure to accomplish stated missions. Leaders at various levels must be selected on the basis of formal education and training, relevant work experience, personal skills and competencies, relevant professional credentials, as well as potential for promoting learning and development in students, applying effective practices to educational processes, and enhancing institutional effectiveness. Institutions must determine expectations of accountability for leaders and fairly assess their performance.

COCLP leaders must exercise authority over resources for which they are responsible to achieve their respective missions.

COCLP leaders must:
- articulate a vision for their organization
- set goals and objectives based on the needs and capabilities of the population served
- promote student learning and development
- prescribe and practice ethical behavior
- recruit, select, supervise, and develop others in the organization
- manage financial resources
- coordinate human resources
- plan, budget for, and evaluate personnel and programs
- apply effective practices to educational and administrative processes
- communicate effectively
- initiate collaborative interaction between

individuals and agencies that possess legitimate concerns and interests in the functional area

COCLP leaders must identify and find means to address individual, organizational, or environmental conditions that inhibit goal achievement.

COCLP leaders must promote campus environments that result in multiple opportunities for student learning and development.

COCLP leaders must continuously improve programs and services in response to changing needs of students and other constituents, and evolving institutional priorities.

Part 4. ORGANIZATION and MANAGEMENT

Guided by an overarching intent to ensure student learning and development, the Commuter and Off-Campus Living Programs (COCLP) must be structured purposefully and managed effectively to achieve stated goals. Evidence of appropriate structure must include current and accessible policies and procedures, written performance expectations for all employees, functional workflow graphics or organizational charts, and clearly stated service delivery expectations.

Evidence of effective management must include the use of comprehensive and accurate information for decisions, clear sources and channels of authority, effective communication practices, decision-making and conflict resolution procedures, responsiveness to changing conditions, accountability and evaluation systems, and recognition and reward processes. COCLP must provide channels within the organization for regular review of administrative policies and procedures.

Part 5. HUMAN RESOURCES

Commuter and Off-Campus Living Programs (COCLP) must be staffed adequately by individuals qualified to accomplish their mission and goals. Within established guidelines of the institution, COCLP must establish procedures for staff selection, training, and evaluation; set expectations for supervision; and provide appropriate professional development opportunities. The program must strive to improve the professional competence and skills of all personnel it employs.

Professional staff members must hold an earned graduate degree in a field relevant to the position they hold or must possess an appropriate combination of educational credentials and related work experience.

Degree or credential-seeking interns must be qualified by enrollment in an appropriate field of study and by relevant experience. These individuals must be trained and supervised adequately by professional staff members holding educational credentials and related work experience appropriate for supervision.

COCLP professional staff should possess the academic preparation, experience, abilities, professional interests, and competencies essential for the efficient operation of the office as charged, as well as the ability to identify and address needs of the commuter and off-campus student population. They should possess the following knowledge and skills:

- ability to work with diverse students
- knowledge of history and current trends in higher education
- knowledge of organizational development, group dynamics, strategies for changes, and principles of community development
- ability to design and evaluate programs to meet desired outcomes
- effective written and oral communication skills
- knowledge of theories of college student learning and development
- knowledge of management and budgeting
- ability to work effectively with internal and external agencies
- ability to serve as an effective advocate

Student employees and volunteers must be carefully selected, trained, supervised, and evaluated. They must be trained on how and when to refer those in need of assistance to qualified staff members, and have access to a supervisor for assistance in making these judgments. Student employees and volunteers must be provided clear and precise job descriptions, pre-service training based on assessed needs, and continuing staff development.

COCLP must have technical and support staff members adequate to accomplish their mission. Staff members must be technologically proficient and qualified to perform their job functions, be knowledgeable of ethical and legal uses of technology, and have access to training. The level of staffing and workloads must be adequate and appropriate for program and service demands.

Salary levels and fringe benefits for all COCLP staff members must be commensurate with those for comparable positions within the institution, in similar institutions, and in the relevant geographic area.

COCLP must institute hiring and promotion practices that are fair, inclusive, and non-discriminatory. The programs must employ a diverse staff to provide readily identifiable role models for students and to enrich the campus community.

COCLP must create and maintain position descriptions for all staff members and provide regular performance planning and appraisals.

COCLP must have a system for regular staff evaluation and must provide access to continuing education and professional development opportunities, including in-service training programs and participation in professional conferences and workshops.

Part 6. FINANCIAL RESOURCES

Commuter and Off-Campus Living Programs (COCLP) must have adequate funding to accomplish their mission and goals. Funding priorities must be determined within the context of the stated mission, goals, objectives and comprehensive analysis of the needs and capabilities of students and the availability of internal or external resources.

COCLP must demonstrate fiscal responsibility and cost effectiveness consistent with institutional protocols.

Fee-paying students should benefit equitably from fee-supported services. This is especially important regarding access to electronic services such as computer/internet and campus cable television systems.

Part 7. FACILITIES, TECHNOLOGY, and EQUIPMENT

Commuter and Off-Campus Living Programs (COCLP) must have adequate, suitably located facilities, adequate technology, and equipment to support their mission and goals efficiently and effectively. Facilities, technology, and equipment must be evaluated regularly and be in compliance with relevant federal, state, provincial, and local requirements to provide for access, health, safety, and security.

The campus must provide adequate facilities for the use of commuter and off-campus students, including recreational, study, and lounge space; computer and internet access; and dining facilities.

Because commuter and off-campus students do not have a residence on campus in which to spend time before, between, and after classes, a variety of comfortable spaces should be provided for their use. These spaces should be in classroom buildings, as well as in college union and student center buildings, and should include individual lockers, computer and copier access, food preparation facilities, and family support services (e.g., infant feeding and changing areas).

Institutions that provide high speed internet access or campus based cable television programming to residential students should also consider options to increase accessibility to such services to commuter and off-campus students.

Part 8. LEGAL RESPONSIBILITIES

Commuter and Off-Campus Living Programs (COCLP) staff members must be knowledgeable about and responsive to laws and regulations that relate to their respective responsibilities. Staff members must inform users of programs and services and officials, as appropriate, of legal obligations and limitations, including constitutional, statutory, regulatory, and case law; mandatory laws and orders emanating from federal, state/provincial and local governments; and the institution's policies.

COCLP staff members must use reasonable and informed practices to limit the liability exposure of the institution, its officers, employees, and agents. COCLP staff members must be informed about institutional policies regarding personal liability and related insurance coverage options.

The institution must provide access to legal advice for staff members as needed to carry out assigned responsibilities.

The institution must inform COCLP staff and students in a timely and systematic fashion about extraordinary or changing legal obligations and potential liabilities.

Part 9. EQUITY and ACCESS

Commuter and Off-Campus Living Programs (COCLP) staff members must ensure that services and programs are provided on a fair and equitable basis. Facilities, programs and services must be accessible. Hours of operation and delivery of, and access to, programs and services must be responsive to the needs of all students and other constituents. COCLP must adhere to the spirit and intent of equal opportunity laws.

COCLP must be open and readily accessible to all students and must not discriminate except where sanctioned by law and institutional policy. Discrimination must be avoided on the bases of age; color; creed; cultural heritage; disability; ethnicity; gender identity; nationality; political affiliation;

religious affiliation; sex; sexual orientation; or social, economic, marital, or veteran status.

Consistent with their mission and goals, COCLP must take affirmative action to remedy significant imbalances in student participation and staffing patterns.

As the demographic profiles of campuses change and new instructional delivery methods are introduced, institutions must recognize the needs of students who participate in distance learning for access to programs and services offered on campus. Institutions must provide appropriate services in ways that are accessible to distance learners and assist them in identifying and gaining access to other appropriate services in their geographic region.

Part 10. CAMPUS and EXTERNAL RELATIONS

Commuter and Off-Campus Living Programs (COCLP) must establish, maintain, and promote effective relations with relevant individuals, campus offices, and external agencies.

COCLP must maintain a high degree of visibility within the campus community through direct promotion and delivery of services, involvement with campus programs, and educational efforts to increase all campus community members' understanding of the needs of commuter and off-campus students.

COCLP should coordinate their activities with all offices and agencies whose efforts directly affect commuter and off-campus students. These include such areas as campus safety and security, transportation and parking, campus information and referral services, and other relevant offices and campus committees.

COCLP should maintain active relationship with various community agencies to ensure the inclusion of the commuter and off-campus student perspective in community decision-making.

Part 11. DIVERSITY

Within the context of each institution's unique mission, diversity enriches the community and enhances the collegiate experience for all; therefore, Commuter and Off-Campus Living Programs (COCLP) must nurture environments where commonalties and differences among people are recognized and honored.

COCLP must promote educational experiences that are characterized by open and continuous communication that deepens understanding of one's own identity, culture, and heritage, and that of others. The programs and services must educate and promote respect about commonalties and differences between individuals in their historical and cultural contexts.

COCLP must address the characteristics and needs of a diverse population when establishing and implementing policies and procedures.

Part 12. ETHICS

All persons involved in delivery of Commuter and Off-Campus Living Programs (COCLP) must adhere to the highest principles of ethical behavior. COCLP must develop or adopt and implement appropriate statements of ethical practice. COCLP must publish these statements and ensure their periodic review by relevant constituencies.

COCLP staff members must ensure that privacy and confidentiality with clients are maintained with respect to all communications and records to the extent that such records are protected under the law and appropriate statements of ethical practice. Information contained in students' education records must not be disclosed without written consent except as allowed by relevant laws and institutional policies. COCLP staff members must disclose to appropriate authorities information judged to be of an emergency nature, especially when the safety of the individual or others is involved, or when otherwise required by institutional policy or relevant law.

All COCLP staff members must be aware of and comply with the provisions contained in the institution's human subjects research policy and in other relevant institutional policies addressing ethical practices and confidentiality of research data concerning individuals.

COCLP staff members must recognize and avoid personal conflict of interest, or appearance thereof, in their transactions with students and others.

COCLP staff members must strive to insure the fair, objective, and impartial treatment of all persons with whom they deal. COCLP staff members must not participate in nor condone any form of harassment that demeans persons or creates an intimidating, hostile, or offensive campus environment.

When handling institutional funds, all COCLP staff members must ensure that such funds are managed in accordance with established and responsible accounting procedures and the fiscal policies or processes of the institution.

COCLP staff members must perform their duties within the limits of their training, expertise, and competence. When these limits are exceeded, individuals in need of further assistance must be referred to persons possessing appropriate qualifications.

COCLP staff members must use suitable means to confront and otherwise hold accountable other staff members who exhibit unethical behavior.

COCLP staff members must be knowledgeable about and practice ethical behavior in the use of technology.

Part 13. ASSESSMENT and EVALUATION

Commuter and Off-Campus Living Programs (COCLP) must conduct regular assessment and evaluations. COCLP must employ effective qualitative and quantitative methodologies, as appropriate, to determine whether and to what degree the stated mission, goals, and student learning and development outcomes are being met. The process must employ sufficient and sound assessment measures to ensure comprehensiveness. Data collected must include responses from students and other affected constituencies.

COCLP must evaluate periodically how well they complement and enhance the institution's stated mission and educational effectiveness.

Results of these evaluations must be used in revising and improving COCLP and in recognizing staff performance.

General Standards revised 2002; COCLP (formerly Commuter Student Programs) content developed/revised 1986, 1997, & 2005

THE ROLE of CONFERENCE and EVENT PROGRAMS
CAS Standards Contextual Statement

A higher education campus is a community where people gather to learn, share, and discuss issues of interest in an open, non-threatening, and enlightened atmosphere. It is a place where topics important to society are addressed freely in a number of formats and settings, in addition to the classroom. Campuses are centers for symposia, lectures, public events, demonstrations, conferences, and other short-duration teaching and learning programs attended by people from all walks of life, generations, occupations, and education levels. These events help to identify the campus as a place where spirited scholarly, cultural, social, artistic, athletic, and other activities can freely occur. As institutions become less constrained by physical borders, they have also become the source of conferences and events occurring on-line and at off-campus locations as well. An administrative department responsible for developing, coordinating, and promoting on- and off-campus conferences and events is typically found at the core this important educational responsibility.

Conference and event programs address a broad range of organizing, hosting, and logistical service needs. Services are provided to a variety of constituents and include program planning; managing conference centers; developing conferences in conjunction with faculty and staff members; providing services and support for summer youth camps; coordinating guest services and special celebrations; scheduling facilities; and organizing donor events, inaugurations, groundbreakings, commencements, homecomings, parents weekends, and other traditional gatherings.

Although the portfolios of program responsibilities will vary from campus to campus, one common element is that of helping institutions expand their activities, presence, and influence beyond the traditional roles of faculty, students, and staff. Conference and events programs make the campus a more effective and user-friendly place for all types of learners. They enhance diverse campus cultures, and conference subject matter often adds depth and variety to campus dialogue. They support institutional efforts to function as a center for celebrations and non-traditional educational activities. They provide venues for free-speech, a forum for cultural events, opportunities for students and scholars to be exposed to research findings, and a chance for more people to observe what higher education is all about.

Conference and event programs provide activities during periods when fewer students are present to optimize efficient use of campus resources. They provide institutions with additional sources of revenue and contribute to the availability and continuity of employment for faculty and staff.

In recent years, institutions have increased their number of short-term learning opportunities for pre-college and professional students, whose support service needs vary greatly. Many of the roles associated with student affairs are now tailored to these students through a single conference and event programs office, designed to serve the unique needs of non-traditional student clientele.

The Association of Collegiate Conference and Event Directors–International (ACCED-I) estimates that more than 1,500 U.S. institutions of higher learning have offices providing conference and event planning. Their operations may include overseeing the summer rental of residence halls and classrooms; year-round management of full-service conference centers; coordination of large public events held in campus arenas and stadiums; and procurement of services and facilities at off-campus locations. Today, conference and event staff members provide everything from multi-department coordination of services to academic support services and professional event planning consultation.

In recent years, a global increase in complex campuses has resulted in a growing need to formalize and standardize conference and event services. Several associations for campus conference and event professionals have come into being, and flourished. As these associations matured, the need for professional standards became abundantly clear in dialogue among members. In the mid-1990s, a study of service practices by the Canadian University and College Conference Officers Association (CUCCOA) culminated in a summary report that called for establishing international standards for practitioners. In 1997 ACCED-I, CUCCOA, the Association of College and University Housing Officers-International (ACUHO-I), and the British Universities Accommodation Consortium (BUAC), now named VENUEMASTERS, collectively agreed on the need for developing professional standards in collaboration with the CAS standards development initiative.

By establishing professional standards in conjunction with CAS, institutional conference and event programs can become increasingly interconnected, forming a basis on which industry-defined service standards may become a reality. The CAS standards and guidelines that follow provide a professional context for the campus conference and event industry and will serve as a useful tool for all who wish to provide conference and event programs in higher education settings.

References, Readings, and Resources

Association of College and University Housing Officers-International (ACUHO-I) http://www.acuho.ohio-state.edu/

Association of Collegiate Conference and Event Directors–International (ACCED-I) http://www.acced-i.com/

Canadian University and College Conference Officers Association (CUCCOA) http://www.cuccoa.org/

United Kingdom: VENUEMASTERS http://www.venuemasters.co.uk/

Contributor: Patrick Perfetto, University of Maryland, ACCED-I

CONFERENCE and EVENT PROGRAMS
CAS Standards and Guidelines

Part 1. MISSION

The primary mission of Conference and Events Programs (CEP) is to provide on and off campus constituents opportunity and access to educational conferences, workshops, events, and activities that are relevant and complementary to the mission of the institution.

The CEP must incorporate student learning and student development in its mission. CEP must enhance overall educational experiences. CEP must develop, record, disseminate, implement, and regularly review its mission and goals. Mission statements must be consistent with the mission and goals of the institution and with the standards in this document. CEP must operate as an integral part of the institution's overall mission.

The program mission must recognize and accommodate, as appropriate, relevant goals of other campus agencies that are integral providers of important services, or are major users of conference and events services.

Part 2. PROGRAM

Conference and Event Programs (CEP) must provide leadership within and for the institution relative to conference and event planning and management.

To accomplish this, the CEP office may:
- serve as a point of contact for multiple campus services
- provide effective coordination of multiple services
- collaborate with clients and service providers to assure that programs have a positive and compatible presence in the campus community
- create opportunities for student affairs and other campus departments to fulfill their programmatic goals for students and other learners
- create opportunities for campus departments to extend employment for employees during periods outside of the regular academic calendar
- provide additional revenue derived from campus income-producing facilities and services
- provide employment and experiential opportunities for students
- ensure that scheduled and routine campus activities are free from undue interference or interruption by activities related to conferences, events, and similar programs
- ascertain the appropriateness and compatibility of conferences, events, and similar activities with the institution's mission

- know, articulate, and exercise state-of-the-art meeting/event planning concepts and procedures
- provide one-stop access to and coordination of services to planners of conferences, events, and similar gatherings
- be a knowledgeable source of information about student services, campus facilities, and support services
- exercise appropriate authority with regard to campus resources necessary to support conferences and events in collaboration with campus service providers, through agreements and memoranda of understanding
- communicate effectively among campus agencies as to specially scheduled or on-going campus activities that might influence or conflict with planned or potential conferences/events
- provide clear description of activities on campus events and calendars

The formal education of students consists of the curriculum and the co-curriculum, and must promote student learning and development that is purposeful and holistic. CEP must identify relevant and desirable student learning and development outcomes and provide programs and services that encourage the achievement of those outcomes.

Relevant and desirable outcomes include: intellectual growth, effective communication, realistic self-appraisal, enhanced self-esteem, clarified values, career choices, leadership development, healthy behaviors, meaningful interpersonal relationships, independence, collaboration, social responsibility, satisfying and productive lifestyles, appreciation of diversity, spiritual awareness, and achievement of personal and educational goals.

CEP must provide evidence of its impact on the achievement of student learning and development outcomes.

The table below offers examples of evidence of achievement of studetnt learning and development.

Student Learning and Development Outcome Domains

Intellectual growth
Examples of achievement indicators
Gains new knowledge from exploring divergent learning opportunities by attending a campus conference/event; Evaluates the institution's academic curriculum and decides to enroll in a degree program

Effective communication

Examples of achievement indicators

Continues dialogue after attending a conference/event and views programs and services as a valuable resource of information on a variety of topics; Articulates learning outcomes of the conference/event experience; Expanded vocabulary and breadth of thinking on a variety of subjects by interacting with institution's faculty and traditionally enrolled students

Enhanced self-esteem

Examples of achievement indicators

Articulates personal growth as a result of a conference/event experience; Is inspired by the community of accomplished and energized thinkers and becomes motivated to participate in open discourse

Realistic self-appraisal

Examples of achievement indicators

Gains enhanced understanding of self and individual abilities from the conference/event experience; Evaluates strengths and abilities through exposure to abundance of disciplines and perspectives that exist in the collegiate environment

Clarified values

Examples of achievement indicators

Gains perspective and insight into personal values and those of persons from other backgrounds and cultures; Achieves insight into learning and education and the opportunity to prioritize it in relation to personal values

Leadership development

Examples of achievement indicators

Uses resources discovered in the academic environment to take action on matters of concern or to resolve perceived problems; Learns to lead, and gains confidence in abilities through interaction with a variety of role models encountered in the collegiate community

Career choices

Examples of achievement indicators

Forms opinions and is motivated to take steps toward advanced education and new career possibilities; makes connections between classroom and out-of-classroom learning; Discovers alternate career options that a formal education can make possible

Healthy behavior

Examples of achievement indicators

Experiences health education and takes opportunities to explore healthy ways of life; Chooses behavior that constructively affects long-term health

Meaningful interpersonal relationships

Examples of achievement indicators

Sustains acquaintances made during campus conference and events; Evidences appreciation and respect for others; Develops sustaining relationships with others

Independence

Examples of achievement indicators

Learns the value of research and is motivated to produce work without unnecessary assistance; Takes advantage of the wealth of resources available within the collegiate community to enhance personal work efforts

Collaboration

Examples of achievement indicators

Shares work responsibilities with others; Articulates benefits gained by working with others; Connects with scholars who could help advance effort and achievement

Social responsibility

Examples of achievement indicators

Participates in a larger learning community by attending a campus conference or event; Forms viewpoints from exposure to social issues at the forefront of higher education

Satisfying and productive lifestyles

Examples of achievement indicators

Achieves a productive balance between education, work, personal, and leisure times while taking part in a campus conference or event; Evidences a value for holistic learning experiences that incorporate elements of the curriculum and the co-curriculum

Appreciating diversity

Examples of achievement indicators

Achieves insight into other cultures and perspectives by interacting with the variety of students and scholars typically present in an academic community; Learns to understand and appreciate lifestyle and cultural differences via the campus living experience

Spiritual awareness

Examples of achievement indicators

Expresses personal beliefs to others in the campus community; Discovers greater openness to spiritual discourse in an academic environment

Personal and educational goals

Examples of achievement indicators

Comprehends and can define educational and other personal goals; Uses the on-campus conference experience to help determine formal education interests; Chooses to enter the institution as a matriculated student in a program of study

CEP must be (a) intentional, (b) coherent, (c) based on theories and knowledge of learning and human development, (d) reflective of developmental and demographic profiles of the student population, and (e) responsive to needs of individuals, special populations, and communities.

Conference and Event Programs must promote student learning and development through the creation, marketing, and staffing of conferences, events, and similar educational activities.

Part 3. LEADERSHIP

Effective and ethical leadership is essential to the success of all organizations. Institutions must appoint, position, and empower Conference and Event Programs (CEP) leaders within the administrative structure to accomplish stated missions. CEP leaders at various levels must be selected on the basis of formal education and training, relevant work experience, personal skills and competencies, relevant professional credentials, as well as potential for promoting learning and development in students, applying effective practices to educational processes, and enhancing institutional effectiveness. Institutions must determine expectations of accountability for leaders and fairly assess their performance.

Leaders of CEP must exercise authority over resources for which they are responsible to achieve their respective missions.

Because of the likely involvement of multiple campus units in the delivery of conference and event services, special attention may be required to properly empower the program leaders to exercise necessary authority over resources.

CEP leaders must:
- articulate a vision for their organization
- set goals and objectives based on the needs and capabilities of the population served
- promote student learning and development
- prescribe and practice ethical behavior
- recruit, select, supervise, and develop others in the organization
- manage financial resources
- coordinate human resources
- plan, budget for, and evaluate personnel and programs
- apply effective practices to educational and administrative processes
- communicate effectively
- initiate collaborative interaction between individuals and agencies that possess legitimate

concerns and interests in the functional area

CEP leaders must identify and find means to address individual, organizational, or environmental conditions that inhibit goal achievement.

CEP leaders must promote campus environments that result in multiple opportunities for student learning and development.

CEP leaders must continuously improve programs and services in response to changing needs of students and other constituents, and evolving institutional priorities.

Special attention should be given to the changing needs of conference and event client and service providers.

CEP leaders should provide guidance on:
- effective and appropriate strategies for communicating with prospective program participants
- student needs, issues, and perspectives
- cultivating relations with academic departments
- working with student, campus, and academic leaders and organizations
- efficient and appropriate use of campus resources
- promoting equal access for all students and program participants

Part 4. ORGANIZATION and MANAGEMENT

Guided by an overarching intent to ensure student learning and development, Conference and Event Programs (CEP) must be structured purposefully and managed effectively to achieve stated goals. Evidence of appropriate structure must include current and accessible policies and procedures, written performance expectations for all employees, functional workflow graphics or organizational charts, and clearly stated service delivery expectations.

Evidence of effective management must include use of comprehensive and accurate information for decisions, clear sources and channels of authority, effective communication practices, decision-making and conflict resolution procedures, responsiveness to changing conditions, accountability and evaluation systems, and recognition and reward processes. CEP must provide channels within the organization for regular review of administrative policies and procedures.

CEP must maintain accurate and current documentation on: operational policies and procedures, agreements and memoranda of understanding with service providers, standards of performance and other expectations of service providers, and access provisions for clients with disabilities.

Other areas for consideration in determining structure and management of conference and event offices may include:
- availability and characteristics of facilities
- size, nature, and mission of the institution
- scope of related academic services
- philosophy and delivery system for services
- variety of delivery methods being employed or available to the institution
- degree of integration with academic disciplines and academic service units

Part 5. HUMAN RESOURCES

Conference and Event Programs (CEP) must be staffed adequately by individuals qualified to accomplish its mission and goals. Within established guidelines of the institution, programs and services must establish procedures for staff selection, training, and evaluation; set expectations for supervision, and provide appropriate professional development opportunities. CEP must strive to improve the professional competence and skills of all personnel it employs.

CEP staff members must be proficient in effective customer service techniques.

CEP staff members should be knowledgeable about services offered directly, and by relevant campus agencies and facilities such as housing, dining, recreation, parking, and technology services.

CEP professional staff members must hold an earned graduate degree in a field relevant to the position they hold or must possess an appropriate combination of educational credentials and related work experience.

Degree or credential-seeking interns must be qualified by enrollment in an appropriate field of study and by relevant experience. These individuals must be trained and supervised adequately by professional staff members holding educational credentials and related work experience appropriate for supervision.

Student employees and volunteers must be carefully selected, trained, supervised, and evaluated. They must be trained on how and when to refer those in need of assistance to qualified staff members and have access to a supervisor for assistance in making these judgments. Student employees and volunteers must be provided clear and precise job descriptions,

pre-service training based on assessed needs, and continuing staff development.

CEP must have technical and support staff members adequate to accomplish its mission. Staff members must be technologically proficient and qualified to perform their job functions, be knowledgeable of ethical and legal uses of technology, and have access to training. The level of staffing and workloads must be adequate and appropriate for program and service demands.

Salary levels and fringe benefits for all CEP staff members must be commensurate with those for comparable positions within the institution, in similar institutions, and in the relevant geographic area.

CEP must institute hiring and promotion practices that are fair, inclusive, and non-discriminatory. Programs and services must employ a diverse staff to provide readily identifiable role models for students and to enrich the campus community.

CEP must create and maintain position descriptions for all staff members and provide regular performance planning and appraisals.

CEP must have a system for regular staff evaluation and must provide access to continuing education and professional development opportunities, including in-service training programs and participation in professional conferences and workshops.

Part 6. FINANCIAL RESOURCES

Conference and Event Programs (CEP) must have adequate funding to accomplish its mission and goals. Funding priorities must be determined within the context of the stated mission, goals, objectives, and comprehensive analysis of the needs and capabilities of students, and the availability of internal or external resources.

CEP must demonstrate fiscal responsibility and cost effectiveness consistent with institutional protocols.

Funds to support the CEP, insofar as possible and desirable, should be self-generated from fees set at fair market rates.

For self-support programs, when higher than expected revenue in any one year results in a surplus, CEP should be authorized to establish reserve funds as a buffer against future shortfalls.

Part 7. FACILITIES, TECHNOLOGY , and EQUIPMENT

Conference and Event Programs (CEP) must have

adequate, suitably located facilities, adequate technology, and equipment to support its mission and goals efficiently and effectively. Facilities, technology, and equipment must be evaluated regularly and be in compliance with relevant federal, state, provincial, and local requirements to provide for access, health, safety, and security.

Housing, dining, and meeting space, as well as athletic, parking, and recreation facilities, sufficient to meet the needs of conference programs, should be available consistent with agreements among and between the institutional collaboratives.

Part 8. LEGAL RESPONSIBILITIES

Conference and Event Programs (CEP) staff members must be knowledgeable about and responsive to laws and regulations that relate to their respective responsibilities. CEP staff members must inform users of programs and services and officials, as appropriate, of legal obligations and limitations including constitutional, statutory, regulatory, and case law; mandatory laws and orders emanating from federal, state/provincial and local governments; and the institution's policies.

CEP staff members should inform conference/event planners, participants, institutional staff and students in a timely, systematic, and forthright fashion, about extraordinary or changing conditions, legal obligations, potential liabilities, risks, and security.

CEP staff members must use reasonable and informed practices to limit the liability exposure of the institution, its officers, employees, and agents. Staff members must be informed about institutional policies regarding personal liability and related insurance coverage options.

Although participation in conferences, events and similar activities is a voluntary action, program leaders should monitor liability for wrongful or negligent acts.

The institution must provide access to legal advice for CEP staff members as needed to carry out assigned responsibilities.

The institution must inform CEP staff and students in a timely and systematic fashion about extraordinary or changing legal obligations and potential liabilities.

Part 9. EQUITY and ACCESS

Conference and Event Programs (CEP) staff members must ensure that services and programs are provided on a fair and equitable basis. Facilities, programs and services must be accessible. Hours of operation and delivery of and access to programs and services must be responsive to the needs of all students and other constituents. CEP must adhere to the spirit and intent of equal opportunity laws.

CEP must be open and readily accessible to all students and must not discriminate except where sanctioned by law and institutional policy. Discrimination must be avoided on the bases of age; color; creed; cultural heritage; disability; ethnicity; gender identity; nationality; political affiliation; religious affiliation; sex; sexual orientation; or social, economic, marital, or veteran status.

CEP should provide services and information through a variety of appropriate formats including web site, e-mail, in person through office hours, telephone, and individual appointments, and customer service systems with a goal of maximizing one stop shopping.

Consistent with its mission and goals, the conference and event program must take affirmative actions to remedy significant imbalances in student participation and staffing patterns.

Staff members should ensure that program services provided through third parties are offered on a fair and equitable basis.

As the demographic profiles of campuses change and new instructional delivery methods are introduced, institutions must recognize the needs of students who participate in distance learning for access to programs and services offered on campus. Institutions must provide appropriate services in ways that are accessible to distance learners and assist them in identifying and gaining access to other appropriate services in their geographic region.

Part 10. CAMPUS and EXTERNAL RELATIONS

Conference and Event Programs (CEP) must establish, maintain, and promote effective relations with relevant individuals, campus offices, and external agencies.

The program should develop institutional support by:
- establishing cooperative relationships with other offices (in addition to direct service providers) such as Alumni, Enrollment Management, Athletics, Institutional Advancement, Communications, Public Relations, Campus

Information Visitor Services, to share information, stimulate program opportunities, and to enhance institutional visibility

- encouraging staff participation in civic and community organizations such as a Chamber of Commerce or Rotary International as well as involvement in professional associations

CEP should adhere to institution-wide processes that systematically involve academic affairs, student affairs, and administrative units such as police, physical plant and business offices.

CEP should collaborate with campus agencies, as appropriate, and meet regularly with service providers to coordinate schedules and facility use, and to review conferences and events under development.

CEP should serve as a resource providing professional advice on conference/event-related issues and activities.

Part 11. DIVERSITY

Within the context of each institution's unique mission, diversity enriches the community and enhances the collegiate experience for all; therefore, Conference and Event Programs (CEP) must nurture environments where commonalties and differences among people are recognized and honored.

CEP must promote educational experiences that are characterized by open and continuous communication that deepens understanding of one's own identity, culture, and heritage, and that of others. CEP must educate and promote respect about commonalties and differences in their historical and cultural contexts.

CEP must address the characteristics and needs of a diverse population when establishing and implementing policies and procedures.

CEP should make reasonable effort to educate the campus community concerning cultural aspects that are unique to individual conferences and events.

Part 12. ETHICS

All persons involved in the delivery of Conference and Event Programs (CEP) must adhere to the highest principles of ethical behavior. CEP must develop or adopt and implement appropriate statements of ethical practice. CEP must publish these statements and ensure their periodic review by relevant constituencies.

CEP should consider the ethical standards of constituents to whom it provides services and with whom it partners.

CEP staff members must ensure that privacy and confidentiality are maintained with respect to all communications and records to the extent that such records are protected under the law and appropriate statements of ethical practice.

Advice and information disclosed by clients, students, faculty, and staff in the course of conducting business should be considered confidential.

Information contained in students' education records must not be disclosed without written consent except as allowed by relevant laws and institutional policies. CEP staff members must disclose to appropriate authorities information judged to be of an emergency nature, especially when the safety of the individual or others is involved, or when otherwise required by institutional policy or relevant law.

All CEP staff members must be aware of and comply with the provisions contained in the institution's human subjects research policy, and in other relevant institutional policies addressing ethical practices and confidentiality of research data concerning individuals.

CEP staff members must recognize and avoid personal conflict of interest or appearance thereof in their transactions with students and others.

CEP staff members must strive to ensure the fair, objective, and impartial treatment of all persons with whom they deal. Staff members must not participate in any form of harassment that demeans persons or creates an intimidating, hostile, or offensive campus environment.

CEP staff members must perform their duties within the limits of their training, expertise, and competence. When these limits are exceeded, individuals in need of further assistance must be referred to persons possessing appropriate qualifications.

CEP staff members must be knowledgeable about and practice the highest principles of ethical behavior in the use of technology.

CEP staff members must use suitable means to confront and otherwise hold accountable other staff members who exhibit unethical behavior.

When handling institutional funds, all CEP staff members must ensure that such funds are managed in accordance with established and responsible accounting procedures, contractual agreements, and the fiscal policies or processes of the institution.

Part 13. ASSESSMENT AND EVALUATION

Conference and Event Programs (CEP) must conduct regular assessment and evaluations. CEP must employ effective qualitative and quantitative methodologies as appropriate, to determine whether and to what degree the stated mission, goals, and student learning and development outcomes are being met. The process must employ sufficient and sound assessment measures to ensure comprehensiveness. Data collected must include responses from students and other affected constituencies.

CEP must evaluate periodically how well they complement and enhance the institution's stated mission and educational effectiveness.

CEP should collaborate with institutional research units to generate data that could project contributions to the local economy, increase student enrollment, or stimulate of additional research or related programs given conference and event activities.

A representative cross-section of appropriate people from campus communities should be involved in reviewing the conference and event program.

CEP should generate and disseminate an annual report identifying overall goals, activities and programs served, financial contributions, regular feedback from participants, and opportunities that contributes to the overall visibility and promotion of the institution.

CEP must assess and evaluate regularly its effectiveness in providing students with quality learning and development opportunities.

Results of these evaluations must be used in revising and improving programs and services and in recognizing staff performance.

General Standards revised in 2002; CEP content developed/ revised in 2002

THE ROLE of COUNSELING SERVICES
CAS Standards Contextual Statement

College counseling represents the union of several movements in higher education and the integration of a helping profession activity with an educational environment (Dean & Meadows, 1995). However, the collegiate environment has moved beyond the physical realm to also include a virtual one, due in part to the rapid technological advances of our culture. The nature and type of the higher educational environment and its effects on students are important tools for college counselors. Steenbarger (1990) noted that college counseling exemplifies the developmental framework that has produced a history of creative outreach and support work on campuses. College counseling is counseling in context that can best be illustrated through exploring the development of the field and the models that have influenced it. The delivery of counseling services to students in higher education has and is evolving to effectively respond to clientele in an ever-changing environment.

Historically, the role and function of college counseling has changed in response to both external and internal factors. Social needs, political environment, national economy, and changing demographics all exert changing influences to which counseling services must respond. Change also occurs in response to internal factors unique to each campus environment (e.g., location of the counseling center within health services versus an office that combines the counseling center with career services or academic advising). As a result, the breadth and depth of counseling services reflect the intersection of these influences. Davis and Humphrey's (2000) comprehensive work provided a thorough review of the history of college counseling roles and service delivery models, the changing demographics of higher education, and implications for the future. It is critical that counseling services respond effectively to these factors. With the rapid technological and cultural changes in our society, the counseling profession among other helping professions has put forth standards of practice to meet the ever changing needs of higher education clientele.

As a result of this rich history, the service delivery of college counseling programs varies extensively across the more than 3,400 accredited institutions of American higher education. As a whole, college counseling services largely reflect the vocational, mental health, and student personnel models of counseling (Oetting, et al., 1970; Davis and Humphrey, 2000). Stone and Archer (1990) highlighted the challenges facing the profession and elaborated specific strategies for effectively addressing the needs in college counseling to ensure high quality services into the next century.

The current challenges are created by external forces including changing ethnic, racial, national, and experiential backgrounds of students; increasing psychological, health, safety, and financial needs of students; increasing competition for resources in higher education; increased emphasis on accountability; new and changing regulations regarding client privacy and the implications of health and mental health care reform (Stone & Archer, 1990; Gallagher & Zhang, 2002; Magoon, 2002). Moreover, the aftermath of 9/11 and other global traumatic events highlight the necessity for college counseling programs to be responsive to unanticipated factors. The level of severity of college students' presenting concerns is much greater than the traditional presenting problems of adjustment issues and individuation that were typically identified in counseling center research from the 1950s through the early 1980s (Pledge, et al., 1998; Heppner, et al., 1994). In the late 1990s and into the 21st century, research indicated that while the level of severity of presenting problems had stabilized, the complexity of problems continued to increase (Benton et al., 2003; Cornish et al., 2000; Pledge et al., 1998). As the severity and complexity of clients' problems expand, it is increasingly important for college counseling professionals to be prepared to work with physicians, community mental health workers, other campus departments, and other health care professionals. An increased focus on retention and outcomes assessment, generated in part by accreditation agencies, has challenged college counseling programs to be more intentional about demonstrating efficacy (Dean & Meadows, 1995).

Based on these challenges, Stone and Archer (1990) stressed a need for counseling centers to (a) clearly define boundaries on the types of problems and degree of severity of those clients for whom the counseling center will provide services and (b) develop and identify extensive referral and outreach services to transition effectively more severe clients to appropriate community resources. At the same time, college counselors strive to maintain the developmental, preventive, and consultative services that are integral to their work. As Stone and Archer (1990) noted, the concepts of working within limits and achieving balance between demands and resources are significant for college counseling services. Archer and Cooper (1998) further recognized the importance of demonstrating to institutions the positive outcomes of helping students maintain psychological health and develop personally in ways that support retention. Humphrey, Kitchens, and Patrick (2000) go one step further to encourage counseling services to expand and embrace the use of interactional and Internet-based technologies for additional service delivery options.

College counseling services work with other student support services to promote students' personal and educational success through activities that complement formal academic programs. College counselors offer remedial, preventive, crisis, outreach, and consultative services, depending on the nature of the campus and students served. Counseling services have changed and adapted over time along with shifts in student demographics. A strong commitment to professional development, whether through conducting research, providing training and supervision, maintaining professional credentials, upholding ethical standards of practice, or actively participating in professional organizations or other scholarly activities, is the catalyst for competent responses to the changing social issues and complex developmental, psychosocial, and mental health concerns of students.

College attendance creates a unique set of circumstances and stresses that can stimulate significant student growth and development, especially when the many student support functions are well coordinated and working together. As students experience change, they often need to address personal issues, work through challenges, and deal with the implications of growth and change. The rapid changes that characterize today's society compounded by the impact of global crisis, catastrophic natural events, and economic decline can exacerbate students' personal and psychological problems (Archer & Cooper, 1998; Davis & Humphrey, 2000). However, students' access to and success in higher education are maximized as counseling services embrace and utilize the medical, technological, and psychological advances of the 21st century. The presence and availability of counseling services is an important support for the education and development of the whole person.

The CAS Counseling Services Standards and Guidelines that follow provide college counselors with criteria to develop, enhance, evaluate, and judge the quality of the campus counseling services offered.

References, Readings, and Resources

Archer, J., Jr., & Cooper, S. (1998). *Counseling and mental health services on campus: A handbook of contemporary practices and challenges*. San Francisco: Jossey-Bass.

Benton, S., Robertson, J., Tseng, W., Newton, F., & Benton, S. (2003). Changes in counseling center client problems across 13 years, *Professional Psychology: Research and Practice, 34*, 66-72.

Cornish, J., Kominars, K., Riva, M., McIntosh, S., & Henderson, M. (2000). Perceived distress in university counseling center clients across a six-year period. *Journal of College Student Development, 41*, 104-109.

Dean, L. A., & Meadows, M. E. (1995). College counseling: Union and intersection. *Journal of Counseling and Development, 74*, 139-142.

Davis, D., & Humphrey, K. (2000). *College counseling: Issues and strategies for a new millennium*. Alexandria, VA: American Counseling Association.

Gallagher, R.P., & Zhang, B. (2002). *National survey of counseling center directors 2002*. Alexandria, VA: International Association of Counseling Services.

Heppner, P., Kivlighan, D., Good, G., Roehlke, H., Hills, H., & Ashby, J. (1994). Presenting problems of university counseling center clients: A snapshot and multivariate classification scheme. *Journal of Counseling Psychology, 41*, 315-324.

Humphrey, K., Kitchens, H., & Patrick, J. (2000). Trends in college counseling in the 21st century. In D. Davis & K. Humphrey, (Eds.) *College counseling: Issues and strategies for a new millennium* (pp.289-305). Alexandria, VA: American Counseling Association.

Magoon, T. (2002). *College and university counseling center directors' 2001-2002 data bank*. College Park, MD: University of Maryland.

Pledge, D., Lapan, R., Heppner, P., Kivlighan, D., and Roehlke, H. (1998). Stability and severity of presenting problems at a university counseling center: A six year analysis. *Professional Psychology: Research and Practice, 29*, 386-389.

Oetting, E. R., Ivey, A. E., & Weigel, R. G. (1970). *The college and university counseling center* (ACPA Monograph No. 11). Washington, DC: American Personnel and Guidance Association.

Sharkin, B. (1997). Increasing severity of presenting problems in college counseling centers: A closer look. *Journal of Counseling and Development, 75*, 275-281.

Steenbarger, B. N. (1990). Toward a developmental understanding of the counseling specialty. *Journal of Counseling and Development, 68*, 435-437.

Stone, G. L., & Archer, J., Jr. (1990). College and university counseling centers in the 1990s: Challenges and limits. *The Counseling Psychologist, 18*, 539-607.

American College Counseling Association (ACCA): http://www.collegecounseling.org.

American College Personnel Association (ACPA): http://myacpa.org; Commission VII: Counseling & Psychological Services: http://www.acpa.nche.edu/comms/comm07/com7hmpg.htm/.

American Counseling Association (ACA) http://www.counseling.org.

American Psychological Association (APA): http://www.apa.org/ and Division 17, Counseling Psychology: http://www.apa.org/about/division/div17.html.

Association for the Coordination of Counseling Center Clinical Services: http://accccs.appstate.edu/

Association of Counseling Center Training Agents (ACCTA): http://accta.ucsc.edu/.

Association of Counselor Education and Supervision (ACES): http://www.acesonline.net/.

Association for the Coordination of Counseling Center Clinical Services (ACCCCS): http://www.ksu.edu/counseling/ACCCCS/index.htm.

Association of Psychology Postdoctoral and Internship Centers (APPIC): http://www.appic.org/index.html.

Association for University and College Counseling Center Directors (AUCCCD): http://www.aucccd.org.

Clearinghouse for Structured/Thematic Groups & Innovative Programs, University of Texas at Austin: http://www.utexas.edu/student/cmhc/clearinghouse/index.html.

Counseling Center Village: http://ub-counseling.buffalo.edu/ccv.html.

International Association of Counseling Services (IACS): An Accreditation Association: http://www.iacsinc.org/.

Resources for College Counselors: http://www.tarleton.edu/~counseling/coresour/cores.htm.

Contributors:
Michelle Stefanisko, Western Carolina University
Laura A. Dean, University of Georgia, ACCA

COUNSELING SERVICES
CAS Standards and Guidelines

Part 1. MISSION

Counseling Services (CS) must incorporate student learning and student development in its mission. CS must enhance overall educational experiences. CS must develop, record, disseminate, implement, and regularly review its mission and goals. Mission statements must be consistent with the mission and goals of the institution and with the standards in this document. CS must operate as an integral part of the institution's overall mission.

The mission of CS is to assist students to define and accomplish personal, academic, and career goals. To accomplish the mission, the scope of CS must include:

- **high quality individual and group counseling services to students who may be experiencing psychological, behavioral, or learning difficulties**
- **programming focused on the developmental needs of college students to maximize the potential of students to benefit from the academic environment and experience**
- **consultative services to the institution to help foster an environment supportive of the intellectual, emotional, spiritual and physical development of students**
- **assessment services to identify student needs and appropriate services and referrals**

A wide variety of counseling, consultative, evaluative, and training functions may be performed by the CS as an expression of its institutional mission.

To effectively respond to the educational needs of the institution and of students, CS should have the following complementary functions:

Developmental. The developmental function is to help students enhance their growth. Developmental interventions help students benefit from the academic environment. To do so, the counseling services promote student growth by encouraging positive and realistic self-appraisal, intellectual development, appropriate personal and occupational choices, the ability to relate meaningfully and mutually with others, and the capacity to engage in a personally satisfying and effective style of living.

Remedial. The remedial function recognizes that some students experience significant problems, ranging from serious adjustment issues to more severe psychological disorders that require immediate professional attention. This function includes assisting students in overcoming current specific personal and educational problems and, in some cases, remedying current academic skill deficiencies.

Preventive. The preventive function is to anticipate environmental conditions and developmental processes that may negatively influence students' well being and initiate interventions that will promote personal adjustment and growth.

While there are basic similarities in the overall goals of various types of institutions, differences in student populations and institutional priorities may affect emphases of functions within individual counseling services. For these reasons, counseling services at two given institutions may emphasize different combinations of personal counseling, academic counseling, career counseling or student development services.

CS should be organized based on institutional characteristics, priorities and organizational structures. Accordingly, not all functions may exist within the same administrative unit. In such cases, coordination among the units is essential to insure a cohesive system of services for students.

Part 2. PROGRAM

The formal education of students consists of the curriculum and the co-curriculum, and must promote student learning and development that is purposeful and holistic. Counseling Services (CS) must identify relevant and desirable student learning and development outcomes and provide programs and services that encourage the achievement of those outcomes.

Relevant and desirable outcomes include: intellectual growth, effective communication, realistic self-appraisal, enhanced self-esteem, clarified values, career choices, leadership development, healthy behaviors, meaningful interpersonal relationships, independence, collaboration, social responsibility, satisfying and productive lifestyles, appreciation of diversity, spiritual awareness, and achievement of personal and educational goals.

CS must provide evidence of its impact on the achievement of student learning and development outcomes.

The table below offers examples of evidence of achievement of student learning and development.

Student Learning and Development Outcome Domains

Satisfying and productive lifestyles
Examples of achievement indicators
> Achieves balance between education, work, and leisure time; Articulates and meets goals for work, leisure, and education; Overcomes obstacles that hamper goal achievement; Functions on the basis of personal identity, ethical, spiritual and moral values

Personal and educational goals
Examples of achievement indicators
> Identifies personal goals for counseling; Recognizes distinction between others' goals and individual goals for psychological health and well-being; integrates self-

142

knowledge with external feedback for personal decision-making; Understands the effect of one's personal and educational goals on others

Healthy behavior
Examples of achievement indicators

Chooses behaviors and environments that promote health and reduce risk; Articulates the relationship between health and wellness and accomplishing life-long goals; Exhibits behaviors that advance a healthy community

Enhanced self-esteem
Examples of achievement indicators

Exhibits self-respect and respect for others; Initiates actions toward achievement of goals; Takes reasonable risks; Demonstrates culturally-appropriate assertive behavior; Functions without need for constant reassurance from others

Realistic self-appraisal
Examples of achievement indicators

Articulates personal skills and abilities; Makes decisions and acts in congruence with personal values; Acknowledges personal strengths and weaknesses; Articulates rationale for personal behavior; Seeks feedback from others and appropriately integrates it into self-appraisal; Learns from past experiences; Exhibits awareness of how he/she is perceived by others

Clarified values
Examples of achievement indicators

Articulates personal values; Acts in congruence with personal values; Makes decisions that reflect personal values; Demonstrates willingness to scrutinize personal beliefs and values; Identifies personal, work, and lifestyle values and explains how they influence decision-making

Independence
Examples of achievement indicators

Exhibits culturally-appropriate self-reliant behaviors; Functions autonomously; Exhibits ability to function interdependently; Accepts responsibility for psychological health and well-being; Manages time effectively

Meaningful personal relationships
Examples of achievement indicators

Develops and maintains satisfying interpersonal relationships; Establishes mutually rewarding relationships with friends and colleagues; Listens to and considers others' points of view; Treats others with respect

Effective communication
Examples of achievement indicators

Writes and speaks coherently and effectively; Writes and speaks after reflection; Effectively articulates abstract ideas

Spiritual awareness
Examples of achievement indicators

Develops and articulates personal belief system; Understands roles of spirituality in personal and group values and behaviors

Appreciating diversity
Examples of achievement indicators

Understands one's own identity and culture; Seeks involvement with people different from oneself; Seeks involvement in diverse interests; Appropriately challenges the abusive use of stereotypes by others; Understands the impact of diversity on one's own experience

Collaboration
Examples of achievement indicators

Works cooperatively with others; Seeks the involvement of others; Seeks feedback from others; Demonstrates reciprocal empathetic responding in group work; Appropriately supports and challenges group members according to group norms; Engages appropriately when in psycho-educational workshop settings

Career choices
Examples of achievement indicators

Articulates career choices based on assessment of interests, values, skills and abilities; Articulates the characteristics of a preferred work environment; Comprehends the world of work; Sets career goals that reflect self-awareness

Social responsibility
Examples of achievement indicators

Understands, abides by, and participates in the development, maintenance, and/or orderly change of community, social, and legal standards or norms; Appropriately challenges the unfair, unjust, or uncivil behavior of other individuals or groups; Recognizes and accepts responsibility for how his/her behavior impacts others and the environment

Leadership development
Examples of achievement indicators

Articulates leadership philosophy or style; Comprehends the dynamics of a group; Exhibits ability to visualize a group purpose and desired outcomes; Recognizes strengths and limitations of group members; Respectfully promotes group involvement and ownership of desired outcomes

Intellectual growth
Examples of achievement indicators

Produces personal and educational goal statements; Employs critical thinking in problem solving; Uses complex information from a variety of sources including personal experience and observation to form a decision or opinion; Obtains a degree; Applies previously understood information and concepts to a new situation or setting; Expresses appreciation for literature, the fine arts, mathematics, sciences, and social sciences

Programs and services must be (a) intentional, (b) coherent, (c) based on theories and knowledge of learning and human development, (d) reflective of developmental and demographic profiles of the student population, and (e) responsive to needs of individuals, special populations, and communities.

To effectively fulfill its mission CS must provide directly, through referral, or in collaboration:

- individual counseling and/or psychotherapy in areas of personal, educational, career development/vocational choice, interpersonal relationships, family, social, and psychological issues
- group interventions (e.g., counseling, psychotherapy, support) to help students establish satisfying personal relationships and to become more effective in areas such as interpersonal processes, communication skills, decision-making concerning personal relationships and educational or career matters, and the establishment of personal values
- psychological testing and other assessment techniques to foster client self-understanding and decision making
- outreach efforts to address developmental needs and concerns of students
- counseling support to help students assess and overcome specific deficiencies in educational preparation or skills
- psychiatric consultation, evaluation, and support services for students needing maintenance or monitoring of psychotropic medications
- crisis intervention and emergency coverage
- staff and faculty professional development programs

In those cases where other campus agencies address similar issues, such as career counseling and educational counseling, CS should establish cooperative relationships and maintain appropriate mutual referrals. In those cases where specialized and needed expertise is not available within counseling services, staff members should make full and active use of referral resources within the institution and the local community.

CS should play an active role in interpreting and, when appropriate, advocating for addressing the needs of students to administration, faculty and staff of the institution. CS can provide a needed perspective for campus administrative leaders, reflecting an appropriate balance between administrative requirements and the special needs and interests of students. CS should interpret the institutional environment to students and intervene to either improve the quality of the environment or facilitate the development of better interactions between the student and environment. CS should be sensitive to the needs of traditionally under-served and special populations.

CS may engage in research that contributes to knowledge of student characteristics and needs and evaluation of student outcomes in its programs. CS may assist students, faculty and staff members who conduct individual research on student characteristics or on the influence of specific student development activities.

CS should provide consultation, supervision, and in-service professional development for faculty members, administrators, staff and student staff members, and paraprofessionals.

Training and supervision of paraprofessionals, practicum students, and interns is an appropriate and desirable responsibility of CS.

Part 3. LEADERSHIP
Effective and ethical leadership is essential to the success of all organizations. Institutions must appoint, position, and empower Counseling Services (CS) leaders within the administrative structure to accomplish stated missions. CS Leaders at various levels must be selected on the basis of formal education and training, relevant work experience, personal skills and competencies, relevant professional credentials, as well as potential for promoting learning and development in students, applying effective practices to educational processes, and enhancing institutional effectiveness. Institutions must determine expectations of accountability for leaders and fairly assess their performance.

Leaders of CS must exercise authority over resources for which they are responsible to achieve their respective missions.

CS leaders must:
- articulate a vision for their organization
- set goals and objectives based on the needs and capabilities of the population served
- promote student learning and development
- prescribe and practice ethical behavior
- recruit, select, supervise, and develop others in the organization
- manage financial resources
- coordinate human resources
- plan, budget for, and evaluate personnel and programs
- apply effective practices to educational and administrative processes
- communicate effectively
- initiate collaborative interaction between individuals and agencies that possess legitimate concerns and interests in the functional area

CS leaders must identify and find means to address individual, organizational, or environmental conditions that inhibit goal achievement.

CS leaders must promote campus environments that result in multiple opportunities for student learning and development.

CS leaders must continuously improve programs and services in response to changing needs of students and other constituents, and evolving institutional priorities.

Part 4. ORGANIZATION and MANAGEMENT
Guided by an overarching intent to ensure student learning and development, Counseling Services (CS) must be structured purposefully and managed effectively to achieve stated goals. Evidence of appropriate structure must include current

and accessible policies and procedures, written performance expectations for all employees, functional workflow graphics or organizational charts, and clearly stated service delivery expectations. Evidence of effective management must include use of comprehensive and accurate information for decisions, clear sources and channels of authority, effective communication practices, decision-making and conflict resolution procedures, responsiveness to changing conditions, accountability and evaluation systems, and recognition and reward processes. CS must provide channels within the organization for regular review of administrative policies and procedures.

Because the functions of CS are essential to the overall mission of an institution, their value and impact should be clearly articulated to the campus and their placement within the organizational structure should be such that it facilitates significant interaction with unit heads in academic and student affairs.

CS should function independently of units directly responsible for making decisions concerning students' official matriculation status, such as judicial actions, academic probation, and admissions or re-admissions actions.

Part 5. HUMAN RESOURCES

Counseling Services (CS) must be staffed adequately by individuals qualified to accomplish its mission and goals. Within established guidelines of the institution, CS must establish procedures for staff selection, training, and evaluation; set expectations for supervision; and provide appropriate professional development opportunities. CS must strive to improve the professional competence and skills of all personnel it employs.

Counseling functions must be performed by professionals from disciplines such as counseling and clinical psychology, counselor education, psychiatry, and clinical social work, and by others with appropriate training, credentials, and supervised experience.

CS professional staff members must hold an earned graduate degree in a field relevant to the position they hold or must possess an appropriate combination of educational credentials and related work experience.

Degree or credential-seeking interns must be qualified by enrollment in an appropriate field of study and by relevant experience. These individuals must be trained and supervised adequately by professional staff members holding educational credentials and related work experience appropriate for supervision.

Student employees and volunteers must be carefully selected, trained, supervised, and evaluated. They must be trained on how and when to refer those in need of assistance to qualified staff members and have access to a supervisor for assistance in making these judgments. Student employees and volunteers must be provided clear and precise job descriptions, pre-service training based on assessed needs, and continuing staff development.

Salary levels and fringe benefits for all CS staff members must be commensurate with those for comparable positions within the institution, in similar institutions, and in the relevant geographic area.

CS must institute hiring and promotion practices that are fair, inclusive, and non-discriminatory. CS must employ a diverse staff to provide readily identifiable role models for students and to enrich the campus community.

CS must create and maintain position descriptions for all staff members and provide regular performance planning and appraisals.

CS must have a system for regular staff evaluation and must provide access to continuing education and professional development opportunities, including in-service training programs and participation in professional conferences and workshops.

CS should maintain an in-service and staff development program which includes supervision, case presentations, research reports, and discussion of relevant professional issues. Institutional budgetary support should be available to provide for in-service and professional development activities.

The director of counseling services must have an appropriate combination of graduate course work, formal training, and supervised experience.

The director of CS should have a doctoral degree in counseling psychology, clinical psychology, counselor education or other related discipline from an accredited institution with a minimum of a master's degree in such areas. The director should hold or be eligible for state licensure or certification where such exists or should pursue such credentials. It is highly desirable that the director has a minimum of three years experience as a staff member or administrator in counseling services within higher education. The director should have received supervision (either pre- or post-doctoral) in counseling within higher education.

The director should have the ability to interact effectively with administrators, faculty and staff members, students, colleagues and community members and should possess all the general qualifications of a counseling staff member.

The responsibilities of the director should include:
- overall administration and coordination of counseling activities

- coordination, recruitment, training, supervision, development and evaluation of counseling and support staff personnel
- preparation and administration of budget
- preparation of annual reports
- provision of counseling information and services to students, faculty and staff in accordance with the mission of CS and the institution, to the community
- evaluation of services
- provision of consultation/leadership in policy formation and program development
- education of staff members regarding legal issues in mental health, medicine and higher education, as well as legal issues governing the delivery of counseling services.

Counseling staff members must have an appropriate combination of graduate course work, formal training, and supervised experience.

The minimum qualification for counseling staff members should be a master's degree from a regionally accredited institution in a relevant discipline such as counseling psychology, clinical psychology, counseling and personnel services, mental health counseling, and clinical social work, with a supervised practicum/internship at the graduate level, preferably in the counseling of students within a higher education setting or should be appropriately supervised until they can transfer their skills to this setting. Counseling staff members should hold, or be eligible for, state or provincial licensure or certification in their chosen discipline (e.g., counseling, psychology, social work), where such exists.

Counseling staff members should have appropriate course work and training in psychological assessment, theories of personality, abnormal psychology or psychopathology, career development, multicultural counseling, legal and ethical issues in counseling, and learning theory. Counseling staff members should keep abreast of current research, including outcome research. Counseling staff members should also demonstrate knowledge of technology, leadership, organization development, consultation, and relevant federal, regional, and state/provincial statutes.

In cases where counseling staff members are responsible for the supervision of colleagues or graduate interns, the counseling staff members should have doctoral degrees or hold degrees commensurate with those being supervised.

Counseling staff members should participate in appropriate professional organizations and should have the budgetary support to do so. Counseling staff members should be encouraged to participate in community activities related to their profession.

Practicum students and interns, as well as paraprofessional assistants, may perform, under supervision, such counseling functions as are appropriate to their preparation and experience.

The level of CS staffing must be established and reviewed regularly with regard to service demands, enrollment, user surveys, diversity of services

offered, **institutional resources, and other mental health and student services that may be available on the campus and in the local community**.

In addition to providing direct services, it is important that staff time be allowed for preparation of interviews and reports, updating institutional information, research, faculty and staff contacts, staff meetings, training and supervision, personal and professional development, consultation, and walk-in and emergency counseling interventions, in accordance with individual staff members' qualifications and task assignments. Similarly, teaching, administration, research, and other such responsibilities should be identified as relevant staff functions.

CS must have technical and support staff members adequate to accomplish its mission. CS staff members must be technologically proficient and qualified to perform their job functions, be knowledgeable of ethical and legal uses of technology, and have access to training. The level of staffing and workloads must be adequate and appropriate for program and service demands.

Clerical employees who deal directly with students should be carefully selected, since they play an important role in the students' impressions of the counseling services and often must make some preliminary client-related decisions.

Part 6. FINANCIAL RESOURCES
Counseling Services (CS) must have adequate funding to accomplish its mission and goals. Funding priorities must be determined within the context of the stated mission, goals, objectives, and comprehensive analysis of the needs and capabilities of students and the availability of internal or external resources.

CS must demonstrate fiscal responsibility and cost effectiveness consistent with institutional protocols.

Part 7. FACILITIES, TECHNOLOGY, and EQUIPMENT
Counseling Services (CS) must have adequate, suitably located facilities, adequate technology, and equipment to support its mission and goals efficiently and effectively. Facilities, technology, and equipment must be evaluated regularly and be in compliance with relevant federal, state, provincial, and local requirements to provide for access, health, safety, and security.

CS must maintain a physical and social environment that facilitates optimal functioning and insures appropriate confidentiality.

CS, when feasible, should be physically separate from administrative offices, campus police, and judicial units.

Individual offices for counseling staff members should be provided and appropriately equipped and soundproof. The offices should be designed to accommodate the functions performed by counseling staff members.

There should be a reception area that provides a comfortable and private waiting area for clients.

CS should maintain or have ready access to professional resource materials.

In those instances where counseling services include a career development unit, there should be a resource center that holds institutional catalogs and occupation and career information.

An area suitable for individual and group testing procedures should be available.

CS should maintain, or have ready access to, group meeting space.

CS should maintain equipment that is capable of providing modern technical approaches to treatment and record keeping and have access to equipment for research and media presentations.

CS with training components should have adequate facilities for recording, and, where possible, for direct observations.

Part 8. LEGAL RESPONSIBILITIES

Counseling Services (CS) staff members must be knowledgeable about and responsive to laws and regulations that relate to their respective responsibilities. CS staff members must inform users of programs and services and officials, as appropriate, of legal obligations and limitations including constitutional, statutory, regulatory, and case law; mandatory laws and orders emanating from federal, state/provincial and local governments; and the institution's policies.

CS staff members must use reasonable and informed practices to limit the liability exposure of the institution, its officers, employees, and agents. Staff members must be informed about institutional policies regarding personal liability and related insurance coverage options.

The institution must provide access to legal advice for CS staff members as needed to carry out assigned responsibilities.

The institution must inform CS staff and students in a timely and systematic fashion about extraordinary or changing legal obligations and potential liabilities.

Part 9. EQUITY and ACCESS

Counseling Services (CS) staff members must ensure that services and programs are provided on a fair and equitable basis. CS facilities, programs and services must be accessible. Hours of operation and delivery of and access to programs and services must be responsive to the needs of all students and other constituents.

CS must be open and readily accessible to all students and must not discriminate except where sanctioned by law and institutional policy. Discrimination must be avoided on the bases of age; color; creed; cultural heritage; disability; ethnicity; gender identity; nationality; political affiliation; religious affiliation; sex; sexual orientation; or social, economic, marital, or veteran status.

Consistent with their mission and goals, CS must take affirmative action to remedy significant imbalances in student participation and staffing patterns.

As the demographic profiles of campuses change and new instructional delivery methods are introduced, institutions must recognize the needs of students who participate in distance learning for access to programs and services offered on campus. Institutions must provide appropriate services in ways that are accessible to distance learners and assist them in identifying and gaining access to other appropriate services in their geographic region.

Part 10. CAMPUS and EXTERNAL RELATIONS

Counseling Services (CS) must establish, maintain, and promote effective relations with relevant individuals, campus offices, and external agencies.

It is desirable that CS develop close cooperation with campus referral sources and with potential consumers of counseling services consultations. CS should also work closely with all other segments of the institution whose goal is the promotion of psychological, emotional, and career development.

CS should work closely with the chief student affairs and chief academic affairs administrators to insure the meeting of institutional goals and objectives.

Within the campus community, CS should establish close cooperation with career services, academic advising, special academic support units (e.g., reading and study skills programs, learning assistance programs) and specialized student services (e.g., services for students with disabilities, international and minority students, TRIO programs, women, veterans, returning adult students).

CS should establish relationships with a wide range of student groups (e.g., student government; gay, lesbian, bisexual, transgender groups; fraternities and sororities) to promote visibility and serve as a resource to them.

CS should establish and maintain a close working relationship with student health services as counseling staff members are often called upon to refer clients for medical concerns or hospitalization, or to serve as consultants to, or to seek consultation from, health services professionals.

CS should foster relationships with academic units and with campus professionals in admissions, registrar's office, student activities, athletics, and residence halls, where appropriate.

CS should establish effective relationships with the institutional legal counsel and the legal staff of relevant professional organizations in order to effectively respond to pertinent legal issues and precedents which underlie the delivery components of CS.

Where adequate mental health resources are not available on campus, CS must establish and maintain close working relationships with off-campus community mental health resources.

CS should have procedures for the referral of students who require counseling beyond the scope of institutional CS.

As the demographic makeup of our campuses change and new instructional delivery methods are introduced, institutions should recognize that students who are at a distance from a physical campus may still need access to the range of counseling functions. Institutions should provide services in ways that are accessible to such learners and assist them in identifying and accessing appropriate services in their own geographic region.

Part 11. DIVERSITY
Within the context of each institution's unique mission, diversity enriches the community and enhances the collegiate experience for all; therefore, Counseling Services (CS) must nurture environments where commonalties and differences among people are recognized and honored.

CS must promote educational experiences that are characterized by open and continuous communication that deepens understanding of one's own identity, culture, and heritage, and that of others. CS must educate and promote respect about commonalties and differences in their historical and cultural contexts.

CS must address the characteristics and needs of a diverse population when establishing and implementing policies and procedures.

Part 12. ETHICS
All persons involved in the delivery of Counseling Services (CS) must adhere to the highest principles of ethical behavior. CS must develop or adopt and implement appropriate statements of ethical practice. CS must publish these statements and ensure their periodic review by relevant constituencies .

CS staff members must recognize and avoid personal conflict of interest or appearance thereof in their transactions with students and others. Staff members must strive to ensure the fair, objective, and impartial treatment of all persons with whom they deal.

When handling institutional funds, all CS staff members must ensure that such funds are managed in accordance with established and responsible accounting procedures and the fiscal policies or processes of the institution.

CS staff members must be knowledgeable about and practice ethical behavior in the use of technology.

CS staff members must not participate in nor condone any form of harassment that demeans persons or creates an intimidating, hostile, or offensive campus environment.

CS staff members must perform their duties within the limits of their training, expertise, and competence. When these limits are exceeded, individuals in need of further assistance must be referred to persons possessing appropriate qualifications.

CS staff members must use suitable means to confront and otherwise hold accountable other staff members who exhibit unethical behavior.

CS staff members must conform to relevant federal, state/provincial, and local statutes which govern the delivery of counseling and psychological services.

CS staff members must be familiar with and adhere to relevant ethical standards in the field, including those professional procedures for intake, assessment, case notes, termination summaries and the preparation, use, and distribution of psychological tests.

Client status and information disclosed in individual counseling sessions must remain confidential, unless written permission to divulge the information is given by the student.

Clients must be made aware of issues such as the limits to confidentiality during intake or early in the counseling process so they can participate from a position of informed consent.

Consultation regarding individual students, as requested or needed with faculty and other campus personnel, is offered in the context of preserving the student's confidential relationship with the counseling services. Consultation with parents, spouses, and public and private agencies that bear some responsibility for particular students may occur within the bounds of a confidential counseling relationship.

All CS staff members must disclose to appropriate authorities information judged to be of an emergency nature, especially when the safety of the individual or others is involved.

When the condition of a client is indicative of clear and imminent danger to the client or to others, counseling staff members must take reasonable personal action that may involve informing responsible authorities, and when possible, consulting with

other professionals. In such cases, counseling staff members must be cognizant of pertinent ethical principles, state/provincial or federal statutes, and local mental health guidelines that stipulate the limits of confidentiality.

General Standards revised 2002; CS content developed/revised 1986, 1997, & 1999

Information should be released only at the written request or concurrence of a client who has full knowledge of the nature of the information that is being released and of the parties to whom it is released. Instances of limited confidentiality should be clearly articulated. The decision to release information without consent should occur only after careful consideration and under the conditions described above.

CS must maintain records in a confidential and secure manner while specifying procedures to monitor access, use, and maintenance of the records.

CS staff members must ensure that privacy and confidentiality are maintained with respect to all communications and records to the extent that such records are protected under the law and appropriate statements of ethical practice. Information contained in students' education records must not be disclosed without written consent except as allowed by relevant laws and institutional policies. CS staff members must disclose to appropriate authorities information judged to be of an emergency nature, especially when the safety of the individual or others is involved, or when otherwise required by institutional policy or relevant law.

All CS staff members must be aware of and comply with the provisions contained in the institution's human subjects research policy and in other relevant institutional policies addressing ethical practices and confidentiality of research data concerning individuals.

Part 13. ASSESSMENT and EVALUATION

Counseling Services (CS) must conduct regular assessment and evaluations. CS must employ effective qualitative and quantitative methodologies as appropriate, to determine whether and to what degree the stated mission, goals, and student learning and development outcomes are being met. The process must employ sufficient and sound assessment measures to ensure comprehensiveness. Data collected must include responses from students and other affected constituencies.

CS must evaluate periodically how well they complement and enhance the institution's stated mission and educational effectiveness.

Results of these evaluations must be used in revising and improving programs and services and in recognizing staff performance.

THE ROLE of DISABILITY SUPPORT SERVICES
CAS Standards Contextual Statement

Students with disabilities have always been present in the college/university environment. Examples range from students with notoriety (Helen Keller entered Radcliffe College in 1900) to the early support programs at the University of Illinois which began with World War II veterans studying through the GI Bill.

Beginning in 1973 with the passage of Section 504 of the Rehabilitation Act, "no otherwise qualified individual with a disability shall, solely by reason of his/her disability, be excluded from the participation in, be denied the benefits of, or be subjected to discrimination under any program or activity of a public entity". As the result of this legislation, colleges and universities receiving Federal funds were required to provide nondiscriminatory, equal access to programs and facilities for individuals with disabilities. The Americans with Disabilities Act of 1990 (ADA) broadened this legislation to include public entities such as restaurants, hotels, stores, transportation, and communication systems. In these areas, oversight of the ADA is not dependent on the receipt of federal funds as it is with institutions of higher education.

Universities and colleges looked to each other to help define the growing need for services. Thus the field of "Disability Services" evolved and in response to that need, a uniquely challenged and experienced cadre of professional disability service providers created what is today the Association on Higher Education and Disability (AHEAD) in 1977.

Colleges and universities worked to design services appropriate to the mission of individual campuses. Disability Services were often housed in student affairs. As a result, many of the earliest service providers were re-assigned from student life, counseling, academic advising, or the Dean of Students' office. Other campuses chose to house the office in affirmative action or in an academic department such as psychology, counseling, special education, or education; however, administrative location is immaterial and remains an institution's prerogative. What is important is that Disability Services offices should have their own financial resources and staff in order to meet the institutional commitment to access and compliance with Federal laws.

The difference in legislative focus between K-12 (IDEA, which is success-oriented) and higher education (Section 504 – Rehabilitation Act, which is access-oriented) often results in students with disabilities who are not prepared to enter higher education as strong advocates for themselves. From the mid-1980s through 2000, most campuses experienced a significant growth in the number of students who self-identified as having a learning disability (LD) and Attention Deficit (Hyperactivity) Disorder (ADD/ADHD) and requested reasonable accommodations. Additionally, current issues facing those who work in disability support services include: advanced technology (screen readers, speech output, etc.), study abroad, distance education, increasing numbers of students with psychological/psychiatric conditions, campus safety, technical standards, and performance demands of graduate and professional schools. These issues are examples of the ever-changing demands of a field that requires a greater comprehension of the impact of medical conditions, assessment of abilities, and programmatic standards/requirements on the part of the Disability Service provider to ensure the institution is able to realistically and reasonably provide access to students with disabilities.

References, Readings and Resources

American Council on Education (1994).*Educating students with disabilities on campus: Strategies of successful projects.* Washington, DC: Author.

American Council on Education. (1995). *College freshmen with disabilities: A triennial statistical profile*. Washington, DC: Author.

Disability Compliance for Higher Education Newsletter. Dan Gephart, Managing Editor, LRP Publications, Horsheim, PA.

Heyward, S. M. (1996). *Frequently asked questions: Postsecondary education and disability*. Cambridge, MA: Heyward, Lawton and Associates.

Kroeger, S., & Schuck, J. (Eds.) (1993). *Responding to disability issues in student affairs*, no. 64. New Directions For Student Services. San Francisco: Jossey-Bass.

Latham, J. D., & Latham, P. H. (1996). *Documentation and the law for professionals concerned with ADD/LD and those they serve.* Washington, DC: JKL Communications.

Ryan, D, & McCarthy, M. (Eds.) (1994). *A student affairs guide to the ADA and disability issues,* Monograph 17. Washington, DC: National Association of Student Personnel Administrators.

Walling, L. L. (ed.) (1996). *Hidden abilities in higher education: New college students with disabilities.* Monograph series no. 21, National Resource Center for the Freshman Year Experience and Students in Transition. Columbia, SC: University of South Carolina.

Association on Higher Education and Disability (AHEAD *P.O. Box 540666, Waltham, MA 02454 USA, tel/tty: 781-788-0003 fax: 781-788-0033,* www.ahead.org

Disability Compliance for Higher Education: Newsletter published monthly by LRP Publishers, http://www.lrp.com/

HEATH Resource Center, National Clearinghouse on Postsecondary Education housed at the George Washington University, www.heath-resource-center.org

Helen Keller: Biographical notes: http://www.rnib.org.uk/xpedio/groups/public/documents/publicwebsite/public_keller.hcsp#P69_9224

Journal of Postsecondary Education and Disability. Association on Higher Education and Disability, Boston, Mass. www.ahead.org

U.S. Department of Education - Office for Civil Rights (OCR) www.ed.gov/offices/OCR

U.S. Department of Education www.ed.gov/policy/speced/guid/idea/idea2004.html

U.S. Department of Justice – ADA Home Page www.usdoj.gov/crt/ada/adahom1.htm

Contributors:
Sam Goodin, University of Michigan
Jim Kessler, University of North Carolina at Chapel Hill
Beth Hunsinger, Community College of Baltimore County, Essex Campus, AHEAD

DISABILITY SUPPORT SERVICES
CAS Standards and Guidelines

Part 1. MISSION

The primary mission of Disability Support Services (DSS) is to ensure equal access for students with disabilities to all curricular and co-curricular opportunities offered by the institution.

In addition, the mission of DSS must:
- Provide leadership to the campus community to enhance understanding and support of DSS
- Provide guidance to the campus community to ensure compliance with legal requirements for access

  Relevant legal requirements may vary among governmental jurisdictions but would include minimally for US institutions the requirements defined under Section 504 of the Rehabilitation Act of 1973, and the Americans with Disabilities Act of 1990.
- Establish a clear set of policies and procedures that define the responsibilities of both the institution and the person eligible for accommodations

DSS must develop, record, disseminate, implement, and regularly review its mission and goals. Mission statements must be consistent with the mission and goals of the institution and with the standards in this document.

DSS must operate as an integral part of the institution's overall mission.

DSS mission and purpose must incorporate student learning and student development in its mission. The program must enhance overall educational experiences.

To accomplish its mission, DSS must:
- Ensure that qualified individuals with disabilities receive reasonable and appropriate accommodations so as to have equal access to all institutional programs and services regardless of the type and extent of the disability
- Possess a clear set of policies and procedures
- Inform the campus community about the location of disability services, the availability of equipment and technology helpful to those with disabilities, and identification of key individuals within the institution who can provide services to students with disabilities
- Define and describe the procedures for obtaining services and accommodations
- Provide guidance and training for institutional staff and faculty members in the understanding of disability issues

  Institutional staff and faculty members should be educated about the stereotypes surrounding people with disabilities as well as appropriate protocols and language.
- Advocate for equal access, accommodations, and respect for students with disabilities within the campus community

Part 2. PROGRAM

The formal education of students consists of the curriculum and the co-curriculum, and must promote student learning and development that is purposeful and holistic.

Disability Support Services (DSS) must be (a) intentional, (b) coherent, (c) based on theories and knowledge of learning and human development, (d) reflective of developmental and demographic profiles of the student population, and (e) responsive to the needs of individuals, special populations, and communities.

If a formal DSS program does not exist, it must be the responsibility of the institution to ensure that the primary mission is accomplished, either through the direct delivery of essential programs and services by the person(s) designated by the institution as the point of contact for students or by assisting other offices in meeting those needs.

DSS must identify relevant and desirable student learning and development outcomes and provide programs and services that encourage the achievement of those outcomes.

Relevant and desirable outcomes include: intellectual growth, effective communication, realistic self-appraisal, enhanced self-esteem, clarified values, career choices, leadership development, healthy behaviors, meaningful interpersonal relations, independence, collaboration, social responsibility, satisfying and productive lifestyles, appreciation of diversity, spiritual awareness, and achievement of personal and educational goals.

DSS must provide evidence of its impact on the achievement of student learning and development outcomes.

The table below offers examples of achievement of student learning and development outcomes.

Student Learning and Development Outcome Domains

Intellectual growth

Examples of achievement indicators

Develops appropriate personal and educational goal statements; Employs critical thinking in problem solving; Uses complex information from a variety of sources including personal experience and observation to form a decision or opinion; Completes educational goals (course work, certificate or degree); Uses acquired knowledge in a new situation; Expands one's knowledge and develops a respect for and appreciation of literature, the fine arts, mathematics, sciences and social sciences; Acknowledges disability and uses strategies, accommodations, and resources in order to achieve intellectual growth

Effective communication

Examples of achievement indicators

Writes and speaks coherently and effectively after reflection using alternate means, if necessary (i.e., sign language, assistive technology, Braille); Effectively articulates abstract ideas; Makes presentations or gives performances; Promotes an understanding of alternate forms of communication with others

Enhanced self-esteem

Examples of achievement indicators

Shows self-respect and respect for others; Initiates actions toward achievement of goals; Takes reasonable risks; Functions without need for constant reassurance from others

Realistic self-appraisal

Examples of achievement indicators

Promotes the development of personal skills and abilities; Makes decisions and behaves in accordance with personal values; Acknowledges and articulates strengths and weaknesses, using accommodations or personal devices to ensure access; Articulates a rationale for personal behavior; Seeks feedback and effectively evaluates feedback from others; Learns from past experiences

Clarified values

Examples of achievement indicators

Articulates personal values; Acts according to personal values; Makes decisions that reflect personal values; Demonstrates willingness to scrutinize personal beliefs and values; Identifies personal, work, and lifestyle values with an understanding of one's disability and can explain how values influence decision-making

Career choice

Examples of achievement indicators

Articulates career choices based on assessment of interests, values, skills, and abilities including disability; Documents knowledge, skills, and accomplishments resulting from formal education, work experience, community service, and volunteer experiences; Makes connection between classroom and out-of-classroom learning; Constructs a resume with clear and appropriate job objectives and evidence of related knowledge, skills, and accomplishments; Makes decisions regarding disclosure of disability to potential employer and requests for reasonable accommodations; Evaluates workplace to assess accessibility in light of needs; Articulates the characteristics of a preferred work environment, including reasonable and appropriate accommodations; Comprehends the world of work and is aware how to approach employers regarding disabilities; Takes steps to initiate a job search or seek advanced education

Leadership development

Examples of achievement indicators

Articulates leadership philosophy or style; Serves in a leadership position in a group or organization either on campus or in the community; Comprehends the dynamics of a group; Exhibits democratic principles as a leader; Exhibits ability to visualize a group purpose and desired outcomes; Serves as a role model for others with disabilities

Healthy behavior

Examples of achievement indicators

Chooses behaviors and environments that promote health and reduce risk; Articulates the relationship between health and wellness and accomplishing life- long goals; Exhibits behavior that advances a healthy community; Appropriately manages disability by effective responses to recommendations of the medical community

Meaningful interpersonal relationships

Examples of achievement indicators

Establishes appropriate relationships with other students, and faculty and staff members; Listens to and considers others' points of view; Demonstrates respect for others

Independence

Examples of achievement indicators

Demonstrates self-reliant behaviors; Uses reasonable accommodations in order to function autonomously; Exhibits ability to function interdependently; Functions without close supervision appropriately but accepts supervision when necessary; Demonstrates effective time management

Collaboration

Examples of achievement indicators

Initiates opportunities for collaboration; Listens to and respects feedback from others; Works cooperatively with others; Contributes to achievement of a group goal

Social responsibility

Examples of achievement indicators

Understands and participates in relevant governance systems; Understands, abides by, and participates in the development, maintenance, and orderly change of campus, community, social, and legal standards or norms; Appropriately challenges the unfair, unjust or uncivil behavior of other individuals or groups; Participates in service or volunteer activities

Satisfying and productive lifestyles

Examples of achievement indicators

Articulates long-term and short-term goals for education, work, and leisure; Works to achieve a balance between education, work, and leisure; Develops a plan for achieving goals; Recognizes obstacles which may interfere with goal achievement; Reassesses goals, if necessary, based on new developments including disability issues; Functions on the basis of personal identity, ethical, spiritual, and moral values

Appreciating diversity

Examples of achievement indicators

Understands the meaning of diversity including its application to race, color, gender, gender identity, religion, sexual orientation, national or ethnic origin, age, disability, marital status, or veteran status; Understands one's own identity; Respects, appreciates, and interacts with people of other experiences; Articulates the advantages and challenges of a diverse society; Challenges appropriately the use of stereotypes by others; Understands the impact of diversity on one's own society

Spiritual awareness

Examples of achievement indicators

Develops and articulates personal belief system; Understands roles of spirituality in personal and group values and behaviors

Personal and educational goals

Examples of achievement indicators

Sets, articulates, and pursues individual goals; Articulates personal goals and objectives; Uses personal goals to guide decisions; Understands how personal goals affect others

Institutions must make effective use of existing administrative structures and resources to avoid unnecessary duplication of services and to ensure that all campus offices and services have as a part of their mission the responsibility to meet the needs of persons with disabilities.

Depending on the institution, students with disabilities should be served within a decentralized system, with a central office providing those services not provided elsewhere on campus.

DSS must identify environmental conditions that negatively influence persons with disabilities and propose interventions that are designed to ameliorate such conditions.

The institution must regularly evaluate the campus for physical access. Maps and signage must reflect accessible routes, handicapped parking, building accessibility, entrances, and restroom facilities. Parking and transportation must comply with applicable accessibility regulations and laws.

The major components of DSS, each of which must be clearly identified to the campus and to the potential and current users of the services, include:

- **a procedure for disclosure**

    Persons with disabilities should be given the opportunity to self-disclose to a disability services provider who is trained to evaluate the information and who understands and respects the confidentiality of the individual.

    Each person requesting services should be screened during an intake interview, should have documentation from a qualified professional, and should ensure that the service provider receives the documentation. The documentation should be current, state a diagnosis, and give evidence to support the impact of the disability and its effect on the academic or work environment. A referral list of qualified and competent professionals should be maintained for students who need more current or new documentation.

- **direct assistance to persons with disabilities**

    Services to qualified individuals should ensure equal access and also meet the requirements as required by current law and institutional policy. The actual services provided will vary among institutions based on the specific disability and on the location of services provided by other campus offices or the community. Staff members provide for accommodations that assist persons with disabilities in the accomplishment of educational, personal, social, and work goals.

    Examples of accommodation can include testing accommodations, readers, scribes, interpreters, note takers, brailed materials, screen magnification systems, text-to-speech, screen reading, voice dictation, and /or optical character recognition systems.

- **consultation to the campus community**

    DSS should act as a consultant and advocate to the campus community in ensuring physical and programmatic access to all institutional resources. This would include collaboration with faculty members about teaching and testing techniques for academic departments. DSS should work to ensure equal access to electronic communication and distance learning materials as well as access to print.

- **advising, counseling, and support for persons with disabilities**
  DSS should assist individuals in devising strategies to adjust to and succeed in higher education. When strategies include reasonable accommodations, the program should provide information about how to acquire them.

- **professional and community education**
  DSS should offer training and educational activities to faculty members, staff, and students and other community members that promotes understanding, awareness, and advocacy.

- **dissemination of Information**
  Information should include access issues, accommodations, and legal rights of persons with disabilities to the campus community. Information regarding the laws, the procedures for receiving services, documentation guidelines, and other related policies should be made readily available in both print and electronic formats. Additionally, general information about location, available hours, contact information, and procedures should be made widely available especially in institutional print and electronic publications including, but not limited to, course schedules, catalogs, bulletins, recruitment materials, student and faculty handbooks, and residence life publications. On-line information about DSS should be accessible with the use of assistive technology and must provide appropriate links to other useful services such as financial aid, admissions, residence life, security, parking, and campus information.

- **collaboration on institutional safety policies and procedures**
  The program should collaborate with appropriate campus offices and community agencies on the development and dissemination of safety, evacuation, and other emergency response plans.

Maps and signage must reflect accessible routes, handicapped parking, building accessibility, entrances, and restroom facilities. The institution must regularly evaluate the physical access of the campus. Parking and transportation must comply with applicable accessibility regulations and laws.

Part 3. LEADERSHIP
Effective and ethical leadership is essential to the success of all organizations. Institutions must appoint, position, and empower leaders within the administrative structure to accomplish stated missions. Leaders at various levels must be selected on the basis of formal education and training, relevant work experience, personal skills and competencies, relevant professional credentials, as well as potential for promoting learning and development in students, applying effective practices to educational processes, and enhancing institutional effectiveness. Institutions must determine expectations of accountability for leaders and fairly assess their performance.

Leaders of Disability Support Services (DSS) must exercise authority over resources for which they are responsible to achieve their respective missions.

Leaders must:
- **articulate a vision for their organization**
- **set goals and objectives based on the needs and capabilities of the population served that will enhance organizational and institutional effectiveness**
- **promote student learning and development**
- **prescribe and practice ethical behavior**
- **recruit, select, supervise, and develop others in the organization**
- **manage financial resources**
- **coordinate human resources**
- **plan, budget for, and evaluate personnel and programs**
- **apply effective practices in educational processes**
- **communicate effectively**
- **initiate collaborative interaction between individuals and agencies that possess legitimate concerns and interests in the DSS**
- **advocate for needs of students with disabilities**

The leaders of a DSS must keep abreast of current litigation, interpretation of case law, changes in the field of medicine and diseases, changes in documenting disabilities, and trends in the field of secondary special education and use this information to advise their institutions and community how to best respond and react to these changes. Also, leaders must be informed of best practices within the field of disability services.

Leaders of DSS must address individual, organizational, or environmental conditions that inhibit goal achievement.

Leaders of DSS must promote campus environments that result in multiple opportunities for student learning and development.

Leaders of DSS must improve programs and services continuously in response to changing needs of students and other constituents, and evolving institutional priorities.

Part 4. ORGANIZATION and MANAGEMENT

Guided by an overarching intent to ensure student learning and development, Disability Support Services (DSS) must be structured purposefully and managed effectively to achieve stated goals. Evidence of appropriate structure must include current and accessible policies and procedures, written performance expectations for all employees, functional workflow graphics or organizational charts, and clearly stated service delivery expectations.

Evidence of effective management must include use of comprehensive and accurate information for decisions, clear sources and channels of authority, effective communication practices, decision-making and conflict resolution procedures, responsiveness to changing conditions, accountability and evaluation systems, and recognition and reward processes. Programs and services must provide channels within the organization for regular review of administrative policies and procedures.

DSS must be situated within the administrative structure to develop and direct program activities effectively. Adequate staff, funding, and resources must be provided.

Such services normally function within divisions of student affairs or academic affairs. The services should involve advisory bodies which include students, faculty and staff members with disabilities.

PART 5. HUMAN RESOURCES

Disability Support Services (DSS) must be staffed adequately by individuals qualified to accomplish its mission and goals.

Within established guidelines of the institution, DSS must establish procedures for staff selection, training, and evaluation; set expectations for supervision, and provide appropriate professional development opportunities. Programs and services must strive to improve the professional competence and skills of all personnel it employs.

Professional staff members must hold an earned graduate degree in a field relevant to the position they hold or must possess an appropriate combination of educational credentials and related work experience.

Designated staff members may serve as practicum instructors or intern supervisors.

Degree or credential-seeking interns must be qualified by enrollment in an appropriate field of study and by relevant experience. These individuals must be trained and supervised adequately by professional staff members who hold credentials appropriate for supervision.

DSS must have technical and support staff members adequate to accomplish its mission. Staff members must be technologically proficient and qualified to perform their job functions, be knowledgeable of ethical and legal uses of technology, and have access to training. The level of staffing and workloads must be adequate and appropriate for program and service demands.

Salary levels and fringe benefits for all staff members must be commensurate with those of comparable positions within the institution, in similar institutions, and in the relevant geographic area.

DSS must institute hiring and promotion practices that are fair, inclusive, and non-discriminatory. Programs and services must ensure a diverse staff to provide readily identifiable role models for students and to enrich the campus community.

Staff assignments should take into account the benefits of employing persons with disabilities.

Sign language and oral interpreters must have appropriate qualifications, including appropriate coursework and certification.

Student employees and volunteers must be carefully selected, trained, supervised, and evaluated. They must be trained on how and when to refer those in need of assistance to qualified staff members and have access to a supervisor for assistance in making these judgments. Student employees and volunteers must be provided clear and precise job descriptions, pre-service training based on assessed needs, and continuing staff development.

Administrative and support staff must be provided with disability awareness training and possess knowledge and understanding of the needs of persons with disabilities.

DSS must create and maintain position descriptions for all staff members and provide regular performance appraisals.

DSS must have a system for regular staff evaluation and must provide access to continuing education and professional development opportunities, including in-service training programs and participation in professional conferences and workshops.

Part 6. FINANCIAL RESOURCES

Disability Support Services (DSS) must have adequate funding to accomplish its mission and goals. Priorities must be determined within the context of the stated mission, goals, objectives, and comprehensive analysis of the needs and capacities of students and the availability of internal or external resources.

DSS must demonstrate fiscal responsibility and cost effectiveness consistent with institutional protocols.

DSS should be funded as a separate institutional budget item. The institution must provide appropriate funding to carry out its stated mission and goals.

The allocation of financial resources must be adequate to meet the obligations of the institution under relevant national, state, provincial, and local laws.

In addition to normal budget categories, the DSS program may have unusual budgetary requirements that can vary from term to term. These may include readers, interpreters, and special equipment such as a TTY/TDD (telephone communication devices for the deaf), screen readers, voice synthesizers, reading machines, device for enlarging print, Braille capabilities, additional technology to provide accommodated exams, and variable speed tape recorders. The institution is not obligated to provide personal equipment such as wheelchairs, hearing aids, or prosthetics. The number and nature of the devices can be determined based on the population of persons with disabilities requesting services.

The decision of whether to purchase mandated devices should not be weighed against competing departmental needs, such as additional computers or staff. Funding for disability accommodations should come from a centralized institutional source rather than from any one individual department.

Part 7. FACILITIES, TECHNOLOGY, and EQUIPMENT

Disability Support Services (DSS) must have adequate, suitably located facilities, adequate technology, and equipment to support its mission and goals efficiently and effectively. Facilities, technology, and equipment must be evaluated regularly and be in compliance with relevant federal, state, provincial, and local requirements to provide for access, health, safety, and security.

Distance learning programs and institutional websites must be constructed to provide full access to persons with disabilities.

Facilities available to DSS units should include:
- offices and programmatic spaces within an accessible facility
- private offices for conducting intake interviews, counseling, or other meetings of a confidential nature
- private and quiet space for tape recording materials, and scribing or taking exams
- a receptionist area with accessible counter heights and TTY/TDD
- storage area to ensure the confidentiality of records
- conference room and training space adequate to accommodate persons in wheelchairs
- nearby availability of accessible rest rooms, water fountains, elevators, and corridors
- adequate handicapped parking convenient to the facility
- coat racks and bulletin boards
- warning devices such as strobe/buzzer fire alarms for emergencies.

Part 8. LEGAL RESPONSIBILITIES

Disability Support Services (DSS) staff members must be knowledgeable about and responsive to laws and regulations that relate to their respective responsibilities. Staff members must inform users of programs and services and officials, as appropriate, of legal obligations and limitations including constitutional, statutory, regulatory, and case law; mandatory laws and orders emanating from federal, state/provincial and local governments; and the institution's policies.

DSS staff members must use reasonable and informed practices to limit the liability exposure of the institution, its officers, employees, and agents. Staff members must be informed about institutional policies regarding personal liability and related insurance coverage options.

The institution must provide access to legal advice for staff members as needed to carry out assigned responsibilities.

Staff members must be aware of and seek advice from the institution's legal counsel on privacy and disclosure of student information contained in educational records, defamation law regarding references and recommendations on behalf of students, affirmative action laws, protective health information laws, and regulations regarding programs and liability issues pertaining to sponsored programs.

The institution must inform staff and students, in a timely and systematic fashion, about extraordinary or changing legal obligations and potential liabilities.

Higher education institutions must adhere to the law in appointing a disability compliance officer.

The DSS staff must, in conjunction with legal counsel, work to develop policies, procedures, and guidelines as required under relevant disability laws.

Interpretation of the laws and their application to the campus should be a coordinated effort with institutional legal counsel.

Part 9. EQUITY and ACCESS

Disability Support Services (DSS) staff members must ensure that services and programs are provided on a fair and equitable basis. Facilities, programs and services must be accessible. Hours of operation and delivery of and access to programs must be responsive to the needs of all students and other constituents. Each program and service must adhere to the spirit and intent of equal opportunity laws.

DSS must be open and readily accessible to all students and must not discriminate except where sanctioned by law and institutional policy. Discrimination must be avoided on the bases of age; color; creed; cultural heritage; disability; ethnicity; gender identity; nationality; political affiliation; religious affiliation; sex; sexual orientation; or social, economic, marital, or veteran status.

Consistent with it mission and goals, DSS must take affirmative action to remedy significant imbalances in student participation and staffing patterns.

DSS must educate the campus community about ensuring opportunities for individuals with disabilities in all facets of the institution. Additionally, as the demographic profiles of institutions of higher learning change and new instructional delivery methods are introduced, institutions of higher education must provide comparable distance education opportunities to students with disabilities.

Part 10. CAMPUS and EXTERNAL RELATIONS

Disability Support Services (DSS) programs must establish, maintain, and promote effective relations with campus offices and external agencies that provide direct support to persons with disabilities.

Such agencies would include vocational rehabilitation, the medical community, veterans administration, school districts, and social services agencies.

DSS must also work to maintain positive relations with students, faculty members, staff, the institutional legal counsel, the administration, all support offices, community agencies, the medical community, diagnosticians, and equal opportunity compliance officers.

DSS should take an active role in the coordination of the institution's response to the needs of persons with disabilities. This is essential to ensure the continuity of services, resource management, consistent institutional policies, and the integration of persons with disabilities into the total campus experience.

DSS should maintain a high degree of visibility with the academic units through the promotion and delivery of services, through involvement in determining what constitutes reasonable accommodations, and through promoting increased understanding of, and responsiveness to, the needs of persons with disabilities.

DSS should be informed about, and actively involved in, influencing and affecting the policies, practices and planning of other units, which directly affect persons with disabilities.

DSS staff members must be available to participate in appropriate campus-wide committees.

Disability support service staff members may act as liaisons between student services, academic services, and community services on the behalf of persons with disabilities.

Part 11. DIVERSITY

Within the context of each institution's unique mission, diversity enriches the community and enhances the collegiate experience for all; therefore, programs and services must nurture environments where commonalties and differences among people are recognized and honored.

Disability Support Services (DSS) must promote education experiences that are characterized by open and continuous communication, that deepen the understanding of one's own identity, culture, and heritage, and that of others. DSS must educate and promote respect about commonalties and differences in their historical and cultural contexts.

DSS must address the characteristics and needs of a diverse population when establishing and implementing policies and procedures.

Part. 12 ETHICS

All persons involved in the delivery of Disability Support Services (DSS) must adhere to the highest principles of ethical behavior.

DSS must develop or adopt and implement appropriate

statements of ethical practice. Programs and services must publish these statements and insure their periodic review by relevant constituencies.

Ethical standards or other statements from relevant professional associations should also be considered.

Staff members must strive to insure the fair, objective, and impartial treatment of all persons with whom they deal. Staff members must not participate in nor condone any form of harassment that demeans persons or creates an intimidating, hostile, or offensive campus environment.

Staff members must use suitable means to confront and otherwise hold accountable other staff members who exhibit unethical behavior.

Staff members must be knowledgeable about and practice ethical behavior in the use of technology.

Staff members must perform their duties within the limits of their training, expertise, and competence. When these limits are exceeded, individuals in need of further assistance must be referred to persons possessing appropriate qualifications.

Staff members must recognize and avoid personal conflict of interest or appearance thereof in their transactions with students and others.

Staff members must ensure that privacy and confidentiality are maintained with respect to all communications and records to the extent that such records are protected under the law and appropriate statements of ethical practice.

Information contained in students' education records must not be disclosed without written consent except as allowed by relevant laws and institutional policies.

Staff members must disclose to appropriate authorities information judged to be of an emergency nature, especially when the safety of the individual or others is involved, or when otherwise required by institutional policy or relevant law. All staff members must be aware of and comply with the provisions contained in the institution's human subjects research policy and in other relevant institutional policies addressing ethical practices and confidentiality of research data concerning individuals.

When handling institutional funds, all staff members must ensure that such funds are managed in accordance with established and responsible accounting procedures and the fiscal policies or processes of the institution.

Part 13. ASSESSMENT and EVALUATION

Disability Support Services (DSS) regularly must conduct regular assessment and evaluations. Programs and services must employ effective qualitative and quantitative methodologies as appropriate, to determine whether and to what degree the stated mission, goals, and student learning and developmental outcomes are being met. The process must employ a sufficient and sound assessment measures to ensure comprehensiveness.   Data collected must include responses from students and other affected constituencies.

Results of these evaluations must be used in revising and improving programs and services and in recognizing staff performance.

Comprehensive, systematic, and periodic assessments should be conducted to address the academic, social and physical needs of students as well as the psychological and physical environments of the campus. In turn, findings should be used to influence how present services should change for future development.

To determine the effectiveness of the organization and administration of the services a data collection system should be developed and implemented. Program evaluations should be obtained from designated staff members, students, faculty members and community.

Analyses of population characteristics and trends in the use of services should be performed regularly. Although not the sole measure of program's success, data may be compiled annually on attrition and graduation rates of students using the services.

DSS must evaluate periodically how well they complement and enhance the institution's stated mission and educational effectiveness.

General Standards revised in 2002; DSS content developed/ revised in 1986, 1997, & 2003

THE ROLE of DISTANCE EDUCATION PROGRAMS
CAS Standards Contextual Statement

Increasingly, *distance learning* has become a major educational issue in recent years. Although it has been defined in various ways by a number of educational authorities, the simplest definition is that "distance learning takes place when the instructor and student are not in the same room but instead are separated by physical distance" (Connick, 1999, p. 3). Distance learning often occurs when the student and instructor are separated by time as well.

Distance education refers to the various methods of instruction that have been intentionally designed to be applied in distance learning settings. Interestingly, distance education has its roots in the correspondence study movement, which began in Europe during the mid-1880s. By 1873, correspondence courses were being offered in the United States, and the University of Chicago had established a strong academic credit correspondence division by 1892 (Watkins, 1991).

Although higher education correspondence courses, sometimes referred to as "independent study programs," remain a viable alternative for many students today, developments in electronic communications have provided new technology-supported options for distance learners. In addition to correspondence study, the most common distance learning technologies include:

- Computer or online courses taught via the Internet or CD-ROM

- Interactive video systems in which two or more locations are connected, allowing student and instructor to see and hear one another from a distance

- Telecourses wherein instructional television courses are videotaped and broadcast over public or cable television stations

Many of these new teaching methods have gained recognition and acceptance throughout higher education, including some of the most traditional academic institutions. Concurrently, regional accrediting bodies are awarding accreditation to both degree programs and institutions that offer instruction completely online. In the "Statement of Commitment by the Regional Accrediting Commissions for the Evaluation of Electronically Offered Degree and Certificate Programs" (Regional Accrediting, 2001b), the accrediting commissions collectively affirmed that although a growing number of colleges and universities are going online with academic programs, the "new delivery systems test conventional assumptions, raising fresh questions as to the essential nature and content of an educational experience and the resources required to support it" (p. 1). Not only are there questions about teaching and learning, but distance education also poses challenges to student affairs programs and related student support services to meet the needs of distance learners even though these students may never set foot on campus.

During the past century, student affairs practitioners have sought to learn how best to provide both resident and commuter students with effective programs and services designed to enhance student learning and personal development. As colleges and universities develop programs that implement distance education technologies, the entire campus community must find ways to serve the special needs of distance learners. In response to the growth of technologically mediated instruction, the Student Support section of the regional accrediting commission's *Best Practices* (2001a) asserts that "the institution recognizes that appropriate services must be available for students of electronically offered programs, using the working assumption that these students will not be physically present on campus" (p 12).

The *Best Practices* were initially developed by the Western Cooperative for Educational Telecommunications www.wiche.edu/telecom/, an organization widely recognized for its expertise in the field of distance learning. Staff members of this cooperative were consulted in the development of the CAS Standards for Educational Services for Distance Learners that follow.

References, Readings, and Resources

Connick, G. P. (Ed.) (1999). *The distance learner's guide*. Upper Saddle River, NJ.: Prentice Hall.

Regional Accrediting Commissions (2001a). *Best Practices for electronically offered degree and certificate programs*. http://www.wiche.edu/telecom/Article1.htm

Regional Accrediting Commissions (2001b). *Statement of commitment by the regional accrediting commissions for the evaluation of electronically offered degree and certificate programs* http://www.wiche.edu/telecom/Article1.htm

Schwitzer, A.M., Ancis, J.R., & Brown, N. (2001). *Promoting student learning and student development at a distance*. lanham, MD: American College Personnel Association.

Watkins, B.L, & Wright, S.J. (eds.) (1991). *The Foundations of American Distance Education*. Dubuque, Iowa: Kendall/Hunt.

Western Cooperative for Educational Telecommunications (1999). *Guide to developing online student services*. http://www.wcet.info/resources/publications/guide/guide.htm

American Association for Collegiate Independent Study, http://www.aacis.org/

Western Cooperative for Educational Telecommunications, P.O. Box 9752, Boulder, CO 80301; 1540 30th Street, Boulder, CO 80303; (303)541-0231; (303)541-0291 (fax) http://www.wiche.edu/telecom/

Contributor: Nancy Thompson, University of Georgia

DISTANCE EDUCATION PROGRAMS
CAS Standards and Guidelines

Part 1. MISSION and PROGRAM

Distance education, for purposes of these standards, refers to any formal educational process provided by or contracted for an institution of higher education in which the student and faculty member are separated by time and/or space.

Distance education may be delivered by a variety of methods including the Internet, radio and telecommunication, CD-ROM, television, video, and/or print. An institution may be a traditional higher education institution, a consortium of such institutions, or other education entity.

Distance Education Programs (DEP) must incorporate student learning and student development in its mission. DEP must enhance overall educational experiences. DEP must develop, record, disseminate, implement, and regularly review its mission and goals. Mission statements must be consistent with the mission and goals of the institution and with the standards in this document. DEP must operate as an integral part of the institution's overall mission.

Institutions providing DEP must offer commensurate educational services as outlined throughout this document to assist distance learners to achieve their goals. Such services must be comparable to educational services provided to conventional learners and they must meet standards comparable to those of other institutional offerings. Institutions must recognize, however, that the students who select distance education might have different needs than those enrolled in campus-based instruction.

Institutions must identify the characteristics of their distance students and adapt services to meet the needs of the particular populations they serve.

Part 2. CONGRUENCY of MISSION and PROGRAMS

The mission of Distance Education Programs (DEP) must be clearly and explicitly stated. Institutional missions must be approved by appropriate governing bodies such as boards of trustees and state/provincial coordinating or governing agencies, and regularly reviewed by the institution and its regional and specialized accrediting agencies. The purposes or mission of distance education must be congruent with its host institution's purposes and must gain explicit approval of the relevant governance bodies of the institution. Primary oversight of the compatibility of distance education purposes and those of the institution rests with the institution and its governance system.

Evidence of effective management must include use of comprehensive and accurate information for decisions, clear sources and channels of authority, effective communication practices, decision-making and conflict resolution procedures, responsiveness to changing conditions, accountability and evaluation systems, and recognition and reward processes. DEP must provide channels within the organization for regular review of administrative policies and procedures.

Guided by an overarching intent to ensure student learning and development, DEP must be structured purposefully and managed effectively to achieve stated goals. Evidence of appropriate structure must include current and accessible policies and procedures, written performance expectations for all employees, functional workflow graphics or organizational charts, and clearly stated service delivery expectations.

Authority over the distance education curriculum must be clearly articulated. Goals of DEP must be stated in terms of outcomes to be achieved by students in the program.

The formal education of students consists of the curriculum and the co-curriculum, and must promote student learning and development that is purposeful and holistic. DEP must identify relevant and desirable student learning and development outcomes and provide programs and services that encourage the achievement of those outcomes.

Relevant and desirable outcomes include: intellectual growth, effective communication, realistic self-appraisal, enhanced self-esteem, clarified values, career choices, leadership development, healthy behaviors, meaningful interpersonal relationships, independence, collaboration, social responsibility, satisfying and productive lifestyles, appreciation of diversity, spiritual awareness, and achievement of personal and educational goals.

DEP must provide evidence of its impact on the achievement of student learning and development outcomes.

The table below offers examples of evidence of achievement of student learning and development.

Student Learning and Development Outcome Domains

Intellectual growth

Examples of achievement indicators

Produces personal and educational goal statements; Employs critical thinking in problem solving; Uses complex information from a variety of sources including personal experience and observation to form a decision or opinion; Obtains a degree; Applies previously understood information and concepts to a new situation or setting; Expresses appreciation for literature, the fine arts, mathematics, sciences, and social sciences

Effective communication

Examples of achievement indicators

Writes and speaks coherently and effectively; Writes and speaks after reflection; Able to influence others through writing, speaking or artistic expression; Effectively articulates abstract ideas; Uses appropriate syntax; Makes presentations or gives performances

Enhanced self-esteem

Examples of achievement indicators

Shows self-respect and respect for others; Initiates actions toward achievement of goals; Takes reasonable risks; Demonstrates assertive behavior; Functions without need for constant reassurance from others

Realistic self-appraisal

Examples of achievement indicators

Articulates personal skills and abilities; Makes decisions and acts in congruence with personal values; Acknowledges personal strengths and weaknesses; Articulates rationale for personal behavior; Seeks feedback from others; Learns from past experiences

Clarified values

Examples of achievement indicators

Articulates personal values; Acts in congruence with personal values; Makes decisions that reflect personal values; Demonstrates willingness to scrutinize personal beliefs and values; Identifies personal, work, and lifestyle values and explains how they influence decision-making

Career choices

Examples of achievement indicators

Articulates career choices based on assessment of interests, values, skills, and abilities; Documents knowledge, skills and accomplishments resulting from formal education, work experience, community service, and volunteer experiences; Makes the connections between classroom and out-of-classroom learning; Can construct a resume with clear job objectives and evidence of related knowledge, skills and accomplishments; Articulates the characteristics of a preferred work environment; Comprehends the world of work; Takes steps to initiate a job search or seek advanced education

Leadership development

Examples of achievement indicators

Articulates leadership philosophy or style; Serves in a leadership position in a student organization; Comprehends the dynamics of a group; Exhibits democratic principles as a leader; Exhibits ability to visualize a group purpose and desired outcomes

Healthy behavior

Examples of achievement indicators

Chooses behaviors and environments that promote health and reduce risk; Articulate the relationship between health and wellness and accomplishing life-long goals; Exhibits behaviors that advance a healthy community.

Meaningful interpersonal relationships

Examples of achievement indicators

Develops and maintains satisfying interpersonal relationships; Establishes mutually rewarding relationships with friends and colleagues; Listens to and considers others' points of view; Treats others with respect

Independence

Examples of achievement indicators

Exhibits self-reliant behaviors; Functions autonomously; Exhibits ability to function interdependently; Accepts supervision as needed; Manages time effectively

Collaboration

Examples of achievement indicators

Works cooperatively with others; Seeks the involvement of others; Seeks feedback from others; Contributes to achievement of a group goal; Exhibits effective listening skills

Social responsibility

Examples of achievement indicators

Understands and participates in relevant governance systems; Understands, abides by, and participates in the development, maintenance, and/or orderly change of community, social, and legal standards or norms; Appropriately challenges the unfair, unjust, or uncivil behavior of other individuals or groups; Participates in service/volunteer activities

Satisfying and productive lifestyles
Examples of achievement indicators
> Achieves balance between education, work, and leisure time; Articulates and meets goals for work, leisure, and education; Overcomes obstacles that hamper goal achievement; Functions on the basis of personal identity, ethical, spiritual, and moral values; Articulates long-term goals and objectives

Appreciating diversity
Examples of achievement indicators
> Understands one's own identity and culture; Seeks involvement with people different from oneself; Seeks involvement in diverse interests; Articulates the advantages and challenges of a diverse society; Challenges appropriately the abusive use of stereotypes by others; Understands the impact of diversity on one's own society

Spiritual awareness
Examples of achievement indicators
> Develops and articulates personal belief system; Understands roles of spirituality in personal and group values and behaviors

Personal and educational goals
Examples of achievement indicators
> Sets, articulates, and pursues individual goals; Articulates personal and educational goals and objectives; Uses personal and educational goals to guide decisions; Understands the effect of one's personal and educational goals on others

DEP must be (a) intentional, (b) coherent, (c) based on theories and knowledge of learning and human development, (d) reflective of developmental and demographic profiles of the student population, and (e) responsive to needs of individuals, special populations, and communities.

Part 3. LEADERSHIP
Effective and ethical leadership is essential to the success of all organizations. Institutions must appoint, position, and empower Distance Education Program (DEP) leaders within the administrative structure to accomplish stated missions. DEP leaders at various levels must be selected on the basis of formal education and training, relevant work experience, personal skills and competencies, relevant professional credentials, as well as potential for promoting learning and development in students, applying effective practices to educational processes, and enhancing institutional effectiveness. Institutions

must determine expectations of accountability for leaders and fairly assess their performance.

Leaders of DEP must exercise authority over resources for which they are responsible to achieve their respective missions.

DEP leaders must:
- **articulate a vision for their organization**
- **set goals and objectives based on the needs and capabilities of the population served**
- **promote student learning and development**
- **prescribe and practice ethical behavior**
- **recruit, select, supervise, and develop others in the organization**
- **manage financial resources**
- **coordinate human resources**
- **plan, budget for, and evaluate personnel and programs**
- **apply effective practices to educational and administrative processes**
- **communicate effectively**
- **initiate collaborative interaction between individuals and agencies that possess legitimate concerns and interests in the functional area**

DEP leaders must identify and find means to address individual, organizational, or environmental conditions that inhibit goal achievement.

DEP leaders must promote campus environments that result in multiple opportunities for student learning and development.

DEP leaders must continuously improve programs and services in response to changing needs of students and other constituents, and evolving institutional priorities.

Part 4. FACULTY QUALITY and SUPPORT
The key ingredient of the quality of academic programs is the caliber of faculty members. The institution must provide adequate faculty support for distance education courses and programs.

Leaders must ensure that faculty members are competent in their disciplines and/or fields of study and capable of teaching students in using a variety of pedagogical methods consistent with qualifications required of non-distance education faculty.

Faculty members must possess demonstrable skill in the appropriate uses of the methods used to deliver instruction.

These methods may include the Internet, CD-ROM, television, video, and/or print.

To assure the quality of instruction, the institution must provide adequate support to faculty in the design and teaching of distance education courses and programs including training in the effective uses of the delivery methods to be used in providing instruction. This support must include access to individuals with special knowledge of the pedagogy of various forms of distance education and to technical personnel.

Faculty members must be educated about the special issues associated with teaching at a distance, including physical, emotional, social, and psychological issues.

In electronically delivered teaching, for example, teachers may need training in how to identify problems of distance students that interfere with learning and how to help students when there is little or no opportunity for face-to-face interaction. The distance education environment poses special challenges with respect to the manner in which educational materials are distributed and shared. Distance education faculty should receive special training on copyright laws and the use of copyrighted materials. Devising ways to assure academic integrity is another area of difficulty in the distance education environment. Institutions should regularly share best practices in this area with all faculty members teaching distance education courses.

Institutional policies concerning teaching load, class size, time needed for course preparation, and sharing of instructional responsibilities must be adapted to appropriately support distributed education models. Because the number of hours required for the preparation and delivery of electronic courses may exceed similar requirements for face-to-face delivery institutional policies must accommodate these requirements.

Faculty members are the primary contact between the institution and the distance student; therefore, they must be able to provide appropriate support and guidance. To accomplish this, the institution must provide faculty access to computer service technicians, advisors, counselors, disability services, student affairs professionals, site administrators, distribution clerks, and library resource personnel

Part 5. RESOURCES FOR LEARNING
Distance Education Programs (DEP) must have adequate funding to accomplish its mission and goals. Funding priorities must be determined within the context of the stated mission, goals, objectives, and comprehensive analysis of the needs and capabilities of students, and the availability of internal or external resources.

DEP must demonstrate fiscal responsibility and cost effectiveness consistent with institutional protocols.

DEP must have adequate, suitably located facilities, adequate technology, and equipment to support its mission and goals efficiently and effectively. Facilities, technology, and equipment must be evaluated regularly and be in compliance with relevant federal, state, provincial, and local requirements to provide for access, health, safety, and security.

Facilities, equipment, and other resources associated with the viability and effectiveness of distance education programs should be reflected in the institution's long range planning, budgeting, and policy development processes.

DEP must have technical and support staff members adequate to accomplish its mission. Staff members must be technologically proficient and qualified to perform their job functions, be knowledgeable of ethical and legal uses of technology, and have access to training. The level of staffing and workloads must be adequate and appropriate for program and service demands.

DEP must be staffed adequately by individuals qualified to accomplish its mission and goals. Within established guidelines of the institution, DEP must establish procedures for staff selection, training, and evaluation; set expectations for supervision, and provide appropriate professional development opportunities. DEP must strive to improve the professional competence and skills of all personnel it employs.

DEP staff positions must be filled based on a defined set of qualifications such as level of education, work experience, and personal characteristics (for example, integrity, communication skills, and leadership ability).

Professional staff members must hold an earned graduate degree in a field relevant to the position they hold or must possess an appropriate combination of educational credentials and related work experience. Degree or credential-seeking interns must be qualified by enrollment in an appropriate field of study and by relevant experience. These individuals must be trained and supervised adequately by professional

staff members holding educational credentials and related work experience appropriate for supervision.

Student employees and volunteers must be carefully selected, trained, supervised, and evaluated. They must be trained on how and when to refer those in need of assistance to qualified staff members and have access to a supervisor for assistance in making these judgments. Student employees and volunteers must be provided clear and precise job descriptions, pre-service training based on assessed needs, and continuing staff development.

Salary levels and fringe benefits for all DEP staff members must be commensurate with those for comparable positions within the institution, in similar institutions, and in the relevant geographic area.

DEP must institute hiring and promotion practices that are fair, inclusive, and non-discriminatory. DEP must employ a diverse staff to provide readily identifiable role models for students and to enrich the campus community.

DEP must create and maintain position descriptions for all staff members and provide regular performance planning and appraisals.

DEP must have a system for regular staff evaluation and must provide access to continuing education and professional development opportunities, including in-service training programs and participation in professional conferences and workshops.

It is especially crucial that administrators, managers, and coordinators possess technical proficiency and a thorough understanding of how distance education programs are linked to institutional mission. These personnel also should be talented in communication skills to prepare them for effective involvement with other administrators, faculty, students, and staff of distance education programs. They also should be able to facilitate collaborative relationships among faculty and staff to achieve program goals and to enable program evaluation.

Adequate library resources must be available and accessible to distance students. Institutions must own the library/learning resources or have formal agreements with other institutions' library/learning resources to ensure adequate access to all distance education students.

Part 6. LEGAL RESPONSIBILITIES
Distance Education Programs (DEP) staff members must be knowledgeable about and responsive to

laws and regulations that relate to their respective responsibilities. Staff members must inform users of programs and services and officials, as appropriate, of legal obligations and limitations including constitutional, statutory, regulatory, and case law; mandatory laws and orders emanating from federal, state/provincial and local governments; and the institution's policies.

DEP staff members must use reasonable and informed practices to limit the liability exposure of the institution, its officers, employees, and agents. Staff members must be informed about institutional policies regarding personal liability and related insurance coverage options.

The institution must provide access to legal advice for DEP staff members as needed to carry out assigned responsibilities.

The institution must inform DEP staff and students in a timely and systematic fashion about extraordinary or changing legal obligations and potential liabilities.

Part 7. EQUITY and ACCESS
Distance Education Program (DEP) staff members must ensure that services and programs are provided on a fair and equitable basis. Facilities, programs and services must be accessible. Hours of operation and delivery of and access to programs and services must be responsive to the needs of all students and other constituents. DEP must adhere to the spirit and intent of equal opportunity laws.

DEP must be open and readily accessible to all students and must not discriminate except where sanctioned by law and institutional policy. Discrimination must be avoided on the bases of age; color; creed; cultural heritage; disability; ethnicity; gender identity; nationality; political affiliation; religious affiliation; sex; sexual orientation; or social, economic, marital, or veteran status.

Consistent with their mission and goals, DEP must take affirmative action to remedy significant imbalances in student participation and staffing patterns.

As the demographic profiles of campuses change and new instructional delivery methods are introduced, institutions must recognize the needs of students who participate in distance learning for access to programs and services offered on campus. Institutions must provide appropriate services in ways that are accessible to distance learners and assist them in identifying and gaining access to other appropriate services in their geographic region.

Part 8. CAMPUS and EXTERNAL RELATIONS

Distance Education Programs (DEP) must establish, maintain, and promote effective relations with relevant individuals, campus offices, and external agencies.

Leaders should pursue partnering opportunities with agencies, remote facility managers, and campus stakeholders to offer and improve distance education services.

Part 9. DIVERSITY

Within the context of each institution's unique mission, diversity enriches the community and enhances the collegiate experience for all; therefore, Distance Education Programs (DEP) must nurture environments where commonalties and differences among people are recognized and honored.

DEP must promote educational experiences that are characterized by open and continuous communication that deepens understanding of one's own identity, culture, and heritage, and that of others. DEP must educate and promote respect about commonalties and differences in their historical and cultural contexts.

DEP must address the characteristics and needs of a diverse population when establishing and implementing policies and procedures.

Part 10. CURRICULUM, COURSE, and DEGREE REQUIREMENTS

Information about courses, programs, and degree requirements must be clear and understandable and accessible to all participants.

Preferably, this information should be published in written form and distributed widely, using a variety of media.

The institutional catalog must clearly state the distance education opportunities available to students. It must present a clear and accurate statement of the instructional delivery systems, learning formats, prerequisites, expected learning outcomes, completion requirements, and other relevant requirements.

Effective distance education programs should employ faculty teamwork, collaborative learning, focused outcomes and shared goals, active creation of knowledge and meaning, and meaningful interaction and feedback. Curriculum design should recognize

these components of quality distance education experiences and provide for them intentionally and systematically.

Part 11. FACULTY/STUDENT INTERACTIONS

Distance education programs must provide for appropriate and effective faculty and student interactions.

These interactions may use one or more media, but should be relevant to the course activities and accessible to all students.

Faculty members must provide for interchange among students, when possible, and with students in all cases.

These interactions must be learning-oriented and ideally should lead to a sense of community among learners and faculty members.

Part 12. TECHNOLOGICAL COMPETENCE of STUDENTS

Distance students must be competent in appropriate technologies or instructional delivery approaches used in the distance education programs of the institution.

Students in distance education programs should possess attributes associated with their ability to succeed in educational programs equal to that of other students admitted elsewhere to the institution.

Part 13. ACCESS TO STUDENT and ACADEMIC SERVICES

Institutions must provide appropriate student services for all students enrolled in distance education programs. These services must be sufficiently comprehensive to be responsive to the special needs of all distance students.

The needs of distance students should be carefully analyzed. Programs and services to aid these students should be carefully designed to meet their particular needs.

Institutions offering distance education programs must provide a fully functioning program of distributed education services.

Distributed educational services are those designed to be delivered in learning environments where student and teacher are separated by time and/or space. These services may be divided into three levels of service. The first level provides comprehensive and thorough information about the institution, programs, and services. The second level includes links to other relevant information sources, frequently asked questions about programs of study, and direct access to human resources including phone numbers and e-mail addresses. The third level should provide access to mechanisms to permit the formation of virtual communities of learners.

Services to students must be of comparable quality to services provided to on-campus students.

In many areas, the services to distance students are nearly identical to those provided to on-campus students. Services in admission, financial aid, and registration, for example, might be indistinguishable from those provided to on-campus students. Other services, however, such as advising, counseling, tutoring, career services, wellness programs, and opportunities to engage in aesthetic and culturally enriching activities, may require significant modification to services provided to on-campus students.

Part 14. EDUCATIONAL SUPPORT SERVICES
The required program of distributed educational services must include at least the following:

14.A Information for Prospective Students
Information must be provided in anticipation that the prospective distance student will need to make decisions about whether to undertake study in this form. This information must include the following:

Subpart 14. AA
Pre-admission. **Information must be no less comprehensive than that available to students during campus visits prior to admission. Information about what it is like to be a distance learner in general, and what it is like to be a distance learner specifically at the institution offering the services, must be accessible and effectively communicated.**

Web pages may be a good vehicle for making information available to distance learners.

Subpart 14. AB
Enrollment. **Certain materials and processes must be described and provided through other suitable and readily accessible formats.**

Among these may be the catalog, academic advising, registration, the student handbook, and information related to services provided specifically for, and expectations of, distance learners.

Policies applicable to all students, such as the academic dishonesty policy and other information mandated by law, must be distributed and include

information concerning how the institution manages such issues for students studying via distance education.

Subpart 14. AC
Academic Program Information. **Prospective students must have access to full descriptive materials about all courses and programs. Requirements of students, including all course prerequisites and technical competence and equipment, must be stated clearly.**

Information should:
- be easily identified and highly visible and clearly organized on web pages
- provide a credible presentation of the institution and its distance learning programs
- provide prospective students with an opportunity to assess their personal readiness for distance learning
- provide students the tools to assess their hardware and software requirements and capabilities
- include costs, transferability, course sequencing, and equipment requirements
- contact sources

14.B Admission
Applications for admission must be provided in a manner that is practical and that can be completed without undue assistance. These applications must be processed in a manner equitable with that of resident students. Application and admission counseling must be made available to distance learners.

The admission process should be described in a detailed, step-by-step fashion. Admission requirements should be specified clearly. Criteria used in admission decisions should be specified clearly. Applications should be provided in several forms (e.g., printed, online), along with clear instructions. Deadlines should be specific and explicit.

14.C Financial Aid
Information about financial aid must be provided to distance students and the application process must be described clearly. Eligibility requirements must be specifically outlined including all institutional financial aid policies. Deadlines for application for financial aid must be clearly stated. Student enrollment in multiple institutions must be recognized and applications for financial aid properly administered.

Distance students applying for financial aid should be provided...
- General information about financial aid
- Clearly described types of financial aid available

- Specified costs of attendance
- Information about average percent of financial need met
- Other relevant forms
- Online information when appropriate, but also available in print form

14.D Registration

Distance students must be provided registration services for each new term or course in a clear, timely, and user-friendly manner. Registration services must accommodate students enrolled in courses and programs taught asynchronously.

Registration policies and processes should be clearly described. Alternative registration methods (e.g., online, print, fax, walk-in) should be identified and provided.

14.E Orientation Services

Orientation to the institution and to the processes of learning required of new distance students must be offered.

The orientation program should be interactive. As with the delivery of instructional services, orientation may employ a variety of methods of communication and should be accessible.

The orientation process should be interactive and must provide opportunities for student-to-student where possible and faculty (or other staff) member-to-student exchanges. Any qualified member of the faculty or staff may deliver this interactive orientation.

All requirements for new distance students must be specified in the orientation program. All services available to new students must be specified.

Prospective learners should be provided a sense of the nature of distance learning along with tips for success.

Academic integrity and related policy issues must be covered in orientation. All applicable student codes must be communicated.

14.F Academic Advising

Academic advising must be readily available throughout the academic year and convenient to both students and advisors.

The academic advising program developed for distance students should be designed around their particular needs.

Advising services must be commensurate with services provided to on campus students in course selection and registration. Additional services to assist students in goal setting and educational and life planning must be provided as needed.

The academic advising services should include:

- One-on-one access to advisors by phone, Internet, or other communication tools
- All general education and major requirements
- Self-help pointers to educational planning and course selection
- Articulation information between programs and institutions
- Advising guidelines, such as curriculum guides
- Access to personal academic records (e.g., courses taken and completed, grades, GPA)

14.G Technical Support

The institution must provide information concerning the equipment, software, and type of Internet service provider students will need to participate fully in their courses and programs.

The institution must take steps to insure that students have the technical skills necessary to participate fully in the academic program and must provide an introduction to the specific applications students will need.

Technical support must be available at times convenient to the students enrolled in distance education courses and programs.

Technical support should include:

- Eligibility for technical support
- Tutorials for dealing with common technical difficulties
- Self-help tools
- A help line/help service

14.H Career Services

Career services must be provided for distance students appropriate to their needs. Their eligibility to receive them must be made clear.

Information about career service processes should be accessible to all students in a form consistent with the format of interaction.

These services may include, but are not limited to, self-exploration, self-assessment, goal setting, decision-making, educational planning, career planning, career information, co-op education, and job search services. Self-help tools for career decision-making and on-line searches for positions should be provided.

Opportunities for experiential learning, such as internships, service learning, cooperative education, and part-time jobs, should be effectively marketed and accessible for distance learners.

14.I Library Services

The institution must provide an orientation to library

services, which includes effective on-line search strategies geared to the programs of study offered at a distance. Service expectations must be defined.

Access to reference materials, periodicals, and books needed to fulfill course requirements must be readily available. Courses with unique or significant needs for library access must provide this information as part of the introduction to the course. Reference services must be available to individual students.

Library services should include:
- Reference support
- Convenient access to document delivery services
- Online tutorials on conducting library research
- Procedures that allow students to obtain necessary books and materials within a reasonable time period should be operable

14.J Services for Students with Disabilities
Accessible services to distance students with disabilities must be provided. The institution's policies concerning reasonable and appropriate accommodations must be provided to the student.

Web pages should conform to World Wide Web (W3C) Content Accessibility Guidelines that explain how to make web pages content accessible to people with disabilities. These guidelines emphasize the importance of providing text equivalents of non-text content such as images, pre-recorded audio, and video.

Assistance in the availability and use of assistive technology must be provided.

14.K Personal Counseling
Counseling services essential to assist distance students to achieve their goals must be provided.

Reasonable efforts should be made to extend comparable counseling services to distance education students. Counseling services, especially in their traditional forms that require face-to-face interaction, cannot be delivered in most distance education formats; however, services that effectively use electronic technologies should be offered when appropriate.

Counseling services for distance education students must be offered in accordance with applicable ethical standards, including ethical guidelines and standards for practice for counseling online. Counselors must develop or adopt ethical standards for their services.

These counseling services should include:
- Descriptions of available counseling services
- For those experiencing a mental health crisis, contact with a

personal counselor on campus, referrals to local emergency care resources, and phone numbers for crisis hotlines
- Self-help tools, including on-line links to appropriate Internet sites and information about finding local referral assistance

14.L Academic Support Services
Information concerning academic support services must be made available.

Distance Learning students should have opportunities for developing learning strategies and getting assistance with content comprehension. Tutoring services, supplemental instruction, and other academic support services should be available to all distance education students. These services should conform to the CAS Standards for Learning Assistance Programs in terms of their quality.

14.M Instructional Materials
Convenient delivery of instructional materials must be provided to all distance students.

Where campus bookstores are available, their services should include:
- Merchandise displayed visually
- Relevant policies about bookstore operations
- Online methods for locating course textbooks and materials
- Alternative methods for ordering books and supplies

14.N Promoting Identity with the Institution
Distance learners must be provided a reasonable opportunity to connect with other students and their instructors. Means of regular communication among students and their instructors must be provided.

Regular communication with distance learners, such as in newsletters, should be offered. Frequent announcements to distance learners though such means as web pages should be provided. Efforts to create virtual communities among distance learners should be made, when appropriate.

Creative use of electronic or other messages that would likely promote an enhanced sense of community such as bulletin boards, special events, institutional news briefs, and opportunities in special interest groups or projects may be provided.

14.O Other Student Services
Additional student services deemed to be necessary or appropriate to the circumstances of each institution's distance education programs must be provided.

Traditional campus services such as leadership development programs and housing services may not be necessarily appropriate or necessary to distance students. Where indicated, however, they should be provided in forms equivalent to those on campus.

Information about health and wellness programs should be made available to distance education students. Referrals to local health-care providers and prescriptions by mail may be examples of services to be provided.

Information about student activities, including organizations, leisure and recreational activities, and cultural and entertainment events may be provided to distance education students when possible.

Part 15. ETHICAL TEACHING and LEARNING

All persons involved in the delivery of Distance Education Programs (DEP) must adhere to the highest principles of ethical behavior. DEP must develop or adopt and implement appropriate statements of ethical practice. DEP must publish these statements and ensure their periodic review by relevant constituencies.

Students must be informed of the applicable ethical standards at the time of their initial enrollment.

Training on ethical principles and guidelines for professionals who deliver the instructional services must be provided. Training on principles and guidelines must be promulgated and enforced by the institution.

Professional association statements of ethical principles and guidelines also are suitable.

DEP staff members must ensure that privacy and confidentiality are maintained with respect to all communications and records to the extent that such records are protected under the law and appropriate statements of ethical practice. Information contained in students' education records must not be disclosed without written consent except as allowed by relevant laws and institutional policies. Staff members must disclose to appropriate authorities information judged to be of an emergency nature, especially when the safety of the individual or others is involved, or when otherwise required by institutional policy or relevant law.

All DEP staff members must be aware of and comply with the provisions contained in the institution's human subjects research policy and in other relevant institutional policies addressing ethical practices and confidentiality of research data concerning individuals.

DEP staff members must recognize and avoid personal conflict of interest or appearance thereof in their transactions with students and others. DEP staff members must strive to insure the fair, objective, and impartial treatment of all persons with whom they deal. Staff members must not participate in nor condone any form of harassment that demeans persons or creates an intimidating, hostile, or offensive campus environment.

When handling institutional funds, all DEP staff members must ensure that such funds are managed in accordance with established and responsible accounting procedures and the fiscal policies or processes of the institution.

DEP staff members must perform their duties within the limits of their training, expertise, and competence. When these limits are exceeded, individuals in need of further assistance must be referred to persons possessing appropriate qualifications.

DEP staff members must use suitable means to confront and otherwise hold accountable other staff members who exhibit unethical behavior.

DEP staff members must be knowledgeable about and practice ethical behavior in the use of technology.

Part 16. ASSESSMENT and EVALUATION

Distance Education Programs (DEP) must conduct regular assessment and evaluations. DEP must employ effective qualitative and quantitative methodologies as appropriate, to determine whether and to what degree the stated mission, goals, and student learning and development outcomes are being met. The process must employ sufficient and sound assessment measures to ensure comprehensiveness. Data collected must include responses from students and other affected constituencies.

DEP must evaluate periodically how well they complement and enhance the institution's stated mission and educational effectiveness.

Results of these evaluations must be used in revising and improving programs and services and in recognizing staff performance.

Program evaluation must address student retention and attrition of distance learners.

Evaluations should be clearly focused. Evaluations should include course content and quality of instruction apart from mode of delivery and use of technologies.

General Standards revised in 2002; DEP content developed in 2000

THE ROLE of EDUCATION ABROAD PROGRAMS AND SERVICES
CAS Contextual Statement

According to the Institute of International Education's *Open Doors* publication, in 2002-2003 a record 175,000 U.S. American college students participated in an education abroad program for academic credit. This figure marks an 8.5% rise from the preceding year and a dramatic 145% increase from 1991-1992 totals. This visible trend toward greater interest and participation in education abroad among college students has happened concurrent to the proliferation of education abroad opportunities. Education abroad participants may now choose from a variety of programs that differ according to program location, type, duration, academic focus, method of instruction, and coordinating entity.

Given the array of programs and the increasing interest in global education among students, their parents, educational institutions, state governments, and federal governments, as well as in other countries throughout the world, the need for Education Abroad Programs and Services (EAPS) offices to have and meet standards can not be overstated.

Over the past 40 years, guidelines and standards for providing EAPS have been developed by various groups, such as NAFSA: Association of International Educators, the Council on International Educational Exchange, the Institute for International Education, accreditation associations such as the Middle States Association, the Institute for the International Education of Students, and more recently The Forum on Education Abroad. NAFSA and The Forum include developing and disseminating professional standards as part of their mission, and The Forum is registered as the Standards Development Organization for education abroad with the Department of Justice and the Federal Trade Commission. CAS drew heavily on the publications of these groups in developing the CAS standards for EAPS. See the Resources section below for access to these organizations and some of their standards materials. They provide essential additional perspectives to any standards assessment of an education abroad office or organization.

On college and university campuses, EAPS responsibilities may be centralized in one office on campus or may be dispersed in multiple schools and departments across the institution. Education abroad directors and advisers must be familiar with a broad spectrum of campus services, processes and systems, including but not limited to academic advising services, financial aid, registration, residence life, health services, counseling services, off-campus regulations and guidelines, disability services, risk management, judicial affairs, career services, alumni services, and development.

In a time of global uncertainties, education abroad directors and advisers must pay special attention to matters of safety and security.

Assessment is a critical aspect of ensuring the integrity of EAPS. EAPS should systematically assess the following areas as identified in the Institute for the International Education of Students' publication <u>The IES Map (Model Assessment Project) for Study Abroad</u>:

- The student learning environment
- Student learning and the development of intercultural competence
- Resources for academic and student support
- Program administration and development (Source:http://www.iesabroad.org/opencms/opencms/IESAbroad/Advisors_and_Faculty/iesMap.html?id=92)

CAS users are encouraged to review the IES assessment definitions.

Some education abroad opportunities are administered by the student's home campus, some by other institutions, and some by organizations. Whenever the programs are not administered by the home campus, the EAPS is responsible for investigating and approving the programs before allowing students to participate in and receive credit through them.

The following standards and guidelines are aimed at home-country campus-based offices, although non-campus based EAPS organizations and overseas institutions will find many of the sections helpful. The provision of Education Abroad Programs and Services has become a global enterprise.

References, Readings, and Resources

Forum on Education Abroad Standards of Good Practice for Education Abroad, 2004. Available at http://www.forumea.org/pdfs/ForumStandards.pdf

Institute of International Education. (published annually). *Open doors report 2004: Report on international educational exchange*. See http://opendoors.iienetwork.org/

IES MAP for Study Abroad: Charting a Course for Quality, published by the Institute for the International Education of Students, Chicago, 2003. Available at http://www.iesabroad.org/iesMAP.do

Martin, P.C., Brockington, J. L., & Hoffa W. W. (2005). *NAFSA's Guide to Education Abroad for Advisers and Administrators, Third Edition*. Washington, D.C.: NAFSA: Association of International Educators.

NAFSA's Code of Ethics at http://www.nafsa.org/content/InsideNAFSA/EthicsandStandards/CodeOfEthics/CodeOfEthics.htm. Originally created in 1989, updated in 2003.

Spencer, S. E., & Tuma, K. (Eds.). (2002). *The guide to successful short-term programs abroad*. Washington, D.C.: NAFSA: Association of International Educators.

NAFSA: Association of International Educators: http://www.nafsa.org/

The Forum on Education Abroad: http://www.forumea.org/

IES MAP (Model Assessment Program) http://www.iesabroad.org/ iesMap.do

Alliance for International Educational and Cultural Exchange: http://www.alliance-exchange.org/

American International Education Foundation: http://www.ief-usa.org/

Association for Studies in International Education: http://www.asie.org/index.htm

Frontiers, The Interdisciplinary Journal of Study Abroad http://www.frontiersjournal.com/

Institute of International Education Annual Report *Open Doors*: http://opendoors.iienetwork.org/

Institute of International Education: http://www.iienetwork.org/

The Center for Global Education: http://www.lmu.edu/globaled/index.html

Contributor: Susan Komives, University of Maryland, ACPA

EDUCATION ABROAD PROGRAMS AND SERVICES
CAS Standards and Guidelines

Part 1. MISSION

Education Abroad Programs and Services (EAPS) facilitate and oversee student participation in educational experiences that occur in countries outside the institution's home country.

EAPS must incorporate student learning and student development in its mission. EAPS must enhance overall educational experiences. EAPS must develop, record, disseminate, implement, and regularly review its mission and goals. Mission statements must be consistent with the mission and goals of the institution and with the standards in this document. EAPS must operate as an integral part of the institution's overall mission.

EAPS' overall mission should address the following:
- whom the program serves
- what the program values
- what the program seeks to accomplish (goals and objectives)
- a commitment to providing an appropriate variety of types of education abroad programs, in a variety of locations for academic credit
- a commitment to supporting students prior to, during, and after their education abroad experience
- a commitment to collaborating with internal and external stakeholders

Part 2. PROGRAM

The formal education of students consists of the curriculum and the co-curriculum, and must promote student learning and development that is purposeful and holistic. Educational Abroad Programs and Services (EAPS) must identify relevant and desirable student learning and development outcomes and provide programs and services that encourage the achievement of those outcomes.

The EAPS should facilitate student participation in a variety of types of education abroad programs such as:
- programs where the student mobility is from the home institution (the school at which the student is seeking the degree) to a host institution (the school outside the institution's home country at which the student receives instruction and services while abroad)
- institutional exchanges where students from the home institution trade places with students from the host institution
- consortia programs that involve two or more institutions
- third-party programs where the program is administered outside the institution

Relevant and desirable learning outcomes of EAPS include: intellectual growth, effective communication, realistic self-appraisal, enhanced self-esteem, clarified values, career choices, leadership development, healthy behaviors, meaningful interpersonal relationships, independence, collaboration, social responsibility, satisfying and productive lifestyles, appreciation of diversity, spiritual awareness, and achievement of personal and educational goals.

EAPS must provide evidence of its impact on the achievement of student learning and development outcomes.

The table below offers examples of achievement of student learning and development outcomes.

Student Learning and Development Outcome Domains

Intellectual growth
Examples of achievement indicators

Produces personal and educational goal statements; Employs critical thinking in problem solving; Increases tolerance for ambiguity; Uses complex information from a variety of sources including personal experience and observation to form a decision or opinion; Obtains a degree; Applies previously understood information and concepts to a new situation or setting; Expresses appreciation for literature, the fine arts, mathematics, sciences, and social sciences; Constructively evaluates the advantages and disadvantages of both the home and host culture

Effective communication
Examples of achievement indicators

Increases proficiency in foreign language ability; Develops intercultural communication skills; Writes and speaks coherently and effectively; Writes and speaks after reflection; Influences others through writing, speaking, or artistic expression; Effectively articulates abstract ideas; Uses appropriate syntax; Makes presentations or gives performances

Enhanced self-esteem
Examples of achievement indicators

Shows self-respect and respect for others; Initiates actions toward achievement of goals; Takes reasonable risks; Demonstrates assertive behavior; Functions without need for constant reassurance from others; Feels confident about having cross-cultural interactions; Comfortable exploring the host environment both independently and with a group

Realistic self-appraisal

Examples of achievement indicators

Reflects on how personal experiences influence growth and development; Articulates personal skills and abilities; Makes decisions and acts in congruence with personal values; Acknowledges personal strengths and weaknesses; Articulates rationale for personal behavior; Seeks feedback from others; Learns from past experiences

Clarified values

Examples of achievement indicators

Reflects on values of various cultures; Understands sources of cultural values; Articulates personal values; Acts in congruence with personal values; Makes decisions that reflect personal values; Demonstrates willingness to scrutinize personal beliefs and values; Identifies personal, work, and lifestyle values and explains how they influence decision-making; Demonstrates an appreciation for different values and belief systems

Career choices

Examples of achievement indicators

Demonstrates awareness of how the education abroad experience may influence career choice; Evaluates the personal merits of both intrinsic and extrinsic work values; Articulates career choices based on assessment of interests, values, skills and abilities; Documents knowledge, skills, and accomplishments resulting from formal education, education abroad, work experiences, community service, and volunteer experiences; Makes connections between classroom and out-of-classroom learning; Constructs a resume with clear job objectives and evidence of related knowledge, skills, and accomplishments; Articulates the characteristics of a preferred work environment; Comprehends the world of work; Takes steps to initiate a job search or seek advanced education

Leadership development

Examples of achievement indicators

Articulates leadership philosophy or style that is culturally sensitive; Serves in a leadership position in a student organization; Comprehends the dynamics of a group; Exhibits democratic principles as a leader; Exhibits ability to visualize a group purpose and desired outcomes; Incorporates curricular and co-curricular knowledge and experiences into ever-evolving leadership philosophy and style

Healthy behavior

Examples of achievement indicators

Chooses behaviors and environments that promote health and reduce risk; Articulates the relationship between health and wellness and accomplishing life-long goals; Exhibits behaviors that advance healthy communities at home and abroad

Meaningful interpersonal relationships

Examples of achievement indicators

Develops and maintains satisfying cross-cultural interpersonal relationships; Establishes mutually rewarding relationships with friends and colleagues at home and abroad; Listens to and considers others' points of view; Treats others with respect

Independence

Examples of achievement indicators

Exhibits self-reliant behaviors; Functions autonomously; Exhibits ability to function interdependently; Accepts supervision as needed; Manages time effectively

Collaboration

Examples of achievement indicators

Works cooperatively with others across cultures; Seeks the involvement of others; Seeks feedback from others; Contributes to achievement of a group goal; Exhibits effective listening skills

Social responsibility

Examples of achievement indicators

Understands and participates in relevant governance systems across cultures; Understands, abides by, and participates in the development, maintenance, and orderly change of community, social, and legal standards or norms; Appropriately challenges the unfair, unjust, or uncivil behavior of other individuals or groups without being ethnocentric; Participates in service or volunteer activities

Satisfying and productive lifestyles

Examples of achievement indicators

Achieves balance between education, work, and leisure time; Articulates and meets goals for work, leisure and education; Overcomes obstacles that hamper goal achievement; Functions on the basis of personal identity, ethical, spiritual, and moral values; Articulates long-term goals and objectives

Appreciating diversity

Examples of achievement indicators

Understands one's own identity and culture; Appreciates and understands norms of and variations in different cultures; Seeks involvement with people different from oneself; Seeks involvement in diverse interests; Articulates the advantages and challenges of a diverse society; Challenges appropriately the abusive use of stereotypes by others; Understands the impact of diversity on one's own society as well as on a global scale

Spiritual awareness

Examples of achievement indicators

Develops and articulates personal belief system;

Understands roles of spirituality in personal, group, and cultural values and behaviors

Personal and educational goals

Examples of achievement indicators

Sets, articulates, and pursues individual goals; Articulates personal and educational goals and objectives; Uses personal and educational goals to guide decisions; Understands the effect of one's personal and educational goals on others

Programs and services must be (a) intentional, (b) coherent, (c) based on theories and knowledge of learning and human development, (d) reflective of developmental and demographic profiles of the student population, and (e) responsive to needs of individuals, special populations, and communities.

To fulfill its mission and goals effectively, EAPS must include the following elements:

- **Clear and consistent academic policies and guidelines for home and host institutions**

Admissions policies and procedures should be clearly articulated to students. Academic policies and procedures for awarding credit and understanding course grade equivalencies should also be clearly articulated to students before they depart for an education abroad program. Guidance with course selection should be offered regarding course transferability and equivalency. Coursework should be appropriately challenging; course requirements and methods of evaluating performance should be clearly stated; feedback should be provided to students periodically, in keeping with host country norms. Opportunities should be provided that allow the learning that occurs as a result of the EAPS experience to be integrated into subsequent educational experiences.

- **Curricular and co-curricular opportunities that are related to the mission and purpose of the specific education abroad program**

The curricular and co-curricular components of each education abroad opportunity should make effective use of the location and resources of the host country; students should be encouraged to engage with the host culture and to reflect on the differences and similarities between the intellectual, political, cultural, spiritual, and social institutions of the home and host countries. Students' curricular and co-curricular experiences should contribute to their appreciation and respect for cultural differences in general. Students should be encouraged to immerse themselves in the host culture, interact with host nationals, practice and

improve their language and intercultural communication abilities, and reflect on their value systems in the context of living in another culture.

EAPS should provide opportunities for internships, service-learning, and other field study experiences that are related to the mission and purpose of the specific education abroad program. EAPS should incorporate opportunities to synthesize the learning that occurs as a result of these out-of-classroom experiences into future educational and life experiences. **Where field opportunities exist, they must be appropriately supervised and evaluated and must relate to the mission of the EAPS and institution. Awarding of credit for internships or field studies must be consistent with the policies of the home institution.**

- **Pre-departure advising and orientation programs**

Pre-departure advising and orientation sessions must inform students about program requirements, academic credit and transfer policies, visa and passport requirements, and housing and travel arrangements, as well as financial, health, liability, insurance, safety, and security information. International students at the home institution must be advised to determine their re-entry status. Students must be asked directly and encouraged strongly to share information about any on-going health concerns before departing for their program locations. Home and host institution codes of conduct that apply to students while abroad must be clearly articulated; consequences of not following these codes of conduct must be clearly defined and communicated. Students must be provided with an introduction to intercultural communication and preparation for the cultural transition, including resources on culture shock and cultural adjustment. Orientation programs must identify resources for students so that they may educate themselves about the culture, customs, and laws of the host countries. EAPS must provide students with the contact the information of their home country's embassy or consulate at their host site.

Students should be advised to utilize the appropriate campus or community resources (travel medicine, financial aid, immigration status, etc.) before departure.

- **Information about student financial assistance**

- **On-going advising and support services for students while they are abroad**

On-going advising and support services throughout the duration of the education abroad program should be provided either through the home or host institution.

- **Re-entry support and orientation programs for returning students**

  Upon return, re-entry programs and services must support re-acculturation to the home country, relationships, and the institution.

  Returning students should be encouraged to integrate their experience abroad into their continued learning, including sharing their stories and experiences with other students, faculty members, and staff members.

Part 3. LEADERSHIP

Effective and ethical leadership is essential to the success of Education Abroad Programs and Services (EAPS). Institutions must appoint, position, and empower leaders within the administrative structure to accomplish stated missions. Leaders at various levels must be selected on the basis of formal education and training, relevant work experience, personal skills and competencies, relevant professional credentials, as well as potential for promoting learning and development in students, applying effective practices to educational processes, and enhancing institutional effectiveness. Institutions must determine expectations of accountability for leaders and fairly assess their performance.

EAPS leaders must exercise authority over resources for which they are responsible to achieve their respective missions.

EAPS leaders must:
- **articulate a vision for their organization**
- **set goals and objectives based on the needs and capabilities of the population served**
- **promote student learning and development**
- **prescribe and practice ethical behavior**
- **recruit, select, supervise, and develop others in the organization**
- **manage financial resources**
- **coordinate human resources**
- **plan, budget for, and evaluate personnel and programs**
- **apply effective practices to educational and administrative processes**
- **communicate effectively**
- **initiate collaborative interaction between individuals and agencies that possess legitimate concerns and interests in the functional area**

EAPS leaders must identify and find means to address individual, organizational, or environmental conditions that inhibit goal achievement.

EAPS leaders must promote home and host campus environments that result in multiple opportunities for student learning and development.

EAPS leaders must continuously improve programs and services in response to changing needs of students and other constituents, and evolving institutional priorities.

EAPS leaders should establish working relationships with institutional agents, including provosts, academic deans, department chairs, risk managers, academic advisors, and student affairs professionals on the home campus to promote programs and engender support.

Part 4. ORGANIZATION and MANAGEMENT

Guided by an overarching intent to ensure student learning and development, Education Abroad Programs and Services (EAPS) must be structured purposefully and managed effectively to achieve stated goals. Evidence of appropriate structure must include current and accessible policies and procedures, written performance expectations for all employees, functional workflow graphics or organizational charts, and clearly stated service delivery expectations.

Evidence of effective management must include use of comprehensive and accurate information for decisions, clear sources and channels of authority, effective communication practices, decision-making and conflict resolution procedures, responsiveness to changing conditions, accountability and evaluation systems, and recognition and reward processes. EAPS must provide channels within the organization for regular review of administrative policies and procedures.

To fulfill its mission and goals effectively, EAPS must:
- **provide leadership for integrating education abroad into the wider administrative and academic structure of the institution**
- **efficiently and effectively administer the programs they coordinate**
- **advise students appropriately, based on their interests, needs, financial ability, language proficiency, and academic background, as they choose an education abroad program**

EAPS should be housed within a centralized unit.

Information about education abroad opportunities and related institutional policies must be easily accessible.

Part 5. HUMAN RESOURCES

Education Abroad Programs and Services (EAPS) must be staffed adequately by individuals qualified to accomplish its mission and goals. Within established guidelines of the institution, EAPS must establish procedures for staff selection, training, and evaluation; set expectations for supervision; and provide appropriate professional development opportunities. EAPS must strive to improve the professional competence and skills of all personnel it employs.

EAPS professional staff members must hold an earned graduate degree in a field relevant to the position they hold or must possess an appropriate combination of educational credentials and related work experience.

EAPS staff should have experience living or studying abroad. Entry into the profession by educators from a variety of academic backgrounds is encouraged.

EAPS professional staff members must be knowledgeable and competent in the following areas:
- cultural sensitivity
- intercultural communication
- culture shock, reverse culture shock, and cultural adjustment
- student advising and counseling
- crisis management
- budgetary and financial management
- collaboration with faculty members and academic departments at home and host institutions
- organizational policies (e.g., admissions, credit transfer, financial aid, travel regulations, immigration policies, insurance)
- pre-departure and re-entry issues
- travel and living abroad
- technology
- country specific health, safety, and security concerns

EAPS professional staff members should be knowledgeable and competent in such areas as:
- foreign language(s)
- countries, cultures, and regions where their students most frequently study (e.g. culture, customs, language, art, geography, political system, economic system, history, traditions, values, laws)
- other countries' educational systems

- human development
- marketing and promoting education abroad programs
- experiential education

Degree or credential-seeking interns must be qualified by enrollment in an appropriate field of study and by relevant experience. These individuals must be trained and supervised adequately by professional staff members holding educational credentials and related work experience appropriate for supervision.

Student employees and volunteers must be carefully selected, trained, supervised, and evaluated. They must be trained on how and when to refer those in need of assistance to qualified staff members and have access to a supervisor for assistance in making these judgments. Student employees and volunteers must be provided clear and precise job descriptions, pre-service training based on assessed needs, and continuing staff development.

EAPS must have technical and support staff members adequate to accomplish its mission. Staff members must be technologically proficient and qualified to perform their job functions, be knowledgeable of ethical and legal uses of technology, and have access to training. The level of staffing and workloads must be adequate and appropriate for program and service demands.

Salary levels and fringe benefits for all staff members must be commensurate with those for comparable positions within the institution, in similar institutions, and in the relevant geographic area.

EAPS must institute hiring and promotion practices that are fair, inclusive, and non-discriminatory.

EAPS must employ a diverse staff to provide readily identifiable role models for students and to enrich the campus community.
EAPS must create and maintain position descriptions for all staff members and provide regular performance planning and appraisals.

EAPS must have a system for regular staff evaluation and must provide access to continuing education and professional development opportunities, including in-service training programs and participation in professional conferences and workshops.

Part 6. FINANCIAL RESOURCES

Education Abroad Programs and Services (EAPS) must have adequate funding to accomplish its mission and goals. Funding priorities must be determined within the context of the stated mission, goals, objectives and comprehensive analysis of the needs and capabilities of students and the availability of internal or external resources.

EAPS must demonstrate fiscal responsibility and cost effectiveness consistent with institutional protocols.

EAPS should offer education abroad programs to students at affordable costs.

EAPS should consider grant writing and fundraising efforts to increase their financial resources, including funding for need-based student scholarships.

EAPS should encourage their institution to create institutional education abroad scholarships and grants, both need and merit-based.

Part 7. FACILITIES, TECHNOLOGY, and EQUIPMENT
Education Abroad Programs and Services (EAPS) must have adequate, suitably located facilities, adequate technology, and equipment to support its mission and goals efficiently and effectively. Facilities, technology, and equipment must be evaluated regularly and be in compliance with relevant federal, state, provincial, and local requirements to provide for access, health, safety, and security.

Office facilities of home and host institutions must be provided to accommodate EAPS goals. Home and host campus facilities must allow for privacy during student advising.

Residential and non-residential student facilities at host institutions must be provided to accommodate program goals, be safe and secure, and be maintained to meet student needs.

Residential and non-residential student facilities should be located conveniently at host institutions.

Host institutions should provide students with services equivalent to the services provided to host institution students (i.e. telephone, computer, Internet) at similar costs.

Part 8: LEGAL RESPONSIBILITIES
Education Abroad Program and Services (EAPS) staff members must be knowledgeable about and responsive to laws and regulations that relate to their respective responsibilities. EAPS staff members must inform users of programs and services and officials,

as appropriate, of legal obligations and limitations including constitutional, statutory, regulatory, and case law; mandatory laws and orders emanating from federal, state/provincial and local governments; and the institution's policies.

EAPS staff members must know where to refer program participants for information on host country laws and host institution policies and procedures. EAPS staff members must make participants aware of home institution consequences of breaking these laws, policies, and procedures.

EAPS staff members must use reasonable and informed practices to limit the liability exposure of the institution, its officers, employees, and agents. EAPS staff members must be informed about institutional policies regarding personal liability and related insurance coverage options.

The institution must provide access to legal advice for staff members as needed to carry out assigned responsibilities.

The institution must inform staff and students in a timely and systematic fashion about extraordinary or changing legal obligations and potential liabilities.

EAPS staff members must ensure that expectations for participant conduct - including but not limited to drug and alcohol abuse, sexual assault and harassment, academic integrity, and social conduct - are clearly articulated in program materials and in pre-departure and onsite orientations.

EAPS must have a clearly defined crisis management program.

The home institution should have a clearly defined crisis management program that integrates and supports the EAPS plan. The home institution should obtain the host institution crisis management plan.

EAPS staff members should develop collaborative relationships with relevant home and host institutional departments (e.g., general counsel, student conduct programs) in order to assess and minimize risk and develop appropriate resources for students.

Part 9. EQUITY and ACCESS
Education Abroad Programs and Services (EAPS) staff members must ensure that programs and services are provided on a fair and equitable basis. Facilities, programs, and services must be accessible. Hours of operation and delivery of and access to programs

and services must be responsive to the needs of all students and other constituents. Each program and service must adhere to the spirit and intent of equal opportunity laws.

Programs and Services must be open and readily accessible to all students and must not discriminate except where sanctioned by law and institutional policy. Discrimination must be avoided on the basis of age; color; creed; cultural heritage; disability; ethnicity; gender identity; nationality; political affiliation; religious affiliation; sex, sexual orientation; or social, economic, marital, or veteran status.

Consistent with their mission and goals, EAPS must take affirmative action to remedy significant imbalances in student participation and staffing patterns.

As the demographic profiles of campuses change and new institutional delivery methods are introduced, institutions must recognize the needs of students who participate in distance learning for access to programs and services offered on campus. Institutions must provide appropriate services in ways that are accessible to distance learners and assist them in identifying and gaining access to other appropriate services in their geographic region.

EAPS should encourage students from underrepresented groups (e.g., gender, ethnicity, age, disability, marital status, socioeconomic status, academic major, religious affiliation, sexual orientation) to apply and participate in education abroad programs.

Part 10. CAMPUS and EXTERNAL RELATIONS

Education Abroad Programs and Services (EAPS) must establish, maintain, and promote effective relations with relevant individuals, campus offices, and external agencies.

EAPS staff members should collaborate with:
- departments on the home campus (i.e., academic departments and programs, Registrar, Academic Affairs, Financial Aid, Financial Services, Student Affairs, International Student and Scholar Services, Admissions, Career Advising, Clinical Health Services, Counseling Services, Institutional Advancement, Disability Support Services, Multicultural Centers, Residential Life)
- consulates of host countries
- home country embassies and consulates abroad
- faculty members at home and abroad who teach or do research in fields related to home institution education abroad opportunities
- administrative staff at the host institution responsible for students from abroad
- external program providers

EAPS staff members should collaborate with third-party program providers as appropriate to sustain existing programs and establish new opportunities to increase the diversity of options for students. Interested individuals (faculty members or other campus personnel) should be encouraged to become involved in education abroad by suggesting possible opportunities, proposing specific programs, or presenting and encouraging discussions about education abroad.

Agreements between EAPS and other institutions to promote education abroad, whether exchange agreements or co-sponsorship of programs, should be supportive of the institution's overall mission and collaborative in regards to academic objectives and standards.

EAPS should ensure that faculty members, administrators, staff members, and students are aware of education abroad opportunities. EAPS should work to ensure that programs are accurately described in advisory and promotional materials and that their purposes, financial implications, and educational objectives are clearly stated.

Part 11. DIVERSITY

Within the context of each institution's unique mission, diversity enriches the community and enhances the collegiate experience for all; therefore, Education Abroad Programs and Services (EAPS) must nurture environments where commonalties and differences among people are recognized and honored.

EAPS must promote educational experiences that are characterized by open and continuous communication that deepens understanding of one's own identity, culture, and heritage, and that of others. EAPS must educate and promote respect about commonalties and differences in their historical and cultural contexts.

EAPS must address the characteristics and needs of a diverse population when establishing and implementing policies and procedures.

EAPS must intentionally foster students' understanding of cross-cultural differences and encourage participants to reflect on these differences at home and abroad.

EAPS must intentionally prepare participants for living and studying in the intended host country.

EAPS staff members must actively work with all interested participants to select an education abroad program suitable to their needs, skills, and eligibility.

EAPS should intentionally seek and promote diversity within education abroad program participants (including underrepresented groups), faculty program leaders, and staff members.

Part 12. ETHICS

All persons involved in the delivery of Education Abroad Programs and Services (EAPS) must adhere to the highest principles of ethical behavior. EAPS must develop or adopt and implement appropriate statements of ethical practice. Programs and services must publish these statements and ensure their periodic review by relevant constituencies.

EAPS staff members must ensure that privacy and confidentiality are maintained with respect to all communications and records to the extent that such records are protected under the law and appropriate statements of ethical practice. Information contained in students' education records must not be disclosed without written consent except as allowed by relevant laws and institutional policies. EAPS staff members must disclose to appropriate authorities information judged to be of an emergency nature, especially when the safety of the individual or others is involved, or when otherwise required by institutional policy or relevant law.

All EAPS staff members must be aware of and comply with the provisions contained in the institution's human subjects research policy and in other relevant institutional policies addressing ethical practices and confidentiality of research data concerning individuals.

EAPS staff members must recognize and avoid personal conflict of interest or appearance thereof in their transactions with students and others.

EAPS staff members must strive to insure the fair, objective, and impartial treatment of all persons with whom they deal. Staff members must not participate in nor condone any form of harassment that demeans persons or creates an intimidating, hostile, or offensive campus environment.

When handling institutional funds, all EAPS staff members must ensure that such funds are managed in accordance with established and responsible accounting procedures and the fiscal policies or processes of the institution.

EAPS staff members must perform their duties within the limits of their training, expertise, and competence. When these limits are exceeded, individuals in need of further assistance must be referred to persons possessing appropriate qualifications.

EAPS staff members must use suitable means to confront and otherwise hold accountable other staff members who exhibit unethical behavior.

EAPS staff members must be knowledgeable about and practice ethical behavior in the use of technology.

EAPS home and host staff members must have ethical and unbiased procedures in place for terminating participants.

Termination procedures should be made public and provided to participants prior to their participation in an education abroad program.

EAPS home and host staff members must have ethical guidelines in place for advising and interacting with students and their families.

In addition to standard records privacy and confidentiality policies, EAPS should develop procedures to assure the long-term protection of students' records.

Part 13: ASSESSMENT and EVALUATION

Education Abroad Programs and Services (EAPS) must conduct regular assessment and evaluations. EAPS must employ effective qualitative and quantitative methodologies as appropriate, to determine whether and to what degree the stated mission, goals, and student learning and development outcomes are being met. The process must employ sufficient and sound assessment measures to ensure comprehensiveness. Data collected must include responses from students and other affected constituencies.

EAPS must evaluate periodically how well they complement and enhance the institution's stated mission and educational effectiveness.

Results of these evaluations must be used in revising and improving programs and services and in recognizing staff performance.

EAPS standards developed in 2005

THE ROLE of STUDENT FINANCIAL AID PROGRAMS
CAS Standards Contextual Statement

According to the American Council on Education, there are three major sources of student financial aid: the federal government, state governments, and colleges and universities. The U.S. federal government is the largest single provider, underwriting 69 % of all financial aid available, mostly through loans. In the 2001-02 academic year, U.S. federal education loans accounted for three-quarters of all federal student aid and more than half of aid from all sources, or over $41 billion. In addition, the 2003 status report on Pell Grants stated that the Pell Grant program provides approximately $11 billion in assistance annually to one-quarter of undergraduates (American Council on Education, 2006). Private sources of aid, such as scholarships from companies and loans from nongovernmental organizations, also are available. In total, approximately $89 billion in financial aid was provided to students in 2001-02, including federal and nonfederal loans, federal and state grants, and institutional grants (American Council on Education, 2006). The mission of the financial aid office focuses on service to students and stewardship of funds. Practically speaking, the financial aid office assumes primary responsibility on behalf of the institution for compliance with government requirements.

An effective and comprehensive aid program must be supported by leaders at the institution who understand the increasing administrative and operational responsibilities, obligations, and the potential liabilities that accompany participation in federal aid programs. It also requires that leaders be aware of the challenges and conflicts imposed on the administration of aid and the delivery of quality services to their students. Leaders can take several steps to ensure that the financial aid program advances the goals of the institution without compromising service quality or program integrity. The consistency between institutional goals and those of the aid program can be evaluated by examining the level of commitment of internal resources, the composition of aid packages, the levels of unmet need, and the extent of commitment to need-based aid.

The establishment and support of goals and measures that ensure high-quality financial aid operations should be a high priority for all institutions. Of equal importance is the leaders' responsibility for educating the institution's community about its goals and mission and the role of financial aid in defining and meeting them. Communicating the importance of financial aid to both internal and external constituencies is critical. Presidents, trustees, and others must understand and support the policies of their financial aid programs and serve as effective advocates at the institutional and governmental levels. These advocacy efforts should . . .

- Provide opportunities for representatives from all academic and administrative areas of the institution to discuss and help formulate institutional goals

- Coordinate with the financial aid office to develop mission statements and strategic goals that consider its relationship with other offices and present its philosophy, purpose, goals, and strategies, and the principles governing financial aid awards; disseminate these statements to demonstrate the leadership's support of them and their complementary relationship to broader objectives of the institution

- Provide forums to make known the impact of pending federal and state developments on the institution and the financial aid office

- Communicate widely the criteria by which financial aid policies are defined and evaluated, and create opportunities to highlight program successes and the positive impact they have on students and the broader community

Institutions committed to these strategies draw upon tools provided by the government, the National Association of Student Financial Aid Administrators (NASFAA), and other non-governmental entities.

References, Readings, and Resources

American Council on Education. (2006). [Online]. *Paying for College.* Available http://www.acenet.edu/Content/NavigationMenu/ProgramsServices/CIP/

National Association of Independent Colleges and Universities (1995). *Federal regulations affecting higher education.* Washington, DC: Author.

National Association of Student Financial Aid Administrators (NASFAA). 1920 L Street, NW, Suite 200, Washington, DC 20036-5020. (202) 785-0453; fax (202) 785-1487; website www.nasfaa.org

Contributors:
Current edition: Jan Arminio, Shippensburg University, NACA
Previous editions: Joan H. Crissman & A. Dallas Martin, Jr., NASFAA

FINANCIAL AID PROGRAMS

CAS Standards and Guidelines

Part 1. MISSION

Financial Aid Programs (FAP) must incorporate student learning and student development in its mission. The program must enhance overall educational experiences. FAP must develop, record, disseminate, implement and regularly review its mission and goals. Mission statements must be consistent with the mission and goals of the institution and with the standards in this document. FAP must operate as an integral part of the institution's overall mission.

FAP shall develop, review, and disseminate financial resources to students to assist them in achieving their educational goals from pre-enrollment through graduation. Many aspects of financial aid are mandated by federal and state entities that define the parameters within which institutional programs must operate. In a manner consistent with the goals of the institution the mission and goals of FAP must address the following:

Students in Transition

Such students move from secondary to postsecondary education, from one postsecondary institution to another including undergraduate to graduate school, and return from a period of non-enrollment to formal learning or re-enrollment in the institution.

Awarding Practices

Such practices establish, promulgate, and implement financial aid criteria that accurately represent the financial needs of the applicant pool, set priorities within this group, and respond with funding to the extent possible.

Financial Counseling

Such counseling provides high quality services to students for (a) the purpose of providing better understanding of financial aid, (b) financial guidance, (c) individual review of situations that may require special consideration, and (d) guidance in academic and financial matters especially as they relates to satisfactory academic progress.

Goal Integration

Goals should be consistent with the mission, goals, policies, procedures and characteristics of the institution and be compatible with the ability of the institution to provide adequate resources to meet the needs and educational goals of the students.

Review of Goals

Institutional goals for financial aid should be developed and reviewed regularly. Such goals should be consistent with statements of good practices articulated by relevant and appropriate professional associations such as the National Association of Student Financial Aid Administrators and the Canadian Association of Student Financial Aid Administrators.

Part 2. PROGRAM

The formal education of students consists of the curriculum and the co-curriculum, and must promote student learning and development that is purposeful and holistic. Financial Aid Programs (FAP) must identify relevant and desirable student learning and development outcomes and provide programs and services that encourage the achievement of those outcomes.

Relevant and desirable outcomes include: intellectual growth, effective communication, realistic self-appraisal, enhanced self-esteem, clarified values, career choices, leadership development, healthy behaviors, meaningful interpersonal relationships, independence, collaboration, social responsibility, satisfying and productive lifestyles, appreciation of diversity, spiritual awareness, and achievement of personal and educational goals.

FAP must provide evidence of its impact on the achievement of student learning and development outcomes.

The table below offers examples of evidence of achievement of student learning and development.

Student Learning and Development Outcome Domains

Intellectual growth

Examples of achievement indicators

Produces personal and educational goal statements; Employs critical thinking in problem solving; Uses complex information from a variety of sources including personal experience and observation to form a decision or opinion; Obtains a degree; Applies previously understood information and concepts to a new situation or setting; Expresses appreciation for literature, the fine arts, mathematics, sciences, and social sciences

Effective communication

Examples of achievement indicators

Writes and speaks coherently and effectively; Writes and speaks after reflection; Able to influence others through writing, speaking or artistic expression; Effectively articulates abstract ideas; Uses appropriate syntax; Makes presentations or gives performances

Enhanced self-esteem
Examples of achievement indicators

Shows self-respect and respect for others; Initiates actions toward achievement of goals; Takes reasonable risks; Demonstrates assertive behavior; Functions without need for constant reassurance from others

Realistic self-appraisal
Examples of achievement indicators

Articulates personal skills and abilities; Makes decisions and acts in congruence with personal values; Acknowledges personal strengths and weaknesses; Articulates rationale for personal behavior; Seeks feedback from others; Learns from past experiences

Clarified values
Examples of achievement indicators

Articulates personal values; Acts in congruence with personal values; Makes decisions that reflect personal values; Demonstrates willingness to scrutinize personal beliefs and values; Identifies personal, work, and lifestyle values and explains how they influence decision-making

Career choices
Examples of achievement indicators

Articulates career choices based on assessment of interests, values, skills and abilities; Documents knowledge, skills and accomplishments resulting from formal education, work experience, community service, and volunteer experiences; Makes the connections between classroom and out-of-classroom learning; Can construct a resume with clear job objectives and evidence of related knowledge, skills and accomplishments; Articulates the characteristics of a preferred work environment; Comprehends the world of work; Takes steps to initiate a job search or seek advanced education

Leadership development
Examples of achievement indicators

Articulates leadership philosophy or style; Serves in a leadership position in a student organization; Comprehends the dynamics of a group; Exhibits democratic principles as a leader; Exhibits ability to visualize a group purpose and desired outcomes

Healthy behavior
Examples of achievement indicators

Chooses behaviors and environments that promote health and reduce risk; Articulates the relationship between health and wellness and accomplishing life- long goals; Exhibits behaviors that advance a healthy community.

Meaningful interpersonal relationships
Examples of achievement indicators

Develops and maintains satisfying interpersonal relationships; Establishes mutually rewarding relationships with friends and colleagues; Listens to and considers others' points of view; Treats others with respect

Independence
Examples of achievement indicators

Exhibits self-reliant behaviors; Functions autonomously; Exhibits ability to function interdependently; Accepts supervision as needed; Manages time effectively

Collaboration
Examples of achievement indicators

Works cooperatively with others; Seeks the involvement of others; Seeks feedback from others; Contributes to achievement of a group goal; Exhibits effective listening skills

Social responsibility
Examples of achievement indicators

Understands and participates in relevant governance systems; Understands, abides by, and participates in the development, maintenance, and/or orderly change of community, social, and legal standards or norms; Appropriately challenges the unfair, unjust, or uncivil behavior of other individuals or groups; Participates in service/volunteer activities

Satisfying and productive lifestyles
Examples of achievement indicators

Achieves balance between education, work and leisure time; Articulates and meets goals for work, leisure, and education; Overcomes obstacles that hamper goal achievement; Functions on the basis of personal identity, ethical, spiritual, and moral values; Articulates long-term goals and objectives

Appreciating diversity
Examples of achievement indicators

Understands one's own identity and culture; Seeks involvement with people different from oneself; Seeks involvement in diverse interests; Articulates the advantages and challenges of a diverse society; Challenges appropriately the abusive use of stereotypes by others; Understands the impact of diversity on one's own society

Spiritual awareness
Examples of achievement indicators

Develops and articulates personal belief system; Understands roles of spirituality in personal and group values and behaviors

Personal and educational goals

Examples of achievement indicators

Sets, articulates, and pursues individual goals; Articulates personal and educational goals and objectives; Uses personal and educational goals to guide decisions; Understands the effect of one's personal and educational goals on others

FAP must be (a) intentional, (b) coherent, (c) based on theories and knowledge of learning and human development, (d) reflective of developmental and demographic profiles of the student population, and (e) responsive to needs of individuals, special populations, and communities.

FAP must assist students by addressing financial issues that may serve as barriers to the achievement of educational goals.

FAP must:

- comply with federal and state law, provincial statutes, and institutional policies
- promote and maintain integrity, accuracy, and timeliness in the delivery of financial aid
- provide adequate information for students and parents to make informed decisions regarding the financing of their education
- promote and provide equal access to eligible students interested in pursuing an education at the institution

Part 3. LEADERSHIP

Effective and ethical leadership is essential to the success of all organizations. Institutions must appoint, position, and empower leaders within the administrative structure to accomplish stated missions. Financial Aid Programs (FAP) leaders at various levels must be selected on the basis of formal education and training, relevant work experience, personal skills and competencies, relevant professional credentials, as well as potential for promoting learning and development in students, applying effective practices to educational processes, and enhancing institutional effectiveness. Institutions must determine expectations of accountability for leaders and fairly assess their performance.

FAP leaders must exercise authority over resources for which they are responsible to achieve their respective missions.

FAP leaders must:

- articulate a vision for their organization
- set goals and objectives based on the needs and capabilities of the population served
- promote student learning and development
- prescribe and practice ethical behavior
- recruit, select, supervise, and develop others in the organization
- manage financial resources
- coordinate human resources
- plan, budget for, and evaluate personnel and programs
- apply effective practices to educational and administrative processes
- communicate effectively
- initiate collaborative interaction between individuals and agencies that possess legitimate concerns and interests in the functional area

FAP leaders must identify and find means to address individual, organizational, or environmental conditions that inhibit goal achievement.

FAP leaders must promote campus environments that result in multiple opportunities for student learning and development.

FAP leaders must continuously improve programs and services in response to changing needs of students and other constituents, and evolving institutional priorities.

The institution should designate a well-qualified senior administrator with appropriate financial aid experience and training to effectively lead the financial aid program staff.

The senior financial aid administrator must be able to advocate for and to represent the financial needs of students, the operation and staffing of the financial aid program, and the institution.

The senior financial aid administrator must ensure the development of:

- a set of policies and procedures that includes descriptions of the administrative processes
- clearly stated criteria used in the decision making process for financial aid and the source of authority for the criteria employed
- steps for appealing evaluating, or revising policies and procedures
- a statement of the institution's mission, goals, and objectives for the financial aid programs
- an effective system to manage the programs, services, and personnel of the financial aid program
- an assessment plan for its programs and services

- **means for coordinating the financial aid program with other institutional agencies**
- **develop criteria for selecting qualified staff and ensuring adequate opportunities for staff development**

Part 4. ORGANIZATION and MANAGEMENT

Guided by an overarching intent to ensure student learning and development, Financial Aid Programs (FAP) must be structured purposefully and managed effectively to achieve stated goals. Evidence of appropriate structure must include current and accessible policies and procedures, written performance expectations for all employees, functional workflow graphics or organizational charts, and clearly stated service delivery expectations.

Evidence of effective management must include use of comprehensive and accurate information for decisions, clear sources and channels of authority, effective communication practices, decision-making and conflict resolution procedures, responsiveness to changing conditions, accountability and evaluation systems, and recognition and reward processes. FAP must provide channels within the organization for regular review of administrative policies and procedures.

Part 5. HUMAN RESOURCES

Financial Aid Program (FAP) must be staffed adequately by individuals qualified to accomplish its mission and goals. Within established guidelines of the institution, the program must establish procedures for staff selection, training, and evaluation; set expectations for supervision, and provide appropriate professional development opportunities. FAP must strive to improve the professional competence and skills of all personnel it employs.

Continued training is essential for all financial aid staff. It is imperative to be alert to change within the field and to be able to integrate changes into daily practice.

Every financial aid staff members should be...

- familiar with federal, state/provincial, and institutional regulations, policies, and practices regarding the awarding of financial aid funds
- willing to seek out and implement new ideas
- able to translate new ideas into practical methods for improving the overall operation of the financial aid program
- respectful of the confidential nature of the profession
- willing to seek out and use new conceptual frameworks and

equipment that bring information to students more clearly and effectively
- aware of relevant developments in the higher education and be able to incorporate these developments

Financial aid staff members should have knowledge and understanding of the mission, programs and services of the institution. Institutional training should be provided for all staff members to include

- a thorough tour of the campus
- familiarization with publications, academic programs, admission policies, and services of the institution
- rights and responsibilities as an employee of the institution

Job descriptions with the duties and responsibilities for each staff member should be developed.

Professional FAP staff members must hold an earned graduate degree in a field relevant to the position they hold or must possess an appropriate combination of educational credentials and related work experience.

Suggested formal training in preparation for professional financial aid employment include such fields as business administration, computer sciences, information systems, college student personnel, higher education administration, counseling and other human behavior disciplines; course work may include computer literacy, research and statistical methods, counseling, legal issues of higher education, and leadership and management.

Professional staff members should be competent to provide assistance to students that may include but not be limited to, the following:

- careful and concerned analysis of each student's need
- knowledgeable guidance and counseling on all financial aid issues and concern
- explanation of federal and state, and, if appropriate, provincial statues of Canada
- interpretation of institutional policies and procedures

Degree or credential-seeking interns must be qualified by enrollment in an appropriate field of study and by relevant experience. These individuals must be trained and supervised adequately by professional staff members holding educational credentials and related work experience appropriate for supervision.

Student employees and volunteers must be carefully selected, trained, supervised, and evaluated. They must be trained on how and when to refer those in need of assistance to qualified staff members and have access to a supervisor for assistance in making these judgments. Student employees and volunteers

must be provided clear and precise job descriptions, pre-service training based on assessed needs, and continuing staff development.

Student employees and volunteers should be trained in public relations, referral techniques, peer counseling, and dissemination of information. They should be knowledgeable in their individual job assignments and understand the confidential nature of their positions.

FAP must have technical and support staff members adequate to accomplish its mission. Staff members must be technologically proficient and qualified to perform their job functions, be knowledgeable of ethical and legal uses of technology, and have access to training. The level of staffing and workloads must be adequate and appropriate for program and service demands.

Support staff members should be skilled in interpersonal communications, public relations, referral techniques and dissemination of information. support staff members with higher technical responsibilities should posses the academic background and experience for effective performance. support staff members should understand the confidential nature of their job.

Salary levels and fringe benefits for all FAP staff members must be commensurate with those for comparable positions within the institution, in similar institutions, and in the relevant geographic area.

FAP must institute hiring and promotion practices that are fair, inclusive, and non-discriminatory. The program must employ a diverse staff to provide readily identifiable role models for students and to enrich the campus community.

FAP must create and maintain position descriptions for all staff members and provide regular performance planning and appraisals.

FAP must have a system for regular staff evaluation and must provide access to continuing education and professional development opportunities, including in-service training programs and participation in professional conferences and workshops.

Part 6. FINANCIAL RESOURCES
Financial Aid Programs (FAP) must have adequate funding to accomplish its mission and goals. Funding priorities must be determined within the context of the stated mission, goals, objectives and comprehensive analysis of the needs and capabilities of students, and the availability of internal or external resources. FAP must demonstrate fiscal responsibility and cost

effectiveness consistent with institutional protocols.

Funding for the financial aid program should cover staff salaries; purchases and maintenance of office furnishings and equipment, including state of the art technology; purchases of supplies and materials; telephone, fax, electronic communication and postage costs; printing and media costs; institutional membership in appropriate professional organizations; relevant subscriptions and necessary library resources; attendance at professional association meetings, conferences, workshops and other professional development activities. In addition to institutional commitment of general funds, other funding sources may be considered including state appropriations, federal resources, student fees, fines, donations and contributions.

The FAP budget must be properly prepared, clearly detailed and defined, continually monitored, and adequately funded for full program support.

Part 7. FACILITIES, TECHNOLOGY, and EQUIPMENT
Financial Aid Programs (FAP) must have adequate, suitably located facilities, adequate technology, and equipment to support its mission and goals efficiently and effectively. Facilities, technology, and equipment must be evaluated regularly and be in compliance with relevant federal, state, provincial, and local requirements to provide for access, health, safety, and security.

The program should have facilities or have access to
- private office or space for confidential counseling, interviewing, and other meetings
- office, reception, and storage space and security sufficient to accommodate assigned staff, supplies, equipment, library resources, and machinery
- conference room or meeting space

The financial aid program should be readily accessible, included on campus maps, and have highly visible signage.

Part 8. LEGAL RESPONSIBILITIES
Financial Aid Programs (FAP) staff members must be knowledgeable about and responsive to laws and regulations that relate to their respective responsibilities. Staff members must inform users of programs and services and officials, as appropriate, of legal obligations and limitations including constitutional, statutory, regulatory, and case law; mandatory laws and orders emanating from federal, state/provincial and local governments; and the institution's policies.

FAP staff members must use reasonable and informed practices to limit the liability exposure of

the institution, its officers, employees, and agents. Staff members must be informed about institutional policies regarding personal liability and related insurance coverage options.

The institution must provide access to legal advice for FAP staff members as needed to carry out assigned responsibilities.

The institution must inform FAP staff and students in a timely and systematic fashion about extraordinary or changing legal obligations and potential liabilities.

Part 9. EQUITY and ACCESS

Staff members must ensure that Financial Aid Programs (FAP) are provided on a fair and equitable basis. Facilities, programs and services must be accessible. Hours of operation and delivery of and access to programs and services must be responsive to the needs of all students and other constituents. FAP must adhere to the spirit and intent of equal opportunity laws.

The program should ensure that its programs, services, and facilities are accessible to and provide hours of operation that respond to the needs of special populations, including traditionally under-represented, evening, part-time, and commuter students.

FAP must be open and readily accessible to all students and must not discriminate except where sanctioned by law and institutional policy. Discrimination must be avoided on the bases of age; color; creed; cultural heritage; disability; ethnicity; gender identity; nationality; political affiliation; religious affiliation; sex; sexual orientation; or social, economic, marital, or veteran status.

Consistent with their mission and goals, FAP must take affirmative action to remedy significant imbalances in student participation and staffing patterns.

As the demographic profiles of campuses change and new instructional delivery methods are introduced, institutions must recognize the needs of students who participate in distance learning for access to programs and services offered on campus. Institutions must provide appropriate services in ways that are accessible to distance learners and assist them in identifying and gaining access to other appropriate services in their geographic region.

Part 10. CAMPUS and EXTERNAL RELATIONS

Financial Aid Programs (FAP) must establish, maintain, and promote effective relations with relevant individuals, campus offices, and external agencies.

Institutional functions and constituencies linked to financial aid typically include admissions, registration and records, athletics, business services, academic advising, counseling services, student affirmative action, outreach programs, educational opportunity programs, career planning and placement, institutional development, and faculty and alumni affairs.

Financial aid documents must be accurate and their confidentiality maintained by all offices at the institution.

Financial aid and admission decisions should be made independently. However, the financial aid program should have access to appropriate information in the student's admission file to assure compliance with applicable rules and regulations.

The financial aid program should maintain relationships with interested groups within the community regarding general and institutional financial aid practices. The community may include grant and scholarship agencies, high schools, and other community outreach programs.

Part 11. DIVERSITY

Within the context of each institution's unique mission, diversity enriches the community and enhances the collegiate experience for all; therefore, Financial Aid Programs (FAP) must nurture environments where commonalties and differences among people are recognized and honored.

FAP must promote educational experiences that are characterized by open and continuous communication that deepens understanding of one's own identity, culture, and heritage, and that of others. The program must educate and promote respect about commonalties and differences in their historical and cultural contexts.

FAP must address the characteristics and needs of a diverse population when establishing and implementing policies and procedures.

Financial aid staff members should be particularly sensitive to the needs of traditionally under-represented students and students with special needs.

Part 12. ETHICS

Students must be provided access to Financial Aid Programs (FAP) on a fair and equitable basis.

All persons involved in the delivery of FAP must adhere to the highest principles of ethical behavior. FAP must develop or adopt and implement appropriate statements of ethical practice. The program must publish these statements and ensure their periodic review by relevant constituencies .

In the formulation of these standards, ethical standards statements adopted by the profession at large or relevant professional associations may be of assistance and should be considered.

FAP staff members must ensure that privacy and confidentiality are maintained with respect to all communications and records to the extent that such records are protected under the law and appropriate statements of ethical practice. Information contained in students' education records must not be disclosed without written consent except as allowed by relevant laws and institutional policies. Staff members must disclose to appropriate authorities information judged to be of an emergency nature, especially when the safety of the individual or others is involved, or when otherwise required by institutional policy or relevant law.

All FAP staff members must be aware of and comply with the provisions contained in the institution's human subjects research policy and in other relevant institutional policies addressing ethical practices and confidentiality of research data concerning individuals.

FAP staff members must recognize and avoid personal conflict of interest or appearance thereof in their transactions with students and others.

FAP staff members must strive to insure the fair, objective, and impartial treatment of all persons with whom they deal. Staff members must not participate in nor condone any form of harassment that demeans persons or creates an intimidating, hostile, or offensive campus environment.

When handling institutional funds, all FAP staff members must ensure that such funds are managed in accordance with established and responsible accounting procedures and the fiscal policies or processes of the institution.

FAP staff members must perform their duties within the limits of their training, expertise, and competence. When these limits are exceeded, individuals in need of further assistance must be referred to persons possessing appropriate qualifications.

FAP staff members must use suitable means to confront and otherwise hold accountable other staff members who exhibit unethical behavior.

FAP staff members must be knowledgeable about and practice ethical behavior in the use of technology.

Financial aid administrators must insure timely and fair administration of policies regarding financial aid decisions and proper notification.

Publications and written communications should include a financial aid deadlines and information on opportunities for financial aid.

Financial aid must be awarded in compliance with applicable rules and regulations governing financial aid.

When appropriate, the senior financial aid administrator and professional staff members may need to exercise professional judgment in making exceptions to established financial aid policies. These decisions should be made in a fair and objective manner with supporting documentation.

Part 13. ASSESSMENT and EVALUATION

Financial Aid Programs (FAP) must conduct regular assessment and evaluations. The program must employ effective qualitative and quantitative methodologies as appropriate, to determine whether and to what degree the stated mission, goals, and student learning and development outcomes are being met. The process must employ sufficient and sound assessment measures to ensure comprehensiveness. Data collected must include responses from students and other affected constituencies.

FAP must evaluate periodically how well they complement and enhance the institution's stated mission and educational effectiveness.

Results of these evaluations must be used in revising and improving programs and services and in recognizing staff performance.

Publications such as the Institutional Guide for Financial Aid Self-Evaluation, published by the National Association of Student Financial Aid Administrators, may be used to evaluate financial aid programs and services.

General Standards revised in 2002; FAP content developed/ revised in 1996.

THE ROLE of FRATERNITY and SORORITY ADVISING
CAS Contextual Statement

Historical Perspective

Fraternal organizations have been part of the college landscape since the establishment of Phi Beta Kappa in 1776 at the College of William and Mary. Today, over 750,000 undergraduates are members of fraternities or sororities. Fraternity and/or sorority chapters exist on over 800 college campuses across the United States and Canada.

A significant growth in fraternity membership following WW II was largely responsible for the establishment of full-time campus fraternity and sorority advisors. From 1975 to the millennium, the existence of the campus fraternity and sorority advisor became even more commonplace. The Association of Fraternity Advisors (AFA), an organization serving student affairs administrators, grew from a few dozen members in 1976 to over 1,400 members by 2006, some 30 years later. Part of the recognizable increase in professional advisors correlates with the 1980s - a remarkable period of growth in undergraduate fraternity and sorority membership. The 1990s were marked by waning membership in established fraternities and sororities; 40% of college campuses saw a decline in membership. At the same time, however, the 1990s saw the growth of many culturally-based fraternities and sororities including both those long established, such as NPHC groups dating back to the turn of the century, and many new groups. Today over 40 different national or regional Latino or Latina oriented organizations exist. Asian oriented fraternities and sororities have emerged as well, establishing their own regional headquarters and colonizing chapters on different campuses. Additionally, several fraternities and sororities have been established for gay and lesbian students. The increasingly diverse and multi-cultural nature of the fraternity and sorority community is solidifying the role of the professional campus advisor – and creating professional demands different from the membership booms of the 1950s and 1980s.

Important Tenets

As a sign of the growing profession of fraternity and sorority advising, in 2003 the Association of Fraternity Advisors established *Core Competencies for Excellence in the Profession* and a Code of Ethics. These documents, together with CAS Standards, provide an excellent framework for institutions and advisors building a programmatic approach to developing their fraternity and sorority community. While variances in institutional approach to advising exist, professionals do share these assumptions regarding the role of the advisor:

1.) The advisor works as an external consultant to individual fraternity and sorority chapters. The advisor encourages autonomy and independence in student decision- making and concurrently provides support that will foster chapter success. In this capacity, the advisor engages undergraduate and alumni leadership toward developing chapter activities that share a connection with the mission of the university.

2.) The advisor serves as a leader in establishing a clear mission for the campus fraternity and sorority community consistent with the institution's mission. This community mission incorporates values of the fraternities and sororities and respects students' interests.

3.) The advisor is actively involved in the development and enforcement of institutional policy relating to fraternities and sororities. The advisor must be adept at consensus building – advocating fraternity and sorority member perspectives while keeping the larger college or university mission at the forefront of discussion and decisions.

4.) The advisor understands current issues that affect college student behavior and educational outcomes. Moreover, the advisor encourages and produces educational programming that draws the student closer to an understanding of behavior and educational outcomes. Such programs would include education on alcohol and drug awareness, multi-cultural sensitivity, leadership education, risk management, and new member education.

5.) The advisor understands alumni and governance structures of the institution and differing fraternal systems and actively educates students about these structures. This understanding would include structural knowledge of the National Association of Latino Fraternal Organizations, Inc. (NALFO), North-American Interfraternity Conference (NIC), National Panhellenic Conference (NPC) and National Pan-Hellenic Council, Inc. (NPHC).

Current Issues

Institutional culture, together with the history, traditions and membership composition of the fraternity and sorority community, will determine the important issues facing a given campus. However, three overriding issues common to professionals across most campuses include:

1.) Addressing High-Risk Alcohol Use Within the Fraternity and Sorority Community
An emerging trend has been to eliminate alcohol in fraternity houses in a manner similar to traditional sorority houses. This practice has received mixed acceptance among various fraternities but has proved successful on a number of campuses. In 2004, an assembly of college and university presidents, inter/national fraternities and sororities and other organizations in higher education, issued *A Call for Values Congruence*, asking for systemic change within the fraternity and sorority community. The assembly identified high risk alcohol use as a systematic problem among fraternities and sororities – a copy of the recommendations for the future are available on the AFA website.

2.) <u>Assessing Educational Outcomes of Fraternity and Sorority Involvement</u>
As the custodians of the out-of-the classroom experience, the advisor is responsible for measuring the impact of that experience, together with the campus programs they support and deliver. Such measurement allows the advisor to ask such questions as: What impact does the fraternity and sorority involvement have on students? Are these experiences desirable? And, how might we shape the fraternity and sorority experience to create a more beneficial effect for students?

3.) <u>Advising & the Role of Multi-Cultural Fraternities and Sororities and the Campus</u>
The variety of approaches to umbrella structures, intake processes, and membership requirements requires advisors to think beyond a traditional fraternity/sorority community comprised only of NPHC, NIC, and NPC member groups. A welcome but new demand is created for the advisor as he or she works to support the interests of a multiplicity of organizations, each celebrating and serving the interests of students that may have been traditionally underrepresented in long established organizations. A list of Latino; Asian; Gay, Lesbian, and Bisexual; and Multi-Cultural fraternities and sororities can be found on the AFA website.

References, Readings, and Resources

Association of Fraternity Advisors; 9640 N. Augusta Drive, Suite 433; Carmel, IN 46032.; 317-876-1632; Fax: 317-876-3891; www.fraternityadvisors.org

AFA encourages the use of resources provided by NALFO, NIC, NPC, NPHC and inter/national fraternities and sororities. Links to these organizations as well as copies of the AFA *Core Competencies for Excellence in the Profession* and Code of Ethics are also available on the website.

Contributors:
Dr. Derick A. Morat, University of the Pacific
Dr. David Ortiz, University of Houston, Clear Lake

FRATERNITY and SORORITY ADVISING PROGRAMS
CAS Standards and Guidelines

Part 1. MISSION

The Fraternity and Sorority Advising Program (FSAP) must incorporate student learning and student development in its mission. The FSAP must enhance overall educational experiences. The FSAP must develop, record, disseminate, implement, and regularly review its mission and goals. Mission statements must be consistent with the mission and goals of the institution and with the standards in this document. The FSAP must operate as an integral part of the institution's overall mission.

The FSAP must promote academic and personal growth and development of students who affiliate with fraternities and sororities and promote the fraternity and sorority community as an integral and productive part of the institution.

To accomplish its mission, the FSAP must:

- promote the intellectual, social, spiritual, moral, civic, and career development, and wellness of students
- provide education and experience in leadership, group dynamics, and organization development
- promote student involvement in co-curricular activities
- promote sponsorship of and participation in community service and philanthropic projects
- promote an appreciation for different lifestyles including cultural and religious heritages
- recognize and encourage the positive learning experiences that are possible in a fraternity and sorority community that has a diversified membership

Participation in a campus chapter represents one of several group affiliation options for college students. Fraternity and sorority affiliation may include: a recruitment process, new/associate member education, initiation (formal induction into the organization), ongoing membership development programming, and lifelong affiliation. Professional staff members should promote student development in all affiliation processes.

Staff members should develop a comprehensive program to promote the education and welfare of participating students and coordinate resources and activities with others in the campus community.

Participation in a fraternity or sorority must promote responsible membership in both the organization and the institution.

Part 2. PROGRAM

The formal education of students consists of the curriculum and the co-curriculum, and must promote student learning and development that is purposeful and holistic. The Fraternity and Sorority Advising Program (FSAP) must identify relevant and desirable student learning and development outcomes and provide programs and services that encourage the achievement of those outcomes.

Relevant and desirable outcomes include: intellectual growth, effective communication, realistic self-appraisal, enhanced self-esteem, clarified values, career choices, leadership development, healthy behaviors, meaningful interpersonal relationships, independence, collaboration, social responsibility, satisfying and productive lifestyles, appreciation of diversity, spiritual awareness, and achievement of personal and educational goals.

The FSAP must provide evidence of its impact on the achievement of student learning and development outcomes.

The table below offers examples of evidence of achievement of student learning and development.

Student Learning and Development Outcome Domains

Leadership development
Examples of achievement indicators

Articulates leadership philosophy or style; Serves in a leadership position in a student organization; Comprehends the dynamics of a group; Exhibits democratic principles as a leader; Exhibits ability to visualize a group purpose and desired outcomes

Intellectual growth
Examples of achievement indicators

Produces personal and educational goal statements; Employs critical thinking in problem solving; Uses complex information from a variety of sources including personal experience and observation to form a decision or opinion; Obtains a degree; Continuously open to learning opportunities; Applies previously understood information and concepts to a new situation or setting; Expresses appreciation for literature, the fine arts, mathematics, sciences, and social sciences

Collaboration
Examples of achievement indicators

Works cooperatively with others; Seeks the involvement of others; Seeks feedback from others; Contributes to achievement of a group goal; Exhibits effective listening skills; Seeks the involvement of others in accomplishing tasks; Serves as a team member to accomplish common goals

Social responsibility
Examples of achievement indicators

Understands and participates in relevant governance systems; Understands, abides by, and participates in the development, maintenance, and/or orderly change of community, social, and legal standards or norms; Appropriately challenges the unfair, unjust, or uncivil behavior of other individuals or groups; Participates in service/volunteer activities

Effective communication
Examples of achievement indicators

Writes and speaks coherently and effectively; Writes and speaks after reflection; Able to influence others through writing, speaking or artistic expression; Effectively articulates abstract ideas; Uses appropriate syntax; Makes presentations or gives performances

Enhanced self-esteem
Examples of achievement indicators

Shows self-respect and respect for others; Initiates actions toward achievement of goals; Takes reasonable risks; Demonstrates assertive behavior; Functions without need for constant reassurance from others

Realistic self-appraisal
Examples of achievement indicators

Articulates personal skills and abilities; Makes decisions and acts in congruence with personal values; Acknowledges personal strengths and weaknesses; Articulates rationale for personal behavior; Seeks feedback from others; Learns from past experiences

Clarified values
Examples of achievement indicators

Articulates personal values; Acts in congruence with personal values; Makes decisions that reflect personal values; Demonstrates willingness to scrutinize personal beliefs and values; Identifies personal, work, and lifestyle values and explains how they influence decision-making

Career choices
Examples of achievement indicators

Articulates career choices based on assessment of interests, values, skills, and abilities; Documents knowledge, skills and accomplishments resulting from formal education, work experience, community service and volunteer experiences; Makes the connections between classroom and out-of-classroom learning; Can construct a resume with clear job objectives and evidence of related knowledge, skills and accomplishments; Articulates the characteristics of a preferred work environment; Comprehends the world of work; Takes steps to initiate a job search or seek advanced education

Healthy behavior
Examples of achievement indicators

Chooses behaviors and environments that promote health and reduce risk; Articulates the relationship between health and wellness and accomplishing life-long goals; Exhibits behaviors that advance a healthy community.

Meaningful interpersonal relationships
Examples of achievement indicators

Develops and maintains satisfying interpersonal relationships; Establishes mutually rewarding relationships with friends and colleagues; Listens to and considers others' points of view; Treats others with respect

Independence
Examples of achievement indicators

Exhibits self-reliant behaviors; Functions autonomously; Exhibits ability to function interdependently; Accepts supervision as needed; Manages time effectively

Satisfying and productive lifestyles
Examples of achievement indicators

Achieves balance between education, work, and leisure time; Articulates and meets goals for work, leisure, and education; Overcomes obstacles that hamper goal achievement; Functions on the basis of personal identity, ethical, spiritual, and moral values; Articulates long-term goals and objectives

Appreciating diversity
Examples of achievement indicators

Understands one's own identity and culture; Seeks involvement with people different from oneself; Seeks involvement in diverse interests; Articulates the advantages and challenges of a diverse society; Challenges appropriately the abusive use of stereotypes by others; Understands the impact of diversity on one's own society

Spiritual awareness
Examples of achievement indicators

Develops and articulates personal belief system; Understands roles of spirituality in personal and group values and behaviors

Personal and educational goals

Examples of achievement indicators

Sets, articulates, and pursues individual goals; Articulates personal and educational goals and objectives; Uses personal and educational goals to guide decisions; Understands the effect of one's personal and educational goals on others

The FSAP must be (a) intentional, (b) coherent, (c) based on theories and knowledge of learning and human development, (d) reflective of developmental and demographic profiles of the student population, and (e) responsive to needs of individuals, special populations, and communities.

The FSAP must include the following elements:

- **Educational programming that enhances member knowledge, understanding, and competencies essential for academic success, personal development, and the exercise of leadership. Educational programming must complement the academic curriculum.**

  Activities that improve the student's chances of academic success are particularly important. Programs should address the maturation and development of students and facilitate the application of knowledge and skills through experiential opportunities.

- **Staff members who provide programs that encourage faculty, staff, and administrator involvement and interaction with students.**

  Leadership programs should help the individual effectively understand and manage group processes, particularly the relevant aspects of self-governance and accountability. Leadership programs also should enable students to gain knowledge about assessing leadership and management skills.

  Good citizenship development programs, including opportunities for self-learning, should assist students in becoming responsible and involved community members.

- **Social and recreational programming that enhances the members' knowledge, understanding, and skills necessary for success and the productive use of leisure time.**

  Social skills programs should assist individuals in developing more mature and satisfying interpersonal relationships.

  Educational programs should promote wellness, teamwork, sportsmanship, and healthy competition.

- **Opportunities for recognition by the institution as appropriate.**

- **The institution and the fraternities and sororities must jointly define their relationship. The relationship statement must be formalized, documented, and disseminated.**

  Campus chapters should participate in the same student organization registration and recognition process as other campus student groups. Additional statements regarding relationships between the institution and its chapters may be defined as appropriate for the campus. Areas of consideration may include:
  - a description of the community
  - historical relationships
  - educational role of fraternities and sororities
  - conditions and responsibilities of affiliation
  - housing and other facilities
  - support and program orientation
  - governance and authority [e.g., national and international organization affiliation and expansion]
  - reference to comprehensive policy documents
  - expectations of the institution and the fraternity and sorority community
  - accountability to other student governing bodies

- **Educational programming that addresses aspects of the fraternity and sorority community that are currently or historically problematic to the institution including housing safety, hazing, alcohol and other drug abuse, sexual harassment, racism, intolerance based on religion or sexual orientation, and other practices and attitudes that diminish human dignity or the physical and social security of the host institution or host community.**

- **Professional staff members who assist students to function productively within the institution and to fully understand the rights and responsibilities of individuals and groups.**

  This may include such activities as interpreting institutional policies, administering a disciplinary system that safeguards due process, conducting performance evaluations, and providing outreach programming to familiarize other departments and community agencies with fraternity and sorority life. Staff members should avoid social situations or appearance of preferential treatment that may pose conflicts of interest.

  The program may include awards for academic and service achievement as well as chapter/community monitoring.

- **Enforcement of applicable laws as well as institutional policies with particular attention paid to housing safety, hazing, the use and possession of alcohol and other drugs, sexual harassment, racism, intolerance based on religion or sexual orientation, and other practices and attitudes that diminish human dignity.**

- **Advising chapters, their individual members, their officers, and their alumni regarding leadership roles and responsibilities.**

Advising services to chapters may include:
- monitoring scholastic standing of chapter members individually and collectively and recommending programs for scholastic improvement
- meeting with chapter leaders to discuss individual and chapter goals and developmental needs;
- assisting student members to understand their responsibilities to the group and to the future of the organization
- attending chapter meetings on a periodic basis
- encouraging chapter members' attendance at regional, and national or international conferences
- evaluating chapter development and recommending programs for improvement
- providing assistance and advice in planning chapter programs (e.g., fund raising, and fiscal management)

Advising services for the fraternity and sorority system (e.g., chapter advisors, house corporation members, chapter presidents, and institutional administrators) may include:
- providing workshops, programs, retreats, and seminars on relevant topics (e.g., human relations, sexual responsibility, and eating disorders/body image)
- coordinating information gathering and dissemination regarding fraternity and sorority life via monthly meetings, newsletters, and/or information bulletins to the various entities involved in fraternity and sorority life
- acquiring resources for and promoting service projects
- advising governing bodies
- providing assistance and advice in the planning of fraternity and sorority community programs (e.g., Fraternity and Sorority Week)
- publishing documents that focus on current events, leadership opportunities, and other information regarding fraternity and sorority life
- developing and distributing a speakers' directory for distribution that focuses on educational programs
- coordinating annual fire prevention and energy conservation programs in conjunction with local agencies for housed organizations
- coordinating cooperative buying efforts in conjunction

with local chapters and/or councils
- monitoring of membership statistics and academic retention by chapter and community

Advising services with other agencies may include:
- collaborating with national or international organizations when applicable/appropriate
- establishing and coordinating communication with local alumni volunteers
- serving as an immediate information resource for students, alumni, and administrators

Part 3. LEADERSHIP

Effective and ethical leadership is essential to the success of all organizations. Institutions must appoint, position and empower Fraternity and Sorority Advising Program (FSAP) leaders within the administrative structure to accomplish stated missions. FSAP leaders at various levels must be selected on the basis of formal education and training, relevant work experience, personal skills and competencies, relevant professional credentials, as well as potential for promoting learning and development in students, applying effective practices to educational processes, and enhancing institutional effectiveness. Institutions must determine expectations of accountability for leaders and fairly assess their performance.

Leaders of the FSAP must exercise authority over resources for which they are responsible to achieve their respective missions.

FSAP leaders must:
- **articulate a vision for their organization**
- **set goals and objectives based on the needs and capabilities of the population served**
- **promote student learning and development**
- **prescribe and practice ethical behavior**
- **recruit, select, supervise, and develop others in the organization**
- **manage financial resources**
- **coordinate human resources**
- **plan, budget for, and evaluate personnel and programs**
- **apply effective practices to educational and administrative processes**
- **communicate effectively**
- **initiate collaborative interaction between individuals and agencies that possess legitimate concerns and interests in the functional area**

FSAP leaders must identify and find means to address individual, organizational, or environmental conditions that inhibit goal achievement.

FSAP leaders must promote campus environments that result in multiple opportunities for student learning and development.

FSAP leaders must continuously improve programs and services in response to changing needs of students and other constituents, and evolving institutional priorities.

Part 4. ORGANIZATION AND MANAGEMENT

Guided by an overarching intent to ensure student learning and development, the Fraternity and Sorority Advising Program (FSAP) must be structured purposefully and managed effectively to achieve stated goals. Evidence of appropriate structure must include current and accessible policies and procedures, written performance expectations for all employees, functional workflow graphics or organizational charts, and clearly stated service delivery expectations.

Evidence of effective management must include use of comprehensive and accurate information for decisions, clear sources and channels of authority, effective communication practices, decision-making and conflict resolution procedures, responsiveness to changing conditions, accountability and evaluation systems, and recognition and reward processes. The FSAP must provide channels within the organization for regular review of administrative policies and procedures.

The FSAP must be organized to encourage positive relationships with students.

The administrative organization of the fraternity and sorority advising program should organized by the size, nature, and mission of the institution. This may include special living arrangements for various levels of affiliation. Fraternities and sororities should be a fully integrated institutional component provided with the necessary resources and support to effect the desired student outcomes. The program should be organized and administered in a manner that permits its stated mission to be fulfilled. The administrative leader of the program should be responsible to the chief student affairs officer or designee.

Part 5. HUMAN RESOURCES

The Fraternity and Sorority Advising Program (FSAP) must be staffed adequately by individuals qualified to accomplish its mission and goals. Within established guidelines of the institution, the FSAP must establish procedures for staff selection, training, and evaluation; set expectations for supervision, and provide appropriate professional development

opportunities. The FSAP must strive to improve the professional competence and skills of all personnel it employs.

FSAP professional staff members must hold an earned graduate degree in a field relevant to the position they hold or must possess an appropriate combination of educational credentials and related work experience.

Appropriate preparatory graduate level coursework may include organizational behavior and development, oral and written communication, research and evaluation, ethics, appraisal of educational practices, group dynamics, budgeting, counseling techniques, leadership development, learning and human development theories, higher education administration, performance appraisal and supervision, administrative uses of computers, legal issues in higher education, and student affairs functions.

Effective management is critical to the success of the program, with expertise often required in the areas of housing, dining, accounting, safety and risk management, alumni relations, and programming. In addition, professional staff members should have experience in the development and implementation of educational programs for students. Staff members should be qualified to work with various internal and external agencies in formulating goals and directions for the chapters and community that are consistent with institutional policies.

Degree or credential-seeking interns must be qualified by enrollment in an appropriate field of study and by relevant experience. These individuals must be trained and supervised adequately by professional staff members holding educational credentials and related work experience appropriate for supervision.

Student employees and volunteers must be carefully selected, trained, supervised, and evaluated. They must be trained on how and when to refer those in need of assistance to qualified staff members and have access to a supervisor for assistance in making these judgments. Student employees and volunteers must be provided clear and precise job descriptions, pre-service training based on assessed needs, and continuing staff development.

The use of graduate assistants and interns may be a way to expand staff capabilities and to provide valuable experience for professionals who have an interest in the field of fraternity and sorority advising.

When appropriate, student employees or volunteers may be utilized and assigned responsibilities for specific projects that are administered or coordinated within the program. Students can lend a valuable perspective to educational programming efforts

The Fraternity and Sorority Advising Program (FSAP) must have technical and support staff members adequate to accomplish its mission. Staff members must be technologically proficient and qualified to perform their job functions, be knowledgeable of ethical and legal uses of technology, and have access to training. The level of staffing and workloads must be adequate and appropriate for program and service demands.

Salary levels and fringe benefits for all FSAP staff members must be commensurate with those for comparable positions within the institution, in similar institutions, and in the relevant geographic area.

The FSAP must institute hiring and promotion practices that are fair, inclusive, and non-discriminatory. Programs and services must employ a diverse staff to provide readily identifiable role models for students and to enrich the campus community.

The FSAP must create and maintain position descriptions for all staff members and provide regular performance planning and appraisals.

The FSAP must have a system for regular staff evaluation and must provide access to continuing education and professional development opportunities, including in-service training programs and participation in professional conferences and workshops.

FSAP professional staff members must engage in professional development opportunities to keep abreast of research, theories, legislation, policies, and developments that affect fraternity and sorority advising.

These activities may include in-service training programs, participation in professional conferences, workshops, and other continuing education activities.

The level of FSAP services must be established and reviewed regularly with regard to demands, enrollment, user surveys, diversity of services offered, institutional resources, and other services available on the campus and in the local community.

Part 6. FINANCIAL RESOURCES
The Fraternity and Sorority Advising Program

(FSAP) must have adequate funding to accomplish its mission and goals. Funding priorities must be determined within the context of the stated mission, goals, objectives and comprehensive analysis of the needs and capabilities of students and the availability of internal or external resources.

The FSAP must demonstrate fiscal responsibility and cost effectiveness consistent with institutional protocols.

When any special institutional or fraternity and sorority funding or expenditure accounts are used, professional staff members should provide for the collection and disbursement of funds and follow the institution's accounting procedures.

Part 7. FACILITIES, TECHNOLOGY, and EQUIPMENT
The Fraternity and Sorority Advising Program (FSAP) must have adequate, suitably located facilities, adequate technology, and equipment to support its mission and goals efficiently and effectively. Facilities, technology, and equipment must be evaluated regularly and be in compliance with relevant federal, state, provincial, and local requirements to provide for access, health, safety, and security.

Contracts with outside vendors must include adherence to ethical and institutional policies.

Houses or common rooms that are owned, rented, or otherwise assigned to fraternities and sororities for their use must be managed in accordance with all applicable regulatory and statutory requirements of the host institution and relevant government authorities.

To effectively carry out essential activities, services, and programs, adequate space should be provided for private consultation, work areas, equipment storage, and resource library. Any space should be accessible and integrated with other institutional student support services.

Part 8. LEGAL RESPONSIBILITIES
Fraternity and Sorority Advising Program (FSAP) staff members must be knowledgeable about and responsive to laws and regulations that relate to their respective responsibilities. FSAP staff members must inform users of programs and services and officials, as appropriate, of legal obligations and limitations including constitutional, statutory, regulatory, and case law; mandatory laws and orders emanating from federal, state/provincial and local governments; and the institution's policies.

FSAP staff members must use reasonable and informed practices to limit the liability exposure of the institution, its officers, employees, and agents. Staff members must be informed about institutional policies regarding personal liability and related insurance coverage options.

The institution must provide access to legal advice for FSAP staff members as needed to carry out assigned responsibilities.

The institution must inform FSAP staff and students in a timely and systematic fashion about extraordinary or changing legal obligations and potential liabilities.

Part 9. EQUITY AND ACCESS

Fraternity and Sorority Advising Programs (FSAP) staff members must ensure that services and programs are provided on a fair and equitable basis. Facilities, programs and services must be accessible. Hours of operation and delivery of and access to programs and services must be responsive to the needs of all students and other constituents. The FSAP must adhere to the spirit and intent of equal opportunity laws.

The FSAP must be open and readily accessible to all students and must not discriminate except where sanctioned by law and institutional policy. Discrimination must especially be avoided on the bases of age; color; creed; cultural heritage; disability; ethnicity; gender identity; nationality; political affiliation; religious affiliation; sex; sexual orientation; or social, economic, marital, or veteran status.

Consistent with their mission and goals, the FSAP must take affirmative action to remedy significant imbalances in student participation and staffing patterns.

As the demographic profiles of campuses change and new instructional delivery methods are introduced, institutions must recognize the needs of students who participate in distance learning for access to programs and services offered on campus. Institutions must provide appropriate services in ways that are accessible to distance learners and assist them in identifying and gaining access to other appropriate services in their geographic region.

The FSAP program must advocate for the needs of specific under-represented populations.

Part 10. CAMPUS and EXTERNAL RELATIONS

The Fraternity and Sorority Advising Program (FSAP) must establish, maintain, and promote effective relations with relevant individuals, campus offices, and external stakeholders.

FSAP staff members must seek out and utilize multiple learning resource opportunities in the delivery of services and programs. These include the national or international headquarters staff, alumni, chapter officers and members, faculty members, institutional administrators, and community resources.

The FSAP must maintain effective contact with its local chapters' national and international representatives.

A team approach in working with students in the local chapters should be a common goal of advisors, alumni, and national or international representatives.

Faculty and staff members are valuable as chapter advisors and role models for students. They may serve on committees that focus on institutional issues affecting the fraternity and sorority community. Further, faculty members can help shape the institutional policy with regard to the fraternity and sorority community. Effective and consistent communications among faculty and staff members, fraternity and sorority chapter members, and chapter advisors can enhance the creation of meaningful learning experiences to improve academic success and increase understanding of educational goals.

Because alumni can serve as valuable resources, program staff members should encourage and enlist a productive level of alumni involvement and assist with information exchange and collaborative programming efforts.

The staff member is typically the principal representative of the administration to the fraternity and sorority community as well as the principal advocate for the fraternity and sorority community within the administration.

Particularly when houses are located in community neighborhoods, good working relationships with neighbors, merchants and community leaders must be maintained to promote cooperative solutions to problems that may arise.

Chapter houses may be governed by the local community and have access to its services and agencies.

The FSAP must assist students in maintaining responsible community living.

Attention should be paid to issues such as fire safety, noise control, parking, trash removal, security, facility and property maintenance and life safety and health code compliance.

Philanthropic activities and community volunteer involvement, which have been traditional components of fraternity and sorority programs, should be developed, maintained, and encouraged.

Part 11. DIVERSITY

Within the context of each institution's unique mission, diversity enriches the community and enhances the collegiate experience for all; therefore, the Fraternity and Sorority Advising Program (FSAP) must nurture environments where commonalties and differences among people are recognized and honored.

The FSAP must promote educational experiences that are characterized by open and continuous communication that deepens understanding of one's own identity, culture, and heritage, and that of others. The FSAP must educate and promote respect about commonalties and differences in their historical and cultural contexts.

The FSAP must address the characteristics and needs of a diverse population when establishing and implementing policies and procedures.

The FSAP must enhance students' knowledge, understanding, skills, and responsibilities associated with being a member of a pluralistic society. The program must provide educational efforts that focus on awareness of cultural, religious, sexual orientation, and gender identity differences.

These efforts should also include assessment of possible prejudices and desirable behavioral changes.

The FSAP must include outreach to underrepresented populations in membership recruitment activities.

Part 12. ETHICS

All persons involved in the delivery of Fraternity and Sorority Advising Programs (FSAP) must adhere to the highest principles of ethical behavior. The FSAP must develop or adopt and implement appropriate statements of ethical practice. The FSAP must publish these statements and ensure their periodic review by relevant constituencies .

Staff members must ensure that privacy and confidentiality are maintained with respect to all communications and records to the extent that such records are protected under the law and appropriate statements of ethical practice. Information contained in students' education records must not be disclosed without written consent except as allowed by relevant laws and institutional policies. FSAP staff members must disclose to appropriate authorities information judged to be of an emergency nature, especially when the safety of the individual or others is involved, or when otherwise required by institutional policy or relevant law.

All FSAP staff members must be aware of and comply with the provisions contained in the institution's human subjects research policy and in other relevant institutional policies addressing ethical practices and confidentiality of research data concerning individuals.

FSAP staff members must recognize and avoid personal conflict of interest or appearance thereof in their transactions with students and others.

FSAP staff members must strive to insure the fair, objective, and impartial treatment of all persons with whom they deal. Staff members must not participate in nor condone any form of harassment that demeans persons or creates an intimidating, hostile, or offensive campus environment.

When handling institutional funds, all FSAP staff members must ensure that such funds are managed in accordance with established and responsible accounting procedures and the fiscal policies or processes of the institution.

FSAP staff members must perform their duties within the limits of their training, expertise, and competence. When these limits are exceeded, individuals in need of further assistance must be referred to persons possessing appropriate qualifications.

FSAP staff members must use suitable means to confront and otherwise hold accountable other staff members who exhibit unethical behavior.

FSAP staff members must be knowledgeable about and practice ethical behavior in the use of technology.

FSAP staff members must be familiar with, adhere to, advocate for, and model relevant ethical standards in the field.

FSAP staff members must demonstrate a high level of ethical conduct. The program must adopt a statement

of ethics that strives to:
- **treat fairly all students who wish to affiliate**
- **eliminate illegal discrimination associated with the selection of members**
- **uphold applicable standards of conduct expressed by the institution and by the respective national or international organizations**

Part 13. ASSESSMENT and EVALUATION

The Fraternity and Sorority Advising Program (FSAP) must conduct regular assessment and evaluations. The FSAP must employ effective qualitative and quantitative methodologies as appropriate, to determine whether and to what degree the stated mission, goals, and student learning and development outcomes are being met. The process must employ sufficient and sound assessment measures to ensure comprehensiveness. Data collected must include responses from students and other affected constituencies.

The FSAP must evaluate periodically how well they complement and enhance the institution's stated mission and educational effectiveness.

Results of these evaluations must be used in revising and improving programs and services and in recognizing staff performance.

The program must seek evaluative feedback from relevant administrative units, community agencies, alumni, students, faculty, and national or international headquarters staff. Selected critical aspects of evaluations should be recorded and maintained by the institution.

Evaluations should address the fraternity and sorority community, programs, services, and activities.

Evaluations should be conducted to determine the strength of leadership, the fulfillment of the community's purposes and priorities, the effectiveness of self-governance procedures, individual chapter congruence with institutional and system purposes, the effectiveness of programs, and the availability and stability of resources.

Periodic assessment and evaluation of chapter needs, goals, and objectives should include chapter vitality and evaluation of each chapter's leadership, self-sufficiency, accountability to purpose, and productive activities.

The living environment of each chapter should be assessed including annual or as-needed safety, sanitation, and quality of life inspections of all housing facilities, kitchens, building electrical systems, heating systems, and fire control equipment.

Research also should be a part of the program. Research topics should include:
- how student development is influenced by fraternity or sorority membership
- influence of participation in members' values
- skill development among members at various stages of membership
- the effect of participation in fraternities and sororities on members' academic performance, retention, and matriculation

General Standards revised in 2002; FSAP content developed/ revised in 1986 & 1996

THE ROLE of HEALTH PROMOTION SERVICES
CAS Standards Contextual Statement

Student learning is both the core goal and the primary outcome of the work of higher education. Several definitions are essential to understanding the functional area of health promotion services on a higher education campus. First, we need to define learning: the document, *Learning Reconsidered* defines learning as a comprehensive, holistic, transformative activity that integrates academic learning and student development, processes that have often been considered separate, and even independent of each other (ACPA/NASPA, 2006). Second, what does it mean to be healthy? Freud said that a person who could love and work is healthy; in the Christian monastic tradition, to be healthy was to pray and to work ("ora et labora")-perhaps they are the same thing. Health may be found in <u>capacity</u> -- the ability to love, to work, to know yourself, and to be, in some way, centered - whether or not you have a chronic illness (Keeling, 1995). And lastly, what is meant by wellness? Wellness is defined as a multi-dimensional model for the understanding of and approach to health that goes beyond the absence of disease or infirmity and includes the integration of social, mental, emotional, spiritual, and physical aspects of health. The concept of wellness was first introduced in the United States in the 1970s as an expanding experience of purposeful and enjoyable living. Wellness refers to a positive state, illness to a negative state (Modeste, 1996). Each of these concepts -- learning, health, and wellness -- are critical to the work of health promotion.

Health promotion services are defined as prevention, education, and wellness policies and initiatives designed to advance the health of students and the campus community in an effort to enhance student learning and create a strong learning environment. Health promotion serves the learning mission of the institution by enhancing students' capability to be effective, engaged learners; by creating healthy, supportive living-learning environments; and by advocating for more socially just campus communities in which every student, regardless of identity or background, is given equitable access to available learning opportunities. A wellness model is used for the promotion of health on some campuses, while other campuses may use an ecological model, a student development model, or a public health model. Regardless of the specific models used, professionals from many different disciplines work to enhance health at the community, campus, and individual levels. It is customary to find health educators; staff from residence life, student activities, campus recreation, orientation and other Student Affairs departments; nurses, physicians, counselors and faculty; as well as students themselves, leading or collaborating on health promotion and wellness initiatives that advance student learning and the mission of higher education. Programs and policies surrounding issues such as alcohol and other drug use, interpersonal violence, sexual health, and mental health are increasingly viewed as campus-wide concerns that affect student success, retention, and academic progress.

In 1996, the American College Health Association (ACHA) appointed the Task Force on Health Promotion in Higher Education to study the scope and practice of health promotion in colleges and universities (Zimmer, Hill, & Sonnad, 2003).. In 2001, ACHA published the culmination of that research as the first edition of *Standards of Practice for Health Promotion in Higher Education* (ACHA, 2005a). Following three years of feedback from professionals, the American College Health Association's Committee on Standards of Practice for Health Promotion in Higher Education presented the second edition, which provided measurable guidelines for enhancing the quality of health promotion programs in institutions of higher education. For the individual practitioner, the *Standards of Practice for Health Promotion in Higher Education* document and the related *Vision into Action* document are designed to guide daily efforts, facilitate the assessment of individual skills and capacities, and assist in decisions to improve practice through professional development, and also delineate a set of indicators to evaluate comprehensive health promotion programs and guide accreditation of those programs (ACHA, 2005b). The standards set forth in this groundbreaking document are guided by several premises about the mission and scope of practice of health promotion or wellness in higher education as well as about health itself.

These premises include the following:

1. Defined health, in the broadest sense, such that health: encompasses the capacity of individuals and communities to reach their full potential; transcends individual factors and includes cultural, institutional, socioeconomic, environmental and political influences; and challenges the prevailing societal view that health is solely a biomedical quality measured through clinical indicators.

2. The mission of health promotion services in higher education is not only to foster wellness focused campus communities by empowering individuals to reach their full potential and taking responsibility for themselves and others, but also to advance the health of students and to contribute to the creation of healthy and socially just learning environment. Thus, health promotion professionals create opportunities, programs and policies to help students and communities: reduce risk for illness and injury, enhance health as a strategy to support student learning, and advocate for safety, social justice, economic opportunity, and human dignity.

3. Because health and social justice are inextricably connected. Therefore, health promotion professionals strive to identify and address the complex social, cultural, economic, and political factors that may contribute to or compromise the health of individuals or communities; advocate for inclusive and equitable access to resources and services; and eliminate health disparities and increase the quality and years of healthy life for all.

4. The scope of practice of health promotion on college campuses includes both individual and environmental approaches. Thus, health promotion professionals develop and implement initiatives, services, programs and policies to: reduce the risk of individual illness and injury as well as help students build individual capacity; and address larger institutional issues, community factors, and public policies that shape health–related decisions that students make.

Health promotion and the academic mission of higher education are natural allies. Health promotion professionals in colleges and universities support the academic mission of student learning by assisting students in leading healthier lives, and engage individuals who will become political, social, and economic decision makers, thereby advancing the collective health of the community.

References, Readings, and Resources

American College Health Association. (2005a). *Standards of practice for health promotion in higher education*. Baltimore: Author. Available online at www.acha.org

American College Health Association. (2005b). *Vision into action: tools for professional and program development.* Based on the Standards of Practice for Health Promotion in Higher Education. Baltimore: Author.

American College Personnel Association and National Association of Student Personnel Administrators. (2006). *Learning reconsidered 2: A practical guide to implementing a campus-wide focus on the student experience*. Washington, DC: ACPA and NASPA. Available online at www.naspa.org

Keeling, R.P. (1995). *The search for sexual health*. Article based on his keynote address at American Social Health Association, Canadian HELP Group Conference in June 1995. Available online at http://www.herpes.com/sexualHealth.html

Modeste, N. (1996). *Dictionary of public health promotion and education: Terms and concepts.* Thousand Oaks, CA: Sage Publications.

Zimmer, C. G., Hill, M. H., Sonnad, S. R. (2003). A scope-of-practice survey leading to the development of standards of practice for health promotion in higher education. *Journal of American College Health*, 51(6), 247-54.

American College Health Association. (2005). The American College Health Association National College Health Assessment (ACHA-NCHA) Spring 2003 Reference Group report. *Journal of American College Health*, 53(5), 199-210.

Glantz, K., Lewis, F. M., & Rimer, B. K. (Eds.). (1997). *Health behavior and health education: Theory, research, and practice* (2nd Ed.). San Francisco, Jossey-Bass.

Green L.W., & Kreuter, M.W. (1999). *Health promotion planning: An educational and ecological approach* (3rd Ed). Boston: Mayfield Publishing Company.

Miller, W.R., & Rollnick, S. (2002). *Motivational interviewing: Preparing people for change*. New York, The Guilford Press.

National Association of Student Personnel Administrators (1998). *Principles of Good Practice for Student Affairs*. Washington, DC: Author.

National Association of Student Personnel Administrators and American College Health Association. (2004). *Leadership for a Healthy Campus: an ecological approach to student success*. Washington, DC: Author.

National Research Council. (Bransford, J., Brown, A., & Cocking, R., Eds.) (2000). *How people learn: Brain, mind experience and school: Expanded edition*. Washington, DC: National Academy Press.

Patrick, K. (Ed.). (1992). Principles and practices of student health (Vol. 3), *College Health*. Oakland, CA: Third Party Publishing Company.

Prochaska, J., Norcross, J. & DiClemente, C. (1994). *Changing for good.: The revolutionary program that explains the six stages of change and teaches you how to free yourself from bad habits.* New York: Avon Books.

Spectrum (November 2005) *Health Education and Health Promotion: Primary Prevention and Student Health*, Caulfield, Stephen C editor, The Chickering Group

Swinford, P. (2002). Advancing the health of students: a rationale for college health programs, *Journal of American College Health, 50*(6), 309-312.

Task Force of the National Advisory Council on Alcohol Abuse and Alcoholism. (2002). *A call to action: Changing the culture of drinking at US colleges.* Washington, DC: National Institutes of Health, US Department of Health and Human Services. Available at www.collegedrinkingprevention.gov.

U.S. Department of Human Services. (2000). *Healthy People 2010, 2nd ed., Understanding and improving health & Objectives for improving health* (Vols. 1-2). Washington, DC: U.S. Government Printing Office.

Zimmer, C. G. (2002). Health promotion in higher education. In *The history and practice of college health.* (ed. Turner, S. & Hurley, J.). Lexington, KY: The University Press of Kentucky.

American College Health Association [ACHA]. ACHA National Office, P.O. Box 28937. Baltimore, MD 21240-8937. (410) 859-1500; Fax (410) 859-1510. www.acha.org

National Association of Student Personnel Administrators [NASPA]. NASPA National Office, 1875 Connecticut Ave., N.W., Suite 418. Washington, DC 20009. (202) 265-7500. www.naspa.org

National Commission for Health Education Credentialing, 1541 Alta Drive, Suite 303, Whitehall, PA 18052-5642. (888) 624-3248. www.nchec.org

Contributors:
Patricia Fabiano, Western Washington University
Susan Kennedy, Pennsylvania State University
Nancy Allen, Michigan State University
Daisye Orr, Washington State Public Health Department
Paula Swinford, University of Southern California
Dixie Bennett, Loyola University Chicago, NIRSA
Cathy Kodoma, University of California at Berkeley
Luoluo Hong, Arizona State University

HEALTH PROMOTION SERVICES
CAS Standards and Guidelines

Part 1. MISSION

The mission and scope of practice of health promotion, sometimes referred to as wellness, must be reflective of the following fundamental assumptions about the role of health in higher education:

- there is a reciprocal relationship between learning and health; as well as, a direct connection between the academic mission of higher education and the well-being of students
- in the broadest sense, health encompasses the capacity of individuals and communities to reach their potential
- health transcends individual factors and includes cultural, institutional, socioeconomic and political influences
- health is not solely a biomedical quality measured through clinical indicators
- health and social justice are inextricably connected
- both individual and environmental approaches to health are critical

Health Promotion Services (HPS) must incorporate student learning and student development in its mission. HPS must enhance overall educational experiences. HPS must develop, record, disseminate, implement, and regularly review its mission and goals. Mission statements must be consistent with the mission and goals of the institution and with the standards in this document. HPS must operate as an integral part of the institution's overall mission.

Part 2. PROGRAM

The formal education of students consists of the curriculum and the co-curriculum, and must promote student learning and development that is purposeful and holistic. Health Promotion Services (HPS) must identify relevant and desirable student learning and development outcomes and provide programs and services that encourage the achievement of those outcomes.

Relevant and desirable outcomes include: intellectual growth, effective communication, realistic self-appraisal, enhanced self-esteem, clarified values, career choices, leadership development, healthy behaviors, meaningful interpersonal relationships, independence, collaboration, social responsibility, satisfying and productive lifestyles, appreciation of diversity, spiritual awareness, and achievement of personal and educational goals.

Health Promotion services (HPS) must provide evidence of its impact on the achievement of student learning and development outcomes.

The table below offers examples of evidence of achievement of student learning and development.

Student Learning and Development Outcome Domains

Intellectual growth

Examples of achievement indicators

Produces personal and educational goal statements; Employs critical thinking in problem solving; Uses complex information from a variety of sources including personal experience and observation to form a decision or opinion; Obtains a degree; Applies previously understood information and concepts to a new situation or setting; Expresses appreciation for literature, the fine arts, mathematics, sciences, and social sciences

Effective communication

Examples of achievement indicators

Writes and speaks coherently and effectively; Writes and speaks after reflection; Able to influence others through writing, speaking, or artistic expression; Effectively articulates abstract ideas; Uses appropriate syntax; Makes presentations or gives performances

Enhanced self-esteem

Examples of achievement indicators

Shows self-respect and respect for others; Initiates actions toward achievement of goals; Takes reasonable risks; Demonstrates assertive behavior; Functions without need for constant reassurance from others

Realistic self-appraisal

Examples of achievement indicators

Articulates personal skills and abilities; Makes decisions and acts in congruence with personal values; Acknowledges personal strengths and weaknesses; Articulates rationale for personal behavior; Seeks feedback from others; Learns from past experiences

Clarified values

Examples of achievement indicators

Articulates personal values; Acts in congruence with personal values; Makes decisions that reflect personal values; Demonstrates willingness to scrutinize personal beliefs and values; Identifies personal, work, and lifestyle values and explains how they influence decision-making

Career choices

Examples of achievement indicators

Articulates career choices based on assessment of interests, values, skills, and abilities; Documents knowledge, skills, and accomplishments resulting from formal education, work experience, community service, and volunteer experiences; Makes the connections between classroom and out-of-classroom learning; Can construct a resume with clear job objectives and evidence of related knowledge, skills, and accomplishments; Articulates the characteristics of a preferred work environment; Comprehends the world of work; Takes steps to initiate a job search or seek advanced education

Leadership development

Examples of achievement indicators

Articulates leadership philosophy or style; Serves in a leadership position in a student organization; Comprehends the dynamics of a group; Exhibits democratic principles as a leader; Exhibits ability to visualize a group purpose and desired outcomes

Healthy behavior

Examples of achievement indicators

Chooses behaviors and environments that promote health and reduce risk; Articulates the relationship between health and accomplishing life-long goals; Comprehends the continuum between illness and wellness; Exhibits behaviors that advance a healthy community

Meaningful interpersonal relationships

Examples of achievement indicators

Develops and maintains satisfying interpersonal relationships; Establishes mutually rewarding relationships with friends and colleagues; Listens to and considers others' points of view; Treats others with respect

Independence

Examples of achievement indicators

Exhibits self-reliant behaviors; Functions autonomously; Exhibits ability to function interdependently; Accepts supervision as needed; Manages time effectively

Collaboration

Examples of achievement indicators

Works cooperatively with others; Seeks the involvement of others; Seeks feedback from others; Contributes to achievement of a group goal; Exhibits effective listening skills

Social responsibility

Examples of achievement indicators

Understands and participates in relevant governance systems; Understands, abides by, and participates in the development, maintenance, and/or orderly change

of community, social, and legal standards or norms; Appropriately challenges the unfair, unjust, or uncivil behavior of other individuals or groups; Participates in service/volunteer activities

Satisfying and productive lifestyles

Examples of achievement indicators

Achieves balance between education, work, and leisure time; Articulates and meets goals for work, leisure, and education; Overcomes obstacles that hamper goal achievement; Functions on the basis of personal identity, ethical, spiritual, and moral values; Articulates long-term goals and objectives

Appreciating diversity

Examples of achievement indicators

Understands one's own identity and culture; Seeks involvement with people different from oneself; Seeks involvement in diverse interests; Articulates the advantages and challenges of a diverse society; Is able to intervene in the abusive use of stereotypes by others; Understands the impact of diversity on one's own society

Spiritual awareness

Examples of achievement indicators

Develops and articulates personal belief system; Understands roles of spirituality in personal and group values and behaviors

Personal and educational goals

Examples of achievement indicators

Sets, articulates, and pursues individual goals; Articulates personal and educational goals and objectives; Uses personal and educational goals to guide decisions; Understands the effect of one's personal and educational goals on others

HPS must be (a) intentional, (b) coherent, (c) based on theories and knowledge of learning and human development, (d) reflective of developmental and demographic profiles of the student population, and (e) responsive to needs of individuals, special populations, and communities.

HPS must advance the health of students and contribute to the creation an institutional and community climate of health and social justice.

HPS must review health promotion research and theories from interdisciplinary sources as a guide for the development of initiatives.

HPS must articulate the theoretical frameworks used in setting priorities and decision-making to the campus community.

HPS must apply professionally recognized constructs, tested theories, and evidence based strategies, to the development of initiatives designed to improve the health of individuals and the campus environment.

HPS must involve students, faculty members, staff members, and community constituents to advance the health of students and to create campus and community environments that support students' health.

HPS professionals should strive to reduce risk, incidence, and severity for individual mental and physical distress, illness and injury; enhance health as a strategy to support student learning; and advocate for safety, social justice, economic opportunity, and human dignity.

HPS must acknowledge that health and social justice are inextricably connected.

HPS professionals should strive to identify and address the complex social, cultural, economic, and political factors that may contribute to or compromise the health of individuals or communities; advocate for inclusive and equal access to resources and services; and eliminate health disparities and increase the quality and years of healthy life for all.

HPS must include both individual and environmental prevention strategies.

HPS professionals should strive to reduce the risk of individual illness and injury, as well as build individual capacity and address larger institutional issues, priority health issues, community factors and public policies that affect the health of students.

HPS professionals must advance the connection between the academic mission of higher education and the well-being of students.

HPS professionals should support the academic mission of student learning by assisting students in leading healthier lives and engaging individuals who will become political, social and economic decision makers, thereby advancing the collective health of the community.

Part 3. LEADERSHIP

Effective and ethical leadership is essential to the success of all organizations. Institutions must appoint, position, and empower Health Promotion Services (HPS) leaders within the administrative structure to accomplish stated missions. Leaders at various levels must be selected on the basis of formal education and training, relevant work experience, personal skills, and competencies, relevant professional credentials, as well as potential for promoting learning and development in students, applying effective practices to educational processes, and enhancing institutional effectiveness. Institutions must determine expectations of accountability for leaders and fairly assess their performance.

Leaders of HPS must exercise authority over resources for which they are responsible to achieve their respective missions.

Leaders of HPS must:
- articulate a vision for their organization
- **set goals and objectives based on the needs and capabilities of the population served**
- **promote student learning and development**
- **prescribe and practice ethical behavior**
- **recruit, select, supervise, and develop others in the organization**
- **manage financial resources**
- **coordinate human resources**
- **plan, budget for, and evaluate personnel and programs**
- **apply effective practices to educational and administrative processes**
- **communicate effectively**
- **initiate collaborative interaction between individuals and agencies that possess legitimate concerns and interests in the functional area**

Leaders of HPS must also:
- **develop health-related programs and policies that support student learning**
- **gather relevant data and review current literature**
- **develop strategic, operational, and resource utilization plans and policies**

Leaders of HPS must identify and find means to address individual, organizational, or environmental conditions that inhibit goal achievement.

Leaders of HPS must promote campus environments that result in multiple opportunities for student learning and development.

Leaders of HPS must continuously improve programs and services in response to changing needs of students and other constituents, and evolving institutional priorities.

Leaders of HPS should advocate for campus wide understanding of the connections between learning, culture, identity, social justice, and health.

Leaders of HPS should support others in strengthening their health promotion skills.

Part 4. ORGANIZATION and MANAGEMENT

Guided by an overarching intent to ensure student learning and development, Health Promotion Services (HPS) must be structured purposefully and managed effectively to achieve stated goals. Evidence of appropriate structure must include current and accessible policies and procedures, written performance expectations for all employees, functional workflow graphics or organizational charts, and clearly stated service delivery expectations.

Evidence of effective management must include use of comprehensive and accurate information for decisions, clear sources and channels of authority, effective communication practices, decision-making and conflict resolution procedures, responsiveness to changing conditions, accountability and evaluation systems, and recognition and reward processes. HPS must provide channels within the organization for regular review of administrative policies and procedures.

The HPS director must be placed within the institution's organizational structures so as to be able to promote cooperative interaction with appropriate campus and community entities and to develop the support of high-level administrators for the creation of safe and healthy campus environments. The placement of HPS within the organizational structure must clearly articulate the value of enhancing well-being and health promotion as essential to the overall mission of an institution.

HPS organizational placement should facilitate significant interaction with unit heads in academic and student affairs.

HPS must be located in an organizational structure to best provide for effective programs and services to achieve its mission.

HPS must play a principal role in creating and implementing institutional policies and programs in response to assessed student needs and capabilities.

HPS should function independent of clinical health services to ensure adequate attention is paid to prevention.

Part 5. HUMAN RESOURCES

Health Promotion Services (HPS) must be staffed adequately by individuals qualified to accomplish its

mission and goals. **Within established guidelines of the institution, programs and services must establish procedures for staff selection, training, and evaluation; set expectations for supervision, and provide appropriate professional development opportunities. The program and service must strive to improve the professional competence and skills of all personnel it employs.**

HPS should encourage professional staff members to participate in regular self reflection, assessment, and professional development planning to improve health promotion practice.

HPS should provide personnel with convenient access to online and other reference services that include materials pertinent to the operational, administrative, institutional, and research services offered by the institution.

Professional staff members must hold an earned graduate degree in a field relevant to the position they hold or must possess an appropriate combination of educational credentials and related work experience.

Professional staff members should have appropriate professional preparation and competencies in both theory and evidence-based practice for promoting health, advancing student learning, and contributing to student development.

The director of HPS should have an advanced degree in health education, public health, higher education administration, or other related discipline from an accredited institution.

The preferred qualification for HPS staff members should be an advanced degree from an accredited institution in a relevant discipline such as health education, public health, higher education administration, counseling, or community development with experience in higher education.

HPS staffing requirements must be established and reviewed regularly with regard to size of campus, institutional resources, student needs, and interdisciplinary health promotion collaborations on campus.

Degree or credential-seeking interns must be qualified by enrollment in an appropriate field of study and by relevant experience. These individuals must be trained and supervised adequately by professional staff members holding educational credentials and related work experience appropriate for supervision.

Student employees and volunteers must be carefully selected, trained, supervised, and evaluated. They must be trained on how and when to refer those in need of assistance to qualified staff members and have access to a supervisor for assistance in making

these judgments. Student employees and volunteers must be provided clear and precise job descriptions, pre-service training based on assessed needs, and continuing staff development.

HPS must have technical and support staff members adequate to accomplish its mission. Staff members must be technologically proficient and qualified to perform their job functions, be knowledgeable of ethical and legal uses of technology, and have access to training. The level of staffing and workloads must be adequate and appropriate for program and service demands.

Salary levels and fringe benefits for all staff members must be commensurate with those for comparable positions within the institution, in similar institutions, and in the relevant geographic area.

HPS must institute hiring and promotion practices that are fair, inclusive, and non-discriminatory. Programs and services must employ a diverse staff to provide readily identifiable role models for students and to enrich the campus community.

HPS staff members must participate in training sessions and professional development that address gender, sexual orientation, racial, cultural, religious and/or spiritual, and ethnic sensitivity.

HPS staff members should be encouraged to demonstrate their commitment to these issues that affect individuals, the campus, and the community by participating in relevant events.

HPS staff members must demonstrate trust when dealing sensitive information and a strict regard for confidentiality.

HPS must create and maintain position descriptions for all staff members and provide regular performance planning and appraisals.

HPS must have a system for regular staff member evaluation and must provide access to continuing education and professional development opportunities, including in-service training programs and participation in professional conferences and workshops.

Specific aspects of professional development should include theories of health promotion, student learning, and student development; assessment and evaluation; service delivery; coalition building; collaboration; and business and financial management.

HPS should maintain and financially support an in-service and staff development program and budgetary support should be available to provide for in-service and professional development activities.

Part 6. FINANCIAL RESOURCES
Health Promotion Services (HPS) must have adequate funding to accomplish its mission and goals. Funding priorities must be determined within the context of the stated mission, goals, objectives and comprehensive analysis of the needs and capabilities of students and the availability of internal or external resources.

HPS must demonstrate fiscal responsibility and cost effectiveness consistent with institutional protocols.

Funding for HPS should be provided and sustained by the institution's budget or through a designated health fee applied to all enrolled students.

Part 7. FACILITIES, TECHNOLOGY, and EQUIPMENT
Health Promotion Services (HPS) must have adequate, suitably located facilities, adequate technology, and equipment to support its mission and goals efficiently and effectively. Facilities, technology, and equipment must be evaluated regularly and be in compliance with relevant federal, state, provincial, and local requirements to provide for access, health, safety, and security.

To promote holistic health, the facilities of HPS should include:
- a safe, functional, effective and conveniently located positive environment for students, faculty and staff members, and community partners
- office space that is functionally autonomous rather than housed as a component of other units on campus
- office space that is physically separate from clinical health services
- quality space to ensure maximum effectiveness in providing health promotion resources for the campus community
- adequate meeting space for training student volunteers and supporting their work
- adequate physical facilities, equipment, and technology to monitor and report population health status data

Part 8. LEGAL RESPONSIBILITIES
Health Promotion Services (HPS) staff members must be knowledgeable about and responsive to laws and regulations that relate to their respective responsibilities. Staff members must inform users of programs and services and officials, as appropriate, of legal obligations and limitations including constitutional, statutory, regulatory, and case law;

mandatory laws and orders emanating from federal, state/provincial and local governments; and the institution's policies.

Staff members must use reasonable and informed practices to limit the liability exposure of the institution, its officers, employees, and agents. Staff members must be informed about institutional policies regarding personal liability and related insurance coverage options.

The institution must provide access to legal advice for staff members as needed to carry out assigned responsibilities.

The institution must inform staff and students in a timely and systematic fashion about extraordinary or changing legal obligations and potential liabilities.

Part 9. EQUITY and ACCESS

Health Promotion Services (HPS) staff members must ensure that services and programs are provided on a fair and equitable basis. Facilities, programs and services must be accessible. Hours of operation and delivery of and access to programs and services must be responsive to the needs of all students and other constituents. Each program and service must adhere to the spirit and intent of equal opportunity laws.

Policies and practices of HPS must be open and readily accessible to all students and must not discriminate except where sanctioned by law and institutional policy. Discrimination must be avoided on the bases of age; color; creed; cultural heritage; disability; ethnicity; gender identity; nationality; political affiliation; religious affiliation; sex; sexual orientation; or social, economic, marital, or veteran status.

Consistent with their mission and goals, programs and services must take affirmative action to remedy significant imbalances in student participation and staffing patterns.

As the demographic profiles of campuses change and new instructional delivery methods are introduced, institutions must recognize the needs of students who participate in distance learning for access to programs and services offered on campus. Institutions must provide appropriate services in ways that are accessible to distance learners and assist them in identifying and gaining access to other appropriate services in their geographic region.

HPS should help identify any social, cultural, political, and economic disparities that influence the health of students so that any disparities may be adequately addressed to improve equity and access to health related services.

Part 10. CAMPUS and EXTERNAL RELATIONS

Health Promotion Services (HPS) must establish, maintain, and promote effective relations with relevant individuals, campus offices, and external agencies.

Sustaining partnerships should include:
- advocating for a shared vision that health promotion is the responsibility of all campus and community members
- developing and participating in campus and community partnerships that advance health promotion initiatives
- utilizing campus and community resources to maximize the effectiveness of health promotion initiatives
- advocating for campus, local, state, provincial, national, and international policies that address campus and community health issues
- institutionalizing health promotion initiatives through inclusion in campus strategic planning and resource allocation processes

To ensure success, HPS must maintain productive relations with students, faculty members, staff members, alumni, the community at large, contractors, and support agencies.

HPS staff members should participate actively with their institutions in designing policies and practices and developing further resources and services, which have direct effects on the health of the campus population.

HPS should work closely with the senior administrators to ensure the meeting of institutional goals and objectives.

HPS should establish relationships with a wide range of constituencies, such as student affairs professionals, faculty members, and student groups to promote collaboration and serve as a resource.

HPS should foster relationships with academic units and campus professionals in residence halls, recreational facilities, student activities, and athletics, where appropriate.

HPS should foster reciprocal relationships with clinical health services and counseling services to refer students for medical concerns and to serve as colleagues and consultants.

Part 11. DIVERSITY

Within the context of each institution's unique mission, diversity enriches the community and enhances the collegiate experience for all; therefore,

Health Promotion Services (HPS) must nurture environments where commonalties and differences among people are recognized and honored.

HPS must promote educational experiences that are characterized by open and continuous communication that deepens understanding of one's own identity, culture, and heritage, and that of others. Programs and services must educate and promote respect about commonalties and differences in their historical and cultural contexts.

HPS must address the characteristics and needs of a diverse population when establishing and implementing policies and procedures.

HPS staff members must demonstrate cultural competency and inclusiveness in advancing the health of individuals and communities.

HPS should identify the social, cultural, and economic disparities that influence the health of students.

HPS should design health promotion initiatives that reflect the social, cultural, and economic diversity of students.

HPS should create health promotion mission statements, program policies, staff member recruitment and retention practices, and professional development goals that reflect the social, cultural, and economic diversity of the campus.

HPS should provide leadership for campus-wide understanding of the connection between culture, identity, social justice, and health status.

Part 12. ETHICS

All persons involved in the delivery of Health Promotion Services (HPS) must adhere to the highest principles of ethical behavior. HPS must develop or adopt and implement appropriate statements of ethical practice. HPS must publish these statements and ensure their periodic review by relevant constituencies.

HPS staff members must ensure that privacy and confidentiality are maintained with respect to all communications and records to the extent that such records are protected under the law and appropriate statements of ethical practice. Information contained in students' education records must not be disclosed without written consent except as allowed by relevant laws and institutional policies. Staff members must disclose to appropriate authorities information judged to be of an emergency nature, especially when the safety of the individual or others is involved, or when

otherwise required by institutional policy or relevant law.

HPS staff members must be aware of and comply with the provisions contained in the institution's human subjects research policy and in other relevant institutional policies addressing ethical practices and confidentiality of research data concerning individuals.

HPS staff members must recognize and avoid personal conflict of interest or appearance thereof in their transactions with students and others.

HPS staff members must strive to insure the fair, objective, and impartial treatment of all persons with whom they deal. Staff members must not participate in nor condone any form of harassment that demeans persons or creates an intimidating, hostile, or offensive campus environment.

When handling institutional funds, all staff members must ensure that such funds are managed in accordance with established and responsible accounting procedures and the fiscal policies or processes of the institution.

HPS staff members must perform their duties within the limits of their training, expertise, and competence. When these limits are exceeded, individuals in need of further assistance must be referred to persons possessing appropriate qualifications.

HPS staff members must use suitable means to confront and otherwise hold accountable other staff members who exhibit unethical behavior.

HPS staff members must be knowledgeable about and practice ethical behavior in the use of technology.

Part 13. ASSESSMENT and EVALUATION

Health Promotion Services (HPS) must conduct regular assessment and evaluations. HPS must employ effective qualitative and quantitative methodologies as appropriate, to determine whether and to what degree the stated mission, goals, and student learning and development outcomes are being met. The process must employ sufficient and sound assessment measures to ensure comprehensiveness. Data collected must include responses from students and other affected constituencies.

Assessment and evaluation should include:
- data gathered from published research on international, national, state/provincial, local, and campus health priorities

- population-based assessment of health status, needs, and assets of students
- environmental assessment of campus-community health needs and resources
- measurable goals and objectives for health promotion initiatives

HPS must periodically evaluate how well the services complement and enhance the institution's stated mission and educational effectiveness.

Results of these evaluations must be used in revising and improving HPS and in recognizing staff performance.

HPS should report evaluation data and research results to students, faculty members, staff members, and the campus community.

HPS Standards were developed in 2006

THE ROLE of COLLEGE and UNIVERSITY STUDENT HOUSING and RESIDENTIAL LIFE
CAS Standards Contextual Statement

Although American institutions of higher learning have provided student housing in one form or another since the first colleges were founded (Frederiksen,1993), the professionalization of those employed in housing was greatly enhanced when the Association of College and University Housing Officers-International (ACUHO-I) held its first annual conference in 1949. This meeting marked a significant step forward in the development of college and university student housing programs as a profession.

Until the middle of this century, college and university residence halls were administered by "housemothers," often under the supervision of deans of men or women. These staff members assumed parental responsibility (*in loco parentis*) for the students housed in the residence halls. During the 1960s, dramatic changes in laws and education produced changes in the operation of residence halls. Housemothers were replaced by full-time staff with professional training in counseling and administration. These student affairs professionals focused on using the residence hall environment as a tool to complement formal classroom education. Since the 1960s, student housing has become increasingly more specialized and complex. However, the concept of utilizing residence halls as combined living-learning environments to enhance classroom learning has remained constant. More recently the quality of campus life, especially the residence halls, is increasingly important in attracting students to a given institution and making a significant contribution to the undergraduate experience.

Many college and university student housing operations employ staff members with wide varieties of skills and functions. Areas administered by institutional housing and residence life programs include such functions as:

- Administration of various electronic media (residential cable TV channels, network access, internal movie and information channels, electronic access systems) and information technology resources (in-room connections, computer labs, learning resources centers, wireless capabilities)
- Apartment housing
- Conference and guest housing
- Education (e.g., leadership development, student government advising, student conduct, joint programs with faculty and academic departments, community and individual development)
- Facilities management and maintenance
- Financial and program planning and administration
- Food services (including catering and cash food operations)
- Identification and "one card" programs
- Marketing
- Off-campus rental referral and related educational services

- Planning and administration of the construction of new facilities
- Research, evaluation and assessment
- Safety and security

Most institutional student housing operations are self-supported auxiliaries that do not receive financial support from the institution or other public sources; in effect, student housing is an education "business." Because of the wide scope and function of student housing, planning is usually initiated institution-wide. Likewise, although housing encompasses many functions, most administrations agree that students are best served when all housing and residence life functions fall under the responsibility of a single administrator, usually the director of housing and/or residential life.

Group living influences maturation by exposing students to a variety of experiences and community-building activities. What distinguishes group living in campus residence from most other forms of housing is the involvement of both professional and paraprofessional staff members in providing intentional, as opposed to random, educational experiences for students. Students living in residence halls participate in more extracurricular, social, and cultural events; are more likely to graduate; and exhibit greater positive gains in psychosocial development, intellectual orientation, and self concept than students living at home or commuting. In addition, they demonstrate significantly greater increases in aesthetic, cultural, and intellectual values; social and political liberalism; and secularism (Schroeder & Mable, 1993).

Residence halls contribute significantly to a student's educational experience. The standards and guidelines that follow provide guidance to those who work in this field and accountability to the public they serve.

References, Readings, and Resources

Association of College and University Housing Officers-International (ACUHO-I) (1992). *Ethical principles and standards for college and university housing Professionals.* Columbus, OH: Author.

Frederiksen, C. F. (1993). A brief history of collegiate housing. In R. B. Winston, Jr. & S. Anchors, *Student housing and residential life: A handbook for student affairs professionals committed to student development goals.* pp. 167-183. San Francisco: Jossey-Bass.

Schroeder, C. C., Mable, P., & Associates. (1993). *Realizing the educational potential of residence halls.* San Francisco: Jossey-Bass.

Winston, R. B, Jr., Anchors, S., & Associates (1993). *Student housing and residential life: A handbook for student affairs professionals committed to student development goals.* San Francisco: Jossey-Bass.

American College Personnel Association. Commission on Housing and Residence Life.
http://www.acpa.nche.edu/comms/comm03/index.html

The Journal of College and University Student Housing. Published by the Association of College and University Housing Officers-International (ACUHO-I), 101 Curl Dr., Suite 140, Columbus, OH 43210. (614) 292-0099; Fax (614) 292-0305; gschwarz@magnus.acs.ohio-state.edu

Contributors:
Previous edition: Mike Eyster, University of Oregon
Current edition: Carole Henry, University of Michigan, ACUHO-I

HOUSING and RESIDENTIAL LIFE PROGRAMS
CAS Standards and Guidelines

Part 1. MISSION

The Housing and Residential Life Program (HRLP) must operate as an integral part of the institution's overall mission. The Housing and Residential Life Program must incorporate student learning and student development in its mission and enhance the overall educational experience.

The mission of HRLP is accomplished through the coordination of several interdependent specialized areas: residence education/programming, business operations, and housing/facilities management.

The standards in this document also apply to additional specialized areas that may include food services, apartment/family housing, special interest housing, conference housing, faculty/staff housing, and off-campus housing services.

The mission of HRLP must address:

- the living environment, including programs and services, that promotes learning and development in the broadest sense, with an emphasis on academic success
- reasonably priced living facilities that are clean, attractive, well-maintained, comfortable, and which include contemporary safety features maintained by systematic operations
- orderly and effective management of HRLP that consists of meeting the needs of students and other constituents in a courteous, efficient, and effective manner
- the provision of a variety of nutritious and pleasing meals, in pleasant surroundings, at a reasonable cost, and related services that effectively meet institutional goals (catering, retail/cash operations, convenience stores), in programs that include food services

The program must develop, record, disseminate, implement, and regularly review its mission and goals. Mission statements must be consistent with the mission and goals of the institution and with the standards in this document.

Part 2. PROGRAM

The formal education of students consists of the curriculum and the co-curriculum, and must promote student learning and development that is purposeful and holistic. HRLP must identify relevant and desirable student learning and development outcomes and provide programs and services that encourage the achievement of those outcomes.

Relevant and desirable outcomes include: intellectual growth, effective communication, realistic self-appraisal, enhanced self-esteem, clarified values, career choices, leadership development, healthy behaviors, meaningful interpersonal relationships, independence, collaboration, social responsibility, satisfying and productive lifestyles, appreciation of diversity, spiritual awareness, and achievement of personal and educational goals.

HRLP must provide evidence of its impact on the achievement of student learning and development outcomes.

The table below offers examples of evidence of achievement of student learning and development.

Student Learning and Development Outcome Domains

Intellectual growth
Examples of achievement indicators

Acquires knowledge; Demonstrates critical thinking in problem solving; Uses complex information from a variety of sources including personal experience to form decisions or opinions; Applies previously understood information and concepts to a new situation or setting; Makes appropriate use of technology to enhance learning processes; Expresses appreciation for the learning process

Effective communication
Examples of achievement indicators

Writes and speaks coherently and effectively; Expresses oneself effectively through a variety of media; Able to respectfully disagree; Writes and speaks after reflection; Able to influence others through writing, speaking or artistic expression; Effectively articulates abstract ideas; Uses appropriate syntax; Makes presentations or gives performances

Enhanced self-esteem
Examples of achievement indicators

Exhibits self-respect and respect for others; Exercises initiative in community; Initiates actions toward the achievement of worthy personal goals; Takes reasonable risks; Demonstrates assertive behavior; Functions without need for constant reassurance from others that advance a healthy residential community

Realistic self-appraisal

Examples of achievement indicators

Develops and confirms a sense of identity; Articulates personal skills and abilities; Makes informed decisions and acts in congruence with personal values; Acknowledges personal strengths and weaknesses; Articulates rationale for personal behavior; Seeks feedback from others; Learns from past experiences

Clarified values

Examples of achievement indicators

Analyzes, develops, and confirms values through activities and opportunities; Acts in congruence with personal values; Makes decisions that reflect personal values; Demonstrates willingness to scrutinize personal beliefs and values; Identifies personal, work, and lifestyle values and explains how they influence residential community development

Career choices

Examples of achievement indicators

Explores career choices and interests based on educational activities and planned opportunities; Can construct a resume' with clear job objectives that documents knowledge, skills and accomplishments resulting from the classroom, co-curricular activities, work experience, community service and volunteer experiences; Makes the connections between classroom and out-of-classroom learning; Able to develop and identify a career choice or direction; Articulates the characteristics of a preferred work environment

Leadership development

Examples of achievement indicators

Participates in student organizations, intramurals, athletics, study groups, learning communities, or hall governance opportunities; Articulates leadership philosophy or style; Serves in a leadership position within a residential community or student organization; Comprehends the dynamics of a group; Exhibits democratic principles as a leader or participant; Demonstrates capacity to be an effective team member and to work with others to accomplish a goal; Exhibits ability to visualize a group purpose and desired outcomes

Healthy behavior

Examples of achievement indicators

Chooses activities, behaviors, and environments that promote health and reduce risk with particular attention to alcohol and drugs; Recognizes mental health and substance abuse concerns and makes appropriate use of resources; Engages in healthy choices with regard to exercise, recreation, nutrition, sexuality, and stress; Articulates the relationship between health and wellness and accomplishing long-term goals; Chooses behaviors

Meaningful interpersonal relationships

Examples of achievement indicators

Exhibits maturity in relating to others; Handles interpersonal and inter-group conflict constructively; Develops friendships; Presents and represents self honestly; Establishes mutually rewarding relationships with friends and colleagues; Listens to and considers others' points of view; Treats others with respect

Independence

Examples of achievement indicators

Exhibits self-reliant behaviors; Functions autonomously; Exhibits ability to function interdependently; Accepts supervision as needed; Manages time effectively; Achieves success in managing personal finances

Collaboration

Examples of achievement indicators

Lives cooperatively with others; Seeks the involvement of others; Seeks feedback from others; Contributes to achievement of a community goal; Exhibits effective listening skills and offers feedback appropriately; Demonstrates reliability

Social responsibility

Examples of achievement indicators

Understands and participates in community governance; Abides by institutional, residential life policies and procedures and local, municipal, state/provincial, and federal laws; Demonstrates respect for self, property, and others; Demonstrates responsible social behavior; Understands, abides by, and participates in the development, maintenance, and/or orderly change of community standards and expectations; Appropriately challenges the unfair, unjust, or uncivil behavior of other individuals or groups; Participates in service, volunteer, and/or community activities

Satisfying and productive lifestyles

Examples of achievement indicators

Achieves balance between education, work, and leisure time; Develops a plan for achieving goals; Reassesses goals and overcomes obstacles that hamper goal achievement; Functions on the basis of personal identity, ethical, spiritual, and moral values; Articulates long-term goals and objectives

Appreciating diversity

Examples of achievement indicators

Understands the meaning of diversity including its application to race, color, gender, gender identity, religion, sexual orientation, national or ethnic origin, age, disability, marital status, or veteran status; Understands own identity and culture and its impact on diversity issues; Appreciates new ideas, cultural, and lifestyle differences; Seeks involvement with people different from oneself; Seeks involvement in diverse interests; Articulates the advantages and challenges of a multicultural society; Challenges abusive use of stereotypes by others; Understands the impact of diversity on society

Spiritual awareness

Examples of achievement indicators

Develops personal belief system; Understands roles of spirituality in personal and group values and behaviors

Personal and educational goals

Examples of achievement indicators

Acquires knowledge and uses information and resources to make educated choices; Engages with faculty in the residential community; Sets, articulates, and pursues individual goals; Obtains a degree; Articulates personal and educational goals and objectives; Uses personal and educational goals to guide decisions; Understands the effect of one's personal and educational goals on others

HRLP must provide educational opportunities for students and other members of the campus community that support the strategic initiatives of the institution.

Partnerships with faculty, academic administrators, and other campus constituents should be developed to utilize student residences as an integral part of the educational experience. These activities may include offering any of the following: partnerships with enrollment management to attract and retain students; faculty-staff interaction with students through workshop and lecture presentations; scholars in residence programs, residential colleges, classrooms (traditional and electronic) and computer labs in the residence halls; opportunities for faculty to hold office hours and meet with students; partnerships with departments and colleges to offer living-learning communities by academic program, theme or special interest; residentially-based tutoring programs, study skills, and related workshops; and activities that contribute to achieving the academic mission.

Staff members must provide a variety of educational opportunities that promote academic success, and the achievement of learning and student development outcomes.

HRLP must be (a) intentional, (b) coherent, (c) based on theories and knowledge of learning and human development, (d) reflective of developmental and demographic profiles of the student population, and (e) responsive to needs of individuals, special populations, and communities.

HRLP should provide an environment that assists residents to remain in good academic standing, earn higher GPAs, and are retained. This may occur through early alert intervention programs, educating staff and students about available campus academic resources, offering living- learning communities which can be linked with course blocking, transition or bridging programs, partnerships with first year experience programs, establishment of first-year interest groups, year-two programs, informal study groups, senior year experience programs, or other academic initiatives.

HRLP must provide access to experiences and services that facilitate:

- **a seamless learning environment**
- **opportunities to interact with faculty and staff members**
- **encouragement and assistance in forming study groups**
- **access to academic resources through technology**
- **opportunities to develop a mature style of relating to others and living cooperatively with others**
- **opportunities for analyzing, forming, and confirming values**
- **activities and educational opportunities that promote independence and self-sufficiency**
- **educational opportunities that assist residents in developing and confirming a sense of identity**
- **experiences that lead to the respect for self, others, and property**
- **experiences that promote a sense of justice and fair play**
- **opportunities to appreciate new ideas**
- **opportunities to appreciate cultural differences and other forms of diversity**
- **opportunities to apply knowledge, skills, and values**
- **opportunities for leadership development and decision-making**
- **opportunities to make career choices through planned activities**
- **opportunities to develop a balanced life style embracing wellness**
- **opportunities to learn life skills, e.g., personal finance and time management**

Educational and community development programming, advising and counseling, and administrative activities of the HRLP staff will vary according to assessed student needs and institutional priorities.

In education and community development programs, staff members must:
- **introduce and orient residents to community**

- expectations, facilities, services, and staff
- document institutional and residential living policies, procedures, and expectations including the potential consequences for violation
- involve students in programming, policy development, and self-governance
- provide educational programs that focus on awareness of cultural differences and self-assessment of possible prejudices
- offer social, recreational, educational, cultural, and community service programs
- promote and provide education about the affects and risks of drug and alcohol use
- encourage residents to exercise responsibility for their community through confrontation of inappropriate or disruptive behavior
- encourage residents to participate in mediating conflict within the community
- encourage residents to learn about their rights as students, tenants, residents, and consumers

  Off-campus housing services should include referrals to available housing opportunities, listings, information about leases, landlord/tenant law, information about local ordinances, community resources, and other related information.

- promote appropriate student use of technological resources

In advising, counseling, and crises intervention, staff members must:

- provide individual advising or counseling support within the scope of their training and expertise, and make appropriate referrals
- create relationships with students that demonstrate genuine interest in students' educational and personal development

In administrative activities, staff members must:

- provide a clear and complete written agreement between the resident and the institution, that conveys mutual commitments and responsibilities

  The agreement should include contract eligibility and duration, room assignments and changes, rates and payment policies, dining options, procedures for canceling, subleasing, or being released from the housing and/or dining agreement, room entry and inspection procedures, and pertinent rules and regulations.

- encourage residents to participate in evaluating the HRLP
- provide information on safety, security, and emergency procedures
- create and maintain an environment and atmosphere which is conducive to educational pursuits

- provide emergency response and crisis intervention management in coordination with relevant campus and community resources
- ensure that the safety and security of the residents and their property are taken into consideration as policies are developed
- assess needs of the housing population annually, specifically addressing the needs for special interest programming and for upgrading or modifying facilities

When food services is included within HRLP, it must include:

- high quality food products
- orderly, secure, and sanitary food storage
- compliance with all pertinent environmental, health, and safety codes as well as sanitation procedures
- timely delivery of services
- high quality customer services
- pleasant environment in dining areas
- materials that educate students about nutrition and its relationship to good health
- suggestions and input from users regarding menu selection, satisfaction, and
- on-going evaluation

When a residential dining program is included within HRLP, it must include the above standards and:

- menu planning to provide optimum nutrition and variety
- recipes and preparation processes that ensure appetizing food
- attention to students' cultural differences and special dietary needs
- hours of dining service operations sufficient to reasonably accommodate student needs
- dining meal plan options that are clear, affordable, and responsive to student needs
- involvement in educational programming that contributes to student learning and resident satisfaction

The standards and procedures developed and published by professional associations should be used for operating institutional food service operations.

Part 3. LEADERSHIP

Effective and ethical leadership is essential to the success of all organizations. Institutions must appoint, position and empower HRLP leaders within the administrative structure to accomplish stated missions. HRLP leaders at various levels must be selected on the basis of formal education and training, relevant work experience, personal skills and competencies, relevant professional credentials, as well as potential for promoting learning and development in students, applying effective practices to educational processes, and enhancing institutional effectiveness. Institutions must determine expectations of accountability for HRLP leaders and fairly assess their performance.

HRLP leaders must exercise authority over resources for which they are responsible to achieve their respective missions.

HRLP leaders must:
- articulate a vision for their organization
- set goals and objectives based on the needs and capabilities of the populations served
- promote student learning and development
- develop strategic, operational, and resource utilization plans and policies
- prescribe and practice ethical behavior
- recruit, select, supervise, and develop others in the organization
- coordinate human resources
- manage financial resources
- manage facility resources
- plan, budget for, and evaluate personnel and programs
- apply effective practices to educational and administrative processes
- communicate effectively
- initiate collaborative interaction between individuals and agencies that possess legitimate concerns and interests in the functional area
- ensure compliance with all institutional, state/provincial, and federal regulations and policies

HRLP leaders must identify and find means to address individual, organizational, or environmental conditions that inhibit goal achievement.

HRLP leaders must promote campus environments that result in multiple opportunities for student learning and development.

HRLP leaders must continuously improve programs and services in response to changing needs of students and other constituents, and evolving institutional priorities.

Part 4. ORGANIZATION and MANAGEMENT
Guided by an overarching intent to ensure student learning and development, HRLP must be structured purposefully and managed effectively to achieve stated goals. Evidence of appropriate structure

must include current and accessible policies and procedures, written performance expectations for all employees, functional workflow graphics or organizational charts, and clearly stated service delivery expectations.

An organizational chart should define both the responsibilities and relationships of staff members with the understanding that HRLP leadership should emphasize fluidity, adaptability and cross-functional collaboration.

Evidence of effective management must include use of comprehensive and accurate information for decisions, clear sources and channels of authority, effective communication practices, decision-making and conflict resolution procedures, responsiveness to changing conditions, accountability and evaluation systems, and recognition and reward processes. HRLP must provide channels within the organization for regular review of administrative policies and procedures.

Where the management of the HRLP is divided among different agencies within the institution, it is the responsibility of institutional leaders to establish and maintain productive working relationships.

A unified organizational structure, including all housing and residential life functions, should be used so as to effectively deliver the services to users and to avoid multiple hierarchical lines of communication and authority.

HRLP must maintain well-structured management functions, including planning, personnel, property management, purchasing, contract administration, financial control, and information systems.

Evaluation of the organization is based on progress toward the achievement of short-range and long-range organizational goals. Planning must be adequate to project and accommodate both immediate and future needs.

Part 5. HUMAN RESOURCES
HRLP must be staffed adequately by individuals qualified to accomplish its mission and goals. Within established guidelines of the institution, HRLP must establish procedures for staff selection, training, and evaluation; set expectations for supervision; and provide appropriate professional development opportunities. HRLP must strive to improve the professional competence and skills of all personnel it employs.

HRLP professional staff members must hold an earned graduate degree in a field relevant to the position they hold or must possess an appropriate combination of educational credentials and related work experience.

There must be at least one professional staff member responsible for the administration and coordination of the department. This individual must be knowledgeable about the goals and mission of the program.

Individual residence halls and apartment areas should be supervised by professional staff that have earned a master's degree from accredited institutions in a field of study such as college student personnel, college counseling, or higher education administration or as appropriate.

Degree or credential-seeking interns must be qualified by enrollment in an appropriate field of study and by relevant experience. These individuals must be trained and supervised adequately by professional staff members holding educational credentials and related work experience appropriate for supervision.

Demonstrated skills of leadership and communication, maturity, a well-developed sense of responsibility, sensitivity to individual differences, a positive self-concept, an understanding of how to promote student learning and academic success, and an obvious interest and enthusiasm for working with students are desirable characteristics for professional, pre-professional, and paraprofessional staff members.

Student employees must be carefully selected, trained, supervised, and evaluated. They must be trained on how and when to refer those in need of assistance to qualified staff members and have access to a supervisor for assistance in making these judgments. Student employees must be provided clear and precise job descriptions, pre-service training based on assessed needs, and continuing staff development.

Resident/community assistants and other paraprofessionals are expected to contribute to the accomplishment of the following functions: (a) educational programming, (b) administration, (c) group and activity advising, (d) leadership development, (e) discipline, (f) role modeling, (g) individual assistance and referral, and (h) providing information.

HRLP must have technical and support staff members adequate to accomplish its mission. Staff members must be technologically proficient and qualified to perform their job functions, be knowledgeable of ethical and legal uses of technology, and have access to training. The level of staffing and workloads must be adequate and appropriate for program and service demands.

Salary levels and fringe benefits for all HRLP staff members must be commensurate with those for comparable positions within the institution, in similar institutions, and in the relevant geographic area.

HRLP must institute hiring and promotion practices that are fair, inclusive, and non-discriminatory. HRLP must employ a diverse staff to provide readily identifiable role models for students and to enrich the campus community.

HRLP must provide procedures for filing, processing, and hearing employee grievances.

HRLP must create and maintain position descriptions for all staff members and provide regular performance planning and appraisals.

HRLP position descriptions should include adequate time for planning as well as for program implementation.

HRLP must have a system for regular staff evaluation and must provide access to continuing education and professional development opportunities, including in-service training programs and participation in professional conferences and workshops.

Training and supervision to accomplish assigned tasks must be provided to HRLP staff.

HRLP staff members should have a written personal development plan that reflects the goals and objectives of the organization and areas for professional growth.

HRLP staff members must have a working knowledge of all relevant policies and procedures, the rationale for policies and procedures, and the relationship of policies and procedures to the organization's mission statement, goals, and objectives.

HRLP policies and procedures are reviewed annually and updated as appropriate.

HRLP staff members must be knowledgeable about and remain current with respect to the obligations and limitations placed upon the institution by constitutional, statutory, and common law, by external governmental agencies and institutional policies.

Part 6. FINANCIAL RESOURCES

HRLP must have adequate funding to accomplish its mission and goals. Funding priorities must be determined within the context of the stated mission, goals, objectives and comprehensive analysis of the needs and capabilities of students and the availability of internal or external resources.

HRLP must demonstrate fiscal responsibility and cost effectiveness consistent with institutional protocols.

Administration of funds must be handled in accordance with established, responsible accounting procedures.

Procedures should be present to ensure reconciliation between goods paid for and goods ordered and received.

Adequate and appropriate internal controls must exist to ensure full accountability of financial processes.

Financial reports must provide and reflect an accurate financial overview of the organization.

Financial reports should provide clear, understandable, timely data on which staff can plan and make informed decisions.

Purchasing procedures must be consistent with institutional policies and be cost effective.

The budget must be used as a planning and goal-setting document that reflects commitment to the mission and goals of the HRLP and of the institution.

Budgets should be flexible and capable of being adjusted during the year.

A portion of fees collected must be dedicated to the immediate support and long-term improvement of housing and residential life programs and facilities. Funding must be available to provide for the continuous upkeep of facilities, equipment and furnishings, on-going repairs, educational programming, and services to residents. Reserves must be available for major maintenance and renovation of facilities, replacement of equipment, and other capital improvements.

Student governance units (e.g., hall or campus-wide residential councils) should have access to accounting offices and services to effectively carry out their functions. Dues collected from

students for programs and services should be managed within the institution.

Representatives of residence hall and apartment housing communities should be given opportunity to comment on proposed rate increases and the operating budget. Rate increases should be announced at least 90 days in advance of their implementation and discussed well in advance of their effective date.

Part 7. FACILITIES, TECHNOLOGY, and EQUIPMENT

HRLP must have adequate, suitably located facilities, adequate technology, and equipment to support its mission and goals efficiently and effectively. Facilities, technology, and equipment must be evaluated regularly and be in compliance with relevant federal, state, provincial, and local requirements to provide for access, health, safety, and security.

The HRLP must ensure the physical environment is attractive, conducive to academic success and other learning opportunities, functional, in compliance with codes, and adequately provided with safety features.

Individual rooms and apartments must be furnished and equipped to accommodate the designated number of occupants.

Adequate space must be provided for student study, recreation, socializing, and group meetings.

Facilities should include private offices for counseling, advising, interviewing, or other meetings of a confidential nature; and office, reception, and storage space sufficient to accommodate assigned staff, supplies, equipment, library resources, conference rooms, classrooms, and meeting spaces.

Public, common, study, recreational areas and computer labs must be adequately furnished to accommodate the number of users.

Housekeeping programs must be required to provide a clean and orderly environment in all housing facilities. All community bathrooms, as well as public areas, must be cleaned and sanitized at least daily on weekdays.

A weekend housekeeping program should be in place.

Sufficient space for custodial work and storage must be available in close proximity to the assigned custodial area.
Maintenance and renovation programs must be

implemented in all housing operations and include four major areas: (a) a preventive maintenance program designed to realize or exceed the projected life expectancy of the equipment and facilities, (b) a program designed to repair or upgrade equipment, facilities, and building systems as they become inoperable or obsolete, (c) a renovation program that modifies physical facilities and building systems to make them more accessible, effective, attractive, efficient, and safe, and (d) a program designed to provide emergency response 24 hours a day.

Periodic inspections must be made to: (a) ensure compliance with fire and safety codes; (b) identify and address potential safety and security hazards including fire extinguishers, exit doors, automatic door closers, outside building lighting, and identify other potentially dangerous spaces. Data from inspections must be used for repair and replacement schedules.

A system of access control must be in place to provide for building security, monitoring of exterior doors, and stringent controls on the use of master keys/access cards.

Systematically planned equipment replacement programs must exist for furnishings, mechanical, fire safety, and electrical systems; maintenance equipment; carpeting; window coverings; and dining equipment where applicable.

Painting must be done on the basis of current need and a preplanned cyclical schedule.

Waste disposal, recycling, and handling and storage of chemicals and hazardous materials must be in compliance with federal, state/provincial, and local health, safety, and environmental protection requirements. HRLP staff must identify work place hazards and strive to minimize the risk to employees through education, training, and provision of personal protective equipment.

Grounds, including streets, walks, recreational areas, and parking lots, must be attractively maintained, with attention given to safety features.

Appropriate parking policies should exist for resident students, be developed collaboratively, and define responsibility and options.

Student housing construction project planning must be responsive to the current and future needs of residents. HRLP staff must be involved in the design and development of new housing construction.

Students should be consulted on the design and development of new housing construction.

A master plan for maintaining and renovating all facilities must exist and include timelines for addressing specific needs.

Laundry facilities should be provided within or in close proximity to living areas, be well-maintained, and reasonably priced.

Suggestions from residents should be regularly and consistently sought and considered regarding physical plant improvements and renovations to college/university housing and dining facilities.

A systematic energy conservation program should be implemented through assessment, programming, education, renovation and replacement.

An up-to-date inventory of housing property and furnishings should be maintained.

Physical plant renovations should be scheduled to minimize disruption to residents and diners.

Acceptable accommodations and amenities should be provided for professional live-in staff members with appropriate consideration provided for the following needs: adequate living space for the staff member and any family, furnishings and equipment, telecommunications package, appropriate access, and parking.

Part 8. LEGAL RESPONSIBILITIES

HRLP staff members must be knowledgeable about and responsive to laws and regulations that relate to their respective responsibilities. Staff members must inform users of programs and services and officials, as appropriate, of legal obligations and limitations including constitutional, statutory, regulatory, and case law; mandatory laws and orders emanating from federal, state/provincial and local governments; and the institution's policies.

HRLP staff members must use reasonable and informed practices to limit the liability exposure of the institution, its officers, employees, and agents. Staff members must be informed about institutional policies regarding personal liability and related insurance coverage options. Staff members must be informed about legal administrative searches.

The institution must provide access to legal advice for HRLP staff members as needed to carry out assigned responsibilities.

The institution must inform HRLP staff and students in a timely and systematic fashion about extraordinary or changing legal obligations and potential liabilities.

Part 9. EQUITY and ACCESS

HRLP staff members must ensure that services and programs are provided on a fair and equitable basis. HRLP facilities, programs and services must be accessible. Hours of operation and delivery of and access to programs and services must be responsive to the needs of all students and other constituents. HRLP must adhere to the spirit and intent of equal opportunity laws.

HRLP must be open and readily accessible to all students and must not discriminate except where sanctioned by law and institutional policy. Discrimination must be avoided on the bases of age; color; creed; cultural heritage; disability; ethnicity; gender identity; nationality; political affiliation; religious affiliation; sex; sexual orientation; or social, economic, marital, or veteran status.

Consistent with their mission and goals, HRLP must take affirmative action to remedy significant imbalances in student participation and staffing patterns.

Policies must be in place to encourage the hiring and promotion of a diverse and multicultural staff.

As the demographic profiles of campuses change and new instructional delivery methods are introduced, HRLP must recognize the needs of students who participate in distance learning for access to programs and services offered on campus. HRLP must provide appropriate services in ways that are accessible to distance learners and assist them in identifying and gaining access to other appropriate services in their geographic region.

Part 10. CAMPUS and EXTERNAL RELATIONS

HRLP must establish, maintain, and promote effective relations with relevant individuals, campus offices, and external agencies.

Particular efforts should be made by the staff to develop positive relationships with campus and off-campus agencies responsible for judicial affairs, counseling services, learning assistance, disability services, student health services, student activities, security and safety, academic advising, admissions, campus mail and telephone services, physical plant services, institutional budgeting and planning, computer center, vendors and suppliers of products used in residence and dining halls, and private housing operators.

Special attention must be paid to the relationships with those units who use housing facilities to carry out their programs, such as conference services.

HRLP staff should be aware of the importance of housing and residential life as a critical institutional asset, its opportunity to contribute to academic programs and the delivery of services, and its effect on attracting and retaining students.

HRLP staff must develop and maintain staff relationships in a climate of mutual respect, support, trust, and interdependence recognizing the strengths and limitations of each colleague.

Part 11. DIVERSITY

Within the context of each institution's unique mission, diversity enriches the community and enhances the collegiate experience for all; therefore, HRLP must nurture environments where commonalties and differences among people are recognized and honored.

HRLP must promote educational experiences that are characterized by open and continuous communication that deepens understanding of one's own identity, culture, and heritage, and that of others. HRLP must educate and promote respect about commonalties and differences in their historical and cultural contexts.

HRLP must address the characteristics and needs of a diverse population when establishing and implementing policies and procedures.

Part 12. ETHICS

All persons involved in the delivery of HRLP must adhere to the highest principles of ethical behavior. HRLP must develop or adopt and implement appropriate statements of ethical practice. HRLP must publish these statements and ensure their periodic review by relevant constituencies.

HRLP staff members must ensure that privacy and confidentiality are maintained with respect to all communications and records to the extent that such records are protected under the law and appropriate statements of ethical practice. Information contained in students' education records must not be disclosed without written consent except as allowed by relevant laws and institutional policies. Staff members must disclose to appropriate authorities information judged to be of an emergency nature, especially when the safety of the individual or others is involved, or when otherwise required by institutional policy or relevant law.

HRLP staff members must be aware of and comply with the provisions contained in the institution's human subjects research policy and in other relevant institutional policies addressing ethical practices and confidentiality of research data concerning individuals.

HRLP staff members must recognize and avoid personal conflict of interest or appearance thereof in their transactions with students and others.

HRLP staff members must strive to insure the fair, objective, and impartial treatment of all persons with whom they deal. Staff members must not participate in nor condone any form of harassment that demeans persons or creates an intimidating, hostile, or offensive campus environment.

When handling institutional funds, HRLP must ensure that such funds are managed in accordance with established and responsible accounting procedures and the fiscal policies or processes of the institution.

HRLP staff members must perform their duties within the limits of their training, expertise, and competence. When these limits are exceeded, individuals in need of further assistance must be referred to persons possessing appropriate qualifications.

HRLP staff members must use suitable means to confront and otherwise hold accountable other staff members who exhibit unethical behavior.

HRLP staff members must be knowledgeable about and practice ethical behavior in the use of technology.

HRLP staff members should remain abreast of ethical codes and practices through involvement in professional associations.

Part 13. ASSESSMENT and EVALUATION
HRLP must conduct regular assessment and evaluations. HRLP must employ effective qualitative and quantitative methodologies as appropriate, to determine whether and to what degree the stated mission, goals, and student learning and development outcomes are being met. The process must employ sufficient and sound assessment measures to ensure comprehensiveness. Data collected must include responses from students and other affected constituencies.

HRLP must evaluate periodically how well they complement and enhance the institution's stated mission and educational effectiveness.

Results of these evaluations must be used in revising and improving programs and services and in recognizing staff performance.

General Standards revised in 2002; HRLP content developed/ revised in 1986, 1992, 1997, & 2004

THE ROLE of INTERNATIONAL STUDENT PROGRAMS
CAS Standards Contextual Statement

In 2004, more than 572,000 international students from over 220 countries studied at institutions of higher education in the United States (US). International students studying in the US pursue undergraduate and graduate degrees as well as English-language training, and are drawn to this country because of the high quality degree programs and the wide range of academic options offered. International students, whether in the US or other host countries, bring with them rich experiences and unique cross-cultural perspectives that help to internationalize the campus and give host country students first-hand opportunities to share learning with individuals from around the world. International students face unique challenges as they attempt to adjust to a different campus life and culture, master written and spoken languages, comply with immigration regulations, meet the requirements of their academic programs, and prepare to return home to begin careers.

The student affairs professionals who work with these students provide information, advising, programs, and services designed to make their experience as positive and productive as possible. They frequently serve as the liaison between international students and all those with whom these students come into contact, including faculty, students, and staff; local citizens; officials of host country and foreign government agencies; and the student's sponsor or family at home, representing the students' best interests and advising them accordingly.

The student affairs professionals who work with these students have a wide range of responsibilities, including advising on immigration, academic, and personal matters; orientation programming offered both at the beginning of the academic term and/or throughout the year; social and cultural programming to help international students learn more about national and local culture and develop friendships with other students; liaisons and problem-solving with offices and groups on- and off-campus; crisis intervention in case of illness or serious legal, financial, or personal problems; and planning, budgeting, and office management.

The student affairs professionals who work with international students should be knowledgeable and articulate about the national culture and how it differs from the cultures of other countries and should understand the social and psychological processes of cross-cultural adjustment. They should be familiar with the educational systems and political, economic, historical, and social issues and trends framing the contexts of the countries from which their students come. The student affairs professionals who work with these students must also be up-to-date on the intricacies of immigration law and regulations, have good counseling and advising skills, understand how to develop effective and creative programming, and be good at setting priorities, managing

time and resources, and communicating effectively with others. Such professionals must also enjoy helping people from diverse cultural backgrounds and learning about cultural differences.

References, Readings, and Resources

Althen, G. (Ed.) (1994). *Learning across cultures.* Cranberry Township, PA: NAFSA Publications.

Althen, G. (1983). *The handbook of foreign student advising.* Yarmouth, ME: Intercultural Press.

Gooding, J. (1995) *The faculty member's guide to immigration law.* . Cranberry Township, PA: NAFSA Publications.

Hall, E. T. (1982). *The hidden dimension.* Yarmouth, ME: Intercultural Press.

Ogami, N. (1987). Cold water [videotape]. Yarmouth, ME: Intercultural Press.

Yenkin, A (Ed.) (1996). *Adviser's manual of federal regulations affecting international students and scholars.* Cranberry Township, PA: NAFSA-AIE Publications.

Intercultural Press, P.O. Box 700, Yarmouth, ME 04096, (207) 846-5168

NAFSA: Association of International Educators,1307 New York Avenue, NW, 8th Floor, Washington, DC 20005-4701; 202-737-3699; Fax 202-737-3657; website: www.nafsa.org

Contributors:
Current edition: Paula Swinford, University of Southern California, ACHA
Previous editions: Bill Carroll, NAFSA

INTERNATIONAL STUDENT PROGRAMS and SERVICES
CAS Standards and Guidelines

Part 1. MISSION
International Student Programs and Services (ISPS) must incorporate student learning and student development in its mission. The program and service must enhance overall educational experiences. The ISPS must develop, record, disseminate, implement, and regularly review its mission and goals. Mission statements must be consistent with the mission and goals of the institution and with the standards in this document. ISPS must operate as an integral part of the institution's overall mission.

The provision of international student programs and services should reflect a strong institutional commitment to the education of international students.

ISPS must promote the academic and personal growth and development of international students. To accomplish the mission, the program must:
- **Assess the needs of international students, set priorities among those needs, and respond to the extent that the number of students, facilities, and resources permit**
- **Provide thorough information on immigration regulations and procedures to advise international students effectively, assure institutional adherence to those regulations and procedures, and interpret host country immigration policy to the campus community**
- **Provide professional services to students in the areas of counseling, advising, and assistance in complying with government regulations**
- **Orient international students to the policies and expectations of the institution, its culture, the host country educational system, and the host country in general**
- **Foster an international dimension within the institution and the community at large**
- **Promote positive interaction among international students, and between international and host country students, the academic community, and the community at large**
- **Facilitate the enrollment and retention of international students**
- **Facilitate re-entry and cultural re-adjustment related to the student's return home**

International student programs and services should facilitate institutional sensitivity to the cultural needs of international community members (e.g., social, religious, dietary , and housing). Programs should be coordinated with academic units and other institutional functional areas that provide programs and services to students, faculty, and staff.

Part 2. PROGRAM
The formal education of students consists of the curriculum and the co-curriculum, and must promote student learning and development that is purposeful and holistic. International Student Programs and Services (ISPS) must identify relevant and desirable student learning and development outcomes and provide programs and services that encourage the achievement of those outcomes.

Relevant and desirable outcomes include: intellectual growth, effective communication, realistic self-appraisal, enhanced self-esteem, clarified values, career choices, leadership development, healthy behaviors, meaningful interpersonal relationships, independence, collaboration, social responsibility, satisfying and productive lifestyles, appreciation of diversity, spiritual awareness, and achievement of personal and educational goals.

ISPS must provide evidence of its impact on the achievement of student learning and development outcomes.

The table below offers examples of evidence of achievement of student learning and development.

Student Learning and Development Outcome Domains

Intellectual growth
Examples of achievement indicators
> Produces personal and educational goal statements; Employs critical thinking in problem solving; Uses complex information from a variety of sources including personal experience and observation to form a decision or opinion; Obtains a degree; Applies previously understood information and concepts to a new situation or setting; Expresses appreciation for literature, the fine arts, mathematics, sciences, and social sciences

Effective communication
Examples of achievement indicators
> Writes and speaks coherently and effectively; Writes and speaks after reflection; Able to influence others through writing, speaking, or artistic expression; Effectively articulates abstract ideas; Uses appropriate syntax; Makes presentations or gives performances

Enhanced self-esteem

Examples of achievement indicators

Shows self-respect and respect for others; Initiates actions toward achievement of goals; Takes reasonable risks; Demonstrates assertive behavior; Functions without need for constant reassurance from others

Realistic self-appraisal

Examples of achievement indicators

Articulates personal skills and abilities; Makes decisions and acts in congruence with personal values; Acknowledges personal strengths and weaknesses; Articulates rationale for personal behavior; Seeks feedback from others; Learns from past experiences

Clarified values

Examples of achievement indicators

Articulates personal values; Acts in congruence with personal values; Makes decisions that reflect personal values; Demonstrates willingness to scrutinize personal beliefs and values; Identifies personal, work, and lifestyle values and explains how they influence decision-making

Career choices

Examples of achievement indicators

Articulates career choices based on assessment of interests, values, skills, and abilities; Documents knowledge, skills, and accomplishments resulting from formal education, work experience, community service, and volunteer experiences; Makes the connections between classroom and out-of-classroom learning; Can construct a resume with clear job objectives and evidence of related knowledge, skills and accomplishments; Articulates the characteristics of a preferred work environment; Comprehends the world of work; Takes steps to initiate a job search or seek advanced education

Leadership development

Examples of achievement indicators

Articulates leadership philosophy or style; Serves in a leadership position in a student organization; Comprehends the dynamics of a group; Exhibits democratic principles as a leader; Exhibits ability to visualize a group purpose and desired outcomes

Healthy behavior

Examples of achievement indicators

Chooses behaviors and environments that promote health and reduce risk; Articulate the relationship between health and wellness and accomplishing life-long goals; Exhibits behaviors that advance a healthy community.

Meaningful interpersonal relationships

Examples of achievement indicators

Develops and maintains satisfying interpersonal relationships; Establishes mutually rewarding relationships with friends and colleagues; Listens to and considers others' points of view; Treats others with respect

Independence

Examples of achievement indicators

Exhibits self-reliant behaviors; Functions autonomously; Exhibits ability to function interdependently; Accepts supervision as needed; Manages time effectively

Collaboration

Examples of achievement indicators

Works cooperatively with others; Seeks the involvement of others; Seeks feedback from others; Contributes to achievement of a group goal; Exhibits effective listening skills

Social responsibility

Examples of achievement indicators

Understands and participates in relevant governance systems; Understands, abides by, and participates in the development, maintenance, and/or orderly change of community, social, and legal standards or norms; Appropriately challenges the unfair, unjust, or uncivil behavior of other individuals or groups; Participates in service/volunteer activities

Satisfying and productive lifestyles

Examples of achievement indicators

Achieves balance between education, work, and leisure time; Articulates and meets goals for work, leisure, and education; Overcomes obstacles that hamper goal achievement; Functions on the basis of personal identity, ethical, spiritual, and moral values; Articulates long-term goals and objectives

Appreciating diversity

Examples of achievement indicators

Understands one's own identity and culture; Seeks involvement with people different from oneself; Seeks involvement in diverse interests; Articulates the advantages and challenges of a diverse society; Challenges appropriately the abusive use of stereotypes by others; Understands the impact of diversity on one's own society

Spiritual awareness

Examples of achievement indicators

Develops and articulates personal belief system; Understands roles of spirituality in personal and group values and behaviors

222

Personal and educational goals

Examples of achievement indicators

Sets, articulates, and pursues individual goals; Articulates personal and educational goals and objectives; Uses personal and educational goals to guide decisions; Understands the effect of one's personal and educational goals on others

ISPS must provide opportunities for discussion and understanding to minimize cultural conflict and to deal with conflict.

ISPS must include the following elements:

- **Counseling and advising in immigration regulations, financial matters, employment, health insurance and health care, personal concerns, and English-language needs**
- **Educational programs to enhance positive interaction between domestic and international students, to develop faculty and staff sensitivity to cultural differences and international student needs, and to assist in the understanding of and adjustment to a host country's educational system and culture**
- **Special orientation programs to enhance knowledge and understanding of the institution, the host country's educational system, and the culture of the host country in general, as well as programs to address issues related to re-entry to the student's home country**
- **Assessment of the educational goals; personal development levels; and social, emotional, and cultural needs of international students**
- **Appropriate and timely referrals to other service and program agencies**
- **Cross-cultural programs addressing cultural problems and issues for faculty, staff, teaching assistants, and students, and dependents of international students;**
- **Liaison with appropriate student organizations**
- **Advocacy within the institution for the needs of international students**

Part 3. LEADERSHIP

Effective and ethical leadership is essential to the success of all organizations. Institutions must appoint, position, and empower leaders within the administrative structure to accomplish stated missions. Leaders at various levels must be selected on the basis of formal education and training, relevant work experience, personal skills and competencies, relevant professional credentials, as well as potential for promoting learning and development in students, applying effective practices to educational processes,

and enhancing institutional effectiveness. Institutions must determine expectations of accountability for leaders and fairly assess their performance.

International Student Programs and Services (ISPS) leaders must exercise authority over resources for which they are responsible to achieve their respective missions.

ISPS leaders must:

- articulate a vision for their organization
- set goals and objectives based on the needs and capabilities of the population served
- promote student learning and development
- prescribe and practice ethical behavior
- recruit, select, supervise, and develop others in the organization
- manage financial resources
- coordinate human resources
- plan, budget for, and evaluate personnel and programs
- apply effective practices to educational and administrative processes
- communicate effectively
- initiate collaborative interaction between individuals and agencies that possess legitimate concerns and interests in the functional area

ISPS leaders must identify and find means to address individual, organizational, or environmental conditions that inhibit goal achievement.

ISPS leaders must promote campus environments that result in multiple opportunities for student learning and development.

ISPS leaders must continuously improve programs and services in response to changing needs of students and other constituents, and evolving institutional priorities.

Part 4. ORGANIZATION and MANAGEMENT

Guided by an overarching intent to ensure student learning and development, International Programs and Services (ISPS) must be structured purposefully and managed effectively to achieve stated goals. Evidence of appropriate structure must include current and accessible policies and procedures, written performance expectations for all employees, functional workflow graphics or organizational charts, and clearly stated service delivery expectations.

Evidence of effective management must include use of comprehensive and accurate information for decisions, clear sources and channels of authority, effective communication practices, decision-making and conflict resolution procedures, responsiveness to changing conditions, accountability and evaluation systems, and recognition and reward processes. ISPS must provide channels within the organization for regular review of administrative policies and procedures.

Institutions enrolling international students must designate a specific office or service unit to coordinate programs and services for this student population.

Part 5. HUMAN RESOURCES

International Programs and Services (ISPS) must be staffed adequately by individuals qualified to accomplish its mission and goals. Within established guidelines of the institution, ISPS must establish procedures for staff selection, training, and evaluation; set expectations for supervision, and provide appropriate professional development opportunities. ISPS must strive to improve the professional competence and skills of all personnel it employs.

Wherever possible, staff members should be representative of the various cultures served in the student population.

ISPS professional staff members must hold an earned graduate degree in a field relevant to the position they hold or must possess an appropriate combination of educational credentials and related work experience. They must be knowledgeable about research and practice in areas related to international student programs and services and stay abreast of developments in policies, laws, and regulations affecting international students.

Professional staff members should be competent in skills such as group facilitation, leadership training and development, crisis intervention, workshop design, report writing, public speaking, social and interpersonal development, individual and group counseling and their cross-cultural aspects. Generally, these competencies are found in persons who graduate from student personnel, counseling, and other higher education graduate programs, as well as from programs such as cross-cultural communication, international studies, and anthropology.

Specific study in the following areas is desirable: multicultural theory, organizational development, counseling theory and practice, group dynamics, leadership development, human development, and research and evaluation. Proficiency in a language other than English and extended travel and/or living experience abroad are also helpful.

Degree or credential-seeking interns must be qualified by enrollment in an appropriate field of study and by relevant experience. These individuals must be trained and supervised adequately by professional staff members holding educational credentials and related work experience appropriate for supervision.

The use of graduate assistants and interns in international student programs and services should be encouraged. These individuals expand staff abilities, provide peer role models, and gain valuable pre-professional experience. Particular attention should be given to preparing assistants and interns to be especially sensitive to cultural differences and the special needs of international students.

Student employees and volunteers must be carefully selected, trained, supervised, and evaluated. They must be trained on how and when to refer those in need of assistance to qualified staff members and have access to a supervisor for assistance in making these judgments. Student employees and volunteers must be provided clear and precise job descriptions, pre-service training based on assessed needs, and continuing staff development.

ISPS must have technical and support staff members adequate to accomplish its mission. Staff members must be technologically proficient and qualified to perform their job functions, be knowledgeable of ethical and legal uses of technology, and have access to training. The level of staffing and workloads must be adequate and appropriate for program and service demands.

Salary levels and fringe benefits for all ISPS staff members must be commensurate with those for comparable positions within the institution, in similar institutions, and in the relevant geographic area.

ISPS must institute hiring and promotion practices that are fair, inclusive, and non-discriminatory. Programs and services must employ a diverse staff to provide readily identifiable role models for students and to enrich the campus community.

ISPS must create and maintain position descriptions for all staff members and provide regular performance planning and appraisals.

ISPS must have a system for regular staff evaluation and must provide access to continuing education and professional development opportunities, including in-service training programs and participation in professional conferences and workshops.

Part 6. FINANCIAL RESOURCES

International Student Programs and Services (ISPS) must have adequate funding to accomplish its mission and goals. Funding priorities must be determined within the context of the stated mission, goals, objectives and comprehensive analysis of the needs and capabilities of students and the availability of internal or external resources.

ISPS must demonstrate fiscal responsibility and cost effectiveness consistent with institutional protocols.

Institutions considering special student fees as a means of supporting international student services and programs should review carefully the ethical issues involved in implementing such fees.

Part 7. FACILITIES, TECHNOLOGY, and EQUIPMENT

International Student Programs and Services (ISPS) must have adequate, suitably located facilities, adequate technology, and equipment to support its mission and goals efficiently and effectively. Facilities, technology, and equipment must be evaluated regularly and be in compliance with relevant federal, state, provincial, and local requirements to provide for access, health, safety, and security.

Part 8. LEGAL RESPONSIBILITIES

International Student Programs and Services (ISPS) staff members must be knowledgeable about and responsive to laws and regulations that relate to their respective responsibilities. Staff members must inform users of programs and services and officials, as appropriate, of legal obligations and limitations including constitutional, statutory, regulatory, and case law; mandatory laws and orders emanating from federal, state/provincial and local governments; and the institution's policies.

Further, staff should also be familiar with constitutional issues of due process and rights of freedom of expression as applicable to residents of the United States and Canada.

ISPS staff members must use reasonable and informed practices to limit the liability exposure of the institution, its officers, employees, and agents. Staff members must be informed about institutional policies regarding personal liability and related insurance coverage options.

The institution must provide access to legal advice for ISPS staff members as needed to carry out assigned responsibilities.

The institution must inform staff and students in a timely and systematic fashion about extraordinary or changing legal obligations and potential liabilities.

Part 9. EQUITY and ACCESS

International Student Programs and Services (ISPS) staff members must ensure that services and programs are provided on a fair and equitable basis. Facilities, programs and services must be accessible. Hours of operation and delivery of and access to programs and services must be responsive to the needs of all students and other constituents. ISPS must adhere to the spirit and intent of equal opportunity laws.

ISPS must be open and readily accessible to all students and must not discriminate except where sanctioned by law and institutional policy. Discrimination must be avoided on the bases of age; color; creed; cultural heritage; disability; ethnicity; gender identity; nationality; political affiliation; religious affiliation; sex; sexual orientation; or social, economic, marital, or veteran status.

Consistent with their mission and goals, ISPS must take affirmative action to remedy significant imbalances in student participation and staffing patterns.

As the demographic profiles of campuses change and new instructional delivery methods are introduced, institutions must recognize the needs of students who participate in distance learning for access to programs and services offered on campus. Institutions must provide appropriate services in ways that are accessible to distance learners and assist them in identifying and gaining access to other appropriate services in their geographic region.

Part 10. CAMPUS and EXTERNAL RELATIONS

International Student Programs and Services (ISPS) must establish, maintain, and promote effective relations with relevant individuals, campus offices, and external agencies.

Professional staff members must coordinate, or where appropriate, collaborate with faculty and staff in providing services and programs for international students.

Part 11. DIVERSITY

Within the context of the institution's unique mission, diversity enriches the community and enhances the collegiate experience for all; therefore, International

Student Programs and Services (ISPS) must nurture environments where similarities and differences among people are recognized and honored.

ISPS must promote educational experiences that are characterized by open and continuous communication that deepens understanding of one's own identity, culture, and heritage, and that of others. Programs and services must educate and promote respect about commonalties and differences in their historical and cultural contexts.

ISPS must address the characteristics and needs of a diverse population when establishing and implementing policies and procedures. ISPS must orient international students to the culture of the host country and promote and deepen international students' understanding of cross-cultural differences.

All institutional units that provide services to students should share responsibility for meeting the needs of international students. Coordinated efforts to promote multicultural sensitivity and the elimination of prejudicial behaviors in all functional areas on campus should be encouraged.

Part 12. ETHICS

All persons involved in the delivery of programs and services for international students must adhere to the highest principles of ethical behavior. International Student Programs and Services(ISPS) must develop or adopt and implement appropriate statements of ethical practice. ISPS must publish these statements and ensure their periodic review by relevant constituencies.

Staff members must ensure that privacy and confidentiality are maintained with respect to all communications and records to the extent that such records are protected under the law and appropriate statements of ethical practice. Information contained in students' education records must not be disclosed without written consent except as allowed by relevant laws and institutional policies, or as mandated by regulations from the US Immigration and Naturalization Service, or the US Information Agency. Staff members must disclose to appropriate authorities information judged to be of an emergency nature, especially when the safety of the individual or others is involved, or when otherwise required by institutional policy or relevant law.

All ISPS staff members must be aware of and comply with the provisions contained in the institution's

human subjects research policy and in other relevant institutional policies addressing ethical practices and confidentiality of research data concerning individuals.

ISPS staff members must recognize and avoid personal conflict of interest or appearance thereof in their transactions with students and others.

ISPS staff members must strive to insure the fair, objective, and impartial treatment of all persons with whom they deal. Staff members must not participate in nor condone any form of harassment that demeans persons or creates an intimidating, hostile, or offensive campus environment.

When handling institutional funds, all ISPS staff members must ensure that such funds are managed in accordance with established and responsible accounting procedures and the fiscal policies or processes of the institution.

ISPS staff members must perform their duties within the limits of their training, expertise, and competence. When these limits are exceeded, individuals in need of further assistance must be referred to persons possessing appropriate qualifications.

ISPS staff members must use suitable means to confront and otherwise hold accountable other staff members who exhibit unethical behavior.

ISPS staff members must be knowledgeable about and practice ethical behavior in the use of technology.

ISPS staff members must balance the wants, needs, and requirements of students, institutional policies, laws, and sponsors, having as their ultimate concern the long-term well being of international educational exchange programs and the students participating in them.

ISPS staff members must demonstrate cross-cultural sensitivity, treating differences between value systems and cultures in non-judgmental ways. The use of pejorative stereotypical statements must be avoided. Staff members must maintain the highest principles of ethical behavior in the use of technology.

Part 13. ASSESSMENT and EVALUATION

International Students Programs and Services (ISPS) must conduct regular assessment and evaluations. ISPS must employ effective qualitative and quantitative methodologies as appropriate, to determine whether and to what degree the stated mission, goals, and student learning and development outcomes are being met. The process must employ sufficient and sound assessment measures to ensure comprehensiveness. Data collected must include responses from students and other affected constituencies.

ISPS must evaluate periodically how well they complement and enhance the institution's stated mission and educational effectiveness.

Results of these evaluations must be used in revising and improving programs and services and in recognizing staff performance.

General Standards revised in 2002; ISPS content developed/ revised in 1996

THE ROLE of INTERNSHIP PROGRAMS
CAS Standards Contextual Statement

In the 1960s, with its social upheaval, a movement to make the college curriculum more relevant and to apply the knowledge of theoretical disciplines to solve societal problems gained considerable momentum. As higher education institutions revamped their curricula, they began to recognize that supervised learning experiences outside the classroom were relevant to the educational process and that ways could be found to evaluate these experiences, possibly for academic credit.

In the early 1970s, two professional associations, the Society for Field Experience and National Center for Public Service Internship Programs, were formed among those involved in college-based field experiences and those involved in policy issues and government-based projects, such as the Urban Corps. These organizations merged in 1978 to form the organization known today as the National Society for Experiential Education (NSEE). Other experiential education organizations include the Cooperative Education and Internship Association (CEIA), the Association for Experiential Education (AEE), NAFSA: The Association of International Educators, and the National Association of Colleges and Employers, among others. A goal of these organizations has been to advocate experiential and related forms of active or engaged learning, both within and outside the classroom or campus setting, and to establish appropriate standards and ethics in the profession.

As a result of the efforts of these organizations, as well as the demand by students and parents for a more career oriented curriculum, internships have become an integral part of a college education. What distinguishes internships from other forms of active learning is that there is a degree of supervision and self-study that allows students to "learn by doing" and to reflect upon that learning in a way that achieves certain learning goals and objectives. Feedback for improvement and the development or refinement of learning goals is also essential. What distinguishes an intern from a volunteer is the deliberative form of learning that takes place. There must be a balance between learning and contributing, and the student, the student's institution, and the internship placement site must share in the responsibility to ensure that the balance is appropriate and that the learning is of sufficiently high quality to warrant the effort, which might include academic credit.

Major questions and concerns arise regarding how colleges and universities can provide an appropriate internship experience, given the various goals of the institution, the academic and student affairs divisions, and the student. For example, some institutions encourage internships but refuse to grant academic credit for them. Some have policies that restrict academic credit to internships only outside the major. Also, accreditation standards within a professional field may conflict with institutional policy. Some may prohibit students from receiving academic credit for internships that provide compensation, although this attitude is declining as quality placements increase. Then there are the variable standards as to what constitutes a credit-worthy internship (i.e.., how many hours equal how many credits) and concern for the liability of students and their institution should mistakes be made.

The kind of internship experience sanctioned by an institution may vary. Some emphasize a form of cooperative education in which compensation for professional work is a high expectation, although credit for the experience is not necessarily expected. Some may involve a heavily supervised semester or summer-long experience either for or not for academic credit, while others might utilize a form of externship, which is similar to short-term, field-based learning with minimal or limited interaction with an organization.

Setting standards for internship programs will establish for administrators, faculty, and staff a set of benchmarks that identify what a quality internship program on a college campus should be. But it is important that we distinguish between an academic internship within academic affairs and the co-curricular internship found in the student affairs division. The CAS Internship Program standards take into account the importance of establishing standards within each of these areas to meet student academic, career and personal goals. It also assumes that there is sufficient communication between the two areas so that the appropriate expertise can be utilized across divisions and throughout the campus.

Of considerable significance is the intent of CAS to include the notion that an internship program is not the sole purview of a career center or off-campus programs office. Academic departments that grant credit for internships, have faculty designated to oversee internships, or have faculty members who accompany students on a short-term or long-term basis to locations off-campus, such as Washington or London, should be considered as having an internship program that are expected to meet these CAS standards.

While professionalism in experiential education has made significant leaps in the past decade, the establishment of these standards is an important milestone within the field. For the first time, a major statement is made that defines an internship within the context of an academic institution of higher education. It emphasizes that careful thought, planning, administration, implementation, and feedback are important in the entire learning process and that sufficient resources should be available to accomplish the established goals of the learning experience. Also, this professionalism must exist within both the academic and the co-curricular areas of the institution.

With the proliferation of internships at the local, state, national and international levels, administrators and faculty have a special obligation not only to ensure the high quality of the learning environment for their students, but also to assess the risk management and safety of students in these settings. Both faculty and staff need to be sufficiently trained to appropriately oversee an internship, to recognize the warning signs, and to take appropriate action. Increasingly, institutions work with third party organizations to place, supervise, and evaluate students because these organizations have dedicated personnel who are expert in these areas. Yet, similar diligence must be paid to the evaluation of their performance as well.

Internships and other forms of experiential education have become much more accepted as part of the college experience. Many new faculty are often former interns who understand the value of an internship and understand the appropriate ways of measuring student performance. More agencies understand how to utilize interns and to give them substantive work and responsibilities. More financial assistance is available either through the institution or the placement site to help cover the student's costs. Technology is providing career centers, internship offices, or off-campus programs with the ability to match the interests of the student with an appropriate placement more efficiently and effectively. Also, the movement toward on-line portfolio systems allows more participation in the development and evaluation of the student by all those involved in the internship experience. Such advances will very likely lead to greater advances in assessment of student outcomes in internships and other forms of experiential learning.

References, Readings, and Resources

Chickering, A. W. (1977). Experience and learning: An introduction to experiential learning. Rochelle, NY: Change Magazine Press.

Inkster, R. P., & Ross, R.G. (1998) The Internship as partnership: A handbook for businesses, nonprofits, and government agencies. Raleigh, NC: National Society for Experiential Education.

Inkster, R. P., & Ross, R. G. (1995). The Internship as partnership: A handbook for campus-based coordinators and advisors. Raleigh, NC: National Society for Experiential Education.

Kendall, J. C., Duley, J. S., Little, T. C., Permaul, J. S., & Rubin, S. (1986) Strengthening experiential education within your institution. Raleigh, NC: National Society for Internships and Experiential Education.

Kiser, P.M. (2000). Getting the most out of your internship: Learning from experience. Belmont, CA: Wadsworth/Thomson Learning.

Kolb, D.A. (1984). Experiential learning: Experience as the source of learning and development. Upper Saddle River, N.J.: Prentice-Hall.

Stanton, T. and Ali, K. (1994). The experienced hand: A student manual for making the most of an internship (2nd ed.). New York: Caroll Press.

Sweitzer, H. Frederick and King, Mary A. (2004). The successful internship: Transformation and empowerment in experiential learning. Belmont, CA: Brooks Cole.

National Society for Experiential Education, 19 Mantua Road, Mt. Royal, NJ 08061; 856.423.3427; fax: 856.423.3420; http://www.nsee.org

Contributor: Gene Alpert, The Washington Center, NSEE

INTERNSHIP PROGRAMS
CAS Standards and Guidelines

Part 1. MISSION

The primary mission of Internship Programs (IP) is to engage students in planned, educationally-related work and learning experiences that integrate knowledge and theory with practical application and skill development in a professional setting.

IP must incorporate student learning and student development in its mission. IP must enhance overall educational experiences. IP must develop, record, disseminate, implement, and regularly review its mission and goals. Mission statements must be consistent with the mission and goals of the institution and with the standards in this document. IP must operate as an integral part of the institution's overall mission.

Part 2. PROGRAM

The formal education of students consists of the curriculum and the co-curriculum and must promote student learning and development that is purposeful and holistic. Internship Programs (IP) must identify relevant and desirable student learning and development outcomes and provide services that encourage the achievement of those outcomes.

Learning goals of the IP must:
- be clear about the educational purpose and expected student learning outcomes of the internship experience
- encourage the learner to test assumptions and hypotheses about the outcomes of decisions and actions taken, then weigh the outcomes against past learning and future implications
- develop and document intentional goals and objectives for the internship experience and measure learning outcomes against these goals and objectives
- maintain intellectual rigor in the field experience

IP must:
- ensure that the participants enter the experience with sufficient foundation to support a successful experience
- engage students in appropriate and relevant internships that facilitate practical application of theory and knowledge
- provide the learner, the facilitator, and any organizational partners with important background information about each other and about the context and environment in which the experience will operate
- articulate the relationship of the internship experience to the expected learning outcomes
- determine criteria for internship sites and train appropriate internship personnel to ensure productive and appropriate learning opportunities for students
- ensure that all parties engaged in the experience are included in the recognition of progress and accomplishment

When course credit is offered for an internship, the credit must primarily be for learning, not just for the practical work completed at the internship. Whether the internship is for credit or not, the focus must be on learning and educational objectives, not just on hours accrued at the site.

Relevant and desirable outcomes include: intellectual growth, effective communication, realistic self-appraisal, enhanced self-esteem, clarified values, career choices, leadership development, healthy behaviors, meaningful interpersonal relationships, independence, collaboration, social responsibility, satisfying and productive lifestyles, appreciation of diversity, spiritual awareness, and achievement of personal and educational goals.

IP must provide evidence of its impact on the achievement of student learning and development outcomes.

The table below offers examples of evidence of achievement of student learning and development.

Student Learning and Development Outcome Domains

Intellectual growth
Examples of achievement indicators
> Produces personal and educational goal statements; Employs critical thinking in problem solving; Uses complex information from a variety of sources including personal experience and observation to form a decision or opinion; Earns a degree; Applies previously understood information and concepts to internship situation or setting; Expresses appreciation for knowledge and new information; Applies knowledge to local, national, and global issues

Effective communication

Examples of achievement indicators

Writes and speaks coherently and effectively; Listens effectively and can engage in controversy or controversial discussions with civility; Writes and speaks after reflection; Able to influence others through writing, speaking or artistic expression; Effectively articulates abstract ideas; Uses appropriate syntax; Makes presentations or gives performances

Enhanced self-esteem and professional development

Examples of achievement indicators

Shows self-respect and respect for others; Initiates actions toward achievement of academic, professional, and/or personal goals; Takes reasonable risks; Demonstrates assertive behavior; Functions without need for constant reassurance from others

Realistic self-appraisal

Examples of achievement indicators

Articulates and demonstrates personal skills and abilities; Makes decisions and acts in congruence with personal values; Acknowledges personal strengths and weaknesses; Articulates rationale for personal behavior; Seeks feedback from others; Learns from past experiences

Clarified values

Examples of achievement indicators

Articulates personal values; Acts in congruence with personal values; Makes decisions that reflect personal values; Demonstrates willingness to scrutinize personal beliefs and values; Identifies personal, work, and lifestyle values and explains how they influence decision-making

Career choices

Examples of achievement indicators

Articulates career choices based on assessment of interests, values, skills, and abilities; Documents knowledge, skills, and accomplishments resulting from formal education, work experience, service-learning, and volunteer experiences; Makes the connections between classroom and internship learning; Makes academic choices based on thoughtful consideration of career goals; Able to articulate clear objectives and evidence of related knowledge, skills, and accomplishments; Articulates the characteristics of a preferred work environment; Understands elements of the work place

Leadership development

Examples of achievement indicators

Understands that leadership is a process rather than a position; Understands that everyone is a potential leader; Comprehends that leadership occurs at all levels of an organization; Articulates leadership philosophy or style in examining own leadership

Healthy behavior

Examples of achievement indicators

Chooses behaviors and environments that promote health and reduce risk; Articulates the relationship between health and wellness and accomplishing life-long goals; Exhibits behaviors that advance a healthy community

Meaningful interpersonal relationships

Examples of achievement indicators

Develops and maintains satisfying interpersonal relationships; Establishes mutually rewarding relationships with friends and colleagues; Listens to and considers others' points of view; Treats others with respect

Independence

Examples of achievement indicators

Exhibits self-reliant behaviors; Functions autonomously; Exhibits ability to function interdependently; Accepts supervision as needed; Manages time effectively

Collaboration

Examples of achievement indicators

Works cooperatively with others; Seeks the involvement of others; Seeks feedback from others; Contributes to achievement of a group goal; Exhibits effective listening skills

Social responsibility

Examples of achievement indicators

Understands and participates in relevant governance systems; Demonstrates civic engagement in campus, local, national, and global communities; Understands, abides by, and participates in the development, maintenance, and/or orderly change of community, social, and legal standards or norms; Appropriately challenges the unfair, unjust, or uncivil behavior of other individuals or groups

Satisfying and productive lifestyles

Examples of achievement indicators

Achieves balance between education, work, and leisure time; Articulates and meets goals for work, leisure, and education; Overcomes obstacles that hamper goal achievement; Functions on the basis of personal identity, ethical, spiritual, and moral values; Articulates long-term goals and objectives

Appreciating diversity

Examples of achievement indicators

Understands one's own identity and culture; Seeks involvement with people different from oneself; Seeks involvement in diverse interests; Articulates the advantages and challenges of a diverse society; Challenges appropriately the abusive use of stereotypes by others; Understands the impact of diversity on one's own society;

Develops an informed perspective on issues of diversity and democracy; Reflects on issues of power and privilege

Spiritual awareness

Examples of achievement indicators

Develops and articulates personal belief system; Understands roles of spirituality in personal and group values and behaviors

Personal and educational goals

Examples of achievement indicators

Sets, articulates, and pursues individual goals; Articulates personal and educational goals and objectives; Acknowledges how internship achieves educational goals; Uses personal and educational goals to guide decisions; Understands the effect of one's personal and educational goals on others

IP must be (a) intentional, (b) coherent, (c) based on theories and knowledge of learning and human development, (d) reflective of developmental and demographic profiles of the student population, and (e) responsive to needs of individuals, special populations, and communities.

IP must offer a wide range of internship experiences appropriate for students at various developmental levels, abilities, and with various life circumstances.

Examples may include older students, commuter students, parents, part-time students, fully employed students, and students with disabilities.

IP must initiate collaborative relations among faculty and staff members within the institution for the design and implementation of internship experiences. They must also develop partnerships with external organizations to meet student learning and development outcomes and the organizations' needs.

Whether integrated into a course, completed as an independent study, or designed for co-curricular learning or personal development, internships should encourage practical application of knowledge and theory, development of skills and interests and exploration of career options in a professional setting. Internships may be for pay or non-pay, for credit or non-credit, and for a variety of lengths or terms. IP experiences could include the following:

Discipline-specific course-based internships: These can be designed to achieve a variety of student learning outcomes relevant to the course and discipline within which the internship

is based, including introducing students to career opportunities as a critical aspect of their college education and their chosen field of study, enabling students to learn what types of work within their chosen field of study best suit their interests, helping students to understand the different career opportunities available to them both inside and outside their curriculum. These experiences should be part of the academic curriculum for credit.

Student-initiated internships: These internships can be designed to enable students to explore internship opportunities within or outside their course of study and their discipline, to apply knowledge learned in their academic program to practice in different situations and venues, and to gain exposure to a broader array of internship experiences than a course- or discipline-based internship might allow. These experiences, if approved in advance, should be considered for academic credit. These experiences could also add to co-curricular learning and personal development.

Short-term internships: These internship programs offer students the opportunity to explore career opportunities through internships without the longer term commitment required by a quarter-term program, academic semester, or year. Typically these occur during week-long breaks or during the short sessions between fall and spring semesters and summer (i.e., Jan or May term). These experiences can be integrated into the academic curriculum or serve as a co-curricular experience, for credit or not-for-credit, in the student's discipline, or in a broader learning context.

Paid internships: Whether integrated into a course, completed as independent-study, or planned during the summer or semester breaks, these internships are designed to provide students with exposure to career opportunities within a paid employment environment. Structured within a real-world context, students are encouraged to apply theory and knowledge in the career setting while receiving financial compensation for their work and time.

Internship experiences must be described in a syllabus or plan.

The internship course syllabus or plan for academic or co-curricular experiences should describe:

- purpose of the internship
- desired learning and development outcomes of the internship for all participants
- assignments that link the internship to academic, career, or personal goals
- opportunities to reflect on one's personal reactions to internship experiences
- logistics (e.g., time required, transportation, materials

required, access to services and resources, credit/non-credit, paid/unpaid, financial costs and benefits)
- roles and responsibilities of students and site personnel
- risk management procedures
- supervision and accommodation requirements by institution personnel and internship site
- evaluation of the internship experience and assessment of the extent to which desired outcomes were achieved
- if for credit, course requirements, including criteria for grading

Part 3. LEADERSHIP

Effective and ethical leadership is essential to the success of all organizations. Institutions must appoint, position, and empower Internship Program (IP) leaders within the administrative structure to accomplish stated missions. IP leaders at various levels must be selected on the basis of formal education and training, relevant work experience, personal skills and competencies, relevant professional credentials, as well as potential for promoting learning and development in students, applying effective practices to educational processes, and enhancing institutional effectiveness. Institutions must determine expectations of accountability for leaders and fairly assess their performance.

IP leaders must exercise authority over resources for which they are responsible to achieve their respective missions.

IP leaders must:
- articulate a vision for their organization
- set goals and objectives based on the needs and capabilities of the population served
- promote student learning and development
- prescribe and practice ethical behavior
- recruit, select, supervise, and develop others in the organization
- manage financial resources
- coordinate human resources
- plan, budget for, and evaluate personnel and programs
- apply effective practices to educational and administrative processes
- communicate effectively
- initiate collaborative interaction between individuals and agencies that possess legitimate concerns and interests in the functional area

IP leaders must identify and find means to address individual, organizational, or environmental conditions that inhibit goal achievement.

IP leaders must promote campus environments that result in multiple opportunities for student learning and development.

IP leaders must continuously improve programs in response to changing needs of students and other constituents, and evolving institutional priorities.

Part 4. ORGANIZATION and MANAGEMENT

Guided by an overarching intent to ensure student learning and development, Internship Programs (IP) must be structured purposefully and managed effectively to achieve stated goals. Evidence of appropriate structure must include current and accessible policies and procedures, written performance expectations for all employees, functional workflow graphics or organizational charts, and clearly stated service delivery expectations.

Evidence of effective management must include use of comprehensive and accurate information for decisions, clear sources and channels of authority, effective communication practices, decision-making and conflict resolution procedures, responsiveness to changing conditions, accountability and evaluation systems, and recognition and reward processes. IP must provide channels within the organization for regular review of administrative policies and procedures.

Part 5. HUMAN RESOURCES

Internship Programs (IP) must be staffed adequately by individuals qualified to accomplish the mission and goals. Within established guidelines of the institution, IP must establish procedures for staff selection, training, and evaluation; set expectations for supervision, and provide appropriate professional development opportunities. IP must strive to improve the professional competence and skills of all personnel it employs.

IP professional staff members must hold an earned graduate degree in a field relevant to the position they hold or must possess an appropriate combination of educational credentials and related work experience.

To facilitate the process of identifying internship sites, professional development of staff and faculty members engaged in IP should include enhancing their ability to:
- identify the compatibility between site needs and student interests
- build relationship with business, organizations, institutions, and other career and professional settings
- establish and maintain collaborative relationships with

academic and other units on campus
- understand career and workforce trends

To ensure goal achievement of the IP experience, the professional development of staff and faculty members engaged in IP should include:

Development of assessment skills:
- access previous evaluations of internship sites and make appropriate recommendations as to the learning value of the internship
- develop, implement, and evaluate internship and learning goals
- ensure the time commitment for the internship is appropriate
- ensure that the time spent at internships produces an appropriate balance between the objectives of the site and the learning objectives of the student
- match the unique needs of students and internship sites

Proper communication with students:
- prepare, mentor, and monitor students to fulfill internship requirements according to legal and risk management policies
- clarify the responsibilities of students, the institution, and internship sites

Enhancement of student learning:
- engage students in internship experiences to enhance student learning and exposure to career opportunities
- use active learning strategies that are effective in achieving identified learning outcomes
- engage students in structured opportunities for self-reflection and reflection on the internship experience
- sustain genuine and active commitment of students, the institution, and internship sites
- educate, train, and support students to apply learning from internship experiences to future endeavors

Management skills:
- foster participation by and with diverse populations
- develop fiscal and other resources for program support

Degree or credential-seeking interns must be qualified by enrollment in an appropriate field of study and by relevant experience. These individuals must be trained and supervised adequately by IP professional staff members holding educational credentials and related work experience appropriate for supervision.

Student employees and volunteers must be carefully selected, trained, supervised, and evaluated. They must be trained on how and when to refer those in need of assistance to qualified IP staff members and

have access to a supervisor for assistance in making these judgments. Student employees and volunteers must be provided clear and precise job descriptions, pre-service training based on assessed needs, and continuing staff development.

IP must have technical and support staff members adequate to accomplish its mission. IP staff members must be technologically proficient and qualified to perform their job functions, be knowledgeable of ethical and legal uses of technology, and have access to training. The level of staffing and workloads must be adequate and appropriate for IP demands.

Salary levels and fringe benefits for all IP staff members must be commensurate with those for comparable positions within the institution, in similar institutions, and in the relevant geographic area.

IP must institute hiring and promotion practices that are fair, inclusive, and non-discriminatory. IP must employ a diverse staff to provide readily identifiable role models for students and to enrich the campus community.

IP must create and maintain position descriptions for all staff members and provide regular performance planning and appraisals.

IP must have a system for regular staff evaluation and must provide access to continuing education and professional development opportunities, including in-service training programs and participation in professional conferences and workshops.

Part 6. FINANCIAL RESOURCES
Internship Programs (IP) must have adequate funding to accomplish its mission and goals. Funding priorities must be determined within the context of the stated mission, goals, objectives, and comprehensive analysis of the needs and capabilities of students and the availability of internal or external resources.

IP must demonstrate fiscal responsibility and cost effectiveness consistent with institutional protocols.

Part 7. FACILITIES, TECHNOLOGY, and EQUIPMENT
Internship Programs (IP) must have adequate, suitably located facilities, adequate technology, and equipment to support its mission and goals efficiently and effectively. Facilities, technology, and equipment must be evaluated regularly and be in compliance with relevant federal, state, provincial, and local requirements to provide for access, health, safety, and security.

Part 8. LEGAL RESPONSIBILITIES

Staff members must be knowledgeable about and responsive to laws and regulations that relate to their respective responsibilities. Internship Programs (IP) staff members must inform users of programs and services and officials, as appropriate, of legal obligations and limitations including constitutional, statutory, regulatory, and case law; mandatory laws and orders emanating from federal, state/provincial, and local governments; and the institution's policies.

IP staff and faculty members and internship site personnel engaged in internships must be knowledgeable about and responsive to laws and regulations that relate to their respective responsibilities.

IP staff members must use reasonable and informed practices to limit the liability exposure of the institution, its officers, employees, and agents. Staff members must be informed about institutional policies regarding personal liability and related insurance coverage options.

IP staff members must establish, review, and disseminate safety and emergency company procedures and policies for the work site and accompanying residential facility.

The institution must provide access to legal advice for IP staff members as needed to carry out assigned responsibilities.

The institution must inform IP staff and students in a timely and systematic fashion about extraordinary or changing legal obligations and potential liabilities.

Part 9. EQUITY and ACCESS

Internship Programs (IP) staff members must ensure that services and programs are provided on a fair and equitable basis. Facilities, programs, and services must be accessible. Hours of operation and delivery of and access to programs and services must be responsive to the needs of all students and other constituents. IP must adhere to the spirit and intent of equal opportunity laws.

The program must be open and readily accessible to all students and must not discriminate except where sanctioned by law and institutional policy. Discrimination must be avoided on the bases of age; color; creed; cultural heritage; disability; ethnicity; gender identity; nationality; political affiliation; religious affiliation; sex; sexual orientation; or social, economic, marital, or veteran status.

IP staff members must select sites that adhere to this non-discrimination standard.

As the demographic profiles of campuses change and new instructional delivery methods are introduced, institutions must recognize the needs of students who participate in distance learning for access to programs and services offered on campus. Institutions must provide appropriate services in ways that are accessible to distance learners and assist them in identifying and gaining access to other appropriate services in their geographic region.

Consistent with their mission and goals, IP staff must take affirmative action to remedy significant imbalances in student participation and staffing patterns.

Part 10. CAMPUS and EXTERNAL RELATIONS

Internship Programs (IP) must establish, maintain, and promote effective relations with relevant individuals, campus offices, and external agencies.

These agencies include government, private business, and nonprofit organizations at the local, national, or international level.

If there is more than one campus unit that facilitates internship experiences, those offices should share information and collaborate as appropriate.

IP should develop productive working relationships with a wide range of campus agencies.

IP must be concerned about issues of risk management and consult with appropriate campus offices and officials to insure proper procedures.

IP flourishes best when the institution as a whole is engaged as part of its surrounding community. IP should advocate for the institution to share its resources with its community and to develop a wide range of mutually beneficial campus-community partnerships. The "community" may include individuals and organizations beyond the immediate physical location of the campus and include state/provincial, national, and international relationships.

Part 11. DIVERSITY

Within the context of each institution's unique mission, diversity enriches the community and enhances the collegiate experience for all; therefore,

Internship Programs (IP) must nurture environments where commonalties and differences among people are recognized and honored.

IP must promote educational experiences that are characterized by open and continuous communication that deepens understanding of one's own identity, culture, and heritage, and that of others. IP must educate and promote respect about commonalities and differences in their historical and cultural contexts.

IP must address the characteristics and needs of a diverse population when establishing and implementing policies and procedures.

Part 12. ETHICS

All persons involved in the delivery of Internship Programs (IP) must adhere to the highest principles of ethical behavior. IP must develop or adopt and implement appropriate statements of ethical practice. IP must publish these statements and ensure their periodic review by relevant constituencies.

IP staff members must ensure that privacy and confidentiality are maintained with respect to all communications and records to the extent that such records are protected under the law and appropriate statements of ethical practice. Information contained in students' education records must not be disclosed without written consent except as allowed by relevant laws and institutional policies. IP staff members must disclose to appropriate authorities information judged to be of an emergency nature, especially when the safety of the individual or others is involved, or when otherwise required by institutional policy or relevant law.

All IP staff members must be aware of and comply with the provisions contained in the institution's human subjects research policy and in other relevant institutional policies addressing ethical practices and confidentiality of research data concerning individuals.

IP staff members must recognize and avoid personal conflict of interest or appearance thereof in their transactions with students and others.

IP staff members must strive to ensure the fair, objective, and impartial treatment of all persons with whom they deal. IP staff members must not participate in nor condone any form of harassment that demeans persons or creates an intimidating, hostile, or offensive campus environment.

When handling institutional funds, all IP staff members must ensure that such funds are managed in accordance with established and responsible accounting procedures and the fiscal policies or processes of the institution.

IP staff members must perform their duties within the limits of their training, expertise, and competence. When these limits are exceeded, individuals in need of further assistance must be referred to persons possessing appropriate qualifications.

All IP faculty and staff members responsible for supervising internship activities must monitor student performance and alter placements as needed.

IP staff members must use suitable means to confront and otherwise hold accountable other staff members who exhibit unethical behavior.

IP staff members must be knowledgeable about and practice ethical behavior in the use of technology.

Part 13. ASSESSMENT and EVALUATION

Internship Programs (IP) must conduct regular assessment and evaluations. IP must employ effective qualitative and quantitative methodologies as appropriate, to determine whether and to what degree the stated mission, goals, and student learning and development outcomes are being met. The process must employ sufficient and sound assessment measures to ensure comprehensiveness. Data collected must include responses from students and other affected constituencies.

IP must evaluate periodically how well they complement and enhance the institution's stated mission and educational effectiveness.

Results of these evaluations must be used in revising and improving IP and in recognizing staff performance.

IP must regularly evaluate, assess, and respond appropriately regarding the extent to which internship sites add to student learning.

IP standards developed in 2006

THE ROLE OF LEARNING ASSISTANCE PROGRAMS
CAS Standards Contextual Statement

Learning assistance programs facilitate student development and academic success. By developing appropriate skills, strategies, attitudes, and behaviors, students increase the efficiency and effectiveness of their learning (Dansereau, 1985). Participation in learning assistance programs can also improve student retention (Ryan and Glenn, 2004; Beal, 1980) by providing the kinds of "rewarding interactions" that seem to foster student intellectual and social growth (Tinto, 1987). These programs may be part of a comprehensive learning assistance center.

Although formal and informal learning assistance has been provided since the opening of the first U.S. colleges (Maxwell, 1996), the first "how to study" books were first published for underprepared entering freshmen in 1900. The reading clinics and study methods laboratories of the 1930s and 1940s and the self-help programs, learning modules, and programmed instruction of the reading and study skills laboratories of the 1950s and 1960s formed part of the historical foundation (Arendale, 2004; Lissner, 1990; Sullivan, 1980; Enright, 1975). By the late 1970s, learning assistance centers often incorporated educational technology, tutoring, and services for the many new nontraditional students (Caverly, 1995; Christ, 1982). Modern learning assistance centers and facilities house such learning support programs as tutoring, Supplemental Instruction, learning and study strategies, reading improvement, writing centers, and mathematics labs (Christ, 1971). A web portal dedicated exclusively to learning support centers in higher education was created in 1998 (LSCHE).

Some learning assistance programs have historically been provided by academic departments such as English, mathematics, psychology, and education. At community colleges and institutions with open admissions policies, remedial courses and related services were usually offered under the auspices of either an academic department or a separate developmental education unit. At more selective colleges and universities, however, learning centers have often been organized under the auspices of student affairs and typically have made services available to all students rather than those viewed as underprepared for college. A wide variety of academic assistance is provided for students by paraprofessional student employees – peer tutors, mentors, and instructors – as well as by professional staff; therefore one function of a learning assistance program is to provide educational and paraprofessional enrichment for student employees.

By the mid-1970s, professionals involved with learning assistance had formed regional, national, and international organizations. One of these groups, Commission XVI: Learning Centers in Higher Education, was charged by its parent organization, the American College Personnel Association (ACPA), to participate in drafting the CAS Standards and Guidelines for Learning Assistance Programs. After five years and numerous drafts, the CAS Standards and Guidelines for Learning Assistance Programs were completed and disseminated for adoption in 1986. This first major document articulating shared concepts, beliefs, and practices for learning assistance practitioners and their programs also suggested that learning assistance programs had become permanent professional components in higher education.

CAS Standards have been instrumental in fostering certification programs and professional development initiatives among learning assistance professionals. In 1989, the College Reading and Learning Association (CRLA) initiated International Tutor Program Certification to assure that minimum standards for tutor training were being met. A few years later CRLA developed International Mentor Program Certification. The National Association for Developmental Education (NADE), with the help of other learning assistance associations including CRLA, Commission XVI of ACPA, the Midwest College Learning Center Association (MCLCA, now the National College Learning Center Association, NCLCA), and the New York College Learning Skills Association (NYCLSA), sponsored initiatives that culminated in the 1995 publication of the *NADE Self-Evaluation Guides: Models for Assessing Learning Assistance / Developmental Education Programs (*under revision for 2007 publication*)*. Using the CAS Standards and Guidelines format as a template, this document applied the CAS process to specific programs, such as tutoring services, adjunct instructional programs such as course-based learning assistance programs, and developmental coursework.

In the early 1990s both CRLA and NADE joined the CAS enterprise and committed to active participation in the revision of the CAS standards and Guidelines for Learning Assistance Programs. The revision process was conducted over a two-year period and involved input from over 150 professional learning assistance practitioners representing numerous professional bodies. This document is the product of that collaboration and represents professional consensus of the role and importance of learning assistance programs in higher education.

References, Readings, and Resources

Arendale, D. R. (2004). Mainstreamed academic assistance and enrichment for all students: The historical origins of learning assistance centers. *Research for Educational Reform*, 9 (4), 3-20

Beal, P. E. (1980). Learning centers and retention. In O. T. Lenning & D. L. Wayman (Eds.), *New roles for learning assistance* (pp. 59-73). San Francisco: Jossey-Bass.

Caverly, D. (1995). Technology in learning centers: past, present, future. In S. Mioduski & G. Enright (Eds), *Proceedings of the 15th and 16th annual institutes for learning assistance professionals*, 15-34.

Christ, F. L. (1971). Systems for learning assistance: Learner, learning facilitators, and learning centers. *Fourth Annual Proceedings of the Western College Reading Association*, 32-41.

Christ, F. L. (1982). Computers in learning assistance centers and developmental education: Beginning to explore. *Journal of Developmental and Remedial Education* (Fall 1982), 10-13.

Christ, F. L. (2002). Academic support. In J. Forest & K. Kinser (Eds.), *Higher education in the United States: An encyclopedia*. Santa Barbara, CA: ABC-CLIO.

Dansereau, D. F. (1985). Learning strategy research. In J. W. Segal, S. F. Chipman, & R. Glaser (Eds.), *Thinking and learning skills*. Hillsdale, NJ: Erlbaum.

Enright, G. (1975). College learning skills: Frontierland origins of the learning assistance. *Proceedings of the Eighth Annual Conference of the Western College Reading Association*, 81-92.

Lissner, L. S. (1990). The learning center from 1829 to the year 2000 and beyond. In R. M. Hashway (Ed.), *Handbook of Developmental Education* (pp. 128-154). New York: Praeger.

LSCHE, Learning Support Centers in Higher Education web portal at http://www.pvc.maricopa.edu/~lsche.

Maxwell, M. (1996). *Evaluating academic skills programs: A sourcebook* (3rd Ed.). Kensington, MD: MM Associates.

Ryan, M. P. & Glenn, P. A. (2004). What do first-year students need most: learning strategies instruction or academic socialization? *Journal of College Reading and Learning*, 34 (2), 4-28.

Sullivan, L. L. (1980). Growth and influence in the learning center movement. In K. V. Lauridsen (Ed.), *Examining the Scope of Learning Centers* (pp. 1-8). San Francisco: Jossey-Bass.

Tinto, V. (1987). *Leaving college: Rethinking the causes and cures of student attrition*. Chicago: University of Chicago Press.

Boylan, H. (1982). The growth of the learning assistance movement. In Boylan, H. (Ed.), *Forging new partnerships in learning assistance* (pp. 5-16). San Francisco: Jossey-Bass.

Boylan, H. (1993). Learning assistance and developmental education: The history and the state of the art. In S. Mioduski & G. Enright (Eds.), *Proceedings of the 13th and 14th annual institutes for learning assistance professionals*, 12-19.

Burns, M. E. (1991). A study to formulate a learning assistance model for the California community college. Doctoral dissertation, Pepperdine University.

Casazza, M. E. & Silverman, S. L. (2000). *Learning & development: Making connections to enhance teaching*. San Francisco: Jossey-Bass.

Casazza, M. E. & Silverman, S. L. (1996). *Learning assistance and developmental education: A guide for effective practice*. San Francisco: Jossey-Bass.

Christ, F., Sheets, R., and Smith, K. (Eds.) (2000). *Starting a learning assistance center: Conversations with CRLA members who have been there and done that*. Clearwater, FL: H&H Publishing.

Clark-Thayer, S. (Ed.) (1995). *NADE self-evaluation guides: Models for assessing learning assistance/developmental education programs*. Clearwater, FL: H&H Publishing.

Enright, G. and Kerstiens, G. (1980). The learning center: Toward an expanded role. In O. T. Lenning and R. I. Wayman (Eds.), *New roles for learning assistance* (pp. 1-24). San Francisco: Jossey-Bass.

Hashway, R. M. (Spring 1989). Developmental learning center designs. *Research and Teaching in Developmental Education*, 5(2), 25-38.

Kerstiens, G. (1995). A taxonomy of learning support services. In S. Mioduski and G. Enright (Eds.), *Proceedings of the 15th and 16th annual institutes for learning assistance professionals*, 48.

Lauridsen, K. (Ed.) (1980-1983). New Directions in Learning Assistance (12 volumes) San Francisco: Jossey-Bass.

Materniak, G. & Williams, A. (1987). CAS standards and guidelines for learning assistance programs. *Journal of Developmental Education*, *11*, 12-18.

Maxwell, M. (Ed.) (1994). *From access to success: A book of readings on college developmental education and learning assistance programs*. Clearwater, FL: H&H Publishing.

Maxwell M. (1997). *Improving student learning skills* (2nd Ed.). Clearwater, FL: H&H Publishing.

New York College Learning Skills Association Ethics and Standards Committee (April 1994). *Statement of ethics and general guidelines for learning assistance programs*. New York: New York College Learning Skills Association.

Peterson, G. T. (1975). The learning center. Hampton, CT: Shoestring Press.

Robert, E. R. & Thompson, G. (Spring 1994). Learning assistance and the success of underprepared students at Berkeley. *Journal of Developmental Education*, 17 (3), 4-15.

Stahl, N.A., Brozo, W. G. & Gordon, B. (1984). The professional preparation of college reading and study-skills specialists. In G. McNinch (Ed.), *Reading teacher education: Yearbook of the 4th annual conference of the American Reading Forum*. Carrollton, GA: West Georgia College. ERIC #248-761.

Stahl, N.A., M. L. Simpson, & C.G. Hayes (1992). Ten recommendations from research for teaching high-risk college students. In *Journal of Developmental Education, 16* (1), 2-4, 6, 8, 10.

Van, B. (1990). *Application of essential developmental education principles by program administrators*. Doctoral Dissertation, University of Connecticut.

White, W. G., Jr., & Schnuth, M. L. (1990). College learning assistance centers: Places for learning. In R. M. Hashway (Ed.), *Handbook of developmental education* (pp. 157-177). New York: Praeger.

White, W. G., Jr., Kyzar, B., & Lane, K.E. (1990). College learning assistance centers: Spaces for learning. In R.M. Hashway (Ed.), *Handbook of developmental education* (pp. 179-195). New York: Praeger.

White, W.G., Jr. (2004). The physical environment of learning support centers. *The Learning Assistance Review*, 9(1), 17-27.

Archives of the LRNASST listserv at http://www.lists.ufl.edu/archives/lrnasst-l.html

Journal of College Reading and Learning: College Reading and Learning Association.

Journal of Developmental Education and *Research in Developmental Education*: National Center for Developmental Education, Appalachian State University.

The Learning Assistance Review: National College Learning Center Association.

NADE Monograph Series: National Association for Developmental Education

Research & Teaching in Developmental Education: New York College Learning Skills Association.

College Reading and Learning Association, www.crla.net.

National Association for Developmental Education, www.nade.net.

National College Learning Center Association, www.nclca.org.

Association of Colleges for Tutoring and Learning Assistance (formerly Association of California Colleges for Tutoring and Learning Assistance), www.actla.info.

New York College Learning Skills Association, www.nyclsa.org.

Contributors:
Karen Agee, University of Northern Iowa
Carol Dochen, Texas State University – San Marcos
Frank L. Christ, University of Texas at Austin

LEARNING ASSISTANCE PROGRAMS
CAS Standards and Guidelines

Part 1. MISSION

The Learning Assistance Program (LAP) must teach the skills and strategies to help students become independent and active learners and to achieve academic success.

The LAP must incorporate student learning and student development in its mission. The LAP must enhance overall educational experiences. The LAP must develop, record, disseminate, implement and regularly review its mission and goals. Mission statements must be consistent with the mission and goals of the institution and with the standards in this document. The LAP must operate as an integral part of the institution's overall mission.

The LAP must collaborate with faculty, staff, and administrators in addressing the learning needs, academic performance, and retention of students.

Models of learning assistance programs vary, but should share the following common goals:
- to make students the central focus of the program
- to assist members of the campus community in achieving their personal potential for learning
- to provide instruction and services that address the cognitive, affective, and socio-cultural dimensions of learning
- to introduce students to the expectations of faculty and the culture of higher education
- to help students develop positive attitudes towards learning and confidence in their ability to learn
- to foster personal responsibility and accountability for one's own learning
- to provide a variety of instructional approaches that are appropriate for the level of skills and learning styles of the student population
- to assist students in transferring skills and strategies they have learned previously to their academic work
- to provide services and resources to faculty, staff, and administrators that enhance and support classroom instruction and professional development
- to support the academic standards and requirements of the institution

Part 2. PROGRAM

The formal education of students consists of the curriculum and the co-curriculum, and must promote student learning and development that is purposeful and holistic. The Learning Assistance Program (LAP) must identify relevant and desirable student learning and development outcomes and provide programs and services that encourage the achievement of those outcomes.

Relevant and desirable outcomes include: intellectual growth, effective communication, realistic self-appraisal, enhanced self-esteem, clarified values, career choices, leadership development, healthy behaviors, meaningful interpersonal relationships, independence, collaboration, social responsibility, satisfying and productive lifestyles, appreciation of diversity, spiritual awareness, and achievement of personal and educational goals.

The LAP must provide evidence of its impact on the achievement of student learning and development outcomes.

The table below offers examples of evidence of achievement of student learning and development.

Student Learning and Development Outcome Domains

Intellectual growth
Examples of achievement indicators

Produces personal and educational goal statements; Employs critical thinking in problem solving; Uses complex information from a variety of sources including personal experience and observation to form a decision or opinion; Obtains a degree; Applies previously understood information and concepts to a new situation or setting; Expresses appreciation for literature, the fine arts, mathematics, sciences, and social sciences

Effective communication
Examples of achievement indicators

Writes and speaks coherently and effectively; Writes and speaks after reflection; Able to influence others through writing, speaking or artistic expression; Effectively articulates abstract ideas; Uses appropriate syntax; Makes presentations or gives performances

Enhanced self-esteem
Examples of achievement indicators

Shows self-respect and respect for others; Initiates actions toward achievement of goals; Takes reasonable risks; Demonstrates assertive behavior; Functions without need for constant reassurance from others

239

Realistic self-appraisal

Examples of achievement indicators

Articulates personal skills and abilities; Makes decisions and acts in congruence with personal values; Acknowledges personal strengths and weaknesses; Articulates rationale for personal behavior; Seeks feedback from others; Learns from past experiences

Clarified values

Examples of achievement indicators

Articulates personal values; Acts in congruence with personal values; Makes decisions that reflect personal values; Demonstrates willingness to scrutinize personal beliefs and values; Identifies personal, work and lifestyle values and explains how they influence decision-making

Career choices

Examples of achievement indicators

Articulates career choices based on assessment of interests, values, skills and abilities; Documents knowledge, skills, and accomplishments resulting from formal education, work experience, community service, and volunteer experiences; Makes the connections between classroom and out-of-classroom learning; Can construct a resume with clear job objectives and evidence of related knowledge, skills and accomplishments; Articulates the characteristics of a preferred work environment; Comprehends the world of work; Takes steps to initiate a job search or seek advanced education

Leadership development

Examples of achievement indicators

Articulates leadership philosophy or style; Serves in a leadership position in a student organization; Comprehends the dynamics of a group; Exhibits democratic principles as a leader; Exhibits ability to visualize a group purpose and desired outcomes

Healthy behavior

Examples of achievement indicators

Chooses behaviors and environments that promote health and reduce risk; Articulate the relationship between health and wellness and accomplishing life-long goals; Exhibits behaviors that advance a healthy community.

Meaningful interpersonal relationships

Examples of achievement indicators

Develops and maintains satisfying interpersonal relationships; Establishes mutually rewarding relationships with friends and colleagues; Listens to and considers others' points of view; Treats others with respect

Independence

Examples of achievement indicators

Exhibits self-reliant behaviors; Functions autonomously; Exhibits ability to function interdependently; Accepts supervision as needed; Manages time effectively

Collaboration

Examples of achievement indicators

Works cooperatively with others; Seeks the involvement of others; Seeks feedback from others; Contributes to achievement of a group goal; Exhibits effective listening skills

Social responsibility

Examples of achievement indicators

Understands and participates in relevant governance systems; Understands, abides by, and participates in the development, maintenance, and/or orderly change of community, social, and legal standards or norms; Appropriately challenges the unfair, unjust, or uncivil behavior of other individuals or groups; Participates in service/volunteer activities

Satisfying and productive lifestyles

Examples of achievement indicators

Achieves balance between education, work, and leisure time; Articulates and meets goals for work, leisure, and education; Overcomes obstacles that hamper goal achievement; Functions on the basis of personal identity, ethical, spiritual, and moral values; Articulates long-term goals and objectives

Appreciating diversity

Examples of achievement indicators

Understands one's own identity and culture; Seeks involvement with people different from oneself; Seeks involvement in diverse interests; Articulates the advantages and challenges of a diverse society; Challenges appropriately the abusive use of stereotypes by others; Understands the impact of diversity on one's own society

Spiritual awareness

Examples of achievement indicators

Develops and articulates personal belief system; Understands roles of spirituality in personal and group values and behaviors

Personal and educational goals

Examples of achievement indicators

Sets, articulates, and pursues individual goals; Articulates personal and educational goals and objectives; Uses personal and educational goals to guide decisions; Understands the effect of one's personal and educational goals on others

Programs and services must be (a) intentional, (b) coherent, (c) based on theories and knowledge of learning and human development, (d) reflective of developmental and demographic profiles of the student population, and (e) responsive to needs of individuals, special populations, and communities.

The LAP must promote, either directly of by referral, the affective skills that influence learning such as stress management, test anxiety reduction, assertiveness, power of concentration, and motivation.

The LAP must refer students to appropriate campus and community resources for assistance with personal problems, severe learning disabilities, financial difficulties, and other areas of need that may be outside the purview or beyond the expertise of the learning assistance program.

The scope of the LAP should be determined by the type and level of skills students require. The format utilized for strengthening academic skills may include mandatory credit-bearing developmental courses or non-credit elective workshops.

The scope of programs and services should also be determined by the needs of the student populations the learning assistance program is charged to serve. These can range from special populations (such as culturally and ethnically diverse students, international and English as a second language students, student athletes, returning students, and students with physical and learning disabilities) to the entire student population.

Formal and informal diagnostic procedures should be conducted to identify skills and strategies that the student should develop to achieve the level of proficiency prescribed or required by the institution or known to be necessary for college learning. Assessment results should be shared with the student to formulate recommendations and a plan of instruction.

The LAP should provide instruction and services for the development of reading, mathematics and quantitative reasoning, writing, critical thinking, problem solving, and study skills. Other programs may include: subject-matter tutoring, adjunct instructional programs and supplemental instruction groups, time management programs, freshman seminars, and preparation for graduate and professional school admissions tests and for professional certification requirements.

Modes of delivering learning assistance programs include individual and group instruction and instructional media such as print, video, audio, computers, and skills laboratories. Instruction and programs may be delivered on site or through distance learning programs.

The LAP should give systematic feedback to students concerning their progress in reaching cognitive and affective goals, teach self feedback methods utilizing self monitoring strategies, and give students practice in applying and transferring skills and strategies learned in the program to academic tasks across the curriculum.

The LAP should promote an understanding of the learning needs of the student population. Some of the ways in which learning assistance programs should educate the campus community:

- establishing advisory boards consisting of members from key segments of the campus community
- holding periodic informational meetings and consulting with staff, faculty, and administrators
- participating in staff and faculty development and in service programs on curriculum and instructional approaches that address the development of learning skills, attitudes, and behaviors
- encouraging the use of learning assistance program resources, materials, instruction and services as integral or adjunct classroom activities
- conducting in class workshops that demonstrate the application of learning strategies to the course content;
- disseminating information that describes the programs and services, hours of operation, procedures for registering or scheduling appointments through publications, campus and local media announcements, and informational presentations
- training and supervising paraprofessionals and pre-professionals to work in such capacities as tutors, peer mentors, and advisors
- providing jobs, practica, courses, internships, and assistantships for graduate students interested in learning assistance and related careers

Part 3. LEADERSHIP

Effective and ethical leadership is essential to the success of all organizations. Institutions must appoint, position, and empower Learning Assistance Program (LAP) leaders within the administrative structure to accomplish stated missions. LAP leaders at various levels must be selected on the basis of formal education and training, relevant work experience, personal skills and competencies, relevant professional credentials, as well as potential for promoting learning and development in students, applying effective practices to educational processes, and enhancing institutional effectiveness. Institutions must determine expectations of accountability for leaders and fairly assess their performance.

LAP leaders must exercise authority over resources for which they are responsible to achieve their respective missions.

LAP leaders must:
- articulate a vision for their organization
- set goals and objectives based on the needs and capabilities of the population served
- promote student learning and development
- prescribe and practice ethical behavior
- recruit, select, supervise, and develop others in the organization
- manage financial resources
- coordinate human resources
- plan, budget for, and evaluate personnel and programs
- apply effective practices to educational and administrative processes
- communicate effectively
- initiate collaborative interaction between individuals and agencies that possess legitimate concerns and interests in the functional area

LAP leaders must identify and find means to address individual, organizational, or environmental conditions that inhibit goal achievement.

LAP leaders must promote campus environments that result in multiple opportunities for student learning and development.

LAP leaders must continuously improve programs and services in response to changing needs of students and other constituents, and evolving institutional priorities.

LAP administrators should:
- participate in institutional planning, policy, procedural, and fiscal decisions that affect learning support for students
- be informed about issues, trends, theories, and methodologies related to student learning and retention
- represent the learning assistance program on institutional committees
- collaborate with leaders of academic departments and support services in addressing the learning needs and retention of students
- be involved in research, publication, presentations, consultation, and the activities of professional organizations
- communicate with professional constituents in the learning assistance field and related professions

Part 4. ORGANIZATION and MANAGEMENT
Guided by an overarching intent to ensure student learning and development, the Learning Assistance Program (LAP) must be structured purposefully and managed effectively to achieve stated goals. Evidence of appropriate structure must include

current and accessible policies and procedures, written performance expectations for all employees, functional workflow graphics or organizational charts, and clearly stated service delivery expectations.

Evidence of effective management must include use of comprehensive and accurate information for decisions, clear sources and channels of authority, effective communication practices, decision-making and conflict resolution procedures, responsiveness to changing conditions, accountability and evaluation systems, and recognition and reward processes. The LAP must provide channels within the organization for regular review of administrative policies and procedures.

The mission and goals of the LAP, the needs and demographics of its clients, and its institutional role should determine where the unit is located in the organizational structure of the institution. Learning assistance programs are frequently organized as units in the academic affairs or the student affairs division. Regardless of where the learning assistance program is organized, it should communicate and collaborate with a network of key units across the institution to assure the coordination of related functions, programs, services, policies, procedures, and to expedite client referrals.

The LAP should have a broadly constituted advisory board to make suggestions, provide information, and give guidance.

The LAP should provide written goals, objectives, and anticipated outcomes for each program and service. Written procedures should exist for collecting, processing, and reporting student assessment and program data.

Regularly scheduled meetings should be held to share information; to coordinate the planning, scheduling, and delivery of programs and services; to identify and discuss potential and actual problems and concerns; and to collaborate on making decisions and solving problems.

Part 5. HUMAN RESOURCES
The Learning Assistance Program (LAP) must be staffed adequately by individuals qualified to accomplish its mission and goals. Within established guidelines of the institution, the LAP must establish procedures for staff selection, training, and evaluation; set expectations for supervision, and provide appropriate professional development opportunities. The LAP must strive to improve the professional competence and skills of all personnel it employs.

Staff and faculty who hold a joint appointment with the LAP must be committed to the mission, philosophy, goals, and priorities of the program and must possess the necessary expertise for assigned responsibilities.

LAP professional staff members must hold an earned graduate degree in a field relevant to the position they hold or must possess an appropriate combination of educational credentials and related work experience.

Professional staff should have earned degrees from relevant disciplines such as reading, English, mathematics, student personnel and student development, guidance and counseling, psychology, or education. LAP professionals should be knowledgeable in learning theory and in the instruction, assessment, theory, and the professional standards of practice for their area of specialization and responsibility. In addition, they should understand the unique characteristics and needs of the populations they assist and teach. LAP professional staff should vary and adjust pedagogical approaches according to the learning needs and styles of their students, to the nature of the learning task, and to content of academic disciplines across the curriculum.

LAP professional staff should be competent and experienced in:
- teaching, advising, and counseling students at the college level
- written and oral communication skills
- working in a culturally and academically diverse environment
- consulting, collaborating, and negotiating with staff, faculty and administrators of academic and student affairs units
- designing and implementing instructional strategies and materials and utilizing instructional technologies
- training, supervising, and mentoring paraprofessionals and pre-professionals
- identifying and establishing lines of communication for student referral to other institutional and student support units

Degree or credential-seeking interns must be qualified by enrollment in an appropriate field of study and by relevant experience. These individuals must be trained and supervised adequately by professional staff members holding educational credentials and related work experience appropriate for supervision.

The LAP should be informed of the policies and procedures to be followed for internships and practica as required by the students' academic departments. The roles and responsibilities of the LAP and those of the academic department should be clearly defined and understood by all involved.

Student employees and volunteers must be carefully selected, trained, supervised, and evaluated. They must be trained on how and when to refer those in need of assistance to qualified staff members and have access to a supervisor for assistance in making these judgments. Student employees and volunteers must be provided clear and precise job descriptions, pre-service training based on assessed needs, and continuing staff development.

The LAP must have technical and support staff members adequate to accomplish its mission. Staff members must be technologically proficient and qualified to perform their job functions, be knowledgeable of ethical and legal uses of technology, and have access to training. The level of staffing and workloads must be adequate and appropriate for program and service demands.

Secretarial and technical staff should be updated on changes in programs, services, policies and procedures in order to expedite smooth and efficient assistance to clients. Appropriate staff development opportunities should be available.

Salary levels and fringe benefits for all LAP staff members must be commensurate with those for comparable positions within the institution, in similar institutions, and in the relevant geographic area.

The LAP must institute hiring and promotion practices that are fair, inclusive, and non-discriminatory. Programs and services must employ a diverse staff to provide readily identifiable role models for students and to enrich the campus community.

The LAP must create and maintain position descriptions for all staff members and provide regular performance planning and appraisals.

The LAP must have a system for regular staff evaluation and must provide access to continuing education and professional development opportunities, including in-service training programs and participation in professional conferences and workshops.

Part 6. FINANCIAL RESOURCES

The Learning Assistance Program (LAP) must have adequate funding to accomplish its mission and goals. Funding priorities must be determined within the context of the stated mission, goals, objectives and comprehensive analysis of the needs and capabilities of students and the availability of internal or external resources.

The LAP must demonstrate fiscal responsibility and cost effectiveness consistent with institutional protocols.

Prior to implementing a new program or service or to significantly expanding an existing program component, a financial analysis should be performed to determine the financial resources required to support the addition or expansion and the appropriate funds made available.

The LAP budget should support its instructional and student support service functions. Adequate funds should be provided for the following budget categories: staff and student salaries, general office functions, student assessment and instructional activities, data management and program evaluation processes, research staff training and professional development activities, instructional materials and media, and instructional and office computing.

Part 7. FACILITIES, TECHNOLOGY, and EQUIPMENT

The Learning Assistance Program (LAP) must have adequate, suitably located facilities, adequate technology, and equipment to support its mission and goals efficiently and effectively. Facilities, technology, and equipment must be evaluated regularly and be in compliance with relevant federal, state, provincial, and local requirements to provide for access, health, safety, and security.

Facilities and equipment should support the instructional, service, and office functions of the learning assistance program. Facility considerations should include flexible space that can be adapted to changes in the delivery of programs, services, and instructional modes; classrooms, labs, resource rooms, media and computer centers, group and one to one tutorial space to support instruction; private, sound proofed areas to support testing, counseling, and other activities that require confidentiality or concentration; adequate and secure storage for equipment, supplies, instructional and testing materials, and confidential records. Attention should be given to environmental conditions that influence learning such as appropriate acoustics, lighting, ventilation, heating and air-conditioning.

Part 8. LEGAL RESPONSIBILITIES

Learning Assistance Program (LAP) staff members must be knowledgeable about and responsive to laws and regulations that relate to their respective responsibilities. Staff members must inform users of programs and services and officials, as appropriate, of legal obligations and limitations including constitutional, statutory, regulatory, and case law; mandatory laws and orders emanating from federal, state/provincial and local governments; and the institution's policies.

LAP staff members must use reasonable and informed practices to limit the liability exposure of the institution, its officers, employees, and agents. Staff members must be informed about institutional policies regarding personal liability and related insurance coverage options.

The institution must provide access to legal advice for LAP staff members as needed to carry out assigned responsibilities.

The institution must inform LAP staff and students in a timely and systematic fashion about extraordinary or changing legal obligations and potential liabilities.

Staff development programs should be available to educate learning assistance program staff of these changes.

Part 9. EQUITY and ACCESS

Learning Assistance Program (LAP) staff members must ensure that services and programs are provided on a fair and equitable basis. Facilities, programs and services must be accessible. Hours of operation and delivery of and access to programs and services must be responsive to the needs of all students and other constituents. The LAP must adhere to the spirit and intent of equal opportunity laws.

LAP must be open and readily accessible to all students and must not discriminate except where sanctioned by law and institutional policy. Discrimination must be avoided on the bases of age; color; creed; cultural heritage; disability; ethnicity; gender identity; nationality; political affiliation; religious affiliation; sex; sexual orientation; or social, economic, marital, or veteran status.

Consistent with their mission and goals, the LAP must take affirmative action to remedy significant imbalances in student participation and staffing patterns.

As the demographic profiles of campuses change and new instructional delivery methods are introduced, institutions must recognize the needs of students who participate in distance learning for access to programs and services offered on campus. Institutions must provide appropriate services in ways that are accessible to distance learners and assist them in identifying and gaining access to other appropriate services in their geographic region.

Part 10. CAMPUS and EXTERNAL RELATIONS

The Learning Assistance Program (LAP) must

establish, maintain, and promote effective relations with relevant individuals, campus offices, and external agencies.

The Learning Assistance Program should:
- be an integral part of the academic offerings of the institution
- establish communication with academic and student services units
- to encourage the exchange of ideas, knowledge, and expertise
- to provide mutual consultation, as needed, on student cases
- to expedite student referrals to and from the learning assistance program
- to collaborate on programs and services that efficiently and effectively address the needs of students
- have representation on institutional committees relevant to the mission and goals of the program such as committees on retention, orientation, basic skills, learning communities, freshmen seminars, probation review, academic standards and requirements, curriculum design, assessment and placement, and faculty development
- solicit volunteers from the local community to contribute their skills and talents to the services of the learning assistance program
- provide training and consultation to community based organizations, e.g., literacy associations, corporate training, and school district based tutorial services

Part 11. DIVERSITY

Within the context of each institution's unique mission, diversity enriches the community and enhances the collegiate experience for all; therefore, the Learning Assistance Program (LAP) must nurture environments where commonalties and differences among people are recognized and honored.

The LAP must promote educational experiences that are characterized by open and continuous communication that deepens understanding of one's own identity, culture, and heritage, and that of others. The LAP must educate and promote respect about commonalties and differences in their historical and cultural contexts.

The LAP must address the characteristics and needs of a diverse population when establishing and implementing policies and procedures.

The program should facilitate student adjustment to the academic culture of the institution by orienting students to the practices, resources, responsibilities and behaviors that contribute to academic success.

The instructional content, materials, and activities of learning assistance programs should provide opportunities to increase awareness and appreciation of the individual and cultural differences of students.

Part 12. ETHICS

All persons involved in the Learning Assistance Program (LAP) must adhere to the highest principles of ethical behavior. The LAP must develop or adopt and implement appropriate statements of ethical practice. The LAP must publish these statements and ensure their periodic review by relevant constituencies.

LAP staff members must ensure that privacy and confidentiality are maintained with respect to all communications and records to the extent that such records are protected under the law and appropriate statements of ethical practice. Information contained in students' education records must not be disclosed without written consent except as allowed by relevant laws and institutional policies. Staff members must disclose to appropriate authorities information judged to be of an emergency nature, especially when the safety of the individual or others is involved, or when otherwise required by institutional policy or relevant law.

LAP staff members must be aware of and comply with the provisions contained in the institution's human subjects research policy and in other relevant institutional policies addressing ethical practices and confidentiality of research data concerning individuals.

LAP staff members must recognize and avoid personal conflict of interest or appearance thereof in their transactions with students and others.

Information and training should be made available regarding conflict of interest policies.

LAP staff members must strive to insure the fair, objective, and impartial treatment of all persons with whom they deal. Staff members must not participate in nor condone any form of harassment that demeans persons or creates an intimidating, hostile, or offensive campus environment.

When handling institutional funds, all LAP staff members must ensure that such funds are managed in accordance with established and responsible accounting procedures and the fiscal policies or processes of the institution.

LAP staff members must perform their duties within the limits of their training, expertise, and competence. When these limits are exceeded, individuals in need of further assistance must be referred to persons possessing appropriate qualifications.

With the prevalence of student paraprofessional and tutorial staff within learning assistance programs, specific attention should be given to properly orienting and advising student staff about matters of confidentiality. Clear statements should be distributed and reviewed with student staff as to what information is and is not appropriate for student staff to access or to communicate.

LAP staff members must use suitable means to confront and otherwise hold accountable other staff members who exhibit unethical behavior.

LAP staff members must be knowledgeable about and practice ethical behavior in the use of technology.

Because LAP staff work with students' academic coursework, they must be knowledgeable of policies related to academic integrity, plagiarism, student code of conduct and other similar policies. All staff members must be cognizant of the implications of these policies.

Statements or claims made about outcomes that can be achieved from participating in learning assistance programs and services must be truthful and realistic.

LAP funds acquired through grants and other non-institutional resources must be managed according to the regulations and guidelines of the funding source and the institution.

Part 13. ASSESSMENT and EVALUATION

The Learning Assistance Program (LAP) must conduct regular assessment and evaluations. The LAP must employ effective qualitative and quantitative methodologies as appropriate, to determine whether and to what degree the stated mission, goals, and student learning and development outcomes are being met. The process must employ sufficient and sound assessment measures to ensure comprehensiveness. Data collected must include responses from students and other affected constituencies.

Qualitative methods may include standard evaluation forms, questionnaires, interviews, observations, or case studies.

Quantitative measurements range from data on an individual student's performance to the impact on the campus' retention rate. Quantitative methods may include follow up studies on students' grades in mainstream courses, GPAs, graduation, re enrollment and retention figures. Comparative data of learning assistance program participants and non participants is also a measure of program effectiveness. Quantitative measures can include data on the size of the user population, numbers utilizing particular services, number of contact hours, the sources of student referrals to the program, numbers of students who may be on a waiting list or who have requested services not provided by the learning assistance program. Quantitative data should be collected within specific time periods and longitudinally to reveal trends.

The LAP must evaluate periodically how well they complement and enhance the institution's stated mission and educational effectiveness.

Results of these evaluations must be used in revising and improving programs and services and in recognizing staff performance.

The LAP should have the ability to collect and analyze data through its own resources and through access to appropriate data generated by the institution.

Periodic evaluations of the learning assistance program and services may be performed by on-campus experts and outside consultants and disseminated to appropriate administrators.

The LAP should conduct periodic self assessments, utilizing self study processes endorsed by professional organizations.

Various means of assessment should be conducted for the purpose of identifying the learning needs of the students and guiding them to appropriate programs and services. Assessment results should be communicated to the student confidentially, honestly, and with sensitivity. Students should be advised directed to appropriate, alternative educational opportunities when there is reasonable cause to believe that students will not be able to meet requirements for academic success.

The LAP should periodically review and revise its goals and services based on evaluation outcomes and based on changes in institutional goals, priorities, and plans. Data that reveals trends or changes in student demographics, characteristics and needs should be utilized for learning assistance program short and long term planning.

General Standards revised in 2002; LAP content developed/ revised in 1986 & 1996.

The ROLE of LESBIAN, GAY, BISEXUAL, and TRANSGENDER SERVICES and PROGRAMS

CAS Standards Contextual Statement

History: It is no longer a matter of whether to provide services for lesbian, gay, bisexual, and transgender (LGBT) college students; rather, it is a matter of when. The talent, energy, and hope with which LGBT students are entering college must be acknowledged and encouraged (Sanlo, 1998). Some students are declaring their bisexual or homosexual orientations in high school, then knocking on institutional doors with expectations of being fully appreciated for who they are in their entirety—including their sexual orientations. Many more students enter college questioning their sexual identities, not yet ready to make pronouncements nor embrace labels, but they deserve the institution's demonstrated acceptance and attention.

When LGBT people refused to allow police to raid the Stonewall Bar in New York City on June 27, 1969, one more time, a stunning message was heard throughout the United States. In response to this singular event, which occurred on the heels of the civil rights movement of the 1960s, numerous Gay Liberation Front groups sprang up on college campuses everywhere, challenging both administration and faculty alike. Marcus (1993) documented the role and involvement of lesbian and gay college students and the importance of these challenges. Sexual orientation issues had finally made their way into the academy.

Public Policy: Homosexuality was often described as a genetic defect, a mental disorder, or a learning disability in early scientific theories. However, Evelyn Hooker's (1963) research found no significant differences in the psychological adjustment of homosexual men when compared to a comparable group of heterosexual men. On the basis of further research by others demonstrating similar findings, the American Psychiatric Association removed homosexuality as a diagnostic mental disorder in 1973. Two years later, the American Psychological Association took the same action and also issued a statement that its member mental health providers must actively stop discrimination against lesbians and gay men. Concurrently, the National Education Association added sexual orientation to its non-discrimination policy. To date, over 200 professional organizations, including the American Educational Research Association, NASPA, ACPA, the American Federation of Teachers, the American Counseling Association, and the National Association of Social Workers, have done the same. The revised standards of the National Council for the Accreditation of Teacher Education (NCATE) now require institutions to recruit and retain a culturally diverse faculty and student body, including individuals with diverse sexual orientations.

However, despite statements of non-discrimination by professional organizations and by institutions, everyday life has not changed dramatically for LGBT people. Given the historical context, many LGBT people choose to remain invisible rather than face the consequences of campus intolerance and hostility (Sanlo, 1999).

The Consortium: The National Consortium of Directors of Lesbian, Gay, Bisexual, and Transgender Resources in Higher Education (the Consortium) was officially founded in San Diego in 1997 to provide support for the professionals in this growing new arena in student affairs. Beyond membership support, the Consortium seeks to assist colleges and universities in developing equity in every respect for lesbian, gay, bisexual, and transgender students, faculty, staff, administrators, and alumni. The Consortium also focuses on developing curricula to enhance its professional goals, to promote improved campus climates, and to advocate for policy change, program development, and the establishment of campus LGBT offices and centers. The Consortium's website—www.lgbtcampus.org—offers valuable information relating specifically to higher education.

Recruitment, Retention, and Numbers of LGBT Students Unknown: Minimal data are currently available as to the number of LGBT students on college campuses. Several reasons exist to explain this fact (Eyermann & Sanlo, 2001). First, some surveys regarding sexual behavior rely on people to self-disclose same-sex interactions, thoughts, or feelings. It is unlikely that people will answer such questions honestly or at all if they do not explicitly trust the anonymity of the process. Second, some surveys rely on people to identity themselves through labels such as homosexual, lesbian, gay, or bisexual. While some LGBT people may use these labels, many others, especially LGBT people of color, may not. Either they have decided to not attach a label to their non-heterosexual identity; or they have not journeyed through the "coming-out" process sufficiently to yet identify with a label; or they use different terminology, all of which are the experiences of LGBT college students. Finally, while some people may have strong feelings of same-sex attraction, it is likely that they remain in heterosexual relationships or become non-sexual and never act on their feelings of such same-sex attraction (Eyermann & Sanlo, 2001).

Consequently, limited empirical data exist to identify numbers of LGBT students. Three factors figure into college data-gathering. First, while surveys may elicit opinions about homosexual issues, few institutions or national polls ask respondents to identify their sexual orientation. For example, neither the General Social Survey (GSS), which surveys the population at large, nor the Annual Freshman Survey conducted by the Higher Education Research Institute (HERI), elicit sexual orientation demographics.

Second, no college or university has sexual orientation or gender identity boxes on admission forms, and retention studies related to LGBT students have not yet been conducted. Therefore, when administrators wish to ascertain the number of LGBT students on campuses, there are few, if any, data bases available to provide such information. Consequently, they find themselves resorting to asking an openly gay student or staff member or simply projecting numbers from LGBT college chat rooms.

Third, student survey respondents may not use the labels used by researchers. Of the few campuses that do ask about sexual identity on campus surveys, most use the traditional terms previously noted. These labels may be offensive to some or too graphic a description for others, depending upon the stage of sexual awareness and development. Either of these opinions may prompt LGB students to falsely answer or to ignore such questions, and few surveys and campuses even consider transgender students in any context.

Violence: Like racism, sexism, and other ideologies of oppression, heterosexism—that only heterosexuality is normal—is manifested in social customs, institutions, and in attitudes and behaviors of individuals. Preserved through the routine operation of institutions, the maintenance of heterosexism is possible because it is in keeping with prevalent social norms. Higher education contributes to the maintenance of institutionalized heterosexism as evidenced by hate crimes directed toward LGBT students, faculty, and staff members (Evans & Rankin, 1998). Given that heterosexism's values underlie higher education, the work involved in proactively addressing violence against LGBT individuals and building communities that are inclusive and welcoming of LGBT persons is both controversial and demanding.

Schuh (1998) noted that campuses are "no longer safe havens for students, faculty, or staff. Violence is a community and societal problem that has found its way into institutions of higher education" (p. 347). Institutions must make concerted efforts to create campus climates where every student is safe and every faculty and staff member is secure in knowing that there will never be another incident such as the one involving Matthew Shepard at the University of Wyoming.

Services: Nearly 100 higher education institutions currently have full-time professionally staffed offices or centers that provide services for and about LGBT students, faculty, and staff (National Consortium website, accessed 2006). Some such services include information and referral; advocacy; support/discussion groups; LGBT student organization advising; safe zones and ally projects; leadership programs; peer counseling; and Lavender Graduation celebrations (Sanlo, 2000). Some campuses have LGBT offices staffed by part-time graduate students, and some campuses with no actual LGBT office or center employ a person who is responsible for providing services to LGBT students (Sanlo, Rankin, & Schoenberg, 2002).

References, Reading, and Resources

Evans, N., & Rankin, S. (1998). Heterosexism and Campus Violence: Assessment and Intervention Strategies. In A. M. Hoffman, J. H., Schuh, & R. H. Fenske, (1998). Violence on campus: Defining the problems, strategies for action. Gaithersburg, MD: Aspen. pp. 169-186.

Eyermann, T., & Sanlo, R. (2002). Documenting Their Existence: Lesbian, Gay, and Bisexual Students in the Residence Halls In R. Sanlo, S. Rankin, & R. Schoenberg. *Our place on campus: Lesbian, gay, bisexual, and transgender services and programs in higher education* (pp.33-40). Westport, CT: Greenwood.

Hooker, E. (1963). Male homosexuality. In N. L. Farberow (Ed.), Taboo topics. (pp. 44-55). New York: Atherton.

Marcus, E. (1993). Making history: The struggle for gay and lesbian equal rights, 1945-1990: An oral history. NY: HarperPerennial.

Sanlo, R. (2000, Spring). The LGBT Campus Resource Center Director: The New Profession in Student Affairs. Washington, DC: NASPA Journal, 37(3). 485-495.

Sanlo, R. (Ed.) (1998). Working with lesbian, gay, bisexual, and transgender college students: A handbook for faculty and administrators. Westport, CT: Greenwood.

Sanlo, R. (1999). Unheard voices: The effects of silence on lesbian and gay educators. Westport, CT: G Bergin & Garvey.

Sanlo, R., Rankin, S., & Schoenberg, R. (2002). *Our place on campus: Lesbian, gay, bisexual, and transgender services and programs in higher education.* Westport, CT: Greenwood.

Schuh, J. (1998). Conclusion. In A. M. Hoffman, J. H., Schuh, & R. H. Fenske, (1998). Violence on campus: Defining the problems, strategies for action. Gaithersburg, MD: Aspen. p. 347.

Contributor: Ronni Sanlo, University of California at Los Angeles

LESBIAN, GAY, BISEXUAL, TRANSGENDER (LGBT) PROGRAMS and SERVICES

CAS Standards and Guidelines

Part 1. MISSION

Lesbian, Gay, Bisexual, Transgender (LGBT) Programs and Services must incorporate student learning and student development in its mission. LGBT programs and services must enhance overall educational experiences. The programs and services must develop, record, disseminate, implement and regularly review its mission and goals. Mission statements must be consistent with the mission and goals of the institution and with the standards in this document. LGBT programs and services must operate as an integral part of the institution's overall mission.

The scope and nature of the programs and services should be shaped by the mission of the institution.

The mission of LGBT programs and services must promote academic and personal growth and development of LGBT students, assure unrestricted access to and full involvement in all aspects of the institution, and serve as a catalyst for the creation of a campus environment free from prejudice, bigotry, harassment, and violence and hospitable for all students.

To accomplish this mission, the goals of the program must be based on assessment of the needs of and campus climate for LGBT students. LGBT programs and services must select priorities among those needs and respond to the extent that resources permit.

To respond to the presence of LGBT students, some institutions create a separate unit. When this is the case, standards outlined here apply. Whether there is a separate unit for LGBT students or not, institutional units share responsibility for meeting the needs of LGBT students. Coordinated efforts to promote the elimination of prejudicial behaviors should be made by all functional areas.

LGBT programs and services should not be the only organized agency to meet the needs of LGBT students. All institutional units share responsibility for meeting the needs of LGBT students in their areas of responsibility. Coordinated efforts to promote the elimination of prejudicial behaviors should be made at every institution by all functional areas.

Part 2. PROGRAM

The formal education of students consists of the curriculum and the co-curriculum, and must promote student learning and development that is purposeful and holistic. Lesbian, Gay, Bisexual, Transgender (LGBT) Programs and Services must identify relevant and desirable student learning and development outcomes and provide programs and services that encourage the achievement of those outcomes.

Relevant and desirable outcomes include: intellectual growth, effective communication, realistic self-appraisal, enhanced self-esteem, clarified values, career choices, leadership development, healthy behaviors, meaningful interpersonal relationships, independence, collaboration, social responsibility, satisfying and productive lifestyles, appreciation of diversity, spiritual awareness, and achievement of personal and educational goals.

LGBT programs and services must provide evidence of its impact on the achievement of student learning and development outcomes.

The table below offers examples of evidence of achievement of student learning and development.

Student Learning and Development Outcome Domains

Intellectual growth
Examples of achievement indicators

Produces personal and educational goal statements; Employs critical thinking in problem solving; Uses complex information from a variety of sources including personal experience and observation to form a decision or opinion; Obtains a degree; Applies previously understood information and concepts to a new situation or setting; Expresses appreciation for literature, the fine arts, mathematics, sciences, and social sciences

Effective communication
Examples of achievement indicators

Writes and speaks coherently and effectively; Writes and speaks after reflection; Able to influence others through writing, speaking or artistic expression; Effectively articulates abstract ideas; Uses appropriate syntax; Makes presentations or gives performances

Enhanced self-esteem
Examples of achievement indicators

Shows self-respect and respect for others; Initiates actions toward achievement of goals; Takes reasonable risks; Demonstrates assertive behavior; Functions without need for constant reassurance from others

249

Realistic self-appraisal

Examples of achievement indicators

Articulates personal skills and abilities; Makes decisions and acts in congruence with personal values; Acknowledges personal strengths and weaknesses; Articulates rationale for personal behavior; Seeks feedback from others; Learns from past experiences

Clarified values

Examples of achievement indicators

Articulates personal values; Acts in congruence with personal values; Makes decisions that reflect personal values; Demonstrates willingness to scrutinize personal beliefs and values; Identifies personal, work and lifestyle values and explains how they influence decision-making

Career choices

Examples of achievement indicators

Articulates career choices based on assessment of interests, values, skills and abilities; Documents knowledge, skills and accomplishments resulting from formal education, work experience, community service and volunteer experiences; Makes the connections between classroom and out-of-classroom learning; Can construct a resume with clear job objectives and evidence of related knowledge, skills and accomplishments; Articulates the characteristics of a preferred work environment; Comprehends the world of work; Takes steps to initiate a job search or seek advanced education

Leadership development

Examples of achievement indicators

Articulates leadership philosophy or style; Serves in a leadership position in a student organization; Comprehends the dynamics of a group; Exhibits democratic principles as a leader; Exhibits ability to visualize a group purpose and desired outcomes

Healthy behavior

Examples of achievement indicators

Chooses behaviors and environments that promote health and reduce risk; Articulate the relationship between health and wellness and accomplishing life long goals; Exhibits behaviors that advance a healthy community.

Meaningful interpersonal relationships

Examples of achievement indicators

Develops and maintains satisfying interpersonal relationships; Establishes mutually rewarding relationships with friends and colleagues; Listens to and considers others' points of view; Treats others with respect

Independence

Examples of achievement indicators

Exhibits self-reliant behaviors; Functions autonomously; Exhibits ability to function interdependently; Accepts supervision as needed; Manages time effectively

Collaboration

Examples of achievement indicators

Works cooperatively with others; Seeks the involvement of others; Seeks feedback from others; Contributes to achievement of a group goal; Exhibits effective listening skills

Social responsibility

Examples of achievement indicators

Understands and participates in relevant governance systems; Understands, abides by, and participates in the development, maintenance, and/or orderly change of community, social, and legal standards or norms; Appropriately challenges the unfair, unjust, or uncivil behavior of other individuals or groups; Participates in service/volunteer activities

Satisfying and productive lifestyles

Examples of achievement indicators

Achieves balance between education, work, and leisure time; Articulates and meets goals for work, leisure, and education; Overcomes obstacles that hamper goal achievement; Functions on the basis of personal identity, ethical, spiritual, and moral values; Articulates long-term goals and objectives

Appreciating diversity

Examples of achievement indicators

Understands one's own identity and culture; Seeks involvement with people different from oneself; Seeks involvement in diverse interests; Articulates the advantages and challenges of a diverse society; Challenges appropriately the abusive use of stereotypes by others; Understands the impact of diversity on one's own society

Spiritual awareness

Examples of achievement indicators

Develops and articulates personal belief system; Understands roles of spirituality in personal and group values and behaviors

Personal and educational goals

Examples of achievement indicators

Sets, articulates, and pursues individual goals; Articulates personal and educational goals and objectives; Uses personal and educational goals to guide decisions; Understands the effect of one's personal and educational goals on others

LGBT programs and services must be (a) intentional, (b) coherent, (c) based on theories and knowledge of learning and human development, (d) reflective of developmental and demographic profiles of the student population, and (e) responsive to needs of individuals, special populations, and communities.

LGBT programs and services must:

- advocate for the creation of a campus climate that is free from harassment and violence
- identity environmental conditions that negatively influence student welfare
- advocate for solutions to be enacted that neutralize such condition
- work to create policies and procedures within the institution that promote and maintain a hospitable climate

LGBT programs and services must work to assure equitable access to and involvement in all educational programs.

Particular attention should be given to financial aid, athletic scholarships, and employment opportunities on campus.

LGBT programs and services must promote institutional understanding for the concerns of LGBT students, faculty, and staff; educating other campus programs and services to be responsive to the unique concerns of LGBT students.

These programs and services must include:

1. individual and group psychological counseling such as:
   1a. coming out support
   1b. services for victims and perpetrators of homophobia
   1c. services to address family issues
   1d. services to address same sex dating issues
   1e. services to address same sex domestic violence
   1f. support for victims and perpetrators of hate crimes
2. health services such as:
   2a. health forms with inclusive language
   2b. LGBT health issues brochures
   2c. safer sex information for same sex couples
3. career services such as:
   3a. resume development
   3b. information on LGBT friendly employers
   3c. employer mentoring programs for LGBT students

3d. information on LGBT issues in the workplace
4. academic advising such as the support of students' educational choices

LGBT programs and services must provide educational opportunities that include:

- examination of the intersection of sexual orientation with race, class, gender, disability, and age
- promotion of self awareness, self-esteem, and self-confidence
- promotion of leadership experiences
- identification of and networking with role models and mentors
- support of students and their families in achieving academic success

LGBT programs and services must educate the campus community when decisions or policies may affect the achievement of LGBT students; publicize services, events, and issues of concern to LGBT students; and sponsor events that meet educational, personal, physical, and safety needs of LGBT students and their allies.

LGBT programs and services may:

- encourage awareness of off campus networks and other support systems for LGBT students including affiliation with state and national organizations
- improve campus awareness of the complex identity issues inherent in the lives of LGBT students
- publicize the accomplishments of LBGT students, faculty, and staff
- represent LGBT concerns and issues on campus-wide committees
- promote scholarship, research, and assessment on LGBT issues
- encourage campus-wide inclusion of LGBT students and avoidance of negative stereotyping in campus media.

The LGBT programs and services should maintain or have ready access to resources regarding LGBT issues.

LGBT programs and services must address the needs of all LGBT students regardless of their ethnicity, race, gender, religion, age, socioeconomic status, disability, and degree or enrollment status. In addition, LGBT Programs and Services must plan for and recognize the diversity among the LGBT student population.

LGBT Programs and Services should advocate for the human rights of LGBT persons.

Part 3. LEADERSHIP

Effective and ethical leadership is essential to the success of all organizations. Institutions must appoint, position and empower Lesbian, Gay, Bisexual, Transgender ((LGBT) Programs and Services leaders within the administrative structure to accomplish stated missions. Leaders at various levels must be selected on the basis of formal education and training, relevant work experience, personal skills and competencies, relevant professional credentials, as well as potential for promoting learning and development in students, applying effective practices to educational processes, and enhancing institutional effectiveness. Institutions must determine expectations of accountability for LGBT program and services leaders and fairly assess their performance.

Leaders of LGBT programs and services must exercise authority over resources for which they are responsible to achieve their respective missions.

LGBT programs and services leaders must:
- articulate a vision for their organization
- set goals and objectives based on the needs and capabilities of the population served
- promote student learning and development
- prescribe and practice ethical behavior
- recruit, select, supervise, and develop others in the organization
- manage financial resources
- coordinate human resources
- plan, budget for, and evaluate personnel and programs
- apply effective practices to educational and administrative processes
- communicate effectively
- initiate collaborative interaction between individuals and agencies that possess legitimate concerns and interests in the functional area

LGBT programs and services leaders must identify and find means to address individual, organizational, or environmental conditions that inhibit goal achievement.

LGBT programs and services leaders must promote campus environments that result in multiple opportunities for student learning and development.

LGBT programs and services leaders must continuously improve programs and services in response to changing needs of students and other constituents, and evolving institutional priorities.

Part 4. ORGANIZATION and MANAGEMENT

Guided by an overarching intent to ensure student learning and development, Lesbian, Gay, Bisexual, Transgender (LGBT) Programs and services must be structured purposefully and managed effectively to achieve stated goals. Evidence of appropriate structure must include current and accessible policies and procedures, written performance expectations for all employees, functional workflow graphics or organizational charts, and clearly stated service delivery expectations.

Evidence of effective management must include use of comprehensive and accurate information for decisions, clear sources and channels of authority, effective communication practices, decision-making and conflict resolution procedures, responsiveness to changing conditions, accountability and evaluation systems, and recognition and reward processes. LGBT programs and services must provide channels within the organization for regular review of administrative policies and procedures.

LGBT programs and services should play a major role in implementing institutional programs developed in response to the assessed needs of LGBT students. Access to the policymakers of the institution should be readily available. The organization should be administered in a manner that permits the stated mission to be fulfilled. LGBT programs and services should be afforded the opportunity to organize in a manner that is efficient and best promotes equity concerns. Emphasis should be placed on achieving an organization in which services are not limited to a specific group of LGBT students (e.g. solely undergraduate students).

Part 5. HUMAN RESOURCES

Lesbian, Gay, Bisexual, Transgender (LGBT) Programs and Services must be staffed adequately by individuals qualified to accomplish its mission and goals. Within established guidelines of the institution, programs and services must establish procedures for staff selection, training, and evaluation; set expectations for supervision, and provide appropriate professional development opportunities. LGBT programs and services must strive to improve the professional competence and skills of all personnel it employs.

Program leaders should possess the academic preparation, experience, abilities, professional interests, and competencies essential for the efficient operation of the office as charged, as well as the ability to identify additional areas of concern about LGBT students. Specific course work in organizational development, counseling, group dynamics, leadership development, human development, LGBT studies, multicultural education, women's studies, higher education, and research and assessment may be desirable.

LGBT program and services professional staff members must hold an earned graduate degree in a field relevant to the position they hold or must possess an appropriate combination of educational credentials and related work experience.

In addition to providing services, staff members should be provided time for advising and reporting, updating institutional information, research, faculty and staff contacts, staff meetings, training, supervision, personal and professional development, and consultation. Similarly, teaching, administration, research, and other responsibilities should be identified as relevant staff functions.

Staff members should have a combination of graduate course work, formal training (including gay/lesbian/bisexual/transgender issues), and supervised experience.

Degree or credential-seeking interns must be qualified by enrollment in an appropriate field of study and by relevant experience. These individuals must be trained and supervised adequately by professional staff members holding educational credentials and related work experience appropriate for supervision.

Student employees and volunteers must be carefully selected, trained, supervised, and evaluated. They must be trained on how and when to refer those in need of assistance to qualified staff members and have access to a supervisor for assistance in making these judgments. Student employees and volunteers must be provided clear and precise job descriptions, pre-service training based on assessed needs, and continuing staff development.

Student staff members should be provided with clear and precise job descriptions, pre-service training, and on-going staff development.

LGBT program and services must have technical and support staff members adequate to accomplish its mission. Staff members must be technologically proficient and qualified to perform their job functions, be knowledgeable of ethical and legal uses of technology, and have access to training. The level of staffing and workloads must be adequate and appropriate for program and service demands.

Support staff should have a thorough knowledge of the institution and be able to perform office and administrative functions, including reception, information giving, problem identification, and referral. Special emphasis should be placed on skills in the areas of public relations, information dissemination, problem identification, and referral.

All LGBT program and services staff members must be responsive to and knowledgeable about LGBT issues.

Salary levels and fringe benefits for all LGBT program and services staff members must be commensurate with those for comparable positions within the institution, in similar institutions, and in the relevant geographic area.

LGBT program and services must institute hiring and promotion practices that are fair, inclusive, and non-discriminatory. Programs and services must employ a diverse staff to provide readily identifiable role models for students and to enrich the campus community.

LGBT program and services must create and maintain position descriptions for all staff members and provide regular performance planning and appraisals.

LGBT program and services must have a system for regular staff evaluation and must provide access to continuing education and professional development opportunities, including in-service training programs and participation in professional conferences and workshops.

Staff development is an essential activity. Additional credit courses, seminars, access to current research are examples of professional development activities that could be made available. Additionally, staff members should participate in appropriate professional organizations and should have the budgetary support to do so. Staff members should be encouraged to participate in community activities related to the student population being served.

LGBT program and services staff members must ensure that the confidentiality of students' sexual orientation and gender identity are protected when appropriate.

The level of services must be established and reviewed regularly with regard to service demands, enrollment, user surveys, diversity of services offered, institutional resources, and other student services available on the campus and in the local community.

LGBT program and services staff must be comfortable and interested in working with gay, lesbian, bisexual and transgender students.

Part 6. FINANCIAL RESOURCES

Lesbian, Gay, Bisexual, Transgender (LGBT) Programs and Service must have adequate funding to accomplish its mission and goals. Funding priorities must be determined within the context of the stated mission, goals, objectives and comprehensive analysis of the needs and capabilities of students and the availability of internal or external resources.

LGBT programs and services must demonstrate fiscal responsibility and cost effectiveness consistent with institutional protocols.

Funding for LGBT programs and devices may come from a composite of institutional funds, grant money, student government funds, and government contracts.

Part 7. FACILITIES, TECHNOLOGY and EQUIPMENT

Lesbian, Gay, Bisexual, Transgender (LGBT) Programs and Services must have adequate, suitably located facilities, adequate technology, and equipment to support its mission and goals efficiently and effectively. Facilities, technology, and equipment must be evaluated regularly and be in compliance with relevant federal, state, provincial, and local requirements to provide for access, health, safety, and security.

LGBT programs and services should maintain a physical and social environment that facilitates appropriate attention to safety factors. In addition it should provide confidential individual and group meeting space.

LGBT programs and services should have access to resources for research including access to private computer space.

Part 8. LEGAL RESPONSIBILITIES

Lesbian, Gay, Bisexual, Transgender (LGBT) Programs and Services staff members must be knowledgeable about and responsive to laws and regulations that relate to their respective responsibilities. Staff members must inform users of LGBT programs and services and officials, as appropriate, of legal obligations and limitations including constitutional, statutory, regulatory, and case law; mandatory laws and orders emanating from federal, state/provincial and local governments; and the institution's policies.

LGBT programs and services staff members must use reasonable and informed practices to limit the liability

exposure of the institution, its officers, employees, and agents. Staff members must be informed about institutional policies regarding personal liability and related insurance coverage options.

The institution must provide access to legal advice for LGBT programs and services staff members as needed to carry out assigned responsibilities.

The institution must inform LGBT programs and services staff and students in a timely and systematic fashion about extraordinary or changing legal obligations and potential liabilities.

Part 9. EQUITY and ACCESS

Lesbian, Gay, Bisexual, Transgender (LGBT) Programs and Services staff members must ensure that services and programs are provided on a fair and equitable basis. Facilities, programs and services must be accessible. Hours of operation and delivery of and access to programs and services must be responsive to the needs of all students and other constituents. LGBT programs and services must adhere to the spirit and intent of equal opportunity laws.

LGBT programs and services must be open and readily accessible to all students and must not discriminate except where sanctioned by law and institutional policy. Discrimination must be avoided on the bases of age; color; creed; cultural heritage; disability; ethnicity; gender identity; nationality; political affiliation; religious affiliation; sex; sexual orientation; or social, economic, marital, or veteran status.

Consistent with their mission and goals, LGBT programs and services must take affirmative action to remedy significant imbalances in student participation and staffing patterns.

As the demographic profiles of campuses change and new instructional delivery methods are introduced, institutions must recognize the needs of students who participate in distance learning for access to programs and services offered on campus. Institutions must provide appropriate services in ways that are accessible to distance learners and assist them in identifying and gaining access to other appropriate services in their geographic region.

Part 10. CAMPUS and EXTERNAL RELATIONS

The LGBT Programs and Services must establish, maintain, and promote effective relations with relevant individuals, campus offices, and external agencies.

The success of the LGBT programs and services is dependent on the maintenance of good relationships with students, faculty, administrators, alumni, the community at large, contractors, and support agencies.

LGBT programs and services should collaborate with campus referral agencies for LGBT students (e.g., multicultural student affairs, women's centers, special academic support units, campus security, health centers, counseling centers, religious programs and career services).

LGBT programs and services should establish relationships with a wide range of student groups (e.g., LGBT student association, student government association, fraternities and sororities) to promote visibility and to serve as a resource.

LGBT programs and services should foster relationships with academic units (especially in LGBT studies, ethnic studies, women's studies, higher education, and college student personnel) and with campus professionals (e.g. student activities, athletics, commuter affairs, and residential life.) Staff should be an integral part of appropriate campus networks to effectively participate in the establishment of institution-wide policy and practices, and to collaborate with other staff and faculty in providing services.

LGBT programs and services should establish effective relations with institutional legal counsel and legal staff of relevant professional organizations in order to effectively respond to pertinent legal issues and precedents, which underlie the delivery components.

Where adequate LGBT resources are not available on campus, LGBT programs and services should establish and maintain close working relationships with off-campus community LGBT counseling and support agencies.

An advisory board made up of students, faculty, staff, alumni, and community members may be established to advise, support, and guide the LGBT programs and services.

Part 11. DIVERSITY
Within the context of each institution's unique mission, diversity enriches the community and enhances the collegiate experience for all; therefore, Lesbian, Gay, Bisexual, Transgender (LGBT) Programs and Services must nurture environments where commonalties and differences among people are recognized and honored.

LGBT programs and services must promote educational experiences that are characterized by open and continuous communication that deepens understanding of one's own identity, culture, and

heritage, and that of others. LGBT programs and services must educate and promote respect about commonalties and differences in their historical and cultural contexts.

LGBT programs and services must address the characteristics and needs of a diverse population when establishing and implementing policies and procedures.

Part 12. ETHICS
All persons involved in the delivery of Lesbian, Gay, Bisexual, Transgender (LGBT) Programs and Services must adhere to the highest principles of ethical behavior. LGBT programs and services must develop or adopt and implement appropriate statements of ethical practice. LGBT programs and services must publish these statements and ensure their periodic review by relevant constituencies.

LGBT programs and services staff members must ensure that privacy and confidentiality are maintained with respect to all communications and records to the extent that such records are protected under the law and appropriate statements of ethical practice. Information contained in students' education records must not be disclosed without written consent except as allowed by relevant laws and institutional policies. Staff members must disclose to appropriate authorities information judged to be of an emergency nature, especially when the safety of the individual or others is involved, or when otherwise required by institutional policy or relevant law.

LGBT programs and services staff members must ensure that the confidentiality of individuals' sexual orientation and gender identity are protected.

Information should be released only at the written request of a student who has full knowledge of the nature of the information that is being released and of the parties to whom it is being released. Instances of limited confidentiality should be clearly articulated. The decision to release information without consent should occur only after careful consideration and under the conditions described above.

All LGBT programs and services staff members must be aware of and comply with the provisions contained in the institution's human subjects research policy and in other relevant institutional policies addressing ethical practices and confidentiality of research data concerning individuals.

LGBT programs and services staff members must recognize and avoid personal conflict of interest or appearance thereof in their transactions with students and others.

LGBT programs and services staff members must strive to insure the fair, objective, and impartial treatment of all persons with whom they deal. Staff members must not participate in nor condone any form of harassment that demeans persons or creates an intimidating, hostile, or offensive campus environment.

When handling institutional funds, all LGBT programs and services staff members must ensure that such funds are managed in accordance with established and responsible accounting procedures and the fiscal policies or processes of the institution.

LGBT programs and services staff members must perform their duties within the limits of their training, expertise, and competence. When these limits are exceeded, individuals in need of further assistance must be referred to persons possessing appropriate qualifications.

LGBT programs and services staff members must use suitable means to confront and otherwise hold accountable other staff members who exhibit unethical behavior.

LGBT programs and services staff members must maintain the highest principles of ethical behavior in the use of technology.

Part 13. ASSESSMENT and EVALUATION

Lesbian, Gay, Bisexual, Transgender (LGBT) Programs and Services must conduct regular assessment and evaluations. LGBT programs and services must employ effective qualitative and quantitative methodologies as appropriate, to determine whether and to what degree the stated mission, goals, and student learning and development outcomes are being met. The process must employ sufficient and sound assessment measures to ensure comprehensiveness. Data collected must include responses from students and other affected constituencies.

LGBT programs and services must evaluate periodically how well they complement and enhance the institution's stated mission and educational effectiveness.

Results of these evaluations must be used in revising and improving programs and services and in recognizing staff performance.

Evaluation of LGBT programs and services facilities, staff, programs, services, and governance must be continuous and implemented within the context of the program's mission.

Both internal and external on-going evaluations are encouraged as part of a thoughtful plan of continuous evaluation of the LGBT's mission and goals. Periodic reports, statistically valid research, outside reviews, and studies exploring student needs and opinions should be utilized.

General Standards revised in 2002; LGBT content developed/ revised in 2000

THE ROLE of MULTICULTURAL STUDENT PROGRAMS
CAS Standards Contextual Statement

The expansion of the civil rights movement begun in the 1960s promoted increased access to students whose attendance in higher education had been highly underrepresented, especially at predominately White institutions. Although some underrepresented student enrollments have increased since the 1960s, enrollment that is representative of the national population as well as the retention and degree completion of students of color continues to be of considerable concern. For example, *The Chronicle of Higher Education* sited the report "A Matter of Degree" that "while 64% of fulltime students at four-year colleges graduate within six years, less than half of black students and less and half of Hispanic students do so in that period of time. The rates from low-income families are only slightly better" (Burd, 2004, p. A19). The report went on to state that the difference in graduation rates between Latino/a and White students is at "the average college" seven percentage points and 15 at a quarter of all four-year institutions.

A contributing factor in the disparity of retention rates has been the initial lack of readiness by institutions to serve expanded student populations. The establishment of Multicultural Student Programs and Services (MSPS) was initially created to respond to this lack of readiness, but more recently to proactively offer programs and services that serve to create environments where all students can thrive. Although MSPS vary in structure and purpose from institution to institution, most advocate for the academic success of students. This often includes advocating for changing policies, practices, and attitudes of the campus and its students and employees that inhibits student confidence and success; mentoring and other community building opportunities including cultural support systems where students can feel comfortable rather than feeling that they have to assimilate into the dominant culture; implementing programs to educate the campus community about various cultures and to promote awareness of multicultural and social justice issues; academic support services including tutoring, special study skills training, supplemental instruction, referral to other learning assistance resources, distinctive orientation programs, academic advising, personal counseling, financial assistance counseling, career development, and graduate school advising; and offering an academic curricula where multicultural perspectives are embedded. On campuses where academic departments for ethnic, women, or queer studies exist, the MSPS sometimes coordinates services with these academic departments. Some MSPS organize services to address specific populations, while others seek to serve all underrepresented and oppressed students collectively. Some have autonomous facilities that include programming, advising, classroom, and counseling space, whereas other MSPS are located in spaces under the management of other campus entities such as the campus union or housing and residence life.

Strong MSPS are essential to the retention and graduation rates of students as well as the multicultural education of the campus. Clearly, institutions exhibit their commitment to providing quality education for all its students through the level of support they provide to MSPS.

Many multicultural offices and centers have been established to serve underrepresented students including students of color, women students, and LGBT students separately. These standards will focus on general programs and services for under-represented and oppressed students. For standards related to programs and services for other underrepresented students see the CAS Standards for Lesbian, Gay, Bisexual, and Transgender Programs; Women Student Programs; and Disability Services.

References, Readings, and Resources

Burd, S. (June 4, 2004). Colleges permit too many needy students to drop out, says report on graduation rates. *The Chronicle of Higher Education,* A19.

Cox, Taylor, Jr. (2001). *Creating the multicultural organization.* San Francisco: Jossey Bass, 2001.

Helms, J. E.(1992). A race is a nice thing to have. Topeka: Content Communications. [available through www.emicrotraining.com]

Komives, S. R. & Woodard, Jr., D. B. (2003). *Student Services: A handbook for the profession* (4th ed.). San Francisco: Jossey-Bass.

McEwen, M K., Kodoma, C. M., Alvarez, A, Lee, S, Liang, C. T. H. (2002). *Working with Asian college students.* San Francisco: Jossey Bass New Directions for Student Services Series.

Pope, R. L. & Reynolds, A. L. (1997). Student affairs core competencies: Integrating multicultural awareness, knowledge, and skills. *Journal of College Student Development, 38,* 266-277.

Pope, R. L., Reynolds, A. L., & Mueller, J. A. (2004). *Multicultural competence in student affairs.* San Francisco: Jossey-Bass.

Talbot, D. (2003). Multiculturalism. In S. R. Komives & D. B. Woodard, Jr., (Eds.), *Student Services: A handbook for the profession* (4th ed.) (pp. 423-446). San Francisco: Jossey-Bass.

Tatum, B. D. (1999). Why *are all the Black kids sitting together in the cafeteria?: And other questions about race.* New York: Basic Books.

California Council of Cultural Centers in Higher Education: www.caccche.org

Contributor: Jan Arminio, Shippensburg University

MULTICULTURAL STUDENT PROGRAMS AND SERVICES
CAS STANDARDS and GUIDELINES

Part 1. MISSION

Multicultural Student Programs and Services (MSPS) must promote academic and personal growth of traditionally underserved students, work with the entire campus to create an institutional and community climate of justice, promote access and equity in higher education, and offer programs that educate the campus about diversity.

Multicultural Student Programs and Services (MSPS) must incorporate student learning and student development in its mission. MSPS must enhance overall educational experiences. MSPS must develop, record, disseminate, implement, and regularly review its mission and goals. Mission statements must be consistent with the mission and goals of the institution and with the standards in this document. MSPS must operate as an integral part of the institution's overall mission.

MSPS must assist the institution in developing shared goals and creating a sense of common community that serves all its constituents fairly and equitably and is marked by:

- access to academic, social, cultural, recreational and other groups and activities
- opportunities for intentional interaction and engagement
- integration

MSPS must encourage the institution to hold units responsible for meeting the needs of traditionally underserved students in their area of responsibility; this includes under-represented or oppressed students, such as students of color, lesbian, gay, bisexual and transgender students, and students with disabilities.

Institutions may have more than one MSPS organization. Each of these MSPS organizations' missions may address the needs of a particular student group or groups. These missions should be complementary. If only one MSPS organization exists, the mission should address the needs of students of the many cultural and oppressed groups.

In addition, MSPS should encourage all units to explicitly include in their mission serving a wide range of underserved students fairly and equitably.

Part 2. PROGRAM

The formal education of students consists of the curriculum and the co-curriculum, and must promote student learning and development that is purposeful and holistic. Multicultural Student Programs and Services (MSPS) must identify relevant and desirable student learning and development outcomes and provide programs and services that encourage the achievement of those outcomes.

Relevant and desirable outcomes include: intellectual growth, effective communication, realistic self-appraisal, enhanced self-esteem, clarified values, career choices, leadership development, healthy behaviors, meaningful interpersonal relationships, independence, collaboration, social responsibility, satisfying and productive lifestyles, appreciation of diversity, spiritual awareness, and achievement of personal and educational goals.

MSPS must provide evidence of its impact on the achievement of student learning and development outcomes.

The table below offers examples of evidence of achievement of student learning and development.

Student Learning and Development Outcome Domains

Intellectual growth
Examples of achievement indicators

Produces personal and educational goal statements; Employs critical thinking in problem solving; Uses complex information from a variety of sources including personal experience and observation to form a decision or opinion; Obtains a degree; Applies previously understood information and concepts to a new situation or setting; Expresses appreciation for diversity in literature, fine arts, mathematics, sciences, social sciences, and global curiosity

Effective communication
Examples of achievement indicators

Writes and speaks coherently and effectively across cultures; Writes and speaks after reflection; Able to influence others through writing, speaking, or artistic expression; Effectively articulates abstract ideas; Uses appropriate syntax; Makes presentations or gives performances; Can work in teams in multicultural settings

Enhanced self-esteem

Examples of achievement indicators

Shows self-respect and respect for others; Initiates actions toward achievement of goals; Takes reasonable risks; Demonstrates assertive behavior; Functions without need for constant reassurance from others

Realistic self-appraisal

Examples of achievement indicators

Articulates personal skills and abilities; Makes decisions and acts in congruence with personal values; Acknowledges personal strengths and weaknesses; Articulates rationale for personal behavior; Seeks feedback from others; Learns from past experiences

Clarified values

Examples of achievement indicators

Articulates personal values; Acts in congruence with personal values; Makes decisions that reflect personal values; Demonstrates willingness to scrutinize personal beliefs and values; Identifies personal, work, and lifestyle values and explains how they influence decision-making; Understands how culture influences one's own values

Career choices

Examples of achievement indicators

Articulates career choices based on assessment of interests, values, skills, and abilities; Documents knowledge, skills and accomplishments resulting from formal education, work experience, community service, and volunteer experiences; Makes the connections between classroom and out-of-classroom learning; Can construct a resume with clear job objectives and evidence of related knowledge, skills, and accomplishments; Articulates the characteristics of a preferred work environment; Comprehends the world of work; Takes steps to initiate a job search or seek advanced education; Comprehends the multicultural dimensions in the world of work

Leadership development

Examples of achievement indicators

Articulates leadership philosophy or style; Serves in a leadership position in a student organization or community group; Comprehends the dynamics of a group; Exhibits democratic principles as a leader; Exhibits ability to visualize a group purpose and desired outcomes

Healthy behavior

Examples of achievement indicators

Chooses behaviors and environments that promote health and reduce risk; Articulates the relationship between health and wellness and accomplishing life-long goals; Exhibits behaviors that advance a healthy community

Meaningful interpersonal relationships

Examples of achievement indicators

Develops and maintains satisfying interpersonal relationships; Establishes mutually rewarding relationships with friends and colleagues; Listens to and considers others' points of view; Treats others with respect

Independence

Examples of achievement indicators

Exhibits self-reliant behaviors; Exhibits ability to function interdependently; Accepts supervision as needed; Manages time effectively, generates ideas, and uses creativity

Collaboration

Examples of achievement indicators

Works cooperatively with others; Seeks the involvement of others; Seeks feedback from others; Contributes to achievement of a group goal; Exhibits effective listening skills

Social responsibility

Examples of achievement indicators

Understands and participates in relevant governance systems; Understands, abides by, and participates in the development, maintenance, or orderly change of community, social, and legal standards or norms; Appropriately challenges the unfair, unjust, or uncivil behavior of other individuals or groups; Participates in service or volunteer activities

Satisfying and productive lifestyles

Examples of achievement indicators

Achieves balance between education, work, and leisure time; Articulates and meets goals for work, leisure, and education; Overcomes obstacles that hamper goal achievement; Functions on the basis of personal identity, ethical, spiritual, and moral values; Articulates long-term goals and objectives

Appreciating diversity

Examples of achievement indicators

Understands one's own identity and culture; Seeks involvement with people different from oneself and with other cultures; Seeks involvement in diverse interests; Articulates the advantages and challenges of a diverse society; Challenges appropriately the abusive use of stereotypes; Understands the impact of diversity on one's own society; Makes an effort to understand other cultures

Spiritual awareness

Examples of achievement indicators

Develops and articulates a personal belief system; Understands roles of spirituality in personal and group values and behaviors

Personal and educational goals
Examples of achievement indicators

Sets, articulates, and pursues individual goals; Articulates personal and educational goals and objectives; Uses personal and educational goals to guide decisions; Understands the effect of one's personal and educational goals on others

MSPS must be (a) intentional, (b) coherent, (c) based on theories and knowledge of learning and human development, (d) reflective of developmental and demographic profiles of the student population, and (e) responsive to needs of individuals, special populations, and communities.

MSPS must be based on models, approaches, or theories that address students across developmental levels.

MSPS must provide educational programs and services for all students that focus on awareness of cultural differences, cultural commonalties, privilege, and identity; self-assessment of cultural awareness and possible prejudices; and changing prejudicial, oppressive, and stereotypical attitudes or behavior.

MSPS may support other institutional functional areas such as recruitment, career services, academic advising, counseling, health services, and alumni relations.

MSPS must promote academic success of students by:
- offering distinctive programs that introduce students to a community network and teach students how to negotiate processes within the institution (e. g., registration, academic advising, financial aid, housing, campus employment)
- assisting them to determine and assess their educational goals and academic skills
- providing support services that assist in achieving educational goals and attaining or refining academic skills
- informing students of educational opportunities, such as internships, special scholarship opportunities, study abroad programs, research, seminar, and conferences
- promoting intellectual, career, social, ethical, and social justice development
- networking with staff and faculty members
- connecting them to campus networks and groups and organizations

MSPS should act as a liaison for referrals and interventions with staff and faculty members and administrators on behalf of students when appropriate.

MSPS must promote personal growth of students by:
- enhancing students' understanding of their own culture, heritage, and identities
- enhancing students' understanding of cultures, heritages, and identities other than their own
- providing opportunities for students to establish satisfying interpersonal relationships
- providing opportunities for interactions, exchange of ideas, and reflection

MSPS must work to create an engaging climate for students by advocating for the following opportunities and encouraging students take advantage of them:
- campus and community service including leadership opportunities
- practice in leadership including training, education, and development
- access to appropriate mentors and role models
- shared inter and intra social experiences

MSPS must work to create a just campus climate by:
- challenging tacit and overt prejudices or discrimination against students
- coordinating efforts to promote multicultural sensitivity and the elimination of prejudicial behaviors
- facilitating desired changes with the cooperation of other campus entities
- identifying and addressing impediments to the growth and development of full participation of students

If institutional practices or policies have prejudicial effects, staff members must bring these facts to the attention of the proper authorities in the institution and work to change them.

MSPS must offer to the campus community programs that increase multicultural awareness, knowledge, and skills by:
- promoting and enhancing the understanding of a variety of cultures and historical experiences
- promoting and enhancing the understanding of privilege, power, and prejudicial and stereotypical assumptions and understanding privilege and power
- promoting and enhancing identity development
- teaching skills on how to combat racism, homophobia, sexism, and other forms of discrimination
- complementing the academic curricula

MSPS must serve as a resource for multicultural training, education, and development.

Educational programs may be provided in collaboration with efforts by academic and student affairs units, and other program support services. Staff members in MSPS should coordinate their efforts with academic, student affairs units, and other support services. Various dimensions of students' cultures, such as history, philosophy, world view, literature, and various forms of communication and artistic expression should be explored. Human relations programs should be designed to assist faculty members, staff members, and students in developing more tolerance, understanding, and ability to relate to others around issues of privilege; age; color; creed; cultural heritage; disability; ethnicity; gender identity; nationality; political affiliation; religious affiliation; sex; sexual orientation; or social, economic, marital, or veteran status.

Activities that attempt to promote students' development should be based upon assessments and should reflect unique dimensions of the multicultural student experience.

MSPS must assist students across the range of their experiences at the institution.

These areas may include:
- monitoring scholastic progress of groups and individual students and recommending strategies for improvement
- providing workshops, programs, retreats, and seminars on relevant topics and encouraging attendance at activities and services sponsored by other campus offices
- encouraging student attendance at conferences, meetings, and programs
- advising student organizations that advance the equality and interests of specific groups (e. g., Black/African American students, Asian/Pacific Islander students, Latino/a students, Native students, LGBT students, and allies), editorial staffs of multicultural publications, fraternal groups, pre-professional clubs, and program councils
- providing assistance and advice in planning multicultural student celebrations (e.g., Black/African American History Month, Kwanzaa, Stonewall Anniversary, Day of Silence, Take Back the Night, Transgender Day of Remembrance)
- assisting multicultural student groups or individuals in identifying and gaining access, where appropriate, to institutional services such as printing, bulk mailing, and computer services
- providing a directory of multicultural faculty and staff members
- providing a directory of faculty and staff who have agreed to provide mentoring and assistance
- publishing a newsletter, website, or other means of focusing on current events, leadership opportunities, and other relevant information

Part 3. LEADERSHIP

Effective and ethical leadership is essential to the success of all organizations. Institutions must appoint, position, and empower Multicultural Student Programs and Services (MSPS) leaders within the administrative structure to accomplish stated missions. MSPS leaders at various levels must be selected on the basis of formal education and training, relevant work experience, personal skills and competencies, relevant professional credentials, as well as potential for promoting learning and development in students, applying effective practices to educational processes, and enhancing institutional effectiveness. Institutions must determine expectations of accountability for leaders and fairly assess their performance.

Leaders of MSPS must exercise authority over resources for which they are responsible to achieve their respective missions.

MSPS leaders must:
- **articulate a vision for their organization**
- **set goals and objectives based on the needs and capabilities of the populations served**
- **promote student learning and development**
- **prescribe and practice ethical behavior**
- **recruit, select, supervise, and develop others in the organization**
- **manage financial resources**
- **coordinate human resources**
- **plan, budget for, and evaluate personnel and programs**
- **apply effective practices to educational and administrative processes**
- **communicate effectively**
- **initiate collaborative interaction between individuals and agencies that possess legitimate concerns and interests in the MSPS.**

MSPS leaders must identify and find means to address individual, organizational, or environmental conditions that inhibit goal achievement.

MSPS leaders must promote campus environments that result in multiple opportunities for student learning and development.

MSPS leaders must continuously improve programs and services in response to changing needs of students and other constituents, and evolving institutional priorities.

MSPS leaders must base their work on models and approaches that are theory-based and data driven.

Part 4. ORGANIZATION and MANAGEMENT

Guided by an overarching intent to ensure student learning and development, Multicultural Student Programs and Services (MSPS) must be structured purposefully and managed effectively to achieve stated goals. Evidence of appropriate structure must include current and accessible policies and procedures, written performance expectations for all employees, functional workflow graphics or organizational charts, and clearly stated service delivery expectations.

Evidence of effective management must include use of comprehensive and accurate information for decisions, clear sources and channels of authority, effective communication practices, decision-making and conflict resolution procedures, responsiveness to changing conditions, accountability and evaluation systems, and recognition and reward processes. MSPS must provide channels within the organization for regular review of administrative policies and procedures.

MSPS must be located in an organizational structure that can best provide for effective programs and services for achievement of its mission.

Wherever located, MSPS should collaborate and form close alliances with student affairs.

In response to assessed student needs, MSPS must play a principal role in creating and implementing institutional policies and programs.

Part 5. HUMAN RESOURCES

Multicultural Student Programs and Services (MSPS) must be staffed adequately by individuals qualified to accomplish its mission and goals. Within established guidelines of the institution, MSPS must establish procedures for staff selection, training, and evaluation; set expectations for supervision, and provide appropriate professional development opportunities. MSPS must strive to improve the professional competence and skills of all personnel it employs.

Professional Staff:

Professional staff members must hold an earned graduate degree in a field relevant to the position they hold or must possess an appropriate combination of educational credentials and related work experience.

Professional staff members must possess the requisite multicultural knowledge, awareness, and skills.

Professional staff should possess the awareness that cultural differences are valuable. Professional staff should value the significance of their own cultural heritage and understand that of different cultures. They should have insight into the interpersonal process of how one's own behavior impacts others. They should be aware of when change is necessary for the realization of a positive and just campus.

Professional staff must have knowledge about identity development and the intersections of various aspects of diversity (i.e., race and class, race and gender, race and sexual orientation) on identity development and the acculturation process. Professional staff must know how various groups experience the campus and what institutional and societal barriers limit their access and their success. Professional staff must know how culture affects verbal and non-verbal communication. Professional staff must be knowledgeable about research and practice in areas appropriate to their programming with students.

Professional staff must be skilled in identifying cultural issues and assessing their impact. Professional staff must be able to develop empathetic and trusting relationships with students. Professional staff must recognize individual, cultural, and universal similarities. Professional staff must be able to make culturally appropriate interventions to seek to optimize learning experiences for students. Professional staff must demonstrate respect for cultural values.

The professional staff of MSPS should reflect the various student cultures involved in MSPS.

In addition to professional staff being knowledgeable in their areas of responsibility, they should be knowledgeable about career planning and development, health promotion, group facilitation, leadership training and development, workshop design, social-interpersonal development, individual and group counseling, and campus resources.

Professional staff should complete specific coursework in organizational development, counseling theory and practice, identity development theory, group dynamics, leadership development, human development, and research and assessment.

Professional staff must have a personal commitment to justice and social change.

Graduate Students and Interns:
Degree or credential-seeking interns must be qualified by enrollment in an appropriate field of study and by relevant experience. These individuals must be trained and supervised adequately by professional staff members holding educational credentials and related work experience appropriate for supervision.

The use of graduate assistants and interns should be encouraged to expand staff abilities, provide peer role models, and give valuable pre-professional experience. Particular attention should be given to preparing all pre-professional assistants to be especially sensitive to cultural differences of focus populations.

Students:
Student employees and volunteers must be carefully selected, trained, supervised, and evaluated. They must be trained on how and when to refer those in need of assistance to qualified staff members and have access to a supervisor for assistance in making these judgments. Student employees and volunteers must be provided clear and precise job descriptions, pre-service training based on assessed needs, and continuing staff development.

Student employees and volunteers from multicultural groups should be utilized.

Student employees must be assigned responsibilities that are within their scope of competence.

Training and activities for student employees could include retreats, leadership classes, and workshops.

Support Staff:
MSPS must have technical and support staff members adequate to accomplish its mission. Staff members must be technologically proficient and qualified to perform their job functions, be knowledgeable of ethical and legal uses of technology, and have access to training. The level of staffing and workloads must be adequate and appropriate for program and service demands.

All Staff:
Salary levels and fringe benefits for all MSPS staff members must be commensurate with those for comparable positions within the institution, in similar institutions, and in the relevant geographic area.

MSPS staff members must institute hiring and promotion practices that are fair, inclusive, and non-discriminatory. Programs and services must employ a diverse staff to provide readily identifiable role models for students and to enrich the campus community.

MSPS staff members must create and maintain position descriptions for all staff members and provide regular performance planning and appraisals.

MSPS staff members must have a system for regular staff evaluation and must provide access to continuing education and professional development opportunities, including in-service training programs and participation in professional conferences and workshops.

Part 6. FINANCIAL RESOURCES
Multicultural Student Programs and Services (MSPS) must have adequate funding to accomplish its mission and goals. Funding priorities must be determined within the context of the stated mission, goals, objectives, and comprehensive analysis of the needs and capabilities of students and the availability of internal or external resources.

MSPS must demonstrate fiscal responsibility and cost effectiveness consistent with institutional protocols.

As programs grow and student diversity increases, institutions should increase financial support.

Part 7. FACILITIES, TECHNOLOGY, and EQUIPMENT
Multicultural Student Programs and Services (MSPS) must have adequate, suitably located facilities, adequate technology, and equipment to support its mission and goals efficiently and effectively. Facilities, technology, and equipment must be evaluated regularly and be in compliance with relevant federal, state, provincial, and local requirements to provide for access, health, safety, and security.

Adequate space should be provided for a resource library, private individual consultations, group workshops, and work areas for support staff. Many of the activities offered by MSPS require the same level of privacy as individual and group counseling.

Wherever it is located, MSPS should provide a safe haven for students. In addition, MSPS should provide a place for all students to learn to become more multiculturally competent.

Part 8. LEGAL RESPONSIBILITIES
Multicultural Student Programs and Services (MSPS) staff members must be knowledgeable about and responsive to laws and regulations that relate to their respective responsibilities. MSPS staff members must

inform users of programs and services and officials, as appropriate, of legal obligations and limitations including constitutional, statutory, regulatory, and case law; mandatory laws and orders emanating from federal, state/provincial and local governments; and the institution's policies.

MSPS staff members must use reasonable and informed practices to limit the liability exposure of the institution, its officers, employees, and agents. Staff members must be informed about institutional policies regarding personal liability and related insurance coverage options.

The institution must provide access to legal advice for MSPS staff members as needed to carry out assigned responsibilities.

The institution must inform MSPS staff and students in a timely and systematic fashion about extraordinary or changing legal obligations and potential liabilities.

Part 9. EQUITY and ACCESS

Multicultural Student Programs and Services (MSPS) staff members must ensure that services and programs are provided on a fair and equitable basis. Facilities, programs, and services must be accessible. Hours of operation and delivery of and access to programs and services must be responsive to the needs of all students and members of campus. MSPS must adhere to the spirit and intent of equal opportunity laws.

The program must be open and readily accessible to all students and must not discriminate except where sanctioned by law and institutional policy. Discrimination must be avoided on the bases of age; color; creed; cultural heritage; disability; ethnicity; gender identity; nationality; political affiliation; religious affiliation; sex; sexual orientation; or social, economic, marital, or veteran status.

Consistent with their mission and goals, MSPS must take affirmative action to remedy significant imbalances in student participation and staffing patterns.

As the demographic profiles of campuses change and new instructional delivery methods are introduced, institutions must recognize the needs of students who participate in distance learning for access to programs and services offered on campus. Institutions must provide appropriate services in ways that are accessible to distance learners and assist them in identifying and gaining access to other appropriate services in their geographic region.

Part 10. CAMPUS and EXTERNAL RELATIONS

Multicultural Student Programs and Services (MSPS) must establish, maintain, and promote effective relations with relevant individuals, campus offices, and external agencies.

Professional staff members must coordinate, or where appropriate, collaborate with staff and faculty members and other staff in providing services and programs to meet the needs of multicultural students.

MSPS must identify and address retention issues of underserved population and advocate for the creation of welcoming surrounding community.

This could include MSPS involvement in community collaborations and coalitions that confront racism, sexism, and homophobia. Community services necessities should be available for all students.

Part 11. DIVERSITY

Within the context of each institution's unique mission, diversity enriches the community and enhances the collegiate experience for all; therefore, Multicultural Student Programs and Services (MSPS) must nurture environments where commonalties and differences among people are recognized and honored.

MSPS must promote educational experiences that are characterized by open and continuous communication that deepens understanding of one's own identity, culture, and heritage, and that of others. MSPS must educate and promote respect about commonalties and differences in their historical and cultural contexts.

MSPS must address the characteristics and needs of a diverse population when establishing and implementing policies and procedures.

Part 12. ETHICS

All persons involved in the delivery of Multicultural Student Programs and Services (MSPS) must adhere to the highest principles of ethical behavior. MSPS must develop or adopt and implement appropriate statements of ethical practice. MSPS must publish these statements and ensure their periodic review by relevant constituencies.

MSPS staff members must ensure that privacy and

confidentiality are maintained with respect to all communications and records to the extent that such records are protected under the law and appropriate statements of ethical practice. Information contained in students' education records must not be disclosed without written consent except as allowed by relevant laws and institutional policies. Staff members must disclose to appropriate authorities information judged to be of an emergency nature, especially when the safety of the individual or others is involved, or when otherwise required by institutional policy or relevant law.

All MSPS staff members must be aware of and comply with the provisions contained in the institution's human subjects research policy and in other relevant institutional policies addressing ethical practices and confidentiality of research data concerning individuals.

MSPS staff members must recognize and avoid personal conflict of interest or appearance thereof in their transactions with students and others.

MSPS staff members must strive to insure the fair, objective, and impartial treatment of all persons with whom they deal. Staff members must not participate in nor condone any form of harassment that demeans persons or creates an intimidating, hostile, or offensive campus environment.

When handling institutional funds, all MSPS staff members must ensure that such funds are managed in accordance with established and responsible accounting procedures and the fiscal policies or processes of the institution.

MSPS staff members must perform their duties within the limits of their training, expertise, and competence. When these limits are exceeded, individuals in need of further assistance must be referred to persons possessing appropriate qualifications.

MSPS staff members must use suitable means to confront and otherwise hold accountable other staff members who exhibit unethical behavior.

MSPS staff members must be knowledgeable about and practice ethical behavior in the use of technology.

Part 13. ASSESSMENT and EVALUATION
Multicultural Student Programs and Services (MSPS) must conduct regular assessment and evaluations.

MSPS must employ effective qualitative and quantitative methodologies as appropriate, to determine whether and to what degree the stated mission, goals, and student learning and development outcomes are being met. The process must employ sufficient and sound assessment measures to ensure comprehensiveness. Data collected must include responses from students and other affected constituencies.

Assessments may involve many methods. Survey instruments, interviews, behavioral observations, or some combination of these methods may be appropriate in a given institution.

General evaluation of the multicultural student programs and services must be conducted on a regularly scheduled basis. MSPS must solicit evaluative data from current multicultural students.

MSPS should solicit evaluative and developmental data from alumni.

Assessments must be conducted in a manner to assure an effective response.

MSPS should consult with the population to be assessed on the nature of the assessment.

MSPS must evaluate periodically how well they complement and enhance the institution's stated mission and educational effectiveness.

Results of these evaluations must be used in revising and improving programs and services and in recognizing staff performance.

MSPS should assess the degree of congruence between students' educational goals and offerings of the institution and communicate the results of the assessment to appropriate decision makers.

General Standards revised in 2002; MSPS (formerly Minority Student Programs) content developed/revised in 1986, 1997, & 2006

THE ROLE of ORIENTATION PROGRAMS
CAS Standards Contextual Statement

To understand current trends in orientation programs, it is helpful to view today's practice within an historical context. The history of orientation programs in the United States is virtually as old as the history of the country's higher education. Harvard College was the first to formalize a system by which experienced students assisted new students in their transition to the institution. In addition to a personalized support system, students also experienced certain rites of passage which, from today's perspective, would likely be considered hazing. While the system was somewhat flawed, it was the beginning of the formalization of orientation as a process that included support of students and their families as the transition to higher education began.

Later in the 19th century, Harvard institutionalized faculty-student contact by assigning faculty members educational and administrative responsibilities outside the classroom. One of these responsibilities was the orientation of new students. Soon other colleges took an interest in the concerns specific to freshman students.

Increases in the number and diversity of college students in the mid-1900s posed issues that many institutions had not previously considered. Today's orientation programs responded to changing demographics by changing institutional agendas across the nation. Programs evolved from simply providing individualized faculty attention to focusing on a multitude of important issues while responding to the needs of an increasingly diverse student and family population.

Today, most orientation programs seek to provide a clear and cogent introduction to an institution's academic community. Orientation is viewed by most as an important tool for student recruitment and retention. Most institutions include academic advising and registration for classes in their orientation programs as an impetus for active participation. Many institutions are implementing continuing orientation programs via a freshman orientation course. Because of such changes, colleges and universities are taking steps to encourage student and parent attendance by formalizing and marketing orientation programs from a decidedly academic perspective, but which address many issues of interest and concern.

One of the most important changes is that orientation is now viewed as a comprehensive process rather than as a minimal program. Colleges and universities nationally and internationally are developing wide-ranging orientation programs that truly address the transitional needs of students and families.

What trends will guide future approaches to orientation programs? It is certain that recruitment and retention will continue to be major forces in the development of orientation programs. Likewise, attempts to foster an environment responsive to the individual needs of students and families will have a significant effect on orientation programming. Additionally, funding for orientation programs will continue as a matter of concern. Demographic changes in institutions of higher education and in society at large will require institutional and programmatic accommodations. Maintaining current orientation programs by reacting to change does little to address the interests of all constituents. New and creative programs and methodologies must be assessed, planned, and implemented if the personal and educational needs of new and transfer students and their families are to be met.

The CAS Orientation Programs Standards and Guidelines that follow have utility for national and international institutions and provide criteria to evaluate the quality and appropriateness of orientation programs.

References, Readings, and Resources

Designing Successful Transitions: A Guide for Orienting Students to College, University of South Carolina, Columbia, SC 29208

National Orientation Directors Association: www.nodaweb.org

National Orientation Directors Data Bank, University of Maryland at College Park,, College Park, MD 20742

The Journal of College Orientation and Transition, Northern Illinois University, DeKalb, IL 60115

Contributors:
Ralph Busby, Stephen F. Austin State University,NODA
Gerry Strumpf, University of Maryland, NODA

ORIENTATION PROGRAMS
CAS STANDARDS and GUIDELINES

Part 1. MISSION

The mission of Orientation Programs (OP) must include facilitating the transition of new students into the institution; preparing students for the institution's educational opportunities and student responsibilities; initiating the integration of new students into the intellectual, cultural, and social climate of the institution; and supporting the parents, partners, guardians, and children of the new student.

OP must incorporate student learning and student development in its mission. OP must enhance overall educational experiences. OP must develop, record, disseminate, implement, and regularly review its mission and goals. Mission statements must be consistent with the mission and goals of the institution and with the standards in this document. OP must operate as an integral part of the institution's overall mission.

Part 2. PROGRAM

The formal education of students consists of the curriculum and the co-curriculum, and must promote student learning and development that is purposeful and holistic. Orientation Programs (OP) must identify relevant and desirable student learning and development outcomes and provide programs and services that encourage the achievement of those outcomes.

Relevant and desirable outcomes include: intellectual growth, effective communication, realistic self-appraisal, enhanced self-esteem, clarified values, career choices, leadership development, healthy behaviors, meaningful interpersonal relationships, independence, collaboration, social responsibility, satisfying and productive lifestyles, appreciation of diversity, spiritual awareness, and achievement of personal and educational goals.

OP must provide evidence of its impact on the achievement of student learning and development outcomes.

The table below offers examples of evidence of achievement of student learning and development.

Student Learning and Development Outcome Domains

Intellectual growth
Examples of achievement indicators

Develops educational goals; Examines information about academic majors and minors; Understands the requirements of an academic degree plan; Examines the core curriculum; Demonstrates knowledge about internships and volunteer opportunities; Develops personal goals; Makes decisions based on complex information from a variety of sources including personal experience, personal values, and orientation programs

Effective communication
Examples of achievement indicators

Examines personal and academic strengths and weaknesses which affect academic plans and communicates that information to academic advisors; Demonstrates the ability to use information on academic policy, student support services, and financial services; Demonstrates the ability to use technological resources; Composes appropriate questions when inquiring about particular requirements, departments, and resources; Appropriately introduces oneself and initiates conversations with others

Enhanced self-esteem
Examples of achievement indicators

Shows respect for self and others; Demonstrates assertive behavior and evaluates reasonable risks with regard to academic course selection and course load when conferring with academic advisors; Produces a schedule of classes in consultation with orientation staff or academic advisors

Realistic self-appraisal
Examples of achievement indicators

Evaluates personal and academic skills, abilities, and interests and establishes appropriate educational plans for the first semester; Ranks academic strengths and weaknesses; Focuses on areas of academic ability and interest and mitigates academic weaknesses; Uses information on course selection, course load, and course schedule in order to construct a schedule; Formulates opportunities for involvement in co-curricular activities

Clarified values
Examples of achievement indicators

Demonstrates ability to evaluate personal values and beliefs regarding relationships, diversity, substance use, academic integrity, and other ethical issues; Analyzes personal, work, and lifestyle values and explains how they influence decision-making in regard to course selection, course load, and level of personal involvement in the campus community; Acts in congruence with values

Career choices

Examples of achievement indicators

Describes career choice options of academic major and minor based on interests, skills, abilities, and values; Identifies the purpose and role of career services in the development and attainment of academic and career goals

Leadership development

Examples of achievement indicators

Demonstrates awareness of leadership opportunities, including those in part-time jobs on and off campus and internships

Healthy behavior

Examples of achievement indicators

Describes personal behaviors and environments that promote health and reduce risk; Identifies services provided to support the advancement of a healthy lifestyle and a healthy campus community; Articulates the relationship between health and the development of life-long goals

Meaningful interpersonal relationships

Examples of achievement indicators

Creates relationships with fellow students, orientation staff, faculty members, academic advisors, and other institution staff to be engaged with the institution in a meaningful way; Demonstrates ability to listen to others' points of view; Treats others with respect

Independence

Examples of achievement indicators

Operates autonomously by attending prescribed student orientation programs while parents and family are attending different programs; Selects, schedules, and registers for academic courses with the advice and counsel of academic advisors and orientation staff; Manages the campus physical environment (i.e., location of buildings, understanding a bus schedule)

Social responsibility

Examples of achievement indicators

Understands the requirements of the codes of conduct; Has knowledge of institution governance systems

Collaboration

Examples of achievement indicators

Works cooperatively with others; Seeks the involvement of others; Seeks feedback from others; Contributes to achievement of a group goal; Exhibits effective listening skills

Satisfying and productive lifestyles

Examples of achievement indicators

Determines the balance between academic course load

requirements, work, and leisure time; Constructs goals for academic course requirements, work, and leisure time activities; Identifies obstacles that hamper the achievement of stated goals; Decides the importance of functioning on the basis of personal, ethical, spiritual, and moral values

Appreciating diversity

Examples of achievement indicators

Becomes aware of the impact of culture on individuals; Becomes aware of educational offerings related to diversity; Demonstrates an appreciation for diversity and the impact it has on society; Seeks involvement with people different from oneself; Challenges appropriately the abusive use of stereotypes

Spiritual awareness

Examples of achievement indicators

Develops and articulates personal belief system; Understands the role of spirituality in personal and group values and behaviors; Identifies campus and community spiritual and religious resources

Personal and educational goals

Examples of achievement indicators

Determines personal and academic goals and objectives; Uses personal and academic goals to guide decisions; Considers the effect of one's personal and academic goals on parents, family, and others

OP must be (a) intentional, (b) coherent, (c) based on theories and knowledge of learning and human development, (d) reflective of developmental and demographic profiles of the student population, and (e) responsive to needs of individuals, special populations, and communities.

OP must aid students and their families (i.e., parents, guardians, partners, and children) in understanding the nature and purpose of the institution, their membership in the academic community, and their relationship to the intellectual, cultural, and social climate of the institution.

OP should introduce students to the learning and development that will occur throughout the collegiate experience.

OP must continue as a process to address, as appropriate, transitional events, issues, and needs. The orientation process must include pre-enrollment, entry, and post-matriculation services and programs.

Components of OP may include credit and non-credit courses, seminars, adventure programs, service learning, summer readings, learning communities, Freshmen Interest Groups (FIGs), web-based educational opportunities, comprehensive mailings, electronic communications, and campus visitations and may be administered through multiple institutional offices.

OP must:
- **be based on stated goals and objectives**
- **be coordinated with the relevant programs and activities of other institutional units**
- **be available to all students new to the institution, as well as to families**

First-year, transfer, and entering graduate students, as well as their families, should be served as distinct populations with specific attention given to the needs of sub-groups such as students with disabilities, athletes, adult learners, under-prepared students, under-represented students, honor students, and international students.

- **assist new students as well as their families in understanding the purposes of higher education and the mission of the institution**

New students should have a clear understanding of the overall purpose of higher education and how this general purpose translates to the institution they are attending. The roles, responsibilities, and expectations of students, faculty and staff members, and families should be included.

- **articulate the institution's expectations of students (e.g., scholarship, integrity, conduct, financial obligations, ethical use of technology) and provide information that clearly identifies relevant administrative policies , procedures, and programs to enable students to make well-reasoned and well-informed choices**

- **provide new students with information and opportunities for academic and personal self-assessment**

OP should assist students in the selection of appropriate courses and course levels, making use of relevant placement examinations, entrance examinations, and academic records.

- **use qualified faculty members, staff, or peer advisors to explain class scheduling, registration processes, and campus life**

- **provide new students, as well as their families, with information about laws and policies regarding educational records and other protected information**

OP should emphasize the independence of students in accomplishing their goals while acknowledging their interdependence with their peers and families.

- **inform new students, as well as their families, about the availability of services and programs**

- **assist new students, as well as their families, in becoming familiar with the campus and local environment**

OP for students and families should provide information about the physical layout of the campus, including the location and purposes of campus facilities, support services, co-curricular venues, and administrative offices. Information about personal health, safety, and security should also be included.

- **assist new students, as well as their families, in becoming familiar with the wide range of electronic and information resources available and expectations for their use**

OP should provide information about technological resources used to conduct institutional business and scholarly work including information about student information systems, electronic databases, email, and online course software. Information about how to manage responsible and ethical use of institutional technological resources should also be presented.

- **provide time for students to become acquainted with their new environment**

- **provide intentional opportunities for new students to interact with fellow new students as well as continuing students, faculty and staff members**

OP should design and facilitate opportunities for new students to discuss their expectations and perceptions of the campus and to clarify their personal and educational goals.

OP should design and facilitate opportunities for new students to meet their peers and begin forming new relationships.

OP must inform students about the history, traditions, and campus cultures to facilitate an identification with and integration into the institution.

Part 3. LEADERSHIP
Effective and ethical leadership is essential to the success of all organizations. Institutions must

appoint, position, and empower Orientation Program (OP) leaders within the administrative structure to accomplish stated missions. Leaders of OP at various levels must be selected on the basis of formal education and training, relevant work experience, personal skills and competencies, and relevant professional credentials. Leaders of OP must promote learning and development in students, apply effective practices to educational processes, and enhance institutional effectiveness. Institutions must establish accountability for leaders and fairly assess their performance.

Leaders of OP must exercise authority over resources for which they are responsible to achieve their respective missions.

Leaders of OP must:
- articulate a vision for their organization
- set goals and objectives based on the needs and capabilities of the population served
- promote student learning and development
- prescribe and practice ethical behavior
- recruit, select, supervise, and develop others in the organization
- manage financial resources
- coordinate human resources
- plan, budget for, and evaluate personnel and programs
- apply effective practices to educational and administrative processes
- communicate effectively
- initiate collaborative interaction between individuals and agencies that possess legitimate concerns and interests in the functional area

Leaders of OP must identify and find means to address individual, organizational, or environmental conditions that inhibit goal achievement.

Leaders of OP must promote campus environments that result in multiple opportunities for student learning and development.

Leaders of OP must continuously improve programs and services in response to changing needs of students and other constituents, and evolving institutional priorities.

Part 4. ORGANIZATION and MANAGEMENT
Guided by an overarching intent to ensure student learning and development, Orientation Programs (OP) must be structured purposefully and managed effectively to achieve stated goals. Evidence

of appropriate structure must include current and accessible policies and procedures, written performance expectations for all employees, functional workflow graphics or organizational charts, and clearly stated service delivery expectations.

Evidence of effective management must include use of comprehensive and accurate information for decisions, clear sources and channels of authority, effective communication practices, decision-making and conflict resolution procedures, responsiveness to changing conditions, accountability and evaluation systems, and recognition and reward processes. OP must provide channels within the organization for regular review of administrative policies and procedures.

All institutional offices involved in program delivery should be involved in the review of administrative policies and procedures.

Coordination of OP must occur even though a number of offices may be involved in the delivery of structured activities.

The size, nature, and complexity of the institution should guide the administrative scope and structure of OP.

Part 5. HUMAN RESOURCES
Orientation Programs (OP) must be staffed adequately by individuals qualified to accomplish its mission and goals. Within established guidelines of the institution, OP must establish procedures for staff selection, training, and evaluation; set expectations for supervision; and provide appropriate professional development opportunities. OP must strive to improve the professional competence and skills of all personnel it employs.

Faculty involvement in the development and delivery of OP is essential to its success. Faculty members should be included as part of the overall staffing.

OP professional staff members must hold an earned graduate degree in a field relevant to the position they hold or must possess an appropriate combination of educational credentials and related work experience.

Degree or credential-seeking interns must be qualified by enrollment in an appropriate field of study and by relevant experience. These individuals must be trained and supervised adequately by professional staff members holding educational credentials and related work experience appropriate for supervision.

Student employees and volunteers must be carefully selected, trained, supervised, and evaluated. They must be trained on how and when to refer those in need of assistance to qualified staff members and have access to a supervisor for assistance in making these judgments. Student employees and volunteers must be provided clear and precise job descriptions, pre-service training based on assessed needs, and continuing staff development.

Student staff must be informed as to the limits of their authority, the expectation for appropriate role modeling, and their potential influence on new students.

OP must have technical and support staff members adequate to accomplish its mission. Staff members must be technologically proficient and qualified to perform their job functions, be knowledgeable of ethical and legal uses of technology, and have access to training. The level of staffing and workloads must be adequate and appropriate for program and service demands.

Salary levels and fringe benefits for all OP staff members must be commensurate with those for comparable positions within the institution, in similar institutions, and in the relevant geographic area.

OP must institute hiring and promotion practices that are fair, inclusive, and non-discriminatory. Programs and services must employ a diverse staff to provide readily identifiable role models for students and to enrich the campus community.

OP must create and maintain position descriptions for all staff members and provide regular performance planning and appraisals.

OP must have a system for regular staff evaluation and must provide access to continuing education and professional development opportunities, including in-service training programs and participation in professional conferences and workshops.

Part 6. FINANCIAL RESOURCES

Orientation Programs (OP) must have adequate funding to accomplish its mission and goals. Funding priorities must be determined within the context of the stated mission, goals, objectives, and comprehensive analysis of the needs and capabilities of students and the availability of internal or external resources.

OP must demonstrate fiscal responsibility and cost effectiveness consistent with institutional protocols.

OP should be funded through institutional resources. In addition to institutional funding, other sources may be considered, including state appropriations, student fees, user fees, donations, contributions, concession and store sales, rentals, and dues.

Overnight programs may require students and their families to stay on campus. Recovering room and board costs directly from participants is an acceptable practice. Resources, such as grants or loans, should be available to those students unable to afford the cost associated with orientation.

Part 7. FACILITIES, TECHNOLOGY, and EQUIPMENT

Orientation Programs (OP) must have adequate, suitably located facilities, adequate technology, and equipment to support its mission and goals efficiently and effectively. Facilities, technology, and equipment must be evaluated regularly and be in compliance with relevant federal, state, provincial, and local requirements to provide for access, health, safety, and security.

Cooperation from the campus community is necessary to provide appropriate facilities to implement orientation programs. Whenever possible, a single office location to house personnel and provide adequate workspace should be conveniently located and suitable for its high level of interaction with the public.

Part 8. LEGAL RESPONSIBILITIES

Orientation Programs (OP) staff members must be knowledgeable about and responsive to laws and regulations that relate to their respective responsibilities. Staff members must inform users of programs, services, and officials, as appropriate, of legal obligations and limitations including constitutional, statutory, regulatory, and case law; mandatory laws and orders emanating from federal, state/provincial and local governments; and the institution's policies.

OP staff members must use reasonable and informed practices to limit the liability exposure of the institution, its officers, employees, and agents. Staff members must be informed about institutional policies regarding personal liability and related insurance coverage options.

The institution must provide access to legal advice for OP staff members as needed to carry out assigned responsibilities.

The institution must inform OP staff and students in a timely and systematic fashion about extraordinary or changing legal obligations and potential liabilities.

Part 9. EQUITY and ACCESS

Orientation Programs (OP) staff members must ensure that services and programs are provided on a fair and equitable basis. Facilities, programs and services must be accessible. Hours of operation and delivery of and access to programs and services must be responsive to the needs of all students and other constituents. OP must adhere to the spirit and intent of equal opportunity laws.

OP must be open and readily accessible to all students and must not discriminate except where sanctioned by law and institutional policy. Discrimination must be avoided on the basis of age; color; creed; cultural heritage; disability; ethnicity; gender identity; nationality; political affiliation; religious affiliation; sex; sexual orientation; or social, economic, marital, or veteran status.

Consistent with their mission and goals, OP must take affirmative action to remedy significant imbalances in student participation and staffing patterns.

As the demographic profiles of campuses change and new instructional delivery methods are introduced, institutions must recognize the needs of students who participate in distance learning for access to programs and services offered on campus. Institutions must provide appropriate services in ways that are accessible to distance learners and assist them in identifying and gaining access to other appropriate services in their geographic region.

Part 10. CAMPUS and EXTERNAL RELATIONS

Orientation Programs (OP) must establish, maintain, and promote effective relations with relevant individuals, campus offices, and external agencies.

OP should be an institution-wide process that systematically involves student affairs, academic affairs, and other administrative units, such as public safety, physical plant, and the business office.

OP should establish policies and practices that address how the institution should interact with parents and families.

Part 11. DIVERSITY

Within the context of each institution's unique mission, diversity enriches the community and enhances the collegiate experience for all; therefore, Orientation Programs (OP) must nurture environments where commonalties and differences among people are recognized and honored.

OP must promote educational experiences that are characterized by open and continuous communication that deepens understanding of one's own identity, culture, and heritage, and that of others. OP must educate and promote respect about commonalties and differences in their historical and cultural contexts.

OP must address the characteristics and needs of a diverse population when establishing and implementing policies and procedures.

Part 12. ETHICS

All persons involved in the delivery of Orientation Programs (OP) must adhere to the highest principles of ethical behavior. OP must develop or adopt and implement appropriate statements of ethical practice. OP must publish these statements and ensure their periodic review by relevant constituencies.

OP staff members must ensure that privacy and confidentiality are maintained with respect to all communications and records to the extent that such records are protected under the law and appropriate statements of ethical practice. Information contained in students' education records must not be disclosed without written consent except as allowed by relevant laws and institutional policies. Staff members must disclose to appropriate authorities information judged to be of an emergency nature, especially when the safety of the individual or others is involved, or when otherwise required by institutional policy or relevant law.

All OP staff members must be aware of and comply with the provisions contained in the institution's human subjects research policy and in other relevant institutional policies addressing ethical practices and confidentiality of research data concerning individuals.

OP staff members must recognize and avoid personal conflict of interest or appearance thereof in their transactions with students and others.

OP staff members must strive to insure the fair, objective, and impartial treatment of all persons with whom they deal. Staff members must not participate in nor condone any form of harassment that demeans persons or creates an intimidating, hostile, or offensive campus environment.

272

When handling institutional funds, all OP staff members must ensure that such funds are managed in accordance with established and responsible accounting procedures and the fiscal policies or processes of the institution.

OP staff members must perform their duties within the limits of their training, expertise, and competence. When these limits are exceeded, individuals in need of further assistance must be referred to persons possessing appropriate qualifications.

OP staff members must use suitable means to confront and otherwise hold accountable other staff members who exhibit unethical behavior.

OP staff members must be knowledgeable about and practice ethical behavior in the use of technology.

Part 13. ASSESSMENT and EVALUATION

Orientation Programs (OP) must conduct regular assessment and evaluations. OP must employ effective qualitative and quantitative methodologies as appropriate, to determine whether and to what degree the stated mission, goals, and student learning and development outcomes are being met. The process must employ sufficient and sound assessment measures to ensure comprehensiveness. Data collected must include responses from students, parents, and families and other affected constituencies.

OP must evaluate periodically how well they complement and enhance the institution's stated mission and educational effectiveness.

Results of these evaluations must be disseminated campus wide and be used in revising and improving programs and services and in recognizing staff performance.

Evaluation of student and institutional needs, goals, objectives, and the effectiveness of orientation programs should occur on a regular basis. A representative cross-section of appropriate people from the campus community should be involved in reviews of orientation programs.

General Standards revised in 2002; OP content developed/ revised in 1986, 1996, & 2005

THE ROLE of OUTCOMES ASSESSMENT and PROGRAM EVALUATION
CAS Standards Contextual Statement

The need for outcomes assessment and program evaluation in higher education has long been acknowledged by the field, and it remains a pressing need today. Early proponents of outcomes assessment included William Rainey Harper, President of the University of Chicago, who in 1889 called on colleges and universities to adopt a program of research with the college student as the subject "in order that the student may receive the assistance so essential to his highest success, another step in the onward evolution will take place. This step will be the scientific study of the student" (Rentz, 1996, p. 28).

Responding to Harper's vision, the Student Personnel Point of View in 1937 challenged the field of student services to employ "studies designed to improve these functions and services" (p. 42). Later in the document, four specific kinds of studies were called for: student out of class life and its connection to the educational mission, faculty and student out of class relationships, financial aid to students, and after college studies to ascertain the effects of college on careers and personal adjustment (American Council of Education, 1937).

The 1949 revision of the Student Personnel Point of View (American Council of Education, 1949) stated the "principle responsibility of personnel workers lie in the area of progressive program development...this means that each worker must devote a large part of time to the formulation of new plans and to the continuous evaluation and improvement of current program (p. 34). This document also stressed the importance of personnel workers being "thoroughly trained in research methods as a part of their professional preparation" (p. 35). Ultimately, the standard for student affairs programs, according to the 1949 document is in "the difference it makes in the development of individual students" (p. 34).

These historical and foundational documents in the field give clear evidence that the role of assessment and program evaluation in higher education and student affairs is important in the education of the "whole" student. While most agree about the importance of conducting research on students and programs, few student affairs divisions have considered it a vital part of their operations. However, the field is paying increased attention to the need for assessment, due in part to increasing emphasis on accountability from accreditation agencies and institutions themselves.

Recent student affairs documents have continued the call for assessment and accountability of program effectiveness as it relates to student learning and development. The Student Learning Imperative (1996) charges student affairs staff to "participate in efforts to assess student learning...and periodically audit institutional environments to reinforce those factors that enhance,

and eliminate those that inhibit, student involvement in educationally-purposeful activities" (p. 6). The Principles of Good Practice for Student Affairs (1996) impresses the need to use systematic inquiry to improve student and institutional performance. Specifically, "student affairs educators who are skilled in using assessment methods acquire high-quality information; effective application of this information to practice results in programs and change strategies which improve student achievement" (p. 3). In the field's most recent document, Learning Reconsidered (2004) the language of assessment and student learning is more comprehensive. "Student Affairs must lead broad, collaborative institutional efforts to assess overall student learning and to track, document, and evaluate the role of diverse learning experiences...assessment should be a way of life—part of the institutional culture" (p. 26).

Recently, student affairs literature has focused on enabling practitioners to utilize assessment. These "how-to" guides provide information about writing outcomes, designing instruments, and performing qualitative as well as quantitative assessment (Bresciani, Zelna, & Anderson, 2004). In addition, professional associations have begun to provide their members with assessment tools. The chief example of this is the CAS standards guide. Multiple assessment and evaluation tools also exist, such as those published by Educational Benchmarking, Incorporated (EBI) (http://www.webebi.com, 2006). Today's assessment programs on campuses may include anything from satisfaction assessment to assessing learning outcomes. Though satisfaction assessment is commonly practiced and is still considered an important tool, it is fundamentally incomplete due to its lack of potential for understanding student learning and development (Bresciani, Zelna, & Anderson, 2004).

Bresciani, et. al., (2004) in their handbook on assessing student learning and development offer a newly updated list of uses and reasons for doing assessment in student affairs. This list is a compilation of several recent works, including the American Association for Higher Education (1994), Bresciani (2003), Ewell (1997a), Maki (2001), Palomba and Banta (1999), and Upcraft and Schuh (1996). These sources note the multiple reasons for carrying out assessment: reinforcing or emphasizing unit missions; improving a program's quality or performance; comparing a program's quality or value to the program's previously defined principles; informing planning, decision-making, and policy discussions at the local, state, regional, and national levels; evaluating programs and personnel; assisting in the request for additional funds from the college or university and external community; assisting in the reallocation of resources; assisting in meeting accreditation requirements; identifying models of best practices and national benchmarks; celebrating successes while reflecting on the attitudes and approaches taken in improving learning and development; and creating a culture of continuous improvement—a culture of accountability, learning, and improvement.

Assessment efforts may take many forms. Assessment is most commonly known as "any effort to gather, analyze, and interpret evidence which describes institutional, divisional or agency effectiveness" (Upcraft & Schuh, 1996). Assessment can employ both qualitative and quantitative techniques such as interviews, focus groups, observations, rubrics, portfolios, surveys and questionnaires. These methods may be aided by on-line survey software helpful in developing personalized assessments.

Assessment activities in student affairs often include assessing student needs and wants, and satisfaction, as well as tracking student use of services, programs, and facilities. The assessment of individual and collective learning outcomes related to programs and services is another crucial aspect of assessment.

Assessment is a tool that can be used to discover an institution's best practices and to bring about continual improvement within the unique context of each institution. Student affairs divisions undertaking assessment efforts should not be discouraged by the seeming enormity of the task. The important thing is to be purposeful, to be systematic, and to use sound research methods that improve operations incrementally.

References, Readings, and Resources

American Association of Higher Education (1994). *Nine principles of good practice for assessing student learning* [On-line]. Retrieved from http://www.iuk.edu/%7Ekoctla/assessment/9principles.shtml

American College Personnel Association (1996). *The student learning imperative: Implications for student affairs* [On-line]. Retrieved from http://www.acpa.nche.edu/sli/sli.htm

American Council of Education. (1937). *The student personnel point of view: A report of a conference on the philosophy and development of student personnel work in colleges and universities* [On-line]. Retrieved from http://www.myacpa.org/pub/documents/1937.pdf

American Council of Education. (1949). *The student personnel point of view: A report of a conference on the philosophy and development of student personnel work in colleges and universities* [On-line]. Retrieved from http://www.myacpa.org/pub/documents/1949.pdf

Bresciani, M. J. (2003). An updated outline for assessment plans. NetResults [Online]. Retrieved from http://www.naspa.org/

Bresciani, M. J., Zelna, C. L., & Anderson, J. A. (2004). *Assessing student learning and development.* Washington, DC: NASPA.

Ewell, P. T. (1997a). From the states: Putting it all on the line—South Carolina's performance funding initiative. *Assessment Update, 9* (1), 9-11.

Maki, P. (2001). *Program review assessment.* Presentation to the Committee on Undergraduate Academic Program. Review at North Carolina State University. Raleigh, North Carolina.

National Association of Student Personnel Administrators & American College Personnel Association. (2004) *Learning reconsidered: A campus-wide focus on the student experience.* Washington, DC: NASPA & ACPA. Retrieved from http://www.myacpa.org/pub/documents/LearningReconsidered.doc

Rentz, A. L. (1996). A history of student affairs. In A. L. Rentz (Ed.), Student affairs practice in higher education (p. 28-55). Springfield, IL: Thomas.

Palomba, C. A., & Banta, T. W. (1999). *Assessment essentials: Planning, implementing and improving assessment in higher education.* San Franciso: Jossey-Bass.

Upcraft, M. L., & Schuh, J. H. (1996). *Assessment in student affairs: A guide for practitioners.* San Francisco: Jossey-Bass.

Williamson, E. G., & Biggs, D. A. (1975). *Student personnel work:* A program of development relationships. New York: John Wiley & Sons.

Banta, T. W. & Kuh, G. D. (1998). A missing link in assessment: Collaboration between Academic and student affairs professionals. *Change,* (March/April), 40-48.

Blimling, G. S. & Whitt, E. J. (1999). *Good practices in student affairs: Principles to foster student learning.* San Francisco: Jossey-Bass.

Schuh, J., & Upcraft, M. L. (1998). Facts and myths about assessment in student affairs. *About Campus,* (Nov/Dec), 2-8.

Schuh, J. H., Upcraft, M. L., & Associates, (2001). *Assessment practice in student affairs: An application manual.* San Francisco: Jossey-Bass.

Contributors:
Current edition:
Joel H. Scott, University of Georgia
Cara Skeat, Gainesville College/University of Georgia

Previous editions:
Roger B. Winston, Jr., University of Georgia

OUTCOMES ASSESSMENT and PROGRAM EVALUATION SERVICES
CAS Standards and Guidelines

Part 1. MISSION

Outcomes Assessment and Program Evaluation Services (OAPES) must incorporate student learning and student development in its mission. OAPES must enhance overall educational experiences. OAPES must develop, record, disseminate, implement and regularly review its mission and goals. Mission statements must be consistent with the mission and goals of the institution and with the standards in this document. OAPES must operate as an integral part of the institution's overall mission.

OAPES efforts must strive to improve student services and development programs, to expand the knowledge base about student development and student services work in general, and to assess the organizational effectiveness of student services. Most institutions do not have a separate student affairs assessment agency. In such institutions the chief student affairs officer must be the advocate for student affairs assessment and program evaluation and must collaborate with, and otherwise provide support to, the institutional assessment efforts so as to accomplish the program. More specifically, the OAPES must:

- describe students in terms of demographics, developmental characteristics, and personal behavior
- conduct periodic needs assessments for use in the design of programs
- study, or use available information about developmental changes of college students
- assess whether student services programs are consistent with and achieve their stated objectives
- assess in terms of behavior changes in students
- study the extent to which students are satisfied with their educational experiences

Student services professionals are responsible for translating a diverse set of service functions into an integrated series of programs and activities designed to encourage students' growth and development. The degree to which these programs and activities are necessary and successful should be measured through periodic assessment of both programs and students. Equally important is the responsibility for continually expanding the knowledge base about the relationship between student development theory and student services practices. The OAPES should seek to provide assessment and evaluation support for all institutional student support service programs. Further, the assessment and evaluation program should strive to increase the institution's knowledge base about its student clientele.

Part 2. PROGRAM

The formal education of students consists of the curriculum and the co-curriculum, and must promote student learning and development that is purposeful and holistic. Outcomes Assessment and Program Evaluation Services (OAPES) must identify relevant and desirable student learning and development outcomes and provide programs and services that encourage the achievement of those outcomes.

Relevant and desirable outcomes include: intellectual growth, effective communication, realistic self-appraisal, enhanced self-esteem, clarified values, career choices, leadership development, healthy behaviors, meaningful interpersonal relationships, independence, collaboration, social responsibility, satisfying and productive lifestyles, appreciation of diversity, spiritual awareness, and achievement of personal and educational goals.

OAPES must provide evidence of its impact on the achievement of student learning and development outcomes.

The table below offers examples of evidence of achievement of student learning and development.

Student Learning and Development Outcome Domains

Intellectual growth
Examples of achievement indicators

Produces personal and educational goal statements; Employs critical thinking in problem solving; Uses complex information from a variety of sources including personal experience and observation to form a decision or opinion; Obtains a degree; Applies previously understood information and concepts to a new situation or setting; Expresses appreciation for literature, the fine arts, mathematics, sciences, and social sciences

Effective communication
Examples of achievement indicators

Writes and speaks coherently and effectively; Writes and speaks after reflection; Able to influence others through writing, speaking or artistic expression; Effectively articulates abstract ideas; Uses appropriate syntax; Makes presentations or gives performances

Enhanced self-esteem

Examples of achievement indicators

Shows self-respect and respect for others; Initiates actions toward achievement of goals; Takes reasonable risks; Demonstrates assertive behavior; Functions without need for constant reassurance from others

Realistic self-appraisal

Examples of achievement indicators

Articulates personal skills and abilities; Makes decisions and acts in congruence with personal values; Acknowledges personal strengths and weaknesses; Articulates rationale for personal behavior; Seeks feedback from others; Learns from past experiences

Clarified values

Examples of achievement indicators

Articulates personal values; Acts in congruence with personal values; Makes decisions that reflect personal values; Demonstrates willingness to scrutinize personal beliefs and values; Identifies personal, work and lifestyle values and explains how they influence decision-making

Career choices

Examples of achievement indicators

Articulates career choices based on assessment of interests, values, skills and abilities; Documents knowledge, skills and accomplishments resulting from formal education, work experience, community service and volunteer experiences; Makes the connections between classroom and out-of-classroom learning; Can construct a resume with clear job objectives and evidence of related knowledge, skills and accomplishments; Articulates the characteristics of a preferred work environment; Comprehends the world of work; Takes steps to initiate a job search or seek advanced education

Leadership development

Examples of achievement indicators

Articulates leadership philosophy or style; Serves in a leadership position in a student organization; Comprehends the dynamics of a group; Exhibits democratic principles as a leader; Exhibits ability to visualize a group purpose and desired outcomes

Healthy behavior

Examples of achievement indicators

Chooses behaviors and environments that promote health and reduce risk; Articulate the relationship between health and wellness and accomplishing life-long goals; Exhibits behaviors that advance a healthy community.

Meaningful interpersonal relationships

Examples of achievement indicators

Develops and maintains satisfying interpersonal relationships; Establishes mutually rewarding relationships with friends and colleagues; Listens to and considers others' points of view; Treats others with respect

Independence

Examples of achievement indicators

Exhibits self-reliant behaviors; Functions autonomously; Exhibits ability to function interdependently; Accepts supervision as needed; Manages time effectively

Collaboration

Examples of achievement indicators

Works cooperatively with others; Seeks the involvement of others; Seeks feedback from others; Contributes to achievement of a group goal; Exhibits effective listening skills

Social responsibility

Examples of achievement indicators

Understands and participates in relevant governance systems; Understands, abides by, and participates in the development, maintenance, and/or orderly change of community, social, and legal standards or norms; Appropriately challenges the unfair, unjust, or uncivil behavior of other individuals or groups; Participates in service/volunteer activities

Satisfying and productive lifestyles

Examples of achievement indicators

Achieves balance between education, work, and leisure time; Articulates and meets goals for work, leisure, and education; Overcomes obstacles that hamper goal achievement; Functions on the basis of personal identity, ethical, spiritual, and moral values; Articulates long-term goals and objectives

Appreciating diversity

Examples of achievement indicators

Understands one's own identity and culture; Seeks involvement with people different from oneself; Seeks involvement in diverse interests; Articulates the advantages and challenges of a diverse society; Challenges appropriately the abusive use of stereotypes by others; Understands the impact of diversity on one's own society

Spiritual awareness

Examples of achievement indicators

Develops and articulates personal belief system; Understands roles of spirituality in personal and group values and behaviors

Personal and educational goals

Examples of achievement indicators

Sets, articulates, and pursues individual goals; Articulates personal and educational goals and objectives; Uses personal and educational goals to guide decisions; Understands the effect of one's personal and educational goals on others

OAPES must be (a) intentional, (b) coherent, (c) based on theories and knowledge of learning and human development, (d) reflective of developmental and demographic profiles of the student population, and (e) responsive to needs of individuals, special populations, and communities.

However organized, OAPES must include studies of students and their development and studies of student services program effectiveness. Furthermore, results of these studies must be disseminated throughout the institution.

Activities of OAPES should include:

- collecting and analyzing student data beginning with pre-enrollment characteristics of first year students and continuing through follow-up studies of former students
- planning, coordinating or conducting periodic studies of the characteristics of students and various student sub-groups
- students may be described in terms of their intellectual, emotional, social, moral, spiritual, and physical development and behavior; such data should be continually collected, updated, and disseminated
- regularly coordinating or conducting student needs assessments to guide program development
- analyzing data indicating trends in student behavior satisfaction retention, and attitudes in terms of the institution's purposes and interpreting the implications of these trends for institutional policies and practices
- assisting in collaborative assessments and planning of programs, activities, and services in the student services/ development division
- collecting and analyzing data to be used for making decisions about the continuation, modification, or termination of student services programs
- assessing on a systematic basis the professional contributions of staff members and providing feedback appropriate to professional development
- coordinating, conducting, or collaborating in accountability and cost effectiveness studies of student services/ development programs
- acting as a resource to faculty and staff regarding assessment and evaluation efforts
- regularly disseminating information about assessment and evaluation findings to concerned members of the campus community
- where appropriate, guiding and evaluating research efforts conducted by students

Part 3. LEADERSHIP

Effective and ethical leadership is essential to the success of all organizations. Institutions must appoint, position and empower Outcomes Assessment and Program Evaluation Service (OAPES) leaders within the administrative structure to accomplish stated missions. OAPES leaders at various levels must be selected on the basis of formal education and training, relevant work experience, personal skills and competencies, relevant professional credentials, as well as potential for promoting learning and development in students, applying effective practices to educational processes, and enhancing institutional effectiveness. Institutions must determine expectations of accountability for OAPES leaders and fairly assess their performance.

OAPES leaders of programs and services must exercise authority over resources for which they are responsible to achieve their respective missions.

OAPES leaders must:
- articulate a vision for their organization
- set goals and objectives based on the needs and capabilities of the population served
- promote student learning and development
- prescribe and practice ethical behavior
- recruit, select, supervise, and develop others in the organization
- manage financial resources
- coordinate human resources
- plan, budget for, and evaluate personnel and programs
- apply effective practices to educational and administrative processes
- communicate effectively
- initiate collaborative interaction between individuals and agencies that possess legitimate concerns and interests in the functional area

OAPES leaders must identify and find means to address individual, organizational, or environmental conditions that inhibit goal achievement.

OAPES leaders must promote campus environments that result in multiple opportunities for student learning and development.

OAPES leaders must continuously improve programs and services in response to changing needs of students and other constituents, and evolving institutional priorities.

Part 4. ORGANIZATION and MANAGEMENT

Guided by an overarching intent to ensure student learning and development, Outcomes Assessment and Program Evaluation Services (OAPES) must be structured purposefully and managed effectively to achieve stated goals. Evidence of appropriate structure must include current and accessible policies and procedures, written performance expectations for all employees, functional workflow graphics or organizational charts, and clearly stated service delivery expectations.

Evidence of effective management must include use of comprehensive and accurate information for decisions, clear sources and channels of authority, effective communication practices, decision-making and conflict resolution procedures, responsiveness to changing conditions, accountability and evaluation systems, and recognition and reward processes. OAPES must provide channels within the organization for regular review of administrative policies and procedures.

Because outcomes assessment and program evaluation efforts are conducted on most campuses in cooperation with other institutional research and evaluation efforts, the chief student affairs officer must be central to the establishment of specific objectives for student services research and evaluation.

Assessment and evaluation objectives should result from a collaborative effort between the chief student affairs officer, those responsible for the various student services programs and others responsible for institutional research evaluation efforts.

Part 5. HUMAN RESOURCES

Outcomes Assessment and Program Evaluation Services (OAPES) must be staffed adequately by individuals qualified to accomplish its mission and goals. Within established guidelines of the institution, OAPES must establish procedures for staff selection, training, and evaluation; set expectations for supervision, and provide appropriate professional development opportunities. OAPES must strive to improve the professional competence and skills of all personnel it employs.

OAPES professional staff members must hold an earned graduate degree in a field relevant to the position they hold or must possess an appropriate combination of educational credentials and related work experience.

Degree or credential-seeking interns must be qualified by enrollment in an appropriate field of study and by relevant experience. These individuals must be trained and supervised adequately by professional staff members holding educational credentials and related work experience appropriate for supervision.

Student employees and volunteers must be carefully selected, trained, supervised, and evaluated. They must be trained on how and when to refer those in need of assistance to qualified staff members and have access to a supervisor for assistance in making these judgments. Student employees and volunteers must be provided clear and precise job descriptions, pre-service training based on assessed needs, and continuing staff development.

OAPES must have technical and support staff members adequate to accomplish its mission. Staff members must be technologically proficient and qualified to perform their job functions, be knowledgeable of ethical and legal uses of technology, and have access to training. The level of staffing and workloads must be adequate and appropriate for program and service demands.

Salary levels and fringe benefits for all OAPES staff members must be commensurate with those for comparable positions within the institution, in similar institutions, and in the relevant geographic area.

OAPES must institute hiring and promotion practices that are fair, inclusive, and non-discriminatory. Programs and services must employ a diverse staff to provide readily identifiable role models for students and to enrich the campus community.

OAPES must create and maintain position descriptions for all staff members and provide regular performance planning and appraisals.

OAPES must have a system for regular staff evaluation and must provide access to continuing education and professional development opportunities, including in-service training programs and participation in professional conferences and workshops.

Within the institution, a qualified professional staff person must be designated to coordinate the outcomes assessment and program evaluation efforts and must work closely with or be responsible to the chief student affairs or academic affairs officer.

The number of staff members assigned to the assessment and evaluation effort will be a function of the size, complexity and purpose of the institution. Institutions unable to assign a full-time professional staff member should devote a portion of their research and evaluation program's resources to this effort.

Staff assigned responsibility for the assessment and evaluation effort should possess effective communication and consultation skills and have an appropriate combination of coursework, training, and experience in the following areas: statistics, research design, assessment, computer literacy, program planning and implementation strategies, human development theory, student subgroup cultures, and student affairs programs. When research staff lack adequate knowledge in any of these critical areas, they should seek expertise from appropriate campus officials.

Part 6. FINANCIAL RESOURCES

Outcomes Assessment and Program Evaluation Services (OAPES) must have adequate funding to accomplish its mission and goals. Funding priorities must be determined within the context of the stated mission, goals, objectives and comprehensive analysis of the needs and capabilities of students and the availability of internal or external resources.

OAPES must demonstrate fiscal responsibility and cost effectiveness consistent with institutional protocols.

Part 7. FACILITIES, TECHNOLOGY, and EQUIPMENT

Outcomes Assessment and Program Evaluation Services (OAPES) must have adequate, suitably located facilities, adequate technology, and equipment to support its mission and goals efficiently and effectively. Facilities, technology, and equipment must be evaluated regularly and be in compliance with relevant federal, state, provincial, and local requirements to provide for access, health, safety, and security.

It is important that the OAPES have secure storage facilities, computer support, sufficient work space, and ready access to appropriate institutional records. Financial resources should be sufficient to support research mailings and data collection, data entry and analysis and printing and distribution of research findings.

Part 8. LEGAL RESPONSIBILITIES

Outcomes Assessment and Program Evaluation Services (OAPES) staff members must be knowledgeable about and responsive to laws and regulations that relate to their respective responsibilities. Staff members must inform users of programs and services and officials, as appropriate, of legal obligations and limitations including constitutional, statutory, regulatory, and case law; mandatory laws and orders emanating from federal, state/provincial and local governments; and the institution's policies.

OAPES staff members must use reasonable and informed practices to limit the liability exposure of the institution, its officers, employees, and agents. Staff members must be informed about institutional policies regarding personal liability and related insurance coverage options.

The institution must provide access to legal advice for OAPES staff members as needed to carry out assigned responsibilities.

The institution must inform OAPES staff and students in a timely and systematic fashion about extraordinary or changing legal obligations and potential liabilities.

Part 9. EQUITY and ACCESS

Outcomes Assessment and Program Evaluation Services (OAPES) staff members must ensure that services and programs are provided on a fair and equitable basis. Facilities, programs and services must be accessible. Hours of operation and delivery of and access to programs and services must be responsive to the needs of all students and other constituents. OAPES must adhere to the spirit and intent of equal opportunity laws.

OAPES must be open and readily accessible to all students and must not discriminate except where sanctioned by law and institutional policy. Discrimination must be avoided on the bases of age; color; creed; cultural heritage; disability; ethnicity; gender identity; nationality; political affiliation; religious affiliation; sex; sexual orientation; or social, economic, marital, or veteran status.

Consistent with their mission and goals, OAPES must take affirmative action to remedy significant imbalances in student participation and staffing patterns.

As the demographic profiles of campuses change and new instructional delivery methods are introduced, institutions must recognize the needs of students who participate in distance learning for access to programs and services offered on campus. Institutions must provide appropriate services in ways that are accessible to distance learners and assist them in identifying and gaining access to other appropriate services in their geographic region.

Part 10. CAMPUS and EXTERNAL RELATIONS

Outcomes Assessment and Program Evaluation Services (OAPES) must establish, maintain, and promote effective relations with relevant individuals, campus offices, and external agencies.

Regular and effective communication systems for the dissemination of results and procuring expertise are particularly important among the full range of academic and administrative offices, institutional governance bodies, and other appropriate constituencies.

Part 11. DIVERSITY

Within the context of each institution's unique mission, diversity enriches the community and enhances the collegiate experience for all; therefore, Outcomes Assessment and Program Evaluation Services (OAPES) must nurture environments where commonalties and differences among people are recognized and honored.

OAPES must promote educational experiences that are characterized by open and continuous communication that deepens understanding of one's own identity, culture, and heritage, and that of others. OAPES must educate and promote respect about commonalties and differences in their historical and cultural contexts.

OAPES must address the characteristics and needs of a diverse population when establishing and implementing policies and procedures.

Part 12. ETHICS

All persons involved in the delivery of Outcomes Assessment and Program Evaluation Services (OAPES) must adhere to the highest principles of ethical behavior. OAPES must develop or adopt and implement appropriate statements of ethical practice. OAPES must publish these statements and ensure their periodic review by relevant constituencies .

OAPES staff members must ensure that privacy and confidentiality are maintained with respect to all communications and records to the extent that such records are protected under the law and appropriate statements of ethical practice. Information contained in students' education records must not be disclosed

without written consent except as allowed by relevant laws and institutional policies. Staff members must disclose to appropriate authorities information judged to be of an emergency nature, especially when the safety of the individual or others is involved, or when otherwise required by institutional policy or relevant law.

All OAPES staff members must be aware of and comply with the provisions contained in the institution's human subjects research policy and in other relevant institutional policies addressing ethical practices and confidentiality of research data concerning individuals.

OAPES staff members must recognize and avoid personal conflict of interest or appearance thereof in their transactions with students and others.

OAPES staff members must strive to insure the fair, objective, and impartial treatment of all persons with whom they deal. Staff members must not participate in nor condone any form of harassment that demeans persons or creates an intimidating, hostile, or offensive campus environment.

When handling institutional funds, all OAPES staff members must ensure that such funds are managed in accordance with established and responsible accounting procedures and the fiscal policies or processes of the institution.

OAPES staff members must perform their duties within the limits of their training, expertise, and competence. When these limits are exceeded, individuals in need of further assistance must be referred to persons possessing appropriate qualifications.

OAPES staff members must use suitable means to confront and otherwise hold accountable other staff members who exhibit unethical behavior.

OAPES staff members must be knowledgeable about and practice ethical behavior in the use of technology.

The privacy of study subjects and the confidential nature of data must not be breached.

Information on individuals should be purged regularly to protect the privacy of current and former students and other subjects.

Part 13. ASSESSMENT and EVALUATION

Outcomes Assessment and Program Evaluation

Services (OAPES) must conduct regular assessment and evaluations. OAPES must employ effective qualitative and quantitative methodologies as appropriate, to determine whether and to what degree the stated mission, goals, and student learning and development outcomes are being met. The process must employ sufficient and sound assessment measures to ensure comprehensiveness. Data collected must include responses from students and other affected constituencies.

OAPES must evaluate periodically how well they complement and enhance the institution's stated mission and educational effectiveness.

Results of these evaluations must be used in revising and improving programs and services and in recognizing staff performance.

General Standards revised in 2002; OAPES content developed/revised in 1986 & 1997

THE ROLE of RECREATIONAL SPORTS
CAS Standards Contextual Statement

Recreational sports programs are viewed as essential components of higher education, supplementing the educational process through enhancement of students' physical, mental, and emotional development. Students who participate in recreational sports tend to develop positive self-images, awareness of strengths, increased tolerance and self-control, stronger social interaction skills, and maturity – all gleaned from recreational sports experiences. The field of recreational sports has grown into a dynamic, organized presence providing quality co-curricular opportunities for the majority of the student body.

The term "intramural" is derived from the Latin words "intra," meaning "within," and "muralis," meaning "walls." Intramurals began in U.S. colleges and universities during the 19th century as students developed leisure time sporting events. Throughout that century, intramural sports were almost exclusively the only form of athletic competition for college males. Originating from intramurals, interest in varsity athletics increased in popularity and institutions assumed responsibility for organizing athletic events.

Until late in the 1800s, intramural sports were perceived by most to be of little instructional or educational value. Near the end of the century, however, colleges and universities began to administer intramural sports for men. In 1913, the first professional staff members were employed to direct intramural programs. Intramurals continued to grow in strength and gain support, until by the 1950s there was a general realization by institutional leaders of the intrinsic educational value of sports participation. Programs expanded and additional facilities were constructed in response to student-led initiatives, and campus facilities were established exclusively for recreational sports activities.

Over time, intramural programs diversified and participation increased. The rise in popularity of aerobic exercise and a societal push toward greater gender equity, including implementation of Title IX of the Education Amendments of 1972, produced an influx of women into collegiate recreational sports, resulting in even higher levels of interest and participation. Consequently, the late 1980s witnessed a second period of rapid growth in programs and the advent of new and better campus facilities for physical activities.

The beginning of the 21st century found even greater expansion of collegiate recreational sports opportunities and facilities, reaching an estimated combined enrollment of 7.1 million students, with an estimated 5.3 million students considered heavy or regular users of established campus recreational sports programs and facilities (NIRSA, 2005). New construction of campus recreational sports facilities, and refurbishing of existing facilities, continues unabated and has helped to provide needed recreational sports services to students. The National Intramural Recreational Sports Association (NIRSA), reported that between 2005–2010, at least $3.17 billion will be spent in new construction and renovations for indoor campus recreational sports facilities at 333 NIRSA Member Institutions, at an average cost of $14.2 million. Total student enrollment for the reporting colleges and universities is 3.8 million (NIRSA, 2005).

Recreational sports programs experienced changing perceptions about their institutional roles and the standards appropriate for their administration as they evolved and expanded. At a majority of institutions, recreational sports programs are placed under the administrative auspices of a division of student affairs, though some programs may be found within a variety of other administrative structures, including athletic departments, physical education programs, and business units. NIRSA suggested that while organizational designs vary among institutions, the full realization for the contribution of recreational sports to any campus depends on institutional commitment to that endeavor. NIRSA (1996) delineated seven primary goals of recreational sports programs:

1. To provide participation in a variety of activities that satisfy the diverse needs of students, faculty, and staff members, and where appropriate, guests, alumni, and public participants can become involved.

2. To provide value to participants by helping individuals develop and maintain a positive self-image, stronger social interactive skills, enhanced physical fitness, and good mental health.

3. To enhance college and university student and faculty recruitment and retention initiatives.

4. To coordinate the use of campus recreation facilities in cooperation with other administrative units such as athletics, physical education, and student activities.

5. To provide extracurricular education opportunities through participation in recreational sports and the provision of relevant leadership positions.

6. To contribute positively to institutional relations through significant and high-quality recreational sports programming.

7. To cooperate with academic units, focusing on the development of recreational sports curricula and accompanying laboratory experiences.

Recreational sports programming significantly impacts student life, development, and learning, as well as recruitment and retention. Hossler and Bean (1990) wrote that "recreational sports (i.e., informal leisure time, relaxation, games, intramurals) have been endorsed by institutions for their value in helping students maintain good physical health, enhancing their mental health by providing a respite from rigorous academic work, and teaching recreational skills with a carryover for leisure time exercise throughout life." NIRSA (2004) found that "participation in recreational sports programs is a key determinant of college satisfaction, success, recruitment and retention." The study also reported that at schools with established campus recreational sports departments, 75% of college students participate in recreational sports programs.

Through participation in recreational sports, students are encouraged to develop critical thinking skills, create new problem-solving strategies, hone decision-making skills, enhance creativity, and more effectively synthesize and integrate this information into all aspects of their lives. In this way, students both perform more effectively in an academic environment and flourish throughout all phases of the co-curricular experience.

References, Readings, and Resources

Hossler, D. and Bean, John P. & Associates. (1990). *The strategic management of college enrollments*. San Francisco: Jossey-Bass.

Keeling, Richard P., Editor. (2004). *Learning Reconsidered: A Campus-wide Focus on the Student Experience*. Washington, DC: American College Personnel Association & National Association of Student Personnel Administrators.

Keeling, Richard., Editor. (2006). *Learning Reconsidered 2*. Washington, DC: American College Personnel Association & National Association of Student Personnel Administrators.

Mull, R.F., Bayless, K.G., and Ross, C.M. (1987). *Recreational sports programming*. North Palm Beach, FL: The Athletic Institute.

National Center for Education Statistics. (October, 2003). *College/University Enrollment as Found in Projections of Education Statistics to 2013*. Washington, DC: Author.

National Intramural-Recreational Sports Association. (1996). *General and Specialty Standards for Collegiate Recreational Sports*. Champaign, IL: Human Kinetics.

National Intramural-Recreational Sports Association. (2004). *The Value of Recreational Sports in Higher Education – Impact on Student Enrollment, Success, and Buying Power*. Champaign, IL: Human Kinetics.

National Intramural-Recreational Sports Association. (2005). *Collegiate Recreational Sports Facility Construction Report*. Champaign, IL: Human Kinetics.

National Intramural-Recreational Sports Association. *Recreational Sports Journal*. Champaign, IL: Human Kinetics.

National Intramural Recreational Sports Association, NIRSA National Center, 4185 SW Research Way, Corvallis, OR 97333-1067. 541-766-8211; Fax 541-766-8284.
e-mail: nirsa@nirsa.org; website www.nirsa.org

Contributors:
Current edition: Kent J. Blumenthal, NIRSA

Previous editions: Dixie Bennett, Loyola University Chicago

RECREATIONAL SPORTS PROGRAMS
CAS Standards and Guidelines

Part 1: MISSION

The Recreational Sports Program (RSP) must incorporate student learning and student development in its mission. The program must enhance overall educational experiences. The RSP must develop, record, disseminate, implement and regularly review its mission and goals. Mission statements must be consistent with the mission and goals of the institution and with the standards in this document. The RSP must operate as an integral part of the institution's overall mission.

The mission of the RSP is to enhance students' fitness and wellness, knowledge, personal skills, and enjoyment by providing:

- **opportunities for a variety of activities that may contribute to individual physical fitness and wellness**
- **opportunities for cooperative and competitive play activity in the game form**
- **a medium through which students can learn and practice leadership, management, program planning and interpersonal skills**
- **access to quality facilities, equipment, and programs**

To accomplish this mission, recreational sports programs should:

- provide a variety of opportunities including informal programs (self-directed), intramural sports (structured), sports clubs (interest groups), instructional programs, special events, outdoor programs, fitness and wellness programs, extramural programs, family and youth programs and programs for people with disabilities
- coordinate effectively the scheduling of events and maintenance of campus sport facilities with other campus units
- provide extracurricular opportunities through participation and leadership roles designed to enhance social, psychological, and physiological development
- contribute positively to public relations efforts of the institution, including the recruitment and retention of students
- when appropriate, work in collaboration with academic units to help teach courses and facilitate laboratory experiences
- assist with the socialization of students into the campus environment

Part 2. PROGRAM

The formal education of students consists of the curriculum and the co-curriculum, and must promote student learning and development that is purposeful and holistic. The Recreational Sports Program (RSP) must identify relevant and desirable student learning and development outcomes and provide programs and services that encourage the achievement of those outcomes.

Relevant and desirable outcomes include: intellectual growth, effective communication, realistic self-appraisal, enhanced self-esteem, clarified values, career choices, leadership development, healthy behaviors, meaningful interpersonal relationships, independence, collaboration, social responsibility, satisfying and productive lifestyles, appreciation of diversity, spiritual awareness, and achievement of personal and educational goals.

The RSP must provide evidence of its impact on the achievement of student learning and development outcomes.

The table below offers examples of evidence of achievement of student learning and development.

Student Learning and Development Outcome Domains

Intellectual growth
Examples of achievement indicators

Produces personal and educational goal statements; Employs critical thinking in problem solving; Uses complex information from a variety of sources including personal experience and observation to form a decision or opinion; Obtains a degree; Applies previously understood information and concepts to a new situation or setting; Expresses appreciation for literature, the fine arts, mathematics, sciences, and social sciences

Effective communication
Examples of achievement indicators

Writes and speaks coherently and effectively; Writes and speaks after reflection; Able to influence others through writing, speaking or artistic expression; Effectively articulates abstract ideas; Uses appropriate syntax; Makes presentations or gives performances

Enhanced self-esteem
Examples of achievement indicators

Shows self-respect and respect for others; Initiates actions toward achievement of goals; Takes reasonable risks; Demonstrates assertive behavior; Functions without need for constant reassurance from others

Realistic self-appraisal
Examples of achievement indicators

Articulates personal skills and abilities; Makes decisions and acts in congruence with personal values; Acknowledges personal strengths and weaknesses; Articulates rationale for personal behavior; Seeks feedback from others; Learns from past experiences

Clarified values
Examples of achievement indicators

Articulates personal values; Acts in congruence with personal values; Makes decisions that reflect personal values; Demonstrates willingness to scrutinize personal beliefs and values; Identifies personal, work, and lifestyle values and explains how they influence decision-making

Career choices
Examples of achievement indicators

Articulates career choices based on assessment of interests, values, skills, and abilities; Documents knowledge, skills, and accomplishments resulting from formal education, work experience, community service, and volunteer experiences; Makes the connections between classroom and out-of-classroom learning; Can construct a resume with clear job objectives and evidence of related knowledge, skills and accomplishments; Articulates the characteristics of a preferred work environment; Comprehends the world of work; Takes steps to initiate a job search or seek advanced education

Leadership development
Examples of achievement indicators

Articulates leadership philosophy or style; Serves in a leadership position in a student organization; Comprehends the dynamics of a group; Exhibits democratic principles as a leader; Exhibits ability to visualize a group purpose and desired outcomes

Healthy behavior
Examples of achievement indicators

Chooses behaviors and environments that promote health and reduce risk; Articulates the relationship between health and wellness and accomplishing life-long goals; Exhibits behaviors that advance a healthy community.

Meaningful interpersonal relationships
Examples of achievement indicators

Develops and maintains satisfying interpersonal relationships; Establishes mutually rewarding relationships with friends and colleagues; Listens to and considers others' points of view; Treats others with respect

Independence
Examples of achievement indicators

Exhibits self-reliant behaviors; Functions autonomously; Exhibits ability to function interdependently; Accepts supervision as needed; Manages time effectively

Collaboration
Examples of achievement indicators

Works cooperatively with others; Seeks the involvement of others; Seeks feedback from others; Contributes to achievement of a group goal; Exhibits effective listening skills

Social responsibility
Examples of achievement indicators

Understands and participates in relevant governance systems; Understands, abides by, and participates in the development, maintenance, and/or orderly change of community, social, and legal standards or norms; Appropriately challenges the unfair, unjust, or uncivil behavior of other individuals or groups; Participates in service/volunteer activities

Satisfying and productive lifestyles
Examples of achievement indicators

Achieves balance between education, work and leisure time; Articulates and meets goals for work, leisure and education; Overcomes obstacles that hamper goal achievement; Functions on the basis of personal identity, ethical, spiritual, and moral values; Articulates long-term goals and objectives

Appreciating diversity
Examples of achievement indicators

Understands one's own identity and culture; Seeks involvement with people different from oneself; Seeks involvement in diverse interests; Articulates the advantages and challenges of a diverse society; Challenges appropriately the abusive use of stereotypes by others; Understands the impact of diversity on one's own society

Spiritual awareness
Examples of achievement indicators

Develops and articulates personal belief system; Understands roles of spirituality in personal and group values and behaviors

Personal and educational goals
Examples of achievement indicators

Sets, articulates, and pursues individual goals; Articulates personal and educational goals and objectives; Uses personal and educational goals to guide decisions; Understands the effect of one's personal and educational goals on others

The RSP must be (a) intentional, (b) coherent, (c) based on theories and knowledge of learning and human development, (d) reflective of developmental and demographic profiles of the student population, and (e) responsive to special needs of individuals, special populations, and communities.

Recreational sports programs must reflect the needs and interests of students, faculty, staff, and other members of the campus community. The RSP must satisfy the particular needs of the campus by balancing team, dual, individual meet, and special event sport experiences.

The overall recreational sports program should include:

- Informal programs to provide for self-directed, individualized approach to participation. This program area accommodates the desire to participate in sport for fitness and enjoyment.

- Intramural sports to provide structured contests, meets, tournaments, and leagues limiting participation to the individuals within the institution. A variety of forms of tournaments should be available, including elimination, challenge, league, and meets. Equitable participation opportunities should be provided for men and women, and when appropriate, co-recreational activity should be offered. Opportunities to participate at various levels of ability should be made available to students (e.g., beginner, intermediate, and advanced).

- Sport clubs to provide opportunities for individuals to organize around a common interest. Opportunities should be available for a variety of interest focused on a sport within or outside the institution. Self-administered and self-regulated groups are normally coordinated and assisted by staff in such areas as governance, facilities, scheduling, safety, budgeting, and fund-raising through sport club coordination. Formation of clubs should be accomplished through appropriate and established channels.

- Instructional programs to provide learning opportunities, knowledge, and skills through lessons, clinics, and work-shops. Depending on type, size, resources, and setting of the institution, the program may include extramural sports, outdoor recreation, fitness and wellness, and special events.

- Special events to introduce new sport or related activities that are unique in approach or nature from traditional programs. These events may be held within or outside the institution.

- Outdoor programs and activities to provide participants with opportunities to enjoy natural environments and experience new challenges.

- Fitness programs to provide opportunities and assistance in personal exercise programs. This voluntary program should motivate individuals to assess their levels of fitness and maintain a positive fitness lifestyle. Individual assessment should be available for participant feedback.

- Recreation and aquatic programs.

- Wellness programs to encourage achievement of one's full health potential. These programs should provide an opportunity to work cooperatively with professionals in health services including counselors and physicians and may be accomplished in concert with others who are similarly oriented.

- Extramural sports to provide structured tournaments, contests, and meets among participants from other institutions. Champions from intramural sports are frequently chosen to represent the institution.

- Family and youth programs for members of the campus community. These activities may include special events, sports, games, instructional programs, fitness and wellness, and outdoor programs.

- Programs for people with disabilities to engage in activities designed to have a positive impact on mobility, socialization, independence, fitness, and community integration.

Program planning and implementation should include consideration of:

- proper facility coordination and scheduling
- rules and regulations that address participant safety
- an environment that minimizes the chance of injuries
- advice to groups and organizations
- accurate interpretation of institutional policies and procedures to program participants
- conflict management issues
- proper supervision of recreational sports activities
- inventory, maintenance, and procedures for participant use of equipment
- participant involvement in program content and procedures through committee structures
- recognition system for participants, employees, and volunteers
- cultural diversity issues
- accurate and adequate publicity and promotion
- volunteerism

Part 3. LEADERSHIP
Effective and ethical leadership is essential to the success of all organizations. Institutions must appoint, position, and empower leaders within the administrative structure to accomplish stated

missions. Recreational Sports Program (RSP) leaders must be selected on the basis of formal education and training, relevant work experience, personal skills and competencies, relevant professional credentials, as well as potential for promoting learning and development in students, applying effective practices to educational processes, and enhancing institutional effectiveness. Institutions must determine expectations of accountability for leaders and fairly assess their performance.

RSP leaders of programs and services must exercise authority over resources for which they are responsible to achieve their respective missions.

RSP leaders must:
- articulate a vision for their organization
- set goals and objectives based on the needs and capabilities of the population served
- promote student learning and development
- prescribe and practice ethical behavior
- recruit, select, supervise, and develop others in the organization
- manage financial resources
- coordinate human resources
- plan, budget for, and evaluate personnel and programs
- apply effective practices to educational and administrative processes
- communicate effectively
- initiate collaborative interaction between individuals and agencies that possess legitimate concerns and interests in the functional area

RSP leaders must identify and find means to address individual, organizational, or environmental conditions that inhibit goal achievement.

RSP leaders must promote campus environments that result in multiple opportunities for student learning and development.

RSP leaders must continuously improve programs and services in response to changing needs of students and other constituents, and evolving institutional priorities.

Part 4. ORGANIZATION and MANAGEMENT
Guided by an overarching intent to ensure student learning and development, the Recreational Sports Program (RSP) must be structured purposefully and managed effectively to achieve stated goals. Evidence of appropriate structure must include current and accessible policies and procedures,

written performance expectations for all employees, functional workflow graphics or organizational charts, and clearly stated service delivery expectations.

Evidence of effective management must include use of comprehensive and accurate information for decisions, clear sources and channels of authority, effective communication practices, decision-making and conflict resolution procedures, responsiveness to changing conditions, accountability and evaluation systems, and recognition and reward processes. The RSP must provide channels within the organization for regular review of administrative policies and procedures.

Institutional leaders should recognize the significant differences in mission among intercollegiate athletics, physical education and recreation academic units, and the recreational sports programs, and act accordingly. The organizational placement of recreational sports within the institution should ensure the accomplishment of the program's mission.

Members of the campus community should be involved in the selection, design, governance, and administration of programs and facilities. Students, faculty and staff and members, and the public, when appropriate, may be involved through committees, councils, and boards.

Part 5. HUMAN RESOURCES
The Recreational Sports Program (RSP) must be staffed adequately by individuals qualified to accomplish its mission and goals. Within established guidelines of the institution, the RSP must establish procedures for staff selection, training, and evaluation; set expectations for supervision, and provide appropriate professional development opportunities. The program must strive to improve the professional competence and skills of all personnel it employs.

RSP professional staff members must hold an earned graduate degree in a field relevant to the position they hold or must possess an appropriate combination of educational credentials and related work experience.

Degree or credential-seeking interns must be qualified by enrollment in an appropriate field of study and by relevant experience. These individuals must be trained and supervised adequately by professional staff members holding educational credentials and related work experience appropriate for supervision.

Student employees and volunteers must be carefully selected, trained, supervised, and evaluated. They must be trained on how and when to refer those in need of assistance to qualified staff members and have access to a supervisor for assistance in making these judgments. Student employees and volunteers must be provided clear and precise job descriptions, pre-service training based on assessed needs, and continuing staff development.

The RSP must have technical and support staff members adequate to accomplish its mission. RSP staff members must be technologically proficient and qualified to perform their job functions, be knowledgeable of ethical and legal uses of technology, and have access to training. The level of staffing and workloads must be adequate and appropriate for program and service demands.

Salary levels and fringe benefits for all RSP staff members must be commensurate with those for comparable positions within the institution, in similar institutions, and in the relevant geographic area.

The RSP must institute hiring and promotion practices that are fair, inclusive, and non-discriminatory. The program must employ a diverse staff to provide readily identifiable role models for students and to enrich the campus community.

The RSP must create and maintain position descriptions for all staff members and provide regular performance planning and appraisals.

The RSP must have a system for regular staff evaluation and must provide access to continuing education and professional development opportunities, including in-service training programs and participation in professional conferences and workshops.

Part 6. FINANCIAL RESOURCES

The Recreational Sports Program (RSP) must have adequate funding to accomplish its mission and goals. Funding priorities must be determined within the context of the stated mission, goals, objectives and comprehensive analysis of the needs and capabilities of students and the viability of internal or external resources.

The RSP must demonstrate fiscal responsibility and cost effectiveness consistent with institutional protocols.

Institutional funds for the recreational sports program should be allocated on a permanent basis. In addition to institutional funding, other sources may be considered, including state appropriations, student fees, user fees, donations, contributions, fines, concession and store sales, rentals, and dues.

Part 7. FACILITIES, TECHNOLOGY and EQUIPMENT

The Recreational Sports Program (RSP) must have adequate, suitably located facilities, adequate technology, and equipment to support its mission and goals efficiently and effectively. Facilities, technology, and equipment must be evaluated regularly and be in compliance with relevant federal, state, provincial, and local requirements to provide for access, health, safety, and security.

The institution must provide adequate indoor and outdoor facilities, technology, and equipment with prioritized blocks of time, for recreational sports programs to accommodate the diverse needs and interest of the campus community.

As a general rule, the larger the population and the more geographically isolated the institution, the greater the need for quality and diversity of facilities. Consideration should be given to a balance of facilities that would provide participation opportunities in team, dual, individual, and meet sports, as well as in fitness and conditioning. Examples of such facilities include swimming pools, gymnasiums, weight rooms and fitness facilities, and general use playing fields.

Part 8. LEGAL RESPONSIBILITIES

Recreational Sports Program (RSP) staff members must be knowledgeable about and responsive to laws and regulations that relate to their respective responsibilities. Staff members must inform users of programs and services and officials, as appropriate, of legal obligations and limitations including constitutional, statutory, regulatory, and case law; mandatory laws and orders emanating from federal, state/provincial and local governments; and the institution's policies.

RSP staff members must use reasonable and informed practices to limit the liability exposure of the institution, its officers, employees, and agents. Staff members must be informed about institutional policies regarding personal liability and related insurance coverage options.

The institution must provide access to legal advice for RSP staff members as needed to carry out assigned responsibilities.

The institution must inform RSP staff and students in a timely and systematic fashion about extraordinary or changing legal obligations and potential liabilities.

Recreational sports professionals should be fully aware of and understand legal areas such as due process, employment procedures, equal opportunity, and civil rights and liberties.

Although participation in recreational sports is a voluntary action, liability of wrongful or negligent acts should be a continuing concern.

Reasonable efforts must be made to insure a safe environment, properly maintained equipment, proper instruction, and adequate supervision.

Part 9. EQUITY and ACCESS
Recreational Sports Program (RSP) staff members must ensure that services and programs are provided on a fair and equitable basis. Facilities, programs and services must be accessible. Hours of operation and delivery of and access to programs and services must be responsive to the needs of all students and other constituents. The RSP must adhere to the spirit and intent of equal opportunity laws.

RSP must be open and readily accessible to all students and must not discriminate except where sanctioned by law and institutional policy. Discrimination must be avoided on the bases of age; color; creed; cultural heritage; disability; ethnicity; gender identity; nationality; political affiliation; religious affiliation; sex; sexual orientation; or social, economic, marital, or veteran status.

Consistent with their mission and goals, the RSP must take affirmative action to remedy significant imbalances in student participation and staffing patterns.

As the demographic profiles of campuses change and new instructional delivery methods are introduced, institutions must recognize the needs of students who participate in distance learning for access to programs and services offered on campus. Institutions must provide appropriate services in ways that are accessible to distance learners and assist them in identifying and gaining access to other appropriate services in their geographic region.

Part 10. CAMPUS and EXTERNAL RELATIONS
The Recreational Sports Program (RSP) must establish, maintain, and promote effective relations with relevant individuals, campus offices, and external agencies.

The recreational sports program should be an institution-wide process that systematically involves student affairs, academic affairs, and other administrative units, such as campus police, physical plant, and the business office.

The recreational sports program should collaborate campus-wide to disseminate information abut their own and other programs and services on campus.

The program staff should serve as a resource to the community, providing expert advice on recreational issues and activities.

Part 11. DIVERSITY
Within the context of each institution's unique mission, diversity enriches the community and enhances the collegiate experience for all; therefore, the Recreational Sports Program (RSP) must nurture environments where commonalties and differences among people are recognized and honored.

The RSP must promote educational experiences that are characterized by open and continuous communication that deepens understanding of one's own identity, culture, and heritage, and that of others. The program must educate and promote respect about commonalties and differences in their historical and cultural contexts.

The RSP must address the characteristics and needs of a diverse population when establishing and implementing policies and procedures.

Part 12. ETHICS
All persons involved in the delivery of the Recreational Sports Program (RSP) must adhere to the highest principles of ethical behavior. The RSP must develop or adopt and implement appropriate statements of ethical practice. The RSP must publish these statements and ensure their periodic review by relevant constituencies.

Ethical standards of relevant professional associations should be considered.

RSP staff members must ensure that privacy and confidentiality are maintained with respect to all communications and records to the extent that such records are protected under the law and appropriate statements of ethical practice. Information contained in students' education records must not be disclosed without written consent except as allowed by relevant laws and institutional policies. Staff members must disclose to appropriate authorities information judged to be of an emergency nature, especially when the safety of the individual or others is involved, or when otherwise required by institutional policy or relevant law.

All RSP staff members must be aware of and comply with the provisions contained in the institution's

human subjects research policy and in other relevant institutional policies addressing ethical practices and confidentiality of research data concerning individuals.

RSP staff members must recognize and avoid personal conflict of interest or appearance thereof in their transactions with students and others.

RSP staff members must strive to insure the fair, objective, and impartial treatment of all persons with whom they deal. Staff members must not participate in nor condone any form of harassment that demeans persons or creates an intimidating, hostile, or offensive campus environment.

When handling institutional funds, all RSP staff members must ensure that such funds are managed in accordance with established and responsible accounting procedures and the fiscal policies or processes of the institution.

RSP staff members must perform their duties within the limits of their training, expertise, and competence. When these limits are exceeded, individuals in need of further assistance must be referred to persons possessing appropriate qualifications.

RSP staff members must use suitable means to confront and otherwise hold accountable other staff members who exhibit unethical behavior.

RSP staff members must be knowledgeable about and practice ethical behavior in the use of technology.

Part 13. ASSESSMENT and EVALUATION
The Recreational Sports Program (RSP) must conduct regular assessment and evaluations.   The RSP must employ effective qualitative and quantitative methodologies as appropriate, to determine whether and to what degree the stated mission, goals, and student learning and development outcomes are being met. The process must employ sufficient and sound assessment measures to ensure comprehensiveness. Data collected must include responses from students and other affected constituencies.

Evaluation of student and institutional needs, goals, objectives, and the effectiveness of the recreational sports program should occur on a periodic basis. A representative cross-section of appropriate people from the campus community should be involved in reviews of the recreational sports program.

The RSP must evaluate periodically how well they complement and enhance the institution's stated mission and educational effectiveness.

Results of these evaluations must be used in revising and improving programs and services and in recognizing staff performance.

General Standards revised in 2002; RSP content developed/ revised in 1986 & 1996

THE ROLE of the REGISTRAR
CAS Standards and Guidelines

The position of registrar evolved from the position of "Bedel" in Europe, which appeared in the 12th century. As the position evolved and the office changed, the "registrar" emerged in the 15th century. With the founding of Harvard, the position of registrar became an integral part of American higher education. In 1910, 15 registrars met in Detroit to discuss the need to share information and develop common practices, a meeting marked the birth of the American Association of Collegiate Registrars (AACR). That group added admissions officers in 1949 and changed its name to the American Association of Collegiate Registrars and Admissions Officers (AACRAO) (Quann, 1979). Over the years AACR and AACRAO and their more than 30 state and regional associations have provided linkages among registrars nationally and internationally, for the exchange of ideas and information that has led to a set of generally accepted policies and practices.

As the role of registrar progressed, it shifted from being essentially the number-two leadership position responsible for handling many aspects of administration, to filling a role more narrowly focused but vital to the life of institutions of higher learning. Today's registrar usually reports to the vice president for academic affairs, student affairs, or enrollment management, and manages a staff that may vary from a few members to more than 100, depending on institution size. The registrar determines the organizational structure for the office; ensures the availability of adequate facilities, equipment, supplies, and services; develops position descriptions for and employs, trains, and supervises office staff; and oversees day-to-day activities.

The office of the registrar is a primary point of contact for students on the college campus. Through the registrar's office, students obtain schedules of classes (including on-line and paper formats), register for courses, drop/add/withdraw, obtain grade reports and transcripts, and receive diplomas. Therefore, accurate and efficient service to students and continuous quality improvement are major objectives for the registrar.

The registrar's office is also a primary point of contact for faculty members for the scheduling of classes and assignment of classroom and laboratory space. In support of faculty members, who often assist in the advising and scheduling processes, the registrar's office provides class rosters and grade rolls, receives and processes grades, and produces grade reports and transcripts. Maintaining a close working relationship with faculty members, department heads, and academic deans is therefore an important role of the registrar.

While duties and responsibilities vary from institution to institution, the registrar is typically responsible for working with academic departments and faculty to determine which courses and sections are offered each term, assigning classroom facilities, producing the catalog and schedule of classes students use to select courses, and implementing a scheduling process.

Today, the registration process by which students select classes each academic term is typically conducted on-line or by touch tone telephone so that students may register from campus or off-campus residences, workplaces, or elsewhere, as long as they have access to a telephone or on-line computer.

The registrar also is responsible for the maintenance of student records. While records are still maintained in paper or on microfilm, most institutions now store student records in electronic data bases. Imaging systems also are used to store former paper records in electronic form.

Other duties of most registrars include the production of class rosters, grade rosters, and grade reports; clearance of students for graduation, preparation of diplomas, and organization of graduation ceremonies; and publication of the college catalog. Registrars also play a vital role in developing and implementing policies and procedures, services, and systems to facilitate student enrollment, maintenance of student records, transfer of records to other institutions, and acceptance of transfer credit.

In addition, the registrar is the individual usually responsible for assuring that the Family Education Rights and Privacy Act (FERPA) requirements are met throughout the institution. Likewise, as student information systems increasingly are becoming more complex, responsibility for oversight of these technologies has gained greater importance as well. Hence, registrars are at the forefront of implementing new technologies on campus.

The pace of change in higher education will increasingly affect the registrar's functions. The standards that follow, in addition to providing basic functional guidelines, are designed to help institutions address such challenges as distance learning; proficiency-based education; assessment; learning opportunities that are not constrained by time, location, or duration; and continuous rapid change in technology.

References, Readings, and Resources

Aucoin, P., & Associates (1996). *Academic record and transcript guide.* Washington, DC: American Association of Collegiate Registrars and Admissions Officers.

Bell, M. M. (1993). *Touchtone telephone/voice response registration: A guide for successful implementation.* Washington, DC: American Association of Collegiate Registrars and Admissions Officers.

Bilger, T. A., & Associates (1987). *Professional development guidelines for registrars: A self-audit.* Washington, DC: American Association of Collegiate Registrars and Admissions Officers.

Lonabocker, L., & Gwinn, D. (1996). *Breakthrough systems: Student access and registration*. Washington, DC: American Association of Collegiate Registrars and Admissions Officers.

Ockerman, E. & Legere, J. (1989). *The role of the registrar*. Washington, DC: American Association of Collegiate Registrars and Admissions Officers (AACRAO).

Perkins, H. L. (1996). *Electronic imaging in admissions, records and financial aid offices*. Washington, DC: American Association of Collegiate Registrars and Admissions Officers.

Peterson, E. D., & Associates (1987). *Retention of records: A guide for retention and disposal of student records*. Washington, DC: American Association of Collegiate Registrars and Admissions Officers.

Preinkert, A. H. (2004). *The work of the registrar: A summary of principles and practices in American universities and colleges: A basis for a proposed manual for registrars*. Washington, DC: American Association for Collegiate Registrars.

Quann, C. J., & Associates (1979). *Admissions, academic records, and registrar services: A handbook of policies and procedures*. San Francisco: Jossey-Bass.

Rainsberger, R. A., & Associates. (1995). *Guidelines for postsecondary institutions for implementation of the Family Educational Rights and Privacy Act of 1974 as amended*. Washington, DC: American Association of Collegiate Registrars and Admissions Officers.

Contributors:
Current edition: Jan Arminio, Shippensburg University
Previous editions: Wayne Becraft, AACRAO

REGISTRAR PROGRAMS AND SERVICES
CAS STANDARDS and GUIDELINES

Part 1. MISSION

Registrar Programs and Services (RPS) must incorporate student learning and student development in its mission. RPS enhance overall educational experiences. RPS must develop, record, disseminate, implement and regularly review its mission and goals. Mission statements must be consistent with the mission and goals of the institution and with the standards in this document. RPS must operate as an integral part of the institution's overall mission.

In support of the overall mission of the institution, and when responsibility is assigned, the mission of RPS must be to:

- develop institutional publications to provide information about courses, programs, policies, and procedures
- develop course schedules to provide information on courses and sections being offered in any given term with their day, time, and location
- schedule appropriate space for all classes
- provide information on regulations, policies and procedures
- develop forms and procedures as required
- provide a registration process for enrolling students in classes each term, which may include the assessment of tuition and fees
- certify student enrollment as required (e.g., veterans services, rehabilitation services, student loans, athletic eligibility)
- provide reports as required (e.g., class rosters, grade rosters, grade reports, transcripts);
- record properly evaluated transfer credit
- administer academic eligibility policies (e.g., graduation, honors, academic probation or dismissal)
- prepare and distribute diplomas
- maintain student record data base and archival files
- ensure that the security and confidentiality of student record data are maintained throughout the university/college
- prepare statistical reports (e.g., enrollment projections, retention, attrition, and graduation rates)

The registrar may also coordinate the arrangements for commencement and provide administrative support to the faculty senate or other governance bodies.

Part 2. PROGRAM

The formal education of students consists of the curriculum and the co-curriculum, and must promote student learning and development that is purposeful and holistic. Registrar Programs and Services (RPS) must identify relevant and desirable student learning and development outcomes and provide programs and services that encourage the achievement of those outcomes.

Relevant and desirable outcomes include: intellectual growth, effective communication, realistic self-appraisal, enhanced self-esteem, clarified values, career choices, leadership development, healthy behaviors, meaningful interpersonal relationships, independence, collaboration, social responsibility, satisfying and productive lifestyles, appreciation of diversity, spiritual awareness, and achievement of personal and educational goals.

RPS must provide evidence of its impact on the achievement of student learning and development outcomes.

The table below offers examples of evidence of achievement of student learning and development.

Student Learning and Development Outcome Domains

Intellectual growth
Examples of achievement indicators

Produces personal and educational goal statements; Employs critical thinking in problem solving; Uses complex information from a variety of sources including personal experience and observation to form a decision or opinion; Obtains a degree; Applies previously understood information and concepts to a new situation or setting; Expresses appreciation for literature, the fine arts, mathematics, sciences, and social sciences

Effective communication
Examples of achievement indicators

Writes and speaks coherently and effectively; Writes and speaks after reflection; Able to influence others through writing, speaking or artistic expression; Effectively articulates abstract ideas; Uses appropriate syntax; Makes presentations or gives performances

Enhanced self-esteem

Examples of achievement indicators

Shows self-respect and respect for others; Initiates actions toward achievement of goals; Takes reasonable risks; Demonstrates assertive behavior; Functions without need for constant reassurance from others

Realistic self-appraisal

Examples of achievement indicators

Articulates personal skills and abilities; Makes decisions and acts in congruence with personal values; Acknowledges personal strengths and weaknesses; Articulates rationale for personal behavior; Seeks feedback from others; Learns from past experiences

Clarified values

Examples of achievement indicators

Articulates personal values; Acts in congruence with personal values; Makes decisions that reflect personal values; Demonstrates willingness to scrutinize personal beliefs and values; Identifies personal, work, and lifestyle values and explains how they influence decision-making

Career choices

Examples of achievement indicators

Articulates career choices based on assessment of interests, values, skills, and abilities; Documents knowledge, skills, and accomplishments resulting from formal education, work experience, community service, and volunteer experiences; Makes the connections between classroom and out-of-classroom learning; Can construct a resume with clear job objectives and evidence of related knowledge, skills ,and accomplishments; Articulates the characteristics of a preferred work environment; Comprehends the world of work; Takes steps to initiate a job search or seek advanced education

Leadership development

Examples of achievement indicators

Articulates leadership philosophy or style; Serves in a leadership position in a student organization; Comprehends the dynamics of a group; Exhibits democratic principles as a leader; Exhibits ability to visualize a group purpose and desired outcomes

Healthy behavior

Examples of achievement indicators

Chooses behaviors and environments that promote health and reduce risk; Articulates the relationship between health and wellness and accomplishing life-long goals; Exhibits behaviors that advance a healthy community

Meaningful interpersonal relationships

Examples of achievement indicators

Develops and maintains satisfying interpersonal relationships; Establishes mutually rewarding relationships with friends and colleagues; Listens to and considers others' points of view; Treats others with respect

Independence

Examples of achievement indicators

Exhibits self-reliant behaviors; Functions autonomously; Exhibits ability to function interdependently; Accepts supervision as needed; Manages time effectively

Collaboration

Examples of achievement indicators

Works cooperatively with others; Seeks the involvement of others; Seeks feedback from others; Contributes to achievement of a group goal; Exhibits effective listening skills

Social responsibility

Examples of achievement indicators

Understands and participates in relevant governance systems; Understands, abides by, and participates in the development, maintenance, and/or orderly change of community, social, and legal standards or norms; Appropriately challenges the unfair, unjust, or uncivil behavior of other individuals or groups; Participates in service/volunteer activities

Satisfying and productive lifestyles

Examples of achievement indicators

Achieves balance between education, work, and leisure time; Articulates and meets goals for work, leisure, and education; Overcomes obstacles that hamper goal achievement; Functions on the basis of personal identity, ethical, spiritual, and moral values; Articulates long-term goals and objectives

Appreciating diversity

Examples of achievement indicators

Understands one's own identity and culture; Seeks involvement with people different from oneself; Seeks involvement in diverse interests; Articulates the advantages and challenges of a diverse society; Challenges appropriately the abusive use of stereotypes by others; Understands the impact of diversity on one's own society

Spiritual awareness

Examples of achievement indicators

Develops and articulates personal belief system; Understands roles of spirituality in personal and group values and behaviors

Personal and educational goals

Examples of achievement indicators

Sets, articulates, and pursues individual goals; Articulates personal and educational goals and objectives; Uses personal and educational goals to guide decisions; Understands the effect of one's personal and educational goals on others

Programs and services must be (a) intentional, (b) coherent, (c) based on theories and knowledge of learning and human development, (d) reflective of developmental and demographic profiles of the student population, and (e) responsive to needs of individuals, special populations, and communities.

The registrar must:
- **have the authority to operate effectively in the academic community**
- **ensure that relevant policies and procedures are communicated widely**
- **ensure the accuracy and reliability of the data collected and distributed**
- **provide for the maintenance, upkeep, security, integrity and proper dissemination of academic records**
- **develop a workable disaster recovery plan that will allow the registrar to function in the event of catastrophic circumstances**
- **educate the institutional community with regard to the security and release of student data**

The registrar should assist in institutional efforts to establish and maintain co-curricular transcripts or other records.

Part 3. LEADERSHIP
Effective and ethical leadership is essential to the success of all organizations. Institutions must appoint, position, and empower Registrar Programs and Services (RPS) leaders within the administrative structure to accomplish stated missions. RPS leaders at various levels must be selected on the basis of formal education and training, relevant work experience, personal skills and competencies, relevant professional credentials, as well as potential for promoting learning and development in students, applying effective practices to educational processes, and enhancing institutional effectiveness. Institutions must determine expectations of accountability for leaders and fairly assess their performance.

Leaders of RPS must exercise authority over resources for which they are responsible to achieve their respective missions.

RPS leaders must:
- **articulate a vision for their organization**
- **set goals and objectives based on the needs and capabilities of the population served**
- **promote student learning and development**
- **prescribe and practice ethical behavior**
- **recruit, select, supervise, and develop others in the organization**
- **manage financial resources**
- **coordinate human resources**
- **plan, budget for, and evaluate personnel and programs**
- **apply effective practices to educational and administrative processes**
- **communicate effectively**
- **initiate collaborative interaction between individuals and agencies that possess legitimate concerns and interests in the functional area**

RPS leaders must identify and find means to address individual, organizational, or environmental conditions that inhibit goal achievement.

RPS leaders must promote campus environments that result in multiple opportunities for student learning and development.

RPS leaders must continuously improve programs and services in response to changing needs of students and other constituents, and evolving institutional priorities.

The registrar's office should:
- develop, advocate, and implement a statement of the mission, goals, and objectives for the unit that is congruent with and complementary to the institutional mission
- be responsible for implementing services congruent with institutional mission, goals, and objectives
- provide accurate information and timely service to all constituencies
- be at the forefront of technological advancement
- be able to justify investment in hardware, by identifying time and cost efficiencies that will accrue to the institution
- be sensitive to the special needs of all students including evening students, commuting students, married students, single parents, students with disabilities, adult learners, and students of various ethnic and cultural groups
- assess decision-making and problem-solving models and select those most appropriate to the institutional milieu
- serve as a catalyst in team building because the activities of the registrar impinge on most other institutional units

Part 4. ORGANIZATION and MANAGEMENT

Guided by an overarching intent to ensure student learning and development, Registrar Programs and Services (RPS) must be structured purposefully and managed effectively to achieve stated goals. Evidence of appropriate structure must include current and accessible policies and procedures, written performance expectations for all employees, functional workflow graphics or organizational charts, and clearly stated service delivery expectations.

Evidence of effective management must include use of comprehensive and accurate information for decisions, clear sources and channels of authority, effective communication practices, decision-making and conflict resolution procedures, responsiveness to changing conditions, accountability and evaluation systems, and recognition and reward processes. RPS must provide channels within the organization for regular review of administrative policies and procedures.

Registrar programs and services must provide channels within the organization for regular review of administrative policies and procedures and document such policies, practices, and procedures in a manual.

The registrar should:
- develop an organizational chart that describes the reporting lines within the office and identifies cooperative interrelationships with other institutional units
- coordinate programs and services with other institutional personnel, offices, functions, and activities;
- develop operational policies and procedures that include the detailed descriptions of responsibilities for each staff member
- ensure that staff responsibilities are consonant with the abilities of designated personnel
- provide for periodic review of policies, procedures, organizational structures, and currency of the office manual
- develop and maintain the office budget
- develop clear and concise criteria for decision making and establish primary responsibility when more than one unit is involved
- assume responsibility for establishing, updating, and evaluating staff training and professional development programs that also include skill improvement, interpersonal, organizational, and tine management components
- identify and be responsive to external constraints and requirements that impact on unit operation (e.g., implications of local, state, and federal regulations, union agreements, accreditation, professional, and athletic

conference requirements); foster communication among the staff by scheduling regular staff meetings
- encourage staff members to participate in state, regional, and national professional activities
- expend significant effort for long-range planning for changes in technology, policy, procedure, and customer service

There should be an office manual that includes: organizational charts showing accountability and reporting lines; interrelationships with other institutional units; applicable operating policies, practices and procedures; unit-specific policies, practices and procedures; external constraints (union, state and federal requirements); ethical standards statements; grievance/appeal procedures; job descriptions and expectations; personnel policies; task and job evaluation forms; and procedures in case of an emergency, natural disaster, or school closure.

Part 5. HUMAN RESOURCES

Registrar Programs and Services (RPS) must be staffed adequately by individuals qualified to accomplish its mission and goals. Within established guidelines of the institution, RPS must establish procedures for staff selection, training, and evaluation; set expectations for supervision, and provide appropriate professional development opportunities. RPS must strive to improve the professional competence and skills of all personnel it employs.

Staff members should be aware of the criteria on which they are to be evaluated at the beginning of each evaluation period. They should be properly trained and their performance monitored so that the evaluation at the end of the period does not contain judgment of criteria that have not been previously discussed.

RPS professional staff members must hold an earned graduate degree in a field relevant to the position they hold or must possess an appropriate combination of educational credentials and related work experience.

The chief administrator of the office should have the capacity to motivate, inspire, and help staff members develop a team atmosphere in the office. Attention should be paid to recognizing and rewarding the efforts of those who have accomplished expected and exceptional work.

Since the registrar works with all sectors of the institution, many of whom have terminal degrees, it would be advantageous if the registrar had a terminal degree as well. Other professional registrar staff may not require a terminal degree, but a master's or bachelor's degree is appropriate. Most degree programs do not specifically prepare individuals to become registrars. Courses of study relevant to the registrar area include: administration, education, business, counseling, curriculum, personnel, sociology, and psychology. Often professional staff are employed in the area after prior teaching or administrative experience. A demonstrated service-oriented philosophy is important since the office will be serving the entire campus population.

The registrar should possess an array of budget management skills: developing budgets, writing proposals for special projects, performing cost benefit analyses, amortizing the cost of major equipment purchases, and preparing analyses of future needs. Additionally, the registrar should be aware of the institution's personnel policies that could affect the budget, of accounting reports that track expenditures, and of policies governing unused funds.

The selection criteria for the registrar's position should include consideration of the match between a candidate's educational, personal, and experiential qualifications and the institution's mission, goals, and objectives. Staff member's selection should attempt to ensure the responsibilities are consonant with abilities.

Typically, the registrar reports to a vice president of academic affairs, student affairs, enrollment management, or comparable senior officer. Specific titles and reporting structures will necessarily reflect institutional mission, goals, and objectives.

Degree or credential-seeking interns must be qualified by enrollment in an appropriate field of study and by relevant experience. These individuals must be trained and supervised adequately by professional staff members holding educational credentials and related work experience appropriate for supervision.

Student employees and volunteers must be carefully selected, trained, supervised, and evaluated. They must be trained on how and when to refer those in need of assistance to qualified staff members and have access to a supervisor for assistance in making these judgments. Student employees and volunteers must be provided clear and precise job descriptions, pre-service training based on assessed needs, and continuing staff development.

RPS must have technical and support staff members adequate to accomplish its mission. Staff members must be technologically proficient and qualified to perform their job functions, be knowledgeable of ethical and legal uses of technology, and have access to training. The level of staffing and workloads must be adequate and appropriate for program and service demands.

The support staff should be skilled in interpersonal communications, public relations, and the dissemination of

information. Personnel should be adept in handling complex and detailed activities and responsibilities. Accuracy is essential because the office is recording the academic history of students.

Development for the support staff should include adequate initial training to be able to represent the institution in their office function in a competent and professional manner. On-going training and staff development should be designed to enhance and broaden understanding of roles and responsibilities within the office and the institution.

Salary levels and fringe benefits for all RPS staff members must be commensurate with those for comparable positions within the institution, in similar institutions, and in the relevant geographic area.

RPS must institute hiring and promotion practices that are fair, inclusive, and non-discriminatory. Programs and services must employ a diverse staff to provide readily identifiable role models for students and to enrich the campus community.

RPS must create and maintain position descriptions for all staff members and provide regular performance planning and appraisals.

RPS must have a system for regular staff evaluation and must provide access to continuing education and professional development opportunities, including in-service training programs and participation in professional conferences and workshops.

Because the office often involves routine and repetitive work, special attention should be given to the accuracy of all work.

Part 6. FINANCIAL RESOURCES

Registrar Programs and Services (RPS) must have adequate funding to accomplish its mission and goals. Funding priorities must be determined within the context of the stated mission, goals, objectives, and comprehensive analysis of the needs and capabilities of students, and the availability of internal or external resources.

RPS must demonstrate fiscal responsibility and cost effectiveness consistent with institutional protocols.

The registrar should have a clear understanding of the office's mission, sources of funding, and the budgeting process used by the institution.

Funds should be provided for salaries and benefits of staff and temporary or part time workers; professional development and staff training; office furnishings; communications and data processing equipment and software; postage, printing, and office supplies; subscriptions to professional and technical publications; membership in appropriate professional organizations; attendance at professional meetings, conferences, and workshops; special projects; and unexpected emergencies.

Part 7. FACILITIES, TECHNOLOGY, and EQUIPMENT

Registrar Programs and Services (RPS) must have adequate, suitably located facilities, adequate technology, and equipment to support its mission and goals efficiently and effectively. Facilities, technology, and equipment must be evaluated regularly and be in compliance with relevant federal, state, provincial, and local requirements to provide for access, health, safety, and security.

The design of the office must guarantee the security of the records and ensure the confidentiality of all sensitive information. The location and layout of the office must be sensitive to the special needs of students with disabilities as well as the needs of the general student population.

Facilities which produce a comfortable, functional, and pleasant work environment encourage staff members to be more productive. The administrative staff members should have private space in which to conduct their business. The offices should be equipped and furnished to support activities. All other employees should have work stations which are well equipped, adequate in size, as private as possible, and appropriately designed for their work.

Offices should be well-lighted, properly ventilated, and heated or cooled to acceptable standards. Adequate space should be allocated for the secure storage of student records and supplies. Space should be provided for meetings with students, conferring with staff, and completing special projects. Ideally a comfortable area within the office or nearby should be available for staff breaks and lunches.

When the registrar is responsible for determining facilities usage outside the immediate office, policies and procedures must be developed and disseminated with respect to the assignment of such space.

Backup copies of important documentation such as transcripts and the student data base must be stored off site in the event of a natural disaster or damage to the records.

Part 8. LEGAL RESPONSIBILITIES

Registrar Programs and Services (RPS) staff members must be knowledgeable about and responsive to laws and regulations that relate to their respective responsibilities. Staff members must inform users of programs and services and officials, as appropriate, of legal obligations and limitations including constitutional, statutory, regulatory, and case law; mandatory laws and orders emanating from federal, state/provincial and local governments; and the institution's policies.

RPS staff members must use reasonable and informed practices to limit the liability exposure of the institution, its officers, employees, and agents. Staff members must be informed about institutional policies regarding personal liability and related insurance coverage options.

The institution must provide access to legal advice for RPS staff members as needed to carry out assigned responsibilities.

The institution must inform RPS staff and students in a timely and systematic fashion about extraordinary or changing legal obligations and potential liabilities.

The registrar must ensure that the institution has written policies on all office transactions which may have legal implications.

The registrar must have procedures to keep staff members informed of all requirements related to the maintenance of academic records. Forms used to implement regulations must be developed and reviewed to assure fulfillment of all institutional requirements.

The registrar should meet with the institution's legal counsel periodically to review all relevant documents for clarity and to determine that current regulations are being followed. Some of the relevant areas that should be reviewed include affirmative action policies; certification of diplomas, degrees, and dates of attendance; court orders; academic and disciplinary dismissals; degree requirements; tuition, fees, and refund policies; fraudulent records; name changes; personnel issues; record keeping practices; residency status determination; requests for information from law enforcement agencies; security procedures; social security number usage; and subpoenas.

RPS must protect students' rights to privacy and access as defined in the legislative statute entitled Family Educational Rights and Privacy Act of 1974 (FERPA).

FERPA, commonly known as the Buckley Amendment, protects the privacy of student records by requiring:

- institutions to limit the disclosure of information from student records to third persons
- notification to students or their parents, if dependency has been established, of their right to review student educational records
- institutions to inform students of their right to seek correction of information contained in their educational records

Part 9. EQUITY and ACCESS

Registrar Programs and Services (RPS) staff members must ensure that services and programs are provided on a fair and equitable basis. Facilities, programs and services must be accessible. Hours of operation and delivery of and access to programs and services must be responsive to the needs of all students and other constituents. RPS must adhere to the spirit and intent of equal opportunity laws.

RPS must be open and readily accessible to all students and must not discriminate except where sanctioned by law and institutional policy. Discrimination must be avoided on the bases of age; color; creed; cultural heritage; disability; ethnicity; gender identity; nationality; political affiliation; religious affiliation; sex; sexual orientation; or social, economic, marital, or veteran status.

Consistent with their mission and goals, RPS must take affirmative action to remedy significant imbalances in student participation and staffing patterns.

As the demographic profiles of campuses change and new instructional delivery methods are introduced, institutions must recognize the needs of students who participate in distance learning for access to programs and services offered on campus. Institutions must provide appropriate services in ways that are accessible to distance learners and assist them in identifying and gaining access to other appropriate services in their geographic region.

Part 10. CAMPUS and EXTERNAL RELATIONS

Registrar Programs and Services (RPS) must establish, maintain, and promote effective relations with relevant individuals, campus offices, and external agencies. RPS staff members must relate effectively with administrators, faculty, students, alumni, and the public.

Part 11. DIVERSITY

Within the context of each institution's unique mission, diversity enriches the community and enhances the collegiate experience for all; therefore, Registrar Programs and Services (RPS) must nurture environments where commonalties and differences among people are recognized and honored.

RPS must promote educational experiences that are characterized by open and continuous communication that deepens understanding of one's own identity, culture, and heritage, and that of others. RPS must educate and promote respect about commonalties and differences in their historical and cultural contexts.

RPS must address the characteristics and needs of a diverse population when establishing and implementing policies and procedures.

Part 12. ETHICS

All persons involved in the delivery of Registrar Programs and Services (RPS) must adhere to the highest principles of ethical behavior. RPS must develop or adopt and implement appropriate statements of ethical practice. RPS must publish these statements and ensure their periodic review by relevant constituencies.

Standards of ethical practice that address the unique problems of managing the day to day maintenance of records and registration processes must be published. These standards must be made a part of the orientation program for each new employee and be routinely reviewed and updated.

Ethical standards statements previously used by the profession at large or relevant professional associations should be reviewed in the formulation of institutional standards.

RPS staff members must ensure that privacy and confidentiality are maintained with respect to all communications and records to the extent that such records are protected under the law and appropriate statements of ethical practice. Information contained in students' education records must not be disclosed without written consent except as allowed by relevant laws and institutional policies. Staff members must disclose to appropriate authorities information judged to be of an emergency nature, especially when the safety of the individual or others is involved, or when otherwise required by institutional policy or relevant law.

The institutional responsibilities of the registrar and records personnel in keeping and releasing student information demands conduct that consistently reflects fairness, common sense, honesty, and respect for the dignity of all persons.

RPS must ensure the institution has a written policy and published statement regarding confidentiality of records and procedures for access, release, and challenge of educational records. The same basic principles of confidentiality must govern electronic data as well as paper documents.

All RPS staff members must be aware of and comply with the provisions contained in the institution's human subjects research policy and in other relevant institutional policies addressing ethical practices and confidentiality of research data concerning individuals.

RPS staff members must recognize and avoid personal conflict of interest or appearance thereof in their transactions with students and others.

RPS staff members must strive to insure the fair, objective, and impartial treatment of all persons with whom they deal. Staff members must not participate in nor condone any form of harassment that demeans persons or creates an intimidating, hostile, or offensive campus environment.

When handling institutional funds, all RPS staff members must ensure that such funds are managed in accordance with established and responsible accounting procedures and the fiscal policies or processes of the institution.

RPS staff members must perform their duties within the limits of their training, expertise, and competence. When these limits are exceeded, individuals in need of further assistance must be referred to persons possessing appropriate qualifications.

RPS staff members must use suitable means to confront and otherwise hold accountable other staff members who exhibit unethical behavior.

The registrar should promote ethical awareness in the academic community as well as within the registrar's office. This can best be accomplished by developing a broad conceptual understanding of higher education, acquiring knowledge of the philosophy and values in the design and application of policies and practices, and implementing the philosophy and values developed for the registrar's office.

RPS staff members must be knowledgeable about and practice ethical behavior in the use of technology.

Part 13. ASSESSMENT and EVALUATION
Registrar Programs and Services (RPS) must conduct regular assessment and evaluations. RPS must employ effective qualitative and quantitative methodologies as appropriate, to determine whether and to what degree the stated mission, goals, and student learning and development outcomes are being met. The process must employ sufficient and sound assessment measures to ensure comprehensiveness. Data collected must include responses from students and other affected constituencies.

RPS must evaluate periodically how well they complement and enhance the institution's stated mission and educational effectiveness.

The evaluation of the operations of the registrar's office may be external or internal. In either case, the registrar's office should have a mechanism in effect that systematically reviews all of its activities and policies. As technology, laws, and regulations change, new activities or policies may need to be implemented. When developing new programs or activities, an evaluation should be a part of the plan to ensure effectiveness, efficiency, and/or appropriateness for future use.

Periodically, the entire office should undertake an extensive self-audit to determine if current activities and policies follow the standards in the profession. The registrar should continuously evaluate the activities of the office to determine if the services meet the needs of its constituents and continue to parallel the mission of the institution.

Results of these evaluations must be used in revising and improving programs and services and in recognizing staff performance.

General Standards revised in 2002; RPS content developed/ revised in 1995

THE ROLE of SERVICE-LEARNING PROGRAMS
CAS Standards Contextual Statement

Service-learning enables colleges and universities to meet their goals for student learning and development while making unique contributions to addressing community, national, and global needs.

Both college students and the communities they serve stand to reap substantial benefits from engaging in service-learning. Among frequently cited benefits to student participants are developing the habit of critical reflection; deepening comprehension of course content; integrating theory with practice; increasing understanding of the issues underlying social problems; strengthening sense of social responsibility; enhancing cognitive, personal, and spiritual development; heightening understanding of human difference and commonality; and sharpening abilities to solve problems creatively and to work collaboratively.

Community benefits include new energy and assistance to broaden delivery of existing services or to begin new ones; fresh approaches to solving problems; access to resources; and opportunities to participate in teaching and learning. Through improved town-gown relationships, colleges and universities also gain additional new learning settings for students and new opportunities for faculty to orient research and teaching to meet human and community needs.

For the purpose of the CAS Standards for Service-Learning Programs, service-learning is defined as follows: "Service-learning is a form of experiential education in which students engage in activities that address human and community needs together with structured opportunities intentionally designed to promote student learning and development." The hyphen in service-learning is critical in that it symbolizes the symbiotic relationship between the service and the learning. The term community in the definition of service-learning refers to local neighborhoods, the state, the nation, and the world community. Service-learning enables all participants to define their needs and interests (Jacoby, 1996).

Reflection and reciprocity are fundamental concepts of service-learning. As a form of experiential education, service-learning is based on the pedagogical principle that learning and development do not necessarily occur as a result of experience itself. Rather, they occur as a result of reflection intentionally designed to foster learning and development. Service-learning programs emphasize various types of learning goals, including intellectual, civic, ethical, moral, cross-cultural, and spiritual. Programs may highlight different combinations of these goals. Service-learning programs are also explicitly structured to promote learning about the larger social issues behind the needs to which the service is responding. This learning includes a deeper understanding of the historical, sociological, cultural, economic, and political contexts of the needs or issues being addressed. Reflection can take many forms: individual and group, oral and written, directly related to discipline-based course material or not.

The other essential concept of service-learning is reciprocity between the server and the person or group being served. Service-learning avoids placing students into community settings based solely on desired student-learning outcomes and providing services that do not meet actual needs or that perpetuate a state of need, rather than seeking and addressing the causes of need. Through reciprocity, students develop a greater sense of belonging and responsibility as members of a larger community.

Service-learning thus stands in contrast to the traditional, one-way approach to service in which one person or group has resources that they share with a person or group that they assume lacks resources. Reciprocity also eschews the concept of service which is based on the idea that a more competent person comes to the aid of a less competent person. Service-learning encourages students to do things with others rather than for them. Everyone should expect to learn and change in the process.

Although service-learning that is embedded in the curriculum provides opportunities for faculty to enhance students' learning by integrating course content with practical experience in a structured manner intended to meet course objectives, powerful opportunities for student learning and development also occur outside the classroom. Student affairs professionals can and do involve students in co-curricular service-learning programs that contribute to their learning and development. While service-learning that is connected to faculty research and community involvement can lead to more broad-based and long-term community enhancement, shorter-term service projects also make considerable contributions to communities in both direct and indirect ways. Even one-time experiences that address community needs and that are designed to achieve specific student learning and development outcomes can appropriately be called service-learning.

References, Readings, and Resources

Campus Compact: www.compact.org.

Eyler, J., and Giles, D. (1999). Where's the learning in service-learning? San Francisco: Jossey-Bass.

Howard, J. (Ed.). (Summer 2001). Service-learning course design workbook. Ann Arbor, MI: University of Michigan.

Jacoby, B. (Ed.) (2003). Building partnerships for service-learning. San Francisco: Jossey-Bass.

Jacoby, B. (Ed.). (1996). Service-learning in higher education: Concepts and practices. San Francisco: Jossey-Bass.

Kendall, J. (Ed.) (1990). Combining service and learning: A resource book for community and public service, Vol. 1. Raleigh, NC: National Society for Experiential Education.

Michigan Journal of Community Service Learning, www.umich.edu/~ocsl/MJCSL.

National Service-Learning Clearinghouse, www.servicelearning.org.

Porter Honnet, E., and Poulsen, S.J. (1989). Principles of good practice for combining service and learning. Racine, WI.: Johnson Foundation.

Contributor: Barbara Jacoby, University of Maryland, NCCP

SERVICE-LEARNING PROGRAMS
CAS Standards and Guidelines

Part 1. MISSION

The primary mission of Service-Learning Programs (S-LP) is to engage students in experiences that address human and community needs together with structured opportunities for reflection intentionally designed to promote student learning and development.

S-LP must incorporate student learning and student development in their missions. In addition, S-LP must enhance the overall educational experience. S-LP must develop, record, disseminate, implement, and regularly review their missions and goals. Mission statements must be consistent with the mission and goals of the institution and with the standards in this document. S-LP must operate as integral parts of the institution's overall mission.

Part 2. PROGRAM

The formal education of students consists of the curriculum and the co-curriculum, and must promote student learning and student development that is purposeful and holistic. Service-Learning Programs (S-LP) must be integrated into and enhance both the academic curriculum and co-curricular programs. S-LP must identify relevant and desirable student learning and development outcomes and provide programs and services that encourage the achievement of those outcomes.

S-LP must:

- allow all participants to define their needs and interests
- engage students in responsible and purposeful actions to meet community-defined needs
- enable students to understand needs in the context of community assets
- articulate clear service and learning goals for everyone involved, including students, faculty and staff members, community agency personnel, and those being served;
- ensure intellectual rigor
- establish criteria for selecting community service sites to ensure productive learning opportunities for everyone involved
- educate students regarding the philosophy of service and learning, the particular community service site, the work they will do, and the people they will be serving in the community
- establish and implement risk management procedures to protect students, the institution, and the community agencies

- offer alternatives to ensure that students are not required to participate in service that violates a religious or moral belief
- engage students in reflection designed to enable them to deepen their understanding of themselves, the community, and the complexity of social problems and potential solutions
- educate students to differentiate between perpetuating dependence and building capacity within the community
- establish mechanisms to assess service and learning outcomes for students and communities
- provide on-going professional development and support to faculty and staff members

When course credit is offered for service-learning, the credit must be for learning, not only for service. Whether service-learning is for academic credit or not, the focus must be on learning and educational objectives, not on hours served.

S-LP must provide evidence of their impact on the achievement of student learning and development outcomes.

Relevant and desirable outcomes include: intellectual growth; effective communication; realistic self-appraisal; enhanced self-esteem; clarified values; professional choices; leadership development; healthy behaviors; civic values, knowledge, and skills; meaningful interpersonal relationships; independence; collaboration; social responsibility; satisfying and productive lifestyles; appreciation of diversity; spiritual awareness; and achievement of personal and educational goals.

The table below offers examples of evidence of achievement of student learning and development.

Student Learning and Development Outcome Domains

Intellectual growth
Examples of achievement indicators

Produces personal and educational goal statements; Employs critical thinking in problem solving; Uses complex information from a variety of sources including personal experience and observation to form a decision or opinion; Earns a degree; Applies previously understood information and concepts to a new situation or setting; Expresses appreciation for literature, the fine arts, mathematics, sciences, and social sciences; Applies knowledge to local, national, and global social issues

Effective communication

Examples of achievement indicators

Writes and speaks coherently and effectively; Listens effectively and can engage in controversy with civility; Writes and speaks after reflection; Able to influence others through writing, speaking or artistic expression; Effectively articulates abstract ideas; Uses appropriate syntax; Makes presentations or gives performances

Enhanced self-esteem

Examples of achievement indicators

Shows self-respect and respect for others; Initiates actions toward achievement of goals; Takes reasonable risks; Demonstrates assertive behavior; Functions without need for constant reassurance from others

Realistic self-appraisal

Examples of achievement indicators

Articulates personal skills and abilities; Makes decisions and acts in congruence with personal values; Acknowledges personal strengths and weaknesses; Articulates rationale for personal behavior; Seeks feedback from others; Learns from past experiences

Clarified values

Examples of achievement indicators

Articulates personal values; Acts in congruence with personal values; Makes decisions that reflect personal values; Demonstrates willingness to scrutinize personal beliefs and values; Identifies personal, work, and lifestyle values and explains how they influence decision-making

Career choices

Examples of achievement indicators

Articulates career choices based on assessment of interests, values, skills, and abilities; Documents knowledge, skills, and accomplishments resulting from formal education, work experience, service-learning, and volunteer experiences; Makes the connections between classroom and community-based learning; Can construct a resume with clear job objectives and evidence of related knowledge, skills, and accomplishments; Articulates the characteristics of a preferred work environment; Comprehends the world of work

Leadership development

Examples of achievement indicators

Understands that leadership is a process rather than a position; Views all students as potential leaders; comprehends that leadership occurs at all levels of an

organization; Articulates leadership philosophy or style in examining own leadership

Healthy behavior

Examples of achievement indicators

Chooses behaviors and environments that promote health and reduce risk; Articulates the relationship between health and wellness and accomplishing life-long goals; Exhibits behaviors that advance a healthy community

Meaningful interpersonal relationships

Examples of achievement indicators

Develops and maintains satisfying interpersonal relationships; Establishes mutually rewarding relationships with friends and colleagues; Listens to and considers others' points of view; Treats others with respect

Independence

Examples of achievement indicators

Exhibits self-reliant behaviors; Functions autonomously; Exhibits ability to function interdependently; Accepts supervision as needed; Manages time effectively

Collaboration

Examples of achievement indicators

Works cooperatively with others; Seeks the involvement of others; Seeks feedback from others; Contributes to achievement of a group goal; Exhibits effective listening skills

Social responsibility

Examples of achievement indicators

Understands and participates in relevant governance systems; Demonstrates civic engagement in campus, local, national, and global communities; Understands, abides by, and participates in the development, maintenance, and/or orderly change of community, social, and legal standards or norms; Appropriately challenges the unfair, unjust, or uncivil behavior of other individuals or groups; Participates in service-learning activities

Satisfying and productive lifestyles

Examples of achievement indicators

Achieves balance between education, work, and leisure time; Articulates and meets goals for work, leisure, and education; Overcomes obstacles that hamper goal achievement; Functions on the basis of personal identity, ethical, spiritual, and moral values; Articulates long-term goals and objectives

Appreciating diversity

Examples of achievement indicators

Understands one's own identity and culture; Seeks involvement with people different from oneself; Seeks involvement in diverse interests; Articulates the advantages

304

and challenges of a diverse society; Challenges appropriately the abusive use of stereotypes by others; Understands the impact of diversity on one's own society; Develops an informed perspective on issues of diversity and democracy; Reflects on issues of power and privilege

Spiritual awareness

Examples of achievement indicators

Develops and articulates personal belief system; Understands roles of spirituality in personal and group values and behaviors

Personal and educational goals

Examples of achievement indicators

Sets, articulates, and pursues individual goals; Articulates personal and educational goals and objectives; Uses personal and educational goals to guide decisions; Understands the effect of one's personal and educational goals on others

S-LP must be (a) intentional, (b) coherent, (c) based on theories and knowledge of learning and human development, (d) reflective of developmental and demographic profiles of the student population, and (e) responsive to needs of individuals, special populations, and communities.

S-LP must offer a wide range of curricular and co-curricular service-learning experiences appropriate for students at all developmental levels and with a variety of lifestyles and abilities.

Examples may include older students, commuter students, students who are parents, part-time students, fully employed students, and students with disabilities.

S-LP must initiate and maintain collaborative relations among faculty members and departments within the institution for the design and implementation of service-learning experiences. They must also develop partnerships with community-based organizations to meet organizations' service needs and to achieve student learning and development outcomes.

Service-learning experiences should include:
- *One-time and short-term experiences.* These can be designed to achieve a variety of student learning outcomes, including introducing students to service-learning as a critical aspect of their college education, enabling students to learn what types of service best

suit their interests, familiarizing students with the community in which the institution is located, and understanding the approaches different agencies take to address community problems. These experiences can be co-curricular or part of the academic curriculum, such as first-year seminars.

- *Discipline-based service-learning courses.* Such courses can be designed to enable students to deepen their understanding of course content, apply knowledge to practice, and test theory through practical application. These courses can be designed for students at all levels. Service-learning internships and capstone courses can provide opportunities for students to consider how disciplinary knowledge can be applied in a socially responsible manner in professional settings.

- *Community-based research.* Whether integrated into a course or done on an independent-study basis, students engage in community-based research work with faculty and community partners to design, conduct, analyze, and report research results to serve community purposes.

- *Intensive service-learning experiences.* Service-learning experiences can immerse students intensively in an unfamiliar setting or culture, whether domestically or abroad. They can engage in dialogue and problem solving with the people most affected by the issues and develop a sense of solidarity with people whose lives and perspectives differ from their own. These experiences vary in length from a one-week alternative break to a semester or a year.

The service-learning course syllabus or plan for co-curricular experiences should describe:
- needs that the service will address
- desired outcomes of the service and learning for all participants
- assignments that link service and academic content
- opportunities to reflect on one's personal reactions to service and learning experiences
- logistics (e.g., time required, transportation, materials required)
- nature of the service work
- roles and responsibilities of students and community members
- risk management procedures
- evaluation of the service and learning experiences and assessment of the degree to which desired outcomes were achieved

S-LP should foster student leadership through service-learning experiences and should encourage student-initiated and student-led service and learning.

Part 3. LEADERSHIP

Effective and ethical leadership is essential to the success of all organizations. Institutions must appoint, position, and empower Service-Learning Programs (S-LP) leaders within the administrative structure to accomplish stated missions. S-LP leaders at various levels must be selected on the basis of formal education and training, relevant work experience, personal skills and competencies, relevant professional credentials, as well as potential for promoting learning and development in students, applying effective practices to educational processes, and enhancing institutional effectiveness. Institutions must determine expectations of accountability for leaders and fairly assess their performance.

S-LP leaders must exercise authority over resources for which they are responsible to achieve their respective missions.

S-LP leaders must:
- articulate a vision for their organization
- set goals and objectives based on the needs and capabilities of the population served
- promote student learning and development
- prescribe and practice ethical behavior
- recruit, select, supervise, and develop others in the organization
- manage financial resources
- coordinate human resources
- plan, budget for, and evaluate personnel and programs
- apply effective practices to educational and administrative processes
- communicate effectively
- initiate collaborative interaction between individuals and agencies that possess legitimate concerns and interests in the functional area

S-LP leaders must identify and find means to address individual, organizational, or environmental conditions that inhibit goal achievement.

S-LP leaders must promote campus environments that result in multiple opportunities for student learning and development.

S-LP leaders must continuously keep up to date with best practices and improve programs and services in response to changing needs of students and other constituents, and evolving national and institutional priorities.

Part 4. ORGANIZATION and MANAGEMENT

Guided by an overarching intent to ensure student learning and development, Service-Learning Programs (S-LP) must be structured purposefully and managed effectively to achieve stated goals. Evidence of appropriate structure must include current and accessible policies and procedures, written performance expectations for all employees, functional workflow graphics or organizational charts, and clearly stated service delivery expectations.

Evidence of effective management must include use of comprehensive and accurate information for decisions, clear sources and channels of authority, effective communication practices, decision-making and conflict resolution procedures, responsiveness to changing conditions, accountability and evaluation systems, and recognition and reward processes. Programs and services must provide channels within the organization for regular review of administrative policies and procedures.

Part 5. HUMAN RESOURCES

Service-Learning Programs (S-LP) must be staffed adequately by professionals qualified to accomplish the mission and goals or by faculty whose responsibilities include service-learning. Within established guidelines of the institution, S-LP must establish procedures for staff selection, training, and evaluation; set expectations for supervision, and provide appropriate professional development opportunities. The program and service must strive to improve the professional competence and skills of all personnel it employs.

S-LP professionals must hold an earned graduate degree in a field relevant to the position they hold or must possess an appropriate combination of educational credentials and related work experience.

Professional development of staff and faculty members engaged in service-learning programs should address how to:
- build relationships with community agencies
- establish and maintain collaborative relationships with campus units
- engage students in community action for the common good
- prepare, mentor, and monitor students to deliver services according to legal and risk management policies
- use learning strategies that are effective in achieving learning outcomes
- engage students in structured opportunities for reflection
- develop, implement, and evaluate service and learning goals

- facilitate the process of identifying student and community needs and interests
- clarify the responsibilities of students, the institution, and agencies
- match the unique needs of agencies and students
- sustain genuine and active commitment of students, the institution, and agencies
- educate, train, and support students to facilitate service-learning experiences for their peers
- ensure that the time-commitment for service and learning are balanced and appropriate
- foster participation by and with diverse populations
- develop fiscal and other resources for program support

Faculty and staff members who integrate service-learning into their courses should receive institutional support (e.g., reduced course load, mini-grants, or teaching assistants.)

SL-P staff should provide professional development for community partners regarding how to work effectively with students, faculty members, and staff in higher education institutions.

Degree or credential-seeking interns must be qualified by enrollment in an appropriate field of study and by relevant experience. These individuals must be trained and supervised adequately by S-LP professional staff members holding educational credentials and related work experience appropriate for supervision.

Student employees and volunteers must be carefully selected, trained, supervised, and evaluated. They must be trained on how and when to refer those in need of assistance to qualified S-LP staff members and have access to a supervisor for assistance in making these judgments. Student employees and volunteers must be provided clear and precise job descriptions, pre-service training based on assessed needs, and continuing staff development.

S-LP must have technical and support staff members adequate to accomplish its mission. S-LP staff members must be technologically proficient and qualified to perform their job functions, be knowledgeable of ethical and legal uses of technology, and have access to training. The level of staffing and workloads must be adequate and appropriate for program and service demands.

Salary levels and fringe benefits for all S-LP staff members must be commensurate with those for comparable positions within the institution, in similar institutions, and in the relevant geographic area.

S-LP must institute hiring and promotion practices that are fair, inclusive, and non-discriminatory. S-LP must employ a diverse staff to provide readily identifiable role models for students and to enrich the campus community.

S-LP must create and maintain position descriptions for all staff members and provide regular performance planning and appraisals.

S-LP must have a system for regular staff evaluation and must provide access to continuing education and professional development opportunities, including in-service training programs and participation in professional conferences and workshops.

Part 6. FINANCIAL RESOURCES

Service-Learning Programs (S-LP) must have adequate funding to accomplish mission and goals. Funding priorities must be determined within the context of the stated mission, goals, objectives, and comprehensive analysis of the needs and capabilities of students and the availability of internal or external resources.

S-LP must demonstrate fiscal responsibility and cost effectiveness consistent with institutional protocols.

Part 7. FACILITIES, TECHNOLOGY, and EQUIPMENT

Service-Learning Programs (S-LP) must have adequate, suitably located facilities, adequate technology, and equipment to support its mission and goals efficiently and effectively. Facilities, technology, and equipment must be evaluated regularly and be in compliance with relevant federal, state, provincial, and local requirements to provide for access, health, safety, and security.

Part 8. LEGAL RESPONSIBILITIES

All faculty and staff members engaged in service-learning must be knowledgeable about and responsive to laws and regulations that relate to their respective responsibilities.

Service-Learning Programs (S-LP) staff members must inform users of programs and services and officials, as appropriate, of legal obligations and limitations including constitutional, statutory, regulatory, and case law; mandatory laws and orders emanating from federal, state/provincial and local governments; and the institution's policies.

All faculty and staff members engaged in service-learning must use reasonable and informed practices to limit the liability exposure of the institution, its

officers, employees, and agents. All faculty and staff members engaged in service-learning must be informed about institutional and community organization policies regarding personal liability and related insurance coverage options.

The institution must provide access to legal advice for all faculty and staff members engaged in service-learning as needed to carry out assigned responsibilities.

The institution must inform all faculty and staff members and students engaged in service-learning about extraordinary or changing legal obligations and potential liabilities in a timely and systematic fashion.

Part 9. EQUITY and ACCESS

Service-Learning Program (S-LP) staff members must ensure that services and programs are provided on a fair and equitable basis. Facilities, programs, and services must be accessible. Hours of operation and delivery of and access to programs and services must be responsive to the needs of all students and other constituents. S-LP must adhere to the spirit and intent of equal opportunity laws.

S-LP must be open and readily accessible to all students and must not discriminate except where sanctioned by law and institutional policy. Discrimination must be avoided on the bases of age; color; creed; cultural heritage; disability; ethnicity; gender identity; nationality; political affiliation; religious affiliation; sex; sexual orientation; or social, economic, marital, or veteran status.

Consistent with their mission and goals, S-LP must take affirmative action to remedy significant imbalances in student participation and staffing patterns.

As the demographic profiles of campuses change and new instructional delivery methods are introduced, institutions must recognize the needs of students who participate in distance learning for access to programs and services offered on campus. Institutions must provide appropriate services in ways that are accessible to distance learners and assist them in identifying and gaining access to other appropriate services in their geographic region.

Part 10: CAMPUS AND EXTERNAL RELATIONS

Service-Learning Programs (S-LP) must establish, maintain, and promote effective relations with relevant individuals, campus offices, and external agencies.

If there is more than one campus unit that facilitates community service and service-learning experiences, those offices should share information and collaborate as appropriate.

S-LP should develop productive working relationships with a wide range of campus agencies, including risk management, transportation, health services, academic departments and colleges, leadership programs, orientation, student activities, and institutional relationships and development.

Service-learning flourishes best when the institution as a whole is engaged as a responsible citizen in its surrounding communities. S-LP professionals should advocate for the institution to share its resources with its community and to develop a wide range of mutually beneficial campus-community partnerships.

Part 11. DIVERSITY

Within the context of each institution's unique mission, diversity enriches the community and enhances the collegiate experience for all; therefore, Service-Learning Programs (S-LP) must nurture environments where commonalties and differences among people are recognized and honored.

S-LP must promote educational experiences that are characterized by open and continuous communication that deepens understanding of one's own identity, culture, and spirituality, and that of others. S-LP must educate and promote respect about commonalties and differences in their historical and cultural contexts.

S-LP must address the characteristics and needs of a diverse population when establishing and implementing policies and procedures.

Part 12. ETHICS

All persons involved in the delivery of Service-Learning Programs (S-LP) must adhere to the highest principles of ethical behavior. S-LP must develop or adopt and implement appropriate statements of ethical practice. S-LP must publish these statements and ensure their periodic review by relevant constituencies.

The faculty members, staff, and students involved in service-learning must be held to the same ethical standards as the SL-P staff members.

S-LP staff members must ensure that privacy and confidentiality are maintained with respect to all communications and records to the extent that such records are protected under the law and appropriate statements of ethical practice. Information contained in students' education records must not be disclosed without written consent except as allowed by relevant laws and institutional policies. S-LP staff members must disclose to appropriate authorities information judged to be of an emergency nature, especially when the safety of the individual or others is involved, or when otherwise required by institutional policy or relevant law.

All S-LP staff members must be aware of and comply with the provisions contained in the institution's human subjects research policy and in other relevant institutional policies addressing ethical practices and confidentiality of research data concerning individuals.

S-LP staff members must recognize and avoid personal conflict of interest or appearance thereof in their transactions with students and others.

S-LP staff members must strive to insure the fair, objective, and impartial treatment of all persons with whom they deal. S-LP staff members must not participate in nor condone any form of harassment that demeans persons or creates an intimidating, hostile, or offensive campus environment.

When handling institutional funds, all S-LP staff members must ensure that such funds are managed in accordance with established and responsible accounting procedures and the fiscal policies or processes of the institution.

S-LP staff members must perform their duties within the limits of their training, expertise, and competence. When these limits are exceeded, individuals in need of further assistance must be referred to persons possessing appropriate qualifications.

All faculty and staff members responsible for supervising service-learning activities must monitor student performance based on training expertise and competence and alter placements as needed.

S-LP staff members must use suitable means to confront and otherwise hold accountable other staff members who exhibit unethical behavior.

S-LP staff members must be knowledgeable about and practice ethical behavior in the use of technology.

Part 13: ASSESSMENT AND EVALUATION

Service-Learning Programs (S-LP) must conduct regular assessment and evaluations. S-LP must employ effective qualitative and quantitative methodologies as appropriate, to determine whether and to what degree the stated mission, goals, and student learning and development outcomes are being met as well as effectiveness of service to the community. The process must employ sufficient and sound assessment measures to ensure comprehensiveness. Data collected must include responses from students, agencies, and other affected constituencies.

S-LP must evaluate periodically how well programs complement and enhance the institution's stated mission and educational effectiveness and meets goals of the community organization and its clients.

Results of these evaluations must be used in revising and improving S-LP and in recognizing staff performance.

S-LP standards were developed in 2005

THE ROLE of STUDENT CONDUCT PROGRAMS
CAS Standards Contextual Statement

Throughout the history of American higher education, colleges have struggled with how to respond to student misconduct. In his letter to Thomas Cooper on November 2, 1822, Thomas Jefferson described the problem of student discipline as "a breaker ahead" which he was not sure that American higher education could weather. In recent years, issues related to student discipline, including sexual assault, use and abuse of alcohol and other drugs, and campus safety have come to the forefront.

Traditionally, the courts viewed the administration of student discipline as an internal institutional matter and did not become actively involved in the process through judicial rulings. However, this position changed in 1961, with the landmark case of *Dixon v. Alabama State Board of Education*, 294 F.2d 150 (5th Cir. 1961), the first of an ever-growing modern body of case law related to the administration of student discipline. The courts have held under the 14th Amendment to the Constitution that public colleges and universities must afford basic due process rights to students accused of violating student conduct codes. However, it is important to note that the rights of due process described in this body of case law differ significantly from those observed in the criminal court system. The limitations placed upon private institutions are substantially less prescriptive. Although the Constitutional rights afforded to students at public institutions are not generally applicable to private institutions, several authors, including Kaplin and Lee (1995), Stoner and Cerminara (1990), and Stoner and Lowery (2004) have encouraged private institutions to bear in mind the restrictions placed upon public institutions and accord their students the same general rights and protections.

In the early American colleges and universities, student discipline was primarily the responsibility of the faculty. As the positions of dean of men and women were established and the field of student affairs evolved, the responsibility for the administration of student discipline shifted. Barry and Wolf (1957) observed, "Despite all of their later disclaimers, most deans of men seem to have been appointed primarily to act as disciplinarians" (p.14). Only in the past twenty-five years has student discipline emerged as a distinct functional area within student affairs. Prior to that time, the responsibility for student discipline was one of a number of duties which fell to an individual or office such as the dean of men or the dean of women and later the dean of students.

In the early 1970s, the American College Personnel Association established Commission XV, Campus Judicial Affairs and Legal Issues, to meet the needs of this emerging profession. In 1988, the Association for Student Judicial Affairs (ASJA) was founded to facilitate the integration of student development concepts with principles of student conduct practice in post-secondary education and to promote, encourage, and support student development professionals responsible for judicial affairs.

ASJA now has a membership of over 1,200 and sponsors conferences attended by more than 600 professionals annually. It also sponsors a summer training institute for campus judicial affairs which began 1993.

Over the past fifteen years, the practice of student judicial affairs has been profoundly affected by the passage of federal legislation. While the Family Educational Rights and Privacy Act of 1974 (FERPA) had implications for judicial affairs, the legislation passed more recently has differed significantly in that it directly targeted aspects of the campus judicial system. For example, the amendments to the Student Right-to-Know and Campus Security Act included in the Higher Education Amendments of 1998 require colleges and universities to include statistics for liquor law violations, drug law, and weapons law violations addressed through the student conduct system. The Higher Education Amendments of 1998 also amended FERPA to allow the release for the final results of a campus disciplinary proceeding when a student is found responsible of a crime of violence or nonforcible sexual offense and to allow parental notification when the institution determined that a student under the age of 21 had violated alcohol or drug policies. In the years between the reauthorization, several pieces of legislation impacting student conduct programs were being introduced into Congress annually as well. This increased governmental involvement demands that student judicial affairs professionals remain knowledgeable about legislative developments and actively work to address legislative proposals which would detrimentally impact the fundamental educational mission of the student conduct system.

The Association for Student Judicial Affairs established three principles for the administration of student conduct programs:

- The development and enforcement of standards of conduct for students is an educational endeavor which fosters students' personal and social development; students must assume a significant role in developing and enforcing such regulations in order that they might be better prepared for the responsibilities of citizenship.

- Standards of conduct form the basis for behavioral expectations in the academic community; the enforcement of such standards must protect the rights, health, and safety of members of that community in order that they may pursue their educational goals without undue interference.

- Integrity, wisdom, and empathy are among the characteristics most important to the administration of student conduct standards; officials who have such responsibilities must exercise them impartially and fairly.

The primary role of student conduct staff members is that of educator. The *ASJA Statement of Ethical Principles and Standards of Conduct* identifies the maintenance and enhancement of the ethical climate on campus and the promotion of academic integrity as the primary purposes for enforcing standards of student conduct. This document further states, "Clearly articulated and consistently administered standards of conduct form the basis for behavioral expectations within an academic community. These standards of conduct for students should be enforced in such manner as to protect the rights, health, and safety of the entire community. "

The student conduct programs standards and guidelines that follow represent the fundamental criteria by which programs can assess their quality and effectiveness.

References, Readings, and Resources

Dannells, M. (1997). *From discipline to development: Rethinking student conduct in higher education.* ASHE-ERIC Higher Education Report Vol. 25, No. 2. Washington, DC: The George Washington University, Graduate School of Education and Human Development.

Dixon v. Alabama State Board of Education, 294 F.2d 150 (5th Cir. 1961).

Hoekema, D. A. (1994). *Campus rules and moral community: In place of in loco parentis.* Lanham, MD: Rowman & Littlefield.

Kaplin, W. A., & Lee, B. (1995). *The law of higher education* (3rd ed.). San Francisco: Jossey-Bass.

Mercer, W. L. (Ed.). (1996). *Critical issues in judicial affairs: Current trends in practice.* San Francisco: Jossey-Bass.

Paterson, G. P., & Kibler, W. L. (Eds.). (1999). *The administration of student discipline: Student, organizational, and community issues.* Asheville, NC: College Administration Publications.

Stoner, E. N., II, & Cerminara, K. L. (1990). Harnessing the "spirit of insubordination": A model student disciplinary code. *Journal of College and University Law, 17,* 89-121.

Stoner, E. N., II, & Lowery, J. W. (2004). Navigating past the "spirit of insubordination": A twenty-first century model student conduct code with a model hearing script. *Journal of College and University Law, 31,* 1-77.

American College Personnel Association Commission for Campus Judicial Affairs and Legal Issues. One Dupont Circle Suite 300 Washington, DC 20036; (202) 835-2272.

Association for Student Judicial Affairs: P.O. Box 2237, College Station, TX 77841-2237; 979-845-5262; Web Page: http://asja.tamu.edu/

Contributors: John Wesley Lowrey, Oklahoma State University, ASJA

STUDENT CONDUCT PROGRAMS
CAS Standards and Guidelines

Part 1. MISSION

Student Conduct Programs (SCP) develop and enforce standards of conduct, an educational endeavor to foster students' learning and development.

SCP must incorporate student learning and student development in its mission. SCP must enhance overall educational experiences. SCP must develop, record, disseminate, implement, and regularly review its mission and goals. Mission statements must be consistent with the mission and goals of the institution and with the standards in this document. SCP must operate as an integral part of the institution's overall mission.

The goals of SCP must address the institution's needs to:

- develop, disseminate, interpret, and enforce campus policies and procedures
- protect rights of students in the administration of the student conduct program
- respond to student behavioral problems in a fair and reasonable manner
- facilitate and encourage respect for and involvement in campus governance
- provide learning experiences for students who are found to be responsible for conduct which is determined to be in violation of institutional standards or who participate in the operations of the student conduct system
- initiate and encourage educational activities that serve to reduce violations of campus regulations

SCP should support appropriate individual and group behavior as well as serve the campus community by reducing disruption and harm. The programs should be conducted in ways that will serve to foster the ethical development and personal integrity of students and the promotion of an environment that is consistent with the overall educational goals of the institution.

Part 2. PROGRAM

The formal education of students consists of the curriculum and the co-curriculum, and must promote student learning and development that is purposeful and holistic. Student Conduct Programs (SCP) must identify relevant and desirable student learning and development outcomes and provide programs that encourage the achievement of those outcomes.

Relevant and desirable outcomes include: intellectual growth, effective communication, realistic self-appraisal, enhanced self-esteem, clarified values, career choices, leadership development, healthy behaviors, meaningful interpersonal relationships, independence, collaboration, social responsibility, satisfying and productive lifestyles, appreciation of diversity, spiritual awareness, and achievement of personal and educational goals.

SCP must provide evidence of its impact on the achievement of student learning and development outcomes.

The table below offers examples of evidence of achievement of student learning and development.

Student Learning and Development Outcome Domains

Intellectual growth
Examples of achievement indicators

Understands consequences of personal actions and purposes of institutional policies; Produces personal and educational goal statements; Employs critical thinking in problem solving; Uses complex information from a variety of sources including personal experience and observation to form a decision or opinion; Obtains a degree; Applies previously understood information and concepts to a new situation or setting; Appreciates literature, fine arts, mathematics, sciences, and social sciences

Clarified values
Examples of achievement indicators

Demonstrates ethical development; Complies with institutional policy; Commits no additional violations of institutional policy; Understands the institutional values reflected in instructional policies; Understands the effect of their behaviors on others; Understands the importance of personal and academic integrity; Articulates personal ethics and values; Acts in congruence with personal ethics and values; Makes decisions that reflect personal ethics and values; Demonstrates willingness to scrutinize personal beliefs, ethics, and values; Identifies personal, work, and lifestyle values and explains how they influence decision-making

Social responsibility
Examples of achievement indicators

Understands and participates in relevant governance systems; Understands, abides by, and participates in the development, maintenance, and orderly change of community, social, and legal standards or norms;

Appropriately challenges the unfair, unjust, or uncivil behavior of other individuals or groups; Participates in service/volunteer activities

Meaningful interpersonal relationships

Examples of achievement indicators

Practices effective conflict resolution; Deals appropriately with interpersonal conflict; Develops and maintains satisfying interpersonal relationships; Establishes mutually rewarding relationships with friends and colleagues; Listens to and considers others' points of view; Treats others with respect

Realistic self-appraisal

Examples of achievement indicators

Articulates personal skills and abilities; Makes decisions and acts in congruence with personal values; Acknowledges personal strengths and weaknesses; Articulates rationale for personal behavior; Seeks feedback from others; Learns from past experiences

Healthy behavior

Examples of achievement indicators

Chooses behaviors and environments that promote health and reduce risk; Articulates the relationship between health and wellness and accomplishing life-long goals; Exhibits behaviors that advance a healthy community

Enhanced self-esteem

Examples of achievement indicators

Shows self-respect and respect for others; Initiates actions toward achievement of goals; Takes reasonable risks; Demonstrates assertive behavior; Functions without need for constant reassurance from others

Effective communication

Examples of achievement indicators

Writes and speaks coherently and effectively; Writes and speaks after reflection; Able to influence others through writing, speaking or artistic expression; Effectively articulates abstract ideas; Uses appropriate syntax; Makes presentations or gives performances

Career choices

Examples of achievement indicators

Articulates career choices based on assessment of interests, values, skills and abilities; Documents knowledge, skills, and accomplishments resulting from formal education, work experience, community service, and volunteer experiences; Makes the connections between classroom and out-of-classroom learning; Can construct a resume with clear job objectives and evidence of related knowledge, skills, and accomplishments; Articulates the characteristics of a preferred work environment; Comprehends the world of work; Takes steps to initiate a job search or seek advanced education

Leadership development

Examples of achievement indicators

Articulates leadership philosophy or style; Serves in a leadership position in a student organization; Comprehends the dynamics of a group; Exhibits democratic principles as a leader; Exhibits ability to visualize a group purpose and desired outcomes

Independence

Examples of achievement indicators

Exhibits self-reliant behaviors; Functions autonomously; Exhibits ability to function interdependently; Accepts supervision as needed; Manages time effectively

Collaboration

Examples of achievement indicators

Works cooperatively with others; Seeks the involvement of others; Seeks feedback from others; Contributes to achievement of a group goal; Exhibits effective listening skills

Satisfying and productive lifestyles

Examples of achievement indicators

Achieves balance between education, work, and leisure time; Articulates and meets goals for work, leisure, and education; Overcomes obstacles that hamper goal achievement; Functions on the basis of personal identity, ethical, spiritual, and moral values; Articulates long-term goals and objectives

Appreciating diversity

Examples of achievement indicators

Understands one's own identity and culture; Understands the impact privilege and oppression have on individuals and society; Recognizes that oppression exists in our society; Understands the privileges of membership; Seeks involvement with people different from oneself; Seeks involvement in diverse interests; Articulates the advantages and challenges of a diverse society; Challenges appropriately the abusive use of stereotypes by others; Understands the impact of diversity on one's own society

Spiritual awareness

Examples of achievement indicators

Develops and articulates personal belief system; Understands roles of spirituality in personal and group values and behaviors

Personal and educational goals

Examples of achievement indicators

Sets, articulates, and pursues individual goals; Articulates personal and educational goals and objectives; Uses personal and educational goals to guide decisions; Understands the effect of one's personal and educational goals on others

SCP must be (a) intentional, (b) coherent, (c) based on theories and knowledge of learning and human development, (d) reflective of developmental and demographic profiles of the student population, and (e) responsive to needs of individuals, special populations, and communities.

SCP must establish the following within the context of its mission and purpose:

1. *Authority*
A written statement describing the authority, philosophy, jurisdiction, and procedures of the student conduct programs must be developed and disseminated to all members of the campus community.

This statement should address (a) how student academic or non-academic misconduct is within the program's jurisdiction, (b) which campus policies and regulations are enforced by these programs, (c) sanctions that may be imposed, (d) a clear description of the relationship between student conduct programs and both campus and external law enforcement agencies, including guidelines regarding when law enforcement authorities will be called in, (e) authority under the policy to address misconduct which occurs off campus including education abroad, and (f) information regarding the impact, if any, of decisions by the criminal courts on the outcome of corresponding student conduct proceedings.

2. *Components*
The institution's policies regarding the administration of student discipline must be clearly described in writing. Elements to be addressed in this policy must include: prohibited conduct; sanctions; boards and administrators with roles in the adjudication of student misconduct; procedures for the investigation and adjudication of allegations of student misconduct; appeal procedures (if provided); procedures for interim suspension (if provided); and policies regarding student disciplinary records.

Generally, the student conduct system should involve significant roles for students in the adjudication of allegations of misconduct; however, membership on boards need not be limited to students. The system should allow sufficient time for an investigation of all allegations prior to a hearing while responding to complaints in a timely fashion.

Procedures and processes must be designed to provide for substantive and procedural due process at public institutions of higher education and fundamental fairness at private institutions of higher education.

SCP should provide students with ample opportunity to receive advice about the process, a general time frame for resolution, and a delineation of individual responsibilities in the process.

Institutional disciplinary action against individual students or recognized student organizations must be administered in the context of a coordinated set of regulations and processes in order to ensure fair and reasonable outcomes and the equitable treatment of students and groups. Allegations of improper behavior originating from both instructional and non-instructional components of the institution must be encompassed in a comprehensive student conduct system for students.

Different procedures may be used to address the various forms of misconduct.

The institution must be clear about which board or individual has jurisdiction over specific conduct regulations.

Students should be assisted in understanding the sources and lines of authority.

The sanctions imposed as a result of institutional disciplinary action must be educationally and developmentally appropriate.

SCP must follow up on cases, including enforcement of sanctions, assessing the developmental processes that have been affected, and ensuring that students are directed to appropriate services for assistance.

The institution must be clear about how it defines student status and the jurisdiction of the system to include whether students can be held responsible for behavior that takes place off campus or between academic sessions.

SCP should maintain written records to serve as referral materials, to document precedents, to provide source material for identifying recurring problems, or to use for appeals.

The institution must clearly state the conduct regulations that apply to student organizations, the procedures that will be followed in the hearing of cases related to student organizations, and the guidelines used to determine if

actions of individual members or small groups within an organization constitute action by the organization.

3. *Information to Campus Community*
The institution must publish information about the SCP.

Publications should contain (a) campus policies, such as those concerning legal representation, the protection of privacy of student disciplinary records, and the destruction of disciplinary records; (b) campus procedures, such as filing a disciplinary action, gathering information, conducting a hearing, and notifying a student of the hearing or appeal board's decision; (c) the composition, authority, and jurisdiction of all student conduct bodies; (d) the types of advice and assistance that the complainant and others can receive about the process; (e) the types of disciplinary sanctions, including interim suspension procedures; and (f) a general explanation of how and when non-campus law enforcement officials are used.

Publications must be distributed through methods that will reach all students.

Dissemination methods may include electronic media; the institutional catalog; the orientation program; the student handbook; admissions, registration, and billing materials.

Published information should include not only descriptions about how the system works, but also the results of the system. By publishing the outcomes of student conduct cases in a manner which protects the privacy of those involved, the institution demonstrates that the system does work and encourages an open discussion of issues related to student conduct.

4. *Hearing Authority*
In addition to a hearing officer, SCP must include a hearing or appellate board composed of representatives of the campus community that is responsible for carrying out student conduct functions delegated by the administration.

Roles and functions of student conduct board members may include (a) reviewing disciplinary referrals and claims; (b) interpreting misconduct allegations and identifying specific charges to be brought against the student(s); (c) conducting preliminary hearings and gathering information pertinent to the charges; (d) advising students on their rights and responsibilities; (e) engaging in substantive discussions with students about relevant ethical issues; (f) scheduling, coordinating, and conducting hearings; (g) reviewing decisions from other hearing bodies, when applicable; (h) notifying the accused in writing about relevant decisions and the board's rationale for such; (i) maintaining accurate written records of the entire proceeding; (j) referring information to an appeal board when applicable; (k)

following up on sanctions to ensure they have been implemented; (1) following up with students who have been sanctioned to ensure awareness of available counseling services; (m) establishing and implementing a procedure for maintenance and destruction of disciplinary records; and (n) assessing student conduct procedures, policies, and outcomes.

A student conduct officer may be assigned responsibility for training student conduct board members, scheduling and facilitating evaluations, and informing faculty, administration, and staff about legal and disciplinary matters.

Student conduct board members should participate on campus government committees associated with student conduct, except when a conflict of interest will result. Student conduct board members may also be involved in the outreach efforts of the SCP.

5. *Training of Student Conduct Board Members*
Initial and in service training of all hearing board members must be provided.

In order for student conduct board members to fulfill their roles and functions, initial training should include (a) an overview of all judicial policies and procedures; (b) an explanation of the operation of the judicial process at all levels including authority and jurisdiction; (c) an overview of the institution's philosophy on student conduct and its role in this process; (d) roles and functions of all student conduct bodies and their members; (e) review of constitutional and other relevant legal individual and institutional rights and responsibilities; (f) an explanation of sanctions; (g) an explanation of pertinent ethics, including particularly the importance of privacy of student disciplinary records and addressing bias and conflict of interest in the student conduct process; (h) a description of available personal counseling programs and referral resources; (i) an outline of conditions and interactions which may involve external enforcement officials, attorneys, witnesses, parents of accused students, and the media; and (j) an overview of developmental and interpersonal issues likely to arise among college students.

In-service training should include participation in relevant and on-going workshops, seminars, and conferences. A library containing current resources about the student conduct system should be maintained and be accessible to student conduct board members.

Part 3. LEADERSHIP
Effective and ethical leadership is essential to the success of all organizations. Institutions must appoint, position, and empower Student Conduct Programs (SCP) leaders within the administrative structure to accomplish stated missions. SCP leaders at various levels must be selected on the

basis of formal education and training, relevant work experience, personal skills and competencies, relevant professional credentials, as well as potential for promoting learning and development in students, applying effective practices to educational processes, and enhancing institutional effectiveness. Institutions must determine expectations of accountability for SCP leaders and fairly assess their performance.

SCP leaders must exercise authority over resources for which they are responsible to achieve their respective missions.

SCP leaders must:
- articulate a vision for their organization
- set goals and objectives based on the needs and capabilities of the population served
- promote student learning and development
- prescribe and practice ethical behavior
- recruit, select, supervise, and develop others in the organization
- manage financial resources
- coordinate human resources
- plan, budget for, and evaluate personnel and programs
- apply effective practices to educational and administrative processes
- communicate effectively
- initiate collaborative interaction between individuals and agencies, both internal and external, that possess legitimate concerns and interests in the functional area

SCP leaders must identify and find means to address individual, organizational, or environmental conditions that inhibit goal achievement.

SCP leaders must promote campus environments that result in multiple opportunities for student learning and development.

SCP leaders must continuously improve programs and services in response to changing needs of students and other constituents, and evolving institutional priorities.

Part 4. ORGANIZATION and MANAGEMENT

Guided by an overarching intent to ensure student learning and development, Student Conduct Programs (SCP) must be structured purposefully and managed effectively to achieve stated goals. Evidence of appropriate structure must include current and accessible policies and procedures, written performance expectations for all employees, functional workflow graphics or organizational charts, and clearly stated service delivery expectations.

Evidence of effective management must include use of comprehensive and accurate information for decisions, clear sources and channels of authority, effective communication practices, decision-making and conflict resolution procedures, responsiveness to changing conditions, accountability and evaluation systems, and recognition and reward processes. Programs and services must provide channels within the organization for regular review of administrative policies and procedures.

Part 5. HUMAN RESOURCES

Student Conduct Programs (SCP) must be staffed adequately by individuals qualified to accomplish its mission and goals. Within established guidelines of the institution, SCP must establish procedures for staff selection, training, and evaluation; set expectations for supervision, and provide appropriate professional development opportunities. SCP must strive to improve the professional competence and skills of all personnel it employs.

SCP professional staff members must hold an earned graduate degree in a field relevant to the position they hold or must possess an appropriate combination of educational credentials and related work experience.

Degree or credential-seeking graduate assistants and/ or interns must be qualified by enrollment in an appropriate field of study and by relevant experience. These individuals must be trained and supervised adequately by professional staff members holding educational credentials and related work experience appropriate for supervision.

Student employees and volunteers must be carefully selected, trained, supervised, and evaluated. They must be trained on how and when to refer those in need of assistance to qualified staff members and have access to a supervisor for assistance in making these judgments. Student employees and volunteers must be provided clear and precise job descriptions, pre-service training based on assessed needs, and continuing staff development.

Students from graduate academic programs, particularly in areas such as counseling, student development, higher education administration, law, or criminology, may assist the student conduct programs through practicums, internships, and assistantships.

Students who participate on conduct boards may be awarded academic credit for proper supervision. Clear objectives and assignments should be outlined to ensure that a student's grade for this participation is in no way influenced by his/her decisions on a particular case.

Each organizational unit must have technical and support staff members adequate to accomplish its mission. SCP staff members must be technologically proficient and qualified to perform their job functions, be knowledgeable of ethical and legal uses of technology, and have access to training. The level of staffing and workloads must be adequate and appropriate for program and service demands.

Salary levels and fringe benefits for all SCP staff members must be commensurate with those for comparable positions within the institution, in similar institutions, and in the relevant geographic area.

SCP must institute hiring and promotion practices that are fair, inclusive, and non-discriminatory. Programs and services must employ a diverse staff to provide readily identifiable role models for students and to enrich the campus community.

SCP must create and maintain position descriptions for all staff members and provide regular performance planning and appraisals.

SCP must have a system for regular staff evaluation and must provide access to continuing education and professional development opportunities, including in-service training programs and participation in professional conferences and workshops.

A qualified member of the campus community must be designated as the person responsible for student conduct programs.

The designee should have an educational background in the behavioral sciences (e.g., college student affairs, psychology, sociology, student development including moral and ethical development, higher education administration, counseling, law, criminology, or criminal justice).

The designee and any other professional staff member in the student conduct programs should possess (a) a clear understanding of the legal requirements for substantive and procedural due process; (b) legal knowledge sufficient to confer with attorneys involved in student disciplinary proceedings and other aspects of the student conduct services system; (c) a general interest in and commitment to the welfare and development of students who participate on boards or who

are involved in cases; (d) demonstrated skills in working with decision making processes and conflict resolution; (e) teaching and consulting skills appropriate for the education, advising, and coordination of hearing bodies; (f) the ability to communicate and interact with students regardless of race, sex, disability, sexual orientation, and other personal characteristics; (g) understanding of the requirements relative to confidentiality and security of student conduct programs files; and (h) the ability to create an atmosphere where students feel free to ask questions and obtain assistance.

Part 6. FINANCIAL RESOURCES
Student Conduct Programs (SCP) must have adequate funding to accomplish its mission and goals. Funding priorities must be determined within the context of the stated mission, goals, objectives and comprehensive analysis of the needs and capabilities of students and the availability of internal or external resources.

SCP must demonstrate fiscal responsibility and cost effectiveness consistent with institutional protocols.

Part 7. FACILITIES, TECHNOLOGY, and EQUIPMENT
Student Conduct Programs (SCP) must have adequate, suitably located facilities, adequate technology, and equipment to support its mission and goals efficiently and effectively. Facilities, technology, and equipment must be evaluated regularly and be in compliance with relevant federal, state, provincial, and local requirements to provide for access, health, safety, and security.

SCP must have access to facilities of sufficient size and arrangement to ensure privacy of records, meetings, and interviews.

The facilities should include a private office where individual consultations and pre-hearing conferences with those involved in disciplinary actions may be held, hearing room facilities, a meeting room for small groups, a library or resource area, and a secure location for student disciplinary records. The facilities should also be designed to promote the personal safety of the individuals involved in the SCP (e.g. multiple methods of egress and panic buttons).

Part 8. LEGAL RESPONSIBILITIES
Student Conduct Programs (SCP) staff members must be knowledgeable about and responsive to laws and regulations that relate to their respective responsibilities. SCP staff members must inform users of programs and services and officials, as appropriate, of legal obligations and limitations including constitutional, statutory, regulatory, and

case law; mandatory laws and orders emanating from federal, state/provincial and local governments; and the institution's policies.

SCP staff members must use reasonable and informed practices to limit the liability exposure of the institution, its officers, employees, and agents. Staff members must be informed about institutional policies regarding personal liability and related insurance coverage options.

The institution must provide access to legal advice and current legal literature and resources for SCP staff members as needed to carry out assigned responsibilities.

The institution must inform SCP staff and students in a timely and systematic fashion about extraordinary or changing legal obligations and potential liabilities.

Appropriate policies and practices to ensure compliance with regulations should include notification to all constituencies of their rights and responsibilities under the student conduct system, a written description, accurate record keeping of all aspects of the student conduct proceedings, and regular reviews of the student conduct policies and practices.

Part 9. EQUITY and ACCESS

Student Conduct Programs (SCP) staff members must ensure that services and programs are provided on a fair and equitable basis. Facilities, programs and services must be accessible. Hours of operation and delivery of and access to programs and services must be responsive to the needs of all students and other constituents. SCP must adhere to the spirit and intent of equal opportunity laws.

SCP must be open and readily accessible to all students and must not discriminate except where sanctioned by law and institutional policy. Discrimination must be avoided on the basis of age; color; creed; cultural heritage; disability; ethnicity; gender identity; nationality; political affiliation; religious affiliation; sex; sexual orientation; or social, economic, marital, or veteran status.

Consistent with their mission and goals, SCP must take affirmative action to remedy significant imbalances in student participation and staffing patterns.

As the demographic profiles of campuses change and new instructional delivery methods are introduced, institutions must recognize the needs

of students who participate in distance learning for access to programs and services offered on campus. Institutions must provide appropriate services in ways that are accessible to distance learners and assist them in identifying and gaining access to other appropriate services in their geographic region.

Part 10. CAMPUS and EXTERNAL RELATIONS

Student Conduct Programs (SCP) must establish, maintain, and promote effective relations with relevant individuals, campus offices, and external agencies.

Representatives of the student conduct system should meet regularly with pertinent campus constituencies (e.g., student government, student development offices, staff, faculty members, academic administrators, public safety, legal counsel) to exchange information concerning their respective operations and to identify ways to work together to prevent behavioral problems and to correct existing ones. Such collaborative efforts might include educational programs and joint publications.

Representatives should also meet periodically with relevant external agencies(e.g., local police, district attorneys, and service providers) to ensure understanding about the student conduct programs as well as address student behavior problems in an effective manner.

Part 11. DIVERSITY

Within the context of each institution's unique mission, diversity enriches the community and enhances the collegiate experience for all; therefore, Student Conduct Programs (SCP) must nurture environments where commonalties and differences among people are recognized and honored.

SCP must promote educational experiences that are characterized by open and continuous communication that deepens understanding of one's own identity, culture, and heritage, and that of others. SCP must educate and promote respect about commonalties and differences in their historical and cultural contexts.

SCP must address the characteristics and needs of a diverse population when establishing and implementing policies and procedures.

Part 12. ETHICS

All persons involved in the delivery of Student Conduct Programs (SCP) must adhere to the highest principles of ethical behavior. SCP must develop or adopt and implement appropriate statements of ethical practice. SCP must publish these statements and ensure their periodic review by relevant constituencies.

SCP staff members must ensure that privacy and confidentiality are maintained with respect to all communications and records to the extent that such records are protected under the law and appropriate statements of ethical practice. Information contained in students' education records must not be disclosed without written consent except as allowed by relevant laws and institutional policies. Staff members must disclose to appropriate authorities information judged to be of an emergency nature, especially when the safety of the individual or others is involved, or when otherwise required by institutional policy or relevant law.

All SCP staff members must be aware of and comply with the provisions contained in the institution's human subjects research policy and in other relevant institutional policies addressing ethical practices and confidentiality of research data concerning individuals.

SCP staff members must recognize and avoid personal conflicts of interest or appearance thereof in their transactions with students and others.

SCP staff members must strive to insure the fair, objective, and impartial treatment of all persons with whom they deal. Staff members must not participate in nor condone any form of harassment that demeans persons or creates an intimidating, hostile, or offensive campus environment.

When handling institutional funds, all SCP staff members must ensure that such funds are managed in accordance with established and responsible accounting procedures and the fiscal policies or processes of the institution.

SCP staff members must perform their duties within the limits of their training, expertise, and competence. When these limits are exceeded, individuals in need of further assistance must be referred to persons possessing appropriate qualifications.

SCP staff members must use suitable means to confront and otherwise hold accountable other staff members who exhibit unethical behavior.

SCP staff members must be knowledgeable about and practice ethical behavior in the use of technology.

Part 13. ASSESSMENT and EVALUATION

Student Conduct Programs (SCP) must conduct regular assessment and evaluations. Programs and services must employ effective qualitative and quantitative methodologies as appropriate, to determine whether and to what degree the stated mission, goals, and student learning and development outcomes are being met. The process must employ sufficient and sound assessment measures to ensure comprehensiveness. Data collected must include responses from students and other affected constituencies.

SCP must evaluate periodically how well they complement and enhance the institution's stated mission and educational effectiveness.

Results of these evaluations must be used in revising and improving programs and services and in recognizing staff performance.

Evaluation of SCP should include:

- performance evaluations of all staff members by their supervisors
- periodic performance evaluations of individual hearing boards
- on-going evaluation of training programs and publications
- periodic review of applicable state/provincial, and federal laws and current case law to ensure compliance

Assessment and evaluation activities may include:

- whether student conduct boards accurately follow the institution's procedural guidelines
- general impressions of the student conduct system according to students, faculty, staff members, and the community
- developmental effects on students and student conduct board members
- annual trends in case load, rates of recidivism, types of offenses, and efficacy of sanctions
- effects of programming designed to prevent behavioral problems
- unique aspects of special function or special population student conduct boards (e.g., student organization or residence hall boards)

General Standards revised in 2002; SCP (formerly Judicial Programs and Services) developed/revised in 1986, 1996, & 2005

THE ROLE of LEADERSHIP PROGRAMS for STUDENTS
CAS Standards Contextual Statement

Many college mission statements contain commitments to develop citizen leaders or prepare students for professional and community responsibilities in a global context. Throughout the history of higher education, however, leadership development has primarily been targeted toward students holding leadership positions, such as student government officials, officers in fraternities and sororities, and resident assistants. Consequently, only a handful of students had a genuine opportunity for focused experience in leadership development.

During the 1970s, many colleges refocused efforts on leadership development when events such as the Watergate scandal caused institutions to ponder how they taught ethics, leadership, and social responsibility. Subsequent initiatives such as the women's and African-American civil rights movements and adult reentry programs, increased access to college, and new forms of campus shared governance, coupled with a focus on intentional student development, led to new forms of leadership development through such programs as assertiveness training, emerging leaders' retreats, and leadership targeted toward special populations.

By the 1970s, professional associations were becoming increasingly interested in broad-based leadership efforts. Several associations, including the American College Personnel Association (ACPA), National Association of Student Personnel Administrators (NASPA), National Association for Campus Activities (NACA), and National Association for Women in Education (NAWE), expanded projects and initiatives with a leadership focus. Burns' seminal book, *Leadership* (1978), brought new energy with its discussion of transformational leadership grounded in values and moral purpose. Thinking about leadership expanded in the 1980s and 1990s to include such perspectives as cultural influences, service learning, social change, and spirituality. Leadership educators focused on developing leadership models with applicability to the college context. Two such models, the Social Change Model of Leadership (SCM) (HERI, 1996)., and the Relational Leadership Model (Komives, Lucas & McMahon, 1996) have been widely adopted.

One college president noted that colleges need to develop not just better, but more leaders, and that efforts should be directed toward the entire student body. Because students experience leadership in many different settings—in and out of the classroom, on and off campus—virtually every student engages in some type of activity that involves the practice of leadership. Regardless of differences in academic discipline, organizational affiliation, cultural background, or geographical location, students must be better prepared to serve as citizen-leaders in a global community. The role of student affairs professionals in this arena is to help students understand their experiences and to facilitate their learning, so they become effective contributors to their communities.

The *CAS Student Leadership Program Standards* can be used to help professionals provide comprehensive leadership programs and enhance students' learning opportunities. Leadership for positional leaders will still occur within specific functional areas such as student activities and residence life; campuses that seek to develop a comprehensive leadership program will recognize the need to make intentional leadership development opportunities available to all students through coordinated campus-wide efforts. Recent research has identified a Leadership Identity Development model (Komives, Owen, Longerbeam, Mainella, & Osteen, 2005) that can guide intentional practice. Further, a 2006 national Multi-Institutional Study of Leadership has established normative data using the SCM (see www.nclp.umd.edu).

Leadership is an inherently relational process of working with others to accomplish a goal or to promote change. Most leadership programs seek to empower students to enhance their self efficacy as leaders and understand how they can make a difference, whether as positional leaders or active participants in a group or community process. Leadership development involves self-awareness and understanding of others, values and diverse perspectives, organizations, and change. Leadership also requires competence in establishing purpose, working collaboratively, and managing conflict. Institutions can initiate opportunities to study leadership and to experience a range of leadership-related activities designed to intentionally promote desired outcomes of student leadership learning.

The Inter-Association Leadership Project brought student affairs leadership educators together in the mid-1980s to create and sustain a leadership agenda. By the end of the decade, higher education's commitment to leadership was clear with over 600 campuses teaching leadership courses; creating special leadership centers such as the Jepson School of Leadership Studies at the University of Richmond and the McDonough Leadership Center at Marietta College; and establishing special programs, including the National LeaderShape Institute. In 1992 the National Clearinghouse for Leadership Programs (NCLP) was established at the University of Maryland, and a co-sponsored series of symposia encouraged leadership educators to identify a leadership agenda for the new millennium. Projects funded by the Kellogg, Pew, and Lilly Foundations; FIPSE; and the federal Eisenhower Leadership grant program have also focused broad-based attention on leadership development. By late 1990s, there were over 800 college leadership programs. The new International Leadership Association (ILA) was established in 1999 to bring a global lens to leadership education. Other leadership institutes serve the leadership educator professional; for example,

NCLP and the NACA host the annual summer leadership educators symposium, and NCLP in partnership with NASPA and ACPA now hosts the Leadership Educators Institute, a bi-annual program for entry and mid-level leadership educators.

References, Readings, and Resources

Astin, H., & Astin, A., (Eds.). (2000), *Leadership Reconsidered: Engaging Higher Education in Social Change*. W.K. Kellogg Foundation.

Boatman, S. (1987). *Student leadership development: Approaches, methods, and models.* Columbia, SC: National Association for Campus Activities.

Boatman, S. (1992). *Supporting student leadership: Selections from the student development series.* Columbia, SC: National Association for Campus Activities.

Brungardt, C. (1996). The making of leaders: A review of the research in leadership development and education. *Journal of Leadership Studies, 3*(3), 81-95.

HERI_(1996)._A social change model of leadership development: Guidebook version III.. Los Angeles: University of California Los Angeles Higher Education Research Institute. *(Available from National Clearinghouse for Leadership Programs).*

Komives, S. R., Lucas, N. , & McMahon, T. (1998) *Exploring leadership.* San Francisco: Jossey-Bass.

Komives, S. R., Owen, J. E., Longerbeam, S., Mainella, F. C., & Osteen, L. (2005). Developing a leadership identity: A grounded theory. *Journal of College Student Development.46,* 593-611.

Komives, S. R., Dugan, J., Owen, J. E., Slack, C. & Wagner, W. (Eds). (2006). *Handbook for Student Leadership Programs.* College Park, MD: National Clearinghouse for Leadership Programs.

Murray, J. I. (1994). *Training for student leaders.* Dubuque:, IA: Kendall/Hunt.

Roberts, D. C. (1981). *Student leadership programs in higher education.* Carbondale, IL: American College Personnel Association.

Rogers, J. L. (2003). Leadership. In S. Komives & D. B. Woodard (Eds.), *Student Services: A handbook for the profession* (4th ed.)(pp. 447-465).

Zimmerman-Oster, K., & Burkhardt, J. C. (1999). *Leadership in the making: Impact and insights from leadership development programs in U. S. colleges and universities.* Battle Creek, MI: W. K. Kellogg Foundation.

Center for Creative Leadership, One Leadership Place, P.O. Box 26300, Greensboro, NC 27438-6300. (910) 288-7210. Publisher of periodic sourcebooks.

Concepts & connections: A newsletter for leadership educators. The National Clearinghouse for Leadership Programs, 1135 Stamp Student Union, University of Maryland at College Park, College Park, MD 20742-4631. (301) 314-7174

Journal of Leadership Studies. Baker College of Flint, 1050 W. Bristol Rd., Flint, MI 48507-9987. (313) 766-4105

Leadership Quarterly. JAI Press, 55 Old Post Road, # 2, P.O. Box 1678, Greenwich, CT 06836-1678. (203) 661-7602

Contributors:
Jan Arminio, Shippensburg University, NACA
Susan Komives, University of Maryland, ACPA
Craig Slack, University of Maryland, NCLP

STUDENT LEADERSHIP PROGRAMS

CAS Standards and Guidelines

Part 1. MISSION

Student Leadership Programs (SLP) must incorporate student learning and student development in its mission. SLP must enhance overall educational experiences. SLP must develop, record, disseminate, implement and regularly review its mission and goals. Mission statements must be consistent with the mission and goals of the institution and with the standards in this document. SLP must operate as an integral part of the institution's overall mission.

The mission of SLP must be to prepare students for leadership roles and responsibilities. To accomplish this mission, the program must:

- provide students with opportunities to develop and enhance a personal philosophy of leadership that includes understanding of self, others, and community, and acceptance of responsibilities inherent in community membership
- assist students in gaining varied leadership experience
- use multiple leadership techniques, theories, and models
- recognize and reward exemplary leadership behavior
- be inclusive and accessible

Student leadership development should be an integral part of the institution's educational mission.

SLP should include a commitment to student involvement in the institution's governance activities. SLP should seek an institution-wide commitment that transcends the boundaries of the units specifically charged with program delivery.

Part 2. PROGRAM

The formal education of students consists of the curriculum and the co-curriculum, and must promote student learning and development that is purposeful and holistic. Student Leadership Programs (SLP) must identify relevant and desirable student learning and development outcomes and provide programs and services that encourage the achievement of those outcomes.

Relevant and desirable outcomes include: intellectual growth, effective communication, realistic self-appraisal, enhanced self-esteem, clarified values, career choices, leadership development, healthy behaviors, meaningful interpersonal relationships, independence, collaboration, social responsibility, satisfying and productive lifestyles, appreciation of diversity, spiritual awareness, and achievement of personal and educational goals.

SLP must provide evidence of its impact on the achievement of student learning and development outcomes.

The table below offers examples of evidence of achievement of student learning and development.

Student Learning and Development Outcome Domains

Intellectual growth

Examples of achievement indicators

Produces personal and educational goal statements; Employs critical thinking in problem solving; Uses complex information from a variety of sources including personal experience and observation to form a decision or opinion; Obtains a degree; Applies previously understood information and concepts to a new situation or setting; Expresses appreciation for literature, the fine arts, mathematics, sciences, and social sciences

Effective communication

Examples of achievement indicators

Writes and speaks coherently and effectively; Writes and speaks after reflection; Able to influence others through writing, speaking or artistic expression; Effectively articulates abstract ideas; Uses appropriate syntax; Makes presentations or gives performances

Enhanced self-esteem

Examples of achievement indicators

Shows self-respect and respect for others; Initiates actions toward achievement of goals; Takes reasonable risks; Demonstrates assertive behavior; Functions without need for constant reassurance from others

Realistic self-appraisal

Examples of achievement indicators

Articulates personal skills and abilities; Makes decisions and acts in congruence with personal values; Acknowledges personal strengths and weaknesses; Articulates rationale for personal behavior; Seeks feedback from others; Learns from past experiences

Clarified values

Examples of achievement indicators

Articulates personal values; Acts in congruence with

personal values; Makes decisions that reflect personal values; Demonstrates willingness to scrutinize personal beliefs and values; Identifies personal, work and lifestyle values and explains how they influence decision-making

Career choices

Examples of achievement indicators

Articulates career choices based on assessment of interests, values, skills, and abilities; Documents knowledge, skills and accomplishments resulting from formal education, work experience, community service, and volunteer experiences; Makes the connections between classroom and out-of-classroom learning; Can construct a resume with clear job objectives and evidence of related knowledge, skills and accomplishments; Articulates the characteristics of a preferred work environment; Comprehends the world of work; Takes steps to initiate a job search or seek advanced education

Leadership development

Examples of achievement indicators

Articulates leadership philosophy or style; Serves in a leadership position in a student organization; Comprehends the dynamics of a group; Exhibits democratic principles as a leader; Exhibits ability to visualize a group purpose and desired outcomes

Healthy behavior

Examples of achievement indicators

Chooses behaviors and environments that promote health and reduce risk; Articulates the relationship between health and wellness and accomplishing life-long goals; Exhibit behaviors that advance a healthy community.

Meaningful interpersonal relationships

Examples of achievement indicators

Develops and maintains satisfying interpersonal relationships; Establishes mutually rewarding relationships with friends and colleagues; Listens to and considers others' points of view; Treats others with respect

Independence

Examples of achievement indicators

Exhibits self-reliant behaviors; Functions autonomously; Exhibits ability to function interdependently; Accepts supervision as needed; Manages time effectively

Collaboration

Examples of achievement indicators

Works cooperatively with others; Seeks the involvement of others; Seeks feedback from others; Contributes to achievement of a group goal; Exhibits effective listening skills

Social responsibility

Examples of achievement indicators

Understands and participates in relevant governance systems; Understands, abides by, and participates in the development, maintenance, and/or orderly change of community, social, and legal standards or norms; Appropriately challenges the unfair, unjust, or uncivil behavior of other individuals or groups; Participates in service/volunteer activities

Satisfying and productive lifestyles

Examples of achievement indicators

Achieves balance between education, work, and leisure time; Articulates and meets goals for work, leisure, and education; Overcomes obstacles that hamper goal achievement; Functions on the basis of personal identity, ethical, spiritual, and moral values; Articulates long-term goals and objectives

Appreciating diversity

Examples of achievement indicators

Understands one's own identity and culture; Seeks involvement with people different from oneself; Seeks involvement in diverse interests; Articulates the advantages and challenges of a diverse society; Challenges appropriately the abusive use of stereotypes by others; Understands the impact of diversity on one's own society

Spiritual awareness

Examples of achievement indicators

Develops and articulates personal belief system; Understands roles of spirituality in personal and group values and behaviors

Personal and educational goals

Examples of achievement indicators

Sets, articulates, and pursues individual goals; Articulates personal and educational goals and objectives; Uses personal and educational goals to guide decisions; Understands the effect of one's personal and educational goals on others

Programs and services must be (a) intentional, (b) coherent, (c) based on theories and knowledge of learning and human development, (d) reflective of developmental and demographic profiles of the student population, and (e) responsive to needs of individuals, special populations, and communities.

SLP must be comprehensive in nature and must include (1) opportunities to develop the competencies required for effective leadership; (2) training, education, and developmental activities; and (3) multiple delivery methods.

- **Opportunities to Develop**

  A comprehensive leadership program must be based on a broad philosophy of leadership upon which subsequent competencies are built. The program must contain components that assist the student in gaining self awareness, the relationship of self to others (differences and commonalties), the uniqueness of the institutional environment within which leadership is practiced, and the relationship to local and global communities. It must advance competencies in the categories of foundations of leadership, individual development, and organizational development.

  Competencies should accrue from both cognitive and experiential development in the following areas:

  Foundations of Leadership
  - Historical perspectives and evaluation of leadership theory
  - Theoretical, philosophical, and conceptual foundations of leadership of several cultures
  - Cultural and gender influences on leadership
  - Ethical practices in leadership
  - Moral leadership
  - Leadership and followership

  Personal Development
  - Awareness and understanding of various leadership styles and approaches
  - Exploration and designing of personal leadership approaches
  - Human development theories
  - The intersections of human development theories, sexual orientation, national origin, and environment
  - Personal management issues such as time management, stress reduction, development of relationships, problem solving, goal setting, and ethical decision-making
  - Oral and written communication skills
  - Critical thinking skills
  - Risk taking
  - Creativity
  - Wellness lifestyle development
  - Supervision
  - Motivation

  Organizational Development
  - Team building
  - Shared leadership
  - Group dynamics and development
  - Organizational communication
  - Group problem-solving and decision making models
  - Planning

  - Conflict management and resolution
  - Methods of assessing and evaluating organizational effectiveness
  - Organizational culture, values and principles
  - Community development
  - Power and empowerment
  - Collaboration
  - Developing trust
  - Organizational politics
  - Leadership in diverse organizations

- **Training, Education, and Development Activities**

  Leadership Training

  Training involves those activities designed to improve performance of the individual in the role presently occupied or that are concretely focused at helping the individual being trained to translate some newly learned skill, or information, to a real and immediate situation. Examples of training include programs for the preparation of residence hall student staff, student government, student judicial board members, community service volunteers, and employment.

  Leadership Education

  Education program elements are designed to enhance participants' knowledge and understanding of specific leadership theories, concepts, and models. Education occurs as students gain information in their present roles that serves ultimately to provide generalized theories, principles, and approaches to prepare them for future leadership responsibilities. The student leadership program should explore the processes by which decisions affecting students, faculty, and staff are made. Examples of education include a course on leadership and politics and a seminar on the evolution of leadership theories.

  Development Activities

  Development requires an environment which empowers students to mature and develop toward greater levels of leadership complexity, integration, and proficiency over a period of time. Developmental activities promote positive behavioral, cognitive, and affective outcomes. Examples of developmental activities include peer mentoring and peer leadership consultant programs.

- **Multiple delivery methods and contexts**

  A comprehensive leadership program must involve a diverse range of faculty, students, and staff members in the delivery of programs and must recognize the diverse contexts of leadership. Regular assessment of the developmental levels and needs of participants must be conducted to implement multiple delivery strategies and contexts.

Examples of delivery methods include internships, panel discussions, movies, lectures, mentor programs, adventure training, and participation in local, regional, and national associations. Examples of contexts for leadership include diverse academic and career fields, campus organizations and committees, employment setting, community involvement, family settings, international settings, and social and religious organizations in both formal and informal positions.

Part 3. LEADERSHIP

Effective and ethical leadership is essential to the success of all organizations. Institutions must appoint, position and empower Student Leadership Programs (SLP) leaders within the administrative structure to accomplish stated missions. SLP leaders at various levels must be selected on the basis of formal education and training, relevant work experience, personal skills and competencies, relevant professional credentials, as well as potential for promoting learning and development in students, applying effective practices to educational processes, and enhancing institutional effectiveness. Institutions must determine expectations of accountability for leaders and fairly assess their performance.

Leaders of SLP must exercise authority over resources for which they are responsible to achieve their respective missions.

SLP leaders must:

- articulate a vision for their organization
- set goals and objectives based on the needs and capabilities of the population served
- promote student learning and development
- prescribe and practice ethical behavior
- recruit, select, supervise, and develop others in the organization
- manage financial resources
- coordinate human resources
- plan, budget for, and evaluate personnel and programs
- apply effective practices to educational and administrative processes
- communicate effectively
- initiate collaborative interaction between individuals and agencies that possess legitimate concerns and interests in the functional area

SLP leaders must identify and find means to address individual, organizational, or environmental conditions that inhibit goal achievement.

SLP leaders must promote campus environments that result in multiple opportunities for student learning and development.

SLP leaders must continuously improve programs and services in response to changing needs of students and other constituents, and evolving institutional priorities.

There should be a person or group of persons designated as responsible for the coordination of direction of the leadership program including allocation and maintenance of resources and developing student leadership opportunities.

Part 4. ORGANIZATION and MANAGEMENT

Guided by an overarching intent to ensure student learning and development, Student Leadership Programs (SLP) must be structured purposefully and managed effectively to achieve stated goals. Evidence of appropriate structure must include current and accessible policies and procedures, written performance expectations for all employees, functional workflow graphics or organizational charts, and clearly stated service delivery expectations.

Evidence of effective management must include use of comprehensive and accurate information for decisions, clear sources and channels of authority, effective communication practices, decision-making and conflict resolution procedures, responsiveness to changing conditions, accountability and evaluation systems, and recognition and reward processes. SLP must provide channels within the organization for regular review of administrative policies and procedures.

SLP are typically organized in a variety of offices and departments both in student services and in academic and other administrative areas. An advisory group with representatives from the involved areas should be established for the purpose of communication.

Part 5. HUMAN RESOURCES

Student Leadership Programs (SLP) must be staffed adequately by individuals qualified to accomplish its mission and goals. Within established guidelines of the institution, programs and services must establish procedures for staff selection, training, and evaluation; set expectations for supervision, and provide appropriate professional development opportunities. The program and service must strive to improve the professional competence and skills of all personnel it employs.

SLP professional staff members must hold an earned graduate degree in a field relevant to the position they hold or must possess an appropriate combination of educational credentials and related work experience.

SLP should have adequate and qualified staff or faculty members to implement a comprehensive program.

Professional staff or faculty involved in leadership programs should possess:

- ability to work with diverse students
- knowledge of the history and current trends in leadership theories, models, and philosophies
- leadership experiences
- followership experiences
- knowledge of organizational development, group dynamics, strategies for change and principles of community
- knowledge of diversity issues related to leadership
- ability to evaluate leadership programs and assess outcomes
- effective oral and written communication skills
- ability to effectively organize learning opportunities that are consistent with students' stages of development
- ability to use reflection in helping students understand leadership concepts by processing critical incidents with students

Degree or credential-seeking interns must be qualified by enrollment in an appropriate field of study and by relevant experience. These individuals must be trained and supervised adequately by professional staff members holding educational credentials and related work experience appropriate for supervision.

Student employees and volunteers must be carefully selected, trained, supervised, and evaluated. They must be trained on how and when to refer those in need of assistance to qualified staff members and have access to a supervisor for assistance in making these judgments. Student employees and volunteers must be provided clear and precise job descriptions, pre-service training based on assessed needs, and continuing staff development.

SLP must have technical and support staff members adequate to accomplish its mission. Staff members must be technologically proficient and qualified to perform their job functions, be knowledgeable of ethical and legal uses of technology, and have access to training. The level of staffing and workloads must be adequate and appropriate for program and service demands.

Salary levels and fringe benefits for all SLP staff members must be commensurate with those for comparable positions within the institution, in similar institutions, and in the relevant geographic area.

SLP must institute hiring and promotion practices that are fair, inclusive, and non-discriminatory. Programs and services must employ a diverse staff to provide readily identifiable role models for students and to enrich the campus community.

SLP must create and maintain position descriptions for all staff members and provide regular performance planning and appraisals.

SLP must have a system for regular staff evaluation and must provide access to continuing education and professional development opportunities, including in-service training programs and participation in professional conferences and workshops.

Program staff should engage in continuous discovery and understanding of emerging leadership models, research, theories, and definitions through disciplined study and professional development activities.

Student organization advisors should be considered as resources to assist both formally and informally in student leadership programs. Advisors can provide information about issues that need to be addressed. The student leadership program staff should assist advisors in conducting leadership training, education, and development for their respective student groups.

Part 6. FINANCIAL RESOURCES

Student Leadership Programs (SLP) must have adequate funding to accomplish its mission and goals. Funding priorities must be determined within the context of the stated mission, goals, objectives and comprehensive analysis of the needs and capabilities of students and the availability of internal or external resources.

SLP must demonstrate fiscal responsibility and cost effectiveness consistent with institutional protocols.

Funding for the student leadership program may come from a variety of sources, including institutional funds, grant money, student government funds, fees for services, and government contracts. Where possible, institutional funding should be allocated regularly for the operation of leadership programs.

Part 7. FACILITIES, TECHNOLOGY, and EQUIPMENT

Student Leadership Programs (SLP) must have adequate, suitably located facilities, adequate technology, and equipment to support its mission and goals efficiently and effectively. Facilities, technology, and equipment must be evaluated regularly and be in compliance with relevant federal, state, provincial, and local requirements to provide for access, health, safety, and security.

Leadership program facilities should be conveniently located on campus. Staff, faculty, and student space should be designed to encourage a maximum level of interaction among students, faculty, and staff.

Part 8. LEGAL RESPONSIBILITIES

Student Leadership Programs (SLP) staff members must be knowledgeable about and responsive to laws and regulations that relate to their respective responsibilities. Staff members must inform users of programs and services and officials, as appropriate, of legal obligations and limitations including constitutional, statutory, regulatory, and case law; mandatory laws and orders emanating from federal, state/provincial and local governments; and the institution's policies.

SLP staff members must use reasonable and informed practices to limit the liability exposure of the institution, its officers, employees, and agents. Staff members must be informed about institutional policies regarding personal liability and related insurance coverage options.

The institution must provide access to legal advice for SLP staff members as needed to carry out assigned responsibilities.

The institution must inform SLP staff and students in a timely and systematic fashion about extraordinary or changing legal obligations and potential liabilities.

Part 9. EQUITY and ACCESS

Student Leadership Programs (SLP) staff members must ensure that services and programs are provided on a fair and equitable basis. Facilities, programs and services must be accessible. Hours of operation and delivery of and access to programs and services must be responsive to the needs of all students and other constituents. SLP must adhere to the spirit and intent of equal opportunity laws.

SLP must be open and readily accessible to all students and must not discriminate except where sanctioned by law and institutional policy. Discrimination must be avoided on the bases of age; color; creed; cultural heritage; disability; ethnicity; gender identity; nationality; political affiliation; religious affiliation; sex; sexual orientation; or social, economic, marital, or veteran status.

Consistent with their mission and goals, SLP must take affirmative action to remedy significant imbalances in student participation and staffing patterns.

As the demographic profiles of campuses change and new instructional delivery methods are introduced, institutions must recognize the needs of students who participate in distance learning for access to programs and services offered on campus. Institutions must provide appropriate services in ways that are accessible to distance learners and assist them in identifying and gaining access to other appropriate services in their geographic region.

Part 10. CAMPUS and EXTERNAL RELATIONS

The student leadership program must establish, maintain, and promote effective relations with relevant individuals, campus offices, and external agencies.

SLP should maintain positive relations through effective communication and encourage participation with a variety of offices, departments, agencies, and constituencies both on and off campus for leadership involvement opportunities.

Part 11. DIVERSITY

Within the context of each institution's unique mission, diversity enriches the community and enhances the collegiate experience for all; therefore, Student Leadership Programs (SLP) must nurture environments where commonalties and differences among people are recognized and honored.

SLP must promote educational experiences that are characterized by open and continuous communication that deepens understanding of one's own identity, culture, and heritage, and that of others. SLP must educate and promote respect about commonalties and differences in their historical and cultural contexts.

SLP must address the characteristics and needs of a diverse population when establishing and implementing policies and procedures.

Part 12. ETHICS

All persons involved in the delivery of Student

Leadership Programs (SLP) must adhere to the highest principles of ethical behavior. SLP must develop or adopt and implement appropriate statements of ethical practice. SLP must publish these statements and ensure their periodic review by relevant constituencies.

SLP staff members must ensure that privacy and confidentiality are maintained with respect to all communications and records to the extent that such records are protected under the law and appropriate statements of ethical practice. Information contained in students' education records must not be disclosed without written consent except as allowed by relevant laws and institutional policies. Staff members must disclose to appropriate authorities information judged to be of an emergency nature, especially when the safety of the individual or others is involved, or when otherwise required by institutional policy or relevant law.

All SLP staff members must be aware of and comply with the provisions contained in the institution's human subjects research policy and in other relevant institutional policies addressing ethical practices and confidentiality of research data concerning individuals.

SLP staff members must recognize and avoid personal conflict of interest or appearance thereof in their transactions with students and others.

SLP staff members must strive to insure the fair, objective, and impartial treatment of all persons with whom they deal. Staff members must not participate in nor condone any form of harassment that demeans persons or creates an intimidating, hostile, or offensive campus environment.

When handling institutional funds, all SLP staff members must ensure that such funds are managed in accordance with established and responsible accounting procedures and the fiscal policies or processes of the institution.

SLP staff members must perform their duties within the limits of their training, expertise, and competence. When these limits are exceeded, individuals in need of further assistance must be referred to persons possessing appropriate qualifications.

SLP staff members must use suitable means to confront and otherwise hold accountable other staff members who exhibit unethical behavior.

SLP staff members must be knowledgeable about and practice ethical behavior in the use of technology.

SLP staff members must ensure that facilitators have appropriate training experience and credentials. Expertise, training, and certification are essential in the administration and interpretation of personality, developmental, and leadership assessment instruments.

Where materials and instruments used in SLP are copyrighted, appropriate citations must be made and permission obtained.

Part 13. ASSESSMENT and EVALUATION

Student Leadership Programs (SLP) must conduct regular assessment and evaluations. SLP must employ effective qualitative and quantitative methodologies as appropriate, to determine whether and to what degree the stated mission, goals, and student learning and development outcomes are being met. The process must employ sufficient and sound assessment measures to ensure comprehensiveness. Data collected must include responses from students and other affected constituencies.

SLP must evaluate periodically how well they complement and enhance the institution's stated mission and educational effectiveness.

Results of these evaluations must be used in revising and improving programs and services and in recognizing staff performance.

Areas to be assessed should include learning outcomes, student satisfaction, goal achievement, and effectiveness of teaching techniques. Particular efforts should be made to conduct longitudinal studies on program evaluations.

General Standards revised in 2002; SLP content developed/ revised in 1996.

THE ROLE of TRIO* and OTHER EDUCATIONAL OPPORTUNITY PROGRAMS
CAS Standards Contextual Statement

Students from low-income and first-generation backgrounds historically have had limited access to higher education. With the realization that the ideals of American higher education include access for all, both state and federal legislation have been enacted to mitigate some of these inequities. Since the 1960s, a variety of educational opportunity programs have been developed at the state and federal levels to increase access and persistence in higher education for students from disadvantaged backgrounds.

The TRIO Programs are federally funded educational opportunity programs designed to motivate and support students from disadvantaged backgrounds to attend and persist in post-secondary education. TRIO includes five outreach programs that target students who are from low-income families and who are the first-generation college students. TRIO serves students from middle school to post-baccalaureate programs. In addition, TRIO's professional development component provides training opportunities for directors and staff of TRIO projects.

The TRIO programs are authorized under the Higher Education of 1965, Title IV, Part A, Subpart 2. FEDERAL TRIO PROGRAMS, as amended in 1998. Programs are administered by the US Department of Education, Office of Post-secondary Education, Division of Higher Education Preparation and Support Service (HEPS). TRIO projects are funded through competitive grant applications. In 2000, there were 2,341 TRIO projects at 1100 institutions of higher education or community agencies, serving approximately 724,735 students.

The Council for Opportunity in Education represents over 7,000 TRIO program staff; sponsors professional development activities including national conferences, symposia; workshops, and publications; sponsors TRIO and educational access research; advocates for TRIO programs and students; and acts as liaison with the US Department of Education.

The initial TRIO programs included Upward Bound, which emerged from the Economic Opportunity Act of 1964 as part of President Johnson's War on Poverty; Talent Search, created in 1965 as part of the Higher Education Act; and Student Support Services, in 1968. The term "TRIO" referred to these original federal programs. The Higher Education Amendments of 1972 added Educational Opportunity Centers and the 1986 Amendments authorized the Ronald E. McNair Post-baccalaureate Achievement Program. The DOE established the Upward Bound Math/Science Program as a subset to Upward Bound in 1990.

Program Descriptions

- Educational Opportunity Centers (EOC) provide counseling and information about college admissions and financial aid with the goal of increasing the number of adult participants who enroll in post-secondary education. Services include advising; counseling; provision of information about educational opportunities and financial assistance; help with completing applications for college admissions; testing, and financial aid; coordination with educational institutions and community partnerships; and provision of referrals, tutoring, and mentoring.

- The Ronald E. McNair Post-baccalaureate Achievement program prepares undergraduates to enter doctoral studies. McNair participants are from disadvantaged backgrounds and have demonstrated strong academic potential. The goal of McNair is to increase graduate degree attainment by students from low-income, first-generation, and under-represented groups. Services include the provision of mentors; scholarly activities to prepare students for doctoral study; summer research internships; tutoring; counseling; assistance with securing graduate program admission and financial aid; preparation for GRE exams; and other activities that enhance successful entry to and persistence in doctoral programs.

- The Student Support Services (SSS) program provides academic support for low-income, first-generation students, and students with disabilities. Support is provided through academic development, assistance with college requirements, and activities that motivate students to complete post-secondary education. The goal of SSS is to increase college retention and graduation rates, and to facilitate two-year college student transition to four year institutions. Services include basic skills instruction and tutoring; academic, financial, and personal counseling; assistance with graduate or professional school admission and financial aid; mentoring; special services for students with limited English proficiency; cultural activities; and accommodations for students with disabilities.

- The Talent Search program identifies, motivates, and assists low-income, first generation youth to complete high school and enter and persist in higher education. Talent Search also serves high school dropouts by encouraging them to reenter the educational system and complete formal education. The goal of Talent Search is to increase the number of youth from disadvantaged backgrounds who complete high school and enroll in post-secondary education. Talent Search serves sixth to twelfth grade students by providing academic, financial, career, and personal counseling; tutoring; information about post-secondary education and college visits; procedures for completing college admissions and financial aid applications; preparation for college entrance exams; mentoring; and middle school student and family involvement activities.

- Upward Bound is an intensive college preparatory support project designed to provide low-income, first-generation high school students with encouragement and the essential skills to complete high school and earn a post-secondary degree. The goal of Upward Bound is to increase post-secondary enrollment and graduation rates of participants. Upward Bound provides instruction and enrichment activities throughout the calendar year. Other services provided include study skill development; academic, financial, and personal counseling; tutoring; cultural and social activities; information about post-secondary education opportunities and college visits, assistance with college entrance and financial aid applications; and preparation for college entrance exams. The Veterans' Upward Bound program serves military veterans who are preparing to enter post-secondary education. The Upward Bound Math Science program authorizes the Department of Education to fund specialized Upward Bound Math and Science Centers designed to strengthen high school students' math and science skills and to encourage students to pursue post-secondary degrees in math and science. Services include intensive summer math and science experiences, counseling and advising, computer instruction, and research activities.

References, Readings, and Resources

Wolanin, T. (April, 1997). The history of TRIO: Three decades of success and counting. *NCEOA Journal,* pp. 2-4.

Council for Opportunity in Education, 1025 Vermont Avenue, N.W. Suite 900, Washington, DC 20005. (202) 347-7430; Fax: (202) 347-0786; Web Page: www.trioprograms.org

National TRIO Clearinghouse, Vermont Ave. N. W., Suite 900, Washington, DC 20005, Phone: (202) 347-2218, Fax: (202) 347-0786 www.trioprograms.org, select TRIO Clearing-house.

United States Department of Education, Office of Post-secondary Education, Higher Education Preparation and Support (TRIO Program Administration): www.ed.gov/offices/OPE/HEP/hepss/index.html

Contributor: Andrea Reeve, Colorado State University

TRIO and OTHER EDUCATIONAL OPPORTUNITY PROGRAMS
CAS Standards and Guidelines

Part 1. MISSION

The mission of TRIO and Other Educational Opportunity (TRIO and OEO) Programs is to encourage and assist people who are traditionally under-represented in post-secondary education because of income, family educational background, disability, or other relevant federal, state, provincial or institutional criteria, in the preparation for, entry to, and completion of a post-secondary education.

To accomplish this mission, TRIO and OEO programs must:

- serve as advocate for access to higher education
- provide services to assist individuals to achieve their educational goals
- facilitate the educational development of individuals served
- provide an environment that recognizes the diversity of backgrounds and learning styles of the individuals served
- develop collaborative relationships with institutions, organizations, and communities to promote an environment conducive to the completion of a post-secondary education

TRIO and OEO programs must incorporate student learning and student development in its mission. TRIO and OEO programs must enhance overall educational experiences. TRIO and OEO programs must develop, record, disseminate, implement and regularly review its mission and goals. Mission statements must be consistent with the mission and goals of the institution and with the standards in this document. TRIO and OEO programs must operate as an integral part of the institution's overall mission.

TRIO and OEO programs should address the developmental needs of the individuals served. Programs and services should enable the individual to acquire the necessary skills and attributes to complete a post-secondary education.

Part 2. PROGRAM

The formal education of students consists of the curriculum and the co-curriculum, and must promote student learning and development that is purposeful and holistic. TRIO and Other Educational Opportunity (TRIO and OEO) Programs must identify relevant and desirable student learning and development outcomes and provide programs and services that encourage the achievement of those outcomes.

Relevant and desirable outcomes include: intellectual growth, effective communication, realistic self-appraisal, enhanced self-esteem, clarified values, career choices, leadership development, healthy behaviors, meaningful interpersonal relationships, independence, collaboration, social responsibility, satisfying and productive lifestyles, appreciation of diversity, spiritual awareness, and achievement of personal and educational goals.

TRIO and OEO programs must provide evidence of its impact on the achievement of student learning and development outcomes.

The table below offers examples of evidence of achievement of student learning and development.

Student Learning and Development Outcome Domains

Intellectual growth

Examples of achievement indicators

Produces personal and educational goal statements; Employs critical thinking in problem solving; Uses complex information from a variety of sources including personal experience and observation to form a decision or opinion; Obtains a degree; Applies previously understood information and concepts to a new situation or setting; Expresses appreciation for literature, the fine arts, mathematics, sciences, and social sciences

Effective communication

Examples of achievement indicators

Writes and speaks coherently and effectively; Writes and speaks after reflection; Able to influence others through writing, speaking or artistic expression; Effectively articulates abstract ideas; Uses appropriate syntax; Makes presentations or gives performances

Enhanced self-esteem

Examples of achievement indicators

Shows self-respect and respect for others; Initiates actions toward achievement of goals; Takes reasonable risks; Demonstrates assertive behavior; Functions without need for constant reassurance from others

Realistic self-appraisal

Examples of achievement indicators

Articulates personal skills and abilities; Makes decisions and acts in congruence with personal values; Acknowledges personal strengths and weaknesses; Articulates rationale for personal behavior; Seeks feedback from others; Learns from past experiences

Clarified values

Examples of achievement indicators

Articulates personal values; Acts in congruence with personal values; Makes decisions that reflect personal values; Demonstrates willingness to scrutinize personal beliefs and values; Identifies personal, work. and lifestyle values and explains how they influence decision-making

Career choices

Examples of achievement indicators

Articulates career choices based on assessment of interests, values, skills, and abilities; Documents knowledge, skills, and accomplishments resulting from formal education, work experience, community service and volunteer experiences; Makes the connections between classroom and out-of-classroom learning; Can construct a resume with clear job objectives and evidence of related knowledge, skills and accomplishments; Articulates the characteristics of a preferred work environment; Comprehends the world of work; Takes steps to initiate a job search or seek advanced education

Leadership development

Examples of achievement indicators

Articulates leadership philosophy or style; Serves in a leadership position in a student organization; Comprehends the dynamics of a group; Exhibits democratic principles as a leader; Exhibits ability to visualize a group purpose and desired outcomes

Healthy behavior

Examples of achievement indicators

Chooses behaviors and environments that promote health and reduce risk; Articulate the relationship between health and wellness and accomplishing life-long goals; Exhibits behaviors that advance a healthy community.

Meaningful interpersonal relationships

Examples of achievement indicators

Develops and maintains satisfying interpersonal relationships; Establishes mutually rewarding relationships with friends and colleagues; Listens to and considers others' points of view; Treats others with respect

Independence

Examples of achievement indicators

Exhibits self-reliant behaviors; Functions autonomously; Exhibits ability to function interdependently; Accepts supervision as needed; Manages time effectively

Collaboration

Examples of achievement indicators

Works cooperatively with others; Seeks the involvement of others; Seeks feedback from others; Contributes to achievement of a group goal; Exhibits effective listening skills

Social responsibility

Examples of achievement indicators

Understands and participates in relevant governance systems; Understands, abides by, and participates in the development, maintenance, and/or orderly change of community, social, and legal standards or norms; Appropriately challenges the unfair, unjust, or uncivil behavior of other individuals or groups; Participates in service/volunteer activities

Satisfying and productive lifestyles

Examples of achievement indicators

Achieves balance between education, work, and leisure time; Articulates and meets goals for work, leisure, and education; Overcomes obstacles that hamper goal achievement; Functions on the basis of personal identity, ethical, spiritual, and moral values; Articulates long-term goals and objectives

Appreciating diversity

Examples of achievement indicators

Understands one's own identity and culture; Seeks involvement with people different from oneself; Seeks involvement in diverse interests; Articulates the advantages and challenges of a diverse society; Challenges appropriately the abusive use of stereotypes by others; Understands the impact of diversity on one's own society

Spiritual awareness

Examples of achievement indicators

Develops and articulates personal belief system; Understands roles of spirituality in personal and group values and behaviors

Personal and educational goals

Examples of achievement indicators

Sets, articulates, and pursues individual goals; Articulates personal and educational goals and objectives; Uses personal and educational goals to guide decisions; Understands the effect of one's personal and educational goals on others

TRIO and OEO programs must be (a) intentional, (b) coherent, (c) based on theories and knowledge of learning and human development, (d) reflective of developmental and demographic profiles of the student population, and (e) responsive to needs of individuals, special populations, and communities.

All TRIO and OEO programs must support the retention and graduation of their students. Activities and services must address the specific objectives of each TRIO and OEO programs.

Programs, services, and activities for students involved in specific TRIO and OEO programs should include academic support services such as academic instruction; tutoring; English as a Second Language (ESL) activities; collaborative learning opportunities; supplemental instruction; development of oral and written communication skills; assessment of academic needs, skills and individual plans to provide appropriate interventions; monitoring of academic progress; preparation for proficiency and entrance exams; academic advising; opportunities for national and international study exchange; research internships; and opportunities to present and publish research.

Programming should also include a variety of mentoring experiences; career development and work internship activities; activities to assist with college admissions and financial aid; activities to prepare students for matriculation into graduate education; coordination with clubs and school activities; academic and cultural field trips; social activities; activities to encourage appreciation of cultural and ethnic diversity; athletic and physical development; leadership development; and other activities that promote matriculation into post-secondary or graduate schools, and support retention, persistence, and graduation.

TRIO and OEO programs should also implement programming with their own institution or agency, and with schools, community, and student families to accomplish their mission.

Part 3. LEADERSHIP
Effective and ethical leadership is essential to the success of all organizations. Institutions must appoint, position, and empower TRIO and Other Educational Opportunity (TRIO and OEO) program leaders within the administrative structure to accomplish stated missions. TRIO and OEO program leaders at various levels must be selected on the basis of formal education and training, relevant work experience, personal skills and competencies, relevant professional credentials, as well as potential for promoting learning and development in students, applying effective practices to educational processes, and enhancing institutional effectiveness. Institutions must determine expectations of accountability for leaders and fairly assess their performance.

TRIO and OEO program leaders must exercise authority over resources for which they are responsible to achieve their respective missions.

TRIO and OEO program leaders must:
- articulate a vision for their organization
- set goals and objectives based on the needs and capabilities of the population served
- promote student learning and development
- prescribe and practice ethical behavior
- recruit, select, supervise, and develop others in the organization
- manage financial resources
- coordinate human resources
- plan, budget for, and evaluate personnel and programs
- apply effective practices to educational and administrative processes
- communicate effectively
- initiate collaborative interaction between individuals and agencies that possess legitimate concerns and interests in the functional area

TRIO and OEO program leaders must identify and find means to address individual, organizational, or environmental conditions that inhibit goal achievement.

TRIO and OEO program leaders must promote campus environments that result in multiple opportunities for student learning and development.

TRIO and OEO program leaders must continuously improve programs and services in response to changing needs of students and other constituents, and evolving institutional priorities.

Part 4. ORGANIZATION and MANAGEMENT
Guided by an overarching intent to ensure student learning and development, TRIO and Other Educational Opportunity (TRIO and OEO) Programs must be structured purposefully and managed effectively to achieve stated goals. Evidence of appropriate structure must include current and accessible policies and procedures, written performance expectations for all employees, functional workflow graphics or organizational charts, and clearly stated service delivery expectations.

Evidence of effective management must include use of comprehensive and accurate information for decisions, clear sources and channels of authority, effective communication practices, decision-making and conflict resolution procedures, responsiveness to changing conditions, accountability and evaluation systems, and recognition and reward processes. TRIO and OEO programs must provide channels within the organization for regular review of administrative policies and procedures.

TRIO and OEO programs must be placed in the institution's organizational structure to promote cooperative interaction with appropriate campus or community entities and to develop the support of senior administrators.

TRIO and OEO programs should be positioned to assure appropriate recognition and visibility.

Part 5. HUMAN RESOURCES

TRIO and Other Educational Opportunity (TRIO and OEO) Programs must be staffed adequately by individuals qualified to accomplish its mission and goals. Within established guidelines of the institution, programs and services must establish procedures for staff selection, training, and evaluation; set expectations for supervision, and provide appropriate professional development opportunities. TRIO and OEO programs must strive to improve the professional competence and skills of all personnel it employs.

TRIO and OEO program professional staff members must hold an earned graduate degree in a field relevant to the position they hold or must possess an appropriate combination of educational credentials and related work experience.

Degree or credential-seeking interns must be qualified by enrollment in an appropriate field of study and by relevant experience. These individuals must be trained and supervised adequately by professional staff members holding educational credentials and related work experience appropriate for supervision.

Student employees and volunteers must be carefully selected, trained, supervised, and evaluated. They must be trained on how and when to refer those in need of assistance to qualified staff members and have access to a supervisor for assistance in making these judgments. Student employees and volunteers must be provided clear and precise job descriptions, pre-service training based on assessed needs, and continuing staff development.

TRIO and OEO programs must have technical and support staff members adequate to accomplish its mission. Staff members must be technologically proficient and qualified to perform their job functions, be knowledgeable of ethical and legal uses of technology, and have access to training. The level of staffing and workloads must be adequate and appropriate for program and service demands.

Salary levels and fringe benefits for all TRIO and OEO program staff members must be commensurate with those for comparable positions within the institution, in similar institutions, and in the relevant geographic area.

TRIO and OEO programs must institute hiring and promotion practices that are fair, inclusive, and non-discriminatory. TRIO and OEO programs must employ a diverse staff to provide readily identifiable role models for students and to enrich the campus community.

TRIO and OEO programs must create and maintain position descriptions for all staff members and provide regular performance planning and appraisals.

TRIO and OEO programs must have a system for regular staff evaluation and must provide access to continuing education and professional development opportunities, including in-service training programs and participation in professional conferences and workshops.

Hiring and promotion practices must ensure diverse staffing profiles.

TRIO and OEO programs professionals must possess a combination of knowledge and experience in working with individuals who are traditionally under-represented in post-secondary education.

Professional staff members should possess:
- effective oral and written communication skills
- an understanding of the culture, heritage, and learning styles of the persons served by the program
- leadership, management, organizational, and human relations skills

Student employees and volunteers from groups traditionally under-represented in higher education should be used and assigned responsibilities that are within the scope of their competencies.

The size, scope, and role of the program staff depend on the mission of TRIO and OEO programs and the populations served. Staffing should be based on the needs of the students or participants and the resources available. When possible, the staff should reflect the characteristics of the population being served.

TRIO and OEO programs should provide continuing professional development opportunities for staff such as in-service training programs, TRIO professional training seminars, participation in professional conferences, workshops, or other continuing education activities.

TRIO and OEO programs staff should contribute to the knowledge and practice of the profession through research and publications.

Part 6. FINANCIAL RESOURCES

TRIO and Other Educational Opportunity (TRIO and OEO) Programs must have adequate funding to accomplish its mission and goals. Funding priorities must be determined within the context of the stated mission, goals, objectives and comprehensive analysis of the needs and capabilities of students and the availability of internal or external resources.

TRIO and OEO programs must demonstrate fiscal responsibility and cost effectiveness consistent with institutional protocols.

Part 7. FACILITIES, TECHNOLOGY, and EQUIPMENT

TRIO and Other Educational Opportunity (TRIO and OEO) Programs must have adequate, suitably located facilities, adequate technology, and equipment to support its mission and goals efficiently and effectively. Facilities, technology, and equipment must be evaluated regularly and be in compliance with relevant federal, state, provincial, and local requirements to provide for access, health, safety, and security.

As applicable, the facilities must include, or the staff must have access to, private offices or spaces for counseling, advising, tutoring, interviewing, or meetings of a confidential nature. Facilities must be accessible to persons with disabilities.

TRIO and OEO programs facilities should be physically located to promote visibility of the programs and to ensure coordination with other campus programs and services.

TRIO and OEO programs should have equal access to the institution's technological resources.

TRIO and OEO programs should advocate for and facilitate access to technology for their students and families. Technology should be employed to promote TRIO and OEO programs, to provide academic and other student services, and to communicate with students including those at outreach locations. Programs should intentionally model for their students the use of technology.

Part 8. LEGAL RESPONSIBILITIES

TRIO and Other Educational Opportunity (TRIO and OEO) Programs staff members must be knowledgeable about and responsive to laws and regulations that relate to their respective responsibilities. Staff members must inform users of programs and services and officials, as appropriate, of legal obligations and limitations including constitutional, statutory, regulatory, and case law; mandatory laws and orders emanating from federal, state/provincial and local governments; and the institution's policies.

TRIO and OEO programs staff members must use reasonable and informed practices to limit the liability exposure of the institution, its officers, employees, and agents. Staff members must be informed about institutional policies regarding personal liability and related insurance coverage options.

The institution must provide access to legal advice for TRIO and OEO programs staff members as needed to carry out assigned responsibilities.

The institution must inform TRIO and OEO programs staff and students in a timely and systematic fashion about extraordinary or changing legal obligations and potential liabilities.

Part 9. EQUITY and ACCESS

TRIO and Other Educational Opportunity (TRIO and OEO) Programs staff members must ensure that services and programs are provided on a fair and equitable basis. Facilities, programs, and services must be accessible. Hours of operation and delivery of and access to programs and services must be responsive to the needs of all students and other constituents. TRIO and OEO programs must adhere to the spirit and intent of equal opportunity laws.

TRIO and OEO programs must be open and readily accessible to all students and must not discriminate except where sanctioned by law and institutional policy. Discrimination must be avoided on the bases of age; color; creed; cultural heritage; disability; ethnicity; gender identity; nationality; political affiliation; religious affiliation; sex; sexual orientation; or social, economic, marital, or veteran status.

Consistent with their mission and goals, TRIO and OEO programs must take affirmative action to remedy significant imbalances in student participation and staffing patterns.

As the demographic profiles of campuses change and new instructional delivery methods are introduced, institutions must recognize the needs of students who participate in distance learning for access to programs and services offered on campus. Institutions must provide appropriate services in ways that are accessible to distance learners and assist them in identifying and gaining access to other appropriate services in their geographic region.

Part 10. CAMPUS and EXTERNAL RELATIONS

TRIO and Other Educational Opportunity (TRIO and OEO) Programs must establish, maintain, and promote collaborative relations with relevant individuals, campus offices, external agencies, project area schools, community organizations, and students' families.

TRIO and OEO programs must include a public relations component to regularly inform the institutions, communities, agencies, and schools about their mission and services.

Part 11. DIVERSITY

Within the context of each institution's unique mission, diversity enriches the community and enhances the collegiate experience for all; therefore, TRIO and Other Educational Opportunity (TRIO and OEO) Programs must nurture environments where commonalties and differences among people are recognized and honored.

TRIO and OEO programs must promote educational experiences that are characterized by open and continuous communication that deepens understanding of one's own identity, culture, and heritage, and that of others. TRIO and OEO programs must educate and promote respect about commonalties and differences in their historical and cultural contexts.

TRIO and OEO programs must address the characteristics and needs of a diverse population when establishing and implementing policies and procedures.

Part 12. ETHICS

All persons involved in the delivery of TRIO and Other Educational Opportunity (TRIO and OEO) Programs must adhere to the highest principles of ethical behavior. TRIO and OEO programs must develop or adopt and implement appropriate statements of ethical practice. TRIO and OEO programs must publish these statements and ensure their periodic review by relevant constituencies.

TRIO and OEO programs staff members must ensure that privacy and confidentiality are maintained with respect to all communications and records to the extent that such records are protected under the law and appropriate statements of ethical practice. Information contained in students' education records must not be disclosed without written consent except as allowed by relevant laws and institutional policies. TRIO and OEO programs staff members must disclose to appropriate authorities information judged to be of an emergency nature, especially when the safety of the individual or others is involved, or when otherwise required by institutional policy or relevant law.

All TRIO and OEO programs staff members must be aware of and comply with the provisions contained in the institution's human subjects research policy and in other relevant institutional policies addressing ethical practices and confidentiality of research data concerning individuals.

TRIO and OEO programs staff members must recognize and avoid personal conflict of interest or appearance thereof in their transactions with students and others.

TRIO and OEO programs staff members must strive to insure the fair, objective, and impartial treatment of all persons with whom they deal. Staff members must not participate in nor condone any form of harassment that demeans persons or creates an intimidating, hostile, or offensive campus environment.
When handling institutional funds, all TRIO and OEO programs staff members must ensure that such funds are managed in accordance with established and responsible accounting procedures and the fiscal policies or processes of the institution.

TRIO and OEO programs staff members must perform their duties within the limits of their training, expertise, and competence. When these limits are exceeded, individuals in need of further assistance must be referred to persons possessing appropriate qualifications.

TRIO and OEO programs staff members must use suitable means to confront and otherwise hold accountable other staff members who exhibit unethical behavior.

TRIO and OEO programs staff members must be knowledgeable about and practice ethical behavior in the use of technology.

Part 13. ASSESSMENT and EVALUATION

TRIO and Other Educational Opportunity (TRIO and OEO) Programs must conduct regular assessment and evaluations. TRIO and OEO programs must employ effective qualitative and quantitative methodologies as appropriate, to determine whether and to what degree the stated mission, goals, and student learning and development outcomes are being met. The process must employ sufficient and sound assessment measures to ensure comprehensiveness. Data collected must include responses from students and other affected constituencies.

TRIO and OEO programs must evaluate periodically how well they complement and enhance the institution's stated mission and educational effectiveness.

Results of these evaluations must be used in revising and improving programs and services and in recognizing staff performance.

Annual program performance reports must be conducted in accordance with federal project guidelines.

Annual evaluation reports should be made available, when appropriate, to the program's various stakeholders, such as relevant campus offices, external agencies, area schools, and community organizations.

General Standards revised in 2002; TRIO/OEO programs content developed/revised in 1999.

THE ROLE of WOMEN STUDENT PROGRAMS AND SERVICES
CAS Standards Contextual Statement

History

In 2006, there are over 400 Women's Student Programs and Services (WSPS) and women's centers housed within colleges and universities across the U.S. While the first women's center was established in 1948 at the University of Minnesota, the vast majority of centers emerged in higher education in the early 1970s. WSPS and women's centers were established on campuses as a direct result of the issues and concerns about gender equity raised by students, administrators, faculty, and staff. Informed by the women's and civil rights movements, programs and services directly aimed at supporting and advancing student women, WSPS and women's centers were developed to respond to individual and institutional needs to support and advance women in higher education. In some institutions, women student programs and services are embedded in the missions and services of divisions of student affairs. In others, women student services and programs are organized as WSPS and women's centers with varied institutional reporting lines.

WSPS and women's centers have varied missions that express the unique cultures and goals of the institutions within which they reside. Most WSPS and women's centers professionals might agree that, generally, their mission includes addressing safety, education, support, equity and community for women students and, in some cases, faculty and staff members as well (Davie, 2002). Centers serve as a resource and advocate for the needs of women and other constituents both on and off campus on issues pertaining to equal access, affordability, recruitment, and retention.

Since their inception, WSPS and women's centers have partnered with on- and off- campus units to deliver services and support students in achieving their educational goals. The unique experiences of women students with campus life require that WSPS and women's centers – regardless of their reporting structure – collaborate with all elements of campus life: all sectors of student affairs, health and mental health services, law enforcement, athletics, academic and co-curricular units. WSPS and women's centers are dedicated to expanding the understanding of gender and social justice issues both on campus and in society and are informed by disciplines and professions such as women's studies, student affairs and higher education, student and public health, social work, and continuing education.

Changing Focus

When WSPS and women's centers were first founded, they tended to focus on questions of access, of getting women into academic institutions. Now that women represent over fifty percent (well over in some cases) of undergraduate students, the focus has changed to supporting women who are in the institutions, while continuing to advocate for equity and advocating for change in the seemingly intractable area of traditional gender roles.

Some consensus exists that women's centers will continue to help their institutions achieve their missions by addressing issues that impact women globally, thus contributing to the important mission of internationalizing campuses. Additionally, WSPS and women's centers can function as a connecting point to a broader range of community, statewide and national agencies, opportunities and resources.

WSPS and women's centers are working to incorporate advanced technology into their own work and into the work of outreach to on- and off-campus partners, by developing the websites, distance education and outreach efforts, video-streaming, specialized programs and accessibility for people with disabilities, and ways to make library, database, and other resources available through the internet.

WSPS and women's centers are examining ways to broaden their purview by partnering with academic areas to conduct research, providing undergraduate and advanced classes, creating internship and practicum opportunities for students, and supporting leadership opportunities for women with an emphasis on leadership development and mentoring for women students within the academy and beyond.

These standards have been updated to reflect the changing focus and missions of women's centers and WSPS.

References, Readings, and Resources

Brooks, K. H. (1988). The women's center: The new dean of women? *Initiatives, 51,* 17-21.

Davie, S. L. (Ed.). (2002). *University and college women's centers: A journey toward equity.* Westport, CT: Greenwood Press.

Clevenger, B. M. (1988). Women's centers on campus: A profile. *Initiatives, 51,* 3-9.

Gould, J. S. (1989). *Women's centers as agents of change.* In C. S. Pearson, D. L. Shavlik, & J. G. Touchton (Eds.), Educating the majority: Women challenge tradition in higher education. New York: American Council on Education & Macmillan Publishing Company.

Kasper, B. (2004). Campus-based women's centers: Administration, structure, and resources. *NASPA Journal, 4*(3), 487-499. Available: http://publications.naspa.org/naspajournal/vol41/iss3/art6.

Kasper, B. (2004). Campus-based women's centers: A review of problems and practices. *Affilia, 19*(2), 185-198.

Miller, A. (1988). Making feminism matter: The revitalization of a campus women's center. *Initiatives, 51,* 37-43.

Parker, J., & Freedman, J. (1999). Women's centers/women's studies programs: Collaborating for feminist activism. *Women's Studies Quarterly, 27,* 114-121.

TenElshof, A., & Searle, S. E. (1974). Developing a women's center. *Journal of the National Association for Women Deans, Administrators, and Counselors, 37*(4), 173-178.

Zaytoun Byrne, K. (2000). The role of campus-based women's centers. *Feminist Teacher, 13*(1), 48-60.

National Women's Studies Association Women's Centers Committee http://www.nwsa.org/centers/index.php

Women's Centers have representation on the NWSA Governing Council as a standing committee. This is more than a symbolic recognition of the important role that women's centers play in feminist education. NWSA recognizes that "women's studies" is broader than what happens in the classroom. NWSA acknowledges women's centers as chief out-of-class feminist educators and encourages participation in the national organization.

Campus-based women's centers have a long history of working together with women's studies to transform the curriculum, the campus environment, and society at large. The Women's Centers Committee of NWSA provides an opportunity for women's center directors, staff and others to gather and share information, ideas, challenges, successes and support. The Women's Centers Committee sponsors an annual pre-conference event as well as sessions during the NWSA annual conference.

NWSA Women's Centers Resources: http://www.nwsa.org/centers/resources.php

Contributors:
Brenda Bethman, Texas A&M University
Ellen Plummer, Virginia Tech
Beth Rietveld, Oregon State University

WOMEN STUDENT PROGRAMS AND SERVICES
CAS Standards and Guidelines

Part 1. MISSION

The purpose of WSPS is to promote a supportive, equitable, and safe environment for women.

Women Student Programs and Services (WSPS) must incorporate student learning and student development in its mission. WSPS must enhance overall educational experiences. WSPS must develop, record, disseminate, implement, and regularly review its mission and goals. Mission statements must be consistent with the mission and goals of the institution and with the standards in this document. WSPS must operate as an integral part of the institution's overall mission.

The mission is accomplished by:

- empowering students to create a campus culture that values all women and their diverse identities and experiences
- providing, coordinating, or participating in comprehensive sexual violence risk reduction programs and services for survivors of sexual violence
- educating all students on the ways in which gender is constructed and shapes social structures and individual experiences
- assessing the climate for women and advocating for the diverse needs of women
- providing information and referrals about issues that disproportionately affect women, such as sexual harassment, relationship violence, rape, and disordered eating
- sponsoring speakers, performers, events, and activities that address gender issues
- creating opportunities for women's voices to be heard

Part 2. PROGRAM

The formal education of students consists of the curriculum and the co-curriculum, and must promote student learning and development that is purposeful and holistic. Women Student Programs and Services (WSPS) must identify relevant and desirable student learning and development outcomes and provide programs and services that encourage the achievement of those outcomes.

Relevant and desirable outcomes include: intellectual growth, effective communication, realistic self-appraisal, enhanced self-esteem, clarified values, career choices, leadership development, healthy behaviors, meaningful interpersonal relationships, independence, collaboration, social responsibility, satisfying and productive lifestyles, appreciation of diversity, spiritual awareness, and achievement of personal and educational goals.

WSPS must provide evidence of its impact on the achievement of student learning and development outcomes.

The table below offers examples of evidence of achievement of student learning and development.

Student Learning and Development Outcome Domains

Intellectual growth

Examples of achievement indicators

Understands the intersection of gender with race, class, sexual orientation, and other identity formations; Explains how feminist, womanist, and other gendered theories inform practice and vice versa; Employs critical thinking in problem solving; Integrates complex information from a variety of sources including personal experience to form a decision or opinion; Expresses an appreciation for how gender informs the production of knowledge and the experience of learning

Effective communication

Examples of achievement indicators

Expresses oneself and influences others through writing, speaking, and/or artistic expression

Enhanced self-esteem

Examples of achievement indicators

Shows respect for self and others; Demonstrates willingness to address challenges and pursue opportunities; Communicates values, needs, and boundaries effectively

Realistic self-appraisal

Examples of achievement indicators

Explores how societal expectations may inform one's self-appraisal; Recognizes personal strengths and challenges; Considers feedback from others; Learns from past experiences

Clarified values

Examples of achievement indicators

Understands influence of societal norms on the construction of personal values; Demonstrates willingness to examine personal beliefs and values and how they influence behavior

Career choices

Examples of achievement indicators

Evaluates workplaces and policies as they relate to gender, race, class, sexual orientation, and ability; Understands how these factors affect the intersection of career choice, personal and professional goals, and the world of work; Develops a vision for professional growth congruent with one's passions, values, and skills

Leadership development

Examples of achievement indicators

Demonstrates initiative, vision, and perseverance; Comprehends group dynamics; Exerts positive influence to create desired outcomes

Healthy behavior

Examples of achievement indicators

Learns about and uses effective self-care strategies; Articulates the relationship between health and wellness and accomplishing life-long goals; Chooses behaviors and environments that promote health and reduce risk

Meaningful interpersonal relationships

Examples of achievement indicators

Develops and maintains interpersonal relationships with others based on respect; Appreciates differences by listening to and considering others' points of view

Independence

Examples of achievement indicators

Exhibits self-reliant behaviors; Functions autonomously; Exhibits ability to function interdependently

Collaboration

Examples of achievement indicators

Develops relationships that lead toward achievement of goals; Seeks wide involvement of others; Demonstrates an openness to feedback

Social responsibility

Examples of achievement indicators

Appropriately challenges the unfair, unjust, or uncivil behavior of other individuals or groups; Participates in community service activities

Satisfying and productive lifestyles

Examples of achievement indicators

Articulates long-term personal and professional goals and objectives based on personal identity, ethical, spiritual, and moral values

Appreciating diversity

Examples of achievement indicators

Seeks to understand one's own multifaceted identity; Seeks involvement with people different from oneself; Articulates the advantages and challenges of a diverse society; Appropriately challenges stereotypes; Understands the impact of diversity on one's own society

Spiritual awareness

Examples of achievement indicators

Develops and articulates a personal belief system; Understands role of spirituality in personal and group values and behaviors

Personal and educational goals

Examples of achievement indicators

Articulates and pursues goals and objectives; Uses goals to guide decisions; Assesses and revises goals periodically; Understands the effect of one's personal and educational goals on others

WSPS must be (a) intentional, (b) coherent, (c) based on theories and knowledge of learning and human development, (d) reflective of developmental and demographic profiles of the student population, and (e) responsive to needs of individuals, unique populations, and communities.

WSPS staff must address the needs of undergraduate and graduate women students by incorporating the dimensions of ethnicity, race, religion, ability, sexual orientation, age, socioeconomic status, and other aspects of identity through programs and services. WSPS must promote unrestricted access for full involvement of women in all aspects of the collegiate experience.

WSPS must provide programs and services that address institutional environment, social justice, campus support services, networking opportunities, and other educational issues of significance to women.

WSPS may address issues of equity for staff members, faculty members, and women in the surrounding community.

To address the institutional environment, WSPS must:

- **advocate for a campus culture that eliminates barriers, prejudice, bigotry, and creates a hospitable climate for all women**
- **assess and monitor the campus climate for women in areas of sexual harassment and sexual violence, and collaborate with on- and off-campus partners to create institutional policies, education, and programs to work toward the elimination of violence against women**

- advocate for assessment of the campus environment for the presence of gender bias in areas including but not limited to employment, educational opportunities, and classroom climate
- advocate for the elimination of institutional policies and practices that result in an inequitable impact on women as students or employees
- promote awareness in ways in which gender bias intersects with racism, classism, and homophobia
- serve as a resource in helping campus constituencies identify and create equitable practices

WSPS must advance social justice through opportunities for involvement in global, national, state/provincial, and local action initiatives related to improving women's lives.

WSPS should provide models of non-hierarchical and collaborative leadership.

WSPS should provide social activism opportunities that allow for the integration of theory with practice.

WSPS must address the provision of campus support services including:
- advocacy, resources, and referrals related to sexual assault, sexual harassment, cyber-harassment, stalking, and relationship violence
- academic support that addresses concerns such as flexible scheduling, the environment for women students in traditionally male-dominated disciplines, and gender equity in the classroom
- resources and referrals for prevention, counseling, medical services, healthcare, disordered eating, physical and mental health, and equitable access to wellness, fitness, and health services
- resources and referrals for underrepresented or underserved communities
- the need for adequate, accessible, affordable, and flexible child and family care

WSPS must facilitate networking opportunities that:
- create support systems and communication networks for women students
- identify role models by recognizing and celebrating the accomplishments of women on and off campus
- encourage liaisons between global, national, state, provincial, and local women's organizations and campus-based women student programs and services

WSPS must provide educational programs that promote awareness of the way in which gender is constructed and shapes social structures and individual experiences. WSPS must offer experiential opportunities that explore oppression, privilege, and racism to increase students' understanding of the intersections of sexism with racism, classism, homophobia, and other forms of oppression.

WSPS should support the promotion of scholarship and research on women and gender in collaboration with a women studies program, if available, as well as with other departments.

Educational programs should focus on women's physical and mental health, personal safety, sexual assault and relationship violence, healthy relationships, leadership, spirituality, current events, and global issues.

WSPS should provide service learning and internship opportunities.

WSPS should advocate curricular change to include women's issues and contribution to society.

Part 3. LEADERSHIP

Effective and ethical leadership is essential to the success of all organizations. Institutions must appoint, position, and empower Women Student Programs and Services (WSPS) leaders within the administrative structure to accomplish stated missions. WSPS leaders at various levels must be selected on the basis of formal education and training, relevant work experience, personal skills and competencies, relevant professional credentials, as well as potential for promoting learning and development in students, applying effective practices to educational processes, and enhancing institutional effectiveness. Institutions must determine expectations of accountability for leaders and fairly assess their performance.

Leaders of WSPS must exercise authority over resources for which they are responsible to achieve their respective missions.

WSPS leaders must:
- articulate a vision for their organization
- set goals and objectives based on the needs and capabilities of the population served
- promote student learning and development
- prescribe and practice ethical behavior
- recruit, select, supervise, and develop others in the organization
- manage financial resources
- coordinate human resources

- **plan, budget for, and evaluate personnel and programs**
- **apply effective practices to educational and administrative processes**
- **communicate effectively**
- **initiate collaborative interaction between individuals and agencies that possess legitimate concerns and interests in the functional area**

WSPS leaders must identify and find means to address individual, organizational, or environmental conditions that inhibit goal achievement.

WSPS leaders must promote campus environments that result in multiple opportunities for student learning and development.

WSPS leaders must continuously improve programs and services in response to changing needs of students and other constituents, and evolving institutional priorities.

Part 4. ORGANIZATION and MANAGEMENT

Guided by an overarching intent to ensure student learning and development, Women Student Programs and Services (WSPS) must be structured purposefully and managed effectively to achieve stated goals. Evidence of appropriate structure must include current and accessible policies and procedures, written performance expectations for all employees, functional workflow graphics or organizational charts, and clearly stated service delivery expectations.

Evidence of effective management must include use of comprehensive and accurate information for decisions, clear sources and channels of authority, effective communication practices, decision-making and conflict resolution procedures, responsiveness to changing conditions, accountability and evaluation systems, and recognition and reward processes. WSPS must provide channels within the organization for regular review of administrative policies and procedures.

In response to the assessed needs of women students, WSPS must play a principal role in creating and implementing institutional policies and programs developed.

In the case of student-run women's programs, student leaders should have access to policy and decision makers of the institution.

Emphasis should be placed on achieving an organizational

placement so that activities of WSPS are not limited to a specific group of women students (e.g., solely undergraduate women) or specific service (e.g., solely counseling services).

WSPS should function as an autonomous unit rather than be housed as a component of other units on campus.

Individual units should be afforded the opportunity to organize in a manner that is efficient and best promotes equity.

Part 5. HUMAN RESOURCES

Women Student Program and Services (WSPS) must be staffed adequately by individuals qualified to accomplish its mission and goals. Within established guidelines of the institution, WSPS must establish procedures for staff selection, training, and evaluation; set expectations for supervision, and provide appropriate professional development opportunities. WSPS must strive to improve the professional competence and skills of all personnel it employs.

WSPS should be staffed by persons with the credentials and ability to forge gender equity on campus to promote the integrity of the unit.

Staff positions must be classified and compensated on a level commensurate with equivalent positions in other units.

WSPS professional staff members must hold an earned graduate degree in a field relevant to the position they hold or must possess an appropriate combination of educational credentials and related work experience.

The leadership must have knowledge of and preferably experience with gender issues and their impact on learning and development

The professional staff should possess the academic preparation, experience, professional interests, and competencies essential for the efficient operation of the office as charged, as well as the ability to identify additional areas of concern for women. Staff members should have coursework in women's studies or demonstrated experience in advocacy on women's issues. Specific coursework may include organization development, counseling theory and practice, group dynamics, leadership development, human development, and research and evaluation.

Professional staff should demonstrate a commitment to improving women's lives and a respect for the diversity of women's identities and experiences.

Professional staff should: (a) develop and implement programs and services; (b) conduct assessment, research, and evaluation; (c) advocate for the improvement of the quality of life for women as students, faculty members, and staff members; and (d) participate in institutional policy and governance efforts to ensure that policies and practices take into account the unique experiences of women.

Degree or credential-seeking interns must be qualified by enrollment in an appropriate field of study and by relevant experience. These individuals must be trained and supervised adequately by professional staff members holding educational credentials and related work experience appropriate for supervision.

Student employees and volunteers must be carefully selected, trained, supervised, and evaluated. They must be trained on how and when to refer those in need of assistance to qualified staff members and have access to a supervisor for assistance in making these judgments. Student employees and volunteers must be provided clear and precise job descriptions, pre-service training based on assessed needs, and continuing staff development.

WSPS should provide student staff with training and development that fosters an understanding of gender, race, class, sexual orientation, religion, ability, and other identity formations. Wherever possible, efforts should be made to ensure that student staff reflects the diversity of women students.

WSPS must have technical and support staff members adequate to accomplish its mission. Staff members must be technologically proficient and qualified to perform their job functions, be knowledgeable of ethical and legal uses of technology, and have access to training. The level of staffing and workloads must be adequate and appropriate for program and service demands.

Technical and support staff should be sufficient to perform office and administrative functions, including welcoming, sharing resources, problem identification, and referral. In the selection and training of technical and support staff members, special emphasis should be placed on skills in the areas of crisis response and management, public relations, information dissemination, problem identification, and referral. A thorough knowledge of the institution, its various offices, and relevant community resources is important.

Salary levels and fringe benefits for all WSPS staff members must be commensurate with those for comparable positions within the institution, in similar institutions, and in the relevant geographic area.

WSPS must institute hiring and promotion practices that are fair, inclusive, and non-discriminatory. WSPS must employ a diverse staff to provide readily identifiable role models for students and to enrich the campus community.

WSPS must create and maintain position descriptions for all staff members and provide regular performance planning and appraisals.

WSPS must have a system for regular staff evaluation and must provide access to continuing education and professional development opportunities, including in-service training programs and participation in professional conferences and workshops.

To remain current and effective in understanding and addressing needs of women students staff members should be encouraged to enroll in credit courses and seminars, and be given access to published research, opinion, and relevant other media.

Part 6. FINANCIAL RESOURCES

Women Student Programs and Services (WSPS) must have adequate funding to accomplish its mission and goals. Funding priorities must be determined within the context of the stated mission, goals, objectives, and comprehensive analysis of the needs and capabilities of students, and the availability of internal or external resources.

WSPS must demonstrate fiscal responsibility and cost effectiveness consistent with institutional protocols.

Although initial funding for WSPS may come from a combination of institutional funds, grant money, student government funds, fees for services, and government contracts, permanent institutional funding should be allocated for the continuing operation of WSPS.

Part 7. FACILITIES, TECHNOLOGY, and EQUIPMENT

Women Student Programs and Services (WSPS) must have adequate, suitably located facilities, adequate technology, and equipment to support its mission and goals efficiently and effectively. Facilities, technology, and equipment must be evaluated regularly and be in compliance with relevant federal, state, provincial, and local requirements to provide for access, health, safety, and security.

Technology and equipment must be updated regularly. In addition, support for technology must be provided to WSPS.

Facilities may be located in prominent, visible areas to visually demonstrate the institution's commitment to WSPS. Facilities should include private meeting areas and welcoming communal space. Facilities should be staffed beyond traditional business hours to ensure access for non-traditional students and other community members.

Part 8. LEGAL RESPONSIBILITIES

Women Student Programs and Services (WSPS) staff members must be knowledgeable about and responsive to laws and regulations that relate to their respective responsibilities. WSPS staff members must inform users of programs and services and officials, as appropriate, of legal obligations and limitations including constitutional, statutory, regulatory, and case law; mandatory laws and orders emanating from federal, state, provincial, and local governments; and the institution's policies.

WSPS staff members must use reasonable and informed practices to limit the liability exposure of the institution, its officers, employees, and agents. Staff members must be informed about institutional policies regarding personal liability and related insurance coverage options.

The institution must provide access to legal advice for WSPS staff members as needed to carry out assigned responsibilities.

The institution must inform WSPS staff and students in a timely and systematic fashion about extraordinary or changing legal obligations and potential liabilities.

WSPS should serve as a resource to individuals and the institution on legal issues, institutional policy, state/provincial, and federal laws related to FERPA, or Canadian Freedom Of Information and Protection of Privacy (FOIPP), the Clery Act (the Campus Security Act), sexual harassment and discrimination, Title IX, and the rights and responsibilities associated with confidentiality.

Part 9. EQUITY and ACCESS

Women Student Programs and Services (WSPS) staff members must ensure that services and programs are provided on a fair and equitable basis. Facilities, programs and services must be accessible. Hours of operation and delivery of and access to programs and services must be responsive to the needs of all students and other constituents. WSPS must adhere to the spirit and intent of equal opportunity laws.

WSPS must be open and readily accessible to all students and must not discriminate except where sanctioned by law and institutional policy. Discrimination must be avoided on the basis of age; color; creed; cultural heritage; disability; ethnicity; gender identity; nationality; political affiliation; religious affiliation; sex; sexual orientation; or social, economic, marital, or veteran status.

Consistent with their mission and goals, WSPS must take affirmative action to remedy significant imbalances in student participation and staffing patterns.

As the demographic profiles of campuses change and new instructional delivery methods are introduced, institutions must recognize the needs of students who participate in distance learning for access to programs and services offered on campus. Institutions must provide appropriate services in ways that are accessible to distance learners and assist them in identifying and gaining access to other appropriate services in their geographic region.

Part 10. CAMPUS and EXTERNAL RELATIONS

Women Student Programs and Services (WSPS) must establish, maintain, and promote effective relations with relevant individuals, campus offices, and external agencies.

WSPS should maintain good working relationships with agencies such as counseling, financial aid, clinical health services, health promotion services, career services, recreational sports, athletics, residential life, multicultural affairs, and public safety. WSPS should maintain a high degree of visibility with academic units through direct promotion and delivery of services, involvement with co-curricular programs, and staff efforts to increase understanding of the needs of women students.

Program staff should be an integral part of appropriate campus networks to participate effectively in the establishment of institution-wide policy and practices and to collaborate effectively with other staff and faculty members in providing services.

WSPS should build effective partnerships with the community to articulate common concerns and share resources.

Part 11. DIVERSITY

Within the context of each institution's unique mission, diversity enriches the community and enhances the collegiate experience for all; therefore, Women Student Programs and Services (WSPS) must nurture environments where commonalties and differences among people are recognized and honored.

WSPS must promote educational experiences that are characterized by open and continuous communication that deepens understanding of one's own identity, culture, and heritage, and that of others. WSPS must educate and promote respect about commonalties and differences in their historical and cultural contexts.

WSPS must address the characteristics and needs of a diverse population when establishing and implementing policies and procedures.

WSPS should be intentional about addressing race, ethnicity, class, sex, religion, sexual orientation, ability, and other aspects of identity in WSPS educational programs and services as well as in institutional policies and practices.

Part 12. ETHICS

All persons involved in the delivery of Women Student Programs and Services (WSPS) must adhere to the highest principles of ethical behavior. WSPS must develop or adopt and implement appropriate statements of ethical practice. WSPS must publish these statements and ensure their periodic review by relevant constituencies.

WSPS staff members must ensure that privacy and confidentiality are maintained with respect to all communications and records to the extent that such records are protected under the law and appropriate statements of ethical practice. Information contained in students' education records must not be disclosed without written consent except as allowed by relevant laws and institutional policies. Staff members must disclose to appropriate authorities information judged to be of an emergency nature, especially when the safety of the individual or others is involved, or when otherwise required by institutional policy or relevant law.

All WSPS staff members must be aware of and comply with the provisions contained in the institution's human subjects research policy and in other relevant institutional policies addressing ethical practices and confidentiality of research data concerning individuals.

WSPS staff members must recognize and avoid personal conflict of interest or appearance thereof in their transactions with students and others.

WSPS staff members must strive to ensure the fair, objective, and impartial treatment of all persons with whom they interact. Staff members must not participate in nor condone any form of harassment that demeans persons or creates an intimidating,

hostile, or offensive campus environment.

When handling institutional funds, all WSPS staff members must ensure that such funds are managed in accordance with established and responsible accounting procedures and the fiscal policies or processes of the institution.

WSPS staff members must perform their duties within the limits of their training, expertise, and competence. When these limits are exceeded, individuals in need of further assistance must be referred to persons possessing appropriate qualifications.

WSPS staff members must use suitable means to confront and otherwise hold accountable other staff members who exhibit unethical behavior.

WSPS staff members must be knowledgeable about and practice ethical behavior in the use of technology.

Part 13. ASSESSMENT and EVALUATION

Women Student Programs and Services (WSPS) must conduct regular assessment and evaluations. WSPS must employ effective qualitative and quantitative methodologies as appropriate, to determine whether and to what degree the stated mission, goals, and student learning and development outcomes are being met. The process must employ sufficient and sound assessment measures to ensure comprehensiveness. Data collected must include responses from students and other affected constituencies.

WSPS must evaluate periodically how well they complement and enhance the institution's stated mission and educational effectiveness.

A comprehensive evaluation of the ongoing program should be carried out in accordance with the general practice of program review for other units of the institution. To assist staff in planning and program formation, WSPS should establish an on-going evaluation process.

Results of these evaluations must be used in revising and improving programs and services and in recognizing staff performance.

WSPS should inform constituencies and the institution of the results of assessment and evaluation. WSPS should engage the institution in climate-related research that addresses issues that might have a disparate effect on women.

General Standards revised in 2002; WSPS content developed/ revised in 1992, 1997, & 2005

THE ROLE OF MASTERS-LEVEL STUDENT AFFAIRS
PROFESSIONAL PREPARATION PROGRAMS
CAS Standards Contextual Statement

Standards for the professional education of student affairs practitioners are of relatively recent vintage, having largely been established during the past two decades. In 1964 the Council of Student Personnel Associations in Higher Education (COSPA) drafted "A Proposal for Professional Preparation in College Student Personnel Work," which subsequently evolved into "Guidelines for Graduate Programs in the Preparation of Student Personnel Workers in Higher Education," dated March 5, 1967. The change in title from "proposal for" in the 1964 version to "guidelines for" in this fourth draft revision exemplifies the movement from a rather tentative statement of what professional preparation should entail to one asserting specific guidelines that should be followed in graduate education programs. A final statement, popularly recognized as the COSPA Report, was actually published some time after the dissolution of the Council (1975).

During this period, others concerned with the graduate education of counselors and other helping professionals were busy establishing counselor education standards and exploring the possibilities for accrediting graduate academic programs. A moving force in this effort was the Association of Counselor Educators and Supervisors (ACES), a division of the American Personnel and Guidance Association (APGA), now the American Counseling Association (ACA). In 1978, ACES published a set of professional standards to be used to accredit counseling and personnel services education programs. APGA had recognized ACES as its official counselor education accrediting body and moved to establish an inter-association committee to guide counselor education program accreditation activity and the review and revision of the ACES/APGA preparation standards. In response to this initiative, the American College Personnel Association (ACPA) established an ad hoc Preparation Standards Drafting Committee to create a set of standards designed to focus on the special concerns of student affairs graduate education. At its March 1979 meetings, the ACPA Executive Council adopted the committee's statement entitled "Standards for the Preparation of Counselors and College Student Affairs Specialists at the Master's Degree Level." ACPA then initiated a two-pronged effort in the area of professional standards. One was a collaborative effort with NASPA to establish a profession-wide program of standards creation and the other was a concerted effort to work under the then-APGA organizational umbrella to establish an agency for the accreditation of counseling and student affairs preparation programs. The former initiative resulted in the creation of the Council for the Advancement of Standards in Higher Education (CAS) and the latter in the establishment of the Council for the Accreditation of Counseling and Other Related

Educational Programs (CACREP), an academic program accrediting agency. Both the CAS and CACREP professional preparation standards reflected the influence of the ACPA standards for student affairs preparation.

The foregoing process was prelude to the *CAS Masters Level Student Affairs Graduate Program Standards and Guidelines*, which follow. A major value of graduate standards is that they provide criteria by which an academic program of professional preparation can judge its educational efforts. Whether used for accreditation or program development purposes, standards provide faculty, staff, administrators, and students alike a tool to measure a program's characteristics against a set of well-conceived criteria designed to ensure educational quality.

The CAS standards for student affairs graduate programs were revised in 2001 and offer standards and guidelines based on profession-wide inter-association collaboration. Topics addressed in the standards include the program's mission; recruitment and admission policies and procedures; curriculum policies; pedagogy; the curriculum; equal opportunity access and affirmative action; academic and student support; professional ethics and legal responsibilities; and program evaluation

Curriculum standards are organized around Foundation Studies, Professional Studies, and Supervised Practice. Foundation Studies pertain to the historical and philosophical foundations of higher education and student affairs. This includes historical documents of the profession such as the Learning Reconsidered I and II (2004, 2006), Student Personnel Point of View (ACE, 1937), Return to the Academy (Brown, 1972), the Student Learning Imperative (ACPA, 1996), Principles of Good Practice (Blimling & Whitt, 1999), Powerful Partnerships (Joint Task Force, 1998), and Reasonable Expectations (Kuh et al, 1994) among others (found at http://www.naspa.org/gradprep/index. cfm?show=6; www.myacpa.org/pub/pub_othermedia. cfm). Professional Studies pertains to student development theory, student characteristics, the effects of college on students, individual and group interventions, the organization and administration of student affairs, and assessment, evaluation and research. Supervised Practice includes practica, internships, and externships under professionally supervised work conditions.

The primary value of the CAS preparation standards is to assist in assuring that an academic program is offering what the profession, through representative consensus, has deemed necessary to graduate prepared student affairs professionals. Two groups that exist to support and promote the preparation of professionals are the Commission of Professional Preparation of ACPA and NASPA's Faculty Fellows.

References, Readings, and Resources

American College Personnel Association [ACPA]. Commission on Professional Preparation. ACPA National Office, One Dupont Circle, N.W., Suite 300. Washington, DC 20036-1110. (202) 835-2272; Fax (202) 296-3286. www.myacpa.org/comm/profprep/comm12.htm.

American College Personnel Association (1996). The student learning imperative: Implications for student affairs. *Journal of College Student Development, 37,* 118-122.

American Council on Education (ACE) (1937). *The student personnel point of view* (Ser. 1, Vol. 1, No. 3,). Washington, DC: Author. [revised in 1949 and 1989].

Association of Counselor Educators and Supervisors (ACES). (1978). Standards for the preparation of counselors and other personnel services specialists at the master's degree level. Washington, DC: Author.

Blimling, G. S. & Whitt, E. J. (1999). *Good practice in student affairs.* San Francisco: Jossey-Bass.

Brown, R. D. (1972). Student development in tomorrow's higher education - A return to the academy. *Student Personnel Series, 16.* Washington, D.C.: American College Personnel Association.

Bryant, W. A., Winston, R. B. Jr., & Miller, T. K. (Eds.) (1991). *Using professional standards in student affairs,* No. 53. New Directions for Student Affairs. San Francisco: Jossey-Bass.

Cooper, D. L., Saunders, S. A., Winston, R. B., Jr., Hirt, J. B., Creamer, D. G., Janosik, S, M. (2002). *Learning through supervised practice in student affairs.* New York: Taylor Francis.

Council of Student Personnel Associations (COSPA). (1964). A proposal for professional preparation in college student personnel work. Unpublished manuscript, Indianapolis: Author.

Council of Student Personnel Associations (COSPA). (March, 1967). Guidelines for graduate programs in the preparation of student personnel workers in higher education. Unpublished manuscript, Washington, DC: Author.

Council of Student Personnel Associations (COSPA). (1975). Student development services in post-secondary education. *Journal of College Student Personnel, 16* (6), 524-528.

Evans, N., & Phelps Tobin, C. (1996). *State of the art of preparation and practice in student affairs: Another look.* Lanham, MD: University Press of America.

Joint Task Force of Student Learning. (1998). *Powerful partnerships: A shared responsibility for learning.* Washington, D. C. American Association for Higher Education.

Kuh, G. D. (1994). *Reasonable expectations: Renewing the educational compact between institutions and students.* Washington, D.C.: National Association of Student Personnel Administrators.

Langseth, M. & Plater, W. (Eds.). (2004). *Public work and the academy: An academic administrator's guide to civic engagement and service-learning.* Boston: Anker Publishing.

Magolda, P & Carnaghi, J. (Eds.). (2004). *Job one: Experiences of new professionals in student affairs.* New York: University Press of America.

National Association of Student Personnel Administrators (NASPA). (1987). *A perspective on student affairs: A statement issued on the 50th anniversary of the student personnel point of view.* Washington, DC: Author. Also available at http://www.naspa.org/gradprep/index.cfm?show=6.

Whitt, E. J., Carnaghi, J. E., Matkin, J., Scalese-Love, P., & Nestor, D. (1990). Believing is seeing: Alternative perspectives on a statement of professional philosophy for student affairs. *NASPA Journal, 27* (3), 178-184.

Winston, R. B. Jr., Creamer, D. G., Miller, T. K., & Associates (2001). *The professional student affairs administrator: Educator, leader, and manager.* Philadelphia: Taylor and Francis.

Contributor: Jan Arminio, Shippensburg University

MASTERS-LEVEL STUDENT AFFAIRS PROFESSIONAL PREPARATION PROGRAMS
CAS Standards and Guidelines

Part 1. Mission and Objectives

The mission of professional preparation programs shall be to prepare persons through graduate education for professional positions in student affairs in schools, colleges, and universities. Each program mission must be consistent with the mission of the institution offering the program.

Program missions should reflect a particular emphasis, such as administration, counseling, student learning and development, student cultures, or other appropriate emphases, as long as the standards herein are met.

The program's mission may include providing in-service education, professional development, research, and consultation for student affairs professional staff members at the institution.

Each professional preparation program must publish a clear statement of mission and objectives prepared by the program faculty in consultation with collaborating student affairs professionals and relevant advisory committees. The statement must be readily available to current and prospective students and to appropriate faculty and staff members and agencies. It must be written to allow accurate assessment of student learning and program effectiveness. The statement must be reviewed periodically.

This review may be conducted with the assistance of current students and faculty, graduates of the program, student affairs professionals, and personnel in cooperating agencies.

The program faculty should consider recommendations of local, state/provincial, regional, and national legislative bodies and professional groups concerned with student affairs when developing, revising, and publishing the program's mission and objectives. The mission and objectives should reflect consideration of the current issues and needs of society, of higher education, and of the student populations served. Personnel in cooperating agencies and faculty members with primary assignments in other disciplines should be aware of and encouraged to support and work toward the achievement of the program's mission and stated objectives.

The mission and objectives should specify both mandatory and optional areas of study and should include a plan for assessing student progress throughout the program of study. The mission and objectives may address recruitment, selection, retention, employment recommendations, curriculum, instructional methods, research activities, administrative policies, governance, and program evaluation.

Part 2. Recruitment and Admission

Accurate descriptions of the graduate program including the qualifications of its faculty and records of its students' persistence, degree completion, and subsequent study and employment must be made readily available for review by both current and prospective students.

Students selected for admission to the program must meet the institution's criteria for admission to graduate study. Program faculty members must make admission decisions using written criteria that are disseminated to all faculty members and to prospective students.

Admissions materials must be clear about preferences for particular student status, such as full-time students, currently employed students or students seeking learning opportunities by distance, and the manner in which such preferences may affect admissions decisions.

Students admitted to the program should have ample intellectual capacities, strong interpersonal skills, serious interest in the program, commitment to pursuing a career in student affairs, the potential to serve a wide range of students of varying developmental levels and backgrounds, and the capacity to be open to self-assessment and growth. Criteria known to predict success in the program for students of various backgrounds and characteristics should be used in their selection. Students from diverse backgrounds should be encouraged to apply.

Students from diverse backgrounds must be given equal opportunity for entry into the program.

Part 3. Curriculum Policies

The preparation program must specify in writing and distribute to prospective students its curriculum and graduation requirements. The program must conform to institutional policy and must be fully approved by the institution's administrative unit responsible for graduate programs. The institution must employ only faculty members with credentials that clearly reflect professional knowledge, ability, and skill to teach, advise, or supervise in the program.

Any revisions to the publicized program of studies must be published and distributed to students in a timely fashion. Course syllabi must be available that reflect purposes, teaching/learning methods, and outcome objectives.

All prerequisite studies and experiences should be identified clearly in course descriptions and syllabi.

The equivalent of two years full-time academic study must be required for the Masters degree.

Ordinarily, to accomplish the goals of the curriculum as outlined later in this document, a program should include a total 42-48 semester credit hours.

Programs must demonstrate that the full curriculum, as outlined in Part 5 of these standards and guidelines, is covered and that graduates reflect relevant proficiency.

Because of the benefits of immersion-like educational experiences characterized by full-time study, full-time enrollment should be encouraged. However to serve those students for whom full-time study is not possible, programs may provide opportunities for part-time study. Part-time enrollment will result in a program of more than two academic years of study.

Appropriate consideration and provisions for admission and curriculum decisions should be made for students with extensive student affairs experience.

Distance learning options may be used in the program.

There must be a sequence of basic to advanced studies. Any required associated learning experiences must be included in the required program of studies.

Associated learning experiences may include comprehensive examinations, degree candidacy, and research requirements.

Opportunity for students to develop understandings and skills beyond minimum program requirements must be provided through elective course options, supervised individual study, and/or enrichment opportunities.

Programs should encourage students to take advantage of special enrichment opportunities and education that encourages learning beyond the formal curriculum, such as experiences in student affairs organizations, professional associations and conferences, and outreach projects.

An essential feature of the preparation program must be to foster an appreciation of spirit of inquiry, in faculty members and students, as evidenced by active involvement in producing and using research, evaluation, and assessment information in student affairs.

Research, program evaluation, and assessment findings should be used frequently in instructional and supervised practical experience offerings. The study of methods of inquiry should be provided in context of elected program emphasis, such as administration, counseling, student learning and development, student cultures, or other program options.

Part 4. Pedagogy
Each program must indicate its pedagogical philosophy in the program literature. In addition, the individual faculty member must identify his or her pedagogical strategies. Faculty members must accommodate multiple student learning styles. Teaching approaches must be employed that lead to the accomplishment of course objectives, achievement of student learning outcomes, and are subject to evaluation by academic peers for the purpose of program improvement.

Such teaching approaches include active collaboration, service learning, problem-based learning, experiential, and constructivist learning. Faculty members should elect to use multiple teaching strategies. Recognition of the student's role in learning should play a significant role in choice of teaching approach.

Part 5. The Curriculum
All programs of study must include 1) foundational studies, 2) professional studies, and 3) supervised practice. Foundational studies must include the study of the historical and philosophical foundations of higher education and student affairs. Professional studies must include (a) student development theory, (b) student characteristics and the effects of college on students, (c) individual and group interventions, (d) organization and administration of student affairs, and (e) assessment, evaluation, and research. Supervised practice must include practica and/or internships consisting of supervised work involving at least two distinct experiences.

Demonstration of minimum knowledge and skill in each area is required of all program graduates.

The curriculum described above represents areas of study and should not be interpreted as specific course titles. The precise nature of courses should be determined by a variety of factors, including institutional mission, policies and practices, faculty judgment, current issues, and student needs. It is important that appropriate courses be available within the institution or from another institution, but it is not necessary that all be provided directly within the department or college in which the program is located administratively. Although all areas of study must be incorporated into the academic program, the precise nature of study may vary by institution, program emphasis, and student preference. The requirements for demonstration of competence and minimum knowledge in each area should be established by the faculty and regularly reviewed to assure that students are learning the essentials that underlie successful student affairs practice. A formal comprehensive examination or other culminating assessment project designed to provide students the opportunity to exhibit their knowledge and competence toward the end of their programs of study is encouraged.

Programs of study may be designed to emphasize one or more distinctive perspectives on student affairs such as educational program design, implementation, and evaluation; individual and group counseling and advising; student learning and human development; and/or administration of student affairs in higher education. Such program designs should include the most essential forms of knowledge and groupings of skills and competencies needed by practicing professionals and should be fashioned consistent with basic curriculum requirements. The wide range of expertise and interest of program faculty members and other involved and qualified contributors to curriculum content should be taken into account when designing distinctive perspectives in programs of study.

Each program must specify the structure of its degree options including which courses are considered core, which are considered thematic, which are required, and which are elective.

A "core" course is one that is principal to the student affairs preparation program. Theme courses are those that center on a common content area (such as introduction to student development theory, the application of student development theory, and using student development theory for environmental assessment).

Programs may structure their curriculum according to their distinctive perspectives and the nature of their students insuring adequacy of knowledge in foundation, professional, and supervised experience studies.

Part 5a. Foundation Studies
This component of the curriculum must include study in the historical, philosophical, ethical, cultural, and research foundations of higher education that inform student affairs practice. The study of the history and philosophy of student affairs are essential components of this standard.

Graduates must be able to reference historical and current documents that state the philosophical foundations of the profession and to communicate their relevance to current student affairs practice.

Graduates must also be able to articulate the inherent values of the profession that are stipulated in these documents in a manner that indicates how these values guide practice.

These values may include educating the whole student, treating each student as a unique individual, offering seamless learning opportunities, and ensuring the basic rights of all students.

This standard encompasses studies in other disciplines that inform student affairs practice, such as cultural contexts of higher education; governance, public policy, and finance of higher education; the impact of environments on behavior, especially learning; and international education and global understanding. Studies in this area should emphasize the diverse character of higher education environments. The foundational studies curriculum component should be designed to enhance students' understanding of higher education systems and exhibit how student affairs programs are infused into the larger educational picture.

Graduates must be knowledgeable about and be able to apply a code of ethics or ethical principles sanctioned by a recognized professional organization that provides ethical guidance for their work.

Part 5b. Professional Studies
This component of the curriculum must include studies of basic knowledge for practice and all programs must encompass at least five related areas of study including (a) student development theory; (b) student characteristics and effects of college on students; (c) individual and group interventions; (d) organization and administration of student affairs; and (e) assessment, evaluation, and research.

Other areas of study, especially when used as enrichment or cognate experiences, are encouraged. Studies in disciplines such as sociology, psychology, political science, and ethnic studies, for example, may be helpful to students depending upon the particular program emphasis. Communication skills and using technology as a learning tool should be emphasized in all the professional studies areas listed above.

Subpart 5b.1. Student Development Theory
This component of the curriculum must include studies of student development theories and research relevant to student learning and personal development. There must be extensive examination of theoretical perspectives that

describe students' growth in the areas of intellectual, moral, ego, psychosocial, career, and spiritual development; racial, cultural, ethnic, gender, and sexual identity; the intersection of multiple identities; and learning styles throughout the late adolescent and adult lifespan. Study of collegiate environments and how person-environment interactions affect student development is also required.

Graduates must be able to demonstrate the ability to use appropriate development theory to understand, support, and advocate for student learning and development by assessing learning and developmental needs and creating learning and developmental opportunities.

This component should include studies of and research about human development from late adolescence through the adult life span and models and processes for translating theory and research into practice. Studies should stress differential strengths and applications of student development theories relative to student age, gender, ethnicity, race, culture, sexual identity, disability, spirituality, national origin, socioeconomic status, and resident/commuter status. Studies should also include specialized theories of development particular to certain populations or groups.

Subpart 5b.2. Student Characteristics and Effects of College on Students

This component of the curriculum must include studies of student characteristics, how such attributes influence student educational and developmental needs, and effects of the college experience on student learning and development.

Graduates must be able to demonstrate knowledge of how student learning and learning opportunities are influenced by student characteristics and by collegiate environments so that graduates can design and evaluate learning experiences for students.

This area should include studies of the effects of college on students, satisfaction with the college experience, student involvement in college, and factors that correlate with student persistence and attrition. This curriculum component should include, but is not limited to, student characteristics such as age, gender, ethnicity, race, religion, sexual identity, academic ability and preparation, learning styles, socioeconomic status, national origin, immigrant status, disability, developmental status,

cultural background and orientation, transfer status, and family situation. Also included should be the study of specific student populations such as resident, commuter, and distance learners, part-time and full-time students, student athletes, members of fraternities and sororities, adult learners, first generation students, and international students.

Subpart 5b.3. Individual and Group Interventions

This component of the curriculum must include studies of techniques and methods of interviewing; helping skills; and assessing, designing, and implementing developmentally appropriate interventions with individuals and organizations.

Graduates must be able to demonstrate knowledge and skills necessary to design and evaluate effective educational interventions for individuals and groups. Graduates must be able to identify and appropriately refer persons who need additional resources.

This curriculum component should include opportunities for study, skill building, and strategies for the implementation of advising, counseling, disciplining, instructing, mediating, and facilitating to assist individuals and groups. The program of study should include substantial instruction in counseling and group dynamics. Students should be exposed to a variety of theoretical perspectives, provided opportunities to practice individual and group interventions, and receive extensive supervision and feedback. Intervention skills are complex and require periods of time to practice under supervised conditions.

In addition to exposure to intervention theory, programs of study should include instruction in individual and group techniques and practices for addressing personal crises as well as problem solving, self-examination, and growth needs. Further, studies should include problem analyses, intervention design, and subsequent evaluation. Studies should emphasize theory plus individual and group interventions that are appropriate for and applicable to diverse populations.

Subpart 5b.4. Organization and Administration of Student Affairs

This component of the curriculum must include studies of organizational, management, and leadership theory and practice; student affairs functions; legal issues in higher education; and professional issues, ethics, and standards of practice.

Graduates must be able to identify and apply leadership, organizational, and management practices that assist institutions in accomplishing their mission.

This curriculum component should include opportunities for the study of student affairs programs and services including but not limited those for which CAS has developed standards and guidelines such as admissions, financial aid, orientation, counseling, academic advising, residence life, judicial services, campus activities, commuter student programs, recreational sports, career services, fraternity and sorority advising, religious programs, service learning, disability services, academic support services, education opportunity programs, multicultural student affairs international student affairs, and health services among others. Studies of organizational culture, budgeting and finance, planning, technology as applied to organizations, and the selection, supervision, development, and evaluation of personnel should be included as well.

Subpart 5b.5. Assessment, Evaluation, and Research

This component of the curriculum must include the study of assessment, evaluation, and research. Studies must include both qualitative and quantitative research methodologies, measuring learning processes and outcomes, assessing environments and organizations, measuring program and environment effectiveness, and critiques of published studies.

Graduates must be able to critique a sound study or evaluation, and be able to design, conduct, and report on a sound research study, assessment study, or program evaluation, grounded in the appropriate literature.

Graduates must be aware of research ethics and legal implications of research including the necessity of adhering to a human subjects review.

This curriculum component should include studies of the assessment of student needs and developmental attributes, the assessment of educational environments that influence student learning, and the assessment of student outcomes of the educational experience particular to student affairs work. This curriculum component also should include studies of program evaluation models and processes suitable for use in making judgments about the value of a wide range of programs and services. Students should be introduced to methodologies and techniques of quantitative and qualitative research, plus the philosophical foundations, assumptions, methodologies, methods, and criteria of worthiness of both. Students should be familiar with prominent research in student affairs that has greatly influenced the profession.

Part 5c. Supervised Practice

A minimum of 300 hours of supervised practice, consisting of at least two distinct experiences, must be required. Students must gain exposure to both the breadth and depth of student affairs work. Students must gain experience in developmental work with individual students and groups of students in: program planning, implementation, or evaluation; staff training, advising, or supervision; and administration functions or processes.

Supervision must be provided on-site by competent professionals working in cooperation with qualified program faculty members. On-site supervisors must provide direct regular supervision and evaluation of students' experiences and comply with all ethical principles and standards of the American College Personnel Association, the National Association of Student Personnel Administrators, and other recognized professional associations.

Qualified student affairs professionals possessing appropriate student affairs education and experience should be invited to sponsor and supervise students for practicum and internship experiences. Typical qualifications include at least a master's degree in student affairs or a related area of professional study, several years of successful professional experience, and experience at that institution. Student affairs professionals serving as on-site supervisors and evaluators of students in training should be approved by the responsible faculty member as competent to accomplish this task.

Site supervisors must be approved in advance by program faculty. Program faculty must offer clear expectations of learning goals and supervision practices to site supervisors.

Supervised practice includes practica and internships consisting of supervised work completed for academic credit in student programs and services in higher education. The exposure of students to diverse settings and work with diverse clientele or populations should be encouraged.

Because individual supervision of students in practica and internships is labor intensive for faculty with this instructional responsibility, supervision must be limited to a small group to enable close regular supervision. Students must be supervised closely by faculty individually, in groups, or both.

When determining practicum and internship course loads, faculty members who provide direct practicum or internship supervision during any academic term should receive instructional credit for the equivalent of one academic course for each small group. Likewise, students enrolled in such internships should receive academic credit.

A graduate assistantship in programs and services in higher education, which provides both substantive experience and professional supervision, may be used in lieu of a practicum or internship. For this to be effective, faculty members responsible for assuring quality learning outcomes should work closely with graduate assistantship supervisors in students' assignment and evaluation processes. Appropriate consideration and provisions should be made for students with extensive experience in student affairs.

Preparation of students for practica and internships is required. Practica and internship experiences must be reserved for students who have successfully completed a sequence of courses pertaining to basic foundational knowledge of professional practice. This must include basic knowledge and skills in interpersonal communication, consultation, and referral skills. Students must comply with all ethical principles and standards of appropriate professional associations.

Preparation of students for supervised practice may be accomplished through special pre-practica seminars, laboratory experiences, and faculty tutorials as well as coursework.

Student membership in professional associations should be expected. Attendance at professional conferences, meetings, or other professional development opportunities should also be encouraged.

Part 6. Equity and Access
A graduate program must adhere to the spirit and intent of equal opportunity in all activities. The program must encourage establishment of an ethical community in which diversity is viewed as an ethical obligation. The program must ensure that its services and facilities are programmatically and physically accessible. Programs that indicate in their admissions materials convenience and encouragement for working students must provide services, classes, and resources that respond to the needs of evening, part-time, and commuter students.

Institutional personnel policies must not discriminate on the the bases of age; color; creed; cultural heritage; disability; ethnicity; gender identity; nationality; political affiliation; religious affiliation; sex; sexual orientation; or social, economic, marital, or veteran status. In hiring and promotion policies, faculty and administrators must take affirmative action that strives to remedy significant staffing imbalance, particularly when resulting from past discriminatory practices; and must seek to identify, prevent, and remedy existing discriminatory practices.

The program should recognize the important educational opportunities that diversity among its students and faculty brings to student affairs preparation. Therefore, programs should encourage the recognition of and adherence to the spirit of multiculturalism by all who are allied with the program's educational enterprise.

Part 7. ACADEMIC and STUDENT SUPPORT
Institutions must provide sufficient faculty and staff members, resource materials, advising, career services, student financial support, facilities, and funding resources for the program.

Outcome indicators to determine whether a program has adequate resources could include student retention.

Part 7a. Faculty and Staff Members
The institution must provide adequate faculty and support staff members for the various aspects of the student affairs graduate program.

The institution must provide an academic program coordinator who is qualified by preparation and experience to manage the program.

The program coordinator or administrative director should have responsibility for managing the program's day to day operations, convening the program faculty as required, developing curriculum, and generally administering the preparation program within the context of the academic unit to which it is assigned. This individual should be the person responsible for guiding faculty teaching assignments, establishing and maintaining connections with student affairs staff members who serve as practicum/internship site supervisors, guiding general program activities, and representing the program to external constituencies.

Faculty assignments must demonstrate a serious commitment to the preparation of student affairs professionals. Sufficient full-time core faculty members must be devoted to teaching and administering the program to graduate not only employable students but also students capable of designing, creating, and implementing learning opportunities. At least one faculty member must be designated full-time to the program.

Faculty members should be available according to a reasonable faculty-student ratio that permits quality teaching, advising, supervision, research, and professional service. A core faculty member is one who identifies principally with the preparation program. Primary teaching responsibility in the program is recognized when core faculty member's instructional responsibilities are dedicated half-time or greater to teaching the program's curriculum. Devoted full-time to the program is defined as a faculty member whose institutional responsibilities are fully dedicated to the program. Teaching loads should be established on the basis of institutional policy and faculty assignments for service, research, and supervision. A system within the program and the institution should exist for involving professional practitioners who are qualified to assist with faculty responsibilities. Collaboration between full-time faculty members and student affairs practitioners is recommended for the instruction, advisement, and practicum and internship supervision of students in the preparation program. Student affairs practitioners should be consulted in the design, implementation, and evaluation of the preparation program, particularly regarding practicum and internship requirements.

Faculty members must be skilled as teachers and knowledgeable about student affairs in general plus current theory, research, and practice in areas appropriate to their teaching or supervision assignments. Faculty members must also have current knowledge and skills appropriate for designing, conducting, and evaluating learning experiences using multiple pedagogies.

Faculty must maintain regular office hours that are clearly listed on course syllabi and in other prominent locations.

Faculty must act in accordance with ethical principals and standards of good practice disseminated by recognized professional organizations.
The institution must provide opportunity and resources for the continuing professional development of program faculty members. To ensure that faculty members can devote adequate time to professional duties, the academic program must have sufficient clerical and technical support staff.

Technical support must be of sufficient quality and quantity to accomplish word processing, data management, scheduling, electronic instructional material development, and distance learning. Equipment sufficient for electronic communications and Internet use is essential.

For more information on distance education standards refer to the CAS Standards and Guidelines for Distance Learning Programs.

Technical support should include regular training in software upgrades and new hardware developments, hardware and software repairs, virus protection, access to the web, on-line journals, courseware, and presentation software.

Classroom facilities should have the capacity to offer classes using electronic technologies.

Adjunct and part-time faculty must be fully qualified and adequately trained to serve as teachers, advisors, and internship supervisors.

Adjuncts and part-time faculty should be provided with information about institutional policies and procedures, access to program resources and faculty, and feedback about their performance.

Part 7b. Resource Materials
Adequate resource materials must be provided to support the curriculum.

Resources may include career information; standardized tests and technical manuals; and materials for simulations, structured group experiences, human relations training, and data-based interventions for human and organization development. In addition, resources may include instruments and assessment tools that measure development and leadership from various theoretical points of view and materials that facilitate leadership, organizational design, management style, conflict management, and time management development. Resources should include software that allows for the analysis of qualitative and quantitative data.

Library resources must be provided for the program including current and historical books, periodicals, on-line journals, search mechanisms, and other media for the teaching and research aspects of the program. Library resources must be accessible to students and must be selected carefully, reviewed, and updated periodically by the program faculty.

The library resources should be available days, evenings, and weekends and should include adequate interlibrary loan services, ERIC and similar data sources, computerized search capabilities, and photocopy services.

Research support must be adequate for both program faculty and students.

Computing services, data collection and storage services, research design consultation services, and adequate equipment should be available in support of research activities of both students and faculty members. The program should provide students with individualized research project development and implementation.

Part 7c. Advising
Faculty members must provide high quality academic and professional advising.

Academic advising should be viewed as a continuous process of clarification and evaluation. High quality academic advising should include, but is not limited to, development of suitable educational plans; selection of appropriate courses and other educational experiences; clarification of professional and career goals; knowledge of and interpretation of institutional and program policies, procedures, and requirements; knowledge of course contents, sequences, and support resources; evaluation of student progress; referrals to and use of institutional and community support services; support for and evaluation of scholarly endeavors including research and assessment; and knowledge and interpretation of professional ethics and standards. Advisors should be readily available to students and should possess abilities to facilitate a student's career exploration, self-assessment, decision-making, and responsible behavior in interactions with others. Advisors should be able to interpret the scores of assessment tools used in the advising process. These might include the Graduate Record Examination, Myers Briggs Type Indicator, and Learning Styles Inventory. The number of faculty advisees should be monitored and adjusted as necessary to ensure that faculty can give adequate attention to all advisees.

Part 7d. Career Services
The institution must provide professional career assistance, either by institutional career services or by the program faculty.

Students should be assisted in clarifying objectives and establishing goals; exploring the full range of career possibilities; preparing for the job search including presenting oneself effectively as a candidate for employment; and making the transition from graduate student to professional practitioner. Faculty members should collaborate with campus career service providers to develop an active program of assistance including acquiring job listings; the preparation of credentials such as recommending applications, correspondence, and resumes; development of employment interview skills; identification of appropriate job search networks including professional associations; selection of suitable positions; and communication of ethical obligations of those involved in the employment process. Ideally, these services should be available to graduates throughout their professional careers.

Part 7e. Student Financial Support
Information must be provided to students about the availability of graduate assistantships, fellowships, work-study, research funding, travel support, and other financial aid opportunities.

Graduate assistantships should be made available to students to provide both financial assistance and opportunities for supervised work experience.

Part 7f. Facilities and Funding Resources
The institution must provide facilities accessible to all students and a budget that ensures continuous operation of all aspects of the program.

A program office should be located in reasonable proximity to faculty offices, classrooms, and laboratory facilities. Adequate and appropriate space, equipment, and supplies should be provided for faculty, staff members, and graduate assistants. There should be facilities for advising, counseling, and student development activities that are private, adequate in size, and properly equipped. Special facilities and equipment may include audio and video recording devices, one-way observation rooms, small group rooms, and computer labs. Adequate classroom, seminar, and laboratory facilities to meet program needs also should be available. Adequate office and technical equipment should be provided including access to e-mail and other relevant technological resources.

Part 8. Professional Ethics and Legal Responsibilities
Faculty members must comply with institutional policies and ethical principles and standards of the American College Personnel Association, the National Association of Student Personnel Administrators, American Association of University Professors, and the CAS functional area ethical standards. Faculty

members must demonstrate the highest standards of ethical behavior and academic integrity in all forms of teaching, research, publications, and professional service and must instruct students in ethical practice and in the principles and standards of conduct of the profession.

Ethical expectations of graduate students must be disseminated in writing on a regular basis to all students.

Ethical principles and standards of all relevant professional organizations should be consulted and used as appropriate. An ethical climate should prevail throughout the preparation program wherein faculty members model appropriate ethical behavior at all times for students to experience, observe, and emulate. Faculty members should present various theoretical positions and encourage students to make comparisons and to develop personally meaningful theoretical positions. Faculty members are expected to ensure that educational experiences focusing on self-understanding and personal growth are voluntary or, if such experiences are program requirements, that reasonable effort is made to inform prospective students of them prior to admission to the program. Students should be held accountable for appropriate ethical behavior at all times with special attention paid to the ethics components of the various CAS functional area standards when students participate in related practicum and internship assignments.

Faculty members must strive to ensure the fair and impartial treatment of students and others.

Faculty members must maintain ethical relationships with students exemplifying respect and the ideals of pedagogy.

Faculty members must not teach, supervise, or advise any student with whom they have an intimate relationship. When a student enters an academic program having a pre-existing intimate relationship with a faculty member, both must notify a third party, such as a department chair, to monitor the pedagogical relationship and assign appropriate teaching, supervisory, and advising responsibilities.

Graduate program faculty members must evaluate annually all students' progress and suitability for entry into the student affairs profession. Evaluation of students' ethical behaviors must be included. Faculty members must keep students informed about their progress toward successful program completion.

Through continual evaluation and appraisal of students, faculty members are expected to be aware of ethically problematic student behaviors, inadequate academic progress, and other behaviors or characteristics that may make a student unsuitable for the profession. Appropriate responses leading to remediation of the behaviors related to students' academic progress or professional suitability should be identified, monitored, evaluated, and shared with individual students as needed. Faculty members are expected in cases of significant problematic behaviors to communicate to the student the problems identified and the remediation required to avoid being terminated from the preparation program. After appropriate remediation has been proposed and evaluated, students who continue to be evaluated as being unsuitable for the profession, making poor academic progress, or having ethically problematic behaviors should be dismissed from the preparation program following appropriate due process procedures. If termination is enforced, faculty members are expected to explain to the student the grounds for the decision.

Faculty members must ensure that privacy is maintained with respect to all communication and records considered to be educational records unless written permission is given by the student or when the disclosure is allowable under the law and institution policy.

Faculty members must respond to requests for employment-related recommendations by students. When endorsement cannot be provided for a particular position, the student must be informed of the reason for non-endorsement.

Faculty members should base endorsements on knowledge of the student's competencies, skills, and personal characteristics.

Each candidate should be informed of procedures for endorsement, certification, registry, and licensure, if applicable.

Faculty members must inform all students of the institutional and program policies regarding graduate student liability.

Program policy should be established to ensure that all students are periodically informed of their liabilities and options for protection. Programs may wish to establish policies requiring students to hold membership in particular professional associations and to purchase liability insurance prior to entering into practica or internships.

Part 9. Program Evaluation
Planned procedures for continuing evaluation of the program must be established and implemented, and the evaluation information must be used for appropriate program enhancements.

Criteria for program evaluation should include knowledge and competencies learned by students, employment rates of graduates, professional contributions to the field made by graduates, and quality of faculty teaching, advising, and research. Evaluation of program effectiveness should reflect evidence obtained from former students; course evaluations; supervisors from institutions and agencies employing graduates of the program; personnel in state/provincial, regional, and national accrediting agencies during formal reviews; and clientele served by graduates.

Review of policies and procedures relating to recruitment, selection, retention, and career services should be included in program evaluations. The timing and regularity of evaluations should be determined in accordance with institutional policy. Generally, the length of time between comprehensive program evaluations by the program faculty should not exceed five years.

General Standards revised in 2002; Preparation Program content developed/revised in 1979, 1986, & 1997

Appendix A
CAS Member Associations - June 2006

Association	Member Since
American Association for Employment in Education (AAEE)	1979
American College Counseling Association (ACCA)	1993
American College Health Association (ACHA)	1995
American Counseling Association (ACA)	1983
Association of College and University Housing Officers-International (ACUHO-I)	1979
Association of College Honor Societies	2004
Association of College Unions International (ACUI)	1979
Association of Collegiate Conference and Events Directors-International (ACCED-I)	1999
Association of Fraternity Advisors (AFA)	1981
Association for Student Judicial Affairs (ASJA)	1990
Association on Higher Education and Disability (AHEAD)	1981
Canadian Association of College and University Student Services (CACUSS)	1994
College Information and Visitor Services Association (CIVSA)	1998
College Reading and Learning Association (CRLA)	1993
College Student Educators International (ACPA)	1979
Council for Opportunity in Education	1994
NAFSA: Association of International Educators (NAFSA)	1989
National Academic Advising Association (NACADA)	1981
National Association for Campus Activities (NACA)	1979
National Association of College Auxiliary Services (NACAS)	1998
National Association of College and University Food Services (NACUFS)	2004
National Association of Colleges and Employers (NACE)	1979
National Association of College Stores	2005
National Association of Developmental Educators (NADE)	1992
National Association of Student Affairs Professionals (NASAP)	2004
National Association of Student Financial Aid Administrators (NASFAA)	1991
National Association of Student Personnel Administrators (NASPA)	1979
National Clearinghouse for Commuter Programs (NCCP)	1980
National Clearinghouse for Leadership Programs (NCLP)	2004
National Consortium of Directors of LGBT Resources in Higher Education	1999
National Council on Student Development (NCSD)	1979
National Intramural Recreational Sports Association (NIRSA)	1981
National Orientation Directors Association (NODA)	1979
National Society for Experiential Education (NSEE)	2004
The Network Addressing Collegiate Alcohol and Other Drug Issues	1999
Southern Association for College Student Affairs (SACSA)	1982

Appendix B

PROTOCOL for DEVELOPING NEW CAS STANDARDS and GUIDELINES

The CAS Board of Directors will move to create new Standards and Guidelines for functional areas as needed. The standards creation protocol is based on a broad based and inclusive process. It encompasses an internal-external-internal drafting procedure that is outlined below.

1. Identify the Functional Area: The CAS Board of Directors identifies and defines the functional area for which a CAS standard is to be written. Functional areas for which standards are developed may be proposed by any professional entity or group of concerned professional practitioners. If other standards created by one or more organizations currently exist outside of CAS, CAS will identify its source and seek its sponsoring agency's cooperation on developing CAS standards and guidelines for that functional area. The CAS Board of Directors must agree by majority vote to sponsor development of a new professional standard.

2. Charging a Drafting Committee for New Standards Creation: When the CAS Board determines that a new CAS Functional Area Standard needs to be developed; a Drafting Committee of three to five CAS Directors (or Alternate Directors) will be formed to guide the development process. At least one person on the committee must be or have been especially connected with the functional area about which the standard is to be written. The chair cannot be a representative of a professional association that has significant interest in the standard. The Committee is encouraged to use every available method of electronic communication, including the conference call service, to facilitate the process of soliciting and receiving input and feedback.

3. Initial Draft: If a professional association connected with the standard area is a member of CAS, that association is asked to write a rough draft of standards. If that professional association is not a member of CAS, the association would be asked to join provided they meet the membership requirement and/or be included in the drafting of the standards and guidelines. If they decide not to join, CAS will continue to move forward with the draft. This rough draft is forwarded to the Drafting Committee that uses it to create a first draft in the CAS standards and guideline format. The CAS General Standards and any other existing standards will be used as the foundation for any newly developed functional area standard.

4. Soliciting Internal Expert Review and Comment: The Drafting Committee then identifies all CAS member associations that have a significant interest in the functional area for which standards are being developed. The first draft will be sent to CAS Directors of identified organizations and asked to provide timely and substantive recommendations of the first draft of proposed standards. One month return time should be allowed for response. The Drafting Committee then creates a second draft based on feedback from CAS Directors. The second draft is posted on the CAS Management site. A minimum of two months should be allowed for the writing of the second draft.

5. Soliciting External Expert Review and Comment: Next, the Drafting Committee identifies expert professionals of both CAS member associations and non CAS member associations for their personal review of the second draft. Such experts could include chairs of ACPA commissions (www.acpa.nche.edu) and NASPA Knowledge Communities (www.naspa.org). It is recommended to consider soliciting feedback from practitioners through an on-line professional list, organizational web pages, and the data base of users collected from purchasers of CAS materials. A CAS designee, such as the graduate assistant, may be appointed to assist the drafting committee in contacting experts in the field and in soliciting their feedback. Also, CAS Directors should be consulted for names of those currently filling positions with interest in standards under review. It would be the goal to receive feedback from at least 5 experts from the field within six weeks.

6. Incorporation of comments into a second draft document: The Drafting Committee will evaluate all substantive recommendations, provide its own well-considered ideas to the standards development process, and prepare a third draft of the functional area standards and guidelines. This draft should be prepared within 6 months after initiation of the process.

7. Submission to the a member of the Executive Committee through the Editor: The proposed revisions to the standards are then forwarded to the CAS Executive Committee for review at least two weeks before their scheduled meeting.

8. Executive Committee Review and Approval: The Drafting Committee chairperson and/or functional area expert who participated on the Drafting Committee will present the draft to the Executive Committee in person or by phone conference as needed. The CAS Executive Committee reviews the draft and formulates a penultimate draft for consideration by the CAS Board of Directors. The CAS Executive Committee votes to send the standards and guidelines to the full Board of Directors. This is sent to the Directors no later than 30 days before a board meeting.

9. Full CAS Board of Directors Review and Approval: The CAS Board of Directors reviews the document and votes to adopt the standards and guidelines.

10. Publication: The newly developed standards, upon adoption by the Board, are then put into the CAS Self Assessment Guide format by the Executive Committee for distribution to the profession at large. Upon completion, the Standards and Guidelines will be published in the Book of Standards along with the appropriate contextual statement.

Appendix B, *continued*

PROTOCOL for REVISING EXISTING CAS STANDARDS and GUIDELINES

The CAS Board of Directors will systematically review approximately six or more CAS Functional Area Standards and Guidelines per year on a projected five year staggered basis. The standards review protocol is based on a broad based and inclusive process. It encompasses an internal-external-internal drafting procedure that is outlined below. Member associations with interest in the functional area(s) under review will be called upon to help assess the need for revision. Members associations may also request consideration for a revision.

It is up to the CAS Director and sponsoring association to collect literature and documentation during a substantive revision of the existing standards.

1. **Review Team**: When it becomes necessary to consider standards for revision a review team consisting of an executive committee member and an expert from the field will be appointed. This team will study the current standards to determine if a substantial revision is necessary or whether an editorial revision will be adequate. Editorial revisions would include: a) basic word and punctuation corrections, b) altering phrases for purposes of clarity, c) updating required changes in general standards, d) presentation/format changes, and e) non-substantive word changes. The review team will make a recommendation to the executive committee.

    If the executive committee concurs that an editorial revision is sufficient, then the revision committee will consist of those two members. Contacting other experts in the field would not be necessary. The revised standards would subsequently need to be reviewed by the executive committee, and then would be a send for full board approval at a regular meeting or through email. This should take place within three months of initiating the review process.

2. **Charging a Revision Committee for Substantial Standards Revision**: The president will appoint and charge a Revision Committee, when the review team recommends to the Executive Committee that a CAS Functional Area Standard requires substantial revision. The charge will include: the members of the Revision Committee, a copy of this protocol, the anticipated timeline for completion of the process, an electronic copy of the current standard, suggested known experts in the field to include during the comment period and the availability of staff support to assist in the process. The composition of the committee will consist of a chair, to guide the revision process, and at least two other CAS Directors or Alternate Directors. The chair cannot be a representative of a professional association that has significant interest in the standard. However, at least one person on the committee must be connected with the functional area. Members of the revision committee who represent professional associations with significant interest in the standard should play a considerable role in ensuring that the revised standards demonstrate contemporary quality practices. The Committee is encouraged to use every available method of electronic communication, including the conference call service, to facilitate the process of soliciting and receiving input and feedback.

3. **Initial Draft**: The Revision Committee members make an initial revisions of the standards and create a draft revised standard. This should be completed within 2 months after initiating the revision charge.

4. **Soliciting Internal Expert Review and Comment:** The Revision Committee will poll all CAS member associations to establish which associations have a significant interest in the functional area standards are under consideration for revision. A notice of revision should be sent to organizations, while sending draft document to specific individuals. The Chair should also follow up with experts to ensure a timely response. Members of the revision committee who represent professional associations with significant interest in the standards should be charged with identifying such colleagues, for example the Chairs and members of ACPA Commissions (www.acpa.nche.edu) and NASPA Knowledge Communities (www.naspa.org).

5. **Soliciting External Expert Review and Comment:** The Chair of the Revision Committee should contact any professional organization that is not CAS members which might have a significant interest in the standards under revision. It is recommended soliciting feedback from practitioners through an on-line professional list, organizational web pages, and the data base of users collected from purchasers of CAS materials. Also, CAS Directors should be consulted for names of those currently serving positions related to the functional area standards under revision. Review and comment from at least ten external or internal experts from the field is suggested.

6. **Incorporation of comments into a second draft document:** A CAS designee sends the revised first draft to the identified experts. From the feedback of expert practitioners the Revision Committee prepares a second draft of the revised functional area standards and guidelines. This should take place within six months of initiating the revision process.

7. **Submission to the a member of the Executive Committee through the Editor:** The proposed revisions to the standards are then forwarded to the CAS Executive Committee for review at least two weeks before their scheduled meeting.

8. **Executive Committee Review and Approval:** The Drafting Committee chairperson and/or functional area expert who participated on the Drafting Committee will present the draft to the Executive Committee in person or by phone conference as needed. The CAS Executive Committee reviews the draft and formulates a penultimate draft for consideration by the CAS Board of Directors. The CAS Executive Committee votes to send the standards and guidelines to the full Board of Directors. This is sent to the Directors no later than 30 days before a board meeting.

9. **Full CAS Board of Directors Review and Approval:** The CAS Board of Directors reviews the document and votes to adopt the standards and guidelines.

10. **Publication:** The newly revised standards, upon adoption by the Board, are then put into the CAS Self Assessment Guide format for distribution to the profession at large. Upon completion, the Standards and Guidelines will be published in the Book of Standards along with the appropriate contextual statement.

Appendix C
Glossary of Terms

accreditation. A voluntary process conducted by peers through non-governmental agencies for purposes of improving educational quality and assuring the public that programs and services meet established standards. In higher education, accreditation is divided into two types - institutional and specialized. Although both are designed to assure fundamental levels of quality, the former focuses on the institution as a whole while the latter focuses on academic pre-professional or specialty professional programs such as law, business, psychology, and education; or services such as counseling centers within the institution. Although the CAS Standards have utility for accreditation self-study, CAS is not an accrediting body.

affirmative action. Policies and/or programs designed to redress historic injustices committed against racial minorities and other specified groups by making special efforts to provide members of these groups with access to educational and employment opportunities. This may apply to students as well as to faculty and staff members.

best practice. A level of professional conduct or practice identified as being necessary for college and university personnel to exhibit in their daily work for the host program or service to be judged satisfactory, sufficient and of acceptable quality. CAS Standards and Guidelines represent best practice.

CAS. The Council for the Advancement of Standards in Higher Education. A consortium of professional associations concerned with the development and promulgation of professional standards and guidelines for student support programs and services in institutions of higher learning. The CAS Board of Directors is composed of representatives from member associations and meets semiannually in the spring and fall. Prior to 1992, the consortium's name was the Council for the Advancement of Standards for Student Services/Development Programs.

CAS Blue Book. The informal name of the publication entitled CAS Professional Standards for Higher Education (previous editions were "The CAS Book of Professional Standards for Higher Education") that presents the CAS standards and guidelines. The first iteration of the CAS standards was published in 1986. Revised editions were published in 1997, 1999, 2001, 2003, and the current 2006 edition. CAS policy calls for an updated revision to be published biannually.

CAS Board of Directors. A body of representatives from professional higher education associations in the U.S. and Canada that have joined the CAS consortium, pay annual dues, and keep their memberships informed about CAS standards and related initiatives. Each member association may designate two official representatives (Director and Alternate) to act on its behalf at CAS Board meetings; each association has one vote on the Council.

CAS consortium. An alliance of professional U.S. and Canadian higher education associations established in 1979 to develop and promulgate professional standards that guide and enhance the quality of student life, learning, and development through support programs and to educate practitioners in this regard.

CAS Executive Committee. A body of elected CAS officers, including president, secretary, treasurer, members at large, and others elected at the discretion of the Board of Directors. This body meets periodically to deal with CAS governance issues and to review penultimate standard statements prior to final review and adoption by the Board of Directors.

CAS Internet URL. http://www.cas.edu The CAS web site at which various CAS initiatives and resources are described, publications may be ordered, and links to CAS member associations are listed.

CAS member association. One of the higher education professional associations that has joined the CAS consortium and is committed to the development and promulgation of professional standards for college student learning and development support services.

CAS preparation program standards. A set of professional standards developed and promulgated for purposes of providing student affairs administration master's level programs with criteria to guide the professional education and preparation of entry-level practitioners in student affairs.

CAS Public Director. An individual appointed to the CAS Board of Directors to represent the public at large. CAS by-laws call for the appointment of public directors who do not represent a specific functional area or professional association.

CAS Standards and Guidelines. Published criteria and related statements designed to provide college and university support service providers with established measures against which to evaluate programs and services. A standard uses the auxiliary verbs "must" and "shall," while a guideline uses the verbs "should" and "may." Standards are essentials, guidelines are not.

certification. Official recognition by a governmental or professional body attesting that an individual practitioner meets established standards or criteria. Criteria usually include formal academic preparation in prescribed content areas and a period of supervised practice, and may also include a systematic evaluation (that is, standardized test) of the practitioner's knowledge.

compliance. Adherence to a standard of practice or preparation. Compliance with the CAS standards implies that an institution or program meets or exceeds the fundamental essential criteria established for a given functional area program and service or for an academic student affairs administration preparation program.

FALDOs. Frameworks for Assessing Learning and Development Outcomes. A companion publication to the CAS Professional Standards for Higher Education, the "FALDOs" are designed to assist practitioners in designing and implementing assessment of outcomes. Based on the outcome domains listed in Part 2, Program, of each functional area standard, the FALDOs include a theoretical description of the learning outcome domain (e. g., leadership development, social responsibility, career choices), assessment examples, list of possible instruments, and additional resources. The FALDOs are published in both book and CD format.

functional area standard. A statement that presents criteria describing the fundamental essential expectations of practice agreed upon by the profession at large for a given institutional function. Standards are presented in bold type and use auxiliary verbs "must" and "shall." Currently there are 35 sets of CAS functional area standards (see Table of Contents).

general standards. Statements presenting criteria that represent the most fundamental essential expectations agreed on by the profession at large for all higher education support programs and services. The general standards are contained within every set of functional area standards; they apply to every area. These "boilerplate" criteria are presented in bold type and use the auxiliary verbs "must" and "shall" as do all CAS standards. The most recent revision of the General Standards, including significant expansion of the section on learning and development outcomes, was adopted in 2002.

guideline. A statement that clarifies or amplifies professional standards. Although not required for acceptable practice, a guideline is designed to provide institutions with suggestions and illustrations that can assist in establishing programs and services that more fully address the needs of students than those mandated by a standard. Guidelines may be thought of as providing guidance in ways to exceed fundamental requirements, to approach excellence, or to function at a more optimal level. CAS Guidelines use the auxiliary verbs "should" and "may."

learning and development outcomes. Change occurring in students as a direct result of their interaction with an educational institution and its programs and services. Part 2 of the CAS standards identifies 16 learning and development outcomes that students should accomplish as a result of their higher education experiences. A number of outcome indicators are also included to guide assessing the outcomes.

in-service (or inservice) education. Educational skill-building activities provided by an institution to staff members within the context of their work responsibilities. A form of staff development designed to strengthen the ability of practitioners to carry out their duties more effectively.

licensure. Official recognition, usually by a government entity, that authorizes practice in the public arena. A license is usually granted only upon the presentation of compelling evidence that the individual is well qualified to practice in a given profession. Granting of a professional license typically authorizes holders to announce their qualifications to provide selected services to the public and attach professional titles to their names. Insurance companies often require individuals to be licensed to qualify for third-party payments.

paraprofessional. An individual who has received an adequate level of training and supervision to work in support of professional practitioners, their offices, and programs. Paraprofessionals may be students, staff members, or volunteers who have not undertaken formal or graduate level professional preparation or earned credentials to function as a professional practitioner.

personal development. Closely related to student development, this term refers to the processes associated with human maturation, especially those concerned with evolving psychosocial, morale, relational, and self-concept changes that influence an individual's quality of life.

pre-professional. An individual who is in the process of obtaining professional education that will qualify her or him for professional practice (e.g., graduate student, intern).

program. Refers to one of two types. (a) organizational, a departmental level administrative unit or sub-unit; (b) activity, an institutional support service such as an invited lecture, a workshop, a social event, or a series of organized presentations over time (e.g., a "lunch and learn" program).

quality assurance. The raison d'tre for the CAS standards and virtually all types of credentialing activities devised to assure the public that educational institutions, programs, and services and those providing them exhibit high levels of competence leading to excellence. Quality assurance initiatives are intended to ensure that those accessing available programs and services will truly benefit from them.

registry. An official record of the names and qualifications of individuals who meet pre-established criteria to function as professional practitioners. The names of professionally licensed and/or certified practitioners are typically listed in a registry. In some instances a professional "register" may be maintained for purposes of providing individuals, institutions, and organizations with the names of those who meet an established level of competence for employment or other activity such as consulting or lecturing. A registry may also be used to identify those judged to possess relevant knowledge or skill outside the context of licensure.

Self-Assessment Guide (SAG). An operational version of the CAS Standards and Guidelines designed to provide users with an assessment tool that can be used for self-study or self-assessment purposes. A SAG is available for each functional area for which a CAS standard exists.

self-study. An internal process by which institutions and programs evaluate their quality and effectiveness in reference to established criteria such as the CAS standards. This process, often used for institutional and specialty accreditation purposes, results in a formal report presenting the findings of the internal evaluation implemented by institutional employees. For accreditation purposes, this report is then validated by a visiting, external committee of peers from comparable institutions or programs. CAS SAGs have great utility for this purpose.

self-regulation. The recommended process by which the CAS Standards and Guidelines can best be used to evaluate and assess institutional support programs and services. This approach calls for institutions and programs to establish, maintain, and enhance the quality of their offerings and environments by using the standards to evaluate themselves. From the CAS perspective, each institution and its programs can and should seek to identify and regulate its own best practices rather than relying on external agencies to do so.

staff development. Refers to the programs, workshops, conferences, and other training related activities offered by institutions, professional associations, and corporate agencies for purposes of increasing effectiveness in accomplishing work responsibilities of staff members.

standard. A statement framed within the context of a professional arena designed to provide practitioners with criteria against which to judge the quality of the programs and services offered. A standard reflects an essential level of practice that, when met, represents quality performance. CAS standards use auxiliary verbs "must" and "shall" presented in bold print.

student development. Refers to those learning outcomes that occur as a result of students being exposed to higher education environments designed to enhance academic, intellectual, psychosocial, psychomotor, moral, and, for some institutions, spiritual development. This concept is based on applying human development theories within the context of higher education. In some instances, the term has also been applied to administrative units (e.g., center for student development).

student learning and development. Refers to the outcomes students realize when exposed to new experiences, concepts, information, and ideas; the knowledge and understanding gleaned from interactions with higher education learning environments. Learning means acquiring knowledge and applying it to life, appreciating human differences, and approaching an integrated sense of self.

Appendix D

FAQ: Frequently Asked Questions about CAS and Its Initiatives

1. Why does CAS write standards?
One criterion for the existence of a profession is the existence of professional standards to guide and judge practice. Without standards there would be few if any criteria established that institutions and their programs and services could use to judge their quality. CAS was established to develop and promulgate the standards necessary to achieve educational excellence.

2. How many CAS Standards and Guidelines are currently in place? Where can I find the list?
As of July 2006, CAS had developed 34 sets of functional area standards and guidelines and one set of student affairs master's level preparation standards. They are listed in the Table of Contents of CAS Professional Standards for Higher Education and on the CAS website at www.cas.edu.

3. What is the difference between a CAS standard and a CAS guideline?
A CAS standard, which is printed in BOLD type, is considered to be essential to successful professional practice and uses the auxiliary verbs "must" and "shall." Compliance with the CAS standards indicates that a program meets essential criteria as described in each standard statement and that there is tangible evidence available to support that fact. A CAS guideline, printed in light-face type, is a statement that clarifies or amplifies a CAS standard. Although not required for achieving compliance, CAS guidelines are designed to offer suggestions and illustrations that can assist programs and services to more fully address the learning and development needs of students. CAS guidelines use the auxiliary verbs "should" and "may."

4. Are institutions in jeopardy if they fail to meet the CAS Standards and Guidelines?
CAS Standards are provided primarily for institutions to use within the context of a "self-regulation" process. That is, although compliance with the standards evidences "good practice" that is recognized profession-wide, there are no external sanctions for non-compliance. However, institutions that do not meet the CAS standards will likely discover that their programs and services fail to function effectively or to meet the needs of their students. Further, institutions that evidence compliance with the CAS standards are virtually assured of receiving "high grades" from regional or specialized accrediting bodies.

5. What utility do the CAS Standards and Guidelines have for practitioners?
The CAS standards are multi-purpose in nature. They can be used to study and evaluate institutional divisions of student affairs and the various functional student support areas common across institutions. Likewise, they can be used for professional development purposes to ensure that staff members comprehend their roles and functions and develop the level of knowledge and skill essential for good practice. Also, the CAS standards can be used to guide the development of new or enhanced functional areas designed to provide students with additional learning and development opportunities.

6. Where will I find the CAS Standards and Guidelines?
CAS publishes two versions of its standards, one in text format and another in workbook format. The CAS Blue Book (CAS Professional Standards for Higher Education, 2006) provides an introduction to CAS, its mission, initiatives, and the principles upon which it was founded. Individual functional area standards accompanied by introductory contextual statements are included, along with Characteristics of Individual Excellence and the CAS Statement of Shared Ethical Principles. In addition, for use with programmatic self-studies, there is a CAS Self-

Assessment Guide (SAG) for each set of standards. These assessment workbooks include the standards and guidelines along with a series of "criterion measure" statements used to judge the level of program compliance with the standard. The CAS SAGs are also available electronically via the CAS web site and in CD-ROM format.

7. How can I obtain the CAS publications and what are their costs?
All available CAS publications, along with current costs and payment options, are listed on the CAS internet web site, www.cas.edu; they may also be purchased from the CAS national office, One Dupont Circle, NW, Suite 300, Washington, DC 20036-1188.   Current publications include the CAS Professional Standards, the SAGs, and the FALDOs, and packaged sets are available.

8. Where will I find information about using the CAS Standards and Guidelines?
An outline of how to put the CAS standards to work is included in the Blue Book, and each functional area SAG has an introductory section that describes how to apply the SAG for self-study purposes. The SAG CD also contains a PowerPoint presentation and E-learning course to help train users.

9. Can a partial program self-study using less than a full functional area standard be implemented?
Each CAS standard is organized into 13 parts. These individual program components can be used on stand-alone bases for program self-studies or for program development purposes. That is, a partial self-study using selected components may be desirable for some programs to consider. Likewise, each component has utility for staff development purposes. One recommended training approach is to hold a series of training sessions in which individual parts are examined in detail. It should be understood, however, that a full program assessment cannot be accomplished using less than the complete functional area standard, and a functional area cannot be considered to be in compliance with CAS standards if all the component parts are not evaluated.

10. How long does a typical division or individual program self-study take to complete?
The time required to complete the self-study process varies greatly with size and complexity of institutions and programs. In most instances, it will take from 6 to 9 months to complete a comprehensive division or campus-wide self-study, while a single administrative unit functional area program self-study may well be completed in approximately 3 months. One of the major time-consuming factors of any self-study is the data collection process in which documentary evidence is obtained and organized into a usable format. More time will be required if the documentary evidence has not already been collected and analyzed.

11. Does CAS offer certification or accreditation?
CAS does not function as a certification or accreditation agency. Rather, CAS encourages institutions and their functional area programs to follow a "self-regulation" approach wherein program evaluation self-studies are implemented for internal assessment purposes.

12. Do the CAS Standards have utility for regional or other accreditation purposes?
Institutions undergoing accreditation self-studies will find the CAS standards most useful. Because CAS functional area standards are invariably more comprehensive than regional accreditation criteria, a self-study using the CAS standards will provide ample documentation that can be used as evidence of compliance with accreditation criteria.

13. How does one become a member of CAS?
Because CAS is a consortium of professional organizations, there are no individual memberships available. The CAS Board of Directors is composed of representatives from member organizations, and each member association has one vote on CAS business. Organizational membership information is available from the CAS national office.

14. Does CAS have a presence at national association meetings?

Because CAS is a consortium of professional associations, each member association is responsible for providing its membership with information about the nature and availability of CAS standards. Most member associations include CAS- related presentations at their conventions. Several CAS officers and directors are available upon request to provide CAS workshops or programs sponsored by professional organizations. CAS-oriented programs have been offered at numerous national and international conferences in recent years.

15. Does CAS provide institutional staff training programs and workshops?

The CAS national office can provide information about CAS officers and board members who are well qualified to provide staff development training workshops and programs for institutions, or to consult about use of the CAS materials.

16. How often are CAS functional area standards and guidelines revised?

CAS policy calls for every functional area standard to be reviewed periodically on a 5-year basis for purposes of determining whether a revision is needed. Individuals or organizations who believe a given standard is in need of revision are invited to contact CAS to make such recommendations.

17. My association has already written professional standards. What can CAS provide that we don't already have?

Several professional associations have established standards for their constituent members, some of which are quite comparable to CAS standards. In general, CAS standards are designed to be used in every type and size of higher educational institution and were created for this broad user base. A primary benefit of the CAS standards is the fact that CAS represents a profession-wide effort to develop, promulgate, and encourage use of its professional standards. Consequently, the professional credibility of the CAS Standards and Guidelines tends to exceed those proffered by a single organization. If an institution or division uses the CAS standards to study more than one functional area, use of CAS ensures that the areas to be examined and the criteria will be consistent across areas.

18. How are CAS projects funded?

CAS membership dues have been maintained at a low annual fee since the Council's inception in 1979. Consequently, CAS has come to rely upon sale of professional publications as its primary source of funding. As a non-profit organization, CAS can accept tax-exempt contributions from individuals as well as grants from philanthropic foundations.

19. Who uses the CAS Standards and how are they typically put to use?

This important question has been studied through a comprehensive, CAS sponsored nation-wide research project. Results, including publication citation, are included in Part I of the CAS Blue Book.

20. Why use CAS standards to evaluate my program rather than using another process (e.g., benchmarks)?

The CAS standards were developed and adopted by knowledgeable representatives from a wide range of higher education organizations. They represent a profession-wide perspective about what constitutes good practice.

Appendix E

CAS Publications Ordering and Website Information

Current publications include:

CAS Professional Standards for Higher Education (6th Ed.), 2006

The 6th edition of CAS Professional Standards includes background information on the CAS approach, functional area contextual statements and functional area standards and guidelines. New standards include College Honor Societies, Education Abroad, Health Promotion, Internships, & Service-Learning; revised standards include Academic Advising, Campus Religious/Spiritual Programs, Clinical Health Services, Commuter & Off-Campus Living, Housing and Residence Life, Multicultural Student Programs, Orientation, Student Conduct, & Women Student Programs, plus the newly developed Statement of Shared Ethical Principles and Characteristics of Individual Excellence.

CAS Self-Assessment Guides – interactive CD (version 3.0)

The 2006 release of the Self-Assessment Guides CD contains 35 sets of functional area self-assessment guides, functional area contextual statements, PowerPoint presentation, and E-learning course for conducting assessments.

Frameworks for Assessing Learning and Development Outcomes, 2006 (FALDOS Book/CD)

The FALDOs are complete with a theoretical description of the learning outcome domain, assessment examples, list of possible instruments, and additional resources. Below is a list of learning domains:

- Career Choices
- Collaboration
- Effective Communication
- Appreciating Diversity
- Personal and Educational Goals
- Healthy Behavior
- Independence
- Intellectual Growth
- Leadership Development
- Satisfying and Productive Lifestyles
- Meaningful Interpersonal Relationships
- Realistic Self-Appraisal
- Enhanced Self-Esteem
- Social Responsibility
- Spiritual Awareness
- Clarified Values

Packaged sets, quantity discounts, international shipping, and expedited shipping are available.

All CAS publications are available for purchase via the CAS website, www.cas.edu, or by contacting CAS:

> CAS
> One Dupont Circle, NW
> Suite 300
> Washington, DC 20036-1188
>
> Phone orders: (202) 862-1400; Fax: (202) 296-3286

For additional CAS information:

CAS website – www.cas.edu

Contact Phyllis Mable, Executive Director, PhyllisMable@aol.com

368